Niall Couper started following Wimbledon in 1982 and became a regular at Plough Lane and, later, Selhurst Park. He became the editor of the alternative matchday programme "Yellow and Blue", which would regularly outsell the official programme three to one and eventually became the official AFC Wimbledon programme. Niall previously wrote the book "Spirit of Wimbledon" (Cherry Red Books) and remains a season ticket holder and now attends games with his daughters Amelia and Lyra.

With thanks to

Jenny Couper for putting up with me
Lyra and Amelia Couper for making me smile
Matt Couper for not writing the book first
Getty Images and in particular Lee Martin and
Mark Trowbridge for all their help with pictures
Rob Smith and John Woodruff for editing
Ashley Grossman for the bulldog clips
Rob Beatty, Terry Buckman, Jerzy Dabrowski,
Robert Dunford, Caroline Kingston-Lynch, Andy Nunn,
Michael Palmer and Martin Tomlin for helping with images
Robert Dale and David McKnight for helping with history
Dave Boyle, Martin Drake, Steve Elson, Mark Lewis
and Robert Cornell for their comments

My Daddy wrote this book. I sometimes go to football with him.
My favourite player was Andy Little, but he hurt his leg.
My Daddy hurt his leg too. I hope they both get better.
Andy was really good and we kept winning when he was playing.
I'm six now and have my own seat. Daddy loves watching the football.
I like it too. But the best bits are Haydon the Womble and chips.
Amelia Couper

THIS IS OUR TIME

The AFC Wimbledon Story

Niall Couper

CHERRY RED
BOOKS

First published in Great Britain in 2012 by Cherry Red Books
(a division of Cherry Red Records Ltd.), Power Road Studios
114 Power Road, Chiswick, London W4 5PY

ISBN 978-1-90144782-8

Design: Nathan Eighty

Printed in the UK by Ashford Colour Press

Front cover image: Andy Nunn

Back cover images: Getty Images (top left), Rob Dunford (top right) and Neil Presland (bottom)

Contents

Prologue

At 5.44pm on 21 May 2011, Danny Kedwell was about to begin the long walk to the penalty spot at the City of Manchester Stadium.

Two hours of football had failed to separate AFC Wimbledon and Luton Town in the play-off final of the Blue Square Premier. After nine penalty kicks the scores were tied at 3-3.

History was thick in the air. Just under nine years earlier, an FA Commission had permitted Wimbledon FC to relocate to Milton Keynes, a decision that was to lead to the formation of AFC Wimbledon. A goal from this kick would propel AFC Wimbledon back into the Football League.

With those thoughts ringing in his ears, Danny – the captain of the club – turned to his team-mates, lined up arm in arm on the halfway line, and uttered the prophetic words: "This is our time…"

Publisher's Introduction

I honestly believe the book you now have in your hands is one of the best and most important football books to come out in recent years. I could be accused of being somewhat biased, being the book's publisher and also an AFC Wimbledon supporter. But the story of this club is unique and, hopefully, an example of what can be achieved by football supporters anywhere if they rally together and put their minds and focus on a common aim.

Most British football fans will know the outline of this story pretty well; Wimbledon FC supporters effectively lost their club when, with FA permission, it was moved 70 miles away to a newish town near Northampton just off the M1. A move somewhere had been brewing for a time but it was still a shock when it happened. Wimbledon had always been a special club in many ways, climbing from non-League to the old Division One (then the top division) in just 10 seasons.

Most of that time they were underdogs and subsequently attracted the kind of supporters that loved that role. It thus wasn't a surprise to me that there were plenty of people who were prepared to do their bit in so many different way when the time came and practical help was needed to help form a new club.

Football supporters generally tend to complain quite a bit. The bigger their club the more they feel success is their right, and if it doesn't happen on a regular basis then something is badly wrong. It is, of course, usually somebody's fault and needs to be fixed – fast. In my view the finances in football have become daft. Not only is the whole business completely unsustainable with many players being vastly overpaid, but it also takes football further and further away from the supporters. Currently we have both Rangers and Portsmouth in huge financial trouble, with the finances of several other clubs looking none too healthy. It is time for a new approach – sustainable football clubs rooted in their local community, owned by, run by and fully accountable to their supporters.

When you actually lose your club the options become very clear very quickly. You need to do something practical if your Saturday afternoons are not going to become soulless. This book is the detailed story of how a new club was born out of the ashes of the old

Wimbledon FC. When the target was set to get AFC Wimbledon into the Football League within 10 years it seemed somewhat optimistic. People, of course, wished us well but most doubted that it could be done. But dreams can come true and this book has a happy ending.

Now, I suppose I am offering you a challenge. If you are not happy with the way your club is run, remember that you and your fellow supporters do have an option – and this book proves that option can become reality. To make it happen is going to take a lot of effort and hard work; it's certainly going to be a steep learning curb with difficult challenges at times, and you are probably going to have to swop your comfortable seat in a smart stadium to stand in the mud and the rain sometimes.

But, believe me, the pride you will feel when your team runs out and you know it is your club you have helped create will be one of the best feelings you have ever had. Football is so often about dreams, and dreams can come true. Wouldn't it be wonderful if, one day, the majority of clubs in the Football League were owned and run by their supporters?

I hope you really enjoy the book and one day we can read your story...

Iain McNay
Chairman, Cherry Red Group, August 2012
iain@cherryred.co.uk

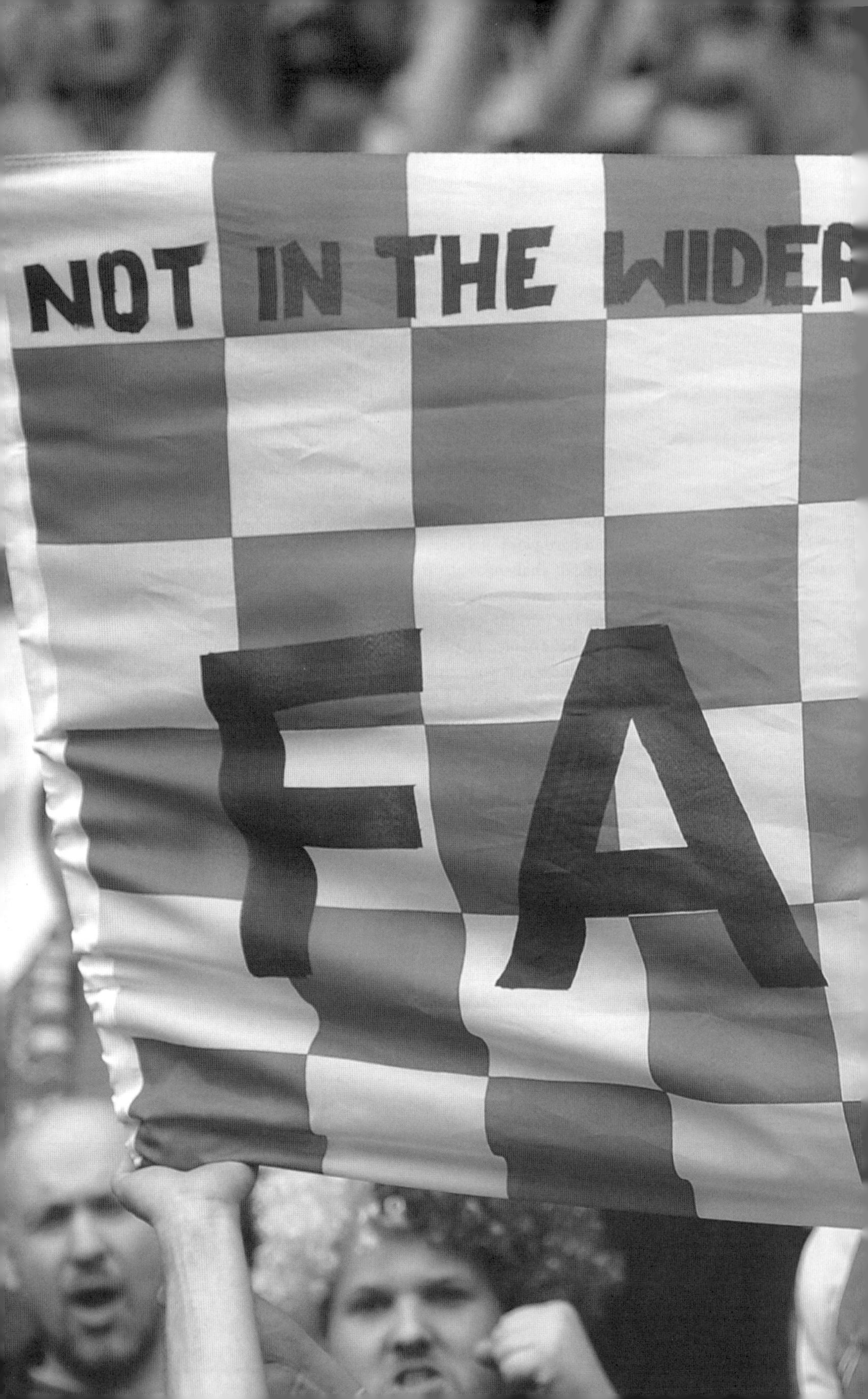
NOT IN THE WIDER
FA

Introduction

The story of AFC Wimbledon is far greater than a simple football tale. It is one of romance and hard work, created mostly by the forgotten heroes of modern football – the fans.

When the club they had loved was ripped away from them, they simply rolled up their sleeves and refused to give up.

There are dozens of heroes who made the journey possible – from the players who donned the yellow and blue and the fans who gave up their afternoon to operate the turnstiles, to the fundraisers and the stewards, to the elected Dons Trust Board members and the club's first directors, to the programme sellers, the scouts and all those who gave their all to chase the impossible.

After all, this was a club that on paper started with nothing. No ground, no players, no money, no manager, no backroom staff, no kit and not even a name. The fans were all that was left. The fans wanted a team to support. They wanted a place to call home. They wanted their history and their memories. They wanted their club back. This book tells how they did it.

AFC Wimbledon's first ever captain Joe Sheerin, right, leads out the Dons on 10 July 2002 (Getty Images)

Y MOTOR SPARES
SUTTON SURREY 644 9894 or 3737 OPEN 7 DAYS A WEEK
YOUR MOTORING NEEDS
BEST
FOR LOCAL SPORT
SUTT
SPORTS D
securicor
Championship MANAGER
HIGH
8642

Chapter One:

How did it end up like this?

1912 The re-formed Wimbledon pose for the first time. The side is a merger of Wimbledon St Andrews, Wimbledon Corporation Employees and a rump of the old Wimbledon (David McKnight)

1894 The last junior Dons - The Wimbledon
Old Centrals (David McKnight)

WIMBLEDON FOOTBALL CLUB (Holders of South London Charity Cup).

1905 The first side to be known simply as Wimbledon. The
club had dropped the Old Centrals suffix months after
winning the South London Charity Cup, their first senior
trophy (David McKnight)

AFC

WIMBLEDON

AFC Wimbledon's history is not just the story of the last 10 years, it is the story of Old Centrals, of Wimbledon Borough, of Wimbledon St Andrews, of Wimbledon Corporation Employees and also of Wimbledon FC. That, in itself, owes a lot to the hard work of a few dedicated Dons fans, notably David McKnight, Mick Pugh and Bert Dale, who, in the aftermath of the decision on 28 May 2002 to allow Wimbledon FC to relocate to Milton Keynes, refused to allow the heritage and history of 113 years to head north to Buckinghamshire without a fight. It is a story of a never-say-die attitude which has continually surfaced time and time again – both on and off the pitch – in the tale of Wimbledon.

Wimbledon's football club began back in 1889 with the Old Centrals. The team of the 19th century was effectively a local park side. Formed by ex-pupils of the Old Central School, they played on Wimbledon Common and used the local pub, the Fox and Grapes, to change in – hardly the stuff of legend.

On 2 November 1889 the Old Centrals played their first known game, a friendly against Westminster, and won 1-0. The games then were all still friendlies, and it was not until 3 December 1893 that the club got its first taste of competitive action when they lost 4-0 to Battersea Albion in the Herald Cup. They would get their revenge a year later, and that 2-1 win in the London Junior Cup also marked their first competitive victory. Wimbledon then flirted with the South London League before joining the Clapham League and the Herald League for the 1895-96 season. They won them both. The Clapham League title, secured just weeks before the Herald, was the club's first piece of silverware.

The Dons would remain trophyless for the next three seasons. In the 1900-01 season, they won the Herald Cup, the South Western Cup and the Clapham League. But success came at a cost. The club could no longer play on Wimbledon Common if their dream of senior football was to be realised, so on 23 August 1901 they moved to a private ground on Worple Road West in Raynes Park.

The next season they scored 100 goals in 33 games and, although they could only finish runners-up to Clapham, the decision had been made: the Old Centrals would kick off the 1902-03 season playing junior football in the Southern Suburban League – a local league that, unlike the Clapham League, had senior divisions.

In 1904 the Dons made the step up to senior football and a year on, on 15 April 1905, Wimbledon Old Centrals won their first senior trophy – the South London Charity Cup – beating Nunhead 2-1. Just two weeks after their cup success, the club took the momentous decision to drop their "Old Centrals" name – from 1 May 1905 the club would be known simply as Wimbledon.

A move to the Mid-Surrey League followed, which they won at the first attempt. And on 22 September 1906 the club made their debut in the FA Cup, losing 2-1 to West Norwood in the first qualifying round. Everything seemed on the up for the Dons, but the fall would be almost as dramatic as the rise and problems with where to play were to prove crucial. They moved to Pepys Road in 1906, but remained there for only a year. During 1907 they tried grounds at Grand Drive in Raynes Park, The Chase off Merton Hall Road, and then Burlington Road in New Malden. None of these proved satisfactory, so there was another enforced move during the 1909-10 season, to Malden Sports Ground. This nomadic existence couldn't continue, and in desperation the club turned to the Council to help them find a permanent home. But there was nowhere suitable, and on 3 September 1910 football was suspended.

Doom and gloom, surely? No, for a stone's throw away two junior sides had been eking out an existence: Wimbledon Corporation Employees in the Wimbledon & District League, and Wimbledon St Andrews in the South Suburban League junior divisions. In 1912, the two merged with a rump of old Wimbledon players and officials to form Wimbledon Borough and joined the senior section of the Southern Suburban League. Less than four months later the "Borough" suffix was dropped. Wimbledon were up and running again.

The side was backed by the old Wimbledon chairman, Frank Headicar, and the Council's crest was adopted as the club's new badge. Meanwhile, Charles Snook, the secretary of Wimbledon Borough, had identified an area of disused swampland once used as a refuse site, and the club bought it and moved in for the start of the 1913-14 season. It was at the corner of Haydons Road and Plough Lane and would be the Dons' home for 79 years.

The start of the First World War slowed progress. By October 1914, 27 Wimbledon players had joined the forces and a year later football was again suspended. The club was restarted just before the end of hostilities, and the Dons were back in action on 14 December 1918, beating Hampstead Town 4-2 in a friendly at Plough Lane.

In a curtailed season, the Dons took part in the United Senior League. A year later they were elected to the Athenian League. WH Keeble, commonly known as Jimmy, became the club's first amateur international when he represented England against Ireland in 1921. Meanwhile, the Athenian League was still deemed too small for the ambitious Dons, and when in 1921 the Isthmian League, the country's top amateur league, announced it was to expand to 14 teams, Wimbledon jumped ship.

The move to the Isthmian League paid few dividends at first. In eight years the club's only success came in the little-heralded Surrey Charity Shield, which they won in 1925, 1926 and again in 1927. The turning point came in 1929. In September of that year, Wimbledon recorded a 15-2 win over Polytechnic in the FA Cup – which to this date remains the club's biggest competitive victory. The Dons would go on to reach the first round, losing 4-1 at home to Northfleet United, and then in March 1930 their run in the FA Amateur Cup ended at the semi-final stage when Bournemouth Gas Works stopped the Dons from reaching the final with a 2-0 win at Portsmouth's Fratton Park.

But silverware was not too far away – and the following season, it arrived by the bucketful. The league title was captured with a record points haul, and for good measure the Dons also won the London Senior Cup, the Surrey Combination Cup,

1923 Wimbledon (in the white sleeves)
in action at Casuals (Getty Images)

the Surrey Charity Shield, the South Western Junior Cup and the South London Charity Cup.

Wimbledon retained the league title the year after. In 1935, they reached the second round of the FA Cup, losing 5-1 to Southend. That year also saw a record crowd of 18,080 squeeze into Plough Lane as the Dons beat HMS Victory 3-0 in the FA Amateur Cup en route to the final at Middlesbrough's Ayresome Park. There they held Bishop Auckland to a scoreless draw before losing the replay 2-1 at Stamford Bridge.

In 1936, the league title was secured once more. But it would be another 23 years before Wimbledon repeated the feat, for the club now entered a period of slow decline. The one bright point came just after the war. The club's former top goalscorer, Doc Dowden, led the Dons as coach to the FA Amateur Cup final in 1947. This time it was Leytonstone who would deny them at the last hurdle in front of a crowd of 47,000 at Highbury. Ron Head, a former prisoner of war, gave the Dons the lead before the East Londoners scored twice to triumph.

In the league, the Dons were on the slide. In 1954 they finished second bottom, and a year later they avoided bottom spot by just four points. Change was needed, and the club's chairman Sydney Black – related to the Crabtree brothers who are AFC Wimbledon regulars nowadays – turned to the former Arsenal and Reading player Les Henley to take over as coach. It was a move that would herald a new golden era for the club.

1931 Record breakers – the Wimbledon side who won seven trophies (pictured here with five) (Shirley Wootton)

1931 Wimbledon entertain London Caledonian on 29 August (Getty Images)

1947 Wimbledon on the attack in the FA Amateur
Cup final at Highbury against Leytonstone.
The Dons lost 2-1 (Andy Watson)

1947 The Wimbledon team (Louise Ellen Martin)

In came the likes of Roy Law, Geoff Hamm, Bobby Ardrey, Les Brown, Brian Martin and John Martin – all of whom would win England amateur caps – and there was also the notable arrival of Eddie Reynolds, a six-foot three-inch Ulsterman. They would all become Wimbledon legends. After a couple of years of transition, as the new replaced the old, Wimbledon clicked.

In 1959, the Dons, inspired by Reynolds' goals, won the Isthmian League title, setting another new points record on the way. They would go close to winning it again in 1960 and 1961. In 1962 they claimed the trophy once more – and that was just the precursor to the heroics of the 1962-63 season.

Led once more by the towering figure of Eddie Reynolds, the Dons beat Colchester United 2-1 in the FA Cup – their first competitive win over a Football League side – and secured the Isthmian League title again, but it was in the FA Amateur Cup that history beckoned. Victories over Southall, Chesham United, Barnet, Bishop's Stortford and Leytonstone took the Dons to a Wembley showdown with Sutton United in which Reynolds scored four goals – all with his head – as Wimbledon triumphed 4-2.

In 1964 the Dons won the title again. The end of that season would also mark the debut of Ian Cooke, whose roles on and off the pitch would prove to be hugely important over the next five decades, but in 1964 all the action was taking place it off the pitch. Accusations of illegal payments to amateur players provoked an FA investigation across the game. Wimbledon refused to sign up to a new amateur code of conduct and, when Clacton Town resigned from the Southern League, the Dons, led by Sydney Black, took their place and turned professional.

It was a controversial move that angered a number of the club's traditionalists – but professionalism it was, and the early signs were promising. The Dons, aided by the finances of Black, won promotion from the Southern League's first division at the first attempt. In the next five years they finished in the top five of the premier division each year, coming closest to the title in 1968 when they narrowly missed out to Chelmsford City – a scenario that would repeat itself nearly 40 years later. In the close season, a young 18-year-old goalkeeper signed for the Dons. His name was Dickie Guy and, many years later, he would become AFC Wimbledon's first life president.

But change was once more on the way. Black died in April 1968 and, despite leaving a legacy to the club – notably, a clause that Plough Lane could only ever be used for sporting purposes – his absence left a huge hole. The Board was restless, and manager Les Henley was to pay the price. He had been at the helm for 15 years and, despite taking the club to their first professional trophy win in 1970, with a 3-0 victory over Romford in the Southern League Cup final, he was sacked halfway through the following season. At the time the Dons were still in with a chance of winning the league, in the last 16 of the FA Trophy and still in the Southern League Cup.

Wimbledon appointed Mike Everitt as Henley's replacement. Home form remained good for the next two seasons, but away from Plough Lane the Dons were appalling and mid-table finishes became the norm. Off the pitch, Bernie Coleman became the majority shareholder. The Dons' 12th-place finish in 1973 was their lowest since 1964 – but strangely that did not deter Brentford who, just before the start of the 1973-74 season, poached Everitt as their new manager.

In came ex-Colchester manager Dick Graham, and if anything he was even worse than Everitt. By the end of March the Dons were one point above the relegation zone,

1952 Wimbledon in action against Walthamstow Avenue at Plough Lane in the FA Amateur Cup (Getty Images)

1959 New Wimbledon manager Les Henley takes training (WISA)

1960 England amatuer internationals
Brian Martin, Roy Law, John Martin pose
at Plough Lane (John Martin)

1963 Eddie Reynolds (behind the post) scores against Sutton in the FA Amateur Cup final (Getty Images)

1963 The victorious Wimbledon side with the FA Amateur Cup in the changing rooms at Wembley (W A Meredith)

and Graham resigned. Trainer Danny Keenan aided by the club's senior professionals took temporary charge and stopped the slide before it was too late, but the club was now in dire trouble – both on and off the pitch.

In May 1974 the club was threatened by closure, and only a £2,500 donation from the Supporters' Club kept Wimbledon alive. It would not be the first time that Dons fans would come to the club's rescue. Meanwhile, after a mess-up with registration forms, the club now had only seven players on its books. The prospects could not have been bleaker.

So God knows quite what persuaded Allen Batsford, boss of Walton & Hersham, to apply for the managerial vacancy. Batsford had led his side to the Amateur Cup in 1973 and a famous FA Cup victory over Brian Clough's Brighton. But apply he did, and the next four years were one of the club's most successful periods. Batsford blended the seven remaining Wimbledon players, led by Ian Cooke and Dickie Guy, with seven of his old Walton & Hersham side headed by Dave Bassett.

In Batsford's first season the Dons secured the Southern League title for the first time. But they were to etch their names in history in the FA Cup. A Mick Mahon goal at Turf Moor against Burnley saw the Dons become the first non-league side in the modern era to win away at a top-flight side. In the next round, a Dickie Guy penalty save enabled Wimbledon to hold that year's European Cup finalists Leeds United to a goalless draw at Elland Road. Only a late Dave Bassett own goal separated the two sides in the replay.

The Dons retained the league title in 1976, a season that saw the debut of a raw 18-year-old Terry Eames who, a quarter of a century later, would become AFC Wimbledon's first manager. Wimbledon won a third successive Southern League title in 1977, and again the FA Cup provided another highpoint. The Dons held First Division Middlesbrough 0-0 at Plough Lane before losing 1-0 in the replay.

With the Dons now claiming to be the nation's top non-league side, the real battles were happening off the pitch. These were the days before direct promotion from the non-league ranks to the Football League. To join the elite 92 you needed to persuade the existing League members to vote you in. The Dons had chanced their arm in the re-election wheel of fortune in 1975 and 1976 and had got royally stuffed both times, getting four and three votes respectively. Tactics needed to change. In 1977 the Dons would be up against Halifax, Southport, Hartlepool and Workington, the sides that had finished in the bottom four of the Football League, and Altrincham from the Northern Premier League.

Bernie Coleman called on local businessman Ron Noades to help. Noades took up the challenge and soon became the new chairman. He created a new committee. One of the committee members – a certain Richard Faulkner – later became a Lord and, in 2002, would make an emotional speech at the launch of the Dons Trust. England cricket captain Tony Greig was also recruited, and the "Dons 4 Div 4" campaign was born. The committee began an extensive lobbying process. However, the strength of the campaign came from the supporters. Noades politicised them, mobilised them and utilised them to their full potential. The fans phoned and wrote to the decision-makers. They turned it into a media crusade and gathered support from all corners. Wimbledon's election to the Football League was becoming a matter of delivering justice.

On 17 June 1977, the Football League's member clubs gathered for the AGM at the Café Royal in central London. The Wimbledon delegation waited anxiously outside.

1970 Wimbledon pose with the Southern League Cup (John Martin)

1975 Dickie Guy, Mick Mahon and Ian Cooke celebrate victory at Burnley in the FA Cup (Paul Willatts)

1977 England cricket captain Tony Greig (second left) lends his support to the Dons 4 Div 4 campaign in April (Paul Willatts)

1978 Wimbledon manager Allen Batsford (Walton times)

1979 New Wimbledon signing Alan Cork with Wimbledon manager Dario Gradi (Getty Images)

Burnley chairman Bob Lord made a key speech. He concluded with the words: "Workington have had their chance, they have finished bottom enough times. It's time to give this lot a go." Then came the vote. The result: Altrincham 12, Halifax 44, Hartlepool 43, Southport 37, Wimbledon 27, Workington 21. Wimbledon were in the Football League.

For the football club it was momentous, but for the supporters it would be far more significant. What Ron Noades had managed to do for the first time was to turn the Dons fans in to an effective campaigning and lobbying force. It was that experience that would provide the perfect grounding for some of the tougher battles that lay ahead.

On the pitch, manager Allen Batsford wasn't sure whether the club was ready for the step up, and on a personal level he was right. After a disastrous start, in January 1978 he was sacked and Dario Gradi put in charge. The slide was halted, but Gradi's reign was one of ups and downs. The club was promoted in 1979 and relegated in 1980. However, he also oversaw the arrival of several legends. It was he who introduced the club's successful youth system that would produce the likes of Glyn Hodges and Andy Thorn. And it was he who signed Alan Cork in 1979 and Dave Beasant a year later.

Meanwhile, Ron Noades was looking at some other options. In the days before restrictions on how many clubs one person could own, Noades brought Milton Keynes City for £1 in 1980. Existing Wimbledon directors Jimmy Rose, Bernie Coleman and Sam Hammam were all appointed advisory members of Milton Keynes City's board, and rumours were growing that the Dons would be relocated to Buckinghamshire. That time it came to nothing, but Noades continued to look. And it wasn't long before he found a new target – Crystal Palace. Noades bought the club, and instantly a merger was on the cards.

Dons fans were incensed, and with the campaigning zeal developed in the battle to get the club in to the Football League, once more they stepped into the breach. This time their wrath was directed at the club's owners. The Batsford Arms, the bar located under the South Stand at Plough Lane, became the centre of the organised protests. The core group of protesters, now AFC Wimbledon regulars known collectively as the Batsford Boys, included a certain Ivor Heller, one of AFC Wimbledon's founders.

The key meeting was on 2 February 1981 at the Nelson's night club – another of Plough Lane's rowdy haunts. Chris Wright of the Palace Action Campaign addressed the audience, along with Eric Willcocks, the club's travel secretary. The fans decided to organise an "Each One, Reach One" campaign to get as many people as possible to demonstrate their discontent with Noades' proposals at the next match. And later that month the two clubs organised a joint coach trip to Solihull to lobby a meeting of Football League chairmen.

The fans' pressure paid off, and the League ruled for the first time that no individual could own two Football League clubs. Noades sold his shares in Wimbledon to Joe McElligott, who was to become club chairman. Noades still hoped that the Dons would agree to a groundshare agreement with Crystal Palace, but the new Wimbledon Board vetoed the plan, and shortly afterwards Sam Hammam paid £40,000 to discreetly became the club's new major shareholder. The fans had won – but at a cost. Noades persuaded Dario Gradi to take over at Crystal Palace, and the Dons were once more without a manager.

1980 Dave Beasant gets treatment from physio Owen Harris (Paul Willatts)

DON'T BURY THE DONS AT 'SEL HEARSE' PA

RN DAMP-PROOFING SERVICES

643-7260 and 01-661-9060

1981 Wimbledon fans stage an anti-merger protest at Plough Lane (Paul Willatts)

Up stepped assistant manager Dave Bassett. It would be the start of a beautiful relationship. Bassett guided the club to promotion in his first full season and, although another immediate relegation followed, this time it was only by a matter of goal difference. Gradi's youth products were becoming the mainstay of Bassett's new team and, coupled with a unique spirit epitomised by the likes of Wally Downes, Alan Cork, Mark Morris, Kevin Gage and Steve Galliers – all of whom would go on to play in the top flight – Wimbledon were on the rise. The 1983 Fourth Division title was secured with a record points total. A year later, the Dons would once more leave the Third Division at the first attempt, but this time as runners-up to champions Oxford United.

It was at about this time that Daily Mirror journalist Tony Stenson described the Dons as "The Crazy Gang" – a label that would stick. Glyn Hodges became the club's first full international, representing Wales against Norway in June 1984. Nigel Winterburn would win the club's Player of the Year award, a feat he would repeat in each of the next two seasons, by which time the Dons were in the First Division. They had made the transition from non-league football to the top flight. It only took nine years.

Wimbledon secured promotion to the First Division with a 1-0 win over Huddersfield, courtesy of a free-kick from Lawrie Sanchez. And then, in September 1986, came the seemingly impossible: Wimbledon beat Charlton Athletic 1-0 and went top of the League. A week earlier, Glyn Hodges and Alan Cork had both found the net, completing a remarkable record of having scored in each of the nation's top four divisions.

Bassett would guide the club to sixth in that first season in the top flight. In his last 12 months in charge, he also signed two players who would come to epitomise Wimbledon: John Fashanu and Vinnie Jones. The Dons, widely tipped as cannon fodder for the nation's elite sides, would record victories at Old Trafford, Anfield and Stamford Bridge. And the action off the pitch was just as dramatic. By the end of the season the Bassett era was over. One row too many with Sam Hammam, and "Harry" was off to take over at Watford. But it wasn't just the managerial staff Hammam was upsetting.

Midway through that season, Hammam revived the idea of a merger from earlier in the decade and revealed his desire to "marry" Wimbledon to Crystal Palace and create a new super-club called Wimbledon Palace or South London United. Again, the Dons fans took up arms. The pinnacle of their protest came before the fifth-round FA Cup tie against Everton. It was Wimbledon's first match to be televised live, and Plough Lane was awash with banners opposing the move. Instrumental in the fans' fight-back was Peter Miller, deputy news editor of the Sunday Mirror who would later become a club director. He persuaded the fans to get organised, and that led to the formation of the Save Wimbledon Action Group – a direct forerunner of the Wimbledon Independent Supporters Association.

A small group of passionate fans orchestrated the campaign – Laurence Lowne, Dennis Lowndes, Richard Faulkner, Paul Willatts and David Lloyd. They set about looking into four key areas: ownership, fan liaison, lobbying and public relations. They produced a regular matchday pamphlet opposing the official club line. It kept asking two key questions: "Where is your evidence that Palace will rally to support this new club? Where is your approval from the football authorities?"

The SWAG campaign lasted for six months. Hammam could have easily ignored the fans but, with the power of the media against him, he eventually buckled. One day he called Laurence Lowne's father, Alf, a veteran of all the great Wimbledon supporters' campaigns. He invited Alf and David Lloyd to his offices in Mayfair. He said he regretted deeply what he had done and admitted he had been naïve. He hadn't fully appreciated the passion of the supporters and the importance that a sense of community plays in a local football team.

Hammam admitted that the fans' campaign had been effective and that he no longer wanted to fight them. "If you really want to campaign," he said, "help me get planning permission for a new ground at Wandle Valley and I will drop the Palace thing." He unveiled a plan for a multi-sports facility with a sliding roof and an artificial pitch near to Plough Lane. He spoke of hosting rock concerts and boxing matches. He believed there was a real desire for such a venue in South-West London. But he wanted an outside developer to help, and that would make Wimbledon tenants in their own stadium.

Two things effectively scuppered the Wandle Valley move. The first was the Football League's decision later that year to ban artificial pitches. The second was Hammam himself. David Lloyd set up a meeting with Hammam and a Mecca Leisure director. In David Lloyd's own words, Hammam was a disaster. "He ranted about the Council and about how they had betrayed the club, when all he needed to do was show them the plans he had shown us and give Mecca the chance to take it all in," Lloyd recalled. The plan died shortly after.

Back on the pitch, Wimbledon were on the brink of their greatest success. Bassett had been replaced by ex-Bristol Rovers manager Bobby Gould, whose first move was among his most significant: he persuaded Don Howe to become the club's coach. With most of the defence departing – Nigel Winterburn joining Arsenal for £400,000 and Mark Morris following Bassett to Watford – Gould brought in a new back four: Clive Goodyear, John Scales, Eric Young and Terry Phelan. All four were plucked from lower leagues, and the last three would become internationals. Up front, Terry Gibson arrived from Manchester United.

Gould and Howe blended the old and new perfectly. A 4-1 win over West Bromwich Albion in the third round of the FA Cup was followed by a 2-1 win at Mansfield and a 3-1 win at Newcastle. That gave the Dons a quarter-final tie against Watford at Plough Lane. Brian Gayle was sent off in the first half, and Watford went in one up. Then an inspired substitution produced a remarkable turnaround. Eric Young came on and made an immediate impact, heading an equaliser within four minutes of the restart. John Fashanu completed the comeback with a 73rd-minute winner.

In the semi-finals the Dons were pitched against fellow top-flight minnows Luton Town (who they would meet 21 years later in the Conference) at White Hart Lane. The Hatters took the lead through future Wimbledon player Mick Harford. John Fashanu brought the scores level from the penalty spot in the second half, before Dennis Wise's late lunge secured the Dons' place in the FA Cup final against "The Team of the Decade", Liverpool. The Dons, 4-1 outsiders, were given the longest odds to win the Cup in living memory.

Within 10 seconds of the kick-off at Wembley, the Dons stamped their authority on the match with Vinnie Jones' crunching tackle on Steve McMahon. Peter Beardsley had the ball in the net for the champions on 30 minutes, but his effort was chalked off for an earlier foul by Andy Thorn. Then came the moment. Terry Phelan won a free-kick on the left, Dennis Wise swung it in, Lawrie Sanchez got a touch and

1988 Dave Beasant dives to his left to deny Liverpool's John Aldridge in the FA Cup final (Getty Images)

1988 Dave Beasant saves John Aldridge's penalty in the FA Cup final (David McKnight)

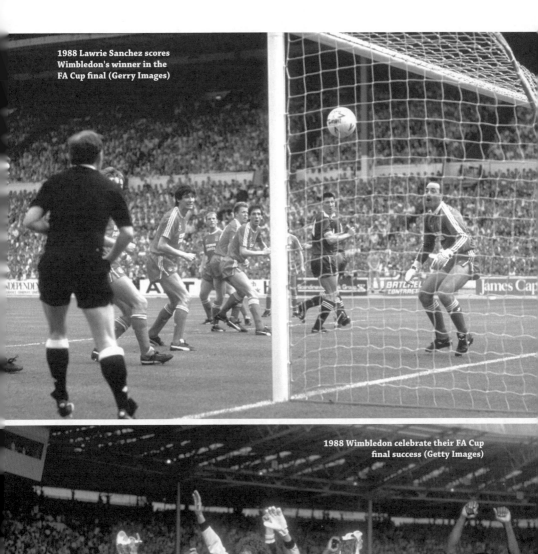

1988 Lawrie Sanchez scores
Wimbledon's winner in the
FA Cup final (Gerry Images)

1988 Wimbledon celebrate their FA Cup
final success (Getty Images)

1989 John Fashanu becomes Wimbledon's
first full England international against
Chile (Getty Images)

Bruce Grobbelaar was left stranded. The Dons, the massive underdogs, had taken the lead.

Liverpool poured forward in the second half, but Wimbledon's defence were a match for everything the Reds could throw at them. Liverpool had the chance to equalise when an outstretched leg from Clive Goodyear brought down John Aldridge. It had seemed a fair challenge, but referee Brian Hill disagreed and awarded a penalty. Dave Beasant had done his homework and guessed right. He saved it – and 23 years later he would be offering advice on penalties to AFC Wimbledon's Seb Brown.

Half an hour later the match was over. In the immortal words of John Motson, "The Crazy Gang had beaten the Culture Club" and captain Beasant was climbing the steps to collect the trophy from Princess Diana. Wimbledon had become only the second club in history to lift both the FA Amateur Cup and FA Cup. Old Carthusians were the first, but that was 94 years earlier. Motson added that "It's a Weird and Wonderful World if you come from Wimbledon." That phrase would become the name of one of the club's most popular websites.

In the months following the final, Dave Beasant and Andy Thorn left the club to join Newcastle. A year later, John Fashanu became the club's first full England international in the scoreless draw against Chile at Wembley – and in the meantime Wimbledon had cemented their place among the nation's top football sides, finishing 12th in 1989 and 8th in 1990. But all the significant action was happening off the pitch.

Bobby Gould refused to extend his contract beyond December 1990 and parted company with the club in the close season. Ray Harford, his assistant, stepped into the breach. The issue of Plough Lane would not go away. Sydney Black had inserted a pre-emption clause stipulating that the ground could be used only for sports, leisure or recreational purposes. He had also inserted a clause that allowed Merton Council to buy the site back for £8,000 if the club went into liquidation.

That clause infuriated Sam Hammam. It stopped him from borrowing money to redevelop the ground which, he insisted, had become an urgent necessity in the light of the Taylor Report and the need for all-seater stadiums. In the summer of 1990 he discreetly approached Geoffrey Smith, Leader of Merton Council, to have the clause removed. According to which report you believe, removing the clause cost Hammam between £300,000 and £800,000. Within a year, Wimbledon would be playing their final game at Plough Lane. The Dons would move to Selhurst Park to groundshare with Crystal Palace.

Hammam announced the decision in the final programme of the 1990-91 season – the opponents that day, ironically, Palace. He had learnt from previous experiences – this time, the move was done and dusted before the fans could do anything about it. He tried to sweeten the pill by insisting that the move was only "temporary". A few years later, Hammam would move the ownership of Plough Lane from Wimbledon Football Club to another company, Rudgwick Ltd, whose directors were Sam and his brother Ned. Wimbledon's youth and reserve sides would continue to use Plough Lane for another seven years, but the new company would charge Wimbledon £50,000 annual rent to use the stadium.

In the final season at Plough Lane, Harford had guided the side to seventh in the table. In preparation for a new start at Selhurst Park, Keith Curle was sold for £2.5m and Robbie Earle signed for £775,000 from Port Vale. Then, in October, came another bombshell: Ray Harford was off to become Kenny Dalglish's assistant at Blackburn.

1993 Everton celebrate their
controversial victory over
Wimbledon (Getty Images)

In the confusion that followed, Don Howe also left – and Wimbledon were suddenly in crisis. The club were seventh at the time.

Joe Kinnear, who was managing the Dons reserves, had seemed the obvious replacement, but instead Hammam turned to the untried former Aston Villa player Peter Withe. The appointment proved nothing short of disastrous. Under Withe, Wimbledon would win just once in 17 games. The final nail in the coffin came with a home defeat to Chelsea, who included ex-Dons Vinnie Jones and Dennis Wise in their starting XI.

Hammam finally appointed Kinnear, and the effect was almost instantaneous, the Dons recovering to finish 13th. The next season they finished one place better, condemning landlords Crystal Palace to relegation in the process with a memorable 4-0 win. The 1993-94 season is remembered as one of the club's finest – they finished sixth, with excellent victories over Liverpool on penalties in the Coca-Cola Cup and a stunning 4-1 win over league leaders Blackburn. But instead it would be marred by allegations of match-fixing.

John Fashanu and goalkeeper Hans Segers would later face charges; both were cleared. At the centre of the allegations was the final match of the season, at Everton. Anything but victory would condemn the hosts to relegation. The Dons roared into a 2-0 lead – and then the controversy began. Everton were awarded a penalty by referee Robbie Hart after Anders Limpar tumbled in the box under pressure from Peter Fear despite the absence of any noticeable contact. The penalty was converted: 2-1.

After the break, Graham Stuart appeared to handle on the line, but Hart waved away the Dons' protests. Barry Horne then rifled home an effort from all of 30 yards to bring the scores level. Then, Stuart collected the ball outside the box and hit what was, at best, a lethargic shot goalbound. Segers, who at the time was renowned as an excellent shot-stopper, inexplicably dived over the ball – and Everton had their winner. The whiff of match-fixing would hang over Segers and Fashanu for the rest of their careers. Fashanu was sold in pre-season to Aston Villa for £1.3m, and the following season the Dons finished ninth.

It was during that year that the Wimbledon Independent Supporters Association was formed by Steve Elson, Marc Jones, Laurence Lowne, Xavier Wiggins and Lee Willett. The quintet had become dissatisfied with the official Wimbledon Supporters Club's inability to push the club more on a move back to the London Borough of Merton. WISA would become hugely influential in the years that followed.

In 1995-96, the Dons finished 14th – their lowest ever placing in the top flight. And after three straight defeats the following season, the first of which had seen David Beckham score from the halfway line, the doom merchants began to mutter. What followed proved them to be wrong – very wrong. After seven straight wins the Dons found themselves top of the Premier League for the first time in 10 years. By Christmas, they had gone 18 games unbeaten and were trailing league leaders Aston Villa by just five points, with three games in hand.

The papers began to talk of a treble. In the FA Cup the Dons dispatched Manchester United, thanks to a last-minute equaliser at Old Trafford by Robbie Earle and a winner by Marcus Gayle in the replay. In the Coca-Cola Cup, victories over Bolton and Sheffield Wednesday took the Dons to the semi-finals. Wembley surely beckoned.

Leicester, in the Coca-Cola Cup, were first up. A 0-0 draw in the first leg at Filbert Street put the Dons in the driving seat. Marcus Gayle gave Wimbledon the lead, but Simon Grayson gave Leicester the vital away goal. Robbie Earle and Efan Ekoku both had late efforts cleared off the line – Wimbledon had fallen at the penultimate hurdle. The FA Cup semi-final against Chelsea at Highbury proved one-sided, and the dispirited Dons were humbled 3-0. A season that had promised so much petered out with Wimbledon finishing in eighth place.

But it was on the strength of that early-season form that Sam Hammam persuaded two Norwegian businessmen, Kjell Inge Røkke and Bjørn Rune Gjelsten, to pay a reported £28 million for an 80 per cent stake in the club. And serious rumours began to surface for the first time of a major relocation. Hull, Basingstoke and Cardiff were all mooted. But it was a proposed move to Dublin that sounded the most ominous.

The news broke in December 1997. It had the backing of Sam Hammam, Joe Kinnear, the new owners, leading Irish politicians, U2 manager Paul McGuinness and Irish property developer Owen O'Callaghan. The Saturday after the news broke – the day of a home game against Southampton – the Wimbledon stands were awash with banners, and chants of "We'll never go to Dublin" echoed round the ground. In the weeks that followed Dons fans, led by WISA, encouraged UEFA, the FA and the Football Association of Ireland to ask serious questions. The FAI were first out of the blocks to oppose the move, and the proposal was finally kicked into the long grass when a plan to build a casino on the proposed new stadium site was rejected.

The Dons finished 15th in 1997-98. And that summer Wimbledon regulars Robbie Earle (Jamaica) and Brian McAllister and Neil Sullivan (Scotland) graced the World Cup finals in France. Robbie would score the Caribbean island's first ever goal at the finals in their 3-1 defeat to Croatia.

Off the pitch, Hammam finally sold Plough Lane to Safeway Stores for a cool £8m.

1997 Robbie Earle celebrates his late equaliser at Old Trafford in the Dons' FA Cup tie against Manchester United (Getty Images)

1997 Wimbledon fans welcome the Norwegian take over (Getty Images)

1998 Robbie Earle scores Jamaica's first ever World Cup goal with a header against Croatia at France 98 (Getty Images)

2000 John Hartson celebrates his late equaliser against Aston Villa (Getty Images)

In just over 15 years, he had made a reported £36m out of Wimbledon from his initial investment of just £40,000. By this time Wimbledon itself was a subsidiary of another Hammam company, Blantyre Venture Ltd, registered in the Virgin Islands.

The following season began well. The Dons reached the semi-finals of the League Cup once again, this time losing 2-1 to eventual winners Tottenham. By March, Wimbledon lay in sixth place and were eyeing up a possible UEFA Cup spot. Then came the trip to Sheffield Wednesday. Wimbledon won 2-1, but Joe Kinnear suffered a heart attack during the match. The shock echoed through the club; Joe would never sit in the Wimbledon dugout again. The Dons failed to win any of their last 11 games and only narrowly avoided relegation.

Terry Burton, who had been Joe's assistant a couple of years earlier, was now in charge of the club's Academy and would have been the natural replacement. Instead, the new Norwegian owners took the opportunity to appoint one of their own. In came welly-wearing former Norwegian national coach Egil Olsen. Out went half the team, and in came a bunch of Norwegians. The famous Wimbledon spirit was wiped away. The history and traditions of the club were being sidelined.

Chris Perry, one of the players to leave, recalled Olsen's first speech: "It wasn't the kind of speech we were used to hearing. There was none of the banter and the passion. I looked around and I knew it was time to leave." Injuries didn't help, either. Record signing John Hartson, a £7m capture from West Ham, could barely manage two games in a row; a serious internal injury ended Robbie Earle's playing career; and Ben Thatcher, a mainstay of the defence, broke his ankle and missed all but the last couple of games.

The Dons' slide began just after Christmas. With just three games to go, Olsen was replaced by Terry Burton – but of course it was too late. A defeat against fellow-strugglers Bradford was followed by a dramatic draw with Aston Villa, leaving the Dons needing only to match Bradford's result on the final day of the season to stay up. But they lost 2-0 at Southampton, while Bradford beat Liverpool, who were chasing a Champions League place, 1-0 at home. After 14 years in the top flight, Wimbledon were down. That summer, Hammam sold his remaining interest in the club. He would take over Cardiff City later that year.

With Hammam gone, South African Charles Koppel was appointed as the club's new chairman. Addressing Dons fans at a pre-season friendly, Koppel promised an immediate return to the Premier League under the stewardship of Terry Burton. The promise failed to materialise as Burton fought unsuccessfully to keep hold of his star players and bed in the latest batch of promising youngsters from the club's Academy. Faint hopes of a play-off place were extinguished at champions-elect Fulham when a controversial last-minute penalty denied the Dons the victory they needed. Hope had finally gone. But the true battle was just about to begin. The ugly spectre of Milton Keynes was about to raise its head once again.

2000 Mick Harford (right) consoles Wimbledon goalkeeper Neil Sullivan after the Dons are relegated (Getty Images)

2000 Distraught Wimbledon fans react to relegation at Southampton (Getty Images)

Chapter Two:

It might as well be Oslo

Koppel, Winkelman and the spectre of MK

In the summer of 2001, feverish activities had begun behind the scenes at Wimbledon FC. The players and managers were kept in the dark. The constant visits of Milton Keynes magnate Peter Winkelman were the only hints of what was to happen. And then came the bombshell...

July 2001
By Terry Burton (Wimbledon FC manager)

The Norwegians had bought Wimbledon FC from Sam Hammam a year earlier, and they had ambitions – there was no doubting that.

I remember going with the chief executive, David Barnard, to their apartment in Norway. There they were discussing their vision for the club. It was all about a culture change. The Milton Keynes thing wasn't on the table at first.

"Can we turn Wimbledon from this Raggedy-arse Rovers team into something more professional?" They talked about setting up a partnership with Ajax. They were looking at new stadiums. But back then they didn't say it was going to be in Kingstonian or somewhere round the M25 – it was just that they wanted a new stadium. But of course they also needed to sell players and they needed to reduce the wage bill.

I was relatively new in the job and players were going out. We'd been relegated from the Premier League in 2000 and this was the start of my second year in charge. The Thatchers, Corts and Euells were all being sold. There was money coming back in and we were trying to invest some of that. It was a tough start for a novice manager going into that situation. It was a bit like the blind leading the blind.

Meanwhile, Winkelman had begun to hang around Selhurst. Then there was the meeting. The whole idea was laid out – the club was going to Milton Keynes. My response was that this was a bit like the Dublin thing, only less romantic.

Dublin had surfaced when I was Joe Kinnear's assistant back in the late Nineties. It was a bit like a fairy tale, a fantasy. Nobody really thought it would come off. But if it did, we'd go along with it. We were football people: we did what we were told.

It was something that was really high in Sam Hammam's thoughts. He was the owner back then. Sam wanted Wimbledon to be challenging for major honours and the only way he could see to do that was to make it a bigger club with a bigger fanbase. He thought Dublin was the answer as they didn't have a football club. But he never really sat down and discussed it with us at any great length. Sam sold his controlling stake to the Norwegians shortly after.

And it was the same thought process that inspired the Norwegians to look at Milton Keynes. Sitting in that meeting in Norway, I thought: "I've heard all this before. This doesn't happen in football, does it? People don't take clubs from where they are supposed to be and move them miles away. This won't ever happen."

I knew all the stuff was going on, but to start with I felt I couldn't influence it or affect it. At that same time, I couldn't put my hand on my heart and say that the new club chairman Charles Koppel was supportive of me, but I didn't really care. On the pitch, I was going to do it how I wanted to.

Charles Koppel reminded me of a salesman. He had this product that he didn't really know anything about, but he was enthusiastic about it and he was going to try and sell it. He didn't really know the ins and outs of the product and he didn't really know the ins and outs of a football club and what made a football club tick.

And like a salesman, he could tell you something which, when you actually read the small print, turned out not to be true.

Bringing back the heroes

The rumours had been rife before the announcement became a reality. The fans moved quickly to ensure that history would be on their side.

Since the Norwegians had taken over the club, Wimbledon FC had become more focused on financial deals and opportunities. The history of the club and its supporters had become sidelined. The fans, in the guise of the Wimbledon Independent Supporters Association, moved into the void. The reclaiming of the club's history by its supporters would become a key part of the battle that was to dominate the next 10 years.

---

26 July 2001
Allen Batsford Testimonial Dinner
By Steve Elson (Wimbledon fan)

By far my proudest act as a Wimbledon fan was being the lead organiser of the Allen Batsford Testimonial Dinner in 2001. Of course, I didn't organise it on my own. People like Sandra Lowne, Laurence Lowne, Marc Jones, Ivor Heller and Chris Phillips played a big part in the evening's success.

I took the idea to the WISA committee after meeting Allen Batsford. Allen had a fascinating story to tell and revealed that he had been promised a testimonial match by Ron Noades that never happened. This seemed like a perfect event for WISA to organise to show that we were more than a protest group. WISA agreed, so off I went.

Eventually we managed to find a venue – the David Lloyd Centre – and I began contacting former players. Once they got over a little distrust of my motives I ended up with people like Dave Bassett, Dickie Guy and Ian Cooke involved. Former club owner Bernie Coleman took a table, and eventually Wimbledon FC took two tables and promised that current players would attend. To be fair, Neal Ardley and Mark Williams did attend and were great value. But the real stars were Allen and the former players. Dickie Guy couldn't make it, but Wally Downes, Keiron Somers, John Leslie, Terry Eames and Billy Edwards did.

In the build-up to the dinner, Marc and I had visited Dickie Guy at home to tell him what we were about. We ended up sitting on Dickie Guy's sofa, watching Dickie Guy's video of the Leeds game, seeing Dickie Guy saving Peter Lorimer's penalty and drinking Dickie Guy's beer – one of those moments that Wimbledon fans of a certain age dream about.

Bassett and Cooke made entertaining and probably slanderous speeches at the dinner before Allen spoke in his own quiet but authoritative manner. Including proceeds from an auction and raffle held that evening, Kris Stewart, the chair of WISA, was able to hand Allen a cheque for £5,000.

More important than the money, though, was bringing people like Allen, Dickie and Ian back into the club. Sam Hammam had sidelined most of our former heroes, even when they had wanted to carry on supporting the club that they had represented so excellently. That night, WISA took the first steps towards bringing them home.

The announcement

Most people had dismissed the rumours linking the club to a move to Milton Keynes. The proposed move to Dublin had been defeated, and this seemed the latest silly scheme to come out of the Wimbledon boardroom. But on 2 August 2001 it became reality. That day, every Wimbledon season-ticket holder and club member received a letter stating simply that the club was going to relocate to Milton Keynes. The club's unofficial websites went into overdrive, and in the months that followed the supporters fought their hardest to oppose the move.

---

1 August 2001
Jay Jays, Wimbledon Broadway
By Kris Stewart (chair of WISA)

The Wimbledon Independent Supporters Association had been told a few times in the weeks beforehand what was coming. We had got leaks from journalists in Milton Keynes and we had been given information from a good source that confirmed it.

We knew to expect an announcement. But we couldn't get anything on record. We wanted someone we could quote, someone who could say that it was happening. We didn't want to jump up and down without any evidence.

We were ready for it. But that didn't take away any of the shock when it appeared in black and white – a letter from club chairman Charles Koppel saying that the club had to move to Milton Keynes to survive.

I remember feeling really sick. I have been politically active, and I didn't have a very high opinion of people like Charles Koppel. Even with all that, I still find myself getting caught out by how appalling people can actually be. There are still some things that make me think: "Bloody hell – I wasn't expecting that!" And moving to Milton Keynes was one of those.

WISA were meeting almost daily then. The whole committee was unanimous in its opposition. I remember the meeting the day before the announcement. I was there with Nicole Hammond, Lee Willett, Laurence Lowne and Kevin Rye in a bar called Jay Jays next to Wimbledon Theatre. There was no doubt whatsoever what was coming – we just sat there and tried to work out how to counter it.

From a purely tactical point of view, the timing of the decision had given us a great opportunity. The Nationwide League started a whole week before the Premiership, so for a week the First Division would be the focus in all the papers. If the decision had been delayed a week or two, we would never have got the coverage that we did.

In Jay Jays, we were all suggesting ideas. Not so much the technicalities, exactly, but general themes. We agreed that protesting at games was a must and that we needed as much publicity as we could get. But there was also the importance of talking to the football authorities.

The first time the idea of moving to Milton Keynes surfaced as a rumour, we spoke to the Football League; that had been back in January 2001. The League pointed us to their rules, and the implication was that the move couldn't happen.

We had also held meetings with David Barnard, the former chief executive of Wimbledon, and the new owner, Bjørn Gjelsten. They said they hadn't done anything about a football ground, but added that lots of people had come to them. And that's when Bjørn said: "If it is Milton Keynes, it might as well be Oslo."

All the way through we had a number of formal meetings, and all the way through they had been refusing to rule out Milton Keynes. It was impossible to work out whether they were denying it because it was ludicrous or because they were working on it.

In the past there had been rumours linking us to Hull or Basingstoke, and this just seemed to be the latest mad idea, so we didn't really take it all that seriously at first. But slowly it began to dawn on us that this time it was for real.

I remember being late for work on the day of the announcement. A friend of mine had got the letter through from Koppel announcing the decision, and he read it to me over the phone at home while I typed it up and posted it on all the websites.

That day at work was spent mainly on the phone talking to the press and other members of the WISA committee, seeing what we could organise in time for the pre-season friendly against Brentford the following night. It wasn't much, really, but we did manage to persuade a lot of people to go.

The gates of Plough Lane after the stadium was demolished (Neil Presland)

Former Wimbledon owner Sam Hammam (Paul Willatts)

Protests at Brentford in 2001
(Rob Dunford)

The final split with Sam

The day after the move to Milton Keynes was announced, Wimbledon travelled to Brentford for a friendly. To the surprise of numerous Wimbledon fans, Sam Hammam was among the attendees. The fans believed that Hammam was responsible for the decision – after all, it was he who had sold the club to the Norwegians. Hammam's view was very different. So when he spoke to Wimbledon fans at a pub before the game, the confrontation became ugly. It was to sour his view of the fans forever.

3 August 2001
Brentford 0 Wimbledon 4 Friendly
By Sam Hammam (ex-owner of Wimbledon FC)

My treatment that night was very, very cruel. What was said about me then still hurts. At this moment it's all behind me and I have accepted it.

The influence was from negative people and not the silent majority. The negative people are the people who love Wimbledon, who love the club, but who see everything in black or dark grey. They dissipated their views and I was the easy target. They blamed me for the club's fall. That evening was the start of the split, and I found it very difficult.

I had been thrown out of the old Wimbledon, and that night I was thrown out by the new Wimbledon, the Wimbledon that was to become AFC Wimbledon.

I remain the father of Wimbledon and I wanted to be their hero. But sometimes your children hurt you, and that is the situation between me and the new Wimbledon. I feel bitter about it and I feel it was unfair. Would those supporters have dreamed, as non-league fans, that they would have all those memories of the Premiership?

I want AFC Wimbledon to be successful and to find a home in Merton. I have a lot of love and happiness for AFC Wimbledon. I am very positive about what they are doing and they are always welcome to talk to me.

People who love Wimbledon, love Wimbledon as long as it is in Wimbledon. I feel strongly about it too, very strongly.

I could see the split happening, and there is a part of me which is AFC Wimbledon. We are together in mind. AFC Wimbledon is part of my life, my history. Everything that is a fragmentation of the old Wimbledon is a part of me. I still feel it is mine even though it will never be again.

Black balloons

The first League game after the announcement was at home to Birmingham City. WISA wanted to make a visual impact – and ordered a thousand black balloons.

---

9 August 2001
Wimbledon 3 Birmingham City 1 Nationwide First Division
By Kris Stewart (chair of WISA)

We started really working hard. We started preparing stuff and talking to the Football League. Then there was the first League game and the black balloon protest. The idea of the black balloons had surfaced on the Weird and Wonderful World website. Balloons always seemed to be a good thing to do, but there was a feeling that it might be a bit tasteless. In the end it worked really well. The wind blew in the right direction, and the air was filled with black balloons.

Then there was the publicity side. Laurence Lowne and Kevin Rye were talking endlessly to the press. We had begun our battle to get our point of view across and get the media to realise that fans mattered.

By Terry Burton (Wimbledon FC manager)

You always hope when you get out on the pitch that you can still perform, irrespective of what's going on. But the whole atmosphere that day was wrong. I had never experienced anything like it before and I never have since.

We could understand the fans' frustrations, we really could, but it didn't help our cause – even though we knew it wasn't directed at the team or myself.

You only have to look at the stats. Our away form that season was fantastic. We beat the likes of Manchester City, we were exceptional away from home. It was promotion form. But at home our form was mid-table at best.

So I'm guessing that all those protests – at almost every home game – did filter down and have some effect.

The vote against and Richmond's error

In the middle of August, the plan to relocate to Milton Keynes seemed doomed when the Football League voted unanimously against it. The League's decision briefly lifted the spirits of Wimbledon fans everywhere. However, Football League Board member Geoffrey Richmond's public support for the fans would sadly prove to be costly.

---

16 August 2001
Football League Board meeting

By Kris Stewart (WISA chairman)

We'd got in touch with the Football League as soon as the rumours about Milton Keynes surfaced. They told us all about the rules – they told us that a club had to take a name from the area it was in, that it couldn't move more than 25 miles, and all that – way before the fateful letter from Charles Koppel hit the doormats.

The Football League kept saying to us that those were the rules. End of. So we knew what our arguments would be, but it didn't remove the shock of seeing Koppel's words in black and white.

When the letter arrived we went straight back to the Football League, and we got the same answer as before – rules were rules. But they added that there hadn't been any formal application to move the club.

We were in regular contact with David Burns, then chief executive of the Football League, and he invited me, Nicole Hammond and Lee Willett to go and see him a day or so before the Board meeting to discuss the move. It was just Burns and a legal advisor in the room at the Football League headquarters, which back then was at Lancaster Gate. He seemed like a nice chap; we would meet him time and time again that year.

He didn't say anything specifically, but the vibe from him was that he seemed fairly convinced that there wouldn't be a vote at that meeting. He seemed convinced that the Board would want to be seen to go through the process properly, that they would want to take their time and not rush into anything.

In the meantime, we had been encouraging people to hassle the individual members of the Football League Board, and it seemed to be working. We seemed to be winning the argument.

Geoffrey Richmond, the Bradford City chairman, had come out publicly against the decision. In response to the flood of letters from Wimbledon fans, he wrote: "I am fundamentally opposed to Milton Keynes. It is my belief that if Milton Keynes want a Football League side they should move up through the pyramid, and in exactly the same way as Wimbledon and others have done so in the past. Please rest assured therefore that my vote will be firmly against the Wimbledon proposal when the matter is discussed by the Football League Board."

In hindsight, perhaps he shouldn't have been so public – Koppel would later argue successfully that Richmond had prejudiced the hearing.

On the night of the actual meeting, I was at Ronan Warde's flat near Haydons Road in Wimbledon. And then Burns called. It was totally unexpected. He said: "Kris, are you sitting down? I have some news for you." And then came the bombshell. "There

Wimbledon fans release thousands of black balloons before the Birmingham City game in August 2001 (Neil Presland)

Dons fans gather at Plough Lane for the start of the Walk from Wimbledon (Neil Presland)

Kris Stewart
(Terry Buckman)

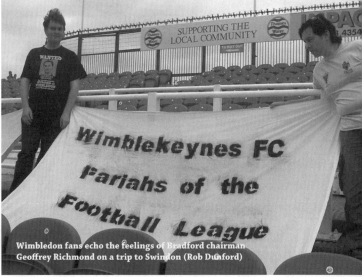

Wimbledon fans echo the feelings of Bradford chairman
Geoffrey Richmond on a trip to Swindon (Rob Dunford)

has been a vote. It was unanimously rejected."

I couldn't believe it. I wanted to know how real it was, how many people had been in the room and whether they had seen our point of view. Burns didn't expand too much. He just added: "That's the decision and that has been communicated to Wimbledon FC."

I think I got out the rum and coke, and then we went for a little celebration in Wetherspoons in Wimbledon.

The Football League statement released the next day said: "Following a long and detailed discussion the Board has concluded that the proposed move by Wimbledon Football Club to Milton Keynes cannot be sanctioned.

"League rules clearly state that clubs should play in the conurbation from which they derive their name or are traditionally associated, unless given the approval to do otherwise by the Board.

"To allow this move would have created a precedent at odds with the heritage of football in this country. Our football clubs are the heart and soul of their local communities and that is something that cannot be transferred from place to place.

"The Football League will now actively encourage Wimbledon Football Club to work in partnership with their supporters and with Merton Borough Council to find a long-term solution to their homelessness."

At the back of my mind, I couldn't help feeling surprised that it looked like it was over so quickly. Beforehand, David Burns had said we should not be hasty, because if we were we could get turned over. He wanted everything in a row – the belt and the braces. And this had all happened so quickly. Surely everything couldn't have been in place already? But that didn't matter, it looked like it was all over. We were happy that night.

Hindsight is a wonderful thing.

The walk from Wimbledon

Sadly, the Football League vote proved futile. The club pledged to battle on in their pursuit of a move to Milton Keynes. The disgust that the club had not even considered a new stadium at Plough Lane as a viable alternative to Milton Keynes was everywhere, and led WISA to organise a walk from the club's old ground to Selhurst Park before the home match with Norwich City. It was to mark 10 years since Wimbledon had last had a home game. Symbolism was thick in the air.

---

25 August 2001
From Plough Lane to Selhurst Park
By Steve Elson (Wimbledon fan)

Walking from Plough Lane to Selhurst Park was just one of those lightbulb ideas that seemed to make perfect sense. We needed something that was more than just a protest, and we were always looking for suitable gestures that would show our contempt for our misguided owners. The proposed walk would be a group effort, highly visible and very symbolic of our plight.

I took the idea to the WISA committee, who liked it. Lou Carton-Kelly agreed to help take it on – and probably wished she hadn't, as the execution of the idea involved a lot more work than I put into just having it. I think Lou had to talk to local councils and the police as well as organise a route and stewards.

I did do the walk, and thoroughly enjoyed it, especially as we approached the Thomas Farley (pub) and other Dons fans flooded out to greet us.

Looking back, it was another grand but ultimately empty gesture. But it was also important because it was another event that brought many Wimbledon fans together. Ultimately that growing collaboration was to play out in the shape of a resurrected football club.

By Lou Carton-Kelly (WISA vice-chair)

The events of August 2001 rocked me to the core. I had followed the Dons for 15 years, and now the club wanted to relocate to Milton Keynes. I was the vice-chair of the Wimbledon Independent Supporters Association at the time, and I was determined to do all I could to help stop the proposed move from happening.

The Walk for Wimbledon took place before the second "home" match of the season and highlighted our homeless plight – it was now 10 years since the Dons had left Plough Lane for Selhurst Park. The walk was a great success and an important milestone for WISA, and Steve Elson deserves a lot of credit for suggesting it.

For years it had been the same faces involved, and now suddenly there were hundreds of people all wanting to do their bit – all wanting to challenge the decision to relocate. We had to keep the momentum going, and we were looking for new avenues to explore. The week before we had organised a "Koppel Out" flypast at Vicarage Road, but this was even more visible.

Two Brentford fans turned up for the Walk for Wimbledon, complete in their colours. Luke Kirton was one of those fans; he was very supportive and advised us on the importance of the Trust movement. The WISA Committee decided that we ought to go and find out more for ourselves.

By Luke Kirton (Brentford Independent Association of Supporters Committee member)

At the time we were in a similar position to Wimbledon. Koppel was busy trying to rip Wimbledon up and take them to Milton Keynes, while our bloke, Ron Noades, was trying to take us to Woking. It was a similar fight.

We first really got in touch with Wimbledon fans at the Brentford Walk, a few months earlier. That went from Hounslow High Street to Griffin Park and a delegation from WISA came along. That's when I first met Lou Carton-Kelly, Simon Wheeler and Kris Stewart. But it was only when we went on the Walk for Wimbledon that we really started sharing ideas.

We had been really naïve at Brentford. We greeted Ron Noades as a hero. We ignored all his history – the threats he had made as owner of Wimbledon and Crystal Palace years before.

He came in as a rich individual and appointed himself as manager. So you knew he had a big ego. But he brought in quality coaches like Ray Lewington and Terry Bullivant. He broke the transfer record fee for a club in the Third Division, paying £750,000 for Herman Hreidarsson. And we used to sing: "He's got white hair, he's a millionaire, Ronnie, Ronnie Noades." We loved him. We had had such bad experiences

The Walk from Wimbledon snakes past the Thomas Farley pub (Neil Presland)

of our previous owner David Webb that anyone would have been welcomed. It later transpired, David Webb was making a percentage out of every player he sold, and had made a tidy profit out of asset-stripping the club. He had one saving grace – the protests against him led to the formation of BIAS and later the organisation would prove vital in the battle against Noades.

Ron wanted to play (computer game) Championship Manager for real, but without the financial risk. He used his various companies to loan money to the club when no one else would. At first, we couldn't see the wood for the trees, but the reality in our eyes was Noades was burdening the club with a generation's worth of debt.

At BIAS, we soon realised that the club was heading into a whole load of trouble. Even after Noades quit as manager, after a shocking defeat to Kingstonian in the FA Cup, the problems continued. There was the issue of the ground. He was talking about the need for a new stadium. He threatened the council continually about leaving the borough. And to be fair the council didn't really care at the time.

And we at BIAS were left fighting on several different fronts, so we effectively broke ourselves in two. We set up sub-groups, looking at governance and finances of the club, and another looking at the council and publicity. One half became the trust, and the other half morphed into the political movement ABeeC. Our trust was full of the lawyers and solicitors – all the clever people. They dealt with the constitution and the legal side of things, how they could make a club work. I was very much in the latter group with the political campaigners. But Brentford needed both halves. We needed to regain the political initiative and we needed to be in a place to take control of the club.

The whole idea of fan power was only just starting to come into play. There were a couple of supporters trusts scattered across the country. Supporters Direct, whose role was to encourage fan involvement in football, was still just a fledgling organisation trying to find its feet. So we were pretty much on our own at the start. It was a lot later that Supporters Direct came in and started to help us, but in August 2001 we already knew how important a trust was. So when it came to the Walk for Wimbledon, all of BIAS was espousing the virtues of the supporters' trust movement. It was a model that appealed to Wimbledon fans and two weeks later a number of the WISA committee went up to their first Supporters Direct conference.

The birth of Yellow and Blue

When Koppel's letter landed on fans' doormats, the websites went into over-drive. Everyone seemed determined to do something to help. Out of those days of despair, the first alternative matchday programme in Britain was born. It was to make its debut on the Walk from Wimbledon. It was full-colour and it contained everything you would expect in a programme – except that this one would have the voice of the fans at its heart.

---

25 August 2001
First Division Wimbledon 0 Norwich City 1
By Niall Couper (Yellow and Blue editor)

I was just an ordinary Wimbledon fan. I had got used to my seat at Selhurst Park. I was on vague nodding terms with the six or so supporters who sat around me. I was not part of any big group. I knew a few other faces from the old days at Plough Lane, but that was it. I was there because I had always been there.

And then came the news that Charles Koppel wanted to move the club to Milton Keynes. It totally destroyed me. I was devastated. I wasn't a member of WISA. I didn't know what to do. I hadn't even been that involved with the protests against the proposed merger with Crystal Palace in 1987 or moving away from Plough Lane in 1991. Both times I was too young to really understand the significance of it all.

But by 2001 I had grown up. I understood what it meant – and I was furious. What I didn't understand was how they could take away my club. I didn't understand the logic of it all. Surely the example of Charlton, who had successfully returned to the Valley after their own exile at Selhurst Park, proved that if there was the will, a return to Wimbledon could be achieved. I had to do something. I hit the websites.

I'm not even sure if I knew of the existence of Weird and Wonderful World before that fateful day of 2 August, but by the end of the day that's where I was camped.

Ideas were flying out from all angles over the next few days, and there was one that caught my imagination: an alternative matchday programme. WISA had already called for a merchandise boycott so this just seemed the next logical step. The idea had come from Ashley Parker-Smith – and it was inspired. Alex Kirk and Ashley were already in discussions about it when I leapt on board. And within a day, seven of us were in email contact: Mark Lewis, Ashley, Alex, Charlie Talbot, Marc Jones, Richard Pope and myself.

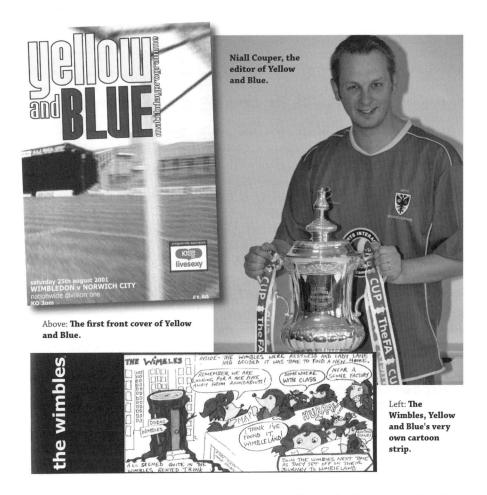

Niall Couper, the editor of Yellow and Blue.

Above: **The first front cover of Yellow and Blue.**

Left: **The Wimbles, Yellow and Blue's very own cartoon strip.**

We were to meet seven days later in Jay Jays on Wimbledon Broadway. Well, I say all – Ashley, whose idea it was, had to stay away as it turned out later he was just 14. We quickly dismissed the idea of getting a programme ready for the first game of the season – that was only two days away. So we targeted the Norwich game on 25 August.

Mark Lewis would organise the distribution and sales, Ashley was to be one of the first programme sellers. I am a qualified journalist. I was on the sports desk of the Independent at the time, and in my previous job I'd helped to edit a series of football magazines about Arsenal. I had the template ready to roll. We had even knocked together a rough pagination.

But the problem was that none of the seven of us had QuarkXPress, the industry standard page-design software. And then, of course, there was the issue of cash. Phone conversations with several printers had made it clear that we would need £1,000 up front to get going. That's where Richard Pope stepped in. He had no real idea who we were. He had no idea what we were capable of producing, but here he was happily writing out a cheque.

The next few days were mayhem. We got a copy of QuarkXPress, and the four designers – myself, Alex, Charlie Talbot and Marc Jones – set to work. We opted for a 32-page full-colour glossy magazine. Pages were sent over the internet to Oxford, where Charlie was studying and editing their student newspaper, to Putney, where Alex, an ex-journalist lived, and to Wimbledon, the home of Marc Jones, the webmaster of Weird and Wonderful World. We printed 2,000 copies, all of which went on sale on the Walk from Wimbledon to Selhurst – the latest WISA-backed protest. We sold out before we reached the ground. Yellow and Blue would later expand to 48 pages.

We were keen to present the alternative view to Charles Koppel's, and over the season we included celebrity columns from the likes of Jonathan Pearce, Jim White and Rodney Marsh. We had columns from WISA, the Dons Trust and Merton Council, interviews with a stream of ex-players, and all the usual content you would expect from a programme. But most amazing of all was that Yellow and Blue would go on to outsell the official matchday programme by three to one.

In a personal capacity, I like to think that in our own way we helped to change the minds of the sceptics in the Wimbledon crowd. For by the season's end, where there had been apathy there was now full support for the protests.

By Mark Lewis (Yellow and Blue business manager)

Looking back now on the launch of Yellow and Blue shows how much technology has moved on. At the time, a small group of people contacted each other via the Weird and Wonderful World Guestbook, agreed on their disgust at Koppel's antics, and decided that producing their own matchday programme would be a good idea.

When it came to meeting up, the most vocal person online, Ashley, turned out to be just 14 and not old enough to meet us in the bar in Wimbledon. The six who did meet were almost complete strangers, unified only by their love of Wimbledon FC and hate of the whole Koppel-generated Milton Keynes doomsday scenario.

I am a frustrated would-be football journalist at heart, but it was soon clear that Niall, Alex and Charlie had the nous and experience to cover that area. So I took on the role of generating funds from page sponsorship and advertising – £150 from Merton Council here, £5 per page from concerned fans there.

Most significantly, on match days I co-ordinated the sales of the new Yellow and Blue programme – lugging boxes from Jonesy's flat in Wimbledon or the Thomas Farley pub in Thornton Heath, the pub Wimbledon fans used before matches at Selhurst Park – then storing the unsold copies in my hallway for months afterwards.

With the notable exception of my wife, all the programme sellers were strangers to me, but we were united in the cause against MK. Some, like Sam Elliott, were still at school; Nigel Higgs' daughters needed him to chaperone them, as we handled hundreds of pounds in loose change after each match. Sam would become a sports journalist for the Non-League Paper, while Nigel would settle for the position of Youth and Community Director of AFC Wimbledon.

Despite being banned from selling Yellow and Blue within the confines of the Selhurst Park stadium, we quickly managed to outsell the official matchday publication and ensure that real Wimbledon fans heard from other real Wimbledon fans about the plight of their club.

As some wise old hack put it, we were "By the fans, for the fans" – and that entrepreneurial spirit was to go some way to galvanising the volunteer efforts that still to this day drive our wonderful club forward.

DONS FANS SAY KOPPEL OUT)

By Matt Couper (Yellow and Blue columnist)

I think we could tell that Niall would be the person writing this book from his experiences with Yellow and Blue. He didn't just dream – he did.

OK, I'm his brother and slightly biased, and he is mine, which is why he let me write the incredibly badly conceived Wimbles cartoon for Yellow and Blue!

As well as having an ad hoc column and the cartoon, I also helped to sell Yellow and Blue. What I remember most was being outside the ground when the club started putting out announcements over the PA telling people not to buy Yellow and Blue as it wasn't the official programme. That was the best matchday publicity we could get – sales doubled!

By Lou Carton-Kelly (WISA vice-chair)

I always felt Yellow and Blue was enormously important. This was far more than a fanzine – it became a "must-read", and it was hugely important in getting our word across.

I remember Anne Eames and Kathy Cook-England would take as many copies of Yellow and Blue as could be spared and would come up to Crystals, yes the night club, where I would be with Trevor Williams and Varney Constantinou selling Dons Trust merchandise. They would ensure that the copies were placed in the Players' Lounge – and those copies would disappear instantly. We knew that it wasn't the club confiscating them, it was the players wanting to read Yellow and Blue to find out what was really going on.

After the game, I used to leg it back to the Thomas Farley pub and would always sell a few copies before the Yellow and Blue team could get back there.

The first step

Central to the development of AFC Wimbledon was the early involvement of Supporters Direct. Supporters Direct had been set up to help fans gain a bigger say in the world of football, but back in 2001 it was a fledgling organisation still trying to find its true voice. A delegation of Dons fans to that year's Supporters Direct Conference was to prove a meeting of minds and the first step to what was to follow in the years ahead.

Wimbledon fans unfurl a banner of intent
(Rob Dunford)

The stage at the first Dons Trust meeting on 25 October 2001 (from left to right) Dave Boyle, Lou Carton-Kelly and Brian Lomax (Martin Drake)

6 September 2001
Supporters Direct Conference Birkbeck College, London
By Dave Boyle (Supporters Direct)

The Supporters Direct Conference in September 2001 was important. WISA took up a large delegation. There was Luke MacKenzie, Lou Carton-Kelly, Mags Hutchison, Nicole Hammond and a few others. It was the first time I had met any of them. And to be honest, I'd been waiting for their call – hoping for them to get in touch.

It was early on in Supporters Direct's life and a lot of people were unsure about what the key issues were in football. Was it ticket prices? Was it conditions in stadiums? Or was it, as I thought, the ownership of football clubs?

I knew there was a definite role for Supporters Direct in shaping the debate, and Wimbledon was perfect for helping that campaign. There couldn't be a clearer example of what happens if your club has bad governance. It said loud and clear that there is a really good reason why you should give a stuff about who runs your football club.

By Lou Carton-Kelly (WISA vice-chair)

I was there with Nicole Hammond, Luke Mackenzie and Mags Hutchison, and we all took part in various workshops; we spoke to fans of other clubs, and, most importantly, discovered how to go about setting up a supporters' trust. I was convinced. I remember going back to the WISA committee and saying: "We need to do this, we need to set up a Supporters' Trust."

We were all so terrified of Wimbledon FC going into administration or, worse still, liquidation. With a trust set up we knew we could be in a position to take over if Koppel decided to carry out his often voiced threat of putting the club into liquidation should the move to Milton Keynes be blocked by the Football League or the FA. The WISA Committee backed the idea, and I was appointed chair of the steering committee which was set up to take the Trust to launch.

The path to the Dons Trust

From the moment Charles Koppel announced the proposed move to Milton Keynes, he stated the club would go into liquidation if the move was not given the go-ahead. Wimbledon's supporters began to look at ways in which they could take over the running of the club – and out of that the Dons Trust was born.

25 October 2001
The first Dons Trust meeting Wimbledon Community Centre
By Lou Carton-Kelly (Dons Trust Steering Committee chair)

The first public meeting was on 25 October 2001 at the Wimbledon Community Centre. The main hall was packed. Myself, and Supporters Direct's Dave Boyle, our caseworker, and Brian Lomax, the organisation's inspirational chair, were all seated on the stage and explained the potential role of a supporters' trust and the work that

Ivor Heller who was approached by Halifax (Michael Palmer)

Wimbledon fans gather outside an Official Wimbledon Fans Forum meeting (Yellow and Blue)

Dons fans make their point (Rob Dunford)

would be required by the fans to bring our own "Dons Trust" to fruition. Years later, Brian Lomax would get a well-deserved OBE for the work he's done for football, football clubs and football fans.

There were also great speeches from Richard Lillicrap of Swansea City's Trust and Steve Powell from the Arsenal Independent Supporters Association. You could sense the feeling in the room that the Dons Trust was a goer.

It was to prove to be the first of regular weekly working group meetings. In the weeks that followed, I would sit upstairs at the Thomas Farley prior to home games collecting membership fees for an organisation that hadn't even been launched yet. We ended up having over 400 pre-launch Trust members.

By Dave Boyle (Wimbledon case worker, Supporters Direct)

The meeting went really well – but I remember feeling like I was the guy with the bad gags.

At Supporters Direct we had loads of start-up meetings back then, and I'd always follow Brian Lomax. Brian would deliver a passionate address about what could be done and the success he had had at Northampton Town. It was all based on reality and full of passion. It appealed to fans and painted a picture of what could be done.

And then I'd come on and stand up and explain all the technicalities: what it would mean, what you need to do, how it would work and what Supporters Direct could do to help. I was as dull as dishwater. I felt like a crappy salesperson.

At the time, we were doing two meetings a week all over the country. Brian was based in Rugby and had to come down to London a couple of times a week anyway, so we really looked forward to this one – for once, we could get home that night.

There was such a buzz in the room – you could sense the electricity about what we were suggesting. I explained that there would have to be a vote to formally set up a trust and that they needed a range a constitutional group, a publicity and marketing group, and a business plan. And they went for it. I remember turning to Brian afterwards and saying: "Do you know, I think this lot will start again."

Nobody else said it. I could just feel the energy in the room. This group of fans had suffered. They had come through the Dublin fiasco, and had already begun to organise against the Milton Keynes move. They were battle-hardened and ready for the challenges ahead. At the formation of the Dons Trust, they were realising that they could be the future of Wimbledon FC.

The working groups were soon set up and were a pleasure to work with – there was so much enthusiasm. It was that experience that made me become an AFC Wimbledon fan. These people had the same passion, the same drive that I did.

I often met up with them in the evening for a pint. I started to get the feeling that these were people I really wanted to know. I had just moved down from Lancaster, and here was a ready-made social circle of like-minded individuals. People you could consider as friends.

Halifax: The other option

The publicity given to the supporters' campaign against the move, and the growing organisation of WISA and the Dons Trust had impressed people across the football world. In late November 2001, Ivor Heller received a remarkable phone call that could have changed everything.

November 2001
By Lou Carton-Kelly (Dons Trust Steering Committee chair)

I do remember there was some talk about it. But it went against everything we stood for, everything we believed in. It was incredible, a complete non-starter as far as I was concerned.

By Kris Stewart (WISA chair)

It was about Halifax Town. I am not sure how serious it ever was, but I had heard about it on the grapevine. I think it was one individual speaking to another. No one talked to me directly about it and no one ever asked my opinion. There was no approach to WISA.

If I am being honest, it sounded like a couple of p***ed-off people thinking tactically. The idea was that if the football world allowed one ridiculous and diabolical act, then all bets were off and we could have this in our back pocket. It was one brief discussion, and I'm not sure how formal it would have been from their side.

If it was all about tactics and trying to be too clever, it wasn't for us. We didn't need to be clever. We needed to be straightforward, not sneaky or tactical.

By Dave Boyle (Wimbledon case worker, Supporters Direct)

I remember vividly coming back from a Dons Trust working group and getting a lift from Ivor Heller. He told me that he had been contacted by another League club. It was an early approach, but they had asked whether the Trust would be interested in buying them and relocating them to Wimbledon.

I couldn't believe what I was hearing. There was no way, after all that had happened to Wimbledon, that this could even be considered. It was never mentioned again.

When the Independent Manchester United Supporters Association looked at setting up a new club, they were contacted by the board of Leigh RMI offering them their own club. They didn't even think twice. How could they keep the moral high ground if they stole someone else's club?

By Ivor Heller (Dons Trust)

I spoke to an official from Halifax. They called me. Halifax were bang in trouble and at the time it looked like they couldn't survive. It was more of a casual conversation than an actual approach. If they were going to take us to Milton Keynes, why shouldn't we take Halifax?

I never took it seriously, but it was a great threat to make. The option was there, it was in our back pocket. It was a spite thing.

It was as if they were saying: "Look what we could do, if you don't have any morals or principles." It was a bargaining chip, but I don't think anyone truly believed we would do it. It was a bit like saying to the FA: "Look what you've started. Once you've done it, you can't stop it." I think the FA were lucky that their precedent didn't set off a football merry-go-round.

I gave a couple of interviews talking about precedence and what had been started. The Halifax option never went public and was never considered seriously, but it was there. It was something to throw at people, to shout about in anger, to say: "Look what you've done. You've opened Pandora's box."

But in reality, at the time there was no other club in the country they could have done it to. We were a small club, sharing a ground away from our natural community. With any other club there would have been riots.

Koppel's Fans Forum backfires

In the first half of the 2001-02 season, the Wimbledon FC chairman, Charles Koppel, repeatedly claimed that the silent majority of Dons fans backed the planned relocation to Milton Keynes. To prove his point he set up the Official Wimbledon Fans Forum (OWFF).

---

12 December 2001
Selhurst Park
By Sean Fox (OWFF elected fans' representative)

We had had the black balloons and the march from Plough Lane to Selhurst Park. Every Dons fan who had been interviewed by newspapers, radio and television had come out against the move.

The Wimbledon Independent Supporters Association, the largest supporters group, had voted not to meet with the club until the Milton Keynes proposal was renounced. Yet chairman Charles Koppel continued to insist that the protests against Milton Keynes came from only a minority of Wimbledon fans. It was out of this insistence that the Official Wimbledon Fans Forum was born.

In a letter to season-ticket holders and club members, Koppel wrote: "The views of some supporters are being aired in public. The views of others are not..." The letter went on to outline his intention to set up OWFF, which he believed would prove his point. All season-ticket holders and club members were invited to join.

The Official Wimbledon Fans Forum was born in September 2001. It was to die in August 2002, when the club ceased to recognise it.

A few weeks after the first meeting, invitations were sent to all OWFF members inviting nominations for the seven elected Council seats. When the manifestos were published, Koppel's delusion was exposed. Of the 30 candidates, only one was pro-Milton Keynes. The results were announced on 12 December 2001: the seven elected candidates were all vociferous opponents of MK, and the pro-MK candidate finished last. I was one of the seven.

The meetings that followed frequently descended into farce. We were promised that two club representatives would attend each meeting. We wanted Koppel to attend, but more often than not he wasn't there. The discussions were not about facilitating the move, as Koppel had hoped, but about rejecting MK and building a new stadium on Plough Lane or some other suitable site.

On one rare occasion when Koppel did attend, the fans' representatives were greeted by the bizarre sight of two policemen waiting in the room to "protect" him. Despite the promises of access to information and directors, little or none was forthcoming. The club's "extensive" study of sites for a new ground investigated in London consisted of a map. The promised "more detailed evidence" was never shown to us.

In March, Koppel said that he would happily sell the club for a pound – but because of the club's financial plight he wouldn't have any takers. Sadly, he declined my outstretched hand with a pound in it.

In the aftermath of 28 May, Koppel lost interest in the OWFF as a method of consultation. He refused repeated requests for a further meeting with fans' representatives.

On the first day of the 2002-03 season, the club refused to attend and published a letter on their website "derecognising" the elected members of the OWFF. In his absence, the Fans Forum voted to back a motion to support AFC Wimbledon, a club that hadn't even been in the offing 12 months earlier.

Politicians rally round

The momentum against the move was growing, and in late 2001 the debate spread to the House of Commons. The Labour MP for Wimbledon, Roger Casale, put down an Early Day Motion.

14 December 2001
House of Commons Early Day Motion
By Roger Casale (Member of Parliament for Wimbledon)

The Early Day Motion was one of the most visible shows of support for the plight of Wimbledon supporters. In the end, 109 MPs signed it. That didn't surprise me – the whole Milton Keynes thing had caused a huge stir in Parliament.

On a local level, I had set up the Wimbledon Civic Forum and as part of that I organised a football task force to tackle the issue. I did everything I could to try to stop the club moving to Milton Keynes.

I brought together the new owners and representatives of the council to try to find a solution to bring the club home to Merton. We met up several times in my constituency office in Nelson Hospital. But at all those meetings, it was becoming clearer that we weren't going to get our club back.

It was all so unprecedented. Two different visions about what a local football club was, were emerging. It's either all about big money, business and finances; or it's about being entrenched in your local community and honouring its history.

For me, the emotions, the love and the history – you couldn't take that away.

Roger Casale, the
Wimbledon MP in 2001

Wimbledon fan Doug
Hammond leads protests
(Getty Images)

Fans of many colours gather for Fans
United Day (Getty Images)

The idea that you could come along with a wad of cash and take the brand, the history and move it to another stadium didn't make sense. It was like treating the club like a branch of Pizza Express. I thought it had to be contested, and there were a lot of people who thought the same too.

Across the country, Wimbledon had become a cause célèbre. They had won the FA Cup, gone all the way to the top from the Southern League – it was the archetypal story of an underdog – and now they were being treated dreadfully.

The fans' plight chimed with other MPs in Parliament, MPs who understood football, MPs who had clubs in their constituencies, MPs who realised how much a role football clubs can play in their communities and how important they are to their constituents. They understood the danger. They realised it was much more than Wimbledon. If franchising was happening there, it could happen anywhere.

I went to all the Dons Trust meetings. I wanted to get involved. As the local MP I did everything I could. At the time, we didn't know we weren't going to be successful, but we just couldn't stand by – we had to throw everything at it.

The EDM was perhaps the most visible political statement, but that was just one of the instruments I used. I also organised a debate in Westminster Hall. I had a question asked at Prime Minister's Questions. I deployed everything at my disposal.

The EDM was easy to put down. Getting the debate at Westminster Hall was much more difficult. I remember that during the debate I accidentally called Tom Watson the MP for West Bromwich Albion rather than West Bromwich East – he was delighted with that!

The PMQ came just after a question on Northern Ireland. Tony Blair's response was short. "I feel your pain," he said. Most people thought that it wasn't a heartfelt response. But later on I found out that he had done his research and that it was truly what he believed.

MPs Andy Burnham and Tom Watson were very supportive. They were shocked about what was going on and helped to rally support throughout the Houses of Parliament. We were trying to demonstrate in Parliament that the wider world did not approve, and that the decision the owners were taking would affect not just Wimbledon: it would open the door to the possibility of football franchising across the country. In the end, I think we did show how unpopular the idea was, but it all fell on deaf ears and didn't make any difference. We lost the battle.

A few months later, on 28 May, it felt like it was all over when the FA Commission made their decision. But what happened afterwards was inspirational. The passion that the supporters showed during the fight lived on. We may have lost the fight, but that decision galvanised the support even more.

I was there supporting the supporters. They were still the same fans with the same links and ties throughout the local community. And from then on, through AFC Wimbledon, their efforts became even more worthy of passion and support.

When AFC Wimbledon won their first trophy, I arranged for the All Party Football Group in Parliament to hold a reception for the team at the Palace of Westminster. Alan Keen and I put on a big event, and we praised them and encouraged them as much as we could. We wanted to send the message that AFC Wimbledon could go on and have a future as glorious as the past had been.

Fans United Day

The protests had begun to escalate. Before a home game against Nottingham Forest, the Dons fans played host to a Fans United Day. It was a mix of colours and cross-football support, and the day turned into a celebration. Fans from over 90 different clubs attended. The home supporters relocated en masse to the Arthur Wait Stand to sit with the supporters of the other clubs.

16 December 2001
First Division Wimbledon 1 Nottingham Forest 0
By Neal Ardley (Wimbledon FC player)

Playing in the shadow of the protests against Milton Keynes was very difficult. Emotions were running high all season, and I remember getting a fair amount of stick from a couple of fans before one game. They were adamant that I had made pro-Milton Keynes comments and they were furious. I had done nothing of the sort, but there was no way of persuading them.

I had every sympathy for the fans. The club was ripping itself apart: the fans wanted one thing, the chairman wanted another and the players were stuck in the middle. I was getting paid to do a job. I had my own views on what was happening, but I couldn't be seen to be giving the fans any sympathy. I tried to sit on the fence and not make any comments on the subject.

It was a no-win situation for the players. The fans, naturally, wanted us to make a stand, but it was our livelihood, and I think some of the supporters failed to realise that. It got a little bit grotty and horrible in the end. I just wanted it all to disappear. I made a conscious decision about halfway through the season not to talk about it.

There were moments when everything felt like it had before. The 1-0 win against Nottingham Forest was one such time. We played really well that day. Chris Wilmott got the winner. Most of the fans were in the Arthur Wait Stand for Fans United Day.

I remember at the end of the game going over and applauding them. I didn't realise how significant that was for the fans, but some of them mentioned it to me later. All I wanted to say was that I knew what they were going through.

The protests were impressive: the black balloons, Fans United Day and the Backs to the Game protest in the final match of the season. But it only added to the pain for the players. Terry Burton was great throughout it all. He made it clear to all of us that we had to respect the fans. He would say: "Let them vent their anger to the chairman, but let's keep playing football on the pitch."

But there was no doubt that our home form suffered that year. If the whole Milton Keynes scenario had never surfaced, I firmly believe we would have gone up. That said, I felt Selhurst Park was not the right place for us. It never had the right atmosphere that a ground of our own would have brought us. When I spoke to the chairman, he made it seem that Milton Keynes was the only option. Whether that was true or not, I don't know.

The fans didn't think so. They vented their anger. They did what they believed in and you can't criticise anyone who does that. They made their point, and when the

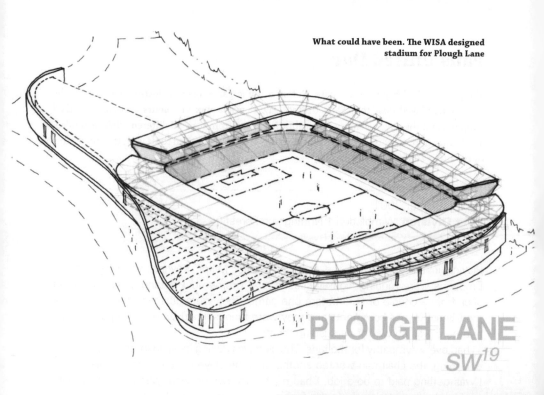

What could have been. The WISA designed stadium for Plough Lane

PLOUGH LANE SW¹⁹

Advertising the launch of the Dons Trust (Rob Dunford)

The Fund Raising Launch of

Join now and become a FOUNDER MEMBER

Have your photo taken with the AXA sponsored FA Cup and AMATEUR CUP

the DONS Trust

Take part in the PRIZE DRAW and GRAND AUCTION

MEET THE PLAYERS (some past, some present)

Sunday 10th February 2002
4:30pm Wimbledon Theatre.
FREE Admittance

WISA press and publicity officer Gail Moss (Mags Hutchison)

decision went against them they didn't give up, they didn't go back. They got off their backsides and did something about it. How many people can say they have done that?

It was a horrible year for me personally, but the fans stood by their convictions and I admire them for it. I wish them all the luck in the world. They deserve it.

By Richard Bugg (Wimbledon fan)

The march from the Farley to the ground on Fans United Day will live long in my memory. The special scarf, the togetherness and the spirit of all the fans were tremendous. That was really the only game I enjoyed that season. The singing and jumping about in the Arthur Wait Stand was electric, and the team winning was a bonus. I was actually really pleased we won. Other results that season were meaningless. But I will always remember that we won that game.

By Dave Boyle (Wimbledon case worker, Supporters Direct)

It was another turning point. I remember after the Fans United Day going back to the Thomas Farley. I was there as a representative of the Football Supporters Federation. I felt privileged to sit on that panel to represent fans from across the country.

This was the biggest fight in football at the time – a fight for the soul of football. I had a sense that this was the start of a movement. Something was starting to build that could change football forever.

The faces that were there were not the usual ones – the move to Milton Keynes had brought together a broad spectrum of people. The fans' movement at Wimbledon was becoming unstoppable.

By Luke Kirton (Brentford Independent Association of Supporters committee member)

We spoke a lot to Dave Boyle over that year. He was our case worker too and he persuaded us to go to Fans United Day – not that it took too much persuading.

We were all wearing our Brentford tops. The Wimbledon fans paid for our tickets and then as we walked in – all these people started to cheer us. "We love you Brentford, we do." It was just brilliant. I knew then that this was going to be a special relationship.

It was a momentous year for both clubs. We went to several of their games. I remember John McGlashan, the chair of the Brentford Trust, spoke at one of the early Dons Trust meetings, and we all offered our support and advice.

Not long after we both Brentford and Wimbledon were on the agenda at a Football Association meeting. Our move to Woking got booted out, but Wimbledon's got referred to a three-man commission. But even then it was far from over for us. Noades was saddling us with debt and he was still at loggerheads with a council that didn't seem to care about the Brentford fans.

And that's how ABeeC started. ABeeC began as a political campaign group. We borrowed from a lot of supporters' groups – WISA included. We wrote letters to councillors and MPs determined to try and make a change. I remember, we got a leaked memo from the leader of the council at the time saying: "Under no circumstances should you respond to these letters."

That infuriated us even more and we took the decision to challenge the council at the ballot box. We got in touch with Charlton fans. They had set up the Valley Party in Greenwich to try and persuade the council to help them return home. And they taught us a lot. They picked up a lot of votes, but came nowhere near to winning an actual seat. In each seat you get three votes and they had put forward three candidates each time and they also chose to contest every seat. They had spread themselves too thin. We choose a much more targeted approach. We stood in just 12 of the 20 seats and put forward only one candidate in each. We gave voters the chance to vote for their normal party, while still being able to show their support for us.

We did all the classic campaigning. We knocked on doors, we leafleted outside train stations. We had hundreds of people working for us. On an average night we would take 60 people to a ward and blitz it. I was standing in the Brentford ward and that was top of the list. We hit it at least three or four times. And you could really sense we were pricking a consciousness there. You would knock on the door and they would say: "Oh, my husband or my dad used to go to Griffin Park, back in the day," or "Oh, my son uses the club's community scheme." There were all these people with ties to Brentford. And it all paid off. I squeezed in by just over a dozen votes.

I was now able to make inroads into the council and persuade key individuals how important Brentford was to the local community. And without that influence we would never have been able to take control of the club.

We eventually wore Ron Noades down and he made an offer to the Brentford Trust. He had seen how organised we were and he offered the club lock, stock and barrel and all its many debts to the Trust for £1. And we took it. But the problem was that we had to look at re-financing deals and it was very difficult, we had to make a lot of very hard decisions. The final piece in the jigsaw was the council. They lent the Trust £750,000 and without that who knows where we'd be now?

I remember not long after that sitting up on the balcony at the club. I was there with John McGlashan. The Trust had just taken over control of the club. He was the managing director and I was an ABeeC councillor. And we were both thinking: "How the hell did all this happen?"

Koppel exposed at secret meeting

As the 2001-02 season developed, the battle between the club's owners and its fans became increasingly ugly. The Wimbledon owners were determined to undermine WISA, and in early 2002 they looked to recruit a local residents' association. It was another low point in relationships between the two sides. It was a move that would backfire spectacularly.

7 January 2002
Haydons Road Bridge Association Meeting
By Gail Moss (WISA press and publicity officer)

The Haydons Road Bridge Residents Association (HBRA) and the 'Koppelgate' tape was one of the more bizarre twists in the story of our campaign against Wimbledon FC's proposed move to Milton Keynes.

A key argument of WISA's campaign had been that the Plough Lane site was big enough to build a new stadium for the club – and we had an architect's design to prove it. This so scared Koppel that on 7 January 2002, he, co-director Matthias Hauger and their adviser Dan Tench attended a secret meeting with a small number of HBRA members at a house near Plough Lane.

Koppel hoped to encourage opposition to the club's return to Plough Lane, and during the meeting a motion written by Tench was passed and signed by the attendees. He made a number of negative remarks about Wimbledon fans, famously saying that: "Football supporters are not necessarily the kind of people you want on your doorstep."

He also said he was confident he could use the media to publicise his belief that Merton residents did not want Wimbledon Football Club to return to the borough. Shortly afterwards, WISA released the results of an ICM poll showing that as many as one in 10 local residents said they would go to matches regularly if the club were to return to Plough Lane.

Koppel then went on to advise those at the meeting how they should approach the campaign to prevent Wimbledon FC returning to Plough Lane, and suggested what they should say. But the proceedings were exposed, thanks to a tape recording of the meeting made by someone sympathetic to the fans' cause. The tape was passed to WISA, who issued a couple of press releases and within a few days had uploaded audio extracts from the tape and the related transcripts to the WISA website.

The situation now turned into farce, with HBRA issuing its own press release defending the meeting as well as Koppel's stance. Their statement included a name and telephone number for press enquiries: these turned out to be the contact details of someone at Brunswick, an international PR consultancy which had worked for Wimbledon FC. Surely HBRA must have been the only residents' association in the country with the budget to hire a top PR firm!

The following Saturday, Wimbledon played Burnley at Selhurst Park, and WISA distributed flyers containing a summary of the HBRA meeting. The result – inevitably – was a sense of outrage, and the sorry tale of Koppel's covert activities mopped up support from many of those fans who still believed his line that there was no alternative to a move to Milton Keynes.

It was now clear that instead of doing all he could to back a return to Merton, Koppel had stooped to helping a small group of residents in obstructing attempts to bring the club home. Moreover, his insulting remarks showed the fans what Koppel really thought of them – his own club's "customers".

The tape left no doubt in anyone's mind that Koppel was intent on moving the club to Milton Keynes come hell or high water, would reject all constructive plans to keep the club in London, and therefore, did not have the fans' interests at heart.

Unfortunately, the FA was not "anyone". Although the revelations severely damaged, if not destroyed, Koppel's credibility with the fans, the battle was still ultimately lost five months later.

By Lou Carton-Kelly (Dons Trust Steering Committee chair)

The WISA flyer detailing what had happened at the HBRA meeting, and how Koppel and Co had employed a PR company to help, was without doubt a benchmark in this sorry saga.

WISA's open-top bus heads down for the launch of the Dons Trust (Martin Drake)

Dave Boyle addresses the audience at the launch of the Dons Trust (Paul Willatts)

Wimbledon legend Dickie Guy at the launch of the Dons Trust (Yellow and Blue)

I handed them out in my stand at Selhurst Park – the Stanley Stephenson Lounge – and that was the moment when I really saw the ordinary Wimbledon fans stand up.

The "sit down and shut up" brigade weren't going to take it any more. They were queuing up to read it and people were leaving the ground and going to photocopy them at the local Tesco – they too now wanted to make a difference.

The launch of the Dons Trust

After Fans United Day and the HBRA debacle, the focus switched to the launch of the Dons Trust. The Trust was to prove instrumental in the months that followed. Its launch was a milestone, and within three months it was to become the largest supporters' trust in the country.

10 February 2002
The launch of the Dons Trust Wimbledon Theatre
By Lou Carton-Kelly (Dons Trust Steering Committee chair)

Take over 1,200 Wimbledon fans, add a liberal sprinkling of VIPs including MPs and members of Merton Council, guest speakers, a passionate MC, over 60 stewards, the FA Cup and a host of ex-players. Place in a theatre for three hours, and gently stir and infuse with emotion. What have you got?

The launch of the Dons Trust on 10 February 2002.

The timescale for the launch was very ambitious, but it was also the only date that Wimbledon Theatre could accommodate us. They gave it to us for free.

As for the night itself, I didn't really know what to expect. We had various working groups working hard to try to make the day a success, and prior to the launch we were all really anxious. We wanted to show the community of Merton that we meant business. Once we knew that the FA Cup and a number of ex-players would be there, we knew we would get a fair crowd, but 1,200... I spent the whole night running on adrenalin. I was excited and nervous all at once.

Chris Philips, from Kiss FM, was the MC, and he was superb. Then there were the speakers. First up was the Mayor of Merton, Stuart Pickover, then ex-players Dickie Guy and Jeff Bryant, and ex-manager Allen Batsford.

Then it was over to Brian Lomax, the newly installed managing director of Supporters Direct. He said that, with their professionalism and skills, the Dons Trust working groups were more than capable of running a football club. How prophetic those words would prove to be.

Then came Dave Boyle, Andrew Judge, the leader of Merton Council, and Wimbledon's MP Roger Casale. Casale had drafted an Early Day Motion opposing the move to Milton Keynes. It was to become one of the most successful Early Day Motions in the history of Parliament.

Finally, we came to Lord Faulkner of Worcester, better known to us as Richard Faulkner, a former director of Wimbledon FC. His speech was passionate and direct. There were a number at that meeting who had known Richard for more than 25 years, and his speech summed up exactly what being a football supporter is all about. It was delivered from the heart.

After the speakers there was a parade of former players, a chance to have a photograph taken with the FA Cup, followed by a fundraising auction of memorabilia, which Jo and Mark Lewis will remember forever for their £3,000-plus bid for a signed picture of Lawrie Sanchez's FA Cup-winning goal.

It was an amazing night and one that will live with me forever. We knew then that the Dons Trust meant business, and we were ready to take over the club.

By Brian Lomax (Supporters Direct managing director)

Of all the memories I have of my time working for Supporters Direct, none is clearer or better than the launch of the Dons Trust. The launch, and the history leading up to it, sent a message of hope to fans everywhere that they are the true owners of the game, and should also be the leading voice within their clubs.

At the launch, I distinctly remember being deeply impressed by the sheer number of people there. If a fire officer had been there, he would undoubtedly have been manhandling people out of the door.

I can't remember what I said, because I didn't write anything down, but I remember the buzz within the room and the determination to get moving. This was a group of people determined to make a difference.

The Trust movement began at my club, Northampton Town, back in 1992. I had been the first chair of Northampton Town Supporters Trust. We took control of the club and, in those early days, we were soon getting enquiries from neighbouring clubs, and then it became clubs a little bit further away and before we knew it we were getting calls from all across the country. When Government decided to fund a national body – Supporters Direct – seven years later in 1999 there were already nearly 100 trusts nationwide. Andy Burnham and Phil French deserve a lot of credit for getting the funding in place. The number of trusts now stands at over 170 and has reached into mainland Europe.

By the time of the launch of the Dons Trust, I had nearly 10 years' worth of experience to play on. I had been chair of the Northampton Town Supporters Trust for its first seven years, and had three years heading up Supporters Direct. In my role at Supporters Direct, I had been to the best part of 100 meetings and each one was different. Sometimes they'd be a big group and at other times there would just be a handful of people – but at each there was the same desire to help their football club. We wanted to encourage people to take a more active role in their clubs. For years, supporters had raised money for their clubs and handed it all over as a simple gift – it was pouring money into a bottomless pit. It was about time they got something back. And the Dons Trust was to become a great example for others to follow, an inspiration.

The first and perhaps the greatest hero of the Dons Trust was, of course, Kris Stewart, who chaired the first meeting. Kris became heavily involved at a national level and came onto the national Committee.

On the stage that night I could sense this was a new departure from anything I had seen before. Even if the vast majority of the audience didn't know it then, I could feel this was all about the creation of a new club. But that night we were also ensuring that no club could ever repeat the horrors that had happened to Wimbledon fans. Being there that night to witness a slice of history was without doubt one of the most memorable and proudest moments of my life.

I remember getting up on the stage straight after Brian Lomax. Brian was the head of Supporters Direct and had just delivered an emotional speech. He told of his experiences of saving his own club, Northampton Town, and his vision of football fans having a greater say in the clubs they love. It was a hard act to follow.

On a personal level, I felt hugely privileged to be asked to speak. I felt then that this could be one of the most significant days in the 113-year life of Wimbledon Football Club, the day when the supporters took the first giant step towards securing the future of their club.

I first saw Wimbledon play in 1963 at Wembley in the Amateur Cup Final. I was at school in north London, and scarcely knew where Wimbledon was. My wife and I moved to Wimbledon when we married, and stayed. I started watching Wimbledon regularly in the mid Seventies, and saw the great FA Cup matches against Burnley, Leeds and Middlesbrough.

I helped with campaigns to win election to the Football League, first unsuccessfully in 1976, and then triumphantly in 1977. I coined the slogan "DONS 4 DIV 4", seen on stickers in the back window of hundreds of cars as fans went around the country seeking the votes to gain election to the League.

I saw the club's board and ownership change many times. We had had battles against mergers, and I lost count of the number of cities where secret talks reportedly took place to relocate the club – Glasgow, Cardiff, Manchester, Belfast, and most significantly Dublin. As a group of supporters, we had become used to the fight, and now, as I addressed a packed Wimbledon Theatre, I could sense we were ready for yet another battle.

I've still got the speech I delivered that night. I talked about the club's history – everything we had achieved, and my own personal involvement. Then I went on to address our current plight.

"Now the owners want to take the club to Milton Keynes," I said. "I have been there, ladies and gentlemen. I went last summer to see the piece of ground where it is proposed that a new stadium will be built.

"It is a fine site. It's near Bletchley railway station, it's by main roads. There's loads of space. There's also a huge local population whose local Football League clubs are some way away in Luton and Northampton.

"But none of these factors is really the point. The overriding attraction of Milton Keynes for today's owners of Wimbledon is that they're being offered the stadium for free, because its construction will be paid for out of the proceeds of adjoining property development.

"So this whole crazy venture is being driven solely by money. The Norwegians know they paid far too much for the club, and they see this as the way to get some of it back.

"Never mind that our club is 113 years old. Or that we are unique in winning both the Amateur Cup and the FA Cup. Or that we are the only club ever likely to progress from non-league football to the top division in just nine seasons.

"Or, above all, that Wimbledon has the most fantastic, dedicated, talented group of fans of any club in the country. You've had to put up with a hell of a lot over recent years, and I salute you.

"This is why I commend today's initiative to establish the Dons Trust, and to say that I have invested in it. I urge you all to do likewise."

At the time I spoke of three options: the club's owners would sell up, liquidate the club or open talks with the supporters. I never even considered that we could start again. In each scenario an effective supporters trust was vital. We needed to have in place an alternative company structure which could credibly take on ownership and management of the club – and quickly.

I was furious at the tactics of the owners. They attempted to argue that local people living close to the old Plough Lane ground had turned against the club, and didn't want it back. In my speech I exposed what we had found out about the Haydons Bridge Residents Association. This was a largely bogus organisation run from the club owners' PR agency.

I said that if they wanted people to believe that there was serious opposition to Wimbledon returning to Plough Lane, they really shouldn't put out press releases purporting to come from the residents with the club's PR agency's phone number as the contact point.

I remember feeling that the momentum was with us. WISA had gathered huge support and had produced a credible design for a stadium on the Plough Lane site. The local MP, Roger Casale, had organised an Early Day Motion in the House of Commons which had attracted over 100 signatures. It had asked the Government to confirm its belief that football clubs must retain their links with their local communities, and that the principle of franchising Football League clubs was unacceptable.

The whole evening was electric. Everyone wanted to sign up to join the Dons Trust. We had laid the gauntlet down to Charles Koppel. Wimbledon fans were ready to take ownership of the club.

Burton turns on Koppel

The protests, the conflicts – it was all getting too much for Wimbledon manager Terry Burton. After being rushed to hospital, he decided that there was only one option left to him: the club chairman Charles Koppel had to go.

Tuesday 12 March 2002
Portsmouth 1 Wimbledon 2 Championship
By Terry Burton (Wimbledon FC manager)

The weeks leading up to the last game at Selhurst were where the problems really started. And that's when I hatched a plan to try to oust Charles Koppel and stop the Milton Keynes move.

We played Portsmouth away. I had been really unwell for about two weeks. I didn't travel down with the team – I drove down later that night. We played really well and won 2-1. But the next day I went to hospital with a burst appendix. It was really serious. The doctor who helped me still goes down to AFC Wimbledon and he really saved my life. It was that bad. It was that close.

The club looked to reassure me. They had continually talked about the need to sell players to balance the books, but they insisted that, as long as I was laid up, under no circumstances would any players be sold. We still had a chance of the play-offs at the

Dons fans make their point clear
(Rob Dunford)

Wimbledon fans echo the sentiments of
manager Terry Burton at a protest at
Selhurst Park (Getty Images)

Simon Wheeler (centre) in the heart of a protest at Selhurst Park (Neil Presland)

time, and we needed to keep the whole squad together. Kevin Cooper, who would go on to be named our player of the season, went while I was lying in my hospital bed. And then, before I was discharged, it turned into a procession of players going out of the door.

David Neilsen was another example of the club's owners not knowing what football was all about. He wasn't in the first-team group at that time, but we were going to loan him out to Norwich to give him some match experience. And I said to Koppel: "Just don't let him play against us as we play them in a couple of weeks." We still had a chance of going up and every point was vital.

But he couldn't understand my reasoning. "Why not?" he asked.

And I said: "It's just an unwritten rule as players always end up playing well against you." And he said: "Don't be stupid." He thought it would be a good idea as we would know all about him and we would know how to stop him. And of course he scored against us.

There were lots of things towards the end of that season that weren't right. I decided that we couldn't go on like this. As I lay there in my hospital bed, it all crystallised, Koppel had to go. I may have been in hospital, but I wasn't delirious. Our away form was the best in the division, yet our home form was dire. It was obvious that things had to change.

Koppel had become such a hate figure that the only way forward was to galvanise the supporters. I had to get rid of Charles Koppel and his henchmen and get this Milton Keynes thing kicked out and use the supporters to lobby and work hard to find us a new stadium. You only have to look at what followed to realise how powerful

Wimbledon supporters could have been back then as a lobbying force.

It was our only hope: get the supporters onside so that we could come together as a club and, with the backing of the supporters, we could get going again. But we couldn't do that with Koppel. So that was the plan.

The boycott

The Dons Trust was growing, the fans were becoming stronger and the season was coming to a close. WISA were keen to send one last firm message to the club's owners that the move to Milton Keynes would not be tolerated. They chose the nuclear option – a season-ticket boycott.

---

6 April 2002
Wimbledon 1 Bradford City 2 Championship
By Kris Stewart (Chair of WISA)

We started thinking about the idea of a season-ticket boycott at the end of the season. It looked like things were going to be happening over the summer and we wanted to put ourselves in as strong a position as possible.

We started talking about what we should do and it was obviously going to be really difficult to get a boycott through. Football is a game of emotions and loyalties. Fans have season tickets for years and years, and it would be a big ask to expect them to give them up. But what was the alternative?

Our money, our season-ticket money, was going to be used to kill our club. The very club we loved. It was going to be spent on expensive lawyers and PR experts in a determined effort to move the club further away from our community. Why should 4,500 people give their £200 or more to kill the thing we loved? It seemed ridiculous. We weren't advocating a boycott of games, but we didn't want to let them have all that money up front.

Sean Fox came up with some suitable wording, and we called an Emergency General Meeting. We were going to ask supporters whether we should ask them not to buy a season ticket. It was a vote on whether we should have a vote. We held the meeting in Crystals at the ground. We had originally wanted to hold it in the Thomas Farley, but it soon became obvious that the upstairs room there was nowhere near big enough.

The result was never really in any doubt, and the proposal to hold a vote was passed easily. But the big thing was the amendment that was added at the meeting. It called on WISA to add a recommendation at the bottom of the ballot paper endorsing a boycott. There couldn't have been a clearer indication of how the mood was going.

The result of the vote itself, held a few days later, was overwhelming in favour and there was a huge turnout. It was yet another nail in the coffin of Franchise and a further show of the growing unity of Wimbledon fans.

By Simon Wheeler (WISA committee member)

To call for a season-ticket boycott was a big decision for WISA to take at the time. I remember the committee meeting when it was all discussed. There were arguments for and against. What would the point be? How much of a difference would it make? But at the time there was nothing else really left open to us.

In hindsight, it might not look that big. But we were asking Wimbledon fans to turn their back on the club in the only way that would really hit the club hard – in the pocket. There was no point in just asking the WISA members to back it – the boycott needed to be wider than that to get legitimacy. So we called an open meeting at Crystals to debate it and vote. We were confident the boycott would go through, but you could never be sure.

Rob Dunford from the website SW19's Army and Niall Couper from Yellow and Blue both spoke – and it was clear that the mood of the meeting was going with the boycott. When it came to the vote, there was a sea of hands in favour. It was on.

In the aftermath, I heard of several fans who, having already ordered a season ticket, demanded a refund. To their credit, the club gave them their money back, but then sent them the ticket anyway. Most were returned torn up in disgust.

That was when the club knew they had lost the battle to win the hearts of the fans.

By Seb Brown (Wimbledon fan)

I was always a Wimbledon fan. So it meant so much to me. My dad's side of the family are all from South-West London. They grew up in Balham and they used to go to the old Plough Lane – my dad Keith and my uncles Gordon and Norman.

I went to my first game when I was little. We were all season-ticket holders at Selhurst and I was there when everything happened. I was 12 or 13 at the time and I didn't really understand all the politics of it. I remembered the talk of Dublin, but that was just the warm-up show to what was going to happen now.

I remember being in the meeting at Crystals to discuss the possible season-ticket boycott. We all knew that the move to Milton Keynes was the end of our club.

The tears of Kevin Cooper

In March 2002, Wimbledon's popular winger Kevin Cooper was sold to Wolves for £1 million. He had been the runaway favourite for the club's Player of the Year award. A WISA poll confirmed it and, with the help of the staff at Wolves, WISA presented Cooper with the award at Molineux. Wimbledon FC were not told in advance.

14 April 2002
Wolverhampton Wanderers 1 Wimbledon 0 First Division
By Kevin Cooper (Wolverhampton Wanderers player)

I was playing the best football of my career, and it was the best year of my life. Receiving the award from the Wimbledon fans at Molineux, having just left, was…well, I can't quite explain how I felt. It was so emotional, it was a wonderful experience.

An emotional Kevin Cooper
approaches the Dons fans
(Aideen Rochford)

Kevin Cooper picks up his player of the
year award (Yellow and Blue)

I remember Kris Stewart giving me the Player of the Year award in front of thousands of cheering Dons fans. I'll be honest – the tears were streaming from my eyes.

The emotion then…it's just so hard to describe. It's better than winning games and scoring goals. To be appreciated by the supporters of the club you have just left in such a way – I just don't think anything in football can better that. It was amazing.

I knew how the fans were feeling, I knew it had been a difficult year for them and I felt for them. I could feel the emotion from the fans as I walked over. And to be honoured like that, I was overwhelmed.

I first got an inkling that I might get the Player of the Year award when I first arrived at Wolves. One of the officials there said he wasn't sure whether I'd still get the award after the move. I knew I'd played well, but I thought the fans would give the award to a player still at the club. And after that there wasn't a whisper until the day of the game itself. I found out later how much work had gone into organising it all, but they kept it all a secret from me.

The whole game had been overwhelming – every time I touched the ball I got a cheer from the Wimbledon fans. It was really nice. I'm glad Wolves won the game, though, as I'm not sure how well they would have reacted to me receiving an award from the opposing fans at the final whistle! That said, I think a lot of Wolves fans developed a soft spot for the Dons supporters because of that game, certainly the ones that I've spoken to.

On the day, the players from Wimbledon were fine. Personally, I had only just left so it was a strange feeling to see them all again. I think the Wolves players were more overwhelmed by the reaction I received than the Wimbledon guys. Most of the Wolves team had never seen anything like it.

I remember Kenny Cunningham saying something similar a few weeks earlier when I got substituted against Stockport and the whole ground rose to applaud me. I had been at Stockport for four years and they had just got relegated, and that was a nice gesture.

Some players claim that they don't hear the fans, but at that game against Stockport I was fully aware that the two sets of fans were on the same side, and that endeared me even more to the fans of Wimbledon and Stockport.

I hadn't wanted to leave Wimbledon. I was 100 per cent happy there. The supporters at Wimbledon were second to none, and my heart is with them. But in the end I was asked to make a choice, and as a professional footballer there are times in your life when you have to do what is right for your family and yourself in the long term. It was the hardest choice I have ever had to make.

It's a difficult subject for me to go into in depth. But in my mind, it would be nice to see a club called Wimbledon playing in Wimbledon and in the First Division.

I have nothing but respect for the fans: they are the bread and butter of the game. And I think it's good for football what AFC Wimbledon are doing.

I'm willing to do anything to help the fans there. After all, the supporters at AFC stood by me, and it's the very least I could do in return. They deserve the best.

By Kris Stewart (Chair of WISA)

It was weird. To be honest, I was really surprised that Wolves were up for it. They could have said no, and I wouldn't have been shocked. After all, why should a League club openly humiliate another? I really didn't think they would buy into it.

My one abiding memory of the day was my T-shirt. I was wearing a neat shirt, but underneath was my "Koppel Wanted for Murder" T-shirt. As I strolled onto the pitch, I unbuttoned my shirt and walked over to give Kevin Cooper the award. A steward came up to me and just said, politely enough: "Sorry, mate, you know you are going to have to keep your shirt on."

Kevin Cooper seemed really touched. He was a lot more down to earth and a lot more genuine than most footballers I had met up to that point.

It was also the only time I ever voted in the Player of the Year poll. I don't believe in it – football is a team game. It was purely a political thing for me that I voted. Koppel had been selling off our best players, and this seemed the perfect way to respond.

The final turn

The final game of the 2001-02 season was a mix of emotions. Five minutes before half-time the fans turned their backs on the play. It was a symbolic gesture. The fans still backed the players and the manager, but the owners had failed to listen to every other protest. At the end of the game, the owners of Wimbledon FC turned their backs on Terry Burton.

---

21 April 2002
Wimbledon 0 Barnsley 1 First Division
By Terry Burton (Wimbledon manager)

After the game, I was sacked. I knew what was coming. They had sold players behind my back. And I'd been trying to let the press know as much as I could without overstepping the mark.

With a couple of games to go, it was over. Mathematically, we could no longer make the play-offs. The points difference was too big. The club's public stance was simple – it was all about results. They told the press that we hadn't won promotion and that wasn't good enough. But if that was the case, 90 per cent of managers would be sacked each year. I didn't get the news officially until after the match. But in the days before it had become more obvious what was going to happen. It really came to a head over Peter Hawkins.

Charles Koppel came down to the training ground a couple of days before the final game of the season. He pulled me aside and said: "We've looked at it, and if you play Peter Hawkins we've got to pay x amount of pounds on a new contract as he has played so many games this season."

I asked: "What's wrong with that? That's what happens in football."

He said: "There's nothing at stake, so why do you need to play him?"

And I said: "He's earned the right, he plays."

A little later on I got a phone call from him: "The owners are not happy about this."

I couldn't believe what I was hearing. This should not just be about my principles, this should be about the club's principles. We want players to come through the youth team and play in the first team. And we need to encourage them to do that – we need to look after them. I asked Koppel: "Do you not think that every other player in the dressing room will not know the reason why he hasn't played? And what will

Wimbledon fans turn their backs on play during the final game at Selhurst Park (Neil Presland)

Niall Couper: **This Is Our Time**

they then think about the club? I'm not doing it for Terry Burton, I'm doing it for the club." And he said: "Well they are not going to be very happy." "Well, they are going to have to be not very happy then," I replied.

I played Hawkins. It should always have been about the ethos of the club. But that was the last straw for them, and I was put on gardening leave.

In over two years I had given 13 players their debuts. At Wimbledon it was about giving the young players their chance, and in Neil Shipperley and David Connolly we had a forward line with prospects. If there had been some investment we would not have been far away from promotion. We had even identified a couple of new players who would have been a perfect fit.

But the owners weren't thinking about football: Milton Keynes was the focus for the club. As for the supporters, they were simply not going to go there. It was the big issue. But it was different for us. We couldn't come out and say what we did or didn't want to do. The club paid our wages.

Those last two seasons were very hard. Playing in the First Division was a massive change for all of us. Half the squad had gone, we were trying to play a new style, we were playing different opponents and financially we were hamstrung. We weren't going to be able to adjust overnight.

I didn't want the club to fall through the divisions, like Barnsley or Sheffield Wednesday. That was my fear: that not only would we lose our top players, but that we would collapse. We tried to keep some stability, but it was a difficult juggling act.

There was a three-year plan. The club wanted to reduce the wage bill and rebuild in the third year. The fans expected us to go straight back up. But if you let half your team go, it's always going to be difficult.

Then came the Milton Keynes announcement. It was a crazy, crazy season, with all the chants about Koppel and not going to Milton Keynes. It was difficult. It did take our eyes off the ball – it was impossible for it not to, but it was something we grew to understand and deal with. It was not the best background, hearing all that barracking at every game. We were thankful that it wasn't aimed at the team and the players. We knew where the criticism was directed, but it didn't help the atmosphere in the ground.

The Backs to the Game demonstration in that final match was just the latest in a long line of protests. All I could do was try to focus on the way we were playing. If only the situation hadn't arisen, we would have benefited from the fans' full support.

Even after that final game, there was still no decision on whether the club would move to Milton Keynes, but at least it was now a problem I wouldn't have to deal with on a day-to-day basis. They put me on gardening leave, but even then I was still convinced that the FA would knock the decision back. I was plotting to remove Koppel and thinking: "How can I get the supporters back onside?" I kept thinking when the FA say no to moving the club 100 miles away, maybe I will get the chance again.

But that never happened and after I voiced my concerns once too often they stopped paying me. It cost me quite a lot of money. I look back on it now and it's like losing your wife and they've been allowed to re-marry, but they've stopped you doing the same. They wanted to keep punishing me, they wanted me to stay lonely. It was all crazy, but then football is crazy sometimes.

By Kris Stewart (Chair of WISA)

I don't know where the idea came from. Throughout the season we had constantly been trying to come up with new ideas and we wanted something big for the last game. We had had sit-ins after games, but we couldn't really stay until midnight. There had been the black balloons, the T-shirts and we had even hired a plane to fly a banner over Vicarage Road when we played Watford.

We wanted something different, something new. But there was always the nagging doubt about how many fans would really be up for it at the crunch. Some people just wanted to sit down and watch football – we just didn't know how many people would join in.

We were not going to do something violent and rush the directors' box or anything silly like that. We wanted to make a statement, we wanted to show that some things are more important than a football match. And turning our backs was it. In the end it was one of those moments when I thought, "Blimey!"

In everyday life, most of us just talk to people who have similar views, and it can be really difficult to know what the feeling is among the wider public. But when the moment came, it was just amazing – pretty much everyone in the home sections of Selhurst Park turned their backs on the game.

The pictures in the media afterwards gave a simple message – we had won the argument with undecided supporters. It was a solid, solid protest. The fact that many of us were wearing "Back to Plough Lane" T-shirts also helped. It made it easier for people to turn.

In that one moment you could see that the fanbase as a whole agreed with what we were doing. We were as one. It was a sign that we, WISA, had run a good campaign, we had put up a good fight. We may have ultimately lost the battle, but we had pulled everyone together, and that prepared the ground for what was to come.

We had agonised over many of the things we had done over the year, but we had hit the ground running. It had been a fight worth fighting. We proved that we could work together and that we had a cause worth fighting for, and that maybe, just maybe, we could still go on to achieve something else – and that's what happened.

Chapter Three:

Not in the wider interests of football

"Not in the wider interests of football"

Since the announcement on 2 August 2001, Wimbledon fans had battled hard against the proposed uprooting of the club. The Football League had even voted 8-0 against the move, but an appeal by Charles Koppel persuaded the Football Association to set up a three-man commission to reconsider the case.

The commission, comprising Ryman League chairman Alan Turvey, Aston Villa secretary Steve Stride and media lawyer Raj Parker, began their deliberations on 14 May 2002. On the same day, Wimbledon fans began a vigil outside the headquarters of the Football Association in Soho Square.

The commission's final report would include the infamous phrase "not in the wider interests of football". These words would become a call to arms for Dons fans. They summed up the commission's opinion on the formation of a new club by disgruntled Wimbledon FC fans.

---

14 May 2002
Slaughter & May, Piccadilly
By Alan Turvey (Ryman League chairman)

I was contacted by the FA's company secretary and asked whether I'd be available on the date. It wasn't really an FA Commission as such. I was there as the FA's representative on the panel, but the other two were independent – I'm not sure how they chose them.

That said, I was there to make an impartial decision. I was under no three-line whip from the FA. I like to think I was chosen for my ability to suspend my prejudices and be fair and impartial. My background was as a referee.

It all began at the headquarters of Slaughter & May in Piccadilly – a huge international law company. Raj Parker chaired the panel. One thing that is clear in my mind was that the process was correct. I had my thoughts and we were not restricted by the chair. We could ask anything we wanted to – and I did.

I knew Steve Stride a little, but I didn't know Raj. And I have to be honest, I've not really seen or spoken to either of them since then.

We arrived basically with a blank piece of paper. All we had was the application from Wimbledon FC – that was it. Our remit was simple: whether they should be allowed special dispensation to "relocate" to Milton Keynes – if that's the right word for it. It was a big issue. My view was that WFC wasn't really in existence at the time. Not the Wimbledon I had known.

It was intense. We might get the chance for a quick sandwich, but there was nothing lavish – there wasn't really time to stop. Each day was long: we would begin first thing and go on late.

It was never just the three of us. There were people taking notes, recording everything. It was a very big room. It had to be: there were loads of witnesses, and sometimes there would be a whole team of people making a presentation. We'd all be sitting at a table, and there would be submission after submission. Then people would come to support what they had written.

There were views from all sides. There was an awful lot of evidence. We heard from the supporters, the owners, other interested partners and that guy from Milton

Keynes, Peter Winkelman. We would discuss each bit of evidence afterwards. Each person had their own views, and we would deliberate carefully. It wasn't really arguing, but we wanted to discuss every aspect. We would discuss every point thoroughly – sometimes one issue would take us all day. What I can say is that at the end of it all it was a thoroughly professional decision. The views of the various people were heard and listened to.

One of the debates that most sticks out in my mind was the issue of a stadium. I remember seeing plans that showed quite clearly that a football stadium could fit on the site of Plough Lane. I can't remember whether it was the fans or the council that put them forward, but both of them were adamant that that could have been the solution.

The club's owners disagreed and kept saying that it would not be big enough. I think the capacity in the plans was over 20,000 – have Milton Keynes Dons ever been close to that at their new ground? I don't think so. I didn't buy that argument at that time, I don't buy it now and I believe I have been vindicated. Wimbledon could have had a stadium in Wimbledon. However, at the time not everyone on the panel agreed with me.

Then there was the issue of the existing team in Milton Keynes – their plight was ignored by the owners. Yet it seemed obvious to me that if Wimbledon FC were allowed to relocate there, their demise would be inevitable.

But you can listen to the same arguments as someone else, the same pros and cons, and come to a completely different decision. It's not uncommon that not everyone can agree. And at the end, a vote was taken and we reached a majority decision. I know it's been widely speculated about how I voted. Most of the reports are probably right. It was generally felt that I was the person that voted against it, but I can't possibly comment.

After the announcement, it wasn't an easy time. When you make a collective decision like that some people want to attack you. I wanted people to know what I thought. I would have loved to say what I thought, but under the legal circumstances…

It didn't end for me on 28 May. I was still receiving papers weeks afterwards. Our written reasons had to be given. I spent most of my holiday dealing with the aftermath – document after document was sent to me.

It was at this time that the words "not in the wider interests of football" were inserted into the report. It definitely wasn't a phrase I put in or even something, in hindsight, I would approve of. But it has to be seen in context. At no point during the two weeks of the hearing did anyone even put forward the suggestion of starting another club. It was all about the future of Wimbledon FC.

Yes, I read the final report – I had to sign it off – but that doesn't mean I agreed with it all. It certainly changed my holiday, but I can't really moan, for Wimbledon fans spent a lot longer dealing with it. I never received a final copy of the report.

What followed has made a few things clear. Fans can run football clubs. And in my view there is space for both ownership models in football. The fans of AFC Wimbledon made their point loud and clear in the years that followed. However, supporters can't just put the best players on the pitch – it's far more complicated than that. I think Erik Samuelson grasped that and got the right people around him.

On a personal level, I would be very wary of dipping into my own pocket to buy into football. However, if you have put £2 million or £3 million into a club you would expect to have a big say in how it is run – but you would be foolish to ignore the supporters.

Milton Keynes move wins approval

Early on Tuesday 28 May the news leaked out: the move had been approved by two votes to one. By 9am it was on the Evening Standard website. It took another four hours for the news to become official. For Wimbledon supporters across the world, it was beginning to sink in.

By Terry Burton (former Wimbledon FC manager)

It was unbelievable. You can't imagine how anyone in their right mind at the FA, who are supposed to be the "guardians" of our game, can be sitting there and making the decision that would take a football club a hundred miles from its natural home.

Has it ever happened before? Has it ever happened since? It just doesn't happen. You just couldn't believe that these men of power could come to this decision. It was just crazy.

By Peter Davis (Wimbledon fan)

Football had ended. The World Cup didn't matter, and all I wanted to do was grab people and shout at them. The Football Association and Charles Koppel had ruined everything. A lawyer and a secretary had decided that Wimbledon Football Club should be allowed to move to Milton Keynes. Where were the football people in this decision-making process?

By Fazal Ahmed (Wimbledon fan)

During the course of that last season, the football had become boring. Trudging to Selhurst was tiresome, and any hope that we'd ever get any sense out of the club owners had vanished. We had our own voice in Yellow and Blue, the best programme the club had ever had. In the last issue, I'd even had a letter published in which I suggested that if we, the fans, were allowed to run our club, we could be bigger than Real – and how soon we'd start living that dream.

It was a bright sunny day. I was working in a dull office next to the Madejski Stadium in Reading. The World Cup was looming. Having recently been on the demo at Soho Square, I was confident. I'd discovered the chatrooms and was eagerly waiting for news.

When I finally got a phone call from my wife about the decision, it felt like part of me had died. Amazingly, I'd turned the whole office to our cause. So when news spread across the building, a crowd gathered offering condolences to me. The only way I can describe it is like a bereavement. All the old names and matches flashed through my mind. I never thought I'd watch football again.

By Erik Samuelson (Wimbledon fan)

I was in a taxi from London Bridge heading for some meeting or other. I was still working for Coopers Deloitte – as they were known then – at the time, and the radio was on.

I heard the club's name mentioned. It distracted me from my thoughts and I asked

the cab driver what it was about. He said: "They have allowed Wimbledon to go to Milton Keynes."

My stomach went through the floor. I couldn't believe it. I didn't want to go to the meeting. I wondered around in a haze. There was nothing else on my mind. I felt physically sick. I couldn't tell you anything about what happened in the meeting – I was elsewhere.

By Neil Presland (Wimbledon fan)

The news broke on the Evening Standard website. I immediately took a half-day holiday and made my way up to Soho Square to join the swell of other supporters who were there praying that the Standard had got it wrong. We waited and waited, but there was no official statement.

Eventually we were forced to "invade" the FA headquarters. That got their attention, and finally we were handed a printed statement confirming that our club was dead. Unbelievable! Here we were, outside the offices of the authority that was supposed to protect football, and they had sold us out to appease a bunch of businessmen. What did I feel? Anger and despair. The despair has now gone, but the anger will stay forever.

By Luke Kirton (ABeeC councillor)

I spent a lot of time showing my support for Wimbledon fans at the vigil at Soho Square. And I was there the day the decision came through. I spent an awful lot of money that day, buying drink after drink for distraught Wimbledon fans.

The atmosphere was awful. It was horrible, absolutely horrible. I could see what the Dons fans were going through. It was all so alien, how could this have been allowed to happen?

I never thought they would do it. And as a Brentford fan, I was scared. Suddenly, overnight it didn't matter what the supporters thought about our possible move to Woking. Ron Noades, the owner of Brentford, didn't have to give a damn about us anymore. He didn't have to worry about what the supporters thought, what the council thought. All bets were off. It was a scary time.

By Ray Armfield (Wimbledon fan)

I was working in and around Central London, so I was able to attend the vigil at Soho Square for at least an hour most days. It was strange initially, just standing around with fellow Dons fans, most of whom I barely knew, corralled into a corner outside the FA headquarters, draped with "Show Me The Way To Plough Lane" and other protest banners.

Soho is a cosmopolitan area, and playing "spot the celebrity" raised the spirits. An eclectic mix of Noddy Holder, Ken Bates and Howard Wilkinson passed by, together with bemused tourists, cheeky van drivers, supporters of other clubs and the odd wino.

(FA chief executive) Adam Crozier stopped for a chat, organising drinks and cakes for us. Although he wouldn't be drawn on possible outcomes, he seemed sympathetic. A visitors' book was started, which deserves a place in any future AFC Wimbledon museum.

Little did we know then that the dirty deed was taking place in a solicitor's office. I did, however, see Alan Turvey, the Ryman League chairman and the panel member who voted against MK, leaving the FA in a taxi one day. I gave him an "I know who you are" nod and a smile, as he passed. He looked embarrassed.

Days went by, and the place began to feel like a mini Greenham Common. A van driver dropped off some bottled water for us and just said: "From Brentford – good luck!" Terry Eames turned up for a couple of hours wearing his red Elonex WFC top.

Eventually, whispers were heard that a verdict would be announced on 28 May. Then rumours of the worst kind began. An article appeared in the Evening Standard followed by feverish activity on the internet, announcing that the MK move had been approved.

Unsurprisingly, a larger than average crowd gathered on the final day. Koppel had expensive lawyers and a glossy brochure on his side; we had hard facts and morality on ours. Wasn't that enough?

I don't know what I expected in terms of an announcement: papal white smoke from the roof of the FA, an announcement by a general election-style returning officer? What we got was a terse statement thrust at us by a minion. Before this, media crews began arriving, all with the same opening line: "You've heard they've voted for MK, haven't you?" The mood became depressed. A few eggs were thrown, and some fans briefly gained entrance to the building, but they were token gestures.

And so to home. My wife, who'd been updating me from Sky News during the day, was a bit cautious around me. My daughter didn't really understand the implications of it all, but just said: "That's not fair, Dad."

Wimbledon fans tuck into cakes provided by the **FA Chief Executive Adam Crozier** at the **Soho Vigil in May 2002 (Martin Drake)**

Dons fans man the barricades during the vigil in May 2002 (from left to right) Graham Timms, Dan Stern, Kevin Rye, Steve Elson, Steve Rowlands and Ray Armfield (Martin Drake)

My 13-year-old son's reaction was the most interesting. If it wasn't for school, he was up for joining me at the vigil, having taken part in all the post-match MK demonstrations. I opened his bedroom door and saw that he'd taken down every single WFC picture and poster that had covered the walls. At that point I wished I had Pete Winkelman next to me so he could explain how "deserving" Milton Keynes was to take our football team away, but I couldn't have vouched for his safety if he'd tried.

By Dean Parsons (Wimbledon fan)

When I heard it on the radio after camping out at the FA headquarters the day before, I couldn't believe it. I remember the exact moment it was announced – I was at work in the warehouse and I had to sit down. I really was in shock that the FA were allowing this tragedy to happen to our club, a club I had loved since my first game against Mansfield in 1981. It was as if my whole family had been shot down in front of me, and I began to cry uncontrollably. It was like when we were relegated, but 10 times worse.

By Alasdair MacTavish (Wimbledon fan)

I left work early to walk from Covent Garden to Soho Square, s***ting myself. I turned into Soho Square and immediately I knew it was bad by the look on people's faces. It was the culmination of the worst year of supporting the Dons. I knew that afternoon that I'd never see WFC play again. They just weren't my team any more.

By Matt Couper (Wimbledon fan)

I clearly remember when I heard the news. It was my JFK moment – I knew exactly where I was, alone at work in my office checking and double-checking various websites.

I'm sure a rumour had come out the day before that the decision had gone against us, and I phoned the FA in a bit of a state to ask if the news was true. I can't remember exactly what they said, but it sounded a bit like "We don't know anything and can you kindly go away before I call the police?"

Back in the office I was getting more and more worked up, then the news came through that the move had been approved. All I knew was that I had to get out, I had to be somewhere else. I think to a lot of people that won't make much sense – it's hardly the action of a responsible employee, and it's difficult to explain to non-footy types. Let's just say I was pretty upset (and also I was a lot younger). I ended up at the Soho Square HQ. I was not the only irresponsible employee there, and I was certainly not the only emotional person.

I found myself talking to Kris Stewart and being asked if I wouldn't mind being interviewed by Simon Bates for LBC the following day. I thought this wouldn't be that hard, and he'd be a sympathetic voice, yet I was grilled by him: "Didn't the players have the right to make a living?" and so on. I was a bit taken back and slightly ashamed that I'd allowed myself to be bullied.

By Mark Chapman (Wimbledon fan)

It was a day I'll never forget. I went to work as usual in the morning, but even now I remember how things didn't feel quite right. I didn't think an announcement was imminent, although talk on the Weird and Wonderful World guestbook the night before had indicated that bad news would be released shortly.

A phone call from a friend relayed the breaking story. In a cliché moment, I dropped the vase I was working on, smashing it to pieces. It didn't bother me – all that mattered was how soon I could get to Soho Square. I knew there would be other people there feeling exactly the same, and it seemed so important that we should all be together.

Arriving at the FA, I found exactly what I'd expected. One thing I remember vividly is cars and vans still beeping their horns as they passed, unaware that the fight was lost. A Crystal Palace fan was there, sympathising, yet he may as well have been talking Swedish for all the attention I paid him.

The tears were for later…

By Clair Richardson (Wimbledon fan)

I only missed one day of the vigil. The amazing response of the passers-by made me feel that not only we were right but we also had the support of the British public.

When I heard the decision on 28 May, I cried. I felt I had been part of the biggest injustice – it was wrong, and everyone knew it. I cried, not for me but for the people who had been watching Wimbledon for decades, people who had just had a huge part of their lives ripped away from them, and for the people who had been campaigning for years to bring Wimbledon back home, where the club belongs.

The day only got worse as I travelled for one last time to Soho Square. I was not the only one who had felt the need to be there. The emotion was thick in the air, my friends were hurt and I was tired and angry. It was over.

By Paul Raymond (Wimbledon fan)

I was sitting at work keeping an eye on the websites, and at about 11.50am the message came up that permission for the MK move had been granted. I was stunned. I don't know how I got through the next 10 minutes. At noon I got up and said: "I'm off to lunch." I went out and walked around, thinking of the good times that I'd had and wondered what I would do in the future.

By Mark Hodsoll (Wimbledon fan)

I always look forward to 28 May. I should do, because 28 May is my birthday, along with Kylie and the late Thora Hird. No prizes for guessing who I'd rather spend a joint party with. And this year was no different, with my 38th year dawning.

I'd spent the preceding weeks with more important things on my mind, sneaking off to Soho Square a few times with my son in full kit to man the barricades. We paraded with the faithful to a chorus of toots from passing drivers, and even had our pictures taken for Jockey Slut magazine, blissfully unaware that for much of the time the dirty deed had already been done. To think I even told my son off for kicking his football against the FA window – if only I'd known.

So there was I, looking forward to an Italian meal for two and everything else you'd expect on your birthday, especially with the kids at the in-laws, when bang! – the news I didn't want to hear. The feeling I had in the pit of my stomach is as indescribable today as it was then.

I spent the evening staring out of the restaurant window, drifting in memories from Windsor & Eton to Andy Sayer to Robbie's header at Old Trafford and Hartson's equaliser…and on and on. Cheers, I thought, happy birthday.

By Adam Russell (Wimbledon fan)

Strangely, I didn't feel anything when I saw the news on Teletext – I just felt blank. It still puzzles me even now. I was extremely angered when I first heard of the plans, spending a few days in an internet cafe in Cesky Krumlow (in the Czech Republic) instead of enjoying my holiday. When the MK move was sanctioned, I felt disappointment at such a poor decision being reached rather than anger.

By Trevor Pearce (Wimbledon fan)

Fittingly, news of the murder – or at least the attempted murder – of my club reached me in a scrappy manner, by rumour and from no official sources.

I logged on at work and went to look at the WISA site, expecting to hear nothing but finding a succession of posts from sources of varying repute saying that the battle had been lost. No official announcement, nothing from the daily papers (they had a broken bone in David Beckham's foot to keep them occupied), no clap of thunder or dimming of the lights.

While I can't actually remember the moment that I actually accepted we'd lost, I do remember being unable to think about anything else all day, unable to hold a coherent conversation, much less concentrate on work. I remember going to the gym at lunchtime and mindlessly pushing weights up and down, not knowing whether I'd lifted 10 kilos or 100, twice or 100 times.

Later that day I played football in the park and went to the pub with fans of other clubs, friends who would send me abusive texts after a 5-0 home defeat by Palace. One of them, a Spurs fan, had vowed revenge when he received a cheery message from me 10 seconds after the final whistle of that year's Worthington Cup final defeat by Blackburn, and I was steeling myself for the banter. But even he could only say: "It's not what you sign up for, is it?" – saying in nine words what I've since said in many, many more.

A few pints later, I walked down to the FA to tape my shirt to the window, with a message reading "Wimbledon FC – RIP. FA Sellout" underneath. And that was 28 May 2002.

I cannot get over the fact that the very people whose privileged existence revolves around my game just capitulated and allowed this to happen; that one man, whose sole claim is that he has more money than I do, can take 113 years of history, can take the team that I had spent my adult life obsessing about, can tell me and thousands – yes, thousands – of others that we don't deserve a professional football team when he'd never been to a football match before 1997; and that the people we relied on to sit him down and quietly tell him exactly what this game is about waved him through and then sat back and washed their hands of the whole thing – it's all beyond belief. It just isn't what you sign up for, is it?

By Richard Bugg (Wimbledon fan)

The day started in good spirits, but the rumour went round that we had "lost". The Sky crew asked us for comments, but I refused and said they should wait for Kris Stewart. When he appeared, ashen-faced, and spoke to them, we knew it was all over.

We never really believed the verdict would go against us. It was like having your guts ripped out. I swear that if Charles Koppel had walked by at that moment he would have been torn to bits by the people there.

But it's what being a Dons fan has always been about. We react best with our backs against the wall. Put us down, and we come back better than before. We never know when we are beaten.

By Mark Lewis (Wimbledon fan)

Strange as it may sound now, I had been looking forward to 28 May 2002 for quite some time. I had spent the past six months working hard on an exhibition my company was running in Germany, and as a German-speaker it was partially my responsibility to ensure that all ran smoothly when the show opened on 28 May 2002.

So, when a friend sent me an innocent text saying: "We have lost...", I was thrown into panic. I was shocked, devastated and surprised. Unlike all my football mates, though, who could get out of work and march to the FA, jam the phone lines of all radio stations and make a vocal protest, I was stuck with 300 international

The Wimbledon FC shop after the decision
on 28 May 2002 (Getty Images)

exhibitors and nine non-football-supporting colleagues in picturesque Lübeck in northern Germany.

Now, Lübeck in late May is pleasant enough, with warm sunshine and a breeze from the nearby Baltic Sea to welcome its tourists. But I would not recommend spending one of the most emotionally traumatic days of your life there. I called home several times to check that the text I had received was right. It was – and I went into autopilot for the rest of the day. What I said to clients and colleagues I have no idea, as my mind and soul were far away, floating somewhere over Plough Lane.

By Callum Watson (Wimbledon fan)

We had protested outside the headquarters of the Football Association in May 2002 for two weeks. I had been there for at least three full days. I had waved to numerous taxi drivers, white van drivers and members of the public who had tooted their horns in support of our cause: to stop Wimbledon moving to Milton Keynes.

I had eaten cakes sent down by Adam Crozier, had laughed with two down-and-outs who had volunteered to storm the roof of the FA in return for two cans of beer and met many fellow Wimbledon fans who I hadn't met before but I now count as good friends. Nothing, however, could have prepared me for the shock of the decision of the FA three-man commission who sanctioned the franchising and destruction of a 113-year-old club I had supported with a passion since 1983.

My support for the Dons began quite late in life when, after completing my degree in Edinburgh, I moved to Kingston upon Thames and started work in London. Being a keen football fan, I went to quite a few games – Charlie Nicholas at Arsenal, the Shelf at White Hart Lane, the West Ham "football academy" – but none of these so-called big clubs felt right. The club I was looking for was in fact only a few stops away by train from Kingston to Wimbledon, followed by a short walk past a graveyard. After watching Wimbledon FC only twice, once at Plough Lane and once away at Orient, I found my passion and the football club I would come to love.

Everything was special: the fans (meeting the Batsford Boys and the Epsom Dons on my first away trips helped), the players (Alan Cork walking into the Sportsman pub with his copy of Sporting Life pre-match still makes me smile), the club staff (Eric Willcocks, the link between the fans and the club, made me so welcome) and an atmosphere between manager, fans, players and club that was special and unique. Wimbledon FC was everything you could ever want in a friendly family club.

So on Tuesday 28 May, why did I feel so bad when the decision to move the club to Milton Keynes was announced? I had never lived in Wimbledon, had no family ties with the area, had started supporting the club aged 21, and now lived 50 miles from Wimbledon in Hampshire. Quite simply, my football club had been destroyed – rubbed out and cancelled at a whim. It didn't feel nice then and it feels just as bad now.

Some of our fans were in tears, some were pretty damn angry, some rather shamefully threw eggs and objects at the FA building. I was just numb and in shock. During the many months of protesting I had never even considered the decision going against us. We were right, and the club and the authorities were wrong to destroy our history and heritage. I slipped away as quickly as possible.

By Peter MacQueen (Wimbledon fan)

A few weeks earlier I'd lost my job as a designer and I was having a pretty torrid time of it. I'd been doing temp work, and now I was the lowest of the low, working for a debt-collection company.

I was sat at work when my girlfriend Audrey phoned me to tell me what had happened. She said: "Wimbledon have got permission." I said: "You must be kidding, don't you mean they turned it down?" And she said: "No, no, it's been granted. They are going to Milton Keynes."

I went on the internet straight away and found out it was true. I was literally shaking after that. I had to go and hide in the toilet. I held my head in my hands for five minutes. Afterwards, everyone at work just laughed – they just didn't understand.

By Adam Procter (Wimbledon fan)

I have only a hazy memory of the actual day. I thought then that I would try to remember it all. It was a strange week, and it had been an even stranger season that seemed to be leading to that day.

That whole season was all about 28 May. If you were to ask me where we finished in the League, I can't remember off the top of my head. If you were to ask me to describe Soho Square that week, then I could.

When the news finally came through I remember feeling numb and in shock. I could not understand how such a decision could be made on the basis of all the lies I had heard all season. I wondered what lengths Koppel had gone to, to make sure his spin machine worked on the three men appointed to decide the future of my club. I think I managed one drink that evening, and wondered what I would do with all that spare time on a Saturday.

I had a strange conversation with my dad as I realised that he would not be making the trip to every home game to sit with me and cheer on the Dons. I wished I had seen more games over the years, or at least some of the games my dad had been to. I remember thinking I would probably only watch the FA Cup final and the World Cup now. "Shock" is the only word I can think of to describe it. I think my dad likened it to losing a family member.

By Martin Drake (Wimbledon fan)

Not a normal Tuesday. Joe Blair texted me late that morning. His text simply read: "Oh s*** :(" I didn't need to ask what that meant.

I was stunned, surprised and very annoyed all at once. How could the FA sanction such a move when it patently went against everything they are supposed to stand for? Hiding behind an independent commission was no excuse.

I couldn't work, so I headed straight for the Central Line and Tottenham Court Road. A brisk walk took me to the FA's soulless corporate-style headquarters in Soho Square. There were already around 50 Dons fans there, and the atmosphere was one of righteous indignation. The decision had been announced to the media, but no one from our wonderful FA had bothered to tell the assorted Dons fans outside.

As our numbers grew, we put posters up and shouted songs, but there was still no official notification. Only when we took over the lobby did the FA provide us with a photocopy of their press release. It was over.

The crowds eventually dispersed, to convene at the Fox and Grapes up on Wimbledon Common, the pub where the original Wimbledon Old Centrals team used to change and drink back in 1889. The general feeling of outrage and disappointment after putting up such an imaginative and intelligent campaign for an entire season soon turned to determination and optimism. Marc Jones was there, full of hope, and people suggested starting a new "Wimbledon" football club that would replace the one whose League place had been franchised to Milton Keynes. This time we would truly own our club, and we would never allow anyone to take it from us.

By Karen Hardy (Wimbledon fan)

I was at work. Someone sent me an email about going to MK. I was so shocked I emailed Niall Couper, who confirmed the awful truth. I couldn't work. I had to tell a few friends. I was sick, cold and in disbelief. Then I asked myself: "Well, what are we going to do?" I'm not a member of WISA but I decided then to go to the momentous AGM on the Thursday.

By Matt Akid (Wimbledon fan)

My memories of 28 May are snapshots, moments of clarity snatched from amid the mundanity of everyone else's lives carrying on as usual.

I remember making my way to the FA HQ at Soho Square in my lunch hour, talking to a few fellow supporters huddled in the rain and knowing instantly from the subdued mood that, even though no announcement had yet been made, the unthinkable was happening.

I walked back to the tube station, through the lunchtime crowds of office workers and tourists, not really knowing what to do with myself. After work I had a drink with a friend and saw the news coverage of the decision on a TV screen in the corner of the pub, but still I could not quite believe what had happened.

My overriding emotion was resignation, defeat, a feeling that part of my life – a hugely important part – was over and that my life would now continue minus my team.

I am so grateful that other people kept the faith and refused to buckle, so that two days later I was able to join more than a thousand fellow Dons at the Wimbledon Community Centre to witness the rebirth of our club.

By Andrew Harris (Wimbledon fan)

I first heard the news from a patient when I was doing my afternoon surgery. He knew I was a Wimbledon supporter, so he asked if I had heard. My reaction was shock, disbelief, anger and horror. Needless to say, after that it was extremely hard to focus on what I should have been doing. I drove home that evening wondering where and who I would be watching next season. Fortunately, two days later AFC Wimbledon was formed – and the rest, as they say, is history.

By Robert Smith (Wimbledon Down Under Supporters Association chair)

On the day of the FA Commission's decision, I wondered what would become of the Wimbledon Down Under Supporters' Association (WDSA). After all, WDSA had been going continuously since October 1985, drawing together Wimbledon FC supporters in this part of the world.

Longstanding friendships had been made, and we all had a common purpose. Now that was in peril. There was a fear that this disparate group of ex-pats, Aussies and Kiwis would become a victim of the shameful FA sellout to franchise football.

But that changed for many of us with the birth of AFC Wimbledon. Disenfranchised Dons fans in Australia and New Zealand now had an alternative to dropping out of the game entirely, or even – perish the thought – following some other team who were once our rivals.

There were a few who no longer wanted to be part of WDSA, and went their separate ways, but the great majority pulled in behind AFC. Why? Because we now had something with which we could identify, even if it was many leagues below where the old Wimbledon played.

By Oliver Cooper (Wimbledon fan)

As I lay in Cyprus soaking up the sun in 2001, I caught a glance of the back page of a newspaper. The key words I noticed were "Dons" and "Milton Keynes". I went into a shop to buy a paper, and indeed there it was: Wimbledon FC planned to relocate to Milton Keynes. I was very blasé about Koppel's plans. My friends (Fulham, Brentford, Arsenal and Spurs fans) asked me what I thought. I confidently predicted: "It's a disgrace, there's no way the FA will allow it."

On 28 May 2002 I received a text from a Fulham-supporting friend. "Will ya go to, will ya go to, will ya go to Milton Keynes. Heard on radio, ur def moving." I switched on the radio at lunchtime, and there it was on the 12.30 news. It was official. If only I had stayed longer at the protests, if only I had volunteered to help WISA, if only I had attended the vigil outside the FA, then I might still have my club.

Two days later at the WISA AGM, its members voted to start a new club. Just five weeks after that, AFC Wimbledon played their first game. Over 4,500 turned up. It was emotional, but I predicted that the support would not last.

Now, I've started to enjoy going to football again. I do still have my club, and I've realised that the FA are useless and I'm crap at predicting things.

Chapter Four:

All I want to do is watch football

The AFC Wimbledon trials get underway at Wimbledon Common Extensions on 29 June 2002 (Neil Presland)

The unfulfilled promise… A Mont Blanc pen, Lou Carton-Kelly's promise to Richard Shaw

Marc Jones, one of AFC Wimbledon's founders (Michael Palmer)

Terry Eames, who was instumental in the early days of AFC Wimbledon (Marcus Massey)

The fightback begins

From the moment the decision was made, several key figures at the Dons Trust and WISA moved into action.

---

28 May 2002
Soho Square
By Lou Carton-Kelly

The night before the commission announced its decision, David Burns, the Chief Executive of the Football League, told us what was going to happen. It was a huge shock. We had run such a brilliant campaign.

It was supposed to be a three-man commission, but when we had first walked into the room there must have been 15 people there, including Charles Koppel. It was one of the most horrible experiences of my life.

We put so much work into preparing the evidence. But all the work that WISA had done, the efforts of Yellow and Blue and all the other people who had stood up to be counted, was in vain.

On the day of the announcement I was outside the FA headquarters at Soho Square with Kris. We were trying to cheer everyone up, telling them all that it would be OK – we could start again. I remember in particular a conversation with Xavier Wiggins. Xav was a huge Wimbledon fan, and he bought into the idea.

But the mood the whole day was really horrible. Kris and I had been fans only since 1986, and most of the people we were talking to had a history with the club going back decades, some even 50 or 60 years. How could we console them?

It was non-stop for both of us. Our phones just kept ringing. We knew we had to get something out there for the media. Richard Shaw lent me his blue Parker pen to write up one of the press releases. I said: "I'll give it back as soon as we're done." He said: "You can get me a Mont Blanc pen when we get into the Football League." Those pens retail at about £150. Needless to say I still need to complete my side of that promise.

Kris and I then went to the cafe on the corner of Soho Square and started writing away. I still have the pen, and it sits on my desk at home as a reminder.

The first steps towards the new Dons

It is well known that AFC Wimbledon was born out of the fateful decision on 28 May 2002. The speed at which it all happened surprised many, but the reality was that the plans for setting up a new club had been hatched six months earlier.

Ivor Heller (AFC Wimbledon commercial director)

In the weeks and months after the letter dropped onto people's doormats, I had been rambling on about a new club to anyone who would listen. Kris Stewart, who was then chairman of WISA thought I was joking. But finally one day he said: "Do you know, Ivor, I think you are serious about this." I remember telling him: "Just imagine how much fun it would be to see our fans winning things again and enjoying their football, and how much it would put us in a good place."

The idea of starting a new club actually first came to me in November 2001, in the middle of that last ghastly season at Selhurst, and I had started to do some research. I wanted to find out whether we would be able to get into a league and what we would need to do. I talked to Trevor Williams about it, and we sounded out a few others and got some positive feedback. So I always knew we had a chance of creating our own club. But it all depended on what the Football Association's three-man commission said.

I knew about the decision the day before it was officially announced. I got a call from someone high up in the FA. I'd heard several rumours before saying we'd lost, but there were loads of rumours flying around then.

Instinctively, I wanted to go up to town and join the vigil at Soho Square and get myself arrested, but my gut feeling was if we wanted to be ready for next season we didn't have a day to waste. We had to get on with building a new club.

That night I put a call into Trev, and we arranged to meet at 8.15 in the morning at my factory on Haydons Road. I knew Trev through the Trust work. Of all the people I knew, he had the best knowledge of non-league football. By the time we met, I was resigned to the fact that I had lost my club. I didn't want to do any more protests. I wanted to do something positive. I'd made up my mind that I wanted to start a new club, and I needed help.

After Trev, I called up Marc Jones, and he joined us later that day. I knew Marc well and he was a good communicator. If ever there was a man you wanted on your side, he was the one. I also called Kris, but he had too much to do at Soho Square to come down to the office, but for the club to have credibility it needed to have Kris on board and I arranged to meet him that night.

Me, Marc and Trev were totally focused. We made a list of things we thought we needed to do to make the club a reality, and within 30 minutes we were making calls. By the end of the day we knew what we needed to do to start a new club, and we also knew that we didn't have long to do it.

I spoke to Terry Eames. Terry told us to get in touch with Nick Robinson from the Ryman League. There's no doubt we wouldn't have got started without him. Nick told us we needed to get a local FA to give us senior status – without that there would be no new club. He told us in no uncertain terms that the London FA was a better bet than the Surrey FA. That's when we made the call to David Fowkes at the London FA – he was immensely helpful. He gave us an awful lot of advice, and it was then that we were told how little time we had.

The last chance we had to get senior status approved for the upcoming season would be at the next London FA meeting. But that meeting was on 10 June – just 12 days away. Nick added that to get senior status we needed a league to play in, a London FA form and a groundshare agreement.

They were the first things we aimed for, and by the end of 28 May we had them all under control. Nick Robinson was fairly confident then that we would get into the Ryman League. I had asked Niall Couper, who I knew lived near the London FA headquarters in Lewisham, to pick up the form. They wouldn't accept a faxed version. He got it to us a day later. I then made an appointment with the Khoslas, the owners of Kingstonian, for Friday the 31st.

And that was why Marc went to the Fox and Grapes that Tuesday night so enthused: he knew it was all falling into place. It's my one regret that I never made it up there that night. I'd arranged to meet Kris Stewart. When he arrived I told him: "Look, this is what we are doing, and we would rather do it with you than without you."

At my factory there was an office put aside for the use of the Dons Trust and WISA, but it was never manned, so I said to Kris: "I'm either shutting it down or you are going to use it to set up the new club. If you want to be on board, you walk in here at 9am and it's all go." To his credit, Kris, loved the idea, rolled up his sleeves and got stuck in. By the time of the crucial WISA meeting on the Thursday we had the AFC Wimbledon office up and running, with computers and phone lines fully operational.

The name itself was the hardest part – we had to get it sorted out by the time of the WISA meeting. David Fowkes came in on the Wednesday and helped us with the form. We wanted to be Real Wimbledon, but David said: "No, the London FA wouldn't sanction that." There were a lot of other names being thrown around. Some were really silly, like "Anti-franchising FC", but we felt that "Wimbledon" had to be the focal part of the name. We plumped for AFC Wimbledon.

The next question on the form was: "What is your start-up date?" Kris didn't hesitate – he said: "1889." David said: "Yes, that's it," and put it on the form. That was a real catalyst for me. We weren't a new club – we were still Wimbledon. Kris had made it sound like a joke, but as soon as David had said we could do it, I just thought: "God, we will have some of that!"

We had to move at a pace. Terry Eames and Nick Robinson were around all the time to advise us. It also helped hugely that Kris and I gelled perfectly in those early days – if we hadn't, AFC Wimbledon may never have happened.

The major stumbling block was the three-year groundshare deal, as without that we would not have been allowed to get senior status. We had to have a legal document in place, and we had 12 days do it.

It was non-stop meetings. It was 24/7. We had a host of volunteers helping: Dan Stern, Pat, Mags Hutchison and loads more. There was a whole procession of people coming in and out. People like Ian Hidden were doing loads of bits and bobs.

In those first few weeks Trevor Williams was hugely important. Trev was doing all our administration, and there was tons of it. We needed to raise £30,000 to pay for the groundshare agreement, and the only way to do that was to sell season tickets. Within a day we had applications flooding in and they all needed to be processed.

It was all coming together, but not everything went smoothly. It took some persuading to get the Dons Trust Board fully onside. All the time we had to keep the Dons Trust informed about what we were doing, but we couldn't wait for them, so to get things moving we had to set the club up in our own names and sell it to them later for £1.

By Nick Robinson (Ryman League vice-chairman and company secretary)

I was first involved in the AFC Wimbledon "birth" when I was telephoned by Ivor Heller to ask for advice about how to proceed. I remember going to Ivor's printing works and being amazed at the progress which had been made in establishing the new club. What was most evident was the passion shown by everyone. Kris Stewart was also present at the first meeting and was prominent among those setting up the new club.

For our part, the Ryman League not only had a vacancy, but we had a history of helping clubs. In 1992 we had been the league which took Aldershot Town on its formation following the demise of Aldershot FC. In addition, our chairman, Alan Turvey, was an FA Councillor and it is a poorly kept secret that he had been the minority vote in the three-man commission which allowed the old Wimbledon to move to Milton Keynes. The original club had joined the Isthmian League in 1921 and only left the league on turning professional to join the Southern League in 1964. Alan and I both wanted to help the new club very much. I told Kris, Ivor and the others that we could not make any promises but we would do everything we could. We got the backing of the League Board of Directors, but time was against us.

"I just want to watch football"

It was arguably the most famous speech in the history of AFC Wimbledon. On Thursday 30 May, two days after the decision had been announced, the Wimbledon Independent Supporters Association held a meeting at the Wimbledon Community Centre which drew a thousand people. The first few speakers were sceptical about the creation of a new club. Then Kris Stewart, the chair of WISA, took the floor...

30 May 2002
WISA AGM Wimbledon Community Centre
By Dave Boyle (Wimbledon case worker, Supporters Direct)

I turned up not knowing what would happen. After the trauma of 48 hours earlier, who knew what to expect?

There was standing room only. Then that filled up. Fans were packed in at the back of the hall and even in the foyer. There was a palpable anger in the room, but a defiance too. Motions to boycott Selhurst Park were passed unanimously. Then came the meat of the night's proceedings – should a new club be formed?

WISA chair Kris Stewart stood down from the platform to speak as an ordinary member. The room fell silent as he began. When he said: "I'm tired of fighting. I just want to watch football," he seemed to echo many people's thoughts. Kris spoke about getting a new team going, and that too seemed to echo many people's thoughts.

The vote was overwhelmingly in favour, but did anyone fully realise what had just happened? I think they did. Previously tired legs, aching from standing for two hours, now had a spring in their step.

It was a reminder that football wasn't about franchising or freeloaders. It was about fans. End of. In the pub afterwards, those fans were smiling – something you'd hardly have thought possible just two days before.

By Seb Brown (AFC Wimbledon fan)

I remember the talks in our house between me and my dad about who we could support instead. Tooting & Mitcham had just got a new ground, and we weren't far from Sutton. Milton Keynes was never an option.

Nicole Hammond (centre), who took the chair to allow Kris to speak on 30 May 2002 (Rob Dunford)

And then came AFC Wimbledon. We heard of it through the media and that was it – decision made. It was a continuation of our club. This is it, we thought, this is our team back. There was no difference: AFC Wimbledon is Wimbledon. The same colours, the same badge, the same people, the same spirit, the same ethos. For me and my dad, it was a no-brainer.

By Nicole Hammond (WISA vice-chair)

Many people recall Kris Stewart's "I just want to watch football" speech at the WISA AGM, timed by chance for two days after the decision, as their turning point – the moment they began to believe in AFC Wimbledon.

The Wimbledon Community Centre was rammed to the rafters that evening. In the late May heat, as ever, it smelt of damp – "the smell of revolution" as I've thought to myself every time I've been there since. But it was a very English revolution, with many cups of tea and no bloodshed. There were many more outside, unable to get in, listening to the proceedings via loudspeakers we had positioned on the window sills.

My memories of the events that evening are a little hazy. I was elected on the night as vice-chair of WISA. I took over from Kris in running the meeting as he took the floor, and procedural duties engaged my mind for a while.

The minutes of the meeting tell a complicated story – many at the meeting were in favour of not starting a new club, wanting instead to continue fighting to stop the move happening – there were still enough potential loopholes and stumbling blocks keeping that hope alive. But once Kris had delivered his speech, the mood changed, and in the vote taken at the end of the meeting the overwhelming majority were in favour of setting up a new club, while fighting to claim back the name, badge, history and colours of Wimbledon FC.

The main thing I recall thinking as I looked at the huge crowd was the thought that, finally, we weren't alone, and the majority were no longer insisting that we "sit down, shut up, and watch the game".

The weeks leading up to the start of AFC Wimbledon had been fraught. The vigil, kept for two weeks outside the FA headquarters while the infamous three-man commission deliberated on Wimbledon FC's fate, became a focal point for supporters of Wimbledon and other clubs showing solidarity. Close enough for me to drop by during lunch, but I felt like a lightweight compared to people like Clair Richardson who were there all day, every day.

Fans had already started to talk about setting up a new club – an idea airily, and now famously, dismissed by the commission as "not in the wider interests of football." Although the idea certainly appealed, airing these thoughts publicly before the commission had made its decision made me feel very uncomfortable, as though we had already given up after all those years of campaigning. It smacked of defeat – sending a message that we were not true football fans and no longer cared about the club – something that some sections of the media, fed by the Koppel and Winkelman publicity machine, were only too ready to believe. This was after months of tedious lecturing by some (no doubt London-based, Manchester United-following) commentators along the lines of "I travel hundreds of miles in a weekend to see my club, what pathetic so-called fans refuse to travel a few miles up the M1 to see theirs?" That neatly bypassed football's essence of belonging to a community and going to see home matches locally.

So for me, the moment the decision was made was the moment that AFC Wimbledon began. We left the FA headquarters and headed for the Fox and Grapes on Wimbledon Common to drown our sorrows, reeling from the shock and knowing that, without a doubt, the wrong decision had been made. The defiant planning of the club we had said we would start if the decision went against us began in earnest. Already there was mention of the Ryman League welcoming a re-born Wimbledon with open arms, although in the end it turned out to be more complicated than that.

I know some others took longer to come around to the idea: Lee Willett, then also on the WISA committee and possibly the most committed campaigner around, was prepared to keep on fighting for Wimbledon FC. As I recall, the description of the camaraderie on terraces – actual terraces, where you could enjoy a drink with your friends in the evening sun – we experienced in our first pre-season friendlies as AFC Wimbledon was enough to start bringing him and others around to the prospect of life at the bottom of the pyramid, recalling happier days from Wimbledon's earlier adventures.

By Kris Stewart (WISA chair)

I decided to make the speech only a few seconds before I stood up. It had been going round in my mind since the FA's decision on the Tuesday. I wanted to be able to say what I thought. As a chair, you're not really supposed to speak out, so when I stood up I asked Nicole Hammond to take the chair.

It is really difficult to judge the mood of a meeting. The first few people who spoke were against the idea of a new club. They were saying it was giving in and it was the wrong time to start afresh. They wanted to continue protesting at Selhurst, to spend another year jumping up and down on the seats. That's what finally swayed me to speak. To me, that was very, very dangerous: Charles Koppel had made it clear in the last year that he had no intention of listening to us. Starting a new club a year later would have been so much harder.

I had nothing written down. The thing I remember most about my speech is that I kept saying: "I just want to watch football." And I really meant it. We would go to games, maybe have a few laughs with friends before or after the match. It was an exciting young side and it should have been a great time to watch the team, but everything else had stopped it being enjoyable.

Sometimes protesting can be fun. At the start of the season it had almost made up for what was going on, but by the end even the protests weren't enjoyable. We could launch black balloons, give out leaflets, organise a Fans United Day, even turn our backs on the play. But in the end, what was the point of protesting when Koppel was never going to listen? Even the normally cynical press were on our side.

All this was in my mind when I came to speak. The Community Centre was packed, and it was actually quite difficult to get to the microphone. I remember having a sense of people listening to me – which is quite nice, particularly when you are talking about something that means so much to you. But it was still hard to know what people were thinking. If my speech encouraged people to join in, then that's great.

After I finished, I wasn't thinking clearly – it had been emotionally draining. I couldn't tell you what happened after that, except that there was a moment when lots of people put their hands in the air.

I never thought the vote would be unanimous in favour of creating AFC Wimbledon, especially after those first few speakers. But somehow, over the course of the meeting, the idea had captured people's imagination. It was going to be hard work, but it was also going to be hugely enjoyable, and I think people clicked onto that.

After the meeting, I just wanted to talk to everyone. It was really important that everybody had voted so strongly in favour. I had already made my mind up that I was going to back AFC Wimbledon whatever happened, even if only a couple of hundred of people came with us, but to have thousands was amazing. I can still picture all those hands in the air.

Then the hard work began. Ivor Heller, Marc Jones and Trevor Williams had actually started on 28 May. I had joined in the day after, but we really went for it after the meeting. AFC Wimbledon was up and running, and for the first time in ages I was looking forward to watching football again.

From Sunderland with love

When ex-Sunderland supporter Erik Samuelson moved from accountants Coopers Deloitte to AFC Wimbledon on a free transfer, it was one of the key signings of those formative days.

---

30 May 2002
WISA AGM Wimbledon Community Centre
By Erik Samuelson (AFC Wimbledon fan)

I went to the Leeds replay in 1975 as many fans did, as a one-off, but I didn't go again until my boys got into football. I was a Sunderland fan so I was only meant to accompany them at first. We had sent our two boys to Beatrix Potter School in Wandsworth where every kid supported either Chelsea or Wimbledon. I didn't try to influence them towards Sunderland and thankfully they chose Wimbledon. I don't know how I would have lived with myself had they chosen a big London team like Chelsea!

I took Pieter to his first ever Wimbledon game against Arsenal in September 1987. Wimbledon were dire, awful. We lost 3-0. I thought that would be that, but I hadn't realised how a seven-year-old sees a game. He was enthralled and loved the whole experience. He wanted a scarf but we were so bad I suggested he leave it a few games, not realising that kids see things through very different eyes. I've never heard the last about my meanness and uncaring parenthood by refusing that request! But that's how it began. He started to ask to go to away games, and then he asked to go to a game on his own, then an away game on his own.

My other son, John, was soon hooked in too, and I went with them quite a lot. And then came the turning point. It was a cup game against Sunderland – my team. And half way through, my boys asked me why I wasn't cheering for Sunderland and it dawned on me that I wanted Wimbledon to win. And that was that. I look back at it now with a bit of irony. After everything that followed, I had deserted my team, but at least I had done it for a good reason. There's nothing more important than your family.

A few years later I was the audit partner for Safeway, who owned Plough Lane. I got on well with their finance director. They were having problems with the Plough Lane site for safety reasons – asbestos or something like that – and had to knock down the Main Stand. He offered me the chance for 20 or 30 people to come to Plough Lane to say farewell to the Main Stand and maybe take a souvenir or two. It was around the time that the first letter from Charles Koppel arrived on our doormats announcing the intention to move to Milton Keynes.

I approached Kris Stewart shortly after the Brentford friendly to tell him about the offer. In the end, I remember that people including Collette Mulchrone and Kris came along to say goodbye to the old ground. It was a desperately sad place. It moved me, and it was from there that I started getting involved in the formation of the Dons Trust. I joined one or two of the working groups, and that was the first time I met Ivor and Luke MacKenzie. I seem to recall that Luke did the website design.

The next big moment for me came a few weeks later at a meeting in a wine bar in Wimbledon. Nicole Hammond was there, and she was worried. The club were threatening to sue her over something she had said about their accounts.

At the time, there were various people, notably Peter Proto who eventually became our auditor, looking into their accounts, and I was one of them. I had written something about them on the WISA forum, and Nicole and Peter had taken it from there, added to it and written an incisive commentary. So I got involved and offered her support and analysis. I remember taking a call at the weekend asking me what they should say.

Then came the commission. Kris and Lou Carton-Kelly were going to go so I built on the analysis that Nicole had used to help them challenge what the club were saying about their financial position.

I was getting used to writing football documents and so I suggested to Kris and Ivor that I should develop a business plan on how a bunch of fans could run a football club. It was based on the club losing the appeal and going into administration – a threat they had repeated time and time again. I was a bit naïve then and the detailed plan wasn't a very good one. But the overall conclusion was right, and it offered a route to survival. We would have to sell all our best players, be prepared to go down a couple of leagues and then build up again. Very similar to what actually happened to the franchised club despite all their ambitions.

Straight after the decision was made, I heard about the plans to start a new club. I approached Kris and offered to tweak the earlier plan into a business plan for a new club.

On the Thursday I went to the WISA meeting at the Community Centre. It was the night of Kris' famous speech, "All I want to do is watch football." I was due to comment on WISA's accounts – so I just said: "You don't want to linger on this tonight. The accounts are OK, now let's move on." But I also had the business plan ready then. It wasn't the greatest document I have ever produced – but it showed that it was possible, that it could work. The main thing I remember about it was that it was worked out on an average gate of 1,000 – I was very conservative, as always.

I was watching the proceedings unfold and I was getting a bit worried so I chose to speak. I got up because I was worried that some people were suggesting we should wait a year and continue protesting – they thought we could still reverse the decision. But I knew we couldn't wait. We had to go for it. And at the end, the vote went for AFC Wimbledon.

I remember being quite pushy. Sometime after the meeting. I pulled Kris and Ivor aside and said: "You need a finance director and I want to be him." To my delight they immediately agreed to it.

A few days later, they came round to my house to flesh out the details. My office is up in the loft and has a heavily slanted roof. They were looking over my shoulder. I'm not one for being sizeist, but I had to ask them to swap round. And Ivor agreed to stand under the eaves as we went through the figures.

I never saw myself as one of the founders of the club – that accolade can go to far more worthy individuals than myself – but I was never more than half a yard behind them. I was there at the start doing the stuff in the engine room, as accountants always do.

All hands on deck

At the start, AFC Wimbledon required a whole range of supporters to step up to the plate and turn a vague concept into a real feasible football club – all in a matter of weeks.

By Luke MacKenzie (AFC Wimbledon fan)

We'd talked about it numerous times at WISA and Dons Trust meetings, but nothing was ever concrete. It was all really about taking over Wimbledon FC, not starting our own club.

It became more of a possibility during the vigil outside the FA headquarters, but the talk only really became serious after the decision. A day or so later I took a call from Ivor. "We need someone to do security and you're it," he said.

By Lou Carton-Kelly (Dons Trust chair)

Lee Willett had built up a great relationship with the police at Norwood, while he was on the WISA Committee. The police had always been kept informed of all our protests. So there was never any issue with the Kingston police – they knew we would never be any trouble, they'd checked with their Norwood counterparts.

I flew off to Japan for the World Cup straight after the famous WISA meeting but I knew things were in good hands. They didn't need me. If there was ever a time for other people to step up to the plate, this was it. There were plenty of good people at WISA and the Dons Trust who could take responsibility plus all the folk who had volunteered their help and services.

I remember meeting Lawrie McMenemy. I was wearing a WFC training top and my Dons Trust baseball cap. We were in the Sapporo Beer Garden and the menu was very Japanese. I heard this very distinctive Geordie voice ordering potato skins. The waitress asked him if he wanted anything to go with the potato skins, and he said: "Chips". It was then that he saw me.

"Hey, Wimbledon, what are you going to do next?" he asked. "We're going to start again from the very bottom," I replied. And he just said: "Good luck" – and you could tell he meant it.

There were many senior football figures out there, and again and again I would bump into people that were full of goodwill. In the weeks that followed I would become Operations Director at AFC Wimbledon, I was chair of the Dons Trust Board, and a part of the WISA Committee. Eventually, I gave up my role with WISA, but did become vice-chair of Supporters Direct.

Doing the deal with Khosla

With just 12 days to secure a groundshare agreement, the race was on – not just to do a deal, but to do the right deal. In the heat of the moment, there was only one man for the job – the ever enthusiastic Ivor Heller. Ivor's first point of call was Rajesh Khosla. He had bought Kingstonian from administration and the club were now leasing their own ground directly from him.

Kingsmeadow, the home of AFC
Wimbledon (Terry Buckman)

31 May 2002
Kingsmeadow

By Ivor Heller (AFC Wimbledon commercial director)

As soon as AFC Wimbledon was founded, people started to speculate about where we were going to play. Very early on we knew that Leatherhead and Dulwich would take us. My opinion was that we needed to be closer to home.

In those early days, there was a lot of pressure to groundshare with Dulwich or Leatherhead by one senior person at the very heart of AFC Wimbledon at the time. But for me, Kingstonian was the only option. I knew that playing there would pay dividends in the long run. It would be close enough to our home community for us to call ourselves Wimbledon. We couldn't be Wimbledon at Dulwich or Wimbledon at Leatherhead.

Let's get one thing straight: Rajesh Khosla is a lot like Nick Robinson – they have both taken a lot of stick from Wimbledon fans over the years, but without either of them we probably would not exist. We were in a race against time. We had just 12 days to get a groundshare deal signed, sealed and delivered.

I made the call to Khosla, and a few days later we pitched up at Kingsmeadow to meet him. He gave us a tour of the ground, not that that really mattered. It was a neat non-league ground and that was all we needed. Everything about him boiled down to money. In the weeks that followed, we had to pick up the legal fees. There always seemed to be expenses, and we always had to pay them.

The first day we spoke to Khosla, he asked how many games we were going to play. At the time, we were fairly confident that we would be going into Division Two of the Ryman League. They only had 16 teams at the time, so we said, including cup ties, 17 games. He paused and then asked how many people did we think would go to games. We could only really guess at how big the club was going to be. The minute I said "Around a thousand", he knew what it meant – hard cash.

He didn't care about the state of the pitch. He wanted the asset he had bought for himself to pay for itself. He had four teams playing at Kingsmeadow, but three of them were midweek – so he could see how it would fit in. If he had been a football man, there would have been no way we could have done a deal. But he was a money man. Khosla has taken a lot of s*** over the years for his attitude, but it was because of that attitude that we would be playing at the best place possible.

Our original deal was for 17 games for a season at a cost to us of £20,000 per annum. There would also be one pre-season friendly against Ks, where they got to keep all the gate money. I remember walking out and saying to Kris: "We got some deal there!" Considering we needed a place to play, somewhere close to Wimbledon and a deal in place in 12 days, this was about as good as we were going to get. Even after that, there were still other clubs throwing their hats into the ring.

The Dons Trust takes over AFC Wimbledon

The passion displayed by Ivor Heller and Kris Stewart could only take AFC Wimbledon so far. They needed financial clout behind them. It came in the form of the Dons Trust.

---

13 June 2002
Dons Trust meeting Wimbledon Community Centre
By Lou Carton-Kelly (Dons Trust chair)

There was never any doubt that the Dons Trust would back the decision to own AFC Wimbledon. Really it was the only option. No Wimbledon fan wanted to have their club stolen from them again, and with a democratically elected body owning the club we could ensure that it could never happen. But even with all that certainty I was still elated that the decision went through. It was the end of a horrible 12 months.

I was devastated by the decision on 28 May. On behalf of the Dons Trust, I had put forward the case against the MK move to the three-man commission. Having spent so many months fighting for our club, I simply could not believe that they ruled in favour of the move. And the decision to back AFC Wimbledon put a line under everything that had gone before.

We had always had in the back of our mind that one day we might have to rescue a football club, namely WFC Ltd – but this was far better. This was building a club that would belong to the fans. We already had bank accounts open and we could start taking donations and season-ticket money from people. And once we had the backing of our members, we started moving.

AFC Wimbledon also made a few other key announcements that night that just added to the euphoria: a kit and a manager.

By Matthew Breach (AFC Wimbledon fan)

The FA announcement really didn't hit home at first. I was numb and just couldn't believe it. The following day I was on a 747 to Japan for the World Cup, and spent the flight wondering if I might never go to a game again. The first couple of days in Tokyo were a blur of new sights, sounds and smells, before the uninspiring England display against Sweden dampened the mood.

I took the bullet train to Sapporo. From my hotel there, I phoned my fiancée back at home, and she read me the letter from the Dons Trust outlining the plan for a new club. After making arrangements to send off the £200 pledge ASAP, I went out into the city with a new sense of hope for the future.

My first port of call was the Sapporo Brewery beer garden for an "eat and drink as much as you like in 180 minutes" barbecue-fest. I spotted a lady across the hall wearing a Dons Trust cap. I rushed over to impart the glad tidings, and to my surprise she told me all the latest insider news – this was none other than Lou Carton-Kelly, the chair of the Dons Trust.

Now on the crest of an emotional wave, I made my way to the Sapporo Dome and screamed England on to an historic win over Argentina. Suddenly, life could hardly be bettered...

The naming of a manager

So by mid-June, AFC Wimbledon was up and running. But who would take charge of team affairs? There were dozens of applicants, but at first the favourite was reluctant even to put his name in the hat.

13 June 2002
Dons Trust meeting (Wimbledon Community Centre)
By Terry Eames (AFC Wimbledon manager)

I had been involved from the very start of the club and I wanted the job, but I still never saw it coming. I got a call from Ivor Heller on 13 June to say there was a meeting of the Dons Trust in Wimbledon that night. He said: "Terry, we really want you to be there tonight. We've got an important announcement to make and we need you there."

I didn't think I could make it. I had meetings until 6pm in Crawley. I couldn't see how I could get to the Community Centre for the start at 7.30pm. So I asked him what the announcement was going to be. "You're going to be the manager," came the reply. I said: "You've got to be joking!" Naturally, I was there for 7.30pm.

I had played for the club in the late Seventies, but I hadn't been involved that much until the Fans United Day in December 2001. My wife had been a season-ticket holder for five years, and she asked me to come down and show some support. It was that day that I first met Kris Stewart and Ivor Heller. I didn't like what was happening to the club I had played for 20-odd years earlier. This wasn't the Wimbledon I knew.

The day the decision to move to Milton Keynes was finally announced, Ivor came to me and asked me what I thought we should do. It was obvious: we would have

to start again. A day after the announcement, I met Kris and Ivor at the Tattenham Corner pub in Epsom. We all agreed that we couldn't let Wimbledon die.

We had made our decision. I had been manager of several non-league clubs and still knew quite a few people in the game. I spoke to the chairmen at Leatherhead and Dulwich, and they were really helpful. I also knew Nick Robinson, the secretary of the Ryman League, quite well, so I gave him a call and put the AFC Wimbledon proposal to him. He was really keen and explained what we needed to do. The first priority was to find somewhere to play.

Ivor contacted Kingstonian about a groundshare. We already knew that Leatherhead and Dulwich would be happy for us to share, but Ks was the ideal location. It was near Wimbledon and it had all the facilities we could want.

The next big decision was to choose a manager. I wanted the job badly, but I decided to sit on the fence for a while and just help out where I could. I didn't want to steal Ivor and Kris' thunder, so I kept quiet and waited. There were many applicants for the job, and a few of them were really talented people. But Ivor and Kris wanted someone whose heart was in Wimbledon. When they asked me, I didn't need to think twice. I just wanted to get the club going. I was part of the history – I had the link with the old times.

At the Dons Trust meeting they called me up to say a few words. I hadn't prepared anything, but I ended up coming out with a speech straight from the heart. The reaction was great, and I remember thinking: "This is me – this is me made for life." I saw the pleasure on all those faces.

In the days that followed I got a lot of backing from the likes of Dickie Guy and

Jeff Bryant. I have never enjoyed myself more than in the days, weeks and months that followed. The first two weeks were mayhem. I'd just had a knee operation, so I wasn't very mobile.

I had to try to get the best individuals. Lee Harwood, who was at Wimbledon as a player in the Seventies with me, was a huge help back then. I hadn't seen him for something like 15 years, but he was the right person at the right time. I needed someone to back me up, someone to support me, and he was perfect.

I recruited Paul Bentley and John Egan, who went on to run the under-11 and under-10 sides. Between them, those two had played over 1,500 games in the Ryman League, and they went round trying to get players interested.

Paul and John helped loads: I would say that around three-quarters of AFC Wimbledon's CCL players came through their recommendations. But in the early days the key was the trials. It was like going to a fete. I was expecting 60 players to turn up, and we ended up with nearly 300. Everything was go. AFC Wimbledon was happening – and I was the manager.

The race to find a league

It was a mad rush to find a league that would take the Dons. The first point of call was the Ryman League and, ironically, another encounter with Alan Turvey, a member of the commission whose decision had led to the club's formation.

---

17 June 2002
Ryman League AGM Le Meridien Hotel, Gatwick
By Nick Robinson (Ryman League company secretary)

In those days we had to give 21 days' notice for an AGM and our papers had already gone out to our member clubs without the required resolution appearing on the papers. We took external solicitors' advice and were told very clearly that we could only pass a resolution which was not on the calling papers for the AGM if 95 per cent of those present and entitled to vote did vote in favour of the proposition. It was either that or we had to call a fresh AGM and give 21 days' notice, when a simple majority of 51 per cent would be sufficient.

But at the same time as this was happening we were concerned for the future of the (Ryman) League. A suggestion had been made at this time that the Football Conference might seek permission for two feeders, North and South in place of the Premier Divisions of the Isthmian, Northern Premier and Southern Football Leagues which were the feeders at that time.

In 2001-02 the Isthmian League had four Divisions, which fed directly into each other and so had four "steps" for clubs to go through. At the 2002 AGM we were looking to merge Divisions One and Two to create Divisions One North and South and this involved a raft of rule changes. We had a fairly complicated voting system at that time because we had full members who had a vote each and associate members who had one vote for every five associate members.

It was all very complicated and we had little choice but to go ahead with the scheduled AGM, we couldn't call a fresh one. We wanted to make sure that the

Fox and Grapes pub, where Wimbledon fans had gathered waiting for the news

principal votes went through, but we decided to put a special resolution "To accept on short notice an application for membership from AFC Wimbledon". The meeting was held at Le Meridien Hotel at Gatwick Airport on Monday 17 June 2002.

On the Saturday before the AGM we had held our Annual Presentation Awards Banquet & Ball at the Copthorne Hotel, Effingham Park and driving down there on the early Saturday afternoon I was listening to Radio London. Tom Watt was hosting a phone-in programme and most callers wanted to talk about AFC Wimbledon. When I arrived at the hotel I received a call on my mobile asking whether I would be prepared to be interviewed on air by Tom. I agreed to this and told Tom everything I had told those who were working so hard to bring the new club to fruition. I explained that we needed 95 per cent of the votes to be in favour of the proposition on the Monday night, that we were hopeful that we could find a place within the Isthmian League for the new club.

By Kris Stewart (AFC Wimbledon chairman)

That day was one of the nastiest ever. It was so horrible. There was a woman following us around with a camera – she had been there to catch the joy as we went from one success to another – but there was no joy to film on this occasion.

The Ryman League AGM took place at some nondescript hotel near Gatwick Airport. Ivor and I had gone along but it wasn't obvious what we were going to be allowed to do. We didn't know what the form was – whether we would be allowed in or whether we would have to sit outside.

We then met up with Nick Robinson, the Ryman League secretary, and he said simply: "I'll come out and speak to you when it's done." He asked us to wait outside. We waited, and we waited. And then we waited some more. And when we got tired of waiting, we had to wait some more. It just went on and on. We wanted to know what the problem was, and we were getting more and more anxious.

We had arrived thinking that the approval of our application was going to be a formality – that was the vibe we had got from Nick Robinson. I thought we were going in and that was that. I didn't think for one moment it would be a "no", but time went on and the doubts began to surface.

By Nick Robinson (Ryman League company secretary)

The AGM started and we agreed the minutes of the last AGM, approved the accounts and the directors' report for the previous season. Then we turned to the future and the question of new clubs to be voted into the league. I stood up and explained the situation to the member clubs.

There were a number of questions from the floor. I recall two clubs principally talking against the idea but we answered all the questions honestly and as well as we could. We knew of the potential for four-figure crowds at grounds which were only used to seeing two or three-figure crowds and we reminded everyone what a success story Aldershot Town had been, what a tremendous boost it had been for clubs which had made so much money in one game against Aldershot that they virtually funded the rest of their season from it; yes, I had seen the papers relating to where the Club would play; yes, I was fully satisfied that the club would be good members of the league; yes we had taken legal advice to say that we could do this and yes, the FA would allow us to have AFC Wimbledon in our constitution. But it all hinged on 95 per cent of those present and voting putting up their hands in favour of the proposition.

By Alan Turvey (Ryman League chairman)

We wanted AFC Wimbledon in the League. It had been our recommendation. But there was always the issue of the constitution. With such a late application, we needed 95 per cent of our member clubs to vote in favour of the motion. It's different now: the FA have a far bigger say in whether clubs can join, but this was 2002 and we had to go with our rules.

By Nick Robinson (Ryman League company secretary)

Eventually the time came for the vote and the question was first asked as to whether clubs were in favour and a great number of hands shot up in the air. The chairman then had to ask if there was anyone against the proposition and we looked nervously around and saw that there were, I think, three votes against which meant that the proposal was defeated. I had to tell those who had worked so hard that there was no happy beginning.

By Alan Turvey (Ryman League chairman)

I was confident that they would get the nod. So when the vote came through I was genuinely surprised. It was upsetting. I don't recall who voted against – and I can't even second-guess why they did it. It could have been for any reason. But I just couldn't fathom it.

By Kris Stewart (AFC Wimbledon chairman)

Eventually Nick Robinson came out and told us: "Because it was a late application you needed 95 per cent of the vote, you got 87 per cent and you're not in." And that was kinda like "f*** it".

We'd had the hopes of thousands of Wimbledon fans on our shoulders. We now had the job of delivering the horrible news. We didn't have a Plan B. There was nothing else to suggest. Could we really survive playing a season of friendlies? We were so sure we were going to be in the Ryman League that we hadn't even thought about Plan B.

We had to phone people to let them know. We knew that fans had been gathering at the Fox and Grapes expecting only good news. I phoned Jonesy and Terry and they told people. It was horrible. We wanted to get out of that hotel and get back as soon as we could. Ivor must have been flashed by every speed camera between Gatwick and Wimbledon.

When we got back, Ivor got a call from Nick Robinson, and it was then that he mentioned the Combined Counties League. But, before then, there had been a long time of "f*** it". We had been completely on the floor – all our hopes had vanished.

By Nick Robinson (Ryman League company secretary)

In the end, thanks to Alan Constable, we were able to help AFC Wimbledon find a place in the Combined Counties League, which was a direct feeder to us in those days. Two years later AFC Wimbledon joined us as Champions of the CCL and we had four tremendous years during which AFC Wimbledon made many friends.

In 2008 we were sad to see them go but they went with our blessing to Conference South and were confident that they would join the ever-growing number of clubs becoming members of the Football League after being members of the Isthmian League.

By Iain McNay (AFC Wimbledon fan)

After the Ryman League vote, everyone was scrambling around for an alternative. At that time my business, Cherry Red Records, sponsored the Hellenic League whose teams were mainly based in Oxfordshire and Wiltshire. The Premier division was Step 5, the same level as the CCL. I knew the league chairman, Michael Broadley, well and had already talked to him to see if the Hellenic League would take the club if our application to join the CCL didn't go through. It wasn't ideal – geographically, the club at that time closest to us was probably Henley Town . But it would have meant that at least we would have got up and running in the pyramid. Michael was 100 per cent positive: "We'll take you, no problem at all. We would love to have you."

By Alan Constable (Combined Counties League secretary)

In the early summer of 2002, rumours had spread about the formation of a phoenix Wimbledon side following the defection to Milton Keynes.

By the time the Ryman League AGM was due to take place in June 2002, which I attended as the secretary of Ashford Town, the rumours had grown, but it was not until the announcement on the night of that meeting that it became clear to me that they had made a late bid to become members of the league. The league secretary Nick Robinson carefully explained that, due to the late application, the Ryman rules required a majority of 95 per cent in favour before the club could be admitted.

It was obvious to me that both Nick and the chairman Alan Turvey wanted the vote to go in the club's favour (both could see the potential). But at the time there was some ill-feeling towards the top table in connection with other matters, especially from some of the larger clubs, and I firmly believe that a few of them used the Wimbledon situation as a tool to show their disapproval. Indeed, although certain clubs (one or two quite local to Wimbledon, which I won't name) spoke out against their election, I do not believe there was any specific or sustained ill feeling towards the new club.

Most, if not all, of the smaller clubs, including my own, were very much in favour, but we only had one vote for every six clubs or so. When the result was announced it showed that while there was a clear majority in favour of the club coming into the League, the necessary majority had not been reached.

The AGM ended rather noisily, but the situation was not lost on me and I quickly asked Nick if he would be happy for the Combined Counties League to take them. He felt that would be a good idea, and I believe he immediately alerted Kris Stewart of the possibility. My immediate thoughts were that, while it would be a real challenge for some of the CCL clubs to stage matches where there would be an attendance far higher than they had been used to, it was an opportunity for the CCL, both financially and in terms of publicity, that simply could not be ignored.

On the way home from the Ryman AGM I phoned Clive Tidey, then secretary of the league, and, like me, he was enthusiastic about the idea. The following day, we contacted Wimbledon and arranged a meeting between the CCL and the club. This was duly held at my own club, Ashford Town. It was positive, and we agreed to recommend to the clubs at our own AGM that AFC Wimbledon should be elected.

Not all of our own clubs, nor indeed one or two of the officers, were initially convinced that it was a good idea. But they were in the minority, and under our rules we only needed a simple majority to get the motion passed.

Frimley Green FC and North Greenford United FC were up for election as well and both were duly elected. It was then AFC's turn, and they made an excellent presentation. Following a number of questions, it was proposed by Withdean 2000 FC and seconded by Hartley Wintney FC that the club be elected. The motion was carried with just two votes against – and we were off on the league's "biggest" adventure.

A Championship sponsor steps forward

The fledgling Dons needed funds – and they needed them fast. The Milton Keynes fiasco had enraged a huge swathe of the football-going public. Among them was a Watford fan. This fan, however, also happened to be a director for one of the nation's most successful computer game companies, SI Games, the creators of Championship Manager. It would lead to a long-lasting relationship that helped to underpin AFC Wimbledon's finances for the coming decade.

AFC Wimbledon announce SI Games as the club's first sponsors with Miles Jacobson, far left (Getty Images)

June 2002
By Miles Jacobson (SI Games director)

I'd been following the franchising of football stories closely ever since Dublin was first mooted, especially as my beloved Watford had been mentioned to me as a possibility for moving there, or to Milton Keynes. A journalist had told me: "Milton Keynes really want a club there." To which I pointed out they already had one, and then I hadn't thought too much more about it.

The Dublin idea failed, and then Wimbledon moving to Milton Keynes was being talked about. I knew how angry I'd be if this happened to Watford, and Watford to MK wasn't far away at all in comparison. So I spent time on some forums, spoke to some friends, and all I saw from everyone was "We're going to fight this."

Shortly after the decision that defied all logic, and everything about the spirit of the game, was made, I heard an interview with Kris Stewart followed shortly by another with Ivor Heller on 5 Live. I picked up the phone, and called our marketing guy at Eidos, our publisher at the time, who are based in Wimbledon.

I told him what I'd just been listening to on the radio and asked him what he thought of the situation. Eidos had just ended its relationship as an England football partner, and we had a new game coming out. "Why don't we sponsor them as part of the marketing campaign?" he suggested.

So I called up a friend of mine at 5 Live to get a number for Ivor and Kris. After a little chat about how much I loved what they were planning, I simply asked if they had a sponsor. "We've had a few calls, but nothing is agreed yet," said Ivor. "How much do you need to run the club for a year?" I asked.

After getting all the info together on what we could offer them, the logos on the kits, the length of deal, etc, I got a call from our marketing guy at Eidos. "We can't do it – there's to be no more football sponsorship." I ranted and raved for a few minutes – I did that a lot in those days. I put the phone down and was about to phone Ivor when I thought: "So what if they won't do it – we still can."

I managed to get hold of Paul and Ov (Oliver) Collyer, the founders and the other two directors of SI at the time, and told them my idea. Of course, they were well versed in the story – we all were at SI. We all passionately opposed what was happening. We wouldn't want it happening to our clubs, so why would we be happy with it happening to another?

I phoned Ivor and told him I was going to fax him over the offer, and I wanted it signed the next day. We were going to try to be a sponsor with a difference. Not one that just had their name on the shirts and made stupid demands about wanting to have their photo taken with the manager on the pitch every month. But one that would get involved, would be part of the club, part of the story. And ever since then we have had what I believe is the best, most open and fairest sponsorship deal in football. Long may it continue.

I'm really lucky. I've been to watch football all over the world. I've seen my hometown club, the one I've always supported, in play-off finals, Europe, promotions, relegations. And still the most emotional football moment I have had was the minute when the final ball was kicked at the City of Manchester Stadium in 2011.

The trials

The club now had a manager, but no players. It would have been almost impossible to build a squad just through contacts, so the decision was made to hold an open trial on Wimbledon Common. Volunteers were on hand to run the proceedings, and even former Wimbledon FC manager Terry Burton lent a hand. But the numbers quickly became overwhelming.

---

29 June 2002
Wimbledon Common Extensions
By Terry Burton (former Wimbledon manager)

David Barnard, who had been chief executive at Wimbledon FC and, like me, had been sacked that previous season, had said to me: "They've got the trials going on down at Wimbledon Common. Do you fancy going down there?" I said: "Great, let's give them our support."

I said to a few press people at the time of the three-man commission: "Look, they have been shafted. But they haven't just accepted it – they are actually trying to do something about it. I think it's fantastic that this group of people are now trying to recreate a football club." At that stage I was still under contract at Wimbledon. So there wasn't a lot I could do in any official capacity.

But, I wanted to be there and show my support for all they had done, the principle of it: "You can kick us, but you can't keep us down." That was great, terrific. But with due respect, this was a group of Sunday footballers at best, so I didn't really give any advice.

Terry Eames had done a fantastic job in just getting these people together and then getting a team together – all of that was just amazing. You couldn't begrudge them having the chance to start again.

By Dickie Guy (former Wimbledon goalkeeper)

I was asked to go down to the trials just to have a look at the goalkeeping situation. I was more than happy to help out, and I went to the first couple of training sessions afterwards as well.

I was still so surprised at how quickly the club got off the ground and how quickly the fans had found out what to do. No one had run a club before, no one had been in touch with the FA before, no one knew how to get into a league – and they had done it all.

The way the club got started and progressed, it was so amazing. AFC Wimbledon caught everyone's imagination, right across the country.

By Sim Johnston (successful trialist)

I found out about the trials two days before they happened, thanks to my mate Eddie Piggott. We work in the same office, and he was listening to Kiss FM when Chris Phillips came on and started plugging them. Eddie came over and asked if I had heard. He knew I was looking for a team. I'd just moved up from Kent, where I had been playing for Otford United, and I thought: "Yeah, I'll give this a try."

I went down there on my own, on my motorbike. I was like Billy No-mates and I was just freaked out seeing all those people. I thought: "How the hell am I going to show what I can do with all these people around?" The organisers had expected 60 people, and they ended up with over four times that. There weren't enough bibs to go round, which made things even more difficult.

I remember walking around, looking to see if any of the players were any good or not. Some people knew each other. There were players of all different standards, but none that I recognised. I heard later that Joe Sheerin, who had played for Chelsea, was there. His presence apparently caused quite a stir, but I was oblivious to it.

The idea of the trial scared me to death. I had always had a nightmare at trials. I'd failed again and again, but this was the first one where I did myself justice. I got picked out by a guy called Brendan, I can't remember his surname. It was a bit of a weird situation: he was also trying out, and yet he was my group leader.

The day began with everyone being split into two groups. Half did ball skills, while the other half played mini-games. I started in the half doing ball skills – it was basically just hanging about in the sun. But when it came to the mini-games I tried really hard, but as a centre-back it's hard to shine. During the day I'd seen that some players had been approached, but no one had come up to me.

Then Terry called everyone over, and I was thinking: "S*** – that's it," and how bad it had been that I had never really been able to show what I can do. It was then that I got a tap on the shoulder from Brendan, asking me what my name was. I went home on a huge high – I was buzzing. It had been madness, but it was also a top day.

The second trial was a few days later at the same place. We did the same kind of things, but this time it was easier to be seen as there were only 60 of us. There were some new faces that Terry had invited down. I thought: "After all that, here's another

Terry Eames and Luke Harwood check over
the details at the trials on 29 June 2002
(Neil Presland)

AFC Wimbledon manager Terry Eames speaks to
the trialists on 29 June 2002 (Niall Couper)

Former Wimbledon manager Terry Burton (left) offers words of advice to Terry Eames at the trials on 29 June 2002 (Neil Presland)

Lord Faulkner of Worcester, who gave a speech on AFC Wimbledon in the House of Lords on 3 July 2002

GIANT KILLERS !

Dave Beasant saves a penalty in the 1988 FA Cup Final.

"We should beat Sutton, but it won't be a landslide. Just a thoroughly professional performance".
Coventry City goalkeeper Steve Ogrizovic prior to a Cup defeat against Sutton United, 1989.

Part of the attraction of the FA Cup is the prospect of smaller teams beating bigger, more favoured opponents. This is known as 'Giant Killing'. Over the years there have been many outstanding results for the 'underdogs'. One of the biggest shocks came in 1901, when Tottenham Hotspur became the only Non-League team to win the trophy.

Here are four more FA Cup shocks that amazed the football world:

In 1879, Darwen were 5-0 down at half time to the all conquering Old

big hurdle to cross." But AFC Wimbledon was the team to join. At the end of each session they would read out a list of names – the ones who would stay on. By the time of the first pre-season game against Sutton they had narrowed it down to 30.

We were all wondering who would play in that first game. The changing room was absolutely rammed. Terry Eames still hadn't picked the starting team. And then came the news that I was in the first ever AFC Wimbledon starting XI. After the nightmare of the trials and being knackered for days after putting all my effort into training, I had made it to the first ever line-up. It was very special – it was like my FA Cup final.

My family were watching, and they just hadn't expected the whole AFC Wimbledon experience to be as big and as huge as it was. They were proud of me and they were amazed. That completed a very special few weeks for me.

Lords a-leaping

Back in the wider world of football, the collapse of ITV Digital had led to a financial crisis among England's Football League clubs. It prompted a debate in the House of Lords. Lord Faulkner of Worcester used the opportunity to appeal to his colleagues to support AFC Wimbledon. Below is his speech.

---

3 July 2002
House of Lords
By Lord Faulkner of Worcester

I start with a little history. Today's football club was founded in 1889 as Wimbledon Old Centrals and played on Wimbledon Common. It moved to Plough Lane in 1912, and stayed there in the heart of the local community until 1991 when it embarked on what was expected to be a temporary groundshare at Crystal Palace's ground in the neighbouring borough of Croydon as it was decided – wrongly, as a recent feasibility study demonstrated – that the Plough Lane ground could not be brought up to the all-seated standards demanded by the Taylor Report after the Hillsborough disaster.

During the 113 years of its existence, the club enjoyed periods of extraordinary success, including winning both the FA Amateur Cup and the FA Cup, and was elected to the Football League in 1977. Within nine years it had been promoted to the highest league, where it stayed until its relegation two years ago. During the Eighties and Nineties the principal shareholder and owner of the club was Mr Sam Hammam, a charismatic though at times controversial figure who sought, often successfully, to motivate his players by unconventional means. Mr Hammam bought the disused Plough Lane ground from the club and then, in 1994, sold it to Safeway for development for £8 million. Most football supporters believe that the gain which was realised, well over £7 million, should have gone back to the club and been invested in a new ground.

In 1997 Mr Hammam sold 80 per cent of his shareholding to a Norwegian company, AKER RGI, for around £25 million. It is believed that the Norwegians, Mr Røkke and Mr Gjelsten, invested in Wimbledon because they believed that the club would move to Dublin and take its Premier League membership with it. To the short-lived relief of its supporters, whose views had not been sought on any of those matters,

Bjorn Gjelsten, owner of Wimbledon FC, and former owner Sam Hammam (Yellow & Blue)

the English and Irish football authorities blocked that move.

The next step came in April 2000, when Mr Hammam sold his remaining interest to a company in which the current club chairman, Mr Charles Koppel, is a shareholder. Relegation from the Premier League followed immediately. There then followed a campaign led by Mr Koppel and backed by expensive lawyers and PR consultants to win support for the club's move from Selhurst Park, not to a ground in Wimbledon, elsewhere in Merton or, indeed, anywhere in London, but to Milton Keynes, over 60 miles away, where developers offered it a ground, effectively for nothing.

The matter was considered by a series of football authority committees and commissions and was finally resolved by a three-man team on 28 May. It received evidence and submissions from a wide range of organisations, including the Football Association, Wimbledon supporters and Merton Council, all of which were vehemently opposed to the move to Milton Keynes.

The commission's report is extraordinary. It bears reading and can be found on the FA's website. It contains these words: "We find the cherished and fundamental principles of football in this country in relation to the pyramid structure and promotion and relegation on sporting criteria alone, admirable. Likewise we respect, value and would seek to uphold the community basis of football clubs. We do not wish to see clubs attempting to circumvent the pyramid structure by ditching their communities and metamorphosising" – that is not a word in my dictionary but it is in the report – "in new, more attractive areas. Nor do we wish, any more than the football authorities or supporters, for franchise football to arrive on these shores."

Yet, despite those admirable sentiments, the commission determined by a two-to-one majority to approve the move to Milton Keynes. It appears that the only piece of evidence which influenced it was the threat by the owners to liquidate the club if the verdict went against it. In what is, frankly, an insult to the intelligence, the commission suggested that in perpetuity there should be a corner of Milton Keynes that would be forever Wimbledon; that street names be changed to represent names similar to those in Wimbledon; that the area of the stadium be called "Wimbledon Park" and that special subsidised trains run from Milton Keynes, and so forth.

The truth is that the commission is allowing the owners to steal the club from its supporters and the community of Wimbledon. It is establishing a precedent which will allow other Football League sides to be relocated by their owners anywhere in the country, and the principle of a franchise is being established for League membership. There is no right of appeal against the commission's decision. The football authorities say they oppose it but can do nothing.

Directors and owners should see themselves primarily as guardians of a public asset, as temporary custodians of an entity in which others, such as supporters and the local community, have a genuine stake. In the case of Wimbledon, the club existed for over 100 years before the present owners took it over. It is therefore not just another investment for them to do with what they like.

The supporters, to their immense credit, are determined to keep senior football going in Wimbledon and through the Dons Trust have formed a new club, AFC Wimbledon, which won election to the Combined Counties League. While there is still uncertainty about where the other Wimbledon club will play next season – incidentally, it is now known mainly as "Franchise FC" not "Wimbledon FC" – AFC Wimbledon will start in August at Kingstonian's ground, just down the road in New Malden. I wish them well and so, I hope, do all Members of this House.

Chapter Five:

AFC Wimbledon 1
Wimbledon FC 0

Above right: **Wimbledon fans march around Selhurst Park on
9 August 2002 (Neil Presland)**

Right: **Wimbledon fans gather outside Selhurst Park for
Party at the Park on 9 August 2002 (Getty Images)**

Champagne and football chairmen

On the morning of AFC Wimbledon's first-ever match, against Sutton United, the Wimbledon Independent Supporters Association took a hired double-decker bus to ambush a protest by Football League chairmen against the collapse of ITV Digital. The expedition was to prove a complete success.

---

10 July 2002
Carlton TV Studios
By Callum Watson (AFC Wimbledon fan)

Six weeks after the fateful decision, I was back at the FA headquarters. A new club had quickly been formed. It was started, run and owned by the fans. AFC Wimbledon had their first game, a friendly against Sutton at Gander Green Lane that night, but first there was a bit of unfinished business.

WISA had hired an open-top bus and were planning to gatecrash the Nationwide League chairmen's protest about the collapse of the ITV Digital deal. The prospect of paying the FA a visit en route was really too good to turn down.

Our double-decker bus circled Soho Square while we handed out our flyers advertising the game and waved at office staff we recognised from the two weeks of the vigil. We put up our banner outside the FA building and sang our songs. We were back. We had not been defeated. We had saved the traditions of the club I loved and we had got rid of the money-men who had never listened to us.

Later, we opened bottles of champagne and joined the crowds heading for Sutton. But first it was to the Carlton Studios on the South Bank, and the Nationwide League chairmen.

By Alex Folkes (AFC Wimbledon fan)

The chairmen were protesting at the decision by Carlton and Granada to shut down ITV Digital and leave all the clubs out of pocket. We were protesting at the decision by the Football League to allow what had been our club to move to Milton Keynes.

I got there and saw a few photographers around, but nobody else. I didn't have to wait long, as an open-top bus soon appeared, bedecked in banners. However, it was not carrying the chairmen, but Dons fans. We had to wait a bit longer for the chairmen, who arrived in a couple of executive coaches and were all given identical placards. More incongruous protesters have never been seen before. These were barons of local industry, owners of Lancashire mills and Yorkshire steelworks. Holding placards and trying to chant in unison while looking embarrassed.

We gave them our protest postcards and asked them to support us. A few of them said that they were on our side and disagreed with the decision which had been taken, but others clearly resented our presence. One told us to "Bugger off" because we'd had our day. Needless to say, we made sure that we stayed and mingled with them so that the press pack could not film them without filming us.

Wimbledon fans ambush a Football League chairmen's protest on 10 July 2002 (Neil Presland)

Wimbledon fans swig champagne on the bus down to Sutton on 10 July 2002 (Niall Couper)

By Dave Boyle (Wimbledon case worker, Supporters Direct)

I hardly slept the night before. It was a surreal day, and it started with the Football League chairmen.

I couldn't help thinking as I looked at the frankly rather grey and uninspiring collection of suits that we had something so much better. The contrast between them, as they shuffled onto their coaches, and us, in our bright yellow T-shirts, was noticeable. On the one side of the road, the past; on the other side, the future – about to get onto their own bus full of hope and vitality.

Our bus was the same open-top affair that had seen regular action throughout the campaign against Milton Keynes. With anti-MK banners tied to it, we made our way towards Sutton.

By Alex Folkes (AFC Wimbledon fan)

The bus wasn't full, but everyone was determined to enjoy the party. We spent most of the journey from Central London trying to figure out new versions of our old songs – you'd be amazed how much difference the extra "A" makes. We stopped at an off-licence in Clapham and bought what seemed like their entire stock of champagne. But not the cheap stuff. Between the 30 or so of us, we must have got through almost three cases of bubbly, including six bottles of Bollinger bought at a wallet-wincing price.

It must have taken about two hours to get to Sutton, but we weren't in a hurry. We sang, we ducked low branches, we waved at bemused motorists and people waiting at bus stops. The low point of the journey was passing Plough Lane. From the top of the bus it was painful to see the rubble where just eight months earlier our stadium had stood.

We arrived at Gander Green Lane just as the crowds that would eventually fill the ground started to gather. This was a new experience for me. Throughout my days of following the Dons we have rarely had large crowds, and even when we have, they've mostly been away supporters. But here we were, ready to fill the place. And smiling. There was nobody involved in this club who we hated. We almost forgot about Franchise and Koppel for a day.

By Dave Boyle (Wimbledon case worker, Supporters Direct)

I went to where the pre-match press conference to announce the sponsors was being held. Everyone was nervous, excited, stunned – and a thousand other emotions. The big guns were in their Sunday best. Kris Stewart was having trouble with his tie, and I offered to help. It wasn't my best effort, but when I later saw the AFC Wimbledon half-season DVD with footage of the press conference, I smiled at my extremely small contribution to the day's events.

The match

And so to the inaugural game: Sutton United v AFC Wimbledon. The atmosphere around the ground was electric and expectations were high. A crowd of 2,000 had been predicted. The official attendance was put at 4,657 – though it was rumoured to be a lot higher than that.

---

10 July 2002
Sutton United 4 AFC Wimbledon 0 Friendly
By Ivor Heller (AFC Wimbledon commercial director)

It was left largely to Trevor Williams to arrange pre-season friendlies – though I made the fateful call to Bruce Elliott, the chairman of Sutton. We had called him several times before to ask for advice. I explained that I thought we should be playing them in our first match. I could tell he was sceptical, and he asked how many I expected to turn up. I had no idea, so I guessed at 1,000 or 1,500. He said: "No, seriously." I could tell he wasn't convinced. So I upped the ante and said: "Well, OK, probably more like 2,000." That's when we got the yes.

There were quite a few people in the office when I made that call, and they all looked at me as though I was barmy. In the end, I was wrong – more than twice that many turned up. So far I have not overestimated anything: this club has always surpassed my wildest expectations. It has gone so far beyond what I dreamt of all those years ago during the dark days at Selhurst.

By David Fry (AFC Wimbledon player)

When I think back to that first game, it sends a shiver down my spine. It was very special for me. When I arrived at about 5.30pm there were already a few fans walking about. It was all part of a crazy day.

I went to Plough Lane for years. I watched Wimbledon when they played teams like Doncaster Rovers and got only a couple of thousand people. As a teenager in the mid Eighties I used to go to every game, home and away. I remember midweek games against Millwall, Gillingham, Orient and Nottingham Forest, and of course the FA Cup final in 1988. I only stopped going when I started playing regularly on Saturdays.

It was always great watching Wimbledon and being part of that crowd, so to actually play in front of those same fans…it was a dream come true. Say you support Portsmouth, and you get to the age of 30 and then you play for Portsmouth. It was incredible. It's like I'd turned into a pro footballer overnight. As a Dons fan, this was too much. Seventeen years after starting my career, I was a Wimbledon player.

And then there was the crowd. I was told to expect about 2,000 fans, and then 3,500. It turned out to be more like 5,000. The kick-off just kept on getting put back. We went out for the warm-up and were promptly told to go back in. Then there was another warm-up, and again we went back to the dressing room. The buzz was getting bigger and bigger. My heart was in my mouth.

I can clearly remember standing in the tunnel. It was just amazing, waiting there while both sides lined up next to each other. I could sense the anticipation of the crowd. Then there was the roar, a massive cheer as we walked out. There were yellow and blue balloons everywhere. It was simply breathtaking.

Even the dressing room was packed. Terry Eames wanted to play two separate teams, one for each half, so there were 24 of us in there. I played in the first half and another team played the second. We didn't even have enough shirts, and had to swap them between us, but I don't think anyone cared.

We had never played together as a team. We didn't know each other. So to be holding a full-strength Sutton side to 0-0 at half-time was an amazing achievement. We ended up losing 4-0, but that didn't really matter. The whole day was for the fans. For me, it was the highlight of my career.

It helped that I "got it". AFC Wimbledon is about Wimbledon reclaiming its identity. But for me it goes back further than that.

I went to Selhurst four times, when I was either injured or suspended, and Ivor Heller had got me a ticket, but it was never like watching at Plough Lane. It didn't feel like Wimbledon FC. You'd drink in the Steve Coppell Bar; you'd be served by people in red and blue stripes. The photos on the wall were all of Palace in various cup finals. It just wasn't Wimbledon FC – where were the photos of 1963, of 1988?

The owners of the club had just forgotten about the fans. But fans make a club: they are the most important part. At AFC Wimbledon the fans would rather have their own identity and watch their own team play Viking Greenford than change identity and watch Crystal Palace. If AFC Wimbledon hadn't started, I wouldn't have gone to another Wimbledon game. All the Dons fans I knew felt the same, and that's why AFC Wimbledon was so important.

After the final whistle we walked round the pitch and applauded all the fans. The fans ran on from everywhere, and I remember looking at their faces – everyone was smiling. Everywhere was yellow and blue. These were the proper Wimbledon fans: the fans I had known from my days at Plough Lane, the fans who had been there against Doncaster Rovers. The club had been re-born.

I did many interviews after the match; I could have stayed there all night. It was breathtaking, the most amazing night of my life. I have played in cup finals, I have won league titles – but none of that can ever compare.

The adrenalin didn't stop flowing. I just couldn't sleep. I kept telling my wife about it all: about all the crazy scenes, about AFC Wimbledon and about the sheer happiness on everyone's faces. Wimbledon were back and I was a part of it.

By Kevin Cooper (Sutton United player)

There's always some excitement surrounding the first pre-season game, but this was off the scale. At Sutton we were hearing stories all the time about the new AFC, things like they'd sold 800 season tickets and they were attracting this and that, but it was all hearsay. We didn't really know what to believe. Personally, I was a bit dismissive. I didn't believe all the rumours.

I had been at a few clubs: Aldershot Town, Charlton and Wycombe. In reserve and testimonial games, I'd played against the likes of Dennis Wise, Matt Elliott, Julian Dicks, Tony Cottee and Alan Shearer. I'd seen a lot in football and I viewed the AFC Wimbledon game as just another pre-season friendly. It was great to be playing football again, but it would be nothing special. I was wrong – very wrong!

I could tell something special was happening from the moment I arrived at Gander Green Lane. There were already loads of people there, and the game wasn't due to

The turnstiles at Sutton United on 10 July 2002 (Neil Presland)

WELCOME TO SUTTON UNITED F.C.
A MEMBER OF THE Ryman FOOTBALL LEAGUE

SECURICOR OMEGA EXPRESS

MAIN SPONSOR securicor security services

FORTHCOMING FIXTURES
WEDS 10 JULY 730 V AFC WIMBLEDON

KI Z
The Football Kit Manufacturer

PROUD TO BE THE SPONSORS of this match

PROUD TO BE THE SPONSORS of this match

SUTTON UNITED F.C.
ADULTS £7.
OAP £4.
JUN. £2.

WIMBLEDON AFC IS BORN

AFC Wimbledon is born. Dons fan Barry James holds up a homemade placard (Getty Images)

BACK TO PLOUGH LANE SW

AFC Wimbledon players, from left to right, Sim Johnston, Drew Watkins and captain Joe Sheerin in action against Sutton United on 10 July 2002 (Getty Images)

Joe Sheerin, right, leads out the Dons on 10 July 2002 (Getty Images)

start for another two hours. And then the rumours of the crowd numbers started to filter through. We were originally told to expect around 2,000. When we first walked out for the warm-up there were about that many in the ground already, and I was thinking: "That's nice, a decent crowd to play in front of."

The PA announced there were hundreds more outside, then that edged up to thousands. It was like being part of a carnival. For most of the team the wait was frustrating. It wasn't so bad for me – I'd only come back from my holiday a few days before, and I knew I was only going to play the second half. It meant I could take in the occasion far more than the other lads.

By the time we kicked off the ground was full, and there were even fans sitting in the trees. I'd never seen anything like it. It just made me want to play as well as I could – and I suspect I probably annoyed a few people that day as I scored twice! The first came courtesy of Matt Hanlon. He headed the ball into my path and I nodded it down before firing it low into the net. The second goal I really enjoyed. I beat two men and then wrong-footed the keeper. It was a good feeling, scoring two goals in front of such a large crowd, but each time only 100 people cheered.

We missed all the scenes that followed on the pitch, as we had gone straight in. I saw it all later on television and it just looked amazing. We could hear it clearly from the dressing room, and the buzz was still there when I left the ground.

At the time my mind wasn't on joining AFC – it was on the next game for Sutton, against Leicester. But I thought to myself: "I wouldn't mind playing in front of that sort of crowd every week." So when Terry Eames spoke to me and asked me to join AFC Wimbledon, I was sold straight away. Who wouldn't be?

By Kevin Bagnall (AFC Wimbledon fan)

"So let me get this right. You're going to drive all the way to London on a Wednesday afternoon, picking up two people you've never met at two places you've never been to, to watch a friendly match between two non-league teams in the middle of summer? And then you're going to drive all the way back here to Stockport after the game so you can go to work the next day? I think you're silly!"

At the risk of sounding sexist, sometimes wives don't quite grasp just how important some things in life are. And there are those events that are important as opposed to important. The call of AFC Wimbledon had to be heeded. How could I face my children in future years and admit that I wasn't there? Simple: I couldn't.

A sunny day. Not a lot of traffic from Manchester to Birmingham (despite the usual M6 antics), and then a quick kip while waiting for Mr Peach. Decision time. "A" road to Leamington, or motorway? Motorway shorter. Wrong choice. End of slip road – gridlock. Two hours to Leamington, including finding the "mansion" inhabited by a certain Leamington Pete. After a tour of the back roads of Leamington we've just over an hour to get to Sutton. Honestly officer, we kept to the speed limit all the way.

The main road to Sutton. Radio 5 Live has a live report from Gander Green Lane as the teams run out. There's a Mr Kris Stewart being interviewed. Blimey! It's hard to describe the feeling of pride and pleasure which that one moment brought to three men in a car who'd never met before that day. If the car itself could have swelled with pride, it would have.

Three miles to go. Kick-off delayed, not once but twice, due to crowd congestion –

at a non-league friendly game. Three miles is a long way when you're late for history. And just for fun, let's try parking the car near the ground.

Queues to get in. It's gone 8 o'clock. Kick-off was supposed to be 7.30. Get those programmes. How do I keep them pristine? I'll manage.

In at last. Our line-up? Who cares? It's our team – AFC Wimbledon. It's not just a match out there on the pitch. It's a new life for us. We score. It was the big bloke up front. Someone says his name's Dean Martin – are they taking the mick? Our first ever goal…is disallowed. We sing, we chant, we laugh, we banter. We are one. In passion. In yellow. And blue. And a borrowed kit.

I've lost Pete and Peachey. I've found others – until now, just names on a guestbook. But we are not just names – we are the club.

Half-time wander. There is such a feeling in the ground. A family feeling. The warmth of the summer night mixes with the warmth of the people.

Second half. They score. Irony of ironies – it's a bloke called Kevin Cooper, the same name as our last player of the season at Selhurst. They score again, and then a couple more. But it doesn't matter – never before has the result of a match mattered so little in comparison with the fact that it was played.

And it never will again. That night something was born that can never die. We were born, and I never thought that would ever happen. It was a long journey home, but nothing compared with the journey ahead.

"Was it worth it?" as I climbed into bed at four in the morning. I think my smile said it all.

By Dave Boyle (Wimbledon case worker, Supporters Direct)

I remember seeing fans wearing other clubs' shirts, I remember being on the pitch at the end. Everyone was smiling, in Stepford Wives fashion. After all the pain and all the despair, it was a joy to behold the joy of others.

By Ian Hidden (AFC Wimbledon fan)

The excitement of what was going to happen that evening had got to me so much that I skived off work a little after lunchtime and made my way to Ivor's office to see if there was anything I could help with. There was. Would I be prepared to drive Kris and Ivor to the ground, collecting Marc Jones and the players' kits en route?

We got to Jonesy's place. There was just enough room in my boot for everything, and we set off for Gander Green Lane. Twenty minutes later we pulled into the car park. Kris and Ivor said their thanks and dashed off to meet the assembled press. Jonesy and I unloaded the boot and had the kit stowed in a room under the main stand for collection by the players.

I dashed home – I live near the ground – for something to eat and a change of clothes. I was halfway through eating when there was a din from a little way down the road. Gander Green Lane gets very busy around 6pm, and my wife called me to the front door. I was as amazed as her when an open-top bus appeared, and I was recognised by some of the fans on the top deck, and they chanted my name. My wife thought we were all mad, but she got caught up in the euphoria.

When I left for the ground, I was amazed at the number of people making their way up the road. Nobody cared about the start being delayed. Nobody even cared about the result, but everybody cared about AFC Wimbledon.

The official attendance was 4,500 or thereabouts, but a senior official at Sutton United told me that they stopped counting after the tickets ran out, and their estimate was a crowd of over 6,000. A hazy day that led to a hazy season.

By Robert Dale (AFC Wimbledon fan)

"Oi!" someone shouted.

I carried on walking down the platform at London Bridge station. It was Tuesday evening, 9 July 2002, and I was on my way home from work, wondering what rubbish was on the box that night.

"Oi!" someone shouted again, "Bert!" and tapped me on the shoulder. It was an erstwhile work colleague, an occasional drinking buddy and Palace fan who I'd bump into three or four times a year at best. It was fate.

We shook hands, exchanged our hellos, and then he asked me the question that was destined to plunge me into a different world. "Are you off to see the new Wimbledon tomorrow night then?"

My match-watching days had ended over a decade previously, but my interest was sufficiently piqued. My friend was in a bit of a rush, but managed to mention "AFC Wimbledon" before shooting off. I spent the 30-minute journey wondering what the hell he was on about. I almost jogged down the road from the station to home and fired up the browser before I'd managed to take my coat off. Search: "AFC Wimbledon".

An hour or so and several websites and chat-rooms later, and I was up to speed. Another hour or so and the arrangements had been made.

And so it came to pass that three Wimbledon fans, three Palace fans, a Chelsea fan and a Man United fan found themselves in a crowded pub in Sutton High Street early the following evening. There was an atmosphere of anticipation I hadn't felt for years. There was also plenty of beer. This was to become a recurring theme as the season progressed! Nobody really knew what to expect. I'd been to a couple of Sutton's pre-season games at Gander Green Lane, and the Chelsea fan lived nearby, so we thought we had an inkling of what to expect. Given the obvious buzz generated by the game, I confidently predicted a crowd of over a thousand, and was laughed down by most of my companions.

As the car nudged yard by yard towards the Borough Sports Ground, they stopped laughing. Everywhere was yellow and blue. And red, green, orange and claret. After half an hour of edging round backstreets we finally found a parking space slightly closer to the ground than the pub was, and set off for a liquid top-up in the Plough. Turning the corner onto the main drag revealed a queue of people halfway down the road, but luckily that was for the ground, so we managed to squeeze up to the bar for a couple more jars. Everywhere I looked there were old Plough Laners proudly sporting their tops, hats and scarves. All the time I was nodding at dimly recognised faces.

I'd been at all our promotion games over the years and, of course, Wembley, and it's no exaggeration to say that the atmosphere inside the ground was at least on a par with anything I'd experienced before. People were shaking hands everywhere, slapping each other on the back, and broad grins were radiating from every face I saw. The match was delayed by half an hour to allow everyone to cram in, speeches were made and balloons let loose, and we played "spot the kit" but gave up when we reached 50 shirts from different football clubs.

The game itself was a bit of a blur, a noisy blur, although not in any anticlimactic way – reminiscent, in fact, of the best Plough Lane days. By the end I'd managed to work out who Joe Sheerin, Dean Martin and Trigger were, and that we'd lost, rather unluckily, to a Ryman Premier team. And it didn't matter in the slightest. If anything, the grins were broader and the back-slapping a little harder. For the first time in history a 4-0 defeat was greeted by a spontaneous pitch invasion.

So that was the rebirth of a football club. Then, next Saturday, it was Dulwich Hamlet...

By Pete Baker (AFC Wimbledon fan)

It was a long time since I'd been to a match, the last having been at Plough Lane in 1991. My kids ribbed me about going back on the terraces, but in the end they came with me. The blue and white strip – the same colours we had worn as a Southern League side – brought a lump to my throat, and for the first time in years I went home hoarse.

By David Honour (AFC Wimbledon fan)

As I joined the train at South Merton that lovely summer evening, memories of the previous few seasons supporting my local football team came rolling past. Most of the memories were none too pleasant. Joe Kinnear's heart attack, his replacement by a Norwegian figure of fun in green wellies, the constant aggro at home games, very little to enjoy on the pitch, and finally the decision that it was OK to take our club away from us.

A notable highlight for me was a confrontation at one game between several supporters and Charles Koppel. Leading the verbal attack was a tiny chap who I'd seen several times before, but I didn't know his name. Little did I realise that he was Ivor Heller and that he would be the salvation of our club and, with others, would restore my faith in the joys of being a football supporter.

All these thoughts went through my mind as the train rumbled on to West Sutton station. I was met by the staggering sight of huge crowds surrounding Sutton's ground and the pub on the other side of the road. AFC Wimbledon banners adorned walls and railings, and it was evident that a massive party was about to begin. Queuing for 15 minutes to see a friendly between clubs that were more or less "amateur" (whatever that means today) seemed a bit ridiculous, but once inside the ground it was well worth while. Balloons, speeches and the teams out on the park signalled the start of the party. OK, so we lost 4-0, but the pitch invasion at the end showed what we had and what Franchise FC had lost. And we've been partying ever since.

By John Woodruff (AFC Wimbledon fan)

It was my first football match for over five years. I was there out of curiosity and to lend support to a new venture. I still counted myself a Dons supporter – I'd been a regular from the last Southern League season until promotion to the old Second

Division – but starting a family and self-employment had put paid to free evenings and weekends.

I went to a handful of Second and First Division games at Plough Lane, and just two or three games at Selhurst. I continued to look out for Wimbledon's results, and was sad (not gutted) to see the club relegated from the Premiership. I was concerned (not angered) at the management blunders, but not at the talk of a move to Milton Keynes: after all, that had first been suggested years ago, and nothing happened then, so why should it now?

I'd always enjoyed lower-level football more, and I didn't like Selhurst Park. I'd moved to Carshalton, and was thinking about going to the occasional game at Carshalton or Sutton. Then came the astonishing FA decision of 28 May – and that did get me angry. But I was seeing events from the outside looking in. I knew little of the communication breakdown between the club and its fans.

But what was this – a kick-about on Wimbledon Common to select players for a new team called AFC Wimbledon? My initial reaction was: "It'll never work."

Anyway, come 10 July, there I was in Gander Green Lane, with Kevin O'Keeffe (another drifted-away Don), one of my daughters, and Kevin's daughter and her boyfriend. The pub opposite the ground was full to bursting, so we relieved the local offy of its remaining cold lagers. The queue for tickets was huge, but we found a turnstile at the back of the ground with no queue and the un-drunk lagers got into the ground undetected.

Inside, there was a real buzz about the place. Lots of vintage Dons apparel, as well as colours from many other clubs. The game itself was what I'd expected – a win for Sutton, but AFC Wimbledon did remarkably well for a scratch team, and the performance by the first-choice XI in the first half was good. The rest of the squad didn't do so well in the second half, but it didn't matter at all. I'd never seen such post-match celebrations for a 4-0 defeat: pitch invasion, lap of honour, the lot.

I was back in the fold.

By Steve Meyer (AFC Wimbledon fan)

I remember my brother-in-law, five minutes after the final whistle of the FA Cup final. He sat on the terracing crying his eyes out. "Martin," I said: "Enjoy this moment – this is as good as it gets." So it proved, until Gander Green Lane on the night of 10 July 2002, when it was my turn to shed tears.

By Kris Stewart (AFC Wimbledon chairman)

It was a game we really wanted to play. There was the shared history of the 1963 FA Amateur Cup final and they were local – it was a perfect fit. Bruce Elliott, their chairman, was up for it, and he spent most of the build-up having long conversations with their groundsman – who wasn't convinced the pitch was ready.

Sutton were a hand-to-mouth club, they were interested in what they could make out of it. But, to be honest, we didn't really know. We started off saying we might get 1,000 there – that's a good gate for a pre-season friendly. And we then agreed a gate share. Ivor was getting more and more excited and I can't remember the amount of times I had to tell him to not get too carried away.

Yes, there was a buzz, and if I listened solely to the people around me, I'd have been like Ivor and expected a gate of around 20 million, such was the enthusiasm. I thought we might get around a thousand. I never imagined, even in my wildest dreams, that there would be over 4,500 there. The police were upset because the road outside was full. The press conference beforehand, announcing the sponsor – that was all a bit mad – but the biggest thing was how many people came.

I remember vividly being interviewed by Radio 5 Live. I was wandering around on the pitch taking it all in at the time. I don't know how many people were listening, but while I was on air the PA boomed out that the kick-off was being put back a second time due to crowd congestion. It was crazy -this was a pre-season friendly between two non-league sides. I think that was the moment when the football world really grasped how big AFC Wimbledon was.

We will never really know the real attendance. I'm not sure if all the turnstiles were working at the end. Bruce knew how much the club had taken, but then there were all the freebies, the match officials, the press and a few others. So we sat down and made up a figure and settled on 4,657.

It was amazing. I walked around the ground and kept bumping into people I hadn't seen for ages or just simply didn't expect to be there. There was an old colleague who supported Stockport and lived in Watford, and he was there. But the ground was full of people like that, people who wanted to be there and be part of history.

The game itself was a blur. I didn't know any of the players. The pitch invasion was hilarious. I remember being with Bruce Elliot and thinking about all the effort he had put into persuading his groundsman that everything would be OK, but he was buzzing too. It was just pure joy to watch all those fans stream onto the pitch.

I was knackered at the end. I just went home to sleep – there was no time for a glass or two.

Solidarity grows against Franchise FC

Wimbledon FC's move to Milton Keynes had rankled the wider football community. There was a growing anger against franchising – an anger WISA would tap into.

Summer 2002
By Simon Wheeler (WISA committee member)

Sean Fox and I were travelling to meetings all over the country, asking fans to boycott games that their own clubs played against the Franchise to show their support for Wimbledon's supporters. I must have missed dozens of games that first season. I remember meeting with Barnet, Swindon and Burnley fans. And then there were the cyber-warriors as well. They hit the message boards of those clubs to try and get them involved.

The amazing thing was that at every club without fail we would find at least one or two individuals who would be very pro the boycott, and they would do all the talking for us. The whole football community it seemed were with us. I would get dozens of emails every day from fans of all colours asking what they could do to make a difference.

WISA's Simon Wheeler at Swindon
(Rob Dunford)

Swindon Town supporters show their support for
WISA's cause (Rob Dunford)

Up and down the land, fans' groups were meeting with their club's owners demanding that their pre-season friendlies against the Franchise be postponed. There was repeated talk of season tickets being returned if the games against the Franchise were not called off. In the end, the likes of Tottenham, Charlton and Aylesbury – even PSV Eindhoven – all cancelled games..

Meanwhile, back at AFC Wimbledon it would become a common sight to see shirts of clubs that were playing Franchise that day down at Kingsmeadow. No one wanted to give them any level of legitimacy.

Trigger hacks a place in history

Eight years later, Glenn Mulcaire would be making headlines all around the world for his phone-hacking activities on behalf of News International, but in 2002 he claimed his first slice of history as AFC Wimbledon's first-ever goalscorer.

---

17 July 2002
Bromley 2 AFC Wimbledon Friendly
By Glenn "Trigger" Mulcaire (AFC Wimbledon player)

I can't quite explain it, but I had a feeling from the moment I woke up that something special was going to happen that day. It's a feeling I had never had before.

Dave Towse went down injured, and we got a free-kick just inside our own half. Andy Sullivan chipped it in. It was headed out and it came back to me.

I knew instinctively what I was going to do. Usually three out of five times when I hit a long-distance shot it either goes in or it hits the post. But I knew this one was going in. I could tell by the leverage and the way my knee was over the ball that Glyn Shimmel in the Bromley goal wasn't going to get to it.

It was such a great way to open the AFC Wimbledon account. So many different aspects have to be in place for the volley to be properly executed: the knee, the leg, the right spot on the foot, the shape of the body.

It is almost impossible to describe how I felt when it went in. I tried to sprint away, but Joe Sheerin held me back. I remember clearly him saying: "You don't know what you've just done. That's the first goal. That's what legends are made of. I would rather have that then any of the next 50."

It was a surreal few seconds. You see it in films, but the world did seem to stop. Everything just panned in, with Joe's words ringing in my ears. It was weird. The only word to describe it is unbelievable. Shims said to me later that he had made history too: the first goalkeeper to let in an AFC Wimbledon goal!

I dedicated the goal to my late brother, Stephen Mulcaire. He died in a car crash in 1981, driving back from watching Chelsea play Shrewsbury in the FA Cup. My dad had always backed me, but it would have been nice if Stephen could have been there too.

My path to AFC Wimbledon was quite an unusual one. I was drinking in the Red Lion pub in Cheam and I got talking with the barman, Mark Lockett. He told me that Terry Eames was the manager of AFC Wimbledon and that he was going to meet up with him a day later. I knew Terry from my Dorking days, so I said: "Just say hello from Trigger."

Niall and Matthew Couper flank Glenn 'Trigger' Mulcaire, moments after he scored AFC Wimbledon's first ever goal against Bromley on 17 July 2002 (Niall Couper)

Glenn Mulcaire, AFC Wimbledon's first ever goalscorer, who would enter the media spotlight years later as the private investigator at the centre of the News International hacking scandal (Alex Folkes)

Mark gave him my number, and that next week I had a series of calls from Terry. It was enough to persuade me to go down to the trials. It was great to be there from the start.

Terry knew what I was about. He knew I could perform in front of crowds. I loved the Sutton game – Trigger loves a stage. Those first few weeks were just an amazing sequence of events. I had fallen in love with the club.

By Paul Jeater (AFC Wimbledon fan)

A drive through the leafy suburbs of Bromley did little to prepare me for my first visit to Hayes Lane. Long before kick-off, Dons fans were arriving clad in the yellow T-shirts that during pre-season became our matchday uniforms.

Once the game began, Bromley took an early lead through a penalty. A diabolical decision, I thought, from a distance of 80 yards. In truth we rarely threatened in the first half, but not long after the restart the ball came over from the right, and there was Trigger on the edge of the box to volley it into the top corner. The Dons had scored.

Behind that goal we celebrated like never before, jumping up and down. The bloke behind me leapt onto a plank of wood masquerading as a bench, and the guy at the other end was launched like a missile into the air.

OK, Bromley got a winner and their keeper had to endure discussions about how his ears resembled a trophy we won in 1988, but he obviously enjoyed the experience because Shims joined us a couple of weeks later. At the end of the game, we had lost, but who cared? We had got a goal!

The arrival of the Bass

Four games played, four games lost. The fifth, away to Walton & Hersham, would be no better: the fledgling Dons were hammered 5-0. But that game saw the arrival of Simon Bassey. A regular in the Ryman League, he couldn't believe what he had let himself in for. Despite all the poor omens, it was to be the start of a beautiful relationship. Ten years on, and he would be the only player from those early days still at the club.

23 July 2002
Walton & Hersham 5 AFC Wimbledon 0 Friendly
By Simon Bassey (AFC Wimbledon player)

I had just retired because of knee problems. I was struggling to play, and it was really difficult to get through 90 minutes. But I was only 26, and John Egan persuaded me to come down. I'd known John since I was a kid and he said that I'd find it a lot easier at a lower level. But that still didn't prepare for my first game.

I'd been on the books at Wimbledon and Charlton, and I'd been playing in the Ryman League since I was 18. I knew quite a lot of the players in the league. And here was Keith Ward. He'd been playing for Banstead, a couple of divisions below me. I knew him as a solid right-back, maybe an occasional centre-back. Terry Eames had him playing centre-forward. Wardy is many things, but he is not a centre-forward.

And it was the same all over the pitch. It was a disaster. After that I really didn't know whether I wanted to play on. Then Kevin Cooper joined, and he was followed by Danny Oakins and Lee Sidwell. No offence to those original guys that came through the trials – and they have their rightful place in the club's history – but things had to change. Slowly, more players were realising that AFC Wimbledon was serious and they wanted to be a part of it.

For me, there were three things that persuaded me to stay. Firstly, it was a bonus just to be playing again. Then there were the crowds. I struggled when I left Aldershot. I played 50 or 60 games for them in front of big crowds and they always gave you a lift. At the time, I was putting in 12 or 13-hour days as a labourer and I really needed that incentive to keep going. Then I went to Carshalton, and I was playing in front of crowds of around 150. I just couldn't motivate myself. So to come to Wimbledon was exactly what I needed. In the years that followed, I've said that to so many players when they look to move on: Wimbledon is a special place, and you'll really struggle to get the same buzz somewhere else.

And then there was the final reason – Wimbledon itself. Wimbledon had been in my blood since I was a kid. I am a Wimbledon fan. I was born in Elephant & Castle, but I moved to Morden when I was five along with one of my best friends. His brother was playing for Wimbledon schoolboys and our two families were close. We all used to go down and watch him play.

And then my best friend died. He was run over. That hit me hard, but I kept watching his brother play and eventually John Phillips, the guy in charge of the Wimbledon schoolboy set-up, asked me to try out. I signed schoolboy terms when I was eight. As an associate schoolboy, I became a regular at Plough Lane and then, later on, at Selhurst Park.

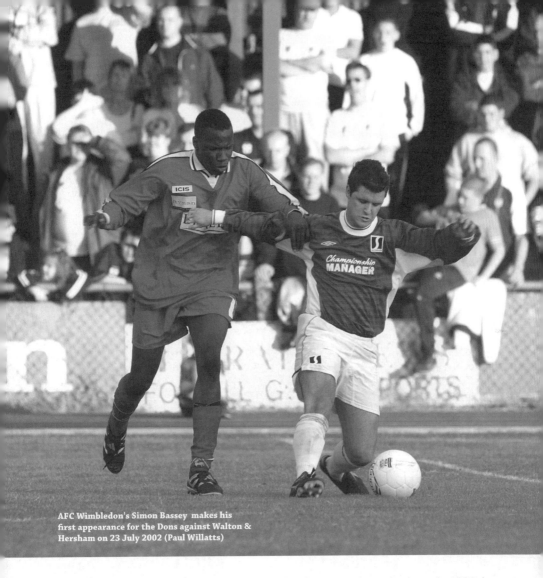

AFC Wimbledon's Simon Bassey makes his
first appearance for the Dons against Walton &
Hersham on 23 July 2002 (Paul Willatts)

It was a great time to be around the club. The first game I watched was in 1986, in our first season in the top flight, when we beat Leicester City 1-0. My first four or five years at Plough Lane were simply fantastic. I picked the best time to be supporting Wimbledon -all those big teams that we beat. Then there was the FA Cup final and everything that went on around that time. I loved Plough Lane and the whole spirit of the place. It was a great time to be a Don.

There's a great picture of me signing associate schoolboy terms when I was 14. I was there with Dennis Wise, and I had this most atrocious bubble perm, but it was all the fashion then. A couple of the fanzines have got hold of that photo since.

I really thought I had a chance of making it at the club, but everything changed when John Phillips moved on and in came Roger Smith. He said I was too small, and I was released at the age of 16. I went on to Charlton and two years later I began my merry-go-round in the Ryman League. Then the injury hit, and it looked like my career was over. But AFC Wimbledon came calling. It was like going home.

AFC Wimbledon's Keith Ward in pre-season action in 2002 (Rob Beatty)

Party at the Park

AFC Wimbledon had begun, but there was still unfinished business at Selhurst Park. WISA wanted to say a final farewell to the club that would become MK Dons. In a symbolic move they invited the football world to turn up on the one proviso that they stayed outside the ground. In the end the journalists present reported that only 668 people had gone through the home turnstiles – 2,000 gathered outside.

9 August 2002
Wimbledon 0 Gillingham 1 Championship
By Kevin Rye (WISA publicity officer)

Although Wimbledon's football club had already died and been re-born by 9 August, the feelings about the franchising of our beloved Wimbledon still ran deep among the fans. If you consider that most people regarded 28 May 2002 as a death, then the Party at the Park was the funeral followed by the wake.

For WISA at the time, though we were most publicly involved in the re-founding of the club as AFC Wimbledon (a role in my opinion all too quickly forgotten by many), we also pledged to keep the pressure up against the product they called the Franchise. Campaigning against franchising in football was part of the mission – and Party at the Park was an important step in that respect to keep the issues alive.

It took a lot of work. Simon Wheeler and myself in particular spent a lot of time planning the event carefully. The police were very understanding of what we wanted to do. If they were pressed, I'm not sure they were that keen on Charles Koppel's Frankenclub either.

A great deal of my time was spent persuading members of the press to attend – something that in all honesty was not that difficult – and setting up interviews with the right people. I particularly remember spending nearly an hour on the phone to Ray Stubbs, then of BBC's Football Focus. He was keen to get all the facts.

The lead-up to kick-off was mostly a blur of interviews, ensuring that our case was on the record. We wanted to make it very clear that AFC Wimbledon wasn't a protest, and certainly not just a fleeting fancy. Football Focus interviewed Michael Taliadoros – better known as Mikey T, a man legendary for his number of consecutive Dons matches he had attended up to that point. He wouldn't be entering the ground as the Wimbledon he supported had just joined the CCL and he would be at their match the week after. That nicely illustrated what we were about.

The other memorable fan was from Gillingham. Alan Liptrott had been banned from his own home ground because he owned a web address that the Gillingham chairman wanted and couldn't have, and so only watched the Gills play away games. This unsung hero refused to enter the ground because of who his club were playing.

The electrifying minute's silence and the later conga round the ground by a couple of thousand Wimbledon fans both showed just what a wonderful bunch of supporters we have, and what dignity in the face of such terrible provocation they – we – all showed. It also gave the lie to the spin from Koppel's camp that our fans were out to cause trouble.

Party at the Park organiser Kevin Rye (holding banner) during protest at Selhurst Park (Martin Drake)

A sparsely populated Selhurst Park as Franchise FC mark their first game on 9 August 2002 (Marcus Massey).

At the end, I remember running through a downpour of rain from the ground to the legendary Thomas Farley for drinks and a debrief. In a way, the rain was the final part of the process, clearing away the last of the grime. For most of that season, our first back in non-league, it always struck me as rather pleasing that our re-born club seemed to play under sunny skies.

By Simon Wheeler (WISA committee member)

AFC Wimbledon had been set up, but we wanted to show the world our disgust at the decision and we wanted to show them what they had lost. It was our last hurrah, the last protest we were ever going to stage.

We had a few meetings with the police beforehand, and they knew what we wanted to do and were helpful. They even managed to get a few assurances from the club to allow us to go through the car park to monitor how many people were going into the ground. I arrived early on the day, and straight away it was obvious the club weren't going to honour that particular deal – it didn't really surprise me. It was only a slight hindrance, and I allowed myself a wry smile.

We thought we would get 500 fans at most. In the end there were around four times that number, and the media all reported that there were far more people outside the stadium than in it.

Many major media figures were there. I remember talking to the likes of Patrick Barclay and Martin Samuel.

We were all there for maybe four hours. We were joined by supporters from all over the country. There were Gillingham, Brighton and Palace shirts outside, and it was largely good humoured. I did confiscate a box of eggs from some kids, but that was about as troublesome as it got.

At the final whistle, we all formed a huge conga and danced around the outside of the ground. It was our final send-off – and then it was back to the Thomas Farley for our last drink there. On the TV there was a live feed from Garth Crooks at the ground. He said: "The football was an irrelevance. The result today was clear: AFC Wimbledon 1, Wimbledon FC 0."

The first win

Nine pre-season games, nine defeats for AFC Wimbledon. When would the first win arrive? The answer came courtesy of the inaugural Supporters Direct Cup final. The opposition were Enfield Town – the first club to be started by disgruntled supporters.

12 August 2002
Enfield Town 2 AFC Wimbledon 3 Supporters Direct Cup
By Andy Sullivan (AFC Wimbledon player)

Losing your first nine games is hardly the greatest of starts for a new club, but it never really worried the players. For the fans, I suspect, it was different.

AFC Wimbledon was so new. The side we had was very raw, and we knew that in every game Terry Eames was going to bring in new players. I had nothing but respect

AFC Wimbledon's Andy Sullivan (Alex Folkes)

for Terry. He had an almost impossible task in pre-season. Sure, all non-league or professional managers get trialists to look at, but they all have a core squad already in place. Terry just had a blank sheet of paper.

By the Enfield match we were still trying to get a nucleus to the side. Given all that, to actually go and beat an established side was an amazing achievement. But for three of us it so nearly didn't happen. I remember Danny Roberts, Tony Readings and myself were all late. We got caught up in traffic on the M25 and only just made it in time for kick-off.

When we got there, we looked around the ground, and the majority of the spectators were wearing the yellow Dons Trust T-shirts with the "I was there" logo on them. I can't quite describe what that means to a player. I just loved the fact that people who had supported what became the Franchise were now watching the Real Dons in large numbers, and I was a part of it. Mental.

My first taste of AFC Wimbledon came after the club's first game against Sutton United. My two best mates, Danny Roberts and Andy Hunt, were at the trials and played in the first game against Sutton. I spoke with Neil Robson the night after, and he explained how amazing the whole experience was and said that I should come down.

I was going through a period where I was fed up with my football. I'd had a disappointing season at Staines and I was now going through the motions with other non-league clubs. So I called Terry and we had a chat about the club and my CV. I'd played in the Conference for Kingstonian and Farnborough, and I'd also won five caps for England schoolboys back in 1994. After that he asked to take a look at me against Dulwich in the second pre-season game.

Come the Dulwich game, I knew I was starting – Terry had told me as much in that first phone conversation. The amazing thing for me was the roar from the Dons fans when both sides came out. It was incredible, and I thought to myself: "God, they haven't seen me play yet, they might boo soon!" Thankfully I had a good game, and Terry kept me on.

The Enfield game itself was a good test for us as they played in a similar league to the Combined Counties. Every other side we had played previously was either a Ryman Premier or Ryman First Division side. As a team, we wanted to win big time. It was also the first time the team met Danny Oakins and Lee Sidwell.

We started strongly and we were constantly at Enfield's defence. Ten minutes hadn't even gone when I received the ball from Lee Passmore out on the left. I only had the right-back to beat. I did a little step-over, dropped my shoulder and beat him, and drilled the ball low into the path of Joe Sheerin for him to stroke it into the net. I was chuffed – 1-0 and I had supplied it. Kevin Cooper then scored a good goal to make it 2-0. I can't remember exactly how the scoring went after that, but I know Lee Sidwell got the winner.

At the final whistle, it was madness. We lifted the Supporters Direct Cup. The fans went crazy. They were coming up to all the players and thanking us for our efforts and wishing us all the best for the season. It just made me want to do more and more for the club.

We were elated. I was delighted for Terry too – he had put his heart and soul into the club, and at last we had given him some reward. Personally, I was on cloud nine and I remember the shivers going down my spine. I just couldn't wait for our first league game against Sandhurst.

We knew the first win was going to be an important milestone. It was great to get it, but you could also feel the sense of relief too.

By Iain McNay (AFC Wimbledon fan)

Our first Combined Counties League match against Sandhurst Town was looming large. I'd been to most of the friendlies and I had been far from impressed with what I had seen. Apart from the second half against Kingstonian, I hadn't felt much of the famous Wimbledon spirit. We had frequently been shambolic and just looked out of our depth.

I felt the Enfield game was the big one. They, too, had been formed by disenchanted fans (of Enfield, who then played in the Ryman Premier), and the Essex Senior League was on a par in the football pyramid system with the CCL. The other nine friendlies had been against teams from higher leagues.

It was a beautiful Monday summer's evening when I set off for Cheshunt, where the match was being played. I was driving in leisurely fashion along the M25 when I hit a traffic jam. Apparently a lorry had overturned several miles further on and blocked the road. I waited for nearly 30 minutes until the next turning. The clock was ticking on and time was running out. I sped through small country lanes, got lost, found Cheshunt and, after stopping twice to ask directions, finally found the ground.

The car park was full, and I ended up parking nearly a mile away and running back to the ground. Breathless, I arrived 15 minutes late and was told we were 1-0 up. I should have been pleased, but all I could think of was that this was the first AFC Wimbledon goal I had missed. But we scored again. We were looking good. We showed spirit, confidence and even some reasonable ability. Enfield pulled one back, but we scored again and eventually won 3-2.

Kevin Cooper (left), who scored AFC Wimbledon's second goal against Enfield Town, in pre-season action in August 2002 (Rob Beatty)

It took a little time for it to sink in. We had won a game! In fact we had even won a trophy. Everyone was ecstatic. After nine straight defeats we had won, and in reasonable style as well.

The nicest touch of all was walking back through the dark car park towards the exit, where several Enfield Town supporters had gathered to wish us the best for the forthcoming season. "See you in the Ryman Premier in two or three years," they shouted. And they meant it. It was a night to touch the heart of true football supporters.

By Dave Boyle (Wimbledon case worker, Supporters Direct)

The great forgotten people in the AFC Wimbledon story are Enfield Town. They had broken the mould. The fans of Enfield had got sick of their owners and they were the first to start a new club.

It was revolutionary at the time. The whole idea had entered the world as a possibility – it had entered the public consciousness.

Before then questions had always persisted: would a breakaway club take enough people with them, would they have the ability to run their own club, could they be a success?

Enfield Town had shown that it could be done. Yes, it was a weapon of last resort, but it was a weapon that could work.

By Paul Millington (Enfield Town chairman)

Enfield Town and AFC Wimbledon have a very similar history. Except that Enfield Town started a year before, on 23 June 2001.

The Enfield Supporters' Trust had fallen out with the regime in charge of Enfield FC, who had sold the club's ground and were now ground-sharing at Boreham Wood, 10 miles away. We had staged protests and got nowhere. We wanted to have a team in our own area – and eventually enough was enough, and we took the nuclear option to start again.

We couldn't have made a better decision. And not long after, through our friends at Supporters Direct, we started making contact with Wimbledon fans. That was in 2001, the time of our first full season. We finished that season winning three cups – the League Cup, the Middlesex Charity Cup and the Cherry Red Trophy – and came runners-up in the Essex Senior League, which is at the same level in the pyramid as the Combined Counties League.

We had shown that fans can run football clubs and that gave encouragement to our friends at Wimbledon. Throughout the summer of 2002 we gave them loads of advice. AFC Wimbledon had been hoping to get into the Ryman League, but they were rejected and I remember speaking to Kris Stewart shortly afterwards.

I told him all about our experience – about the simple joys of finally being able to watch football. We had had two years of demonstrations and protests, and the football itself had become a side issue. It was such a relief to get back to it and start enjoying games again. It was all about the performances on the pitch – that was the main thing, it didn't matter which league you were in.

I couldn't recommend it enough. I said to Kris: "Don't mess about with protesting any more – go out and start enjoying your football again." I told him about the forms, the paperwork, the ground-share agreements and everything like that. There was one other bit of advice I gave him: don't forget the corner flags. In our first friendly we thought we had organised everything, but as we walked out we realised that it was the one thing we had forgotten. It didn't matter too much about players – AFC Wimbledon were never going to have a problem finding them.

There was still the issue of the first win – and we even helped them there. Supporters Direct organised the match. Dave Boyle was behind it: he wanted the two fans-run clubs to face each other, and he set up the Supporters Direct Cup. You never want to lose a match, but I suppose it was good to have our name tied in with their history. It gave them a lift – and look where they are now.

Picking the dates

Having finally got into a league, the tricky next step was to organise the fixtures.

By Alan Constable (Combined Counties League secretary)

Summer 2002

For us at the Combined Counties League, the next thing was to plan the fixtures. Whoever entertained AFC Wimbledon first was guaranteed a gate that would be huge, certainly by CCL standards. It could have been any of our clubs. I try never to

Alan Constable, the Combined Counties League secretary, who helped set AFC Wimbledon's first fixtures

Wimbledon fans wait for the start of their first game in the Combined Counties League away at Sandhurst (Getty Images)

show fear or favour, but in the end I chose Sandhurst Town as the new Dons' first destination.

This was partly because I had every confidence that Sandhurst, as a well-run club, would handle things efficiently – and it was important to get off to a good start – but also because their secretary, Tony Ford, had done the League and myself a favour the previous season by agreeing to make a particular trip in midweek (to allow AFC Wallingford, who would have had a far longer trip to the same club, to play them on a Saturday). It was a small matter, and I usually receive full co-operation from all the clubs anyway, but I felt that this was a favour I could return. So Sandhurst became the chosen club, and my trust in them was justified as they organised matters magnificently.

AFC Wimbledon's first home game was then against Chipstead, which I attended. The massive crowd of over 4,000 seemed unbelievable for a CCL match. It was a tight game, as I recall, with AFC Wimbledon mostly on top but unable to push home their advantage, and Chipstead snatched it right at the death. At that point, though, most involved with AFC Wimbledon were just pleased to have their own side back again, and the result was less important.

AFC Wimbledon were now in motion and all the clubs in the League that season benefited hugely in financial terms. We decided to allow any club to move their home game to a larger ground, although not many did and there were very few problems, with only one or two minor incidents. Indeed, AFC supporters were generally accepted as well-behaved and sporting.

The club won many of their games but were not quite able to achieve a top two finish that first season, with two strong outfits in AFC Wallingford and Withdean 2000 up against them. It is quite sad these days to see Wallingford now back in junior football and Withdean not even in existence at adult level.

Chapter Six:

The Eames era

The perfect start

After the pain of 28 May 2002, all the hard work over the summer and all the pre-season friendlies, this was it: AFC Wimbledon's competitive debut. A glorious hot sunny day. Sandhurst away in the League. A huge crowd – and a win.

17 August 2002
Sandhurst Town 1 AFC Wimbledon 2
Combined Counties League Premier Division
By Keith Ward (AFC Wimbledon player)

After all that had happened in the two months before – all the emotions, all the training – now everything was focused on this one game. I remember getting on the coach at Kingsmeadow to head off for the game. You could feel the sense of anticipation. We were all hyped up. The friendlies had been great, but they were more often than not just another chance for Terry to try something out. This one, however, would count.

There was a lot of nervous banter on the way to the game. When we got there, everywhere was yellow and blue. We all expected some sort of crowd, but this was overwhelming.

There were 2,500 people there, basically standing in a field. I have no idea how the fans must have felt. A year earlier they had been watching Nationwide football in state-of-the-art stadiums, and here they were crowded six or seven deep around a metal railing in a ground with no seats to speak of.

It was a boiling hot day, and we started off really well. Kevin Cooper scored almost immediately. I ran the ball down the line and fed it into him, and he just slid it under the goalkeeper. Then there was my second. The contact was superb – it just flew into the net. It came five minutes after the first one. We had a corner, the ball went from left to right, it went over all of us and back to Coops. He crossed it back in and I got between two defenders and just powered it in.

When it hit the net I just didn't know what to do. I remember there was a split second where I was just stunned. This was our first league game and here we were 2-0 up inside the first 25 minutes. Then the roar of the crowd got into my ears and I just ran into them. It seemed the only place to go.

The biggest thing for me was the supporters. I have played against a few teams with big support. I played for Tooting against Wycombe in front of 3,500 and I played in an FA Vase semi-final at Whitley Bay for Banstead, but before AFC Wimbledon I had never had a big crowd cheering me on. It makes the world of difference.

During the game, I was thinking: "We just have to get the win, we just have to get the win and get the three points under our belt."

When they got a goal back, we really got the jitters. The pressure on us was immense, but we held out. At the final whistle, the crowd celebrated as though we had won the Premier League. The songs, the chants and the passion at that Sandhurst match will live with me forever.

The celebrations that night were also legendary. We ended up in Wimbledon Village until the small hours, celebrating with the supporters. I don't remember a great deal

Kevin Cooper is mobbed by his team-mates after scoring AFC Wimbledon's first ever league goal in the 2-1 win at Sandhurst (Paul Willatts)

AFC Wimbledon's Kevin Cooper in action against Sandhurst (Getty Images)

AFC Wimbledon fans celebate Keith Ward's goal at Sandhurst (Paul Willatts)

Danny Oakins is congratulated by Wimbledon fans as he comes off the pitch at Sandhurst on 17 August 2002 (Getty Images)

about the night, but it must have been a good one as I woke up with curry all down me. That night helped us bond as a team and a club.

With all the press coverage the next day I got quite a lot of stick from my mates. They were all asking how to spell my surname so that they could put it on the back of their shirts. My workmates took the p*** too. I walked in on the Monday and they were all chanting my name. Of course it had been a gamble to join a totally new team, but I saw it as a new challenge. I liked what I saw at the club, and after the Sandhurst game I knew I hadn't made a mistake.

In a way it seemed inevitable that I'd end up at Wimbledon. The Wimbledon connection has kept reappearing throughout my life. I was born in Tooting and the estate I lived on was full of Chelsea fans, so I became one myself. But I used to go and watch Wimbledon with my dad when they were in the Southern League.

I made my debut at the age of 18 for Tooting & Mitcham against Hitchin Town – I scored the winner and we won 1-0. The manager that day was Dave Donaldson and his assistant was Jeff Bryant, both Wimbledon legends. And now I, too, was part of the legacy.

By Dean Parsons (AFC Wimbledon fan)

It was a lovely sunny afternoon. I managed to find a space by the corner flag, and while the lads warmed up we sang "AFC Wimbledon" as if our lives depended on it. But it wasn't until the lads ran out before kick-off that we got to see them in our new yellow and blue kit in all its glory. I was so glad that we had gone back to that lighter blue, as it was how I remembered our kit from when I first fell in love with the club.

I've never had such an emotional day since, well, the FA Cup final or when we beat Huddersfield to get promoted. And when 'Uncle' Keith Ward powered in the winner, the atmosphere, the emotion was just like '88. Except that it was better, because this was our club winning.

By Matt Rickard (AFC Wimbledon fan)

On 17 August 2002 Wimbledon FC, the team I had worshipped for over 20 years, visited Vicarage Road. The year before 2,000 of us had used this match to protest against the folly of moving our local club 70 miles north to Milton Keynes. We had even hired a plane to fly over the ground throughout the game proudly displaying our MK NO WAY slogan.

Except it wasn't a folly. Not to the commercial director (sic) of Aston Villa and some faceless lawyer. These two men had been allowed to sit in judgement and, incredibly, felt that Charles Koppel's terrible investment decision was a more pressing concern than 113 years of history and the aspirations of football fans everywhere.

So Vicarage Road on 17 August was an eerie place, with just 35 remaining Wimbledon fans in attendance. Fifty miles away in the Surrey village of Sandhurst, the mood was somewhat different. A huge beer tent was straining under the demand of a thousand summer thirsts, the clubhouse of the local village football club had been renamed the Batsford Arms in honour of Allen Batsford – the man who had indelibly stamped his mark on Wimbledon history by winning promotion to the Football League in 1977 – and some 2,500 fans were rejoicing in the rebirth of Wimbledon FC as AFC Wimbledon.

I felt at home at Sandhurst. The same people I had stood shoulder to shoulder with at Plough Lane, at Wembley and latterly at Selhurst Park were there. The community camaraderie that had first drawn me to my local team was in evidence and the traditional badge was back, emblazoned on our shiny new yellow and blue kit.

The only thing missing was the players – the spineless, believe-in-nothing players who took their money and lapped up the adoration. But when we needed their support, the silence was deafening.

By 3 o'clock the crowd was some 10 deep around the metal railing that surrounded the pitch. I and eight others had perched on a park bench which we christened "the executive lounge". As the action unfolded, all the old emotions returned: incredible surges of passion and despair, anger and ecstasy. The same jokes and songs echoed around the field, and the referee was every bit as inadequate as his professional predecessors.

And then we scored. Not a work of art by any means, but as the ball nestled in the back of the net involuntary actions took over: a leap into the air, arms flailing and a lap of the far end of the pitch – embracing strangers as I went, screaming and roaring. The goal was celebrated harder and more intensely than that Lawrie Sanchez header 14 years earlier.

When it happened again, moments later, the idea that we were going to romp this non-league business fleetingly entered my head. Even a soft goal conceded failed to bring me back to earth (that happened the following Tuesday, when Chipstead failed to understand the romance of the situation), and I spent the rest of the day basking in the August sun and the righteous glow that I wouldn't want to be anywhere else in the world – and especially not in Watford.

By Nicole Hammond (WISA vice-chair)

Attendances at the pre-season friendlies were encouraging, but would the fans keep coming? If half of us came to AFC Wimbledon, and the other half continued, blinkered, going to Selhurst Park, could we still declare success? Fears were dispelled the week before our first fixture, at the club now known as Franchise FC's first league fixture of the season. Thousands of us turned up to protest outside, in a party atmosphere. Barely a handful went through the home turnstiles.

The following week at our first league fixture at Sandhurst, I saw 'Mr Angry', a miserable bloke who for years had happened to have the seat next to mine at Selhurst. Mr Angry used to spend most of the matches berating the team and anyone else associated with the club. As far as I could tell, he rarely joined in the WISA protests except occasionally as a chance to express yet more rage, but on that sunny afternoon in Surrey he was beaming from ear to ear. Well, that settled it. If Mr Angry was following AFC Wimbledon and was smiling, some kind of miracle must have occurred.

The feeling that we'd reached everyone was compounded by reports of pathetic attendances at the Franchise, which the press gleefully compared to ours, six levels lower down the system. I saw this at first hand, working on the turnstiles at Kingsmeadow: I noticed how we seemed to have attracted everyone – the older generation, many of whom didn't get involved in the protests and who I thought might have continued going to Selhurst through habit as long as Franchise FC continued playing there, came through my turnstile in their hundreds.

Lee Sidwell, Glenn Mulcaire and Andy Sullivan take to the pitch for AFC Wimbledon's first competitive match, away at Sandhurst on 17 August 2002 (Getty Images)

Some of them stopped to say that they had never gone to Selhurst in the first place in protest, but coming to Kingsmeadow was like the old days at Plough Lane. Even more surprisingly, the teenage lads came too – kids who I thought would be susceptible to peer pressure to support a "proper" club not only came to games (easy enough at £2 for under-16s) but wore the shirt on the bus – they were Wimbledon fans, not Chelsea kids who couldn't afford to go to the big club that most other local kids automatically support.

If anyone ever caught me wiping an eye as they came through my turnstile, it could have been a recurrence of that overwhelming feeling from the community centre on 28 May 2002 – the agitators who had been moaning and protesting for years were now the majority, had taken the moral high ground and they were running their own club.

A sellout and a dose of reality

AFC Wimbledon's first home game will always be remembered as a momentous occasion. There were the thousands of fans locked out and the amazing buzz inside the ground – but there was also the first league defeat.

21 August 2002
Combined Counties League Premier Division
AFC Wimbledon 1 Chipstead 2

By Joe Sheerin (AFC Wimbledon captain)

I was expecting a big crowd, but I wasn't expecting that many. The official attendance was put at 4,262, but I heard later that there may have been many more than that inside. While I was still about two miles away from the ground I started to see the odd couple of fans heading towards the game. A mile later there were dozens. By the time I had turned into Kingston Road, everywhere was yellow and blue.

I had played in a pre-season friendly for Chelsea against Kingstonian in 1997 and that had had a big gate, but this was huge. It was amazing. People were waving to me as I drove in. It got the old nerves going. I remember walking in and everyone was wishing me good luck. It was such a huge occasion.

The Sutton game had been big too, but I had arrived two hours before kick-off then and had missed all of the build-up to the game outside the stadium. I didn't get the same buzz then as I did for the first home game at Kingsmeadow.

I suppose in a lot of ways I was lucky. I knew Kingsmeadow well, as I had driven down there so many times to play for Chelsea's reserves. I was there almost every Monday night. But in those games we were lucky to get 100 people watching. Against Chipstead, the ground was packed.

Even by the time of the warm-up the ground looked full, and yet there were thousands still outside. And then we were told that the kick-off was being delayed. It was then that we started to realise that this was going to be a unique occasion.

I remember being in the changing room waiting to go out. I didn't want to let on I was nervous. I was the captain – I was supposed to be composed, but I was s***ting myself. I had missed the Sandhurst game so I knew less than the others about what to expect. But looking around the dressing room it was clear that I was among the more relaxed players. You could tell by the looks on some of their faces that they were petrified.

I had never led a side out to that kind of roar before. It was deafening. Kingsmeadow is a small, compact ground and it was packed, and all these cameras were flashing. It was also an evening game, and that always adds to the atmosphere. The hairs on the back of my neck were standing up. The whole captain's experience was so new to me as well. I remember that even putting on the captain's armband felt weird. I wasn't used to wearing an armband and it felt uncomfortable.

And then there was the mascot. He was a 10-month-old baby called Elliott Brown. His dad came into the dressing room before the match; I remember him telling us all that he had been the last ever Southern League mascot for Wimbledon, and that touched quite a lot of the players. It made us realise that little bit more what AFC Wimbledon was about. I was really quite nervous about carrying little Elliott. I was so worried about dropping him, but in the end, thanks to the noise of the crowd, I think Elliott was more scared than I was.

The worst part of the night was the result. Considering we were quite nervous, we had played fairly well, but we didn't take our chances and we made silly mistakes. Chipstead won the game with a last-minute winner. I was gutted. But in a way the defeat was almost inevitable. There was such a big expectation, but we had only been

Wimbledon fans queue to get in for AFC Wimbledon's first league game, against Chipstead on 21 August 2002 (Neil Presland)

The long queue to get in on 21 August 2002 (Getty Images)

AFC Wimbledon captain Joe Sheerin carries the club's first mascot 10-month-old Elliott Brown on to the pitch on 21 August 2002 (Niall Couper)

together as a side for a month. There were a lot of people thinking we were going to win every game, and losing brought a lot of people down to earth. It was helpful for our development. It was a release and lifted a burden from all the players.

But my one lasting memory of that night was the reception we got from the fans at the end. It was superb. We had lost, but the love was still there and that spoke volumes about what we meant to the fans. After that, I vowed that I would not let them down again.

By Kris Stewart (AFC Wimbledon chairman)

Given how many people had come to the Sutton game, I had always thought we might have a sellout. But it was only the week before that we began to realise how big the game was going to be. We were keeping in touch with the police and we were really worried.

Four or five days before the game, we took the decision to try and dampen things down because we knew it was going to sell out. We were saying: "If you haven't got a season ticket, then we can't guarantee you can get in." And we were telling people to get there as early as they could. In hindsight, we should have made the match all-ticket, but by the time we realised that it was too late.

On the night itself, it just got bigger and bigger. We had expected a crowd but not that many. Around the time we delayed kick-off for the first time, the senior police

AFC Wimbledon fans read the club's first official programme before the Chipstead match (Getty Images)

offer turned to me and said: "That's it: you have to shut the gates and tell everyone to go home." There were still thousands outside.

I went out with him to the gates and we were counting back from the turnstiles. When we got to a certain number, he said: "You can have up to there but no more." It was left to me to tell everyone beyond that point in the queue that they couldn't come in.

I borrowed a megaphone and said: "I'm really sorry. The ground is full and you guys are not going to get in." No one wanted to miss the game, and it was really tough to send people home. In the end I had to go into the queue and tell people face to face what was happening. It was horrible. Everyone had a reason to be there, and it was really painful turning them away.

There was one guy who had brought his son and had driven all the way down from the Midlands. It was a birthday treat for his son. It was really difficult to turn them away, but I couldn't show any favouritism and I couldn't break the rules as the police and the local council were watching us really closely, especially as this was the first match we had ever put on. I found it heartbreaking, but the ground was full, really full. You couldn't walk around it. It was a massive event.

I remember very little about the match itself, apart from losing. But it was a great night. It showed that AFC Wimbledon could be a success and, of course, personally I was glad we beat Chipstead in the return.

Revealing the fan power behind AFC Wimbledon

Buoyed by early successes on and off the pitch, WISA went en masse to the inaugural Fans' Parliament held at the NEC Birmingham. The message they spread to the wider football-supporting world was simple – fans are a club's greatest resource.

---

13 October 2002
Football Supporters' Federation Fans' Parliament NEC Birmingham
By Nicole Hammond (WISA chair)

The Football Supporters' Federation held its inaugural Fans' Parliament in Birmingham in October 2002. Representatives of WISA attended, and pretty good we were feeling too – AFC Wimbledon had not only been formed, but were having a great start to their first season.

The conference had a real buzz, and I think the fact that everyone was thinking "they actually did it" after all our years of being in trouble was a big part of that buzz. The conference agenda was full of doom, gloom and clubs in crisis – but we were there proving that fans could do amazing things and, perhaps, it was no longer safe for club owners to ignore their supporters.

I drove up with Lou Carton-Kelly and Dave Boyle, a typically giggly early-morning start. Everyone wanted to talk to AFC Wimbledon. As the day went on, there was a lot of talk of taking action by fans of other clubs in various kinds of trouble, and I suddenly realised that I had something to say.

We had held a Fans United day at Selhurst Park the previous season on a bitterly cold December day. After our huge publicity efforts for the event, and with relations with Wimbledon FC at an all-time low, we were certain that the club would find a spot of frost on the pitch and call the match off just to spite us. They didn't, and while I was wandering around the away end where we were hosting the visiting fans with an Oxford United-supporting friend I'd brought along, he remarked on how I seemed to know everyone. I had always thought that bumping into and greeting lots of familiar faces was part of the matchday experience, but he said he didn't know a soul at Oxford. How strange, I thought.

My first experience of WISA had been a few years before that. Dear old Sam Hammam was trying to move the club to Dublin, to the dismay of Wimbledon's small but passionate fanbase. Leaflets protesting against the move had been passed around at a game, and we had all stayed behind afterwards to join in an impromptu demo. I was wondering how it was all going to end when the PA announced something about a meeting at the Prince of Wales pub in Wimbledon. Everyone politely filed out and my brother and I caught a train to Wimbledon.

In the pub we started chatting to a Wimbledon fan, Stig from Norway, who had been at the match and would become a good friend. It turned out that we had all misheard the announcement: the meeting wasn't until later in the week. And so started a cycle of grim meetings in the Phoenix Hotel in Wimbledon with the likes of Laurence Lowne, Lee Willett, Marc Jones, Steve Elson, Xavier Wiggins – already

tired from campaigning and unaware of quite how many more years of struggle lay ahead.

The latest threat was a proposal to move us to Belfast. Eamonn Holmes had written a piece in the *Daily Mail* supporting the idea. A volunteer was needed to write in, putting our point of view. I put my hand up, bought a copy of the paper on the way home and sent a response that night. Two days later it appeared in print, in full. I had become a campaigner!

More and more meetings followed. In fact, my memory of the late Nineties and early Noughties is pretty much nothing but meetings. WISA needed a significant boost to its membership if it was to be taken seriously. At the next home game we launched a membership campaign, dropping the membership fee to get in as many people as possible. "A pound at the ground," said Steve Elson, and we were off.

So began my long and proud career of handing out leaflets outside football grounds. My brother and I teamed up – he had a talent for getting the attention of passers-by: "Sir! Yes, you sir in the smart shirt! Can I interest you in today's exclusive offer?" But after two hours of being ignored by most of the crowd, we had gained only 20 new members, and went into the match disheartened.

At the following week's meeting, Laurence stood up and said: "We have a couple of stars here! Nicole and Douglas pulled in a record 20 new members on Saturday!" We were pleased but also dismayed – 20 was impressive? How could people be so apathetic? A credible threat to take our club away, and so few people willing to stump up a measly pound? The small WISA minority would encounter this apathetic "Sit down, shut up, watch the game" attitude time and time again as we tried,

Cassandra-like, to tell the unheeding masses what was going on under their noses.

Having said that, a Premier League survey of fans that was carried out around that time revealed that as well as being more educated than the average, Wimbledon fans' membership of an independent supporters group stood at seven per cent of its overall fanbase, far higher than for any of the other clubs. I remember this particularly well because I wrote a statistical summary of those results for the WISA newsletter while I was holed up at one of the nerve-centres of the campaign, Tim Hillyer's back office in Epsom. Happy days.

The point I'm making is that we knew each other incredibly well, and we knew each other's skills and resources. And this was the point I made when I stood up at the Fans' Parliament in Birmingham and spoke to all the other fans of clubs in crisis – all this talk of action means next to nothing if you don't know each other or know what you can do. AFC Wimbledon took off so quickly partly because we were already a gang. Someone who knows someone at the council who can find us some practice pitches? I've got his number. A graphic designer? He's over there. Someone to put together a programme? There's already a team and they're already doing it! A manager? Here's an ex-Wimbledon player who's been coming to all the meetings and is just itching to do the job! An architect? Here's three of them. An accountant? How many do you want?

A thousand cheese rolls

In a season of welcomes, the arrangements made by Merstham FC surpassed all others. The club's chairman was so overwhelmed by the occasion that he took it upon himself to shake the hand of every AFC Wimbledon supporter.

---

9 November 2002
Combined Counties League Premier Division
Merstham 0 AFC Wimbledon 2
By Ted Hickman (Merstham FC chairman)

It was a wonderful, wonderful day. I was so proud. I had a feeling it would be a great day, but not everyone was as convinced as I was. People in our neighbourhood were really worried about it -they were concerned that football thugs would invade their town. They had read the newspapers and watched the TV and seen pictures of Millwall and Birmingham fans causing loads of trouble. They thought all football fans were a load of thugs. In the weeks and months before the game, everyone was coming up to me and saying: "Are things going to be all right, Ted? We're not going to have the thugs, here are we?"

There were also worries about car parking and congestion. Fears were being voiced that were just unfounded. In the end, the biggest problem on the day was the trains. They were running late, so we took the decision to delay the kick-off by 15 minutes.

It was a damn lot of hard work to organise everything, but it was a fantastic day. Our home pitch is part of an open park, so we had to close in the ground. We hired

fencing that slotted into large concrete blocks – without that we wouldn't have been able to collect the gate money. It was going to be a bonanza. The money itself was a big concern. We had to organise a way of looking after it. Fears were creeping in that someone might steal it.

Then there was the catering. We had a small social club, but that was too small, so we hired the hospitality suite connected to the local Age Concern Centre, and it was there that we made the famous cheese rolls. We had an army of ladies making them from 6.30 in the morning: cheese and onion, cheese and pickle, ham and pickle, ham and tomato – the list was endless. Our club secretary was up even earlier than that to pick up all the rolls. The ladies were running a production line: one would cut the rolls, the next would butter them, the next would fill them and the next would wrap them. They were at it for hours and hours.

We also had a huge marquee erected in the ground to sell teas, coffees, chocolates, soft drinks and those cheese rolls. We hired a hamburger stall and portable toilets. It was an organisational nightmare, but in the end everything went smoothly.

We had to deal with the local police. We knew our beat policeman Steve quite well, and he was involved with everything all the way through. We also had a few specials in. At the start they hung around the hospitality suite, but they had bugger all to do so they all trotted off to watch the match.

I was so proud of everything everyone had done, and I was so proud that all these people had come down to visit us. The Dons fans were superb. I walked around the edge of the pitch and I remember all the big smiles on everybody's faces. I introduced myself to everyone: "I am Ted Hickman, I am the chairman of Merstham FC, welcome." I shook hands with all the fans. It was just something I wanted to do.

It was a pleasure to have people participate in the event. I wanted to thank everyone. It was the biggest thing that had ever happened in the history of Merstham FC and it proved that we could put on a show.

I had such a wonderful time with the Wimbledon fans, players and officials. I will always remember Kris Stewart and my little friend Ivor. They were really, really superb.

If football was to ever become like that... Forget the £200 to take your family to a big game. This was what football should really be like. We may have lost the game 2-0, but we won so many friends that the score was irrelevant.

At the final whistle the fans were coming up to me and to anyone connected with Merstham to say thanks. The mere thought of it brings a lump to my throat. I cannot remember meeting so many nice people in such a short space of time. There was even hardly any rubbish to clean up. It all just went perfectly. I used to be a press photographer, but I had so much to do and had so much fun that I didn't have the chance to get my camera out.

A few weeks later, I stopped at the traffic lights round the corner from the ground. I saw a motorcyclist with a Wimbledon sticker on his number plate. I stopped him and asked him if he was an AFC Wimbledon fan. He was, and he said: "Bloody hell, you're the chairman of Merstham FC!" We had a good natter; the lights must have changed two or three times.

I have had similar experiences a number of times since and I had a wonderful time when we came to Kingsmeadow. I spoke to our players and they all said that those two games against AFC Wimbledon will live with them forever. It was simply wonderful.

The gloom at Wallingford

The match had promised so much: a top-of-the-table meeting between AFC Wimbledon and the unbeaten league leaders, AFC Wallingford. However, it was to be marred by a sending-off and an ugly fight between 'supporters' at half-time. The match ended with a police helicopter buzzing overhead. It was hardly the ideal background for Sean Daly to make his debut.

23 November 2002
Combined Counties League Premier Division
AFC Wallingford 3 AFC Wimbledon 0
By Sean Daly (AFC Wimbledon player)

I only really got involved because of Simon Bassey's suspension. Terry was looking for a left-back, and ironically it was Bass, along with Neil Robson, who recommended me to him.

Terry rang me up on the Wednesday and asked if I could play on Saturday. I signed on the Thursday and that was that. But it was a bit of gamble. An ankle injury meant I hadn't played for a year and a half. I had only just started kicking a ball again. And I hadn't even met the players before I got on the coach.

Bassey told me what to expect. So I was a bit prepared, but to see a crowd of 2,000-plus in an Oxfordshire village still takes some getting used to. The whole place was buzzing.

AFC Wimbledon's Sean Daly,
who made his debut away at Wallingford on
23 November 2002 (Neil Presland)

An isolated Joe Sheerin at Wallingford on 23 November 2002 before his early dismissal changed the game (Rob Dunford)

Then there was this family who recognised me from my time at Wimbledon, which was really strange. That was over 10 years before, yet they still recognised me. I had been on schoolboy terms with the club from age nine to 14. Wimbledon then sent me up to Lilleshall, and when I came back they wanted me to sign associate schoolboy terms, but I wanted to get a proper contract. I had Arsenal, Chelsea, Tottenham and West Ham interested in me. But I finally opted for Crystal Palace. I should have gone to Arsenal. It didn't work out at Palace, or at Fulham after that. So I ended up drifting round the non-league circuit. I had more clubs than Nick Faldo.

I went on to Carshalton, where I picked up my ankle injury. I tried to rest it but that didn't help. And after a failed pre-season with Tooting & Mitcham, I finally had an operation. I was just getting my fitness back up to scratch when Terry called.

As for the match itself, we were disappointed that we didn't win. The turning point came with Joe Sheerin's dismissal. We were on top before that and we even created more chances than they did afterwards, but it just wasn't our day. They had three breakaways and scored each time.

The magnitude of the club only really began to hit home the following week. I am an electrician by trade, and we do a lot of loft conversions. Two days after the Wallingford game, I went round to this house full of mad Wimbledon fans. The wife was there and she kept asking me about everything to do with the club, the players, the league, everything. And that's when it clicked that this was really big.

By Andy Nobes (Wallingford fan)

It's difficult trying to explain the strange mix of feelings I felt after the election of AFC Wimbledon to the Combined Counties League. Although I was a passionate supporter and committee member of my local side, AFC Wallingford, I had followed Wimbledon since 1995 and the days of Earle, Holdsworth, Jones and Perry. I regrettably never made it to a live game, but I wore my three replica kits with pride (even when the white third kit was mistaken for a Spurs top) and I had a red Elonex shirt that had been worn by Gary Elkins.

Gary was at the time the only link between Wimbledon FC and AFC Wallingford, having been born in Wallingford and lived locally when he was playing for Wimbledon in the Premiership. He came to play for his hometown club when he retired from professional football.

Although my interest in Wimbledon slipped somewhat in the disastrous Egil Olsen/ relegation season and the frustrating season in the First Division that followed it, I thought the fans' decision to form AFC Wimbledon was one of the most daring and exciting moves in football. It was an adventurous new chapter in the already fascinating history of Wimbledon Football Club. But I never expected for a second that I would end up watching AFC Wallingford v AFC Wimbledon, and that very season.

When the fixture list was announced, I could barely wait. After three months of hype, 23 November finally arrived. This was like a dream – the legacy of the famous Wimbledon, with the bulk of its hardcore fanbase, visiting the Hithercroft, the ground where I had spent most of my youth, watching hundreds of AFC Wallingford games, sweeping the stands before the game, playing in the goals (and getting bollocked by the groundsman), smoking fags in the stand late at night and so on.

And this visit was not a big club sending their reserve team down for a friendly, but a crucial, much-hyped, competitive top-of-the-table clash, with my team the unbeaten league leaders. The atmosphere was fantastic. The ground was absolutely packed with 2,350 people, easily the biggest crowd in our history. The visiting fans were making plenty of noise, but we managed to rustle up about 300 home fans and even managed to sing a couple of songs.

We won the game 3-0, a scoreline which probably flattered us after AFC Wimbledon had missed several chances. The game had swung heavily in our favour with the controversial sending-off of Joe Sheerin. Andy Shildrick scored with a cracking scissor-kick to make it 2-0 just before half-time. To be honest, I wanted AFC Wimbledon to score in that first half because it would have made for a much closer and more exciting game that would have done justice to the occasion.

The violence in the bar outside the ground (which involved 'fans' not related to either club) spoilt the occasion for some people, but for me it was a memorable day. One of my most vivid memories is from near the end of the match. With the somewhat anticlimactic second half petering out, an eerie atmosphere filled the ground with the rain pouring down on the dispirited, wet and muddy-footed Wimbledon fans. A sound began to rise from the far side of the ground, starting as a half-hearted murmur, but growing into a passionate and defiant "AFC Wimbledon, AFC Wimbledon, AFC Wimbledon..." I have to admit, that moment gave me goose pimples. I felt a kind of allegiance with the visiting fans and wished they could have enjoyed the day as much as I did.

In the end, though, I was delighted with the victory and happy with the way Wallingford put away their chances. At the end of the day the creation and arrival of AFC Wimbledon reminded me even more about the importance of following my local team, and following them through thick and thin.

By Kris Stewart (AFC Wimbledon chairman)

I hardly saw the game. The violence in the bar at half-time spoiled everything. We had gone there full of high hopes and bubbling with enthusiasm.

We were told later that the violence was caused by a group of people not connected with either club. The police explained that they were local idiots who just saw the opportunity for a ruck. But after seeing scenes like that, it was little consolation that both clubs were innocent. The concept of searching out violence is pretty sick and it ruined everything.

It was a surreal day. The ground was full – very full – and it was very wet. You could feel the tension around the ground. In the first half there had been a problem with one of our fans getting attacked and his friends were getting upset. There was a lot of needle in the atmosphere which I hadn't felt before.

I was walking through the bar at half-time when it kicked off. I was right in the middle of it. The surprising thing was how long it went on for. It may have been only a couple of minutes, but it felt like ages. I remember some chairs and a table got broken, and then there was blood and broken glass. My mum was in the bar when it kicked off and she was petrified. There were people put off going to away games after that.

It took a long time to calm people down, and there were a lot of people who were quite upset. As chairman of AFC Wimbledon it was horrible for me. There were lots of people who come to our games who have never seen a nasty fight in a pub, and I was one of them – just ordinary people who love football.

I just wanted to go home, but there was still the second half and I had to wait for the coach. The game then was pointless – we were losing and a man down. The hype and enthusiasm before the game had gone so flat.

It was a really low experience. I spoke to their chairman afterwards. It was a communal head-shaking. We stood and commiserated with each other. At the time, it was easily the hardest day I'd had to deal with as chairman of AFC Wimbledon. Thankfully a lot of people knew nothing about it until later.

The match was to end in a surreal atmosphere. Dark clouds above, a police helicopter hovering overhead, a car park packed with police and thousands of dejected fans who cared little about the result. This was not what AFC Wimbledon was about.

The last defeat and a tie-up with St Pauli

In the short term, the home defeat by fellow title-chasing Withdean would end any hope of AFC Wimbledon winning promotion. But it was also the last time the Dons were to lose a League match for 78 games – a British record. The game also marked a link-up between AFC Wimbledon and German side St Pauli.

22 February 2003
Combined Counties League Premier Division
AFC Wimbledon 0 Withdean 2000 2
By Niall Couper (Editor of Yellow and Blue)

Withdean 2000 at home. It was a match of milestones. It was a match full of what-ifs. It was also to be the last time we were to lose in a league match for nearly two years – taking in a British record 78 matches.

AFC Wallingford were soaring away at the top of the table, but they had decided not to apply to join the Ryman League. A top two finish and we'd be up. Victory over Withdean, who had about a thousand games in hand over us, was a must.

The sun was out and a crowd of 3,203 looked on in nervous anticipation. I was in the press box then as the editor of the club's matchday programme. It was do-or-die. The attitude of the players on both sides leaned heavily towards the latter. To describe the game as dirty would be a massive understatement – there were more cards on display than you'd find in Clintons.

Withdean players were tumbling over at the slightest of touches. The visitors took the lead after about 20 minutes from the penalty spot – the only surprise was that the Dons No 1 Glyn Shimmel wasn't sent off for that indiscretion. Danny Oakins had an effort disallowed, and Kevin Cooper and Andy Sullivan both had chances to level the score but missed. However, to be honest Withdean were having the better of it.

The cards continued to fly and shortly after the break a mass brawl broke out – which wasn't all that an uncommon event in those early days of AFC Wimbledon. Danny Oakins started it and everyone else joined in. The Withdean keeper threw a punch and got away with it. Several players were booked and Withdean's Shaun Grice was sent off.

Sean Daly made it a 10-a-side game five minutes before the end. He had taken a dislike to one of their wingers and headbutted him, and as we chased the game, they added a second. And with that our hopes of promotion were over.

The defeat was to prove more costly than we thought. A year or so later the Football Association inserted a new tier into non-league football, the Conference North and South. It pushed us one step further down the pyramid. Had we got promoted that first season and gone up again (as we almost certainly would have done), we would have made the Conference South by 2005. But that's just another "what if". There might then have been no British record, no heartache in the Ryman Premier Division play-offs, and no Terry Brown – and perhaps no promotion to the Football League.

The match also marked the home debut of Matt Everard. He would become a mainstay of the Wimbledon defence and one of the club's first real legends. This would be the only league game in which he would taste defeat in the blue of Wimbledon. His last game for the Dons would come 78 league matches later when injury ended his playing career.

By Dave Boyle (Wimbledon case worker, Supporters Direct)

How did a small club in the Combined Counties League get involved in a love-in with a bunch of anarcho-syndicalists playing in Germany?

It all started several years earlier when I was doing a master's degree in cultural studies. I decided somewhat spuriously to do my dissertation on the cultural aspects of watching Euro '96 in pubs, which was a joy to research. In the course of my studies I'd read about fan culture in other countries and come across this team from Hamburg who played in brown – a brave choice, aesthetically and historically – and had the best slogan I'd ever seen: "Never again racism. Never again fascism. Never again the Second Division." Their main messageboard had a section called "for our visitors from abroad", which was in English. I immediately adopted them as my German team.

St Pauli are the outsiders of German football, loathed for their propensity to defy the odds and resented for their refusal to get with the slickness of the Bundesliga. Their fans are renowned for being, well, unhinged. They care about more than just their team, and to them football isn't just about watching 11 men kicking a ball around. They have a real sense of community and have lots of fun into the bargain.

I started to post on their messageboard, and mentioned what had happened at Wimbledon and what we'd done with AFC Wimbledon. I suspected that it might just be right up their alley – fans taking on the established order, doing it their way and damn the consequences. It's also a bit of a mad story, too, and I was sure that aspect would appeal to them.

And so it did. Soon afterwards, a fellow poster contacted me to say that there was a posse of St Pauli fans coming over the see the game against Withdean at Kingsmeadow. Sofas and floor space in Clapham, Walthamstow and Blackheath were secured, and then here they were. They loved it. They loved the bars. They loved the atmosphere, despite the defeat. They managed to get served in an off-licence on Wimbledon Broadway at 1am. And they promised they'd be back.

Since then St Pauli fans have been back several times and AFC Wimbledon fans have been to Hamburg as well.

Tempers flare between AFC Wimbledon and Withdean in the crunch league match on 22 February 2003 (Paul Willatts)

The Dons find a home

In 1991 Wimbledon FC left Plough Lane. In 2002 an FA commission granted the club a move to Milton Keynes on the grounds that their continuing homelessness made them a "special case". The club chairman, Charles Koppel, had insisted that no site was available inside the M25. But within nine months of their formation, AFC Wimbledon had put in place a deal that would secure them a stadium that was just two miles from Wimbledon Common, where the club had first played in 1889.

---

24 March 2003
Dons Trust Special General Meeting Wimbledon Theatre
By Lou Carton-Kelly (Dons Trust chair)

It was a momentous night. I was nervous, of course, but I was also confident. The Dons Trust Stadium Working Group (SWG) had put in a lot of time and effort, and I was convinced that what we were putting forward was the best option: to buy the lease at Kingsmeadow.

The SWG had looked at all the other options available, but one by one they were ruled out. The dream, of course, was to return to Plough Lane, but realistically it was too expensive. The land itself was too pricey, and there would have been the stadium-building costs on top of that.

We considered six other options, but for one reason or another they were all ruled out. The only serious alternative to buying the lease at Kingsmeadow was a groundshare with Tooting & Mitcham, which had a lot going for it. The romance of a return to the London Borough of Merton, our spiritual home, was of course the biggest appeal, and we considered the groundshare very seriously. The Dons Trust Board even approved a payment for traffic studies to support Tooting & Mitcham's application which, if successful, would have allowed Merton Council to lift the restriction of only one club playing at their ground, Imperial Fields.

We had wanted to give people both options to consider, but 11 days before the SGM, Merton Council's planning committee vetoed the idea of the groundshare, so we were left with Kingsmeadow. For most of us on the Dons Trust Board it was the preferred option, but we wanted to have both available to help our bargaining position.

It was hard work getting a deal with the Khoslas, the owners of the Kingsmeadow lease. Ivor Heller, Kris Stewart, Erik Samuelson and I worked endlessly to get the best deal for the club. Throughout, we continued to refer to our financial working group to see what was feasible and what was not.

And so to the night itself. I suppose I feared that we might get a more negative response, and I expected a few more dissenting voices, but when the vote was taken it was almost unanimous: the members of the Dons Trust wanted us to buy the lease at Kingsmeadow.

It would take three months of hard work, and after a successful share issue that raised £1m in three weeks we took control of Kingsmeadow in mid July 2003 – and in the process secured the future of Kingstonian FC. After 12 years of pain, we finally had a place we could call home. Who would have thought 12 months earlier when we were just starting out that this would be possible?

Dons Trust members queue up to get in to the Special General Meeting on 24 March 2003 (Alex Folkes)

The decisive vote... Dons Trust members vote in favour of buying the lease at Kingsmeadow (Alex Folkes)

By Tom Adam (Dons Trust Board member)

Before we were able to take control of Kingsmeadow, we were interviewed by Kingston Council to check our suitability. So myself, Lou Carton-Kelly and Kris Stewart found ourselves being questioned by various members of the council, including the council leader.

We were asked how long we envisaged being at Kingsmeadow. I thought about 15 years and that's what we told them. They wanted to see whether we had a long-term view. They didn't want us to come in as fly-by nights and disappear again without a care about the local community. They wanted us to reassure them. The 15-year promise gave them that level of reassurance. But it was still up to the members to have the final say.

Dons answer doubters

AFC Wimbledon had won dozens of matches, but when the big challenges arrived the side failed to live up to expectations and had lost. Questions were being asked about the club's big-match temperament. The victory over Wallingford answered them all. And after the vote to buy the lease at Kingsmeadow, it completed a perfect week.

29 March 2003
Combined Counties League Premier Division
AFC Wimbledon 3 AFC Wallingford 2
By Matt Everard (AFC Wimbledon player)

The Wallingford game was far and away the most enjoyable game I've ever played in. I remember my goal, the winner, clearly. We won a free-kick out on the left. I think Andy Sullivan put a deep ball across. Coops peeled off on the back post, took it down well and then chipped a sweet ball to the opposite post, where I just backed off my marker and got matched up with one of their smaller defenders. I got the jump on him and knocked it in.

The crowd went mad, but I didn't celebrate much. I've never really been one to celebrate my goals – I give it more of a Stuart Pearce celebration. It was a massive victory for the club. It proved to a few of the doubters that we were a side to be reckoned with, that we could compete in the big games, fight for each other, play well and get the right result.

I hadn't played in the first game at Wallingford, so it wasn't really dominating my thinking as much as the other guys. But I distinctly recall the players talking about what went wrong at their place and how much they were looking forward to this game. They felt the pressure more than I did. We had just lost to Withdean, and the question marks were there: could we really beat the big clubs?

I remember the atmosphere clearly, not just from the Kingston Road End – which was then the home end – but from the whole of the ground. The noise was relentless for the whole game and the place was just rocking. We desperately wanted to win for the fans as well as Eamo and ourselves, just to get the buzz going, especially after we had let ourselves and everyone else down during the Withdean game.

One... Andy Sullivan's corner goes straight in against Wallingford on 24 March 2003 to level the scores (Alex Folkes)

Two... Joe Sheerin's deft header gives the Dons the lead (Martin Tomlin)

Three... Matt Everard powers in AFC Wimbledon's winner against Wallingford (Alex Folkes)

AFC Wimbledon players celebrate against Wallingford (Martin Tomlin)

I was determined to get that result out of the system. But I could sense how big the Wallingford game was. We didn't need to get pumped up for it, and in the end we just totally dominated.

At the time, I had no idea my goal was going to be the winner. That said, I didn't think Wallingford would score again as we'd done a good job of containing them. Apart from the two free-kicks and the one scuffed shot in the first half, they didn't have a shot on target the whole game. I just thought, with the way we were playing, there were definitely more goals in it for us, and we had three or four good chances to make sure of it in the last 15 to 20 minutes. But in the end I think we were just happy to take the win.

It was really satisfying to score. I had a lot to make up for. I was totally to blame for their first goal – I was all over their player, and the referee had no choice but to give the free-kick. It was still quite a difficult angle, but Shane Small-King went and put it in the top corner.

Thankfully Sully equalised almost immediately, direct from a corner. I'm not quite sure how it went in. I suppose a lot of it was down to Danny Oakins, who just stood in front of the keeper and backed him further away from the ball, allowing it to creep in at the near post.

And then Joe scored to put us ahead. It was a great header. We had a corner which Sean Daly sent over to the back stick. I contested it with Andy Shildrick, who got the jump on me and knocked it back out to Sean. He got it back in, and Joe got up well and got a real deft flick on it that sent it into the top corner. The whole Kingston Road End went mental.

"That makes up for my foul," I thought, but I was wrong. I got a clean header on the ball with about four minutes left of the first half, and two of their players collided with each other and the referee gave a free-kick. I couldn't believe it. It was 30 yards out, but after the first one, I just knew what was coming. And there it was, Small-King again, 2-2. Gutted.

And it nearly got even worse for me. In the dying seconds of the half, our goalkeeper Ray Merry and I went up for the same ball. I got a late shout from Ray to get it away, but by that time I was already in the process of trying to knock it back to him. I got the flick on it and looked up, and Ray was about a yard away. It went over him. It looked like an own goal all the way, but Wardy came out of nowhere, got back and hooked the ball over his shoulder, and I managed to hoof it away.

To be honest, from where I was standing the ball looked at least half a yard over the line. Wardy hooked it backwards and it still hit the underside of the bar on its way out. I suppose after what had happened before we were due our slice of luck. To go in 3-2 down would have been devastating.

That scare woke us up, and we totally dominated the second half. After I scored, we had loads of chances. Ally missed a sitter. He tried to lob the keeper but ended up lobbing the stadium. Coops went through on goal – the angle was getting a bit tight for him – and he blazed his shot across the goal. Then Gavin Bolger had a good chance but he hit the ball straight at the keeper. They had a man sent off at the end, but by then the game was already over.

The celebrations that night were superb. We left the bar when we got kicked out at about 8pm, and I was absolutely hammered.

The Wallingford game had it all. Before that season I had never even heard of Wallingford, but here I was, acutely anticipating a game against them as if Chelsea and their lavish assemblage of exotic, ball-juggling, slightly-past-their-prime mavericks had just rolled into town. In fact, Wallingford was second only to Sandhurst for the event of the season.

It had atmosphere. Some 3,500 people were packed into Kingsmeadow, most of them seemingly wedged onto the Kingston Road End – a terrace not well designed for watching football, but acoustically up there with Roker Park.

It had a victory…for Wimbledon. OK, we had 36 of them that season, but this was against a good side, in a game we had to win. I had witnessed every abject surrender by various Wimbledon teams in the previous 10 years and fully expected us to continue in this fine tradition. In fact, after falling a goal behind after just 10 minutes, I was waiting for four of the players to hail cabs, and a couple to nip back to the changing room to start running the bath, leaving the other five to wander about aimlessly, huffing and puffing.

It had a sending-off. Admit it, no game could ever be complete without one. Ignore the po-faced commentator who decries that it has ruined the game. All sending-offs are entertainment of the highest kind. If your team suffers the loss of a man, it unites the crowd, galvanises the team and sometimes leads to a glorious victory against all the odds – Watford in the FA Cup quarter-final, anyone? Whereas, if the opposing team loses a man, the hilarity that ensues is up there with sharing a beer with Tommy Cooper.

It had great goals. Joe Sheerin's leap to flick home a Lee Sidwell cross was spectacular – Fashanu-esque, even – though he probably has a phobia about that sort of thing now. Meanwhile, Shane Small-King enjoyed his swerving 25-yard free-kick into the top left corner so much that he did it again half an hour later, Ray Merry not even moving during the repeat so as not to miss anything.

This game really did have it all.

The perfect send-off

AFC Wimbledon's season ended in a festival of football and fun. The match sold out 20 minutes before kick-off. The team won 5-1. Dozens of old Wimbledon players turned up. Kevin Cooper scored with a header. Lee Sidwell won the Player of the Year award. The antics off the pitch reached new levels. Even the Womble was back, and smiles were everywhere.

---

5 May 2003
Combined Counties League Premier Division
AFC Wimbledon 5 Raynes Park Vale 1
By Terry Eames (AFC Wimbledon manager)

It was an amazing day from the moment I turned up at Kingsmeadow to the journey home from the Hand in Hand pub on Wimbledon Common over 12 hours later.

It all began at 10.30am with the revival of an old Plough Lane tradition. In the old days on the final day of the season, all the staff, volunteers and players would gather together for a big photo session, and it was great to recreate that moment at Kingsmeadow. The club would have been nothing without its legions of volunteers, and this was just a small way of saying thank you. It meant as much to me as it meant to anyone else.

That first season was the greatest period of my footballing life. AFC Wimbledon began on day one with nothing, yet by the end of the season we had achieved so much. Key to all our success was keeping our tradition and rediscovering the spirit that had served Wimbledon so well for decades.

By 11am there were loads of people milling about and the ground was already buzzing in a way I had not known all season. Then there was the presentation of the future youth teams on the pitch. Watching them as they paraded around the ground made me feel so proud. These kids wanted to be part of AFC Wimbledon. They were smiling and they were chasing autographs. They were cuddling the Womble that had just swapped allegiances from Wimbledon FC to AFC Wimbledon. You could tell they "got" AFC Wimbledon. There were moments like that throughout the day.

When the news filtered through that the game had sold out 20 minutes before kick-off, I took some time to look around the ground. The crowd had fluctuated all year between 2,500 and 4,000, but they all wanted to be there for the final game. I remember walking round and seeing faces I hadn't seen for years, some of them not since my days at Plough Lane.

By Lee Dobinson (Raynes Park Vale manager)

It was just one solid noise – you just couldn't hear the specifics. In a normal game in the CCL you can hear individuals really clearly, especially the one guy from Ash United!

After the first game we expected quite a lot of barracking, but it was a good feeling all day and it was a great vibe. I knew there were going to be a lot of people there, but it far exceeded my expectations. It took me several minutes just to get into the ground. I had posted a few times on the Weird and Wonderful World guestbook, and people were stopping me and introducing themselves. There was a real buzz about the place and I thoroughly enjoyed it.

It was a big game for them, but we wanted to win too. We played well and the result didn't do us justice – 5-1 flattered AFC Wimbledon. Perhaps 2-1 would have been fairer.

By Terry Eames (AFC Wimbledon manager)

The game itself wasn't the greatest. We won 5-1, but it was about the day more than the match. The scenes after the final whistle were fantastic and two or three of the boys were in tears. Tom Watt on Radio London was dumbfounded.

After the game, Lee Sidwell picked up his well-deserved Player of the Year award. Lee was a player who no one had given a second look before, but he's a fighter. And what he lacked in ability he gave in passion and spirit. It didn't surprise me that the Wimbledon crowd warmed to him. They saw in Lee what they had seen in Wimbledon players down the ages, and that was why it was so important to me that Dickie Guy presented the award – from one passionate Wimbledon hero to another.

The return... The Womble is welcomed by AFC
Wimbledon's commercial director Ivor Heller
on 5 May 2003 (Alex Folkes)

By Lee Sidwell (AFC Wimbledon player)

I didn't expect to be named Player of the Year. I thought Coops or Danny Oakins would win it. The whole day was overwhelming. The atmosphere was the best I have ever known.

Getting the award at the end was a proud moment for me. The squad had all these players with a lot more experience than me, so to come in from a league lower than the CCL and win the award was unbelievable.

By Kevin Cooper (Wimbledon FC 2001 player of the year)

All the old boys who were at Kingsmeadow were the real heroes. The ones who won the FA Amateur Cup, the ones who took the club into the Football League and the ones who won the FA Cup. And then there were the fans – they too were heroes. I was just honoured to be in the same company.

I had wanted to come down for months and months, and as soon as I heard that this match was on a Monday when the kids were off school, I knew I was going to be there. After that day at Molineux the year before when the fans honoured me, I wanted so badly to show my appreciation to them.

I kept an eye on what was going on on-line. The Wolverhampton Wanderers fans also kept me informed. The day proved to be everything I'd hoped for – and more. It was such a wonderful time. AFC Wimbledon has the whole spirit of the club I played for. It is Wimbledon.

It was also the first time I ever heard the song: "There's only two Kevin Coopers"!

By Roy Law (1963 FA Amateur Cup-winning side captain)

The atmosphere was brilliant, and I was so proud to be part of the day. I have so many good memories of the day, it's impossible to list them. It was so nice to meet up with so many of my old colleagues: Bobby Ardrey, Dickie Guy, George Coote and so many of the 1963 team.

It was a full programme of events. It epitomised perfectly what AFC Wimbledon was all about.

By Dave Beasant (1988 FA Cup-winning side captain)

It was a good day. The football wasn't the greatest, but that wasn't the point. It was a celebration of the amazing achievements of AFC Wimbledon. These were the fans of Wimbledon who had supported the club through thick and thin. They were saying: "This is our stance, we're here at AFC and we're proud."

There were 4,500 inside the stadium and loads more locked outside. I just found it all amazing and I have nothing but respect for the fans. They were typical Wimbledon fans, the ones I knew from my days at the club. They were humorous with their chants and their songs. It took me back to my days at Plough Lane. It was emotional.

The header… AFC Wimbledon top goalscorer
Kevin Cooper scores a rare header in a post-
match set-up beating one-off goalkeeper Ivor
Heller (Martin Tomlin)

AFC Wimbledon players gather at the final whistle
on 5 May 2003 (Alex Folkes)

Wimbledon FC Player of the Year Kevin Cooper meets his AFC Wimbledon namesake on 5 May 2003 (Alex Folkes)

Lou Carton-Kelly shows Simon Bassey a red card as he poses for the club's naked 2003-2004 calender (Paul Willatts)

AFC Wimbledon managerTerry Eames signs off the club's first season with a speech on the pitch (Alex Folkes)

By Glenn Mulcaire (AFC Wimbledon's first goalscorer)

The final day of that season epitomised everything the club stands for. The whole is bigger than the sum of its parts. The Wimbledon fans are intelligent and caring people, and for me that's what shone through.

While the awards were going on, Robbie Earle came over to me and said: "I may have got the first World Cup goal for Jamaica, but I didn't score the first AFC Wimbledon goal with a 30-yard volley." That was just unbelievable.

By Noel Frankum (AFC Wimbledon player)

I was a schoolboy at Wimbledon FC. I was in the same year as Neal Ardley, Stewart Castledine, Justin Skinner and Chris Perry. I've always known what Wimbledon is supposed to be about. It's about being a community, enjoying yourself and having fun.

In my years at Wimbledon FC we were just kids, but there was still all this banter going on. We liked having a laugh. It was just the culture of the club. We'd be doing our own session and we'd see all the professionals mucking about. They used to set fire to training bags, cut up people's clothes. Anything and everything was happening. The whole club was mad. I learnt from that and I've mucked about ever since!

AFC Wimbledon in that first season was as mad as anything I've ever known, and never more so than on that final day of the season. Loads of stuff was going on. We just wanted to enjoy ourselves.

Danny Oakins kicked it all off by showing his arse to the crowd midway through the game. We knew from then on that everything was fair game. Once we got back into the changing room I tried to shave off Kevin Cooper's hair, but that just backfired on me. Keith Ward and Danny Oakins pinned me down I ended up with a St George's cross shaved into my chest hair. And that was just the start of it. Within a matter of minutes hair was all over the floor. We shaved off Ally Russell's chest hair. Then it was on to goalkeeper Ray Merry. You just had to take it.

There was a bit of the Crazy Gang about us – in fact we were probably crazier than the Crazy Gang. I was serious once. I think it was back in October '87 – it lasted about 20 minutes.

By Joe Sheerin (AFC Wimbledon captain)

It was a perfect end to a perfect year. We had been used to big crowds and even huge roars. The Wallingford game sticks out in my mind, but this was even better. There was an excellent buzz around the game – it was a carnival atmosphere.

Even though we finished the season in third place, we had improved throughout the year. We had broken club records – highest points tally, most goals scored – and, most importantly of all, we had proved that we weren't a flash in the pan. Attendances didn't drop off, as some had predicted. The whole day turned into a huge celebration of everything that everyone had achieved over the previous 11 months.

The team had developed, and the dressing room was the best one I had ever known. There were no prima donnas. Everyone was out for a laugh – Noel Frankum, Simon Bassey, Gareth Graham, Danny Oakins.

A couple of weeks earlier, we all agreed to do a naked calendar. We rolled up on the Sunday morning still drunk from the night before. They provided us with loads of beer and it just turned into one big laugh. They got us to do all these dodgy poses, but by the end of it we couldn't take anything seriously and it ended up with us all running around the pitch at Kingsmeadow naked and lagered-up. The residents must have been getting a right eyeful! It was one of the funniest days. But that final game surpassed even that.

We had the best bunch of lads. Maybe we weren't quite up to Crazy Gang level, but we were getting there.

By Terry Eames (AFC Wimbledon manager)

The first season at AFC Wimbledon epitomised perfectly the spirit of Wimbledon. There was the ability to defy the odds, the determination to succeed and, most importantly, there was the passion of a community. AFC Wimbledon was born out of the will of the supporters. It thrived because of the togetherness of the club: the supporters and the players. It was very much like the old Wimbledon.

Together we defied the sceptics. Back in August 2002, there were many people saying that by November our attendances would die off. But that never happened. The fans that came down grew to love the club more and more. But it was not an easy year. Sometimes I found it really hard to be manager of AFC Wimbledon and hold down a full-time job as well.

The icing on the cake came in mid-July 2003, when we finally took over the lease at Kingsmeadow. That was one of the proudest days of my life. How many other clubs could have raised £1 million in three weeks? And after 12 years of pain, Wimbledon had a home base once more.

The Dons grow up

The final game of AFC Wimbledon's first season was also the final time Yellow and Blue was published. The programme had been launched as a protest against the move to Milton Keynes. It had campaigning at its core, but now, a season in, AFC Wimbledon needed to grow. Yellow and Blue had served its purpose.

Summer 2003
By Niall Couper (Yellow and Blue editor)

There was a little doubt for me that 5 May 2003 was probably my footballing highlight. There were all the heroes on the pitch, and AFC Wimbledon had shown the world what could be achieved by a bunch of football fans. And then Ivor took the microphone – as he always liked to.

He started a long stream of thank-yous, and then he came to us – the Yellow and Blue team – who were up in the press box. Me, Alex Kirk, Charlie Talbot and Marc Jones. He thanked us, and the crowd launched into a chorus of "Yellow and Blue". It made the hairs on the back of my neck stand up. It was awesome. I will happily live on that moment for ever.

But it was also the last time Yellow and Blue would go to print. Our time was over.

The end... The Yellow and Blue team (from left to right) Niall Couper, Alex Kirk, Marc Jones, Charlie Talbot and Matthew Couper with the programme's last edition on 5 May 2003 (Niall Couper)

The Yellow and Blue team (from left to right) Jill Stratton, Jo Lewis, Charlie Talbot, Aideen Rochford, Kevin Rye, Martin Drake, Niall Couper, Mark Lewis, Dave Boyle and Alex Folkes (Niall Couper)

In the months that followed, I fell out with Marc Jones, with Charlie Talbot, with the programme's promotions manager Heather Jackson, even with Ivor Heller. The club wanted to take the programme in-house and we no longer fitted the bill. The problem was, I was a campaigner. I liked the cause, I liked the fight – and that's what Yellow and Blue was. The club had grown since the dark days of Selhurst Park. What it needed now was a matchday programme, not a call to arms.

I have spoken to Alex many times about it since. His view is simple. We had had fun. We had had our time in the sun. We had managed to escape legal proceedings from Charles Koppel – although we were threatened twice. We had had some of the best columnists – I still miss Chris Phillips' musings. We had been edgy. But now was the right time to go.

We had become more like When Saturday Comes than an "official mouthpiece". Yellow and Blue's days were over. Wimbledon was growing up.

Dons hold off Fulham to capture Merton

In the aftermath of Franchise FC's getting permission to relocate to Buckinghamshire, they also decided to give up their Football in the Community Schemes in London. Football in the Community is a national body, but each borough can decide who runs the scheme in their boundaries. At its peak Wimbledon's Football in the Community Scheme operated in seven London boroughs. By 2003, it was down to just Merton and Franchise FC now decided to abandon it as well. Viewed as the top prize in South West London, Fulham had their eyes on it.

3 July 2003
By Nigel Higgs (Dons Trust Board member)

The Community Scheme is one of the unsung success stories of AFC Wimbledon. The year AFC Wimbledon started, we got wind of the fact that Franchise were pulling out of Merton. Historically, Wimbledon's community scheme had been one of the best in the country. They had been active in seven London boroughs, and now they were down to one – Merton. And now they were leaving there too. The future now rested with the council.

We desperately needed to do something and I said as much to the club's then chairman Kris Stewart. If we wanted to ensure AFC Wimbledon had a long-term presence in Merton, we needed to be running the community scheme.

It was then that we got a little bit of luck. We were approached by a few of the old Wimbledon Football in the Community Scheme guys. They had Steve Allen, the old club's physio on board. They had formed a company called Soccer Skills and they said they could help re-create what Wimbledon had. "You can outsource it to us and we will take 50 per cent of the profit." And that seemed fair enough. To help strengthen our bid we worked with Tooting & Mitcham, who were based in the borough. But it was no shoo-in and it so nearly didn't happen. Fulham wanted it. The Merton scheme included Wimbledon Park and that's the real jewel in the crown in south-west London. It regularly attracts 150 kids. The PFA favoured Fulham and were lobbying the council heavily on their behalf. We had a hard sell on our hands.

AFC Wimbledon's community scheme takes to the pitch at Kingsmeadow (Terry Buckman)

We met with the parents, the coaches and the council, and we explained what we could do. In hindsight you can excuse their scepticism. Fulham were sniffing around and we were a small non-league club with no real pedigree. The agreement with Soccer Skills helped because of the links to Wimbledon FC. But it was still difficult to predict how things would go and that summer we waited nervously to see who the council would prefer. In the end it was left to the council leader at the time, Andrew Judge, to announce the decision. We'd won. We had managed to hang on to Merton by the skin of our teeth. Wimbledon came very close to being wiped off the map of Merton.

Now we are in the Football League the goalposts have changed completely. The funding is there now. It's a 9 to 5 business taking bookings, going into schools and delivering football schemes. We have a new website, a blog, the whole scheme is really flying.

Paul Foley is a great Senior Community coach – effectively he's the manager. And then there's Dan Stevens, the administrator; he's a huge fan and that helps too. But we came so close to having nothing.

The joy of the Combined Counties

AFC Wimbledon's failure to gain promotion in their first season had a slightly sour outcome, but for the Combined Counties League it offered another year in the limelight.

Summer 2003
By Alan Constable (Combined Counties League secretary)

There was a fear that the Ryman League would attempt to "pull rank" in that first close season and try to pinch AFC Wimbledon, even though they hadn't finished in a promotion place. But they didn't, and everyone welcomed Wimbledon back for a second season.

There was a slightly sour note when I found myself the subject of criticism from some Wimbledon fans, because when they saw the fixture list for their second season they felt they had a surfeit of midweek home matches. I had genuinely believed that this policy would have been welcomed. It was taken on police advice, because there was concern about upwards of 2,000 people leaving some of the smaller grounds late on a Tuesday evening. So the complaints were unexpected – indeed, I thought that if there were going to be any, they would come from other clubs having to go to AFC Wimbledon in midweek, as some CCL clubs struggle to field their best sides in midweek. I was quite upset by one email which suggested that "I wanted to shaft Wimbledon again" – which, to say the least, didn't take into account my enthusiasm to get them into the league in the first place. It was no big deal, though, and after speaking with Trevor Williams, the AFC Wimbledon secretary, we put an article on the club's official website explaining the reasoning, which hopefully was accepted by most, and the matter was soon forgotten.

As everyone knows, everything ended extremely well for the club that second season, with the league won without losing a match, and the League Cup secured with victory at Woking against North Greenford United – the sight of so many AFC supporters filling the magnificent Woking main stand will never be forgotten.

The Caveman cometh

The first season of AFC Wimbledon had been full of romance. The second season was a time for the players to roll up their sleeves and deliver. A victory in Kent was among the most memorable that year – sealed by a last-minute winner from Matt Everard, who would quickly earn the nickname of Caveman.

18 October 2003
Herne Bay 2 AFC Wimbledon 3 FA Vase, second round
By Matt Everard (AFC Wimbledon player)

It was all in slow motion. It was deep in injury time. Ryan Gray was jinking away on the left wing and sent in an outswinger.

Wimbledon fans celebrate the late winner at
Herne Bay in the FA Vase on 18 October 2003
(Rob Beatty)

I can still picture the ball coming over. They had a lanky centre-half, I got the nudge on him as he was going up and the ball hit my forehead perfectly. I headed back in the direction it had come and it looped over the keeper. He got a hand to it but couldn't keep it out. Cue mayhem.

Nowadays an injury-time victory in Kent in the FA Vase might not seem much, but back then there was no FA Cup and not even the FA Trophy to go for. And we'd be nailed on for the League title. The Vase was what we wanted – it was our big motivator. Yes, winning leagues means a lot, but nothing can beat a cup tie.

The whole moment, the goal, the celebrations are still so vivid. I ran to my wife – I was going to run into the crowd, but I saw her and off I went. The whole team bundled in. Zoe was completely smothered!

It was just a huge relief. We had a good drink after the game. At that level you could get away with it. For the players we had then it was brilliant. Such a superb atmosphere.

I'd actually got us off to a great start scrambling in the ball from a Danny Oakins throw-in. They levelled just before the break, before Joe Sheerin put us back ahead early in the second half. To be honest, we were coasting then and I think a lot of us thought it was a case of how many we'd get. But that complacency can come back and bite you – and it very nearly did.

From nowhere they scored with a shot from miles out. Goals like that are a real kick in the teeth, you can't do anything about it. But this time it set up that brilliant finale – and one of my greatest memories in football.

By Mark Lewis (AFC Wimbledon fan)

By this point in AFC Wimbledon's fledgling history, the team and its supporters were getting used to winning almost every game. The FA Vase, however, involving teams from other regional leagues, was different. The Herne Bay game proved to be one of many difficult trips to Kent the Dons would ever face.

The team didn't have much opposition to overcome in the CCL that season, so they may not have taken Kent League side Herne Bay seriously enough. The Dons contrived to blow their lead twice as Matt Everard seemed to forget he actually did have to do some defending for a change. But the "Caveman" legend was truly born that afternoon when Everard looped home an injury-time header in stoppage time to clinch a dramatic cup victory.

As Everard's winner fell into the net mass hysteria broke out among the hordes of travelling Dons fans. Standing directly behind the goal, my six-foot-plus frame was swept up into the air and tossed sideways as jubilant supporters surged forward in triumph. It was an epic goal celebration, unrivalled in AFC Wimbledon history until that moment in the City of Manchester Stadium in May 2011.

It will only take 10 years

On the pitch, AFC Wimbledon was on a roll. The club's organisation was in place, but it needed a fresh focus and new objectives. Fundamental questions were being asked: What should the club aim to achieve? How ambitious could it really be? In January 2004, a meeting of the Dons Trust would lead to the setting of a new set of aims, including one 'ridiculously ambitious' one – to achieve Football League status within 10 years.

Dons Trust Workshop

January 2004
Kingsmeadow
By Tom Adam (Dons Trust chair)

The club had been making tremendous strides on the pitch, but we thought we needed to become more focused about our aims and objectives as a club.

We are privileged at AFC Wimbledon to have supporters with such a wide skill set. Among them is David Hall. David is an expert in business management and was vital in the process. In latter years, he would stand a couple of times for the Dons Trust Board – each time he failed to get on. But in the 2003-04 season, he had a different role to play. The Dons Trust Board called him into act as a facilitator and it was he who helped co-ordinate the workshop at Kingsmeadow that would lead to the 10-year target being set.

There were a number of us there: Marc Jones, Kris Stewart, Ivor Heller, Nigel Higgs and a few others – that was in the days before membership of the Dons Trust Board and the AFC Wimbledon Board was split. I remember Marc wasn't sure what a workshop was. He thought we were going to do a bit of carpentry – he was joking of course.

David took control of the meeting early on, and set up a brainstorming exercise and listed all the important things we were trying to achieve. There were dozens and dozens of ideas, some more ambitious than others, but after a while it was clear that they were beginning to fall into set groups. They are all reflected in the aims we still have now. There was one about diversity and equality. There were some around the role we wanted to play in the wider football world and others about our reputation. Of course the stadium and the location of the club came into it – we all wanted to be back in Merton eventually.

There was also the issue of fundraising and that for me was essential. We had a line in our aims about financial prudence, but underpinning that was the need to raise our own revenue. We set ourselves a fundraising target of £100,000 a year – and we have pretty much reached that now. The Dons Draw, which was Niall Couper's brainchild, now makes around £70,000 a year. And in the first 10 years Roger Dennis took around £120,000 from Golden Goals. The fundraising team, led for four years by Mark Davis, has raised £1 million for the club all told. Where would we be without them?

But back to the aims, and the brainstorm. A final set of ideas centred around the football. How ambitious could we really be? How far could we really go?

And that's where David Hall came into his own. For each aim and objective, he wanted to be realistic, to have people responsible, and to have timelines and targets for each one. He said: "You can't just have objectives for the sake of objectives." Our dream was to get our Football League place back. And he said simply: "Well, you are going to have to put a timescale next to it." And I said: "10 years is about right." It felt correct. We had to set something feasible, and we had to also be ambitious. One or two thought we were over egging it, but we went for it. And in our aims we set the target to reach the Football League by the 2013-14 season.

Although the club now had new aims, on the training pitch tensions had been growing, Wimbledon's record run was still unchallenged, but the club's board and its management had developed different approaches. Something had to give – and in the middle of February 2004 it did. Manager Terry Eames was suspended on Friday the 13th and formally sacked a few days later. It was left to club chairman Kris Stewart to address an angry Kingsmeadow crowd.

18 February 2004
AFC Wimbledon 5 Raynes Park Vale 0 Premier Challenge Cup
By Luke MacKenzie (Dons Trust Board member)

Terry had threatened to resign several times. In the early days after games we had lost, he would storm in and threaten to quit. Each time we had to spend ages talking him out of it. It was ridiculous. And that was the start of those of us involved in running the club losing faith in him.

It was a really difficult time. The Dons Trust Board was changing: Tom Adam had replaced Lou Carton-Kelly as chair, and one of the new Board members was Anne Eames, Terry's wife. Every time we needed to discuss anything involving Terry, which was a lot as he was manager of the club, she would have to step out of the room. It was hardly an ideal situation.

We'd ask Terry to do something, and there was no certainty it would happen. There were issues with the reserves and the youth team – in fact, there were problems all over the place. Terry felt he was the Number 1 man at the club, and he had his own agenda (as the independent hearing by Stephen Powell later confirmed). He may have been our manager, but we didn't want to jeopardise the future of the club for the sake of one person. AFC Wimbledon was not solely about Terry Eames.

It all came to a head at a Dons Trust Board meeting in the President's Lounge. We had all heard various stories from Kris and Trevor and numerous other sources. It was all terribly sad. We had put him there in the first place. The shock of it all was a wake-up call for us. The honeymoon was over: it was now time to deal with real football issues. It wasn't an easy decision to make, but we had no choice.

To an outsider it looked ludicrous. Here was a manager in the middle of a huge unbeaten run, taking the club towards its first title. But it wasn't about results.

I remembered the speech Terry had made at Wimbledon Theatre months before. He said that if he was to ever get sacked, he would come down to watch us from the terraces. And that's the saddest thing – I haven't seen him at a game since.

It was hard for Kris. Straight after the hearing, he took the brave decision to make an announcement from the stands. It was a Wednesday-night cup game. He took loads of stick and endless abuse. It was brutal. It all became personal. It was awful to watch – here was an individual who had done so much for the club. And he just took it. I don't know whether it played a part in his decision to step down later, but it can't have helped his position.

It was such a difficult and sad time, but it was also a time when the club finally grew up. We had people leave that night and never come back. It was the first time we realised that running a football club wasn't going to be a bed of roses.

By Erik Samuelson (AFC Wimbledon finance director)

When we made the decision to suspend Terry we called him to a meeting. We told him he was suspended and why, although he left before we could finish everything we wanted to say. A story went around that Terry had thrown his coffee over the board when we suspended him. I don't know where this story came from but Terry didn't do that, nor is it the sort of thing I think he would ever have done.

We were unprepared for what happened next – before we could put a statement together the news had broken on Weird and Wonderful World (then the chat site of preference). Immediately we were getting calls and emails from fans asking what was going on. It is fair to say we weren't anywhere near as prepared as we should have been.

By Nicky English (AFC Wimbledon assistant manager)

I was really gutted for Terry when he got sacked. I just couldn't understand it. I wasn't that close to the AFC Wimbledon board, but Erik, Ivor, Kris and Jonesy were all friends with Terry. They were all Wimbledon through and through. The way it was all dealt with did leave a bad taste in my mouth.

I had first got involved with AFC Wimbledon through a friend of mine, John Egan, when the club was first formed. John knew Terry Eames. I knew the local football scene really well. I'd been a youth-team coach at Chipstead and helped develop players like Steve Sidwell. I'd won numerous league titles and cups, so I knew the players who were available locally. And Terry needed players quickly.

He would tell me a position he needed filled, and I would try to help him fill it. The likes of Danny Oakins, Lee Sidwell, Ray Merry and Gareth Graham – all came directly through my contacts.

Then there was Alex Tapp. He's my nephew, and at the time he was one of the top prospects, having played for England at a number of youth levels. The one problem was that he was playing for the deadly enemy in Milton Keynes, but thanks to his tips we contacted a few other players to get them on board. We missed out on a couple, but that's how Gavin Bolger and Seb Favata signed up.

It was obviously working well as, halfway through that first season, Terry asked me to come on board as his assistant – and together we built a good squad from nowhere. I'd been in charge at Netherne, and as we didn't have a reserve side we arranged to use them as one. It would be a bit of an anticlimax for several of the players we brought in: they'd expect to be playing for AFC Wimbledon, and they'd end up playing in the middle of the countryside for Netherne.

On a personal level it was a great opportunity for me. I went to Wimbledon and enjoyed it straight away – it was one of the best times of my life. Each week I'd sit down with Terry. We'd discuss what had happened in training, look at the options and then pick the side. Normally it would be Terry who won the arguments, but we had a good team which by and large picked itself.

Terry also showed great faith in me. We didn't really know each other, yet he stuck by me in those early days. I remember taking a training session on the athletics track behind the ground. Simon Bassey had joined up. He was an ex-Aldershot player and came with a great reputation. He had a few problems with his knees and was always carrying some sort of knock. Anyway, he and another of our experienced players,

Neil Robson, were far from happy with the running regime we were doing around the track. It was 100 metres at full pelt, then 100 metres jogging and then three-quarters speed on the back straight, and so on.

Bassey said to me: "I've never run 400 metres to get the ball in my life" (except his language was a bit more colourful than that). I told him and Robbo that if they had a problem with that they could bloody well take it to Terry and tell him. And off they marched. I was dead worried – here were the two most experienced players, players who knew how training works at a much higher level, going off to tell the manager what they thought of me.

I honestly expected an ear-bashing from Terry. Instead, the pair of them came back with their tails between their legs and got on with it. The whole experience must have worked wonders for Bass as he is still there years later, long after everyone else went.

Off the pitch, everything was flying forward at 150mph. The morale, the team, everything – all being swept up by the enthusiasm and determination of the fans. It was amazing. Forget Alex Ferguson or José Mourinho – the bond the players had with the fans back then was second to none. The atmosphere in the bars was electric. It was amazing. The players all knew what it was about. They'd be there every Tuesday and Thursday night for training without fail. They were determined to push on and take Wimbledon back to where they belonged.

During all my time at the club, I can think of only two games where we didn't do ourselves justice – away at Banstead and at home to Colne in the FA Vase. But most of the time we knew we'd come through and win. We could be two down with 10 minutes to go and still win 4-2. That's just how it was. And we played some really good stuff.

Terry loved AFC Wimbledon, and Wimbledon FC before that. You could cut him and he would bleed yellow and blue. He supported them as much as Ivor or Jonesy did. He was a big-time supporter. I could see that Terry was trying to do his best, and he wanted to do things his way – after all, he was the manager. But the Board wanted to make the decisions.

I was always of the view that if it isn't broken, don't change it. Terry was plotting for the year ahead – he knew what he wanted to do. And part of that was to secure the future of some of our best players. He verbally offered the likes of Matt Everard and Danny Oakins more cash. And Matt Everard is probably the best centre-half I've ever worked with. As a partnership, those two were brilliant. Terry also wanted some security for himself and a commitment from the board.

But all of that was out of sync with how the club wanted things run. Terry is very hot-headed, and the disagreements rumbled on for weeks, with row after row and things getting increasingly strained. It was like a runaway train – the crash was inevitable. He had one row with the Board too many, and within 10 minutes he was gone.

It was a very difficult time for me. The crowd were massively in his favour – he was their god. He was Wimbledon personified. We were something like 10 points clear, unbeaten and coasting towards the title. His dismissal threatened to destroy everything the club had built.

By Dave Boyle (Wimbledon case worker, Supporters Direct)

I never really knew everything that happened. But it was clear there was an issue that needed to be addressed. The fans held Terry Eames in complete adulation, but when you spoke about him to people like Kris they would roll their eyes skyward.

It was a difficult period. The first-year love-in was over. AFC Wimbledon was turning into a "proper" football club, and people were becoming more critical of the club's board. Kris was getting continually asked how much was he earning. I was on the board of WISA at the time, and I remember talking to Nicole Hammond, who was the chair – we had real concerns about the fallout if Terry was sacked. It was about the right process and the right PR.

When the decision came, it split the club – several well-known people were heavily critical of the process. The problem was that Terry's suspension was not being seen from the outside as an act by reasonable people making a considered decision. And there was the whole problem of governance: who could Terry appeal to? In normal circumstances that would be the Dons Trust Board – but half of them had been in on the decision, and they would have had to get up and leave the room.

It was then that I suggested they set up an independent panel that Terry could appeal to. I mentioned it to Nicole and she took it to Kris. The club had already taken legal advice and had come to a similar conclusion. I suggested Stephen Powell from Arsenal Independent Supporters Association run it and I was pleasantly surprised that the club agreed. He was a union man, but more importantly he was independent of the club. It really helped, and within minutes of the hearing Stephen had his report up on the website. It killed all further criticism stone dead.

AFC Wimbledon had conducted the process in a fair and balanced way. Yes, it hurt, and it did strain a few relationships, but this was a process that would be unheard of at any other club. The whole story that Terry Eames was shafted and that something was fundamentally wrong with AFC Wimbledon was killed overnight.

That night there was an evening game at Kingsmeadow. Kris took the microphone, took a few boos as well, and explained what had happened. That must have taken some bottle.

By Erik Samuelson (AFC Wimbledon finance director)

I went to the game with my elder son and, as usual, we wandered off into the crowd on the terrace. Ivor and Kris went into the boardroom (I didn't always go in the boardroom in those days) and then the bar. I heard later that they had been subjected to some awful abuse from a number of fans and I know that Ivor in particular felt very badly treated.

I remember warning my son that if any unpleasantness arose on the terraces then he should make himself scarce and leave me to deal with it, but in fact there was hardly anything. I recall one fan saying that: "You had better have a very good reason for this," but that was all – and it wasn't said in an unpleasant way. I didn't even find out that Terry, Anne and family had been in the crowd that day until I got home – I really only wanted to watch the game and I didn't see them.

When it came to Kris' moment to read the statement to the crowd he did so obviously under great strain but clearly and firmly.

He was abused by a small number of angry fans while he was doing so, but he stuck to it. Later, I saw him in the car park being bellowed at by one very angry fan, right in his face, but he kept cool and dealt with it very well.

I hated the whole process from beginning to end and I'm sure Kris did too, but he showed brave leadership for which I greatly admired him. I'm not sure I would have been able to do the same.

By Kris Stewart (AFC Wimbledon chairman)

We had a meeting with Terry Eames, and after that we met as a Board to decide what to do. We talked about the various scenarios. The original directors all had the same ethos then – Ivor was a bit different, but underneath he was ultimately the same – we wanted to do things right and be decent. It was really important to us.

We had an employee that we had a situation with. As the employer, we couldn't go washing all our dirty laundry in public. And that's not just from a point of view of legal issues such as potential libel actions, but the desire to be a decent employer. But we knew we were on a hiding to nothing – we couldn't explain our reasoning.

We had to be decent, we wanted to do things right. AFC Wimbledon is not only a football club, but a football club that is owned by the fans. The fans were in effect my boss – I had to show them that we were doing the right thing. I took a lot of advice. I wanted to know what we should do.

We had to tell the fans as much as we could, and we had to be honest about what we couldn't say and why we couldn't say it. But the question was how. And it came to us that there was a match that very night, presenting us with the perfect opportunity. So we decided to write something, but then there was the question of what exactly we were going to do with it.

There was one person in particular, who I won't name, and he said simply that I had to tell people personally. I had to speak directly to the fans. And he wouldn't let me do anything different. As soon as he'd said that, it just clicked: we all knew that that was what had to be done. I thought: "F***, I don't really want to do that!" But I knew I had to.

We worked on the practicalities to make sure it could be done. We checked the PA, we printed the speech out and I went out and did it. As for the game, I don't remember what the score was or even who we played – that was all an irrelevance that night. I was totally consumed.

Afterwards, lots of people said it was brave, but what else could I have done? Hide behind a bit of paper? If you are Charles Koppel or Ken Bates you can do that, but if you are the chairman of AFC Wimbledon you don't have that option.

I'd heard what people were saying, and it wasn't pleasant. But it had to be done, and I got through it and I am really glad I got through it. It was f***ing horrible, but it was the right thing to do. If we are about anything, we are about doing the right thing.

If you have principles, you have to show those principles during the difficult times as well as the good. Otherwise there's no point in having them.

By Robert Dunford (Webmaster, SW19's Army)

There's a certain irony that Terry Eames was ousted on Friday the 13th. It may be no more than footnote in the club's history now, but at the time it seemed like a nightmare for many.

If anyone was Mr Wimbledon back then, it was the man known as Eamo. A vocal opponent of the move to Milton Keynes, his appointment as first-ever AFCW era manager was perfect. When he bawled at a player, he was doing it for us as well. So when it was announced on the official website on that cold Friday that he had been "suspended pending a formal disciplinary meeting", everyone was shocked. Not to mention pinching themselves too – we didn't do that sort of thing these days, surely?

Conspiracy theories abounded. Perhaps he had got caught doing something he shouldn't after the recent Colne post-match brawl (a particularly niggly FA Vase game at Kingsmeadow a month or so earlier). Following the announcement, opinion was split – were you on the side of a manager, who was one of "us", or were you on the side of the club's Board?

It's no exaggeration to say that emotions were running high, although results on the pitch helped to smooth things. The day after the announcement the Dons thrashed Chessington United 9-0 down at Leatherhead. Ironically, considering it was Valentine's Day, there wasn't much love shown that afternoon to Board members, who were openly abused by more than a couple of fans in what is probably still the most toxic atmosphere of an AFCW-era game. The pro-Eames chants at the end showed where the collective hearts lay.

After a few more days of arguments and all-round bloodletting, we faced Raynes Park Vale at home in the Premier Challenge Cup (the CCL league cup). We won 5-0, but it was an eerily subdued contest – and with good reason, as the club had finally sacked Eames. But in the days before Twitter and smartphones, the club felt the need to announce the sacking over the PA after the game. A sombre Chris Phillips passed the mic to a nervous-sounding Kris Stewart, who proceeded to read out the club's statement.

Nobody needed to call the riot police, though. True, there were some boos and jeers, but most people listened quietly. Whether it was shock or resignation, there wasn't going to be mutiny. People just sighed and shrugged their shoulders.

It later became clear why Eames had left. It was not what we expected from a hero. If anyone had "won", it was the Board, who we could now see had acted properly after all. In the blink of an eye, Eamo was persona non grata. For most people, anyway. Some long-standing WFC fans, friends of the Eames clan as well, were so disgusted at his ousting that they left and have hardly been seen since.

As for the man himself, he had said when he first took the job that, should he leave, he would be back on the terraces the next game. He appeared just one more time, at the last game of that season against Wallingford. Some shook his hand, but just as many kept their distance. He felt like a gatecrasher, hardly the Mr Wimbledon of those idealistic days of two years before.

Maybe Eames cared too much for his own good? We will never know, but what we did now know was not to get too attached to a manager or player again. Especially the ones you support the most.

By Nicky English (AFC Wimbledon assistant manager)

After Terry had gone, Kris Stewart and Erik came to me. They were desperate. "Don't walk away," they pleaded. They were really worried. We were in the process of winning the league. These were Terry's players, and they could have walked. "It could all spiral downhill," they said. "We can't have another year in the CCL, we could lose half our support, it could be the end of us." They were really worried.

I was torn, really torn between my loyalty to Terry and my desire to help the club. But in the end it was too big an opportunity to turn down. I became the caretaker manager.

Disquiet on the Board

The Terry Eames saga had brought everything to a head. The fairytale was over, and for the first time Wimbledon supporters had begun to realise that running your own football club was a serious business. The workshop a month earlier had asked the Board to focus and a battle of principles had begun to bubble over.

February 2004
By Dave Boyle (Wimbledon case worker, Supporters Direct)

I wasn't at the heart of it all, but you could sense that there were difficulties.

Lou Carton-Kelly was on the board of Supporters Direct at the time, and there was a feeling that some of the people at the heart of AFC Wimbledon were reluctant to turn to us for help because they felt that would strengthen Lou's position.

Kris and Lou would come along and talk to other trusts to encourage them, but no one else from the club had much to do with us. There was a definite "corporate side" of the club that felt they could do it all by themselves. AFC Wimbledon was not as well represented among the fans' movement as they perhaps should have been, unlike, say, FC United of Manchester a few years later.

The problem was that AFC Wimbledon was a double-headed creature. On the one side were the creative ideologues; and on the other side those who believed that AFC Wimbledon was there purely out of necessity. That caused problems. I never got that close to it, and I never really wanted to be. Once you get close to the politics of it, you have to take sides. And AFC Wimbledon was too important for me to do that.

By Lou Carton-Kelly

There were suggestions that the whole Terry Eames debacle was the reason I stepped down, but it was nothing to do with that: It was external pressures that eventually took their toll.

I was the Operations Director of AFC Wimbledon, I was on the board of both Supporters Direct and the Dons Trust, and I was a committee member of WISA. It was non-stop, seven days a week for three years. Wimbledon had been my morning, noon and night. I didn't have a job, I was going through a divorce and buying a new house. I needed to pay the mortgage and I couldn't do AFC Wimbledon and the Dons Trust as well. I needed to start earning again.

Yes, there were differences on the Dons Trust Board. I always wanted to check everything with the fans, but some of the other members of the Board wanted to just get on with it.

There was Ivor. He is very gung-ho, a walking dynamo. He does everything at 100mph. He put his life and soul into getting AFC Wimbledon off the ground. He may never admit it, but his company must have really suffered because of his endeavours for the club. We didn't agree on everything, but there would be no AFC Wimbledon without him.

And then there was Erik. What an amazing man. If he wanted something done, he would find a way of doing it. He wanted to do everything and it's clear that there is no way that AFC Wimbledon would have got as far as they have without him. It will be a very sad day when he decides to stand aside.

Personally, I had given up three years of my life. I had done my bit and now I had to move on.

By Niall Couper (Dons Trust Board member)

I'd got elected onto the Board at a by-election. It was a dream come true: here I was, right at the heart of the club. I loved the idea of being involved in its day-to-day running. But I was utterly naïve – there was so much more to it than that.

I was an ideologue. I viewed AFC Wimbledon as this whiter-than-white creation – out to right all the wrongs in the corporate world of football. I was a sports journalist at the time, used to decisions being made yesterday and working to constant short deadlines. The reality of the Dons Trust Board of 2004 couldn't have been more at odds with both my experience and my expectations.

Some people on the Board were like me, but there were others who were used to making decisions by committee – and I found that all painfully slow. I also wanted to represent the community spirit of Wimbledon, while others were determined to make it more corporate – and that was a dilemma that was tearing the club apart.

There were a number of great friendships that I had built over the previous three years of battling Koppel that were ruined during my brief spell on the board. We simply couldn't see eye to eye, and I regret that now. From the inside it was poisoning my love of AFC Wimbledon. Board meetings would drag on beyond midnight. I was living on the other side of London without a car at the time, and that made it increasingly difficult for me to attend. I lasted barely a year before I had to step down.

I felt relieved to be out of it, but also content to see a Board moving from disunity towards harmony. The Dons Trust was at last starting to come of age.

Trouble at the Lane

In the first couple of seasons, AFC Wimbledon had been a novelty welcomed by most. But the size of the club's travelling support meant that sooner or later the issue of stewarding would come to the fore. It arrived in brutal fashion when Bromley allowed near-neighbours Coney Hall to use their ground for a cup tie against the Dons.

16 March 2004
Coney Hall 2 AFC Wimbledon 2 (match abandoned)
Premier Challenge Cup
By Kris Stewart (AFC Wimbledon chairman)

Everything felt wrong as soon as we got to the ground. It seemed as though there wasn't anything planned. It felt like chaos. Back then for away games we would normally help out with stewarding, but they turned us down. If it had been six of

THE JOHN FIORINI STAND

Hitting the floor... AFC Wimbledon's cup tie
against Coney Hall on 16 March 2004, which was
to be cut short by crowd trouble (Rob Beatty)

them and 800 of us, as it quite often was, it would have been OK – we would have got away with it. But that night that wasn't the case.

There was no segregation – it was a disaster waiting to happen. There were a large number of fans who had had a few too many and were clearly after trouble – I don't suspect for one moment they were Coney Hall regulars – and sadly some of our fans reacted.

There were a number of misunderstandings. I couldn't point the finger of blame at any one person – a number of things went wrong that night. I don't think we were really responsible, except for the Wimbledon fans who were fighting.

From the beginning, you could sense how it would all unfold. We shouldn't have played the game; my regret is that I should have told Nicky English and the ref not to even start the game. It wasn't safe.

I'm not sure whether it would have stopped the fighting, but to call it off wouldn't have made things any worse. Yes, there would have been consequences for both clubs, but we should have put people's safety first – that's far more important than a game of football.

I hope that if something like that ever looks as though it might happen again, those in charge would have the balls to pull the game. Sadly, that night I didn't have the balls, and I will regret that forever.

Nicky English is chaired by the fans after the CCL title is secured at Walton Casuals on 12 April 2004 (Paul Willatts)

Sealing the title

With the Dons on such a long unbeaten run, it was always just a matter of time before the title was secured, but it was still a huge relief when the moment finally arrived. It was also the moment when Dickie Guy – a legend from the Seventies – became president of the club.

---

12 April 2004
Walton Casuals 0 AFC Wimbledon 3
Combined Counties League Premier Division
By Matt Everard (AFC Wimbledon player)

I got the first really early on. Ryan Gray swung in a corner. I made a little move on the defender – I was never one for late runs – I connected with my head and the ball sizzled in.

It may seem strange, but I'd had a lot of pre-match nerves. Yes, it was a matter of when rather than if we'd win the league, but still I had butterflies and I think it was the same for a lot of the team. That goal, just four minutes in, settled everything.

We were going to be champions – the only shame was that it wasn't going to be sealed at home. We had nearly 2,000 fans there, but there would have been even more at home. And everything at AFC Wimbledon is always about the fans. Coops got two more and we were home and dry.

It was around that time that Aldershot came in for me. I'd be lying to say I didn't think about the chance of becoming a professional footballer. And maybe if I'd been three or four years younger I would have gone for it, but I was 30 at the time and it didn't seem right.

I didn't really fancy playing for them. I'd lived in Aldershot nearly all my life, but it was never really a contest. I wanted to stay at Wimbledon and see how far I could go.

By Dickie Guy (AFC Wimbledon president)

I felt humbled and delighted when they asked me to become club president. It was after our first promotion.

I was in the Alexandra pub in Wimbledon, and I was about to walk up to Ivor and Kris and to say a big thank you to them for the way they had treated me and my family during that season. Instead, I saw them walking up to me. They asked me straight: "Dickie would you do us the big honour of becoming president?" I was gobsmacked – and I was absolutely over the moon.

A world of adventures

In what was to prove to be AFC Wimbledon's final season in the Combined Counties League, it had become clear that the Dons were now a level above the opposition. Nothing could stand in their way, and in mid-April that even included being two goals down after three minutes and ending the match with nine men. It was typical of the team's boundless spirit.

24 April 2004
Chessington & Hook 3 AFC Wimbledon 5
Combined Counties League Premier Division
By Gareth Graham (AFC Wimbledon player)

It was one of those crazy games that just went to show what AFC Wimbledon was all about. We were two down within three minutes – so that wasn't the best of starts. But it was all about the ref. He was just awful. To be honest, we were used to getting everything. I suppose it was a just huge shock for referees at that level to cope with crowds in the thousands.

But that day everything was ridiculous, everything went against us. The ref just lost it. Nicky English was sent from the dugout for calling the ref poor after he missed a blatant penalty. Our physio was sent off for treating Matt Everard for a head injury. It was chaos.

At least Paul Quinn had managed to get one goal that the ref did decide to count before the break. The problem was that I was fuming by then. As we came off at half-time, I said to the ref: "I'm having a bad game, but you are f***ing dreadful!"

I shouldn't have sworn, but that sort of thing happens every week. I was used to refs just swearing back, but he went straight for the red card. I couldn't believe it. I've been sent off a few times and I normally deserve it. Trevor Williams was walking beside me at the time, and he couldn't believe it either. He went mad and got sent off as well!

Chessington & Hook take the lead against AFC
Wimbledon on 24 April 2004 (Rob Beatty)

Kevin Cooper scores his 100th goal for AFC
Wimbledon at Chessington & Hook (Martin Tomlin)

I was gutted when I got back to the dressing room. I felt I'd really let the team down, and I told them to go out and win it. We wanted to keep our unbeaten run going – and to be honest, they probably did better without me.

In the second half we were battering them, but we kept getting pulled up for one thing or another, and then they'd hit us on the counter. We were 3-1 down with less than 15 minutes to go. We'd always known we were going to win the league, so for us the unbeaten run had become the motivator. When you're that far behind with so little time, things do tend to look bleak, but there was something special about Wimbledon back then.

Ryan Gray nodded one in. And then it became the Coops show. It was always Coops. He got tripped in the area – and even this ref couldn't miss that one. Coops got up and whacked the ball in. He didn't mind telling us afterwards that that was his 100th goal for the club.

Before he got the 101st, Shane Small-King (signed from AFC Wallingford the month before) got himself sent off along with one of their players. I didn't have a clue what that was for. Then it became nine against nine, when one of their players made a superb diving save. Off he went, and Coops whacked in the penalty. I think Ryan added one more to seal it at the death.

It was crazy – you shouldn't really get games like that, but that was AFC Wimbledon. We had a great spirit, a great bunch of lads. There were the likes of Danny Oakins, Simon Bassey, Noel Frankum and Joe Sheerin. We were all cut from the same cloth. I still keep in touch with a number of the lads from those days.

The banter was just unbelievable. And you couldn't dare leave your stuff alone for a second. Towards the end I used to take to the pitch without any pants on as the lads used to constantly rub Deep Heat into them – and I tell you, that pain can last for days!

Some of the nights were amazing. There were occasions when I went missing for a couple of days, normally after we were celebrating some cup or league success. It would be the Peel and then the Grove to silly o'clock and then God knows where. It was the same route some of the fans took, and we just followed them.

For me, it was always about the fans – the Fans' Club – and that's what made it special. The atmosphere was amazing.

The Wonderful world of Woking

After the straw bales at Sandhurst and the cheese rolls at Merstham, this was to be the club's first real taste of a return to the big time – a final at Woking and that stand. AFC Wimbledon were still prone to nerves in the big games, and this was no different. It took a Kevin Cooper effort to settle the side and secure a league and cup double.

---

30 April 2004
AFC Wimbledon 4 North Greenford United 1
Premier Challenge Cup Final
By Kevin Cooper (AFC Wimbledon player)

It was the goal that sealed it. Matt Everard had put us ahead, but we were nervous

COMBINED COUNTIES
CUP FINAL
A.F.C WIMBLEDON
V
NORTH GREENFORD
FRIDAY APRIL 30TH K.O. 7.45PM

FIDE ET DILIGENTIA

WELCOME TO WOKING F.C.

The entrance to Woking marks AFC Wimbledon's first cup final (Martin Tomlin)

Kevin Cooper scores AFC Wimbledon's third goal in the Premier Challenge Cup final against North Greenford United (Paul Willatts)

The AFC Wimbledon team celebrate their cup success on 30 April 2004 (Paul Willatts)

The Dons fans get their hands on the Premier Challenge Cup after the club's 4-1 success (Rob Beatty)

– really nervous. Jamie Taylor had surged forward – he was like a little Jack Russell – but no one else had gone up with him. We were all hanging back to protect our 2-1 lead.

So I hit the box, and he squared the ball back to me. I struck it first time and it went in. The crowd exploded. All credit to Jamie – I would have shot if it had been me. That third goal just killed the game off, and it was a party atmosphere from that moment on.

North Greenford pushed on, but right at the end Gavin Bolger beat the offside trap and, like a repeat of my first, he set me up and I couldn't really miss. I ran into the crowd. The league and league cup double was ours.

Of everything I achieved at the club, this topped it all. It is the one game that stands out a mile. We'd gone the whole year unbeaten, but the setting, the build-up, the fans – this game had everything. It may have been just the CCL league cup, but it felt like a big cup final. The buzz that day was just something else.

We'd had a pre-match meal at Kingsmeadow, before setting off on the team coach with our families and friends in another coach behind us. Then came the fans in open-top buses. And then we got there – and there was that stand. We must have had 98 per cent of the support inside the ground – everything was yellow and blue. And at the end, when we climbed the steps to pick up the trophy, the whole pitch was covered with Dons fans.

I just didn't want that night to end. After everything that had happened to the club and the fans, this was what they really deserved. It said to the football world: "We are Wimbledon, we are up and running."

I had eight pints given to me within four minutes of getting back to Kingsmeadow – I'm normally a two pint a night man! The fans were just so friendly, then there was the music, and all of us getting on the stage to do our bits. Looking back on the whole story of AFC Wimbledon, it was one of those moments when you realised what AFC Wimbledon really means.

It proved to be one of my last games for the club. In the summer I sat down with the new boss, Dave Anderson. I wanted a contract, but he had set himself a policy of only offering contracts to players under 25. I was 27. He promised that if I stayed on I would have played, but that wasn't enough for me at the time. Hindsight is a wonderful thing, and I still regret that decision now. I love Wimbledon.

By Nicky English (AFC Wimbledon caretaker manager)

Kevin Cooper was an amazing player. He had some sort of sixth sense as to where the goal was. He never did any work, but he could score goals. It was unbelievable. God knows how far he could have gone if he had picked up his workrate.

English departs

AFC Wimbledon ended their Combined Counties League life with victory over bogey side AFC Wallingford. The game could have been a stepping stone to greater things for caretaker manager Nicky English, but the Board had become tired of the players' antics off the pitch and wanted a new approach. So instead of a celebration, the match was to prove to be his epitaph.

AFC Wimbledon parade the League and Cup
Double at Kingsmeadow (Jerzy Dabrowski)

8 May 2004
AFC Wallingford 1 AFC Wimbledon 2
Combined Counties League Premier Division
By Nicky English (AFC Wimbledon caretaker manager)

We had already won the league and we were just relaxing. It was easy. Jamie Taylor scored early on, and from there it was just game over. We went back to a pub in Wimbledon and it was good fun – one of those great nights in the history of AFC Wimbledon. I didn't know then that it would be my last game in charge.

I was put in as caretaker manager. I had kept asking what they were going to do. They wouldn't say whether I'd got the job for 18 months or even till Christmas. It was deeply frustrating.

And then after the Wallingford game, they said: "We're going to advertise for a manager." That left a really sour taste in my mouth. When you stick by people, you expect them to do the same back. I'd made a decision to stay with Wimbledon when I could have walked away. This felt like a kick in the teeth.

They tried to soften the blow and asked me to apply and kept saying, "Nicky, you're our No. 1 choice." I knew the strength of our squad, I knew I'd be given more resources, and I was convinced that under my guidance we would have gone straight through the Ryman First Division. I expected not only to get the job, but to deliver as well.

I had two interviews, and then out of the blue Dave Anderson got the job. I felt hard done by. Every one of the supporters had been tremendous to me. None of them ever had a cross word, not even when I took over from Terry Eames.

WISA members at the protest at Carshalton (from left to right)
Hugh, Simon Wheeler, Michael Maidment, Peter Bowles, Clair
Richardson, Martin Drake (sitting), Sean Fox and Peter Jones
(Rob Dunford)

Chapter Seven:

AFC
WIMBLEDON

The Anderson years

So here's to you, Mr Anderson

Back on the pitch, with Nicky English gone, the task of pushing the team further up the pyramid fell to Hendon's Dave Anderson. It was a challenge he would relish.

May 2004
By Erik Samuelson (AFC Wimbledon finance director)

We got Ian Cooke (former Wimbledon FC player and now an AFC Wimbledon non-executive director) involved in the interview process. We didn't have the football understanding he did. We met him in the President's Lounge early in the process. The curtains were open, and soon rumours started flying around that we were interviewing him for the job. Everyone was speculating who would be the next Wimbledon manager.

There were a number of people involved in the first stage of the process but I wasn't one of them. Kris Stewart was initially aided by football support managers Lee Dobinson and Steve Brindley. They all gave written feedback, and proposed a shortlist of people we wanted to ask back for second interviews and Nicky English wasn't on the list. Kris then took the list to the Dons Trust Board – and there was a rumbling of discontent. It led to Nicky's name being added to the shortlist.

The second interviews took place in the President's Lounge. We were provided with detailed assessments on all of them. I remember that we interviewed Dave Anderson, Nicky English and John Raines, the Sutton manager. But Dave was the standout candidate. He was credible, engaging and persuasive. He was well prepared, and I remember vividly Ian Cooke saying after we had finished: "He's the guy. He has a view on how to put a promotion team together. I'm not as convinced that the others know how to do that. He's the one."

By Dave Anderson (Hendon manager)

I knew all about what had happened to AFC Wimbledon – it was almost impossible not to. I'd followed their form in the Non League Paper and I knew they were looking for a new manager.

So I went to Kingsmeadow with John Morris, my reserve-team manager at Hendon, to take a gawp. It was a midweek game, and they'd had to put the kick-off back 15 minutes to get the crowd in. This was the Combined Counties League – it was just unbelievable.

This was before the improvements to the ground, and we stood in the corner of what is now the Tempest End – it had no roof on it then. And we just tried to take it all in. It wasn't hard to be persuaded. I must have spent most of the game putting my CV together in my head. I couldn't get out of the game fast enough to start writing it.

I had been at Hendon for five years. We were having a great year in the Ryman Premier. It was the year before they introduced the Conference North and South, so you only had to finish in the top 12 or so to get promoted.

We were going to finish third or fourth, but the chairman wasn't prepared to

Dave Anderson, who replaced Terry Eames as AFC Wimbledon's new manager, in July 2004 (Terry Buckman)

Little Chef, the location of Dave Anderson's first interview with AFC Wimbledon

Gareth Graham, one of the players who left ater Dave Anderson's arrival in 2004 (Rob Beatty)

make the jump up. It seemed like the right time for me to move on. So I applied for the Wimbledon job. I had the first interview at a Little Chef just off the M25. It was all a bit surreal – I arrived in my work van and changed into a suit in the back. Then I went in and met them. Kris Stewart, was there, and a couple of others too. It was very informal. We had a couple of cups of tea and I couldn't help thinking how weird it was sitting in a Little Chef with a suit on. But we connected well and I got a second interview.

The second interview couldn't have been more different. It was in a Hilton Hotel just off the A3. It went on for about an hour and a half. I remember coming out of it thinking I had done well and that I couldn't have done anything better. Afterwards Kris called me to tell me the timetable of how the decision would be made. And there was a problem straight away: I was in Portugal, and I would be playing golf when the decision was going to be announced.

So he told me the decision there and then, but swore me to secrecy. He wanted to do the decent thing and tell the other candidates before it became public. I couldn't really get the smile off my face. I told the lads I was away with. In hindsight it was ideal: I was glad to have a few days just to let it all sink in.

The big irony of it all was where I was when I got the news. It was in a stunning villa in Portugal. The next time I was there was seven years later – almost to the day. And it was then that I heard Wimbledon had been promoted to the Football League.

...and farewell

Anderson's arrival forced Nicky English backstage. It was a situation that suited neither man, and after a long drawn-out process, English would finally call it a day. But Anderson's revolution didn't stop there: on their way too were some of the club's original stalwarts.

By Nicky English (ex-AFC Wimbledon caretaker manager)

They asked me to take charge of the youth team. I did it, and I did really well – I think we won the league – but it was still a very difficult year.

Straight after the club appointed Dave Anderson, they held a reception at Merton Civic Centre where they introduced him as the manager without even a nod in my direction for what we had achieved.

It was very awkward working with Anderson. He didn't make me feel welcome. Naturally there was going to be a turnover of players. He brought in the spine of his old Hendon side, and most of my team had just gone.

We spoke very little. He didn't ask my advice on local players, on how the youth team was progressing, or even what worked with the players he already had. He kept calling me "Son", even though I was a year older than him. It was basically an unmanageable situation. Something had to be done, and in the end Erik sided with Anderson. They treated me well then. They paid up my contract and I was released. It was a sad day, but that's football.

In hindsight, if Anderson and I had got on, I really think I could have helped him. But we were both a bit arrogant. I didn't understand why I didn't get the job, and he must have been worried about me still being there, ready to step in at a moment's notice. I must have been a threat to him.

There were a lot of decisions back then that weren't made well, but let's face it, the people in charge were quite inexperienced at the time. They had never run a football club before, but they were learning fast.

By Gareth Graham (AFC Wimbledon player)

Over the summer Dave Anderson came in. We sailed through the next season – and at the end of the campaign it was decision time. Dave didn't want me to go, but I got injured in pre-season. I have no qualms about it. I can't grumble.

Dave was a fellow Northern Irishman like me and he gave me every chance, but the reality was I wasn't fit. I'm a bit of a chunky monkey, and I needed a full pre-season. With the injury, I just never gave myself the chance.

A song and a dance

Terry Eames and Nicky English may have gone, but to the wider world the Wimbledon story had already become a fairytale. In the summer of 2004 the story reached a new stage: the Wimbledon Theatre, courtesy of Matt Couper's production A Fans' Club. A revamped version would even go the Fringe in Edinburgh a year later.

6 June 2004
A Fans' Club Wimbledon Theatre
By Matt Couper (playwright)

I'd wanted to write a book about my experiences as an AFC Wimbledon fan, a kind of Nick Hornby-esque story but for proper fans. I even penned a few chapters. However, after a couple of knock-backs I stopped. Then I had an Eureka moment, after watching Jerry Springer: The Opera. Why not AFC Wimbledon: The Musical? Well, there were several reasons, so I decided to script a play with music, rather than a musical.

In 2003 I started writing. The first decision I made was to use fictional characters rather than focus on real people such as Kris Stewart. So many people had made a contribution to the establishment of AFC Wimbledon that it would have been unfair to focus on just a few. So the characters in the play became a mishmash of all the people that helped set up the club.

My hope was that any Wimbledon fan watching the play would have been able to identify with one of the characters and recognise their own contribution. I named the Wimbledon fans in the play after former Wimbledon FC heroes. The lead character Dave was named after Dave Beasant; Alan after Alan Cork; Eddie after Eddie Reynolds. The tricky one was the female character, who I called Chrissy, after Chris Perry.

For both shows in 2004 and 2005 I managed to draw together an excellent artistic team who helped produce and direct the show. I was also exceptionally lucky that I could bring in Chris Barlow to write and direct the music.

Early in 2004 I booked the Wimbledon Studio Theatre and anxiously awaited the first night. The first night wasn't that busy, but word seemed to get out and suddenly

you couldn't buy a ticket for love or money! The venue held 80 people, but I swear some nights we almost had 100 in.

I loved the experience of the 2004 performance, but it was clear from the reviews outside of Wimbledon (I still haven't brought a copy of Time Out since!) that I would need to make some changes to give the show wider appeal. So for the 2005 production I removed the clown characters (Mr Fran and Mr Chise) and replaced them with an old-style Greek chorus, people who could comment on the action from the outside. These were the Football Gods.

My inspiration for the Football Gods, were the Mayan gods the Monkey Twins (Hun-Batz and Hun-Choen – thanks go to www.godchecker.com). The Monkey Twins appeared to be the original football commentators, which made them perfect for the show. It is great fun writing such absurd characters. I still wanted the comedy element that Fran and Chise brought, but also a bit of objectivity (although I would never claim that the production was anything other than partisan) and the Football Gods seemed to fit the bill.

My aim in 2005 was to put the show on the main stage at Wimbledon, sell out and use the proceeds to take the show to Edinburgh – my advice here is never let your ego get the better of you! The show didn't sell out. The tragic events on the London tube (7/7) the day before the first night didn't help, but it wasn't the sole reason. However I had already made a commitment to go to Edinburgh – where it soon became clear that shows about the war in Iraq were more attractive to the paying public than a show about AFC Wimbledon. We got some good reviews, but not the audiences. It would also have helped if I'd have been in Edinburgh, but I was stuck doing a job I hated with a passion!

I made a huge loss. But my biggest regret, and one that will haunt me forever, is that Big Fat Cat (legendary Wimbledon supporter and now Radio WDON stalwart Geoff Hawley) lent me all his old Wimbledon shirts in 2004 – and after the last show they went missing. I have been trying to track them down ever since, so if you come across an old Wimbledon shirt with "BFC" written on the label please let me know. Until then I will continue to gather up as many old shirts as possible.

Bass moves backstage

Injuries had curtailed Simon Bassey's career. He tried to carry on, but his knee couldn't take any more. On a pre-season away trip, Dave Anderson broke the news to him that his playing days were over. But there was to be an alternative…

Summer 2004
AFC Wimbledon team coach
By Simon Bassey (AFC Wimbledon player)

I remember it vividly. We were on the coach heading for a pre-season friendly. Dave Anderson had only been manager a short time. I had got to know him really well. We had hit it off straight away. We were similar characters, both forthright and to the point.

I had played the first two seasons in the CCL. My knee had held up for most of that time. That was until the league game away at North Greenford United, two days before the cup final against them. The game should never really have gone ahead. It was raining heavily and there was water all over the pitch. I went to turn on the grass and I felt my knee go. And that was it: I had torn my cartilage, and I missed the cup final.

I had an operation in the summer and I tried to get fit. I didn't know Dave Anderson well then. I had been introduced to him and had maybe five minutes with him, but I wanted to impress. I knew I had to get fit, but I just couldn't get through games. Every time my knee would blow up.

And so it came to that coach journey. Dave told me straight: "You are not going to be playing for me." And then came the big news: "I like what you have to say, and the way that you say it. I want you to help John Morris with the reserves and work for me." I could have tried to see if I could get another club, but this was the best option I had and obviously it kept me involved with Wimbledon.

I don't like to move about. If I'm happy somewhere, I like to stay there. It's not about the money – it never has been for me. It's about being happy and giving myself the best chance. I get the real hump if I'm in a place I don't like – it really gets to me. I enjoy being at AFC Wimbledon and this gave me the best chance to stay.

I worked with the reserves and then eventually, under Terry Brown, I became first-team coach.

Anderson's start

Dave Anderson's first competitive game in change was against Ashford Town (the Middlesex variety). The game began badly, but his new signings came to the rescue and the Dons fans left with a new hero.

14 August 2004
AFC Wimbledon 5 Ashford Town (Middlesex) 1
Ryman League Division One South
By Dave Anderson (AFC Wimbledon manager)

It was a couple of weeks after I got the job that I took my first training session, but I had already begun the process of looking at the squad.

I had made a deal with the board that we would get out of the Ryman Division 1 South in one year and out of the Ryman Premier two years after that. I brought five or six Hendon players with me because I knew they would have the ability to win the division.

The big problem was that the squad I inherited just wasn't right. There was no real work ethic, the discipline wasn't there and there were some big egos in the dressing room. It had got to a point that the club were struggling to get a coach company to take them to away games, so bad was their reputation. I dealt with that with an iron fist. I think any decent non-league manager would have had to do the same.

I had to juggle all that and turn AFC Wimbledon into a semi-professional club. If I look back at it now that was easily my biggest success at the club and laid the foundations for what was to come. And there were other things I changed. I brought in Mike Rayner, a physio, to help bring even more professionalism to the club. And he may well have been my best ever signing.

But I'm not sure if all that really prepared me for my first ever game, against Ashford United. We were playing well, but against the run of play Matt Bower scored and we were 1-0 down. Jon Turner, my assistant, turned to me and said he had just realised how many people were in the ground because he could suddenly hear a pin drop. It was one of those nervous jokes, but there was an element of truth behind it.

It was the moment when I realised how big a job I had taken on. At moments like that, the best thing you can do is take a deep breath. We had to let our players do that too – a lot of them weren't used to playing in front of such big crowds.

But there was never any need to worry. Two minutes later, Richard Butler levelled and we were away. Rob Ursell played brilliantly – he was simply too good for Ashford. Jamie Taylor got two, Richard Butler got one more and we won 5-1. We were off and running. That first season was about being ruthless. Style meant nothing – we just wanted to get the points on the board and seal the title.

Richard Butler was an essential signing. Then there was the whole Kevin Cooper thing. You don't lose a striker who has got 100 goals in 100 games without a few grumbles. We wanted to get someone in who the fans would buy into, someone who would typify the new Wimbledon and the new work ethic and ethos of the club. And that was Richard Butler.

It was a bit strange signing him. I always tell prospective players to bring someone with them – an agent, a friend or a member of the family. It helps them bounce ideas off someone. Richard Butler brought his father, who turned out to be a very old friend of mine. We hadn't seen each other for about 15 years, but we were soon nattering away like it was yesterday. I remembered seeing Richard when he was three or so. We just talked and talked about the old times. We almost forgot the reason while we were all there.

In the end he signed, and he proved his worth. But I was really surprised that he didn't stay on when I left. He was pivotal to the new ethos, the new workrate. He was part of all of that. But although he would take a lot of the headlines, he wasn't my key signing.

The three players who were vital for me were Steve Butler, Jon-Barrie Bates and Martin Randall. They never got the appreciation they deserved, but they were men's men. They were loved in the dressing room. I trusted them, they were really everything I wanted from a player. I knew that when I needed them they would roll up their sleeves and get stuck in. All three of them were happy to take stick if it meant that the fans left the young lads – like Richard Butler – alone.

By Richard Butler (AFC Wimbledon player)

There was a buzz around the ground, and it was a bit of a new atmosphere for me. There were a bunch of new players and a new manager. The expectations were high, very high. We had no real choice – we had to win the game.

And the start couldn't have been much worse. To go one down wasn't in the script. So I was glad, not just for me, but for Dave Anderson too when I equalised. He had

New AFC Wimbledon manager Dave Anderson calls the shots for his first league game in charge on 14 August 2004 (Terry Buckman)

New boy Richard Butler, second left, fires in a shot against Ashford Town on 14 August 2004 (Terry Buckman)

shown faith in me by making me his first signing and that goal began the payback. From then on it was all one-way traffic. I got another as we swamped them for a nice 5-1 win. It got everyone's confidence going.

I had been playing for Ashford Town and I didn't expect the call from Dave. He had obviously watched me a few times, and he asked me to come down and have a look at the place and let him know what I thought. So I went down. I didn't sign straight away – I like to think about these things first. I came back and signed a few days later – and that's one decision I didn't regret for a moment.

Ursell rejects Franchise to sign

One of Dave Anderson's first signings was a little-known player from Harefield United. Rob Ursell was to become a Wimbledon legend, but what made his capture even more significant was that he turned down a trial with a certain team in Buckinghamshire to make the switch to Kingsmeadow.

Summer 2004
By Rob Ursell (AFC Wimbledon player)

A lot has been written about my route to Wimbledon. There was so much happening at the time, and of course there was the offer of the trial at MK Dons.

I had been at Harefield in the Spartan South Midlands League. Foolishly I'd signed a two-year contract there, but when it ran out options appeared everywhere. I started by training with Hayes, and I played there against Crewe in pre-season. Then John Morris called and I was given the chance to train at Wimbledon on the Thursday. So I went.

Then the Hayes manager called. He was a bit upset that I'd gone down to Wimbledon, but he still wanted me to play for them on Saturday in a pre-season friendly. But he said: "You do whatever you want to do." Then Dave Anderson asked me to play for AFC Wimbledon on the same day. He was so full of enthusiasm that I chose the yellow and blue of Wimbledon.

I couldn't believe the crowd, the game and the passion of the fans – I didn't want to lose that opportunity. I was numb playing in front of such a big crowd. I knew then that's what I wanted.

Then there was the trial. I was supposed to go for a trial at the MK Dons on the Thursday. I had spoken to their manager, Stuart Murdoch, and agreed to go. But I remember someone telling me in no uncertain terms that if I took that trial there would be no way back to playing for AFC Wimbledon.

I was aware of the history, but I didn't realise then how deep the emotions were, how the fans really felt. I would have kicked myself if I'd not got back to Wimbledon, so I turned it down. Honestly, it wasn't so much of a moral issue at the time, but I see it so much clearer now and I'm so glad I made that decision.

History means so much to the fans. Years later my dad ran into the Wimbledon team at South Mimms service station. Terry Brown came over to him and said how much I was still in the hearts of Wimbledon fans everywhere. He didn't have to do that.

The '88 rematch

In the latter years of Wimbledon FC the former players and the history of the club had been largely ignored by the club's management. AFC Wimbledon was different. History mattered, and the new Dons were determined to claim all the heritage of Wimbledon FC. One of the first milestones in that crusade was the 1988 FA Cup final rematch in September 2004.

12 September 2004
Wimbledon Masters 1 Liverpool Masters 1 Kingsmeadow
By Niall Couper (match organiser)

It seemed like the perfect fusion. AFC Wimbledon needed funds to help pay off the debt taken on by buying Kingsmeadow, and at the same time we wanted to prove to the world that we were the true continuation of Wimbledon FC.

So, I thought, what could be better than recreating our greatest slice of history – the '88 FA Cup final? It began with the idea of just a fans/celeb match with a few of the old Dons boys watching, but my problem is that if I go unchecked my thoughts tend to escalate. And escalate. And escalate.

I thought, why not get a few of the old Wimbledon players to actually take part? And then I thought perhaps we could even get the original referee. And if we were going to get a couple of the old Wimbledon players along, I might as well try to get some of the 1988 side to take part. And in that case I might as well go for the 1988 Liverpool team as well. Insanity – but then such was the world of fundraising for AFC Wimbledon in those early days.

We'd already had our successes. Paul Jeater, Chris Phillips, Peter MacQueen (Moleking) and I had already come up with the concept of the Dons Draw. I'd spent ages putting together a proposal for it and doing all the legal research on lotteries for a presentation to the Dons Trust Board. Moleking designed the logo. The Trust went with it, and the Draw must now be one of the club's biggest fundraisers.

But the '88 rematch was on a different scale in terms of logistics. With David Hamilton, Anna Slade and Jill Stratton, I worked hard on getting ex-Wimbledon players involved. We wanted to make it a parade of our old heroes. There were going to be players from the last five decades attending and even some ex-AFC Wimbledon players. It was our moment to truly claim the history of Wimbledon FC. And those who were capable of playing were asked to lace up their boots one more time.

On a personal level, I can't describe how momentous it was to see the likes of Dickie Guy, John Scales, Warren Barton, John Leslie, Wally Downes, Efan Ekoku and Kieron Somers all in an AFC Wimbledon shirt. And there were also those in the stands who were no longer fit enough to take the field, such as Roy Law, Dave Beasant, Lawrie Sanchez and Robbie Earle.

These were Wimbledon legends, all saying in the clearest way possible that AFC Wimbledon is Wimbledon FC. The one disappointment was that there weren't that many members of the actual 1988 team on display. But we had managed to get good wishes from most of them.

The Wimbledon Masters team for the Weird and Wonderful
Re-match on 12 September 2004 (Terry Buckman)

However, the big problem was who they were going to play against. And a lot of the credit for that must go to Glenn Mulcaire. Glenn would later gain notoriety as the man at the centre of the News International phone-hacking scandal. But before all that he had been the AFC Wimbledon reserve-team manager, and it was in that role that I had got to know him. The season before I had been the editor of the club's programme, and we had worked closely together on his regular column. So I knew he was connected.

Glenn put his company, Nine Consultancy, behind the project, and they put an early call into Phil Neal and David Fairclough, who ran the Former Liverpool Players' Association. And 24 hours later Glenn was up at Anfield discussing the whole proposal. They were persuaded, and then he worked on filling in the holes. He contacted Ray Houghton, John Aldridge, Steve McMahon and numerous other Liverpool legends. In the end, the Liverpool side that took the field contained more of the '88 generation than the Wimbledon team.

Terry Burton agreed to manage the Dons team, while Phil Neal managed the Reds. The proceeds would be split between the Dons Trust and The Hillsborough Justice Campaign. After all that, getting the original referee, Brian Hill, to officiate was a doddle.

It was still a big challenge to get the game on. And that's where my naïvety hit home: I had no idea how difficult it was to run a matchday. I had to take a step back. The likes of Erik Samuelson came in, and then there were the dozens of volunteers. They basically rescued the whole concept. It all became a bit awkward and it got to me.

Around 3,000 people turned up to watch, and there were smiles everywhere as Jack

John Scales in AFC Wimbledon colours
(Terry Buckman)

Liverpool legend Steve McMahon
(Terry Buckman)

Dickie Guy faces John Aldridge in the
'88 re-match (Terry Buckman)

Goodchild Way morphed into Wembley Way for the afternoon. We had auctioned off a place in each team – Ian Morgan and Nigel Shannon were the lucky winners – and we also staged a fans/celeb match beforehand. I think we raised around £30,000 in all.

In the rematch itself, Dean Thomas got the better of Steve McMahon in midfield. Warren Barton and John Scales were masterful – and then there was the inevitable Kevin Cooper goal to put the Dons one up. I wasn't quite sure how fair it was to field a player who had only just left the year before. But then he'd been plying his trade in non-league, whereas most of the opposition were former internationals.

Then came Liverpool's redemption. They won a penalty, and who should step up to take it, but none other than John Aldridge. Back in 1988, Dave Beasant had saved Aldridge's spot-kick, confirming Beasant's immortal status among Dons fans and securing the FA Cup for the Dons. However, this time Dave was in the stands, and standing in Aldridge's way was Dickie Guy. Dickie is famed for his own FA Cup penalty-saving heroics, denying Leeds United's Peter Lorimer, when the Dons were a non-league side and Leeds were European champions. But that was back in 1975 and this was only the second time in 10 years that he had played in goal. There were to be no heroics this time. Dickie got a hand to it, but it was not enough and the match ended 1-1.

I don't think I enjoyed even a single second of the day. I couldn't relax, I was so involved with the organisation. It was only much later that I realised what we had achieved. It wasn't just the moment when dozens of old Wimbledon players declared their loyalty to AFC Wimbledon and the Wimbledon Old Players Association was born, it was also the moment a swathe of Wimbledon fans realised that AFC Wimbledon is Wimbledon FC.

The magic of the Wizard

In that first season in the Ryman South, Rob Ursell was flourishing. His skills quickly earned him the nickname the Wizard, and he would go on to become a regular in the England Futsal (indoor five-a-side) team. The one game that sealed his place in Wimbledon folklore was an away trip to Dunstable in the FA Cup. Ursell scored all three goals, including one wonder strike.

---

2 October 2004
Dunstable Town 0 AFC Wimbledon 3 FA Cup third qualifying round
By Rob Ursell (AFC Wimbledon player)

On paper this was set to be a very tough game against a higher-division team. Despite that we were quite confident, but no one expected us to win 3-0. We scored early, and that made it a lot easier. We then scored just before and just after half-time – and that knocked the stuffing out of them. Psychologically, they were all perfectly timed goals.

I remember every game I played in, and all the Wimbledon games I remember really clearly. Wimbledon fans still talk about my final goal that afternoon. And yes, it was definitely one of my best goals of my career. It was a long ball. Jon-Barrie Bates flicked it on. I wouldn't usually shoot from there. It was miles out, but when

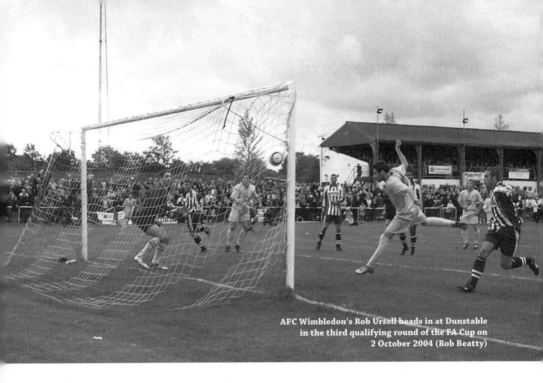

AFC Wimbledon's Rob Ursell heads in at Dunstable
in the third qualifying round of the FA Cup on
2 October 2004 (Rob Beatty)

you've scored two already... I can picture the flight of the ball now – it looped up and dipped in off the bar. They don't usually go in, but it was just one of those days where everything went right.

I never really celebrate goals, and I wasn't going to make any exception that day. I remember Ryan Gray coming over and shouting at me. But I still made little of it. I celebrate more when other people score. It was a great way to complete a hat-trick, but while most Dons fans will talk about the third, neither I nor Dave Anderson thought it was the pick of the three.

He always says my first goal was the best I scored that afternoon, but I disagree. I can be a bit of a perfectionist. I cut in and hit it hard from about 20 yards out, and it went in. Everyone was going mental, but I just came away thinking the goalie should have saved it.

For me it was the second goal that was the most memorable – it was a header. Gibbo put in a great cross and it just hit me on the head. Even I couldn't miss from there. I used to get a lot of ribbing about not being able to head the ball from Dave, the players, the coaching staff and the fans. So personally that meant more.

I still have the ball from the game. Everyone signed it. However, my dog got hold of it and it's a bit chewed now – but you can still make out the signatures!

That year we were in Ryman One and to most people it was obvious we were above everyone at the level.

People like Steve Butler and Frankie Howard were very influential. They created a great atmosphere in the dressing room. We were such a united unit – everyone got on. But there were still two different types of player at AFC Wimbledon then – those who had experience of a higher level and those, like me, who hadn't. And beating the likes of Dunstable proved to the players like me that not only could we compete at a higher level, but we deserved to be there and there could be no doubts that we were going to go up, and that we were going to win the League.

Breaking the record

It had all begun against Chessington United on 26 February 2003, but no one knew then that that 3-1 victory would be the start of something so special. It would be 78 league games before the Dons tasted defeat again in a league match. On the way they would set a new British record – that milestone would come away at Bromley in November 2004.

---

13 November 2004
Bromley 1 AFC Wimbledon 1 Ryman First Division South
By Rob Ursell (AFC Wimbledon player)

Dave Anderson had been on Sky Sports News before the game talking about the record. We all knew about it. It had started to become a millstone around our necks. I used to get a lift with Dave, and around that time he was always going on about it, moaning how much it was affecting us all.

The game didn't start too well. We were 1-0 down early on, and it wasn't the best game. I took several corners and each one found Matt Everard – normally he'd bury them, but each time the ball went just over. It must have been nerves. And then came my moment. I don't score boring goals – I always tell people that. I don't do tap-ins.

There was someone closing me down. I didn't have the pace to get away from him. He was going to dive in, so I dragged the ball back past him – he should have stood up. I didn't think about it, I just looked up and curled the ball in. I was never really conscious about what I was doing, it just happened. I only ever scored one goal better than that – but that was in pre-season, against Barnet. This meant so much more.

It was a huge relief when the final whistle went. The fans behind the goal were excellent, and I remember Dave sending us all over to them. It was a great feeling. The changing room afterwards was one big celebration – weird for a draw. The pictures from that went everywhere – I remember picking up FourFourTwo a few weeks later and seeing it in there. It is an honour to have played a part in it.

The Caveman endeth

Central to Wimbledon's historic unbeaten run was the presence of captain Matt Everard. He played in nearly all of the 78 games, a rock at the centre of the Dons' defence, but an injury away at Bashley brought his Wimbledon career to a premature end. The Dons' unbeaten run came to an end a week later.

---

27 November 2004
Bashley 1 AFC Wimbledon 2 Ryman First Division South
By Matt Everard (AFC Wimbledon player)

My Wimbledon career came to an end in late November 2004, though I didn't realise it at the time. It was away at Bashley. We had just set a new unbeaten record run.

AFC Wimbledon celebrate breaking their British unbeaten league record at Bromley on 13 November 2004 (Paul Willatts)

AFC Wimbledon's Matt Everard, No. 5, gets the plaudits at Bashley after scoring on 27 November 2004. It was to be his last game for the Dons (Paul Willatts)

Early in the game I jarred my knee. It hurt, but at the time I didn't think much of it. We came in at half-time, got the usual ear-bashing from Dave Anderson for being one down, and then we went out for the second half.

In hindsight, God knows how I managed to keep going. I even got the equaliser with a header from a corner. But I knew my knee wasn't right, and Dave took me off with about 10 minutes to go. Martin Randall got the winner in the last minute, which helped to ease my personal pain. But even then I didn't realise how serious it was. It was only the next week that it dawned on me.

Mike Rayner gave me a few tests and fiddled about with the knee the next Tuesday night at training. He didn't say anything straight away, but you could see it in his face. He got me to do some flexing exercises, and that was it. It was my cruciate – I was out.

I never came back. I was close in July the following year, but after one straightforward run the knee went again. Between 2004 and 2006 I had 11 operations on my knee, including two cruciate and two cartilage operations. It was all over.

I take great pride in the fact that I played the bulk of the games in Wimbledon's 78-game unbeaten run of league games, under three managers. The next game after Bashley was away at Cray Wanderers. We lost 2-0.

78 and out

The unbeaten run had to come to and end at some point. With the team hit by injuries, including centre-forwards and centre-backs, the trip to Hayes Lane in December 2004 proved a step too far.

---

4 December 2004
Cray Wanderers 2 AFC Wimbledon 0 Ryman First Division South
By Dave Anderson (AFC Wimbledon manager)

Bromley. It's a funny place for me. A couple of weeks earlier we'd set the new English league unbeaten record with a 1-1 draw there – thanks in no small part to a peach of a curler from Rob Ursell. That took us to 76 games unbeaten. I'd gone to that game with black hair and left it with grey, such was the pressure to beat that record.

Bromley was also the place I was told to head down to have a look at a certain striker. I didn't get my act together, and by the time I was ready he had moved on to Tonbridge Angels. That striker was Jon Main. Dons fans will all know about him.

Then, of course, there was the Ryman Premier play-off there. And later, as manager of St Albans, I went there having lost two games in a row – never in my managerial career had I lost three league games in a row. I thought we had no chance against Bromley, who were flying high at the time. But we came away with a 4-3 win.

I suppose there is just something about Hayes Lane. It was also the home of Cray Wanderers.

We could have played for a month and never scored. Nothing went right for us; we were plagued with injuries and in the end the better side on the day won. Our form had been patchy for a while and all good things have to come to an end eventually.

AFC Wimbledon's Joe Sheerin looks on as the
Dons' unbeaten League run comes to an end at
Cray Wanderers on 4 December 2004 (Rob Beatty)

But the truth was it was a relief. It lifted a huge weight off our shoulders, there was so much pressure on us. Yes, of course, I was disappointed that it was over, but we'd already written our name into the history books and, at last, every game was a normal game once more.

A pipe and slipper day

Dave Anderson had promised the club that he would win the Ryman League First Division South at the first attempt. Promotion had been secured six weeks earlier with a 3-0 home win over Dorking, and on 9 April 2005 he delivered on his promise.

---

9 April 2005
AFC Wimbledon 1 Metropolitan Police 0 Ryman First Division South
By Dave Anderson (AFC Wimbledon manager)

I wanted the title and that was it. We had made sure of promotion a month or so before, but I couldn't tell you anything about that game. All I wanted was the title. And I remember the game against the Met Police vividly. It was the worst game of football I have ever watched.

Even our goal wasn't all that. I remember Stuart MacKenzie was in goal for them. He was about the same age as me – and he played a blinder. All over the pitch our players were nervous. The surface back then was absolutely dreadful too. We weren't a Barcelona passing team, but it didn't help. It was dreadful, like watching paint dry, but I was realistic – at the time it was the most important game of my career.

It was a big night for the club afterwards. I remember "Yellow and Blue Wombles" to the tune of "Hey Jude" ringing out in the bar. It was one of those great moments.

AFC Wimbledon's Richard Butler, on the floor, fires in a shot against the Metropolitan Police on 9 April 2005 (Rob Beatty)

AFC Wimbledon players celebrate sealing the Ryman League South title (Paul Willatts)

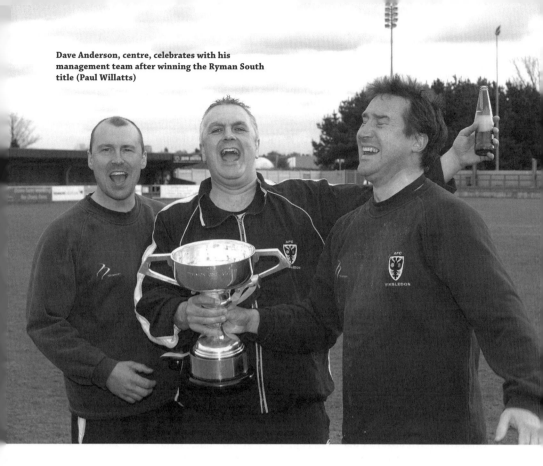

Dave Anderson, centre, celebrates with his management team after winning the Ryman South title (Paul Willatts)

Jon Turner calls them "pipe and slipper" days. They are days that will live with you when you are old and sitting in a comfy chair with a pair of slippers on and a pipe in your hand.

Flying the flag

There is little doubt that AFC Wimbledon supporters are a creative bunch, and for any new visitors to Kingsmeadow one of the standout memories will be the colourful flags that decorate the back of the Tempest End. The first flag appeared back in 2005. There are now over 50 different designs. Their creator is Clive Yelf (alias Fleydon).

Easter 2005
Kingsmeadow
By Clive Yelf (AFC Wimbledon fan)

The first flag was made as a minor matchday distraction for my then young children, giving us all something to play around with and focus on before kick-off. It was a straightforward yellow and blue effort with the crest in the middle and, although I was reasonably happy with it, I started thinking of various ways to improve on it. So, despite the fact there was no sign of any demand from the children, I decided to make them another, just to see. That one was quicker to make but the lettering was still a pain. What if I made a third, just to try a slightly different way? That was it really – once I started I was on a roll and the flags started appearing at regular intervals. The Tempest End was looking a bit brighter and on the whole the supporters seemed to enjoy them – so I just carried on.

Over time the designs have become more abstract as I basically took everyone else's images and AFC Wimbledon-ised them – John Cleese, Canadian WW2 posters, Irish tobacco ads, (Pop Art pioneer) Roy Lichtenstein and the opening sequence from Dad's Army for example. There have been about 50 or so over the years and they've featured in newspaper photos, FA Cup television broadcasts and, after I created a 'mockumentery' blog to document each flag in March 2009 Time Out magazine picked up on that and featured the flags in a full-page spread, which was a bit bizarre.

I try to take a couple of flags to most home games but I usually only go for hanging a full set of flags at 'big' games as it takes so long to get them all hung up and then taken down afterwards. Plus I've a suspicion that there might be an unofficial competition among the players to see if they can knock them down during penalty practice in the warm-ups. Either that or their shooting is painfully erratic!

The flags have also been a real boon on the community side as well, starting with High Path day centre in September 2009, where we helped them create their own flag. This led on to the 'Flying the Flag for Haydon' community arts project with Merton schools and that in turn led to successful exhibitions at Wimbledon library in July 2010 and a year later at Morden Hall Park. The flags also graced the end-of-season celebrations at the Civic Centre in Merton in 2011. Meanwhile, the club, who have always been very supportive of the flags, turned some of them into merchandise, producing flag-themed fridge magnets and mugs, and now a local cubs group produce a flag as part of their artist badges. Raising funds through the merchandise and friends through the arts projects is the real bonus and has become such a focus that I haven't really had the time to do any flags of my own recently. That may not be a bad thing, though, as, with about 55 flags in total, storage is becoming a bit of an issue!

I do have it in my mind to try to push the 'mock blog' with the Fleydon persona to its extreme, though, with the fancy of putting on an exhibition in a proper gallery with notes 'explaining' the deeper meanings and symbolism of each flag in copious detail. It's all quite amazing for something that started off as little more than a temporary distraction, a single sheet and some pots of emulsion paint!

Opposire page, Clockwise: **Flying the flag... Ladies Night; A Better Class of Team; The Devil is a Don – all Clive Yelf creations**

Butler serves up the silver

Having secured the title a month earlier, the Dons were about to return to Woking for another cup final. This time the atmosphere was even more tense, and it took an extra-time winner from Richard Butler for the Dons to triumph.

3 May 2005
Walton & Hersham 1 AFC Wimbledon 2 Surrey Senior Cup final (at Woking)
By Dave Anderson (AFC Wimbledon manager)

Reaching the final was all part of an amazing run. We'd beaten Sutton in the semi-finals, and they were three divisions above us. That was a phenomenal achievement. But there was one thing that would make the final at Woking special. It was that stand. What a sight! I kept it on video and would show it to any prospective new players. I'd say to them: "How could you not want a bit of that?"

Seeing that huge stand at Woking full of AFC Wimbledon fans awash with yellow and blue was amazing. The hairs on the back of my neck stood up as I watched it fill up in the warm-up. And when I came out with the team it was just awesome. By that time as a manager there's not much more you can do except just take it in. I had a mate over from Belfast that night, and he just couldn't believe it.

As for the game itself, Walton & Hersham had tonked us in the league a week or so before, so the pressure really was on us. Shane Smeltz gave us the lead with an absolute screamer. In hindsight, he must have been the bargain of the decade. We got him for nothing. He was a good lad and he had a drive in him, a determination to succeed. He was one of those players who you can tell would be able to cut it at a much higher level, so it was no surprise to me where he went on to.

Anyway, they equalised and the game went into extra time. Step forward Rob Ursell. He went on a mazy run, beat three or four and laid it back to Richard Butler. I'm convinced to this day that he mis-hit it. Had he hit it cleanly it would have gone straight at the keeper, but no matter – it went in, we won, and the place went mad.

I doubt there's ever been a county cup final like that one. And I doubt there will ever be one like it in the future.

By Rob Ursell (AFC Wimbledon player)

It was the best game of my Wimbledon career. End of.

I had a lot of energy that night – I don't know where it came from. To still be going at the end of extra time. Once the final whistle went, my legs went. I was dead on my feet. I'd given everything and we'd won.

I had an extra spring in my step. I was picking up loose balls, chasing down players – none of that was part of my normal game. I liked people to get the ball to me. But that night I was causing problems for Walton all over the pitch. I was running everywhere.

I helped set up the winner. We won a throw-in on the left, and it came to me. I headed the ball past their defender. And then I was one-on-one with their centre-back. I always back myself in those situations. I got round him and cut it back for

AFC Wimbledon's Shane Smeltz, with his shirt over his head, celebrates putting the Dons ahead in the Surrey Senior Cup final against Walton Casuals on 3 May 2005 at Woking (Terry Buckman)

Richard Butler's extra-time winner in the Surrey Senior Cup final (Terry Buckman)

AFC Wimbledon's Richard Butler celebrates
(Terry Buckman)

Dons fans celebrate Richard Butler's winner
(Terry Buckman)

Richard Butler. His first shot was saved, but the ball came back to me – I found him again, and this time it went in. We all went nuts.

But I'd been inches away from winning it in normal time. At 1-1, I hit a volley and somehow their defender managed to scramble the ball off the line.

That was the best game I have ever played in, the atmosphere, the tension and everything. I had seen pictures from the final from the year before, but that did no justice to the reality. This was so different – seeing all those yellow and blue balloons pouring down from the stands and everyone singing. It was a great motivator. Playing in front of Wimbledon fans was motivation enough, but this was something different. If you couldn't be lifted by that…

It was a mad atmosphere at the final whistle. I remember thinking of the level and the surroundings I had played in the year before. This was all completely surreal.

By Shane Smeltz (AFC Wimbledon player)

The ball came back to me. I must have been 25 metres out or more and I caught it sweetly on the volley. Less than quarter of an hour gone, 1-0. They equalised just before the break and I recall having a chance early in the second half to restore our lead, but it went just wide. So it was left to Richard Butler to claim the glory.

It was a great day. I remember the atmosphere and the game clearly. It was certainly the biggest game I played for AFC Wimbledon. The Wimbledon supporters were great, they packed the stadium out. Three-quarters of the ground looked a hundred years old and then there was that large new grandstand with 2,000-odd seats. It was packed with Wimbledon fans. It was a fantastic atmosphere – you had to pinch yourself to remember what level of football this was. I don't think there are any other supporters like that. It was great.

I had arrived at the club only a couple of months earlier. I'd been playing in Australia for MetroStars and there was a nine-month gap before the leagues for the old NSL and the Australian A-League re-started, so I thought it would be a good time to go overseas. So I came to England. I didn't really know anyone. I ended up staying with a mate who was playing for Barnsley at the time. It was all a bit off the cuff. I got a couple of games at Mansfield and, after a few other trials here and there, I found myself at AFC Wimbledon. It all started pretty well. I scored twice on my debut as we beat Newport County 5-0. But the cup final was certainly the pinnacle. Several Dons fans said afterwards that my goal that night was my best goal for the club, and to be honest it's hard to argue with that.

By Richard Butler (AFC Wimbledon player)

It's difficult not to get taken in by a game like that. When you walk out onto the pitch and see a stand full to the rafters with yellow and blue, it's amazing. And the atmosphere that night was just on a different level. We had a vague idea what to expect, as we always had a good following, but to see it…

As for the game itself, we were confident, very confident. At the time we had the best players at that level. And it turned out to be one of the best days of my career.

I don't remember goals I score very well, and the one I got in the final is no different. I do remember it being late on, but how it went in I couldn't tell you. But the reaction that followed…now that does sticks in my mind – I'll remember it forever. The whole place erupted. It was like a bomb had just gone off inside the stadium. The noise, the colours...unforgettable.

At the final whistle everyone flooded onto the pitch from all four corners of the ground. You can't forget moments like that. When we went up to get the trophy the pitch was awash with yellow and blue. It was like everyone in the ground was on the grass.

After that we had a few drinks, but it wasn't insane.

There were so many influential players back then. Steve Butler was the key to the side – he got everyone going. Then there was Rob Ursell – when he was on form he was simply untouchable. Shane Smeltz was good too – and you can see that by where he went on to. Frankie Howard was great. We were just a great team.

We had a lot of talent in the side. I thought of myself as just one of 11 men. I didn't see myself as anything special. So to get all three Player of the Year awards...well, I was really chuffed. I was really overwhelmed. I still have the trophies. They are in a glass cabinet just outside my kitchen, in pride of place, and it's rare that a day goes by without me looking at them.

I often talk about my time at Wimbledon, even now. Anyone who has played there or been involved with the club in even the smallest way will never forget it.

The history battle

Off the pitch, the Wimbledon fans' determination to reclaim their heritage continued to gather pace. Meanwhile, supporters of MK Dons were equally determined to gain acceptance in the wider football world. The conflict would come to a head in the summer of 2005 in Cardiff.

4-5 June 2005
Football Supporters Federation Annual Conference
By Gerry Hever (WISA Committee member)

It had been three years since that terrible decision, and despite maintaining the moral high ground there was a sense that the situation we found ourselves in and the continued existence of the abomination from Buckinghamshire were in danger of becoming the norm.

The anger was still there on our part, of course, but it was still necessary to maintain the public pressure on the parties responsible for the loss, to ensure that they and the FA were reminded of the wrong that needed righting, and that the club's history and honours belonged to the Wimbledon community. To that end it was imperative that WISA maintained the pressure on the franchised entity and allow them no quarter until our aims were achieved. With the club's focus on achieving our aims on the field, it was only right that WISA continued, as it had started, to act in the best interests of Wimbledon supporters.

Every opportunity had been taken to discourage other clubs from encouraging the Franchise. This included the highly successful campaigns to get their pre-season friendly games cancelled or boycotted. But they wanted legitimacy. In June 2005 the Football Supporters Federation (FSF) Annual conference was taking place in Cardiff,

and on the agenda was the proposal to admit as members the MKDSA, a supporters' group representing customers of the National Hockey Stadium.

The view was that apathy would allow their acceptance. We could not let that happen. As the voting process allowed one vote for each member or organisation, if we joined and attended in numbers we felt we would be able to block their application.

So, a mini-bus was organised and driven by Simon Wheeler. Also on board were Lou Carton-Kelly, Jill Stratton, Aideen Rochford, Collette Mulchrone, Ross Maclagan, Gail Moss, Dennis Lowndes, Ronan Warde, Sean Fox and several more. Other Wimbledon-supporting FSF members would also attend the conference. Spirits were high as we set off and even higher when we arrived. We had caught them unprepared – they hadn't expected a large group of true Dons.

Passionate speeches were made by both sides. After intense debate, the Football Supporters Federation membership approved a motion that would not allow the MKDSA association to join the FSF until the FA and the Football League tightened up the rules on football franchising.

Then came the coup de grâce and a second motion proposed by Sean. The motion was simple. The MKDSA could not join the FSF until the history and honours of Wimbledon FC from before 28 May 2002 were returned to AFC Wimbledon or the community of Wimbledon, and that two years must elapse before the MKDSA could apply to join the FSF, subject to the criteria above being met. Sean made a very emotional speech supporting the motion. It even made Aideen cry – mind you, that's not that difficult. It worked and it was ratified.

The three-strong MK delegation was very upset. Afterwards, they were still trying to justify the inexcusable. We left very happy with a double victory that shortened the journey home from Wales considerably.

A Little taste of supporter power

In the North of England a disgruntled group of Manchester United fans, angered by the Glazers' takeover at Old Trafford, decided to follow the example of AFC Wimbledon and Enfield and start their own fans-run club. FC United of Manchester were born, and one of their first friendlies was a trip to Kingsmeadow. The match was an eye-opener for AFC Wimbledon's new No. 1, Andy Little.

---

23 July 2005
AFC Wimbledon 1 FC United of Manchester 0 Supporters Direct Cup
By Andy Little (AFC Wimbledon player)

When Dave Anderson called to try to sign me, he didn't have to tell me anything. The club, in effect, sells itself if you are motivated by what football is truly about. Dave spent most of the time telling me about how good a goalkeeper he had been in his day. He didn't need to say any of that. I was already sold on the club – he was basically wasting his breath.

However, he wanted all the new lads he had just signed – me, Matt York and Barry Moore – to really understand what AFC Wimbledon was about. So he sent us down to Wimbledon Theatre to watch A Fans' Club – the play about the club. It really made me think. I was a Sheffield Wednesday fan as a kid. I used to go all the time. If it had happened to my club…

The play just brought it home. It really told us what it was all about and then to get involved in the whole story it was all a little surreal. But even that didn't properly prepare me for running out onto the pitch in an AFC Wimbledon shirt at Kingsmeadow. I'd been playing non-league football for years. I thought I knew what to expect.

The game against FC United turned all that we had learnt at the play into reality. It hit me straight between the eyes. This was a pre-season friendly, yet there were 3,000 people there – all those United fans and all those Wimbledon fans.

The Sky Sports cameras were there too. It was like Wimbledon v Manchester United. These were the same sets of fans who just a few years earlier would have been at Old Trafford in the Premiership.

I remember thinking clearly: "Bloody hell, this is big!" I had played for Crawley, in front of reasonable crowds, but this was a whole different level. Seeing the highlights on Sky Sports News that night was unbelievable. I knew a bit about the story from when I met Dave and from the play, but you don't believe it until you see it. It was only then that it became a reality.

We won 1-0. It wasn't a great goal; Ricci Crace got a deflection in the second half. But the result wasn't what it was about. This was supporters claiming football back for themselves, and I was now part of the story.

AFC Wimbledon players, including new goalkeeper Andy Little, take the field to face FC United of Manchester in the Supporters Direct Cup on 23 July 2005 (Getty Images)

FC United of Manchester fans at Kingsmeadow on 23 July 2005 (Getty Images)

Winkelman admits '70 miles' is too far

Just a few weeks after the Fans Supporters Federation Annual Conference, WISA and MKDSA would come face to face again – this time at a pre-season friendly in Surrey. It would also lead to a momentous admission from Peter Winkelman, the chairman of Franchise FC.

---

28 July 2005
Carshalton Athletic v Milton Keynes Dons Colston Avenue
By Simon Wheeler (WISA chair)

It was a hugely busy summer for us at WISA – and it led to my first face-to-face confrontation with Peter Winkelman, the chairman of Franchise FC.

We were determined to up the ante in our push to regain the history and honours of the club for Merton and/or AFC Wimbledon. We once again targeted pre-season friendlies and the response, as it had been back in 2002, was overwhelming supportive. Time and time again clubs were pulling out of pre-season friendlies.

They were left with Carshalton Athletic. We couldn't believe they had agreed to a pre-season friendly, particularly as so many bigger clubs had refused to even contemplate playing them.

Then of course they were so local to us – if any club should understand our emotions then surely it would be our near-neighbours. It didn't make any sense, but then local friendlies always throw up the potential for things to get out of hand.

Their players and management team didn't help one bit. I think their manager had some connection with Franchise FC – he might have been a scout of something for them – and I recall he and some of his players made some disparaging remarks about AFC Wimbledon and that just incensed us even more.

It didn't take long to decide to hold a protest outside the ground – although we planned it as more of a vigil than a protest. In the end there was around 25 of us there making our point.

A tiny handful of Franchise fans attended and there were a few exchanges. There was also the issue of some of our undesirable supporters who wanted to get into the ground, but we were able to control them. And then suddenly this big Jaguar turns up with a personalised number plate. Peter Winkelman, the chairman of Milton Keynes Dons, had arrived.

We had been speaking to the police in the days before and we were in constant contact with them on matchday – they knew how incendiary his presence was. He couldn't attend the match and I was next to the policeman when he walked up to Winkelman to turn him away. Winkelman was livid. I remember clearly him saying: "I've just travelled 70 miles to get here. Do you realise how difficult that is? It's taken me two hours to get here."

He clearly didn't understand the irony of what he had just said. "Now you know exactly why we didn't want you to steal our club," I shouted back.

There were a few more exchanges. I asked him for a meeting about the history and honours but he wasn't listening. Meanwhile, his wife was taking picture after picture. She was terrified. But the reality is they should never have come, and the police eventually sent them packing.

The real difficulty came in the days after. The chairman of their supporters association reported WISA and myself to the Football Supporters Federation. He claimed we had organised a group of thugs. It led to a formal investigation and over the next month or so they spoke to all sides. I remain convinced to this day that it was just an attempt to get us kicked out of the FSF and speed their own entry into the organisation. In the end we were cleared. The police and Carshalton made very positive comments about how we had conducted ourselves, how we had organised the vigil and how we had put our point across peacefully. It was yet another defeat for Franchise.

The hidden benefactor and a question of morals

AFC Wimbledon's progress through the leagues had begun to stall. In the Main Stand, several directors and board members were voicing their concerns, it was enough to stir one man into action.

---

20 December 2005
AFC Wimbledon 0 Hendon Town 1 Westview League Cup
By Mike Richardson (AFC Wimbledon supporter)

I am a lifelong Wimbledon fan. I was born in Wimbledon Park. I saw my first Wimbledon game when I was five. I saw them in 1963 when they won the FA Amateur Cup final and again in 1988 when they won the FA Cup final.

When Wimbledon FC was given permission to move to Milton Keynes, I turned my back on them in disgust. I'd given up on Wimbledon, but I didn't think anyone could set up a new club and run it well. For the first two or three years of AFC Wimbledon I didn't go at all. I live on the Isle of Man, and for me it was about £250 a throw to come down and watch games. I didn't believe it could work.

And then slowly I started to come back down. I started to turn up and watch the game from the terraces, but then at my great age I decided I needed to get a seat. I got one in the directors' section, directly in front of Erik Samuelson and Iain McNay.

I got used to Iain chatting away to Erik at games giving him his views. One bitter cold Tuesday night when we played Hendon for some reason Ivor was sitting in Erik's seat next to Iain. We played badly, they played badly and it was obvious that the club needed some money to help move it along.

Ivor and Iain were talking away behind me about what we could do so I said I could put in a few pence to help the club. I think they were a bit stunned by that. They didn't expect anything from this old man. So then I had a meeting with Kris Stewart, Ivor, Erik and Nigel. We went to the Cannizaro House Hotel on Wimbledon Common.

I said I could put in £50,000 a year. We were in the Ryman League at the time, and it was obviously a substantial amount of money. I had set up two big insurance companies from scratch and had moved on. I now run another company which has about $1bn under management. It's profitable, and I live in an area with low tax, it's about 20p in the pound. So I thought I might as well put the tax I would have paid in the UK into the football club.

AFC Wimbledon fan Mike Richardson, left, and Jon Main, centre, one of the players his investment helped the club buy (Paul Willatts)

Jon Main, No. 10, in Tonbridge colours at Kingsmeadow shortly before his record move to AFC Wimbledon (Martin Tomlin)

I'm just a supporter. All I wanted in return was a car-parking space and a title – and that's how the vice-president's label came about. I fly in on a Saturday morning to Gatwick and come in by car. I need to be able to get in and out quickly and so I needed a car-parking space.

I wasn't asking for any influence in the club or any say in how the club runs it affairs. I believe 200 per cent in a fans-run club now. I don't believe politics should get involved in it. I don't care whether you are red, blue, green or whatever – all that should matter first and foremost is the football club. (Personally, I'm slightly more right-wing than Attila the Hun.)

And although it should not be about influence, you still need to make people who can put money into the club feel important. You don't need to give them power, but you need to make them important and the Dons Trust isn't quite there yet.

Iain was a big benefactor as well, and the more money I put in the more he put in. He didn't want to appear second-tier. But I still believe there is much more potential investment out there. The Dons Trust needs to be more decisive about getting it. For example, I do a lot of international travel, and I often go to China and South America. A friend of mine was heading the marketing for the Shanghai Grand Prix and was keen to put some money in.

I tried to get a clear decision from the Dons Trust about what sort of people could put money into the club, but it didn't happen. There are a lot of big betting companies in the Isle of Man. They would be happy to promote AFC Wimbledon, but is that against our ethos or not? We need a clear answer. In my view they are perfectly legal: they are not dealing in drugs or doing anything wrong. If it's cigarettes or betting, then as long as it's legal that's fine in my book.

AFC Wimbledon still has to grow up. What's wrong with accepting sponsorship money from such companies? If you can't get a clear line from the Dons Trust Board about that, you won't get the big sponsorship in. No one is going to risk getting embarrassed in front of their board by putting forward a proposal without the knowledge that their company is going to be deemed "acceptable".

All I want to do is make sure the club succeeds. I have got the odd penny to rub together. All I have done is quietly help the club financially.

By Iain McNay (AFC Wimbledon PLC chair)

That Hendon game was awful. It was a cold, miserable evening and we were dreadful. Ivor and I were talking about how much we needed a decent striker in the first half, and Mike Richardson, who I had hardly talked with before, turned round and said he would be willing to pay for one.

Ivor spoke to Mike at half-time and suddenly the playing budget had increased by £20,000. The following season Mike upped his financial support to £50,000 and was made the club's first vice-president. This move turned out to be the start of a vital component to the club's future success. Mike and I later paid the Jon Main transfer fee between us, and, along with a third person, we paid for Danny Kedwell as well. Both these signings were the key to the club's subsequent success.

AFC Wimbledon's Shane Smeltz in action for New Zealand in Chile. Smeltz was to score and become the Dons' first international goalscorer (NZF)

The first international goal

Shane Smeltz's arrival at AFC Wimbledon caused quite a stir. The Kiwi had represented his country and now he had joined the Dons. In June 2005, he became AFC Wimbledon's first full international in a friendly against Australia in Craven Cottage. But his big breakthrough came in Chile, when he scored his first international goal. It would spark a goalscoring run that would peak in a remarkable draw with world champions Italy in the 2010 World Cup in South Africa.

---

25 April 2006
Chile 4 New Zealand 1 Estadio El Teniente, Rancagua, Chile
By Shane Smeltz (AFC Wimbledon player)

I made my debut for the national team against Shandong FC on 23 June 2002 and my full international debut against the USA a year later. The first time I wore the All Whites shirt as an AFC Wimbledon player came against Australia in a friendly at Craven Cottage, but that was as an 89th-minute substitute. But this was different. This was my first international goal. This was a big game. Chile. And a great atmosphere.

I remember the goal really well. It came after 14 or 15 minutes and put us 1-0 up, we were buzzing. It was amazing. But they came back hard and played some good football. We ended up getting beaten quite comfortably in the end.

Chile was a long way to go, but there was never an issue of not going. Whenever you get a call-up for your international team you are going to go. As a Kiwi you are used to travel, so it didn't really bother me and the journey from the UK to Chile was a lot easier than the journey for the boys from New Zealand.

Back at Wimbledon, yes, I got some stick for it. They couldn't believe that here I was having to jet off to foreign shores on international duty. And then there was also all the sponsorship deals. I was being looked after by Nike at the time. The rest of the team had to buy their own boots, so they tended to spend most of the time trying to steal mine.

The club was also immensely proud. At every opportunity they'd mention it. There was nothing handed over physically to actually mark the fact that I had become the club's first full international, and then later the club's first international goalscorer, but they recognised it.

The goal was a huge breakthrough for me. I played about half a dozen games for New Zealand by then and, as a forward, pressure was starting to grow on me to get a goal. Once I scored the pressure was off and I went on to average roughly a goal every two games for New Zealand.

However, as much as that first goal might mean a lot to AFC Wimbledon fans and me as well, my 17th international goal in my 33rd game for my country easily eclipsed it. I'd left AFC Wimbledon years before and was back playing Down Under and that goal came in the Mbombela Stadium in Nelspruit, South Africa. The opponents were Italy at the World Cup, the reigning world champions. To score the first goal of the game and to come away with a draw for us – New Zealand, who no one expected to do anything was probably the biggest achievement I will ever have in football.

I look back at it all now and it's amazing what football can do. I'm proud of my time at AFC Wimbledon. I kept my head down, I kept going. I worked hard and look at what happened to me.

Dons caught out by Fisher

A long, hard season had seen the Dons reach the play-offs, and the promised land of the Conference South was in sight. But Fisher Athletic had spent big, and the Dons were beset by injuries. The trip to Champion Hill was only ever going to produce one winner – and it was not the side in yellow and blue.

2 May 2006
Fisher Athletic 2 AFC Wimbledon 1 Ryman Premier play-off semi-final
By Andy Little (AFC Wimbledon player)

We had done what we had set out to do – we had reached the play-offs, but it had been hard work and by the end of the season it felt like we were running on empty. There were people out there who shouldn't have played, and half of the team were in the stands. But it was still football – 11 against 11 – and we fancied our chances in a one-off game.

But then there was Leroy Griffiths. He's one of those players who runs hot and cold, and that night he was hot. He had an excellent game. He scored the first for them in the first half and they added a second midway through the second half.

Frankie got one back for us with about 10 minutes to go, and from then on all I remember is constantly wanting us to get a corner. I wanted to go up there and score. I kept picturing the dream again and again. I wanted to get the chance, but the opportunity never came and in the end, to be fair, we were second best on the night.

The one consolation that season was that I was named Player of the Year. It wasn't the first time in my career I had got that accolade. I had it two years in a row at Croydon and once at Crawley, but the award from Wimbledon is the only one I have out on show at home.

I didn't know anything about it. I didn't have a clue – and to be honest, I felt a bit sheepish going up to get the award. But it wasn't like at Croydon where only 20 or so people voted for it. When you get that kind of accolade from Wimbledon you know that a lot of people appreciate what you have done. It was a real pleasure to be recognised in that way.

By Antony Howard (AFC Wimbledon player)

It was a tough, tough game. The end of the season had hit us so hard – we had injuries upon injuries. And Fisher were so big and physical. I remember looking at our squad and thinking how young our bench was. I knew it was going to be an uphill struggle.

After going 2-0 down, there was no real way back. I got one back, but then I took a knock, my ankle was screwed and I had to go off. We just didn't have anything left.

As a player I just had to let it go, you have to bounce back. We had to flush it out

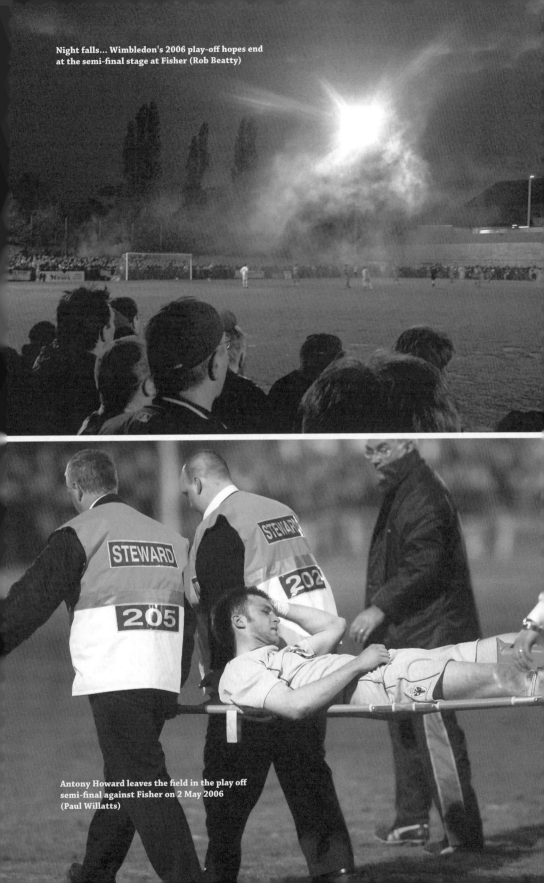

Night falls... Wimbledon's 2006 play-off hopes end at the semi-final stage at Fisher (Rob Beatty)

Antony Howard leaves the field in the play off semi-final against Fisher on 2 May 2006 (Paul Willatts)

Multi-millionaire Darragh MacAnthony, who in the summer of 2006 tried to buy AFC Wimbledon (Getty Images)

Kingsmeadow, the home of AFC Wimbledon, which came close to getting new owners in summer 2006 (Terry Buckman)

and move on. That's one bit of advice that sticks with me from my days at Fulham. I remember the coach there asking all us young boys to recall their worst game, and no one could. And he looked us in the eyes and said: "That's the best way: hang on to your best game and forget the bad ones."

I can recall loads of my great games, but the Fisher one has now mostly faded away.

Safe in your hands: The MacAnthony approach

Defeat in the play-offs had left a bitter taste: it was the club's first real failure. AFC Wimbledon desperately wanted a new hope – something to cling on to – and the arrival of multi-millionaire Darragh MacAnthony offered the chance of a new impetus. It would also question the fundamental ethos of the club.

3 July 2006
Kingsmeadow
By Kris Stewart (AFC Wimbledon chairman)

I didn't know fully what to expect. All I knew was that he was going to talk to us about something. I wasn't sure how likely it was to be something we were going to be interested in. But when someone has a lot of money, it's worth talking to them. They might come up with something you hadn't thought about, and equally you might come up with something they hadn't thought about.

At that first meeting with Darragh MacAnthony were Erik, Ivor, Iain McNay and me, and also Xav Wiggins. It was Xav who knew Darragh MacAnthony. Darragh made it clear very early on that he wanted to buy the club, and I just thought: "You are kinda missing the point of what the club is about." But for us it was never that clear-cut. We all came into the meeting with different ideas: some of us wanted to convert him into a sponsor, some of us were going along for the ride, others wanted to make sure we didn't mess it up and end up selling the club.

I remember his introduction, a "This is the kind of person I am" speech. Psychologists always talk about the fact that you make decisions about people very quickly. And I am no different. I put him in a box very early on. I didn't think that this was a guy we could do anything with. He was a very determined guy, very driven and very much convinced about his own way of doing things. I remember the word "dictator" was bandied about, and he didn't seem to object to it.

For me, I was there to see what this was about, and very quickly it became obvious that there wasn't anything else to talk about. After about five minutes, I was thinking: "Well I've not got anything else planned for today, so it might be interesting to listen to someone who is a bit different."

The best thing we could do was get out of the room relatively quickly without appearing to be rude and then talk about it among ourselves. Erik was p***ed off. It was very unusual for him. He's normally very good at switching off his emotions in key meetings. Ivor is a bit different. He will keep going until he's sure he can't get anything good for the club out of it. Either way, it was obvious it had to go back to the Dons Trust Board.

We had a long conversation there. It was reasonably straightforward to reject the selling of the club. What took time was the discussion about our principles and what we intended to do the next time something like this happened. It got us thinking about a lot of things we hadn't thought about in the past.

There was the question about whether the Board should just reject it outright or whether it should go to the members. Were the Board overstepping the mark? These were fundamental questions that we needed to address.

By Iain McNay (AFC Wimbledon PLC chair)

The meeting was held in an office in Richmond, just around the corner from the station. MacAnthony had flown in from Spain in a private plane and told us that he had come over especially to meet us all. He came across as very dynamic and enthusiastic. He has just watched the club DVD on the plane which had fired him up. It became apparent very quickly that his agenda and ours were very different. He was clear that if we were to take his money he wanted control of the club and would run it his way. The Dons Trust would be relegated to, at best, an advisory body and would have no real power.

I felt he didn't really understand the principles on which the club was run and also didn't fully appreciate the implications of our history. It was clear to me very quickly that this was never going to work. Erik challenged him early on, the two of them locked horns, and the meeting was going nowhere from that point. I asked him a couple of questions about how he saw our future and he didn't, for me anyway, really seem to understand how the mind of a football supporter worked. He had obviously been incredibly successful at a young age in a short space of time and had great business instinct, energy and vision.

I have to say I actually quite liked him; you could see why he had been so successful, but he wasn't for us; he wanted to be in total control and that was completely against what we stood for as a club. It was two different worlds that were never going to come together.

By Erik Samuelson (AFC Wimbledon director)

I always like to think of myself as rational, able to put my own personal feelings to one side and judge things on their merits. But this was different. I couldn't imagine why we were even talking about selling the club. I felt outraged.

Originally, I remember Ivor saying: "I think I've got someone who is interested in putting a lot of money into the club." At the time, I recall he was thinking that it might be about sponsoring the stadium or something on that scale. He was very excited – and in those circumstances you just let Ivor get on with it.

Darragh MacAnthony had been introduced to the club via long-term supporter Xavier Wiggins. It was Xav who set up the first meeting. Between the first approach and the meeting, things had changed. MacAnthony had a Mr Fix-It, a go-to man. And he had his ear. He had said to him: "You will never settle for just sponsorship, you won't be happy, you won't be satisfied. You will want more than that, you will want control." I didn't know any of that at the time.

Iain McNay, Ivor, Kris and I were at the meeting and Xav was there to do the introductions. We had been told we would be made a substantial offer, but I wasn't

Darragh MacAnthony, right, with Peterborough United's Barry Fry after taking over the Posh shortly after his bid for AFC Wimbledon was turned down (Getty Images)

AFC Wimbledon's commercial director, Ivor Heller, who was in favour of further discussions with prospective new owner Darragh MacAnthony (WDSA)

sure what to expect and what form it would take – there had been a hint that he might want to take ownership. So we went in without really knowing what to expect and we were interested to see what they might be putting forward.

And then came the bombshell. MacAnthony said: "AFC Wimbledon has been a fantasy, a dream." I don't recall exactly what he said next, but to me the thread was simple. He was effectively saying: "I want to continue the dream by buying the club and making it mine." I thought: "That's not continuing the dream, that's destroying it."

He went on to talk about his vision. He said that within three years he envisaged negotiating with Merton Council for a new ground in Wimbledon and to be knocking on the door of the Premier League within seven years.

Iain was his usual measured self and asked all the right questions. I was livid. I said: "You just want to take over the club – that's not what I'm prepared to talk about. It's not what our members believe in." Then I asked him about his style of management. He replied: "I delegate completely." So I asked him: "What about the big decisions?" And he said: "I make all those." And someone said (I think it might have been me): "That sounds like a dictator."

I kept interrupting him and after a few more challenges he said to me: "You and I are not going to agree. So I think it's best that you don't say anything more." The next time I interrupted him he said: "I thought we had agreed that you weren't going to speak." I said: "That's what you said we agreed, not what I agreed to." Needless to say, the meeting didn't progress too well after that. But he finished his pitch and the meeting ended amicably with handshakes.

The whole experience left me livid. I was fuming inside. This wasn't the meeting I had expected to attend, but that wasn't MacAnthony's fault.

We went back to the President's Lounge, Kris, Ivor and me. Kris felt an immense burden on his shoulders. As chairman of the club he was very conscious of his responsibility to the fans. He felt this was a massive decision – and the weight of it all concerned him. For me it was very simple. A year or so after AFC Wimbledon had begun, we had proposed a list of aims and these had been voted on and overwhelmingly approved by the club's owners, the Dons Trust members. And first or second on the list was that we should always remain under fan ownership. I couldn't understand why we were even discussing giving that up.

Not long after the meeting, we were forwarded an email by Xav setting out in more detail what MacAnthony was proposing, and that went to a Dons Trust Board meeting. At that meeting I was gobsmacked and dismayed by the discussions.

It's there in the minutes, exactly as I remember it. Two Board members wanted to hear more details. I couldn't believe it.

I said: "You want to sell the club!" "No, no," they replied. "We want to see more details." But we already had the key proposal, which was that we had to give control to Darragh MacAnthony and surely there was nothing more to know. I just couldn't understand why anyone would want to hear any more unless they were willing to contemplate selling the club. After what happened with Plough Lane, what on earth would make anyone think it would be any different this time? Whatever safeguards we might demand, someone, someday could and probably would find a way round them. I kept thinking: "Don't people learn from the past?"

A third member of the Board also wanted to see more details, but they were absolutely clear and said: "We should not sell the club." But they were curious to hear what MacAnthony had to say.

I am reasonably sure that Xav had asked to be at the meeting but the board had refused. Afterwards his reaction was understandable. He had wanted the proposal taken to the members and he was disappointed that we weren't going to agree to that. I think he felt that we should be democratic and ask the members. For me that didn't make any sense. We had our stated aims, formally approved by the Dons Trust members, so we'd already got their view and our job was to represent that view. Why even talk about it?

The rest of the Board was also against taking it further. But it had revealed a problem that needed addressing. We decided that we had to develop a strategy for how to deal with these types of issues. So the board decided to tell MacAnthony: "Thank you, but no." We added that we were developing a plan for our longer-term development and if things changed we would get back to him. To his credit, MacAnthony took it well and appeared to understand. He went on to take control of Peterborough and he has done a pretty good job there. Xav was a director there for a couple of years.

It was a complete eye-opener for me. It was awkward and difficult at the subsequent Dons Trust AGM. John Owen got up and said: "There have been some people promoting the idea of selling the club. We need to change our constitution to make sure it can never happen again." And from that the board went on to develop the 'Restricted Action' clauses.

These have potentially huge consequences. The new clauses mean we would have to get a vast number of members to take part in decisions on really big changes such as changing stadium, even if it is to move back to Merton. So when we are ready to move to Wimbledon we will have to work really hard to get enough people to participate. We will have to knock on doors to get everyone out to vote. I agreed with the principle of the new clauses. My only hope is that we haven't gone too far and made it too hard to do what we want, which is to go home under fans' ownership.

The reaction

Shortly after the fateful meeting with Darragh MacAnthony, Xavier Wiggins published an open letter to the boards of AFC Wimbledon PLC and the Dons Trust. With permission from Xavier Wiggins, below is an edited extract of the letter. The whole debate would change the future governance of the Dons Trust.

By Xavier Wiggins (AFC Wimbledon fan)

OPEN LETTER TO THE BOARDS OF AFC WIMBLEDON PLC AND THE DONS TRUST

Dear All,

I am writing to you as both an AFC Wimbledon supporter and a founder member of WISA. I am also an appointed representative of the businessman [Darragh MacAnthony] with whom some of you recently met. This open letter is in response to the statement issued by you on 17 July.

It is important to emphasise from the outset that I hold the boards of both the club and the trust in enormous regard. What we have achieved thus far with your passion, commitment and intelligence has been phenomenal and long may the success continue.

This letter is in relation to a specific situation that is particularly unusual and therefore one that is bound to create a broad range of opinion.

However, I do feel that the statement issued deserves a response to give the story some balance.

The reason for bringing the businessman to meet a group of four board members was to discuss an outline approach for a large-scale involvement by the businessman in the football club.

What we hoped for subsequent to the meeting was for the board members to discuss this first basic approach and to ask us to make a full and formal proposal to the board and the trust members.

We felt that the general proposal hanging on the following key elements would have been sufficient to warrant this:

1. The businessman would "invest" £1 million into the club in year one to go towards the playing budget, the general playing and non-playing staff infrastructure, some improvements to Kingsmeadow including the addition of some seats and improvement of the bars and common areas.

2. He would put additional funds into the club in future years no less than £1m per year and probably much more.

3. He would not want to take ownership of Kingsmeadow away from the supporters.

4. He would work with the fans to implement an agreeable exit route in the event of his departure that would return the club to the supporters.

5. He would commit to a future of the club at Kingsmeadow or in Merton.

6. He would begin discussions immediately with the council and relevant land owners in Merton with a view to buying a plot and funding development of a new community stadium with zero rent and an indefinite arrangement with AFC Wimbledon.

It was made clear that these would be CONTRACTUAL points. To this day we have had no request from the board to make a full proposal. Indeed you have chosen to throw it out at the very first stage.

Now for some comments on the actual statement.

1. Heading: "Safe in your hands" should mean that we, the supporters, would be asked our opinion on an approach of this significance and that we should vote on the route to take. Instead we have a situation where a board has listened to one version of events from four people without the full proposal being heard. Having sat in the meeting and been party to the atmosphere I speculate that the outline approach was conveyed to the rest of the board with negativity and with a lack of objectivity.

2. Having already discussed naming rights of the stadium at an earlier date, it was made very clear that the meeting on 28 June was called specifically to discuss a potential approach to acquire the club. It was certainly not in relation to "discussing a commercial sponsorship deal". This is a fairly fundamental point and the error does confuse me.

3. The money was to be spent on evolving the staff structure not "installing a professional management team". The businessman remained extremely respectful of the current team.

4. "It was very clear that he wanted ownership and total control of the club" is not the full story. The plan was always to leave sacrosanct key contentious issues to the fans such as where we play and other points made earlier. Once these key decisions had been ring fenced other secondary decisions would ultimately lie with the investor though there would be proper

supporter representation on the board. The thinking was three supporters on a board of seven, though admittedly this figure was not mentioned in the meeting. I must note that there was a full understanding and with zero reluctance that the businessman agreed to ring-fence such crucial points.

5.   He did admit that he was an impatient personality and that he would like to move quickly. A time frame of seven weeks was given as "difficult but achievable" by the board.

6.   The way the paragraph beginning "although he was willing..." is worded as if he didn't care who he bought. This was simply not the case.

There are two key points from the "On 3 July" paragraph:

1.   Who was asking the Dons Trust to give up control of AFC Wimbledon? We certainly weren't. We were giving an outline proposal that we wanted comments on prior to making a full and detailed proposal to the board and the members. We said how key decisions would be made by the fans and reinforced that these would be contractual points.

2.   How was there "little appetite to recommend"? Based on what?

I remain convinced that the board should have requested a full proposal prior to giving or not giving their backing to the members.

Regardless of whether or not the boards backed the approach I am adamant that the members should have been called on to decide.

It is also interesting to note that at no point did the businessman mention profit. It was made very clear during the meeting that his motives were two-fold:

1.   To have fun
2.   To raise his and his company's profile

Ask yourselves how he would have had fun or raised his profile positively if he were to make regular unpopular decisions?

It was stressed that the future would be one where he worked closely with the fans and the community. This was a genuine approach from an extremely wealthy, successful and intelligent businessman. While I return to my opening paragraphs in my general support of your work as boards of the club and trust, I do believe that you have acted totally inappropriately on this.

I would urge you to reconsider the way in which significant issues such as this are dealt with. I would welcome the opportunity to get involved in and help shape the strategy document you mention in the statement. This debate will, I am sure, run a little longer. I hope that those reading this feel slightly more informed.

Yours,

Xavier Wiggins

By Dave Boyle (Supporters Direct)

The whole Darragh MacAnthony affair really defined AFC Wimbledon. It was a wake-up call and made a lot of people realise how vulnerable the club was.

I first heard about it while I was waiting for a train at City Thameslink station. I got a phone call. It was Ivor – and he was really excited. He said: "I just spoke to this bloke and he wants to buy the club – and it would be f***ing brilliant." He explained that

he'd already met him and shown him the first-year DVD, and he'd loved the idea of what the club was about. He loved the idea of a fans-owned club so much that he wanted to buy it. And he was minted.

Ivor hadn't really stopped to think about it. MacAnthony had Xavier Wiggins in his corner, and Xav and Ivor go back years and years. If Xav was OK with it, Ivor must have thought, then it can't be bad. My fear was that once you sell the club, then that's it. It's out of your control. In Wimbledon's history Sydney Black was a great owner, he wrote a clause into the Plough Lane lease stating that the ground could never be sold for anything other than sporting use. But he died, and we all know what Sam Hammam did.

The whole issue made the internal divisions within the Dons Trust Board resurface. There was one constituency that just wanted to get a ground back in Wimbledon, a place in the Football League and say a big "F*** you!" to the football world. And there was another that wanted to ensure the club remained fans-owned forever more. The key question was how big was the first constituency, how many of them were willing to sell up so soon.

In the end it was pretty decisive. There were only three people who wanted to see more of what MacAnthony had to offer – Ivor Heller, Marc Jones and Geraldine Messenbird. The majority refused to go any further without the backing of the whole Trust membership.

But MacAnthony's offer had exposed a problem. The Board could have accepted it there and then. Even if the membership had subsequently passed a vote of no confidence in the entire Board, it would have been too late -the club would have gone. David Cox, the chair of the Board, knew that was a problem and he moved to fix it. With the help of Mark Davis, the club changed its governance and the Board now has its hands tied when it comes to selling the club. That was the right move, but it would never have happened if it hadn't been for the MacAnthony approach.

It also asked deeper questions. What sort of club did AFC Wimbledon want to be? What were its ambitions? Where did it see its future? But those questions would come later, with the survey overseen by Nicole Hammond, which would set benchmarks for everything the club stands for.

But the battles will continue. Every generation needs to re-fight all the battles that have been won before.

By Luke Kirton (Brentford Independent Association of Supporters Committee member)

In the end, the debate about football finances all comes down to ideals. At Brentford an individual came in with a big wedge of cash and we took it. You could write hundreds of books on the idealism versus reality. But it was the only real option for us.

Football is not an even playing field and we struggled as a fans-owned club. We had the lowest playing budget, we were fighting relegation and at the same time trying to get a new stadium.

I don't think it's possible to compete in the higher levels of English football as a purely fans-owned club. It's all moved on so much. To make it in the modern game you need money. When the Premier League started, having the millions Jack Walker had was enough to deliver the title for Blackburn Rovers. Now those colossal sums of money he had are just about enough to sustain a good Championship side.

In England you need someone with more money than sense. They have to say "I don't mind losing all this money." It needs someone who is a fan. Investors are meaningless – there's no money to be made in football – and before you know it the ground is a Tescos and the club is homeless. You only have to look at the likes of Brighton, Wimbledon and Chester to see that.

For me the interest in the financial side of the game has waned. I used to avidly read all the analysis of the financial plight of football. But I don't want to know whether we're going to go bust for this reason or that any more. I just want to watch the football now.

At Brentford, we have this bloke that has put in £12 million just to make us an average League One club. But I've not totally given up on the fans-owned model. Hopefully one day, there will be a successful fans-owned club competing at the higher level, following the Barcelona model. Just right now I don't think England is ready for it.

By Mark Davis (Dons Trust Board Secretary)

The AFC Wimbledon website made the announcement about the governance changes on 17 July 2006, under the simple title "Safe in your hands: Ownership of AFC Wimbledon."

I should probably be saying that it was always obvious to me that the club would be successful, that any model apart from supporter ownership was always off-limits, and that any approach to buy the club was bound to fail. But that wouldn't be entirely truthful.

I don't remember the email that, as Dons Trust secretary, I presumably sent out at the end of June 2006 summoning Board members to a meeting to discuss Darragh MacAnthony's proposal to buy the club. Nor do I remember how much detail of the proposal I knew in advance of our Board meeting on 3 July. I do remember spending the train ride to the meeting trying to piece my own feelings together.

Was I indignant that someone had the effrontery to want to buy us? No. Intrigued? Definitely. Open-minded? Reasonably. And if I'm honest, I was just a little exhilarated that something big was happening that I, as a recently co-opted Board member, would be involved in.

At the time, the club was only four years old. Our birth had made a big splash in the football world and kept alive the dreams of Wimbledon supporters devastated by the relocation of the club. We had secured two promotions and a play-off position in the Ryman Premier. We had purchased Kingsmeadow – a decision that has proved so important to our sustainability. These were big achievements, and we could rightly cock a snook at those who said fans couldn't run a football club.

And yet...

There was also, in my mind, a worry that maintaining the momentum was not going to be easy. Each successive promotion was going to be harder than the last, and we couldn't be completely sure that all our supporters – and volunteers – were in it for the long haul. Home attendances were down 10% on our first season. The governance of the club was definitely experiencing growing pains. All in all, the risk of the club gradually withering on the vine, although a pessimistic scenario, couldn't be completely discounted. Could I say, hand on heart, that I would be there, week in, week out, if our long-term prospects were a few hundred hard-core supporters watching Ryman League football?

So what of this alternative? A rich businessman tantalising us with Premier League football and a shiny new stadium in Merton – apparently with some safeguards for the Trust. That had a certain allure. After all, when I started supporting Wimbledon FC they were in the Premier League. I hadn't believed then that fan ownership was the only desirable model for a football club, and I wasn't sure now that it would be the right model for all stages of AFC Wimbledon's development.

And was it an all-or-nothing decision we were to be presented with anyway? What might those safeguards be? And why couldn't I get the Who's "Won't Get Fooled Again" out of my head?

I don't know whether similar thoughts went through the minds of other Board members as they made their way to Kingsmeadow that evening. What I do know is that the Dons Trust Board – despite its exasperating tendency back then to drift into rambling and inconclusive discussions of second-order issues – had this strange knack of being focused, perceptive and constructive when there was something really important and urgent to address.

People sometimes say that the Trust Board lacks transparency and that Board members hide their opinions behind collective agreement. Having helped set those rules, I'm not going to criticise – or break – them here. In fact, looking through the minutes published on the official website, you get a pretty good picture of the discussions that took place, and you don't have to read too far between the lines to see that the approach from MacAnthony ("Mr Smith" in the minutes) was both emotive and divisive.

In essence, what happened was this. Darragh MacAnthony, a young Irish businessman who had made his fortune in the overseas property market, had approached the club's management, via AFC Wimbledon supporter Xavier Wiggins, to express an interest in buying it. He talked about Premier League football within eight years and a new stadium, probably in Merton. He wanted total control of the club and didn't believe that it should be run by volunteers. He was, however, willing to contemplate some sort of safeguards – it wasn't entirely clear what they were but perhaps some right for the Trust to take over the club and the stadium in the event he moved on. If a deal was to be done, it was to be done very quickly indeed. There was very little detail on the table beyond that, although those who had been present at the initial meeting with MacAnthony did their best to describe what had been said.

It was quickly evident to those around the table that the probability of doing a deal with MacAnthony was pretty low. Whatever the views of Board members on the idea of selling the club at all, or of this opportunity in particular, any such deal would have been highly controversial with the membership, and complex and time-consuming to negotiate. If MacAnthony really was in a hurry to buy a football club, then it would probably have to be another club. Nonetheless, we needed to decide how to handle the overtures that had been made to us and how to involve the Trust's membership in any process that resulted from that. And, less urgently, we needed to think through what our position would be if similar circumstances arose in the future.

We came up with three options. The first was to reject MacAnthony's proposal outright and to tell the membership this was what we had done. The second was to invite a more detailed proposal that could be put to the membership. The third was to tell MacAnthony that we wanted the time and space to work with our membership on the future strategic direction of the club before we could entertain further discussions with him. If he was willing to wait for that process to unfold, then fine. If not, then so be it: he was welcome to pursue other opportunities.

As so often happens in complex situations, people can arrive at similar conclusions for different reasons. No one favoured the option of rejecting MacAnthony's offer outright, although it was clear that some were against the possibility of selling the club on principle. Three board members – Ivor Heller, Marc Jones and Geraldine Messenbird – wanted to know more about MacAnthony's offer and voted for the second option, for varying reasons. Everyone else was in favour of the third option, which won a majority vote.

My own reasoning was as follows. While the details of MacAnthony's offer might become clearer, it seemed to me that we didn't have a good understanding of what the future looked like if we remained as we were. The fears I had harboured on the train were, after all, just one possibility. Unless we as supporters had a better idea of what the future could and should look like, we had nothing to compare MacAnthony's offer with. And if it became apparent, after we had thought this through, that supporters really did wish to relinquish control of the club in order to fuel our ambitions on the field, there was no pressing need to jump at this particular approach. To this day, I think we took the right decision.

It took a week or two longer, and a further meeting, before it was clear that the MacAnthony deal was dead. He gave us a little more information about his ideas, but nothing very concrete. Some Board members still hankered after a full proposal, and the second meeting was perhaps a little bit tetchier than the first. But anyway, MacAnthony went on his way (buying Peterborough, who have since enjoyed a roller-coaster ride) and we got on, eventually, with our strategy review.

When we announced what had happened, reactions from supporters were mixed. Some felt we should have solicited a detailed proposal and let the membership decide. Rather more, I think, questioned why, as a fans-owned club, we hadn't simply dismissed MacAnthony's offer out of hand. Overall, I think most people were reasonably understanding of the course of action we had pursued. And participation in the subsequent (rather protracted) strategy process was very healthy.

So, what can we take from the Mr Smith episode? First, I think we're stronger for having gone through a strategy process and become clearer about our goals. Second, we have adopted some further safeguards in the Trust's constitution to prevent the club being sold without a period of proper reflection and an enhanced majority vote in favour. Third, we've learned – as on a number of occasions in the short history of this club – that we can resolve differences of opinion amicably and in a civilised manner. And, of course, we've learned that, despite my earlier fears, we really can be a well supported, fans-owned club that can take its place in the Football League.

Of course, this may not be the last time we will have faced such a situation. How will people feel in the future if a lack of investment is holding us back from a return to Merton or, after the novelty of League Two has worn off, from going on to further promotions? My own view is that super-majority provisions in the Trust's Constitution will count for far less than having a proper, ongoing conversation between the Board and supporters about what the realistic choices are. Given where we have reached to date, I don't lose much sleep over the possibility that that will mean giving up, for years to come, supporter control of all that we have worked so hard to create.

It would take until February 2008 before the Dons Trust changed its constitution to ensure that actions that threaten the ownership structure of AFC Wimbledon, and similar major decisions, can be approved only if an enhanced majority of Trust members votes for them. There are four categories of these so-called restricted actions. The most heavily restricted category (category A) applies to actions such as selling the club, selling Kingsmeadow or changing the name of AFC Wimbledon.

For a category A action to be approved, there would need to be two separate meetings of the Trust's membership within the space of one month. At least half of the Trust's membership would need to be present or represented at each meeting. At the first meeting, at least three-quarters of the votes (and 40 per cent of the total membership) would need to be in favour of the action. At the second meeting, a two-thirds majority would be required to confirm the decision. The effect of this is to stop a small number of members rushing such decisions through without the wider membership participating in the decision.

Reclaiming the Womble

A giant Womble had made a guest appearance at AFC Wimbledon at the end of the club's first season, but that was a one-off. Dons fans wanted their Womble back, and they wanted it back for good. It was another piece in the jigsaw of reclaiming the club's legacy. Years before, Wimbledon FC had had Wandle the Womble. Now came the arrival of Haydon.

July 2006
By Dean Parsons (aka Haydon the Womble)

It was March 2006 when the Womble Underground Press (WUP) fanzine, in its fourth year of publication, asked what the funds they had recently raised should go towards. In previous years they had paid for the trophy cabinet and the training gear

Haydon the Womble prepares for the Mascot
Grand National (Rob Beatty)

AFC Wimbledon mascot Haydon the Womble.
The Womble returned to Kingsmeadow on a
permanent basis in July 2006
(Terry Buckman)

for the ladies' team. They were looking for new suggestions. The top two ideas were a scoreboard and a mascot. With a scoreboard needing planning permission, the vote for a mascot shone through.

As soon as it was decided that we would have a mascot, there was only one choice – we had to have a Womble. Thanks to the hard work behind the scenes by Mags Hutchison, Ivor and the WUP team, the club was soon granted a licence by the Beresfords – the family of Elisabeth Beresford, who created the Wombles – to go ahead.

Near the end of the season, WUP advertised for contestants for "Mascot Idol" – and the winner would be the mascot. I had to apply. I was turned down by Charles Koppel for the role of Wandle the Womble years earlier, and this was too good an opportunity to miss.

So after the last home game of the season, I was waiting by the stage in the main bar, ready to do whatever it was I had to do to win the chance to be our club's mascot. Rob Aitkenhead, one of the people behind WUP, came over and told me that although they had been other applicants, as soon as they heard that I had applied they'd all withdrawn. So by default, I would be the person inside AFC Wimbledon's official mascot. Ivor announced the news to all those still in the bar. It was a very proud moment for me!

Over the close season drawings went back and forth getting the look just right, and the club asked the Junior Dons to suggest names for the mascot. It was left to Elisabeth Beresford herself to pick from the suggestions, and she chose Haydon the Womble.

I went to the club the night before the unveiling at the home game against Boreham Wood to get used to the costume, but we were still waiting for the head to arrive. It arrived with just an hour to spare on the day of the match. It was a lot harder to see out of than I'd imagined, and also a lot warmer inside, but that didn't matter. The moment I had waited for had arrived, and Ivor introduced AFC Wimbledon's first mascot to the crowd. Outside in the sun, it was roasting hot inside the costume and I only lasted until half-time for the first few games.

It wasn't long before I was invited to take part in the Mascot Grand National at Huntingdon on 4 October, raising money for the Children's Trust in Tadworth. I travelled up not knowing what to expect. I needn't have worried – Captain Blade of Sheffield United and City Gent of Bradford were already there and introduced themselves. I soon got acquainted with the others, and when it came to doing a lap of the parade ring before the race I had such fun having play water fights that I forgot to conserve my energy for the race. Well, that's my excuse – I finished 45th out of 68 runners! But I did raise the most money, and it was said that I would have won the best turned-out mascot award if I hadn't raised the most money. So I'd spread the word about AFC Wimbledon, and raised a lot for charity – I was hooked. Since then I have ran in the Mascot Grand National four times, and my best finish was 17th! I have always been in the top three for most money raised, which makes me very proud.

I have also taken part in mascot cricket matches, egg and spoon races and even a 100 metres "sprint" at a BUPA athletics meeting – finishing second, being beaten only by the official mascot for the Athletics Association.

It was at that first Grand National that I met Tadworth the Hound, the mascot for the Children's Trust. He invited me to visit the Trust, so I went along one evening to meet the children and spent three hours visiting every ward, every room. I had a fabulous time, and when I was leaving a mum said thank you to me. I said it was a pleasure, she held my arm and said: "No, seriously, thank you – you have given me hope." Apparently when I put my furry hand on her daughter's, she lifted her finger to touch me back, and that was the first movement she had shown since the accident that had hospitalised her. That really touched me and made me realise that a big furry Womble can make a difference. That is why I ran the London Marathon wearing the costume, why I went on the fourth plinth in Trafalgar Square for the Antony Gormley project and why I am seriously thinking of doing a sponsored coast-to-coast walk – 128 miles.

But obviously my main role is on match days, and I absolutely love banging my wheelie bin and getting the crowd singing. I am so honoured to be the official mascot for our great club. I look forward to the day when we are in a cup final again at Wembley. Well come on, with AFC Wimbledon there is no such word as unthinkable!

Stewart steps down

Kris Stewart had been at the very heart of everything AFC Wimbledon had achieved right from the off. It finally took its toll, and in September 2006 the man who had coined the phrase "I only want to watch football" stepped down.

4 September 2006
Kingsmeadow
By Kris Stewart (AFC Wimbledon chairman)

I decided to step down the day before I actually did. It was just too much. I was just knackered. I had thought for a while that I was coming to the end of my time. Now I was thinking: "Just one last season."

It was the most enjoyable job I had ever had. It was a dream, and I learnt more from it than any other job I've done. I learnt a lot about so many things and a lot about myself, but there was no switching off – it was 24/7. I think that anyone who does that job shouldn't do it for more than a couple of years. It's too much.

As a chairman of a football club, there's no room for you. The whole Terry Eames thing first surfaced on my birthday. I was out with my friends – most of whom weren't connected with football – when I took the call. I had to step outside and I was gone for hours. I had to be. And then there were holidays. I had to still be in touch, reachable. You could never relax. Everything was to do about football. You can never be off duty and you can't express a personal opinion about anything, even if it's just to a mate. Every time you speak, you speak as the chairman of a football club.

If this was my own football club, where I could do whatever I wanted to do and there was no comeback, and we were drawn in the FA Cup against the Franchise, I wouldn't play the game. But as chairman of AFC Wimbledon I couldn't do that. There would be too much comeback from the FA, the media and even supporters.

The whole role makes people who aren't Wimbledon fans – and I do still know some – look at you differently. And yes, I was becoming very one-dimensional. It was

all-consuming. It would have been nice to have something else to talk about.

And then there were times when I had to do things I really didn't enjoy at all – like the whole Terry Eames affair.

It was all starting to wear me down. And in the end it came down to one bad day at the office. It was nothing serious, but everything crystallised in one moment. I didn't want to get to the point where I hated going to work, hated working with Erik, Ivor and Nigel. It was then that I decided to jack it in. I probably should have gone earlier. I had reached my sell-by date.

Face to face with Winkelman

Off the pitch, the battle to reclaim Wimbledon FC's heritage was getting more intense. In August 2006 it finally came to a head, when for the first time WISA sat down with representatives of Milton Keynes Dons.

---

9 September 2006
By Simon Wheeler (chair of WISA)

After the 2005 Football Supporters Federation conference, the campaign against Milton Keynes began to shift into overdrive. I was leaving the UK in August to work in New Zealand for a year, and I was keen to continue to make life as challenging as possible for Milton Keynes.

WISA and like-minded fans had continued the previously successful campaign of cancelling and boycotting Franchise's pre-season fixtures. In quick succession games against Charlton, Ipswich, Colchester and Tottenham were called off. An email from one irate Milton Keynes supporter moaned that a friendly with QPR was now under threat – that had replaced the one against Colchester that had replaced

The Football Supporters Federation's Malcolm Clarke who helped broker a deal between Franchise FC and WISA

Luton fans at Kingsmeadow. One of many anti-franchising protests (Rob Beatty)

the one against Ipswich! It was more than evident that the continued pressure being applied was creating havoc with Milton Keynes' pre-season friendlies, and there was no sign of it abating.

At the 2005 FSF Conference, it has been agreed that the MK Dons Supporters Association (MKDSA) could not join the FSF until the history and honours of Wimbledon FC from before 28 May 2002 were returned to AFC Wimbledon or the community of Wimbledon. But it had taken a long time to get a meeting organised to discuss this as the two sides were poles apart. WISA had sent Peter Winkelman, the chief executive and chairman of Milton Keynes Dons, letter after letter with no reply. When we finally received an acknowledgment from Winkelman he emphasised the fact that they were a continuation of Wimbledon FC and were not willing to discuss the matter any further.

But we didn't give up, and the WISA committee agreed to continue to make life as challenging as possible for them. Eventually they conceded to a meeting. Milton Keynes were keen for the boycotts to end as they were finding it difficult to find teams to play against either home or away in pre-season, and other clubs' fans were refusing to travel away to games in Milton Keynes.

The FSF agreed to facilitate and act as mediators. A neutral venue was selected, a law firm in central London, and finally we all came face to face. It took two meetings to come to an agreement, and it would be fair to say that they were extremely challenging from all parties' points of view.

The FSF were represented by Malcolm Clarke and Steven Powell. They did an excellent job in facilitating and encouraging dialogue between WISA, represented by me and secretary Ross Maclagan, and John Brockwell, the chairman of the MKDSA, and Peter Winkelman. An argument broke out right at the beginning and we moved into separate rooms, with Malcolm and Steven shuttling between with various propositions.

At the end of the first meeting it looked as though a deal was more or less on the table. But by the start of the second meeting the positions had changed, and the whole deal seemed to be off. The "Dons" name was the stumbling block. Both parties needed to take something back to their members that would be acceptable, if not totally ideal. It was evident that some compromise was needed to take place if the status quo was not to remain. A tentative agreement was finally reached.

We got them to agree to relinquish the history and honours of Wimbledon FC.

They would not go directly to AFC Wimbledon, but to the Borough of Merton, where they would remain with Merton Council. In lieu of the "Dons" name not being dropped by Milton Keynes, the trademarks, badge, domain names and logos of Wimbledon FC, including the Crazy Gang logo, would also be transferred, with immediate effect, to Merton Council. But this time there was no proviso about the Council retaining them. Merton immediately handed them over to AFC Wimbledon.

In return WISA agreed that it would no longer actively ask its members to encourage boycotts and fixture cancellations and would not oppose MKDSA's application to join the FSF.

The accord was announced on 9 September 2006 on the WISA website, but it still needed formal approval. Both parties agreed to go back and ballot their members. MKDSA had a strong vote in favour. Of 1,064 WISA and AFC Wimbledon Fans who voted, 1,023 were in favour and only nine against. The other 32 ballot papers were spoilt. By then I was in New Zealand, but I had played my part in reclaiming Wimbledon's history for the Borough of Merton.

We maintained the right to object to Milton Keynes referring to themselves as the "Dons" and continue to encourage Milton Keynes to drop the stigma of franchising by developing their own identity.

A dose of the big time – Devon style

In years gone by, an away trip to Devon in October would not have appealed too much, but this was different. This was the FA Cup and this was Exeter, who were all set to return to the Football League. It was a taste of the big time and a chance to see what the future might hold.

---

28 October 2006
Exeter City 2 AFC Wimbledon 1 FA Cup fourth qualifying round
By Roscoe Dsane (AFC Wimbledon player)

It was the noise that I remember best. Hundreds of miles from home, we heard this noise as we came out of the tunnel: AFC Wimbledon fans in full voice. It was all you could hear. There may well have been more Exeter fans in the stadium, but the 1,500 Dons fans who made the trip sung and sung.

That's the reality with Wimbledon, and it's what makes the club so special. There's an inner drive, an inner sense of injustice that drives the fans on, and as a player it becomes impossible to escape that raw emotion.

Their team all looked bigger and stronger. I think that's the big difference as you go up the divisions. Our big mistake was to give them too much respect. By half time we were 2-0 down and frankly out of it.

After the break, Byron Bubb headed the ball on and I was through. I tried to slip it to the keeper's left, mis-hit it slightly and it went through his legs. I have no reason to lie about it – it happens all the time in the game. It was just a bit of luck – it doesn't really matter as long as the ball goes in. It gave us all a lift, and for a while I think we all felt we could go on and get something out of the game, but it wasn't to be.

I loved being at AFC Wimbledon. The fans were amazing. There was such a good

Roscoe Dsane on the ball in front of the Dons
faithful at Exeter in October 2006 (Martin Tomlin)

AFC Wimbledon players take the field to face
Exeter City in the fourth qualifying round of the
FA Cup on 26 October 2006 (Martin Tomlin)

feel about the whole place. There was such determination from everyone from the stewards to the manager and everyone in between. All the players felt the importance of the history and the need to right a wrong. I would recommend a spell at AFC Wimbledon to any up-and-coming player.

That pre-season I didn't have a club, and Steve Watson suggested I go down to AFC Wimbledon. I scored a few goals – I played brilliantly against Leyton Orient. After that I spoke to Dave Anderson, and he said: "Yeah, let's do a deal." It had been a frustrating time for me. I had been out injured and I had watched a lot of my friends make a good go of being professional footballers. I really wanted to catch them up. I was really hungry to be successful and I wanted to score a lot of goals.

It's going to sound egotistical, but I knew I was better than some of my friends who were playing at a higher level, and that just drove me on even more. But it doesn't always work out. I left Wimbledon after a year to move up a level. I went to Accrington followed by Torquay, but I was never as happy as I was at AFC Wimbledon.

I was close to rejoining at the start of 2011. I spoke to Terry Brown and I'd have loved to come back – it would have been a dream. But at the time the system he was playing just didn't suit my game.

By Dave Anderson (AFC Wimbledon manager)

I had several friends over from Belfast for the trip to Exeter. They hired a car from Bristol and headed into town to spend the day drinking with the Wimbledon fans. The support we took there was just unbelievable. It was something like 1,500 people. Many League sides can only dream of taking that many to an away game.

We conceded almost immediately and we were being run ragged. I said to Simon Bassey that we'd be laughing if we went in just one down – and that was exactly the time they added a second. But even 2-0 flattered us – it could have been six by half-time. The second half was different: we scored a goal and gave it a go, but it wasn't to be.

Ivor managed to get my mates on the bus back. We used Grays' coach. It used to be the England cricket coach. It was utter luxury, and some of my friends said it was better that many hotels they'd stayed in. And we had a bit of a party on the way back.

Bassey had got a 20-year-old bottle of whiskey, and each of the players had a wee nip. Then he called us to join them, and it all took off from there. Normally I let the players get on by themselves, but we all had a good sing-song on the way back to Kingsmeadow. Ivor, my players and my mates. The driver was the only one sober by the time we got back to the ground and I'm not even sure about that!

The big thing for me was the call I got from the Grays chairman a few days later. The driver had said we were an absolute credit and he would have no problem driving us anywhere else. We may have been drunk, but we tidied up after ourselves – and for me that proved just how far we had come. We did things right.

Gell will tear you apart...

In 2006, AFC Wimbledon finally put a marker down on how far they could go. The victory over Aldershot was their first against a Conference side in a competitive game. The Dons trailed 1-0 at half-time. Midfielder Chris Gell scored the vital equaliser. And the match had added significance – the manager of the opposing side was one Terry Brown, who in years to come would a play a pivotal role in AFC Wimbledon's rise through the leagues.

---

16 December 2006
Aldershot 1 AFC Wimbledon 2 FA Trophy first round
By Chris Gell (AFC Wimbledon player)

It was all a bit of a blur. The ball was pinging around the edge of the box, and I slid in to win it. It went out wide and then came back to me and I just hit it. I didn't know where to run, everyone was heading for me. So I just gave up and got bundled. It was a great feeling.

I've seen that goal dozens of times since on YouTube. The ball swerved a bit – it must have been windy! I put the clip on my Facebook page for a bit, and I still get comments from my friends about it.

To score against Terry Brown was brilliant. I was banging on his door afterwards, screaming: "Have that, Browny!" We had some history – me and Terry. I played against his teams dozens of times when I was at Northwood, and he had always seemed to get one over on me. So it was very sweet.

Before the match we couldn't have been bigger underdogs, I remember some of the supporters telling us they'd put money on us to win. I can't quite remember what I said, but I really thought we didn't have a chance.

We were one down at half-time. Yes, they were outplaying us, but we weren't doing that badly. That didn't stop Dave laying into us. I hadn't played that well in the first half, and we picked it up massively in the second half. He told us to stop giving them space and we would get our chances.

And it all changed. Suddenly, we were tackling all over the park, winning every 50-50, winning every header, winning everything. We were up for it and you could sense suddenly that we could really do it. To heck with the divisions between us – AFC Wimbledon of the Ryman League could go to Aldershot and turn them over.

My goal levelled it, and when Scott Fitzgerald put us ahead five minutes later everything erupted. I turned around and looked at the huge mass of Dons fans at the other end. It was just mayhem. I'll remember that for ever more. The last five minutes was like the Alamo. Forget the idea of having any forwards – it was 11 defenders, and all clearances went straight to row Z. It was desperate stuff, but we did it. That day we grew a little bit more. It was just unbelievable on the coach after. I'd love to have the DVD of that game.

Then of course there was that song...I love that song! None of my friends or family believed me – a bunch of them really weren't into football. So I dragged them down to Kingsmeadow. I remember fearing that the fans wouldn't sing it. But in the warm-up it trickled down the stands: "Gell will tear you apart..." It was superb. Every time I hear that song now, I think: "That's special." I got some stick for it, but I don't mind.

Goalkeeper Andy Little celebrates with AFC Wimbledon manager Dave Anderson after the 2-1 win at Aldershot in 2006 (Paul Willatts)

AFC Wimbledon celebrate their 2-1 win at Aldershot (Paul Willatts)

Those days at Wimbledon were like a dream come true. From the top to the bottom it was a great club. Dave Anderson was a special character. He had his way of doing things. I remember having to call him once to say that I couldn't make training. He was livid, and in his lovely Irish tones told me in no uncertain terms that if I didn't get my arse down to training he'd send the IRA after me. Needless to say, I went.

By Dave Anderson (AFC Wimbledon manager)

It was some game. I remember Gelly's goal well. Seconds before, he went down like he'd been shot by an AK47. Then he got up, the ball came back to him, he took a couple of steps and blasted it in. It was one of those games where our game plan worked perfectly.

By Terry Brown (Aldershot manager)

For Dave it was a massive game – the pressure was on him. And I remember the ecstasy on his face. The Dons fans will tell you that they out-sung the Aldershot fans, but I remember it being a wall of noise from both sets of fans. But what a scalp it was for them, coming to Aldershot and going away with a win. Aldershot had a cup pedigree at the time – we'd reached the semi-finals of the Trophy the year before.

I have to own up, Dave won the tactical battle and Andy Little had a fantastic game. I remember thinking: "God, how good is he?" Roscoe tormented us. We had let him go the previous year. He had been plagued with injuries and he didn't kick a ball for me for a whole season, but I knew he was talented. He came back to haunt us.

By Andy Little (AFC Wimbledon player)

No one had given us a chance – and as a team we had a feeling that Dave was under pressure. We did OK in the first half – or at least I thought we had. But as we came into the dressing room, you could feel a bit of atmosphere. Dave laid into me, and we didn't see eye to eye over that. It was the first time he barked out: "Give yourself a shake" – that was to become a bit of a catchphrase for him. But I wasn't the only one who felt his wrath during the break.

It must have worked, because in the second half we turned in one of the most accomplished performances of his reign. When we ran out we were met by a wall of noise. The end I ran to was split between Dons and Aldershot fans – they were both singing at each other. It was intense, and the Dons songs kept getting louder and louder. When we scored the second I turned around and just thought "Wow!" The Dons end was just erupting. At the final whistle, I was being hugged by everyone.

It was one of those games. It seemed like none of the Dons fans wanted to go home. They just stayed and sang. I stayed on the pitch for quite a while – I wanted to soak it all up. When I eventually went into the changing room, you could still hear the fans singing and singing. I will never forget it.

On to the Breach...

Off the pitch, things were starting to change. In December 2006 Matt Breach was elected to the Dons Trust Board. It was the start of a transformation of the Board, and four years later Matt would be elected as chair of the Dons Trust.

By Matt Breach (Dons Trust Board member)
Dons Trust AGM
18 December 2006

After being a volunteer for four years I took the plunge and stood for election to the Dons Trust Board in 2006. From my position as one of the more senior stewards, I thought I could help to bring a bit of practicality and urgency to the Board; the overriding impression I had from "the outside" was that the Board then was more interested in constitutional and political matters than actually helping run the club.

I was quite surprised to be elected from a fairly large field of candidates, but before any feelings of satisfaction could begin to form I had a phone call from Erik that put me into the picture about what would become known as "Darlogate". My first few months on the Board were a bit of a blur as I was thrown straight into helping to deal with the Jermaine Darlington international clearance affair, soon followed by a second failure in the play-offs and the replacement of Dave Anderson as manager with Terry Brown.

In the summer I got a chance to reflect on how things were going. I decided that the work involved and the attendant aggravation – suddenly all things "wrong" at the club appeared to be my fault – were worth putting up with for that indescribable feeling I got whenever I saw us play: in some small part I knew it was as a result of my efforts. I worked hard to move the Board from being a debating society that could talk itself to death to actually undertaking the role it was set up for – to oversee the running of the club.

During that period we were extraordinarily lucky to have a core team of executives who ran the club well and with the best interests of the fans at heart. I can now see how some of the other fans-owned clubs foundered through poor governance – and that could have happened to us. I believe we did make progress – the separation of the football-club executives from the Trust Board being a key step – but as a Board we were far from what we needed to be. I knew we had to keep pushing forward, looking to better ourselves.

The booking that changed a season

On 56 minutes Roscoe Dsane scored to put AFC Wimbledon one up against Conference side Gravesend & Northfleet in the FA Trophy. It would prove to be a winner that secured another notable scalp for the Dons. But the booking three minutes later of the Dons' Jermaine Darlington was to have far more serious consequences.

AFC Wimbledon's Jermaine Darlington in action against at Gravesend on 13 January 2007 in the FA Trophy. His 59th minute booking would have grave consquences for the club (Paul Willatts)

Roscoe Dsane, who scored the winner at Gravesend (Martin Tomlin)

13 January 2007
Gravesend & Northfleet United 0 AFC Wimbledon 1
FA Trophy second round
By Roscoe Dsane (AFC Wimbledon player)

The FA Trophy had really brought our season alive. The Aldershot game the round before had been immense. It was a great atmosphere, and for me with all my Aldershot connections it meant an awful lot. The victory over Gravesend & Northfleet – another Conference side – should have been another high-water mark.

We were on form and starting to prove that we could compete at a higher level. Dave Anderson was a really bubbly character and had created a team with the right blend of youth and experience. I had built up a great understanding with Wes Daly. Every time I made a run I knew that he would find me. And that was the case against Gravesend. Mickey Haswell, who didn't play that day, could pick me out too.

I got the winner that day, but I can barely remember it. Everything was overshadowed by what happened with Jermaine Darlington. I scored about 10 minutes into the second half, but it was Jermaine's booking a couple of minutes later that changed our entire season.

Jermaine was another of the players in the team I had built up an understanding with. He was a real humble guy. It wasn't his fault that the club didn't have the right paperwork. It all turned into a bit of a disaster and we were all gutted. But it was never Jermaine's fault. And I do wonder how far we could have gone.

By Dave Anderson (AFC Wimbledon manager)

The best compliment for that game came from a friend of mine who'd watched it. He said simply: "You couldn't tell which club was from the Conference and which was from the Ryman League." That's how good we were that day. But the win was made meaningless by the booking of Jermaine Darlington and everything it led to.

The Darlington affair

The euphoria of the victory over Gravesend & Northfleet was rapidly wiped away by the controversy that followed Jermaine Darlington's booking. When it was reported to the FA, as all bookings are, they found they had no record for him: he was still registered with the FA of Wales. That oversight was to have catastrophic consequences.

30 March 2007
FA Tribunal
Soho Square
By Erik Samuelson (AFC Wimbledon chief executive)

"Oh f***, I've screwed the club." Those were the words of Trevor Williams in the President's Lounge seconds after he found out. He sunk to the floor, his back against the bar and his head buried in his hands. He was inconsolable.

He had just opened the letter from the FA explaining what had happened. Jermaine Darlington, who had been on Cardiff City's books, had not got international clearance to move to Wimbledon. Then, I didn't understand the consequences of not having the right paperwork. It didn't sound that serious. Trev knew immediately.

It had crossed his mind when we first made our move to sign Jermaine to look into the issue of international clearance, but for some reason he had just never got round to it. He just couldn't believe it. We rang a few people to ask for advice, and everyone said: "You're dead in the water."

David Barnard introduced us to lawyer Jim Sturman, who still acts for Chelsea. He really helped us, and we went into overdrive to see what we could do. (I have an email folder called "Complaints and praise". It has a sub-folder called "Jermaine Darlington", which has 267 emails in it.) We had to deal with the FA, because the infringement that had led to the discovery had occurred in a Trophy game; and then we had to deal with the Ryman League.

First up was an FA panel, where we were charged with all sorts of heinous things. I took responsibility for it. Trev was in too much distress, and it was potentially so damaging to the club's prospects that, as chief executive, I had to take responsibility.

We were up in front of a three-man panel. Jim was our advocate. He was facing three FA councillors: one from the North-East, one from the South-West and one other. Various other FA officers were on hand to offer legal advice. It was all very formal. The charge was read out, and we were asked if we understood it. The chair then invited questions and, it was at that point that I thought: "We're on a hiding to nothing."

The first question wasn't a question – it was a lecture. The official launched into a long diatribe about how we had broken this rule and that rule and how it was an utter disgrace. I was livid, not so much with the points that he was making but with the process. This was supposed to be a question, and this was just one long statement. I was fuming. Jim knew I was fuming, but he wouldn't let me say anything in case I made matters worse, I suppose. After all the questions we left the room and waited, and then eventually we were called back in and we were told straight – we

Clear that... The Clive Yelf flag inspired by the
18-point deduction imposed on AFC Wimbledon

The Norwich City chief executive, Neil
Doncaster, who sat on the appeal board

The FA headquarters, where the FA Tribunal
sat on 30 March 2007

had been kicked out of the Trophy. I wanted to say something. I was desperate to say something, but again Jim stopped me.

Then it was the turn of the Ryman League. There was Martin Ede from Fisher Athletic, Dean Fisher from Croydon Athletic, Alan Turvey was the chair and Nick Robinson was there to interpret the rules. The case was put to us and Jim made our defence. I deferred to Jim again. He knew how these things worked. I had looked into several different cases of clubs that had gone through the same thing. We voiced our mitigating circumstances, but it all came to nothing and we were told we would be given an 18-point deduction (all the points we'd won in games where Jermaine had played) and a £400 fine. It was a shock. We then waited for the written report. We read it, and Jim was incensed by the injustice of it. He said: "I want to fight this. We are going to fight this." And I said: "Yes, let's go for it." And that's where the work really began.

Everything went into overdrive, while the fans were in uproar. Letters and emails were being sent off in every direction. Alan Turvey had an anonymous threatening letter put through his letterbox and Ryman board members got rude emails sent to them. Turvey seemed to think we could control our fans but of course we couldn't. In fact I had asked Bruce Badcock, the Ryman League administrator, to forward the abusive emails and I wrote to the senders to point out that they were not helping our cause.

Then there was the politics and the lobbying. Someone launched an online petition, and then I was introduced to Phil French. Phil was Dave Boyle's predecessor at Supporters Direct. He worked for the then Labour minister Andy Burnham. Phil was brilliant. He guided me through the process. He knew what needed to be done. He knew we had to be sensible. Yes we had been wronged, but there was a right way to go about things – we needed to be professional. He took me through the public relations part of it too.

We worked hard to get our message across to journalists like Richard Williams of the Guardian and Martin Samuel to make sure we were getting our message out in the press. I wrote to Richard Caborn, the Sports Minister, and just about everyone else. We engaged our local MPs, and that led to a question being asked in the House of Commons by Siobhan McDonagh, the Labour MP for Mitcham and Morden. At Prime Minister's Questions she asked Tony Blair what he thought about the decision. He said: "It sounds like a daft rule and someone should change it." At the time a lot of people could have dismissed this as an off-the-cuff comment to appease one of his MPs, but Siobhan assured us it was genuine – he knew about the case and genuinely thought the decision was wrong.

The whole campaign – the politics, the media – was sending certain people in various circles apoplectic. Alan Turvey was livid. Meanwhile we were tipped off by those on the inside that whatever we did, the decision had already been made – the result would not change. We managed, by means I'd rather not say at the moment, to get our message to a few key people, and in my view that was the key to our success. Those key people made sure that for our appeal we got a panel which was willing to look at the issue afresh.

When Jim and I got to the appeal hearing at Soho Square, the headquarters of the FA, David Henman was there, as chair of the Sanctions and Registration Committee, along with an FA councillor and Neil Doncaster, then the chief executive of Norwich City. Jim presented our case. We were professional and thorough. We put forward all our mitigating circumstances. And then it was the Ryman League's turn.

They were asked to present. They looked at each other and didn't seem to know who was going to present – which didn't reflect well on them, I thought. I'm probably not allowed to say exactly what was said in the meeting but the general thrust was to see if Alan and Nick felt that perhaps the punishment was disproportionate – which made me hope that this might be the panel's view. And then we were all asked to sit outside while they deliberated.

Jim was in the hall being sociable with Alan and Nick. That was totally the right thing to do, I knew that, but I wanted to be alone with my thoughts. Then we were called back in, and they read out their decision. It began badly: "The panel confirms that the Ryman League was correct and appropriate in making its decision." My heart sank – but there was a "but"… "However," the statement continued, "we have decided to reduce the points deduction from 18 points to three. The penalty of £400 remains."

I could see Alan Turvey looking stunned. So was I – I couldn't believe it. Jim and I thanked everyone and came out. I rushed upstairs to the lobby and rang Kris as we had pre-arranged. He couldn't believe the news either, and asked me to repeat it. Then he got to work. The FA said their statement would be up on their website in an hour, but we wanted to have something up before them. I summarised the decision of the hearing and Kris set about getting it up on the club's site.

I popped outside and told the Dons fans who had gathered there, and they were absolutely delighted. I went back inside, and Neil Doncaster walked by. I asked him if I had heard right, and he burst out laughing and said, "Yes!"

Alan Turvey was doubly upset. Not only had he suffered all that abuse from some of our fans, but now he had also lost. He was furious but we'd won, fair and square – and that was all that mattered.

Howzat for a Howard hat-trick

There could be few better ways to celebrate the success of the appeal than a confident victory. AFC Wimbledon had many big wins in their climb through the non-league divisions, but none would be bigger than the 9-0 win over Slough. For captain Anthony Howard the game was even more memorable: the central defender got a hat-trick.

---

31 March 2007
AFC Wimbledon 9 Slough 0
Ryman Premier Division
By Antony Howard (AFC Wimbledon player)

It sounds selfish, but it would have been great if it had finished 3-0. I'm a defender. I'd always got the odd goal here and there, but never a hat-trick. And certainly not what they call the perfect hat-trick – one with my left, one with my right and one with my head. That's some feat for a forward – let alone a defender like me. So to win 9-0 takes some of the shine off it. But it was still some game.

I remember it really well: it was against one of my old clubs. I still had a lot of old friends there, and that made it a bit more emotional. I felt a bit sorry for them.

AFC Wimbledon's Antony Howard head goalwards against Slough on 31 March 2007. The 9-0 win would be the Dons' biggest in their history (Rob Beatty)

Slough goalkeeper leaps into action at Kingsmeadow on 31 March 2007 (Rob Beatty)

Slough were really struggling – they'd lost five or six on the bounce and we were on a really amazing run. We were due a game where we were going to really explode on someone and poor Slough were on the receiving end. It was a walkover, really: they were dead and buried from the moment I scored after two minutes and we just hammered them.

The pick of the goals was my second one. I went on to became a coach in the States, and the kids I was coaching would all go away and look me up on the internet. And the first hit is that goal – it's there for everyone to see on YouTube. It's served me really well on the East Coast. It was a sweet left-foot volley. Normally, my left foot is purely for standing on, but I couldn't have hit this one any better. Normally, the ball would have sailed over the stand and landed on the running track. But it just flew into the net. I went a bit mad – I took off my shirt and went running off. I got booked for that. I guess the referee wasn't quite as impressed as I was.

What made the game even more unusual was that my grandmother was there. She was a Bromley fan, and at that time we played them quite often. Both teams were always up there challenging, but this was the only time she went to Kingsmeadow. And that meant a lot to me. My whole family has always kept a close eye on my career. The newspaper cuttings, the medals and even the ball from the Slough game – they are all back home in my old bedroom. My mum's nuts about all that stuff. The nice yellow flag I got from the club when I left is there too.

Joining AFC Wimbledon was a no-brainer for me. It was a simple move. Dave Anderson was my manager at Hendon, and he had left there to take the AFC Wimbledon job. He didn't have to work to hard to persuade me to follow him. Dave's a special character – he could talk the hind legs off a donkey. He got me down to Kingsmeadow and we had a meeting in the centre circle. He started talking about playing in front of 3,000 or even 4,000 fans each week and what a special club AFC Wimbledon is. I just said: "Dave, job done."

He wanted young, dedicated players, and I fitted that mould. I wasn't earning the most at Hendon and I wasn't earning the least, but I think I was his sort of player. Once I knew about all the other players who were coming in, I just knew we were going up. We were head and shoulders above everyone that first season.

I was named Player of the Year, and that was without doubt my biggest achievement in soccer. Was I the best player at AFC Wimbledon that year? Probably not. We had Roscoe Dsane, who was unbelievable, and Richard Butler and loads of other quality players. But I played most of the games that season. And then getting the Players' Player award as well was out of this world. To be recognised by your peers – that really means something.

Playing in front of 4,000 people at that level was amazing. The last time I went back to Kingsmeadow, my wife just couldn't believe it. The fans made me feel so special – like a little celebrity. And I think that was when she realised what sort of club AFC Wimbledon is and how much it means to the fans. I've played at several different clubs, and nothing will ever be like Wimbledon. AFC Wimbledon has seeped into my blood.

I sometimes wonder whether people will remember me in 10 or 20 years' time – but this is a club that does remember its history. Look at Dickie Guy. The guy is a legend. I won't ever be like him, but whenever I've come back to the club I've been made welcome at the bar, and it just feels so special.

I loved my time at AFC Wimbledon. My best memories are of after the games. We were all down-to-earth players, and there was nothing I liked more than spending time with them and the fans in the bar after a game. I just loved it. A nice shower, some time in the players' lounge, then into the main bar to listen to Ivor make his little speech. A couple of times I'd be up there getting a Man of the Match award. And then it was the rest of the evening with the fans. The amount of times I'd have to leave my car in the car park and get the train back to Dartford... Getting back to the ground on the Sunday was always a nightmare, but it never stopped me doing the same the week after. That was my life at Wimbledon. Whatever went on on the field was a blur, but the memories of the fans – that's what it was all about.

I was just a non-league player, but maybe if I'd stayed I might have made it into the League – who knows? At the end of the 2006-07 season, though, I left. Terry Brown had taken over and the club was in transition. I had to be realistic. I was in my mid- twenties, and I asked myself: "Can I help this club push on? Could I really be a League player with Wimbledon?" Possibly. But Terry needed young, hungry kids, who had the desire, the drive to push Wimbledon on. And he got them in. I had to get on with my life. Being a part-time footballer just wasn't going to pay the bills. So when the chance came to coach in Connecticut, I took it.

Since then, of course, the team has gone from strength to strength. I don't regret my decision – I had four and a half great years at Wimbledon. And what has been achieved is brilliant. The fans deserve every second of their success. Football is a better place for the existence of AFC Wimbledon. It was a fairytale the first time round, and it's a fairytale all over again.

When it all began with those trials on Wimbledon Common, most people would have thought: "These guys are nuts." But they did it. I think back to people like Simon Bassey. He was there right at the start, and he has become the cornerstone. I can't think of a nicer person in football – for the information he gave me as a player and the work he did to get us all to gel together off the pitch. He deserves every single bit of credit he gets.

The Samuelson era begins

When Kris Stewart stood down, Erik Samuelson was given the chief executive role on a temporary basis. In April 2007 he was formally appointed.

---

21 April 2007

By Erik Samuelson (AFC Wimbledon acting chief executive)

Kris called me on Sunday in early September 2006 and said: "I need to resign." It was a bit of a body blow. But I've been in business for a long time, and when someone says that you have to take it seriously.

My view is that resignation has to be the best course for the person concerned – not for the business, not for me, but for them. It was a little different with Kris as he was technically my boss, but I still wanted him to convince me that it was the right thing for him to do. If it was, I told him, he would get my full support. And at the end of the call, he had my support.

Kris had come through several difficult situations, and I had been really impressed

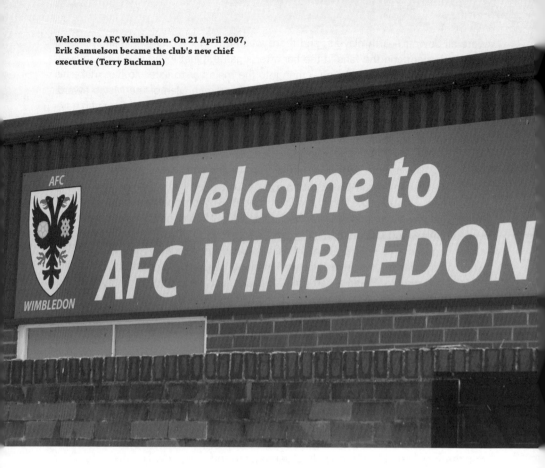

with him as a chief executive. He was absolutely magnificent, when it came to the Terry Eames affair. He doesn't like confrontation, but he was brilliant. It was his finest hour. I doubt he enjoyed any part of the process, but the way he conducted himself was superb.

When Kris went I took over the role temporarily. I wanted to keep the ship steady and make sure everyone was happy. There were a number of little things that I wanted to change, but nothing major. I wanted to ensure that the transition was smooth. I had been working as finance director from the start and I loved it so much I retired from PricewaterhouseCoopers four years early to free myself up to be able to help even more. So I was well placed to take over the operational stuff. Eventually I convinced the Dons Trust Board that I wanted the role permanently. Most people were fully supportive, which in football I have subsequently learnt is very unusual. Although I do recall one fan who described me as "megalomania gone mad" – a phrase my sons like to throw at me every now and then.

When it came down to the negotiations, I was in the fortunate position of not needing to get paid – I had earned enough in my career. But Kris had been paid, and had had a contract, and the Dons Trust Board was insistent that I have a contract too. However, for a contract of employment to be valid there has to be a minimum payment, and normally that is £1. But I thought that sounded a bit ordinary, and I asked for a guinea instead as it was posher. They all laughed but agreed to it. And that amused me – I negotiated hard for that five per cent rise.

The end of Mr Anderson

When Dave Anderson agreed to become manager of AFC Wimbledon, he promised that by the end of the 2006-07 season the club would have gained promotion to the Conference South. Beaten in the play-offs the year before, luck would be against him once more in the 2007 end-of-season lottery. And he would pay the ultimate price for defeat.

---

1 May 2007
Bromley 1 AFC Wimbledon 0
Ryman Premier Division play-off semi-final
By Andy Little (AFC Wimbledon player)

I thought we should have won the league that year. We had an excellent record – we lost only six out of 42 – but we just drew too many games. People talk about the ref at Bromley – and certainly Dave knew his earlier comments about him didn't help – but that shouldn't have played a part in it.

We were really confident. We felt we wouldn't get beaten. We had been docked points and had that reduced. We felt like we'd had the world against us, and that made us more than determined than everything. Then Wes got done for two bookings, but even then Bromley never really threatened. Then Nic McDonnell, who I knew well, scored for them. The reaction was typical Wimbledon – a wall of noise from our supporters encouraging us on. We threw everything at them, even with 10 men.

At the end I was up there in the penalty area, and I nearly set one up for Richard Jolley. I thought the ball was in – I had my hands up in the air to celebrate – but it hit the roof of the net. I was so gutted. I thought we had levelled, and even with 10 men the momentum would have been with us. I am convinced even now that we would have won it in extra time.

And that remains my biggest regret at Wimbledon: that we didn't go up that year.

By Richard Butler (AFC Wimbledon player)

I really rated Dave Anderson. I liked him as a manager – he got us really motivated. But he was also a very hard man to impress. I felt so sorry for him after the Bromley game.

Wes Daly got sent off after only about 30 minutes. But we were still in it. Then Richard Jolley missed a sitter late on that would have made it 1-1, and I would have backed us to go on and win it from there. It was bad luck – nothing went right for us and Dave paid for it. He hadn't achieved what the club wanted him to do, but he had come so very close.

I haven't spoken to him for a few years now, but Dave is the sort of man that I'd happily have a chat and a laugh with.

By Erik Samuelson (AFC Wimbledon Chief Executive)

After the final whistle I looked down and saw Dave alone in the dugout. I guess he was having a quiet smoke or something like that. He knew what was coming.

AFC Wimbledon goalkeeper Andy Little
(Terry Buckman)

Time sets on the anxious AFC Wimbledon
support at Bromley in the Ryman League
play-offs (Rob Beatty)

Niall Couper: **This Is Our Time**

He knew the deal. Promotion from the Ryman First in year one, then promotion to the Conference South two years after that. He had done the first part, but this was the end of year three.

We'd had a conversation back in February, when the results weren't going too well for us. I pulled him aside then and told him: "We do need to get promotion this year." And he said: "Give me a target number of points." But I'm not a believer in setting that sort of target: as soon as you do that, it's the beginning of the end. I could have given him three games to improve or set a points target, but I didn't see any benefit in doing that. He knew what he had to do.

When we lost – and Bromley should be grateful to Wes Daly for that – it was over. I left Dave alone that night. He needed to be with his players and gather himself.

I called him the next day, and he told me this wonderful story about his childhood. He was brought up in Belfast during the Troubles, and back then the communities were effectively ruled and policed by the paramilitaries. If you did something wrong, they would be the ones to deliver justice, whatever it might be. However, it was your responsibility to hand yourself in. If you failed to do so, the retribution would be even worse – and you didn't want that. "Last night," he said, "that story came back to me. I've been expecting your call."

It was a terribly difficult call for both of us. I had only been officially the club's chief executive for 10 days, and this was the first big job I had to do. Dave helped me by bringing a lot of humour to it. I said at the end: "I think we need to move on." But we needed to do things properly. We agreed terms and parted amicably. Dave was "sacked by mutual consent". He was so gracious about it – far more than I would have been.

Dave had achieved so much for Wimbledon. He made us so much more professional, on and off the pitch. He had moved the club forward, but he also knew and respected the terms of the agreement.

By Dave Anderson (AFC Wimbledon manager)

I never really had the luck. The year before at Fisher, I had seven of my first-team squad in the stands so I never really had a chance. I wasn't too disappointed by that defeat – I got over it quite quickly. Bromley was different. In football, there are two things you can't control – injuries and luck. And both times they went against me at a crucial stage.

I'd been worried that we hadn't been playing that well going into the Bromley game. And then I saw who the ref was: It was the same ref who had been in charge against Hampton & Richmond a month earlier and sent off Lee O'Leary after half an hour. We lost 2-0, and I'd laid into him after that one. So perhaps it was no surprise that we were once again down to 10 after 30 minutes. To be fair, Wes Daly committed bookable offences, and once he had pulled their player back I knew what was coming.

But to be honest, my biggest disappointment that night was not the sending-off, but their goal. A moment or two before they headed it in, Frankie Howard had been blatantly fouled in the corner, but the ref ignored it and they scored from the cross. It should have been a free-kick. Once Wes was gone we did as well as we could, but it was always going to be an uphill battle.

After we lost, I knew what was going to happen next. I'd made the promise to Kris and Erik to get us up within two seasons and I had not delivered. AFC Wimbledon was a juggernaut, and I couldn't stop it. I knew what the deal was. The whole season had been surreal – there was the possible 18-point deduction hanging over us, and that distracted us a bit. Sometimes I wonder whether, if it had not been reduced to three points, I might have been allowed to stay on.

But I completely understood the situation: the club needed to move on. The official line was "mutual consent", but it wasn't really like that. Erik said he wanted to make a change, and I totally understood – that was the "mutual" part of it. I was proud of my record at AFC Wimbledon. I was in charge of something like 160 games in all competitions and lost maybe no more than 20.

A year later, Terry got the luck that had deserted me. One down with 10 minutes to go, and the keeper dropped the ball. I've known Browny for a long time and he deserved it. And if you look where the club are now, it was the right decision. It takes you a while to get over managing a club like that. Four or five weeks later I felt a little bit lighter and a little bit less stressed.

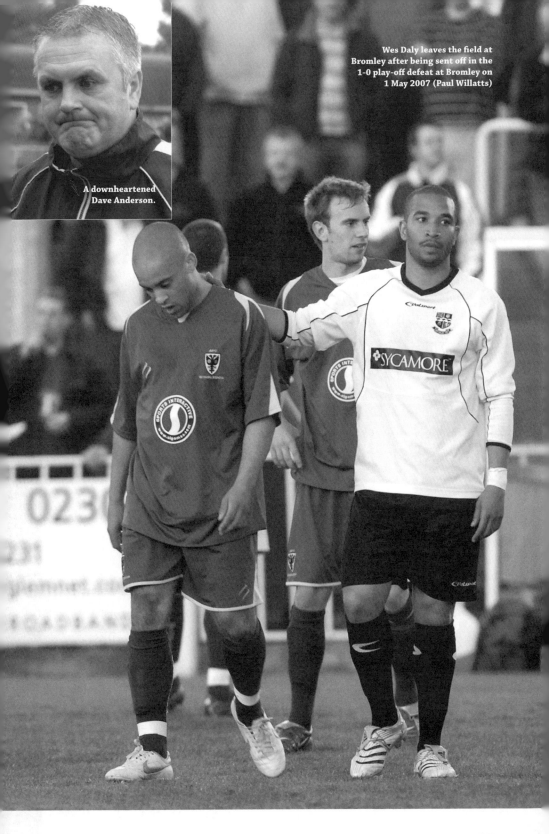

A downheartened
Dave Anderson.

Wes Daly leaves the field at
Bromley after being sent off in the
1-0 play-off defeat at Bromley on
1 May 2007 (Paul Willatts)

Chapter Eight:

I can't help falling in love with you

AFC Wimbledon players charge at the Tempest End in celebration on 25 April 2009 (Paul Willatts)

Brown and Cash step in

Two weeks after the official departure of Dave Anderson, Wimbledon appointed a new double act to take his place. The pair had a great track record at Aldershot and elsewhere and were to beat off a strong shortlist to take the hot seat at Kingsmeadow.

---

15 May 2007
Kingsmeadow
By Terry Brown (AFC Wimbledon manager)

My next-door neighbour Russell Smith happened to be an absolute fanatical Wimbledon supporter and I was out of work at the time, having just left Aldershot. Russell kept telling me how wonderful AFC Wimbledon was and he knew Ivor Heller and various other people at the club.

At the time my wife was just recovering from leukaemia and I was just at the point where I needed to get back into work. Stuart Cash had also got in touch with me and was keen on the role too. We had worked together well at Aldershot and he thought that if we put in for it together we would make a good proposition.

We had a couple of interviews. The first one was in some hotel in Kingston. It was a pretty low-key affair, nothing classy. I think there were about three or four of us that were being interviewed that day and if I remember rightly we faced John Faulkner and Erik Samuelson. Erik got John in to be his football expert on the panel. John had all the experience, he'd played at a high level and had been a first-team coach at Luton, so he asked all the football questions. Erik asked all the financial ones, but generally it was left fairly open. It was basically left to me to sell myself.

It was fortunate that the job spec was almost identical to what I had done at Aldershot. Then I had taken on a big club that had started again and was in the Ryman League, where everyone wants to beat you and every game is like a cup final. I would hate to go back to the Ryman League. You play against highly motivated teams. There was the standard of the pitches, some of them were absolutely dreadful. And then, of course, you would send a scout to watch someone like Heybridge Swifts one week and the scout would say they were awful, but they would have rested a couple of people and those who had played would be unrecognisable from the previous week. And then there would be the crowd. It would go from a couple of dozen and a dog to just over a thousand.

That wouldn't make much of a difference at Combined Counties level where, with respect, most players could hardly kick a ball, but in the Ryman League there are a couple of players who can actually play – and those sorts of crowds spur them on even more. It is like playing in the FA Cup every week. So I knew what AFC Wimbledon was facing. It was enough to say, I had been there, done that and got the T-shirt. The only thing I hadn't done was take the club into the Football League. I had even guided Aldershot from part-time to full-time. I knew the challenges AFC Wimbledon would have to face, and that was a massive selling point. There were few people in football who had taken the same journey as me. I was ticking all the boxes without having to say very much. But there was another element to the interview, capturing the ethos of Wimbledon.

Terry Brown, right, and Stuart Cash.
The pair took charge of AFC Wimbledon
on 15 May 2007 (Martin Tomlin)

Russell filled me in with a lot of the background – the venom felt towards MK. I made sure that they knew I knew who the enemy were before I stepped in the front door. That was a key part of the process. Before any interview, you need to do your research, get the information you need. I knew what MK meant to AFC Wimbledon.

For the second interview, I think Ivor Heller and Nigel Higgs were there too. Ivor and I got on really well. Stuart and I had a good vibe about the job and how the interview went and we were more or less given the job there and then. It was then that we were given the budget. It was a real accountant's budget. We went back to Stuart's house and then to the pub to look it over.

We looked over it again and again and kept coming to the same conclusion: we really can't do this on that budget. Yes, we wanted the job, but we would be hanging ourselves if we accepted the job on that budget. It was a budget for getting out of the CCL. It was a hideous budget. If you can't be successful, there's no point in taking the job however much you want it. Yes, Wimbledon was a big draw, but we would have been on a hiding to nothing. We could never have attracted the likes of Jason Goodliffe or Jake Leberl or Quinny on that sort of budget.

We were literally seconds away from phoning Erik to say we can't take it when the phone rang. It was Erik and he said: "Look, I got you a little bit more."

By Erik Samuelson (AFC Wimbledon chief executive)

We had sports psychologist John Faulkner working for us at the time and he had a good football pedigree. He had played for Leeds, Norwich and Luton, and he undertook the role Ian Cooke had done when we appointed Dave Anderson during the interview process.

It was a fairly straightforward process: first interviews, second interviews, then a recommendation to the Dons Trust Board.

Loads of great candidates put their names forward. I particularly remember Glenn Cockerill being one of them. He had already applied when I got a call from Lawrie McMenemy. Lawrie asked us to consider Glenn and I said he had already put his name forward. It was then that Lawrie picked up on my north-east accent, so I explained how I had swapped my allegiances from Sunderland and how my boys had chosen Wimbledon ahead of Chelsea. I will remember his reply forever: "Bloody good job they chose Wimbledon as you would never have made CEO of Chelsea!"

There were several good people we interviewed: Glenn; Brian Statham, the Heybridge Swifts manager; Graham Westley, who was unemployed at the time, but went on to manage Stevenage; and the ex-Wimbledon players Dean Holdsworth and Scott Fitzgerald.

There was the political problem with Dean. He had played for Franchise. He was very impressive, and I didn't expect him to be. He talked about his views on the world – the football world – his management strategy, and what he learnt from Sam Allardyce from his time at Bolton. On pure technical ability he came second. If he had been top, it would have made it really difficult for us – we would have had to deal with the whole Franchise thing.

Graham Westley was also impressive. He came in with a CD presentation. He was well prepared and he ticked all our boxes – and he was the only one to do so. But culturally the fit wasn't there. I liked his style, the way he did things, but his views and his personality would not have fitted into AFC Wimbledon.

And so to Terry Brown. I didn't know Terry at all. I had never met him. Everyone else I spoke to was bubbling about him. They said he was the man. It helped hugely that Terry came as a double act with Stuart Cash. Stuart had applied when Dave got the job, so we already knew all about him. We were impressed with him back then, and I admit we had kept an eye on his progress.

When I first met Terry I thought he was quiet and unassuming, but then he took control of the interview and said what he wanted to say. He did it in a nice way, and that really impressed me. I remember sitting back and admiring his style. But Terry also came with a good track record, and he came with Stuart, so he had had a flying start. Was he clearly the best? Well, in the end, yes.

After the second interview we had pretty much made up our minds. And after we made the offer, we revealed the budget. Stuart and Terry didn't say much, but you could see they were troubled by how small it was. I could sense their fears, so we went away looked at the budget again, made a few calls and released enough funds to make them happy to join us.

Hatton's brace brings joy for Brown

Promotion from the Ryman Premier Division was vital. Victory in the opening game was essential to start the season on the right note. And a double for debut boy Sam Hatton delivered just that for new boss Terry Brown.

18 August 2007
AFC Wimbledon 2 Ramsgate 0 Ryman Premier Division
By Terry Brown (AFC Wimbledon manager)

I inherited a very good football team from Dave Anderson. And Dave and I remain good friends to this day. I had some extra names I wanted to add in, and the extra money Erik had found allowed us to get them.

Jason Goodliffe was the first name on my list. He is a leader on the pitch and in the dressing room. I wanted him as my captain. I brought in winners. There was Jake Leberl from Dagenham, who had just won the Conference, and Rob Quinn from Stevenage. Then there was Sammy Hatton, who came in on the back of a recommendation from Jason Goodliffe. And Tony Finn from the Met Police – he was a very talented young winger. We were building a squad that could handle the Ryman League. And then there were the good players who were already there, the likes of Andy Little.

I knew it was tough and we needed to get off to a good start. I remember being told all about Ramsgate. Dave had had his problems against them. I remember being told how big they were. They were absolutely enormous – they all seemed about 6ft 6in tall.

"Welcome," I thought, "to the Ryman League."

Sam Hatton celebrates scoring his second against Ramsgate (Paul Willatts)

By Sam Hatton (AFC Wimbledon player)

The Ramsgate game was big for both me and Terry Brown. It was my debut and Terry's first competitive match in charge of AFC Wimbledon. I'd joined from Stevenage – I'd been there with Jason Goodliffe. I got released and had nowhere to go. It was Jason who recommended me to Terry. I agreed a year contract, and after a month and a half they got me to sign a longer contract, so I must have done something right.

When it came to the Ramsgate match I was really nervous. It was my first proper game of football – I had never played for the first team at Stevenage. Terry helped massively – he's a great man manager. He talked me up. He kept saying that if I played like I had in pre-season, I would go places. "People want a goalscoring midfielder," he said. And that's what I was back then. Clubs would be in for me, he added.

I scored twice in the first half. It was the perfect way to start my Wimbledon career, and it repaid some of the faith Terry had shown in me. Both goals came from random runs, and each time the ball popped out for me and I hit it. The first came after six minutes and the second around half an hour in. It would have been nice to get a hat-trick, but two on your debut isn't bad.

The worst part of the whole day came afterwards. I was named Man of the Match, which meant I had to go up for the presentation after the game. I don't do public speaking – everyone at AFC Wimbledon knows that. But the presentations are an essential part of an AFC Wimbledon match day. It's done in front of the fans in the main bar. I was really nervous – far more so than before the game. I hated every moment of it – I think they got maybe three words out of me!

When I joined AFC Wimbledon I didn't really know what to expect. I knew all about the old Wimbledon, but I didn't know much about the new Wimbledon. Every pre-season the players get a chat from Browny or Erik about the history of the club, for the benefit of the new boys. With some players it gives them extra motivation, while others come to AFC Wimbledon just to play their football. I fall into the latter category.

Personally, it helped me that Jason Goodliffe was here when I joined. He is the best captain I have ever played under, a natural leader. He knows the players who need a word of encouragement and he knows the ones who need to be told what to do. He was a huge help in those early days at AFC Wimbledon.

The victory in that first game was just a tiny indication of what was to come, but it was still just one game – we still had a whole season to go. Browny was expecting us to go up, so I just listened to him.

It was the start of a long journey for me. Everything has moved on from when I first started. We became more professional, we trained every day. There was no drinking in the bar after matches, the old non-league ways had gone. We ate properly – although we were still allowed the occasional Nando's. I never expected to be at AFC Wimbledon for so long. I took each season one at a time, but to be part of three promotions wasn't bad!

Better than Gerrard

Luke Garrard was one of a small number of players who truly typified the spirit of Wimbledon. The combative midfielder had filled most positions, and in November he completed the set by donning the keeper's gloves. For goalkeeper Andy Little, the match signalled the end of his Wimbledon career.

---

10 November 2007
AFC Wimbledon 1 Hornchurch 0 Ryman Premier Division
By Luke Garrard (AFC Wimbledon player)

Terry Brown had come into the changing room a couple of weeks before and asked if anyone had ever played in goal. I played for Barnet's youth team as a goalkeeper from 10 to 14 before moving outfield. Two or three weeks before the Hornchurch game I had started doing goalkeeping sessions. It meant getting to training at six rather than seven, but I enjoyed it, messing around with Andy Little and the young Jack Turner.

At half-time against Hornchurch, Andy Little came in with two fingers pointing one way and two pointing another way. Browny asked if he could continue, and it was a shake of the head. The manager took the gloves and threw the gloves at me – one went one way, the other went another way. I caught them both, and he said: "You'll do!"

I reckon I must have caught 400 crosses and stopped 500 one-on-ones in that game. It was great fun. There was a lot of banter afterwards. To be honest, I had a great defence in front of me and there was little to do. I have loads of pictures of the game. There's a great one of me taking the ball off Jason Goodliffe's head.

In the first half I had played really well and played a part in our winner. I took a quick throw, and Rob Quinn got the ball to Wayne Finnie, who slotted it home. I got the Man of the Match award. But it was just one of those great games at Wimbledon, and I loved it. The fans in the Tempest End were amazing – they cheered everything I did. And I was delighted to keep a clean sheet. I've got to have the best goalkeeping record in Wimbledon's history!

I played just about everywhere during my time at Wimbledon. Dave Anderson signed me as a central midfielder. I'd played there at Bishop's Stortford, mainly because I'd got bored playing in defence and wanted to have more time on the ball. And that was where I was at Northwood when Dave came in for me.

I remember being invited to come down and watch AFC Wimbledon play against Chelmsford in March 2006. I arrived about 1.30pm, and there was already a carnival atmosphere, with thousands of people there. Dave Anderson started to show me round. I stopped him after five minutes and just said: "Let's sign." I would have signed for half the money he offered me. By 2.10, I had been named as a substitute.

I sat on the bench and knew I had made the right decision, Mickey Haswell was playing for Chelmsford then. They were really strong and won, and that was the start of the real rivalry between us and Chelmsford. I made my debut the week after.

There were some real lows – the play-off defeats against Fisher and Bromley. At Fisher we had so many injuries and they were the better side. At Bromley, Dave

Anderson always said from the moment he knew who the referee was that we never had a chance. The whole team learnt a lot from that one – from then, on we were never bad to referees.

No offence to Dave Anderson, but the big catalyst was the arrival of Browny and Cashy: they made us so much more professional. They brought in a new fitness coach, Jason Moriarty. Gone was all the straight-line running – what we did now was more advanced and right at the forefront of developments. We became the fittest club in the league.

And when Terry took over he asked me about my playing history, and I owned up that I'd played as a full-back at Swindon. I played at centre-half, centre-back, right midfield and full-back – and goalkeeper of course – while I was with Wimbledon. But it was as a full-back where I thrived. Terry brought in a new formation that allowed the full-backs to get on the ball and push forward. I loved that – me on one side and Haswell (and then later, Chris Hussey) on the other side given licence to attack.

Those were great times, and I've kept in touch with a lot of the boys from back then. Keds, Sam Hatton, Jake Leberl, Quinny and the rest – it was a special crop of lads, one of the best teams I've ever played for. Not just in terms of ability but in terms of a unit.

On the way to home matches, 11 of us would meet up at Waterloo station – that's absolutely unheard of. Haswell and a couple of others from Essex, Leberl, Quinn and Mainy from Kent, the South London boys, and a couple of us from North London. On the way back it would be a good bet that one of us would have picked up the Man of the Match bottle of champagne, and we'd all be swigging that on the train before hitting a few bars around Waterloo. It was a proper tight-knit group.

Those couple of years I spent at the club were just phenomenal – I got two promotions while I was there and loved every moment. But equally important to the development of the club was when Browny and Cashy realised how important Simon Bassey was to the club. Bass constantly rings all the old boys. I still speak to him regularly now. He's determined not to burn any bridges – but that's part of the whole ethos of the club anyway. Bass is the glue that kept the spirit of Wimbledon alive and the players grounded in the special history of AFC Wimbledon.

But all good things have to come to an end. I got a bad injury, and while I felt physically fit, my ability on the ball just wasn't there. I wasn't doing myself justice. It was Jay Conroy in one week, and then me the next. There was no consistency. It just wasn't working – Terry Brown and I both knew it.

Then Sam Hatton came in. He was phenomenal from the off and has gone on to become a great player. It was then that Terry told me I was third choice at right-back. He wanted me to stay, but I knew I had to move on. I could have gone to Hayes and stayed in the Conference, but I liked what was being offered at Boreham Wood, so I went there. There was no animosity between me and Terry. We'd always been honest with each other, and these things happen in football. If I saw him now, we'd share a beer – I have no doubt about that.

There were some real special moments for me at Wimbledon: the Hornchurch game, the Staines play-off final – I've got all my shirts framed from those games. I love the club. And I love the song: "Luke Garrard, Garrard. He's better than Steve Gerrard. Luke Garrard, Garrard." I remember one of the lads saying they were singing a song about me. I didn't believe it at first, and then I heard it. It was absolutely amazing! The boys loved it in the changing room too. It's a great song – whoever

Luke Garrard grasps the ball against Hornchurch on 10 November 2007 (Luke Garrard)

Luke Garrard prepares to punch clear (Luke Garrard)

Jason Goodliffe embraces Luke Garrard
(Luke Garrard)

made it up is heroic and I'd love to meet them. But I have to let Wimbledon fans into a secret. I am, in fact, not as good as Steve Gerrard – I'm not even good enough to lace his boots!

By Andy Little (AFC Wimbledon player)

It was one of the freak things. The cross came in, I went up for it and I landed awkwardly. I was a bit dazed. I looked for where the ball was and saw we had cleared it, and then the referee blew up for half time.

And as we came off I remember thinking something didn't feel right. I took off my glove and showed my hand to Mike Rayner, the physio. He took one look at it and said: "Bloody hell, I'm not touching that!" He sent the doctor in. The doctor took a look and asked me if I wanted him to try to put my fingers back in. I said yes – and it was bloody agony. Cashy kept asking if I thought I could play, but Mike said I needed to go to hospital.

And then a star was born in Luke. I still see him regularly, and every time he keeps saying: "45 minutes, clean sheet!" To be honest, you couldn't pick a better character to go in goal. He's a cocky little sod, and that helps as a goalkeeper. He wasn't going to be overawed by the moment.

However, my fingers were all over the place. I remember going down to the hand clinic at St George's in Tooting, and I got this big round of applause from all the staff there. They said it was the best hand X-ray they'd ever seen – the fingers were all at right angles to each other.

I had physio for months after, and it took far longer that we all thought it would to get back. A year later I did my cruciate, and that was that. At least I was able to stay with the club and do some coaching.

Bassey signs off with a Casual win at Wembley

In a break from the chase for promotion, AFC Wimbledon were invited to face Corinthian-Casuals at the new Wembley Stadium. The match was to mark the 125th anniversary of the Corinthians. In the early days of international football, the Corinthians had twice provided the full XI for England and it was land owned by the club that would become the site of the national stadium. The Corinthians would later merge with the Casuals. The 2008 friendly was a once in a lifetime experience for two sides that took to the new Wembley turf. It would also be the last time the Dons faithful would see a veteran of the club's CCL days in action.

---

13 April 2008
Corinthian-Casuals 1 AFC Wimbledon 8 Friendly Wembley Stadium
By Simon Bassey (AFC Wimbledon first-team coach)

It was a really special occasion for me: the last time I would lace up my boots to play in the blue of Wimbledon – and at Wembley too! I had retired because of my persistent knee problems, but I made a comeback for this game.

I had a new pair of boots for the game. A mate of mine had given them to me along with a pair of moulded-rubber boots ages before, but then the knee problems kicked

Jason Goodliffe leads out the Dons at Wembley
against Corinthian-Casuals on 13 April 2008
(Jon Main)

Simon Bassey prepares to come on at Wembley
against Corinthian-Casuals (Paul Willatts)

in. The rubber ones I'd used in training, but the studs had remained under my bed unused. They are back there now, but with Wembley mud on them.

It was some feeling to run out on the pitch. But I'll admit I was a bit slower than I used to be. I really enjoyed the whole day. Fair play to Terry for letting me have a game. I'd like to say there was a long speech from Terry about how important it was that I played in the match, but that would be far from the truth. He said: "You'll have a game, won't ya?" And that was that.

You dream about playing at Wembley, so it was a great way to end my playing days. To be honest my knees weren't great, but I couldn't moan, and Corinthian-Casuals were the best sort of opposition I could face. We won 8-1 and that's still the highest ever score at the new Wembley. People may mock it, saying it wasn't the real thing, but it was still Wembley. Nowadays in training a few of us often gang up on some of the lads if they get a bit cocky and say: "So when did you play at Wembley?"

As for the game itself, I have issues with Chris Hussey. He played in my usual position at full-back, so I filled in at centre-back. And he ended up messing up for their goal. He cost me my Wembley clean sheet!

It was just a fantastic day. We had a good win at Ashford Town the day before. We stayed in a nice hotel and got the coach to Wembley. It was great for all the boys – they all had their camera-phones out, recording it all. And I was no different. I've got all the footage on my old phone and there's no way I'm throwing that out.

The day before we had been in Ashford Town's dressing room. It was painted brown and had a five-watt light bulb in it, 24 hours later we were at Wembley. Every player had their own wardrobe and their own shower, and there were something like five hairdryers in there too. Meanwhile, the coaching staff had their own suite with a settee, plasma-screen TVs and everything. It was all a million miles away from Ashford Town.

It was a dream to play there. It really was something special. Every child dreams about it. The pitch may have moved about, but as I came out I thought back to where I had stood for the '88 Cup final, cheering on Wimbledon as a 12-year-old boy.

It was great and I was glad my children were there. I have the DVD. And now, whenever there is a game at Wembley on telly, I tell my son: "Daddy played there." I miss out the bit that it was against Corinthian-Casuals. He will rumble me soon.

By Sam Hatton (AFC Wimbledon player)

It was hard to take seriously. It was amazing to be on the pitch, which was unreal, like a carpet. It was so perfect. It was a pretty one-sided game – we won 8-1.

One of our fans, Mario Rajakone, won a prize draw to come on the pitch and played for us for a few minutes in the second half. There was also around 5,000 fans watching, but at Wembley they were rattling about.

My one abiding memory was my goal. The ball was played out wide to Tony Finn, he picked me out and I headed it in. Everyone wants to play at Wembley. It's every English schoolboy's dream – and then to score, well…

But this felt just like a taster. It made me thirsty to play there again in a serious cup game, in a game that means something.

The route to the final

The capture of Jon Main was to prove vital for Wimbledon as they shot through the non-league ranks. He was the club's most expensive signing to date at around £20,000. Over the next three and a half years he would pay back that fee with dozens of goals. And it was his goals that would propel the club to its first-ever play-off final.

---

29 April 2008
AFC Wimbledon 3 Hornchurch 1 Ryman Premier play-off semi-final
By Jon Main (AFC Wimbledon player)

The night of the play-off semi was pretty special. The crowd was electric, and I was absolutely buzzing. Play-offs bring that out in me. I'd been involved the year before with Tonbridge Angels, so I knew what kind of tension to expect. But the ground that night was something special. There are times when Wimbledon fans really transform a stadium, and that was one of those nights.

Luis Cumbers put us one up early on, and just before the break Jason Goodliffe flicked one on and I volleyed it home. At 2-0 we felt comfortable, but in the second half they threw everything at us. It was non-stop, and they pulled one back with about 15 minutes to go. You could really feel the pressure mount. It was a cup-tie atmosphere.

Then Steve Ferguson cleared the ball, I ran about 15 yards back to pick it up. I was waiting to get clattered, but their defender stayed off me. He gave me a little bit of space to control it. He was some old boy, so I knew I could get past him. I could see Finnie on the right all by himself, screaming for the ball, but I knew I could beat the last man. I got round him and tucked it under the keeper. It was an amazing feeling – it was the 90th minute, and there was no way back for Hornchurch then. I remember being totally out of breath and everyone piled on top of me.

I joined the club in the November of that season. I knew of Wimbledon's interest two weeks before I signed. Tonbridge had just got a new manager, but as soon as I found out about Wimbledon's interest that was it. We may have been in the same division, but Wimbledon were on a different level – they were a big club going places. It was an easy decision.

Everyone knew I was going, but the club insisted I didn't leave until after we had played Wimbledon. And that was really weird. All the Tonbridge players knew what the deal was, and I suspect most of the Wimbledon lads knew as well. There was never a question of me not giving 100 per cent, and I scored. But I remain convinced that Jason Goodliffe was ordered not to kick me!

I wanted to get the goals that would get Wimbledon up. The play-offs were the perfect time to do that, but it was really touch and go whether I'd make it. I had been out for nearly three months with a broken metatarsal. I got the injury against my old club, Tonbridge Angels, back in January that year – I had scored twice but went off after an hour. I was desperate to return for the business end of the season. My aim was to get a run-out in the friendly at Wembley and then be fully fit for the play-offs.

It was a real race to get back in time, but I made it. Three days before the play-off semi I made my first start since the injury – ironically that, too, was against

Jon Main celebrates scoring the Dons' second against Hornchurch in the play-off semi-final on 29 April 2008 (Paul Willatts)

Hornchurch. I scored as we drew 1-1. But that felt like a bit of a warm-up game – both sides had one eye on the play-offs. However, the game proved to Terry Brown that I was back and ready to go. In the end the whole team delivered.

At the final whistle the ground erupted, and afterwards the changing room was buzzing. But it wasn't all done yet. We knew there was still a game to go, and we all had to get the train home and go to work the next day. The celebrations would have to wait until the job was done.

Ten minutes that changed the Dons

Few games in Wimbledon's history were more significant. Twice the Dons had reached the Ryman Premier play-offs and twice they faltered. A third failure could prove catastrophic. The Dons needed to escape the Ryman Premier, but with 20 minutes to go it was looking bleak – Staines were leading 1-0. It was then that Terry Brown turned to Mark De Bolla. It was to prove an inspired substitution. Within 10 minutes, Luis Cumbers had scrambled home an equaliser leaving the stage set for De Bolla's finale.

3 May 2008
Staines Town 1 AFC Wimbledon 2 Ryman Premier play-off final
By Mark De Bolla (AFC Wimbledon player)

With the score level at 1-1 and five minutes to go, Nic McDonnell got fouled and here it was – a free kick about 25 yards out. I'd been on the pitch for less than 10 minutes, but I had been given one clear instruction – take all the free kicks and change the game. Sam Hatton was floating around it, but there was absolutely no question. This free kick was mine.

I just had this feeling – I can't say where it came from – that I was going to score. Marcus Gayle was at the end of the wall, and I told him to move. I hit the ball low and really well, the keeper didn't really see it and I just knew it was going to go in. I wheeled away to celebrate before it had even hit the net.

I'd been suspended and then had been out on loan at Bromley, and this was my first game back. It had been a difficult time, but Simon Bassey kept faith in me. He kept telling me that he knew I'd be involved in the play-offs. He kept on encouraging me, and when it came to it, he said: "Go on and make a name for yourself." And with that strike, with that goal, I suppose I did. I ran straight to Bass to celebrate.

Before the game, we were all buzzing. At the time this was easily the biggest game in AFC Wimbledon's history. Everything the fans had fought for had come down to this. And it got to the players: for the first 70 minutes we didn't do ourselves justice. Staines had taken the lead just before half-time and they must have thought they had the game sown up. They were full of confidence.

I was itching to get on. I felt fresh, and I played well. And then with less than 10 minutes left, Luis Cumbers scrambled the ball in and suddenly we were back in it. The crowd lifted us, and the game was there for the taking. Then came my goal, and at the final whistle it was total mayhem: I remember getting thrown in the air. We could hear the songs booming out from the pitch when we went briefly into the changing room before coming out to get the trophy.

It was an unforgettable experience. I remember being pulled aside to do a TV interview and Jake Leberl pouring a pint of beer over my head – I still owe him for that. The coach journey back to the ground, the huge celebrations there – it was all such a buzz. That all changed a couple of days later when I was released. It was a bit of a come-down.

I'd joined from Ebbsfleet United, where I was in my second season. But I felt I wasn't getting on well with the management there, so I asked to go out on loan. It was then that I spoke to Rob Quinn, and he said he had been talking to Terry Brown about me. I knew the history of AFC Wimbledon, and Quinny sold the club to me. It seemed the right move for me at the time – and looking back, I wouldn't have changed a thing. I would love to have stayed longer.

It all started to go sour a few weeks before the play-offs. At the beginning, I had a good understanding with Terry. He wanted the players to give me the ball as much as possible. He knew I could use it and spread the ball around and score goals as well. And then he brought in Jon Main and changed the formation. Everything was going through him, I was being used on the wing – and I'm no winger. I was being sidelined.

I had no problems with Jon, and we're still friends now. But the writing was on the wall for me. And then Terry dropped me altogether. At that point in my career I just wanted to play games, and I went on loan to Bromley, who were in the league above us at the time. Looking back, I have no hard feelings about it. I am just one player, and players come and go. It was tough for me, but to every fan Terry Brown is a hero, you only have to look at his record – he did brilliantly.

By Terry Brown (AFC Wimbledon manager)

It was a massively important game. Everyone at Wimbledon kept saying: "Please not the play-offs." They were dreading them – especially after the two failures under Dave Anderson, but I was confident.

That whole first season I needed my strong players, my leaders, to get us through and the likes of Jason Goodliffe and Jake Leberl delivered.

I can remember the first few months being very difficult. We were expected to walk away with the league and win every match, but it wasn't that easy. Chelmsford had put together a real quality side with Jeff King in charge, and they had a far bigger budget than we had. Four games in and we were held 1-1 at home to Staines and this chap came out of the crowd. He was livid with the way we were playing and threw his season ticket at me. It didn't get much better, we went five games without a win and I remember being told at Leyton by one fan that I might as well f*** off now the amount of use I was.

Winning didn't seem to make much of a difference either. We thrashed Dagenham 5-1 in the FA Cup and I was still getting endless abuse. "Jesus," I thought, "What the hell have I let myself in for?" Here I am, a brand spanking new manager, taking all this stick. I was getting castigated nearly every week.

AFC Wimbledon is a big club with big ambitions. I loved my time at Aldershot and I was loved by the fans there, but that counted for nothing when I came to AFC Wimbledon. The fans wanted an ex-Wimbledon player in charge, so it was never going to be an easy first year. We had to take an awful lot of flak. The whole year was very, very uncomfortable. It wasn't pleasant and I didn't enjoy it.

And then it came to the play-off final. Staines had played so many games in a short space of time. They were determined to finish above us, but it didn't matter one iota to me where we finished as long as we were in the play-offs. I had been there before with Aldershot, it was all about being fresh and ready.

People talk about Mark De Bolla, but for me it was Sam Hatton who changed the game. He created the first goal and Mark came on after that. Both the substitutions were about getting fresh legs on.

Mark De Bolla was an interesting one. I was umming and aahing about whether to bring him back from his loan spell. But Simon Bassey was in no doubt. He said to me: "Listen Terry, it's a no-brainer. He's a proven goalscorer at this level and he can take great free kicks."

The match itself was touch and go for a long time. The first goal was disputed, but I think it was a fair enough challenge – though I doubt you'll find a single person at Staines who will say the same. But then you always need your bit of luck in big games. They may have finished above us, but in my mind we were always the second best team in the league that season. Then came De Bolla's free kick and that was it.

It would have been a very difficult second year. The Ryman League is all about winning ugly. It's about going away to places like Heybridge Swifts on a Tuesday night and digging out a result.

There was no real plan as far as the club was concerned for that first year. It was all about getting out of that God-forsaken league in whatever way possible.

By Jason Goodliffe (AFC Wimbledon captain)

I've played in an FA Trophy final and a Conference play-off final, both with Stevenage, and both times I played really well and we lost. But nobody will remember that. I wasn't feeling great before the game against Staines and I didn't play that well. Yet it will live long in the memory for both me and the thousands of Dons fans who watched it all unfold.

Marcus Gayle and I were just not as good as we had been in the previous 10 games. We had been a solid unit and in control, but against Staines the game was so open, and that didn't suit either of us or the rest of the team. We really struggled, but just when all looked lost, our superior fitness began to kick in.

Physically they were getting tired, you could sense it all over the pitch. And when we equalised, there was only ever going to be one winner. Yes, it took a special strike from Mark De Bolla, but by then it was all one-way traffic. Personally, I didn't enjoy the game until those last five minutes.

The celebrations afterwards were unbelievable. I was carried off on the shoulders of hundreds of fans. The crowd was all over the pitch. We went back into the changing room, and when we came out to get the trophy the pitch was one big sea of yellow and blue. I remember standing on the presentation table to show everyone the trophy. It was immense.

And then we went back to Kingsmeadow. God knows how many fans were there. It must have been a couple of thousand, but it felt like 50,000, and to get into that sea of people was one big buzz. It was moments like that that made you realise how special this club was and appreciate everything everyone had been through.

I had been at Stevenage for six years, and then I went to York briefly on loan, but

AFC Wimbledon fans prepare for kick-off against Staines in the Ryman League play-off final on 3 May 2008 (Martin Tomlin)

Luis Cumbers dives to level the scores at Staines on 3 May 2008 (Paul Willatts)

Mark De Bolla scores the winner at Staines on 3 May 2008 (Paul Willatts)

Mark De Bolla celebrates his winner
(Paul Willatts)

AFC Wimbledon players celebrate
Mark De Bolla's winner (Getty Images)

Joyous AFC Wimbledon fans celebrate their
play-off final victory over Staines (Getty Images)

AFC Wimbledon manager Terry Brown is embraced after the final whistle of the Ryman League play-off final (Getty Images)

AFC Wimbledon captain Jason Goodliffe makes his way through the crowds with the Ryman League play-off final trophy (Martin Tomlin)

AFC Wimbledon captain Jason Goodliffe is
embraced by the club's commercial director
Ivor Heller (Martin Tomlin)

at the age of 32 I didn't really want to up sticks and move north. I went briefly to Rushden & Diamonds, but that didn't feel right either. I decided that at my age I should look at playing part-time and think about what else I should be doing with my life.

I had worked with Terry for nine years at Hayes. I knew the man and I really appreciated what he wanted to do. I knew all about AFC Wimbledon and what they wanted to achieve. And I wanted to buy into that. When Terry offered me the chance to be captain, I was really grateful – it was a fantastic opportunity for me. And memories like the Staines one made it all worthwhile.

By Marcus Gayle (AFC Wimbledon player)

I felt sick that morning, like I was going to throw up. It was the first time in my career that I'd felt sick and nervous at the same time. It was a hot day, the atmosphere was great, expectations were high. We knew what was at the end of it if we won.

And it was huge for me personally. I knew it was going to be my last game for the club. I had said throughout that year that I would call it a day at the end of the season and concentrate on coaching. So I knew this was it. I had come really close to retiring almost as soon as I started at AFC Wimbledon. My hamstring kept pulling – three times in three months. I thought: "My career at AFC Wimbledon is never going to take off."

I said to Erik, Terry and the physio Mike Rayner: "If this doesn't clear up I don't want to waste your time. I don't want to just be on the treatment table, so let's part ways now." But Mike persevered and found out eventually what the problem was – it was down to the way I was positioning my feet when I was running, and he helped cure it. Without him, I would never even have got going at AFC Wimbledon.

It was great to come back to the Dons. I took to the pitch with all the history behind me, but I never really thought about it. When I looked in the mirror, I didn't see someone famous with all this Wimbledon history, I just saw me. If a tackle came in I took it. But age was catching up with me, and I knew I couldn't keep going for much longer. Staines was it. It was going to be my swansong.

We went one down, and the pressure was on. We managed to regroup a bit, and then Mark De Bolla came on. His goalscoring record at the time was pretty good, and I thought that if he got half a chance, he'd probably take it. And then in the space of a couple of minutes Luis Cumbers scored to put us back in it, and Mark struck a great free-kick to win the match.

My legs were killing me at the end. I was shattered and at the final whistle all the fans were pulling and shoving. A bunch of them were trying to pick me up. It was a tough league, really physical. Not much football was played, but we made it through. The post-match celebrations were amazing. We were up. It was great to finish on a high note.

By Alan Turvey (Ryman League Chairman)

I thought it was very unfortunate for Staines. They had finished above AFC Wimbledon in the league, but that's the play-offs for you. But there were no complaints from Staines afterwards. I remember they said: "Look, we had the home draw and we didn't take advantage of it."

By Nicky English (ex-AFC Wimbledon caretaker manager)

I kept following what was happening with AFC Wimbledon. It was impossible not to. Once you've been involved with the club it gets under your skin. And I have no doubt that those last 10 minutes were the most important in the club's history. Forget the play-off final in Manchester: those last 10 minutes were crucial. I don't think Wimbledon could have coped with another season in the Ryman Premier.

I was getting calls and text messages all the time from Salad, a larger-than-life AFC Wimbledon fan. I remember being told they were losing with 10 minutes to go, and then it all turned round. Mark De Bolla sealed it. I knew Mark from his days in youth football. I was chuffed that it was him who got the winner. Without that strike, who knows where the club would be now?

By Erik Samuelson (AFC Wimbledon Chief Executive)

There is no doubt in my mind that the Staines game was the watershed moment in AFC Wimbledon's history. In my office I have an old Wimbledon calendar on the wall. It's stuck on February 2009. Almost every time my accountant comes in she makes a mistake about some date or other because of it. But I will never replace it or turn it over. That month has a series of photographs from the Staines game.

There's Mark De Bolla scoring from the free-kick, and Mark De Bolla celebrating. There's Luis Cumbers diving in for the header and in the middle is a group of 70 or 80 Dons fans celebrating at the final whistle. My younger son is in the middle of that group, on the phone and waving to me. It was simply the best day in the club's history.

I was very worried for our future if we failed to get promotion that year. I remember turning to Ivor with 10 minutes to go and saying: "Ivor, I think this is slipping away from us." Ivor is normally the most optimistic of people, but he didn't say anything. His silence spoke volumes. He'll deny it to this day, but he was worried.

I was so excited when we scored – I knew that would be the turning point. I remember speaking to our scout Lionel Meade before the game. Staines had pipped us to second place after a phenomenal run of victories in a very short space of time. But Lionel said: "If we are still in the game after 60 minutes, we will win – by then they will be dead in the legs." He was right.

I am not a demonstrative man, everyone knows that. I like to keep things to myself. My elder son was away travelling with his future wife. But my younger son was at the game, and he sent me a simple text at the final whistle that read: "Well done Dad." I was overcome by emotion. I don't do emotion, but that really got to me. It was a sudden release of tension after all the hard work that so many different people had put in over the years.

Later that night I went back to Kingsmeadow. I sat on one of the concrete bollards in the car park, just watching everyone else enjoying themselves, and that made me immensely happy.

I'm teetotal, and after a while I headed home to celebrate. I tucked into a massive plate of ice cream – it's a tradition I have when we win. When we lose, I have to try and cheer myself up, and have a massive plate of ice cream. And if we draw, I think: "What the hell" – and have a massive plate of ice cream.

By Leigh Rumbelow (AFC Wimbledon fan)

When we played Staines Town in the Ryman play-off final, they, as the higher-placed team, were the hosts. The match wasn't segregated as it would have been at Kingsmeadow, and most of the time the banter round the ground was good-natured. Not behind the goal where we were standing, though.

Two supporters, one from each team, had spent the whole match having a go at each other. The nasty stuff kicked off just after we equalised in the 82nd minute. Something was said by one of the two, and it was obvious that they were about to start fighting. My daughter and I looked at each other and went and stood between the two of them, me facing our supporter, my daughter facing the Staines guy. I really can't remember what I said to our guy, but it was something along the lines of us being in with a real chance of winning and did he really want to miss us competing in the Blue Square South.

It really was one the longest two minutes of my life. The bloke was standing there huffing like an angry bull, but I guess he didn't want to risk hurting a woman. He was half watching the match, and suddenly he rushed off yelling and screaming – it dawned on me that we'd scored. I was so intent on stopping the fight that I didn't register what was happening on the pitch. I have no idea what happened to the Staines bloke, but the next thing I knew my much taller and stronger daughter had picked me up and was swinging me round in relief and celebration.

The next season we both signed up for stewarding – which I continue to do. My daughter has taken Security Industry Authority training and now works as a security guard.

By Jerzy Dabrowski (AFC Wimbledon fan)

I have always disliked play-offs. We'd lost in the play-offs the previous two seasons, so I wasn't exactly looking forward to the Staines game. Having no run of the ball in the first 80 minutes didn't help. Losing 1-0 with less than 10 minutes left, all the talk around me was of another year in the Ryman Premier. Then after an error by the Staines keeper, two loanees – Nic McDonnell and Luis Cumbers – combined to get us back on level terms.

But even then, no one was confident until that free-kick from Mark De Bolla. The ground erupted, strangers hugged and tears flowed. At the final whistle it was only the third time I had cried at a Wimbledon game – the FA Cup final in 1988, the Sutton game in 2002 and now, in Staines. The main talking point about that game now is: "What if we had lost – where would we be now?" Thank God we don't have to answer that.

By Matt Breach (Dons Trust Board member)

The Staines play-off final – an emotional rollercoaster that I was resigned to losing right up until the moment that Mark De Bolla hammered home that free-kick. Enjoyable? Yes. Did I dance around like an idiot after the final whistle? Yes. But though I was happy, my overriding feeling was pure relief that we had finally done it.

They say that the darkest time of night is just before the dawn. My lowest moment as a Wimbledon supporter, even allowing for the wretched performances at the end of our Premier League relegation season, was the 90th minute of our home game against East Thurrock United just a month earlier.

Cruising along with a 1-0 lead against a team in the relegation zone who were reduced to 10 men, we conceded a sloppy goal with only three minutes to go. Frantically chasing the game, we then let their sub Ben Boyce have a sight of goal from 25 yards, and the sweetest strike he is ever likely to hit gave them all three points with pretty much the last kick of the game.

I stood watching the tiny knot of their supporters celebrating and just knew we weren't good enough to go up. That feeling of dread grew as our season petered out, and then my mood just continued to darken at Wheatsheaf Lane as Matt Flitter was spared a nailed-on red card and then scored to put Staines ahead.

Cue Cumbers and De Bolla. Relief was finally at hand.

By Niall Couper (AFC Wimbledon fan)

It had been a real struggle to get tickets. I couldn't get to the ground, and there was a limit for away fans which meant there was no guarantee that season-ticket holders would get their mitts on one.

But that was the least of my worries. I had made a promise. To my wife. Camping. New Forest. Two-year-old Amelia in tow and about a dozen friends there too. This weekend was taken. There was no choice. This was AFC Wimbledon. This was the play-off final. This was the biggest game in our short history. I was going. End of. A few calls. Favours pulled. Tickets secured. And a mad dash up the M3 for an absent dad. Was it worth it? Luis Cumbers, Mark De Bolla, the celebrations on the pitch, being there with my brother, the pure joy – God, yeah.

I left with a smile larger than the Cheshire Cat's. It was beautiful. And on the journey back to the campsite the immortal Wimbledon anthem started to play on the car radio. Elvis: "Can't Help Falling in Love With You". Perfect. I can't remember what everyone said to me when I got back to the tent – I was in my own happy world. Thank you, Wimbledon.

Gayle blows into reserve

Marcus Gayle had been a Wimbledon legend and was welcomed with open arms when he moved to AFC Wimbledon. His popularity knew no end at Kingsmeadow, but age had caught up with him. His playing career was over, but now a new path presented itself.

June 2008
By Marcus Gayle (AFC Wimbledon reserve team manager)

I got a phone call shortly after the end of the season, offering me a role with the reserves. "Who else would do a better job than you to inspire the lads?" they said. I was delighted – I didn't hesitate for a moment.

I had learnt a lot during my short time at AFC Wimbledon. It is a special club, and I tried to instil that in my team. I told them to remember who they are fighting for. I told them what the club represents, how much has gone before. "Look at the

shirt you're wearing. It's not just a piece of cloth. It's a history. It's a battle. You are representing the fans, me, the club. The people who founded the club worked hard. They've done a lot. They've sacrificed a lot to put those shirts on your back. You put those shirts on, you repay them."

I constantly reminded them how the club was founded and what it meant to people. AFC Wimbledon is not a social club, it's a club with ambition. It's a club with a journey to complete. A mission to right a wrong.

I'd love to be manager of AFC Wimbledon one day. I'd love to fulfil that ambition. Why not? I'm still learning – man management, motivation skills, tactics and a whole lot of things. But to lead this club one day…

Dons lay down a marker

The Dons' arrival in the Conference (Blue Square) South made many Wimbledon fans a little nervous. Consolidation was on the lips of most, and an away trip to title favourites Newport County on the opening day was a daunting prospect. The result changed everyone's expectations.

---

9 August 2008
Newport County 1 AFC Wimbledon 4 Blue Square Bet South

By Terry Brown (AFC Wimbledon manager)

Over the summer we knew we had to have a clearout. The Conference South is a very different league to the Ryman and we now had time to start planning for a different style of football and we had already scouted a few good youngsters.

Erik never stretches the club financially. He plans for having a budget based on not

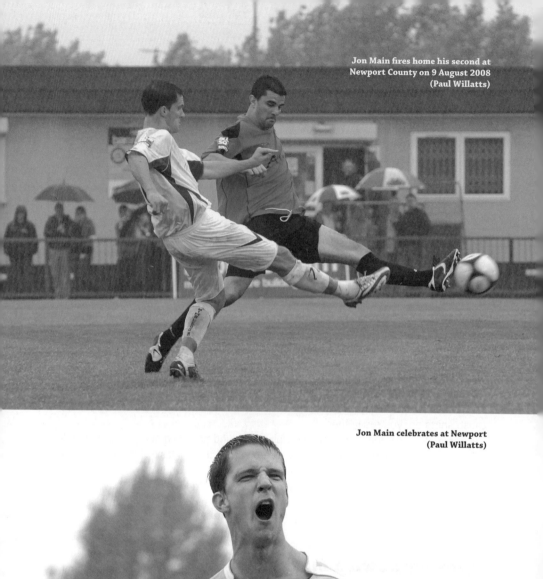

Jon Main fires home his second at
Newport County on 9 August 2008
(Paul Willatts)

Jon Main celebrates at Newport
(Paul Willatts)

having a single cup win, but over the years we have played Exeter and Wycombe in the FA Cup and they may not have been pretty to watch but they were money spinners. And it also helped that Erik, Ivor, Nigel and then later on David Charles were all supporters. So when I said we need a goalscorer, they'd say: "Bloody hell, you do."

And that's how we got the likes of Jon Main, he cost me £20,000, and then later that season Danny Kedwell, who cost us £10,000. I'm not going to have two better signings than that in my life. When we added Danny we created the most potent attacking force in the division. But Newport County was before Danny arrived and it was all about Jon Main. He had been great the year before and pushed us on, and at Newport he was tremendous. They couldn't live with him. He got a hat-trick, but it wasn't all Jon Main. At the back Alan Inns headed and kicked absolutely everything that day. There was no getting past him.

The victory at Newport was the real catalyst for our whole season. We had played beautifully in pre-season, we had been terrific, but that had been on sunny afternoons on beautiful pitches. At Newport the heavens opened; the conditions were horrendous, it was a bog of a pitch. And we absolutely spanked them. We were a different class. I would have been happy if we came away with a draw. Everyone had thought they would be up there challenging. Our supporters came away buzzing and thinking the impossible. We were all thinking: "If that's the best this league can offer then we are not going to be a million miles away come the end of the season."

By Jon Main (AFC Wimbledon player)

It was my first overnight stay as a footballer. You could tell then that we were going places. Gone were the constant trips to local grounds – this was serious.

It's a routine I got used to, but back then everything was new. We met early, got the coach down there, had a light meal, went for a walk and then back to bed. And then breakfast in the morning. I went for it. It was a buffet and it was too hard to resist. I had the full fry-up. Mickey Haswell was horrified. He took one look at my plate and said: "You can't have that!" It wasn't my fault that it was there! I've learnt a bit since then and, after that, breakfast became light scrambled eggs and toast. But this was the first time, and I always love a fry-up. Given the final result, I can't say that it affected me too much.

It was a huge game. Newport were one of the favourites for the league. They had the heritage too – they were a big club. Even though it was the middle of August, it was raining really heavily. Yet I just couldn't believe how many Wimbledon fans were there – there must have been well over a thousand that made the long trip.

I was nervous, really nervous. It was a big step up for me, but it was games like this that had persuaded me to sign for Wimbledon. I remember thinking I had to really turn it on. I had read their programme before kick-off, and gone through all their player profiles in it. They had all seemed to come from League clubs, players from Arsenal and the like. And here was I from Tonbridge.

We were on top right from the start, passing the ball really well. It wasn't all one-way traffic, though – Andy Little had to make one good save from range. I ended with a hat-trick, but it could have been even more. I missed a couple of good chances early in the first half. My first goal was a header – that was quite rare for me. Mickey Haswell whipped the cross in and I remember seeing it coming across and thinking:

"That's going to hit my head." I stretched back to get my head on it. I knew I was going to get a good connection, and the keeper didn't really have a chance.

The second killed the game. It came with just over half an hour to go. Terry had told us just to keep going and doing what we were doing. Kennedy Adjei got the ball around the halfway line. He's all left-footed, but I shouted at him and pointed to where I wanted the ball. And he slid the ball through sublimely with his right. It was an inch-perfect pass that evaded the last defender. My first touch put me in, and I hit the ball with everything I had. It flew into the top corner, 2-0. I remember sliding over to all the Wimbledon fans massed on the big side terrace. It was special.

My third was a bit of a scramble. When Luke Pigden hit the ball back in it bounced through a crowd of players. I checked to see if I was onside and then slotted it home. Tony Finn added a fourth a couple of minutes later, and although Newport pulled one back it was really all about us.

Not bad, I thought. Opening day, new league, new challenges and a hat-trick. I gave the match ball to my nephew Harry. He's got a few now!

On the coach home we were all singing and it was a great feeling. From that moment we realised we could do something. We weren't in the Conference South to make up the numbers. We set the standard that day. That, and the Chelmsford game later in the season, were our markers for everyone else.

A proper first for the Dons

AFC Wimbledon had achieved so much in six years. Victory at Maidstone would secure another first – the debut appearance in the first round of the FA Cup.

25 October 2008
Maidstone 0 AFC Wimbledon 1 FA Cup fourth qualifying round
By Sam Hatton (AFC Wimbledon player)

It was a neat ball played in by Tony Finn. I got in and popped it over the keeper. At first I thought I was offside, but the flag didn't go up and I celebrated.

It's always great to score and get the winner, but the FA Cup is special. It's a great competition. You can travel anywhere in the world and people know about the FA Cup. It's the best cup competition to play in, in my eyes.

And then of course there's the history element of it for this club. And that's where Terry comes into his own. He told us what it would mean to reach the first round of the FA Cup. He reminded us of how special the FA Cup was to our fans. He talked about Burnley away, the Leeds game and of course the 1988 Cup final.

But things have moved on since then. We still have the history, but AFC Wimbledon in 2008 was a different vintage from the Wimbledon of 1988, from the old Crazy Gang who ran around kicking people. We liked to pass the ball around and keep it.

Marcus Gayle had told us a few stories about the antics from the old Wimbledon. But this was a different generation. We were more organised, more sensible – but the team spirit was still there. We were one unit. We had our characters too: Rob Quinn and Jake Leberl, and the joker of the team, Luke Garrard. It was a great atmosphere in the changing room.

Sam Hatton slots home the winner at Maidstone on 25 October 2008 to send AFC Wimbledon into the first round of the FA Cup for the first time (Paul Willatts)

Sam Hatton, centre, celebrates his goal at Maidstone (Paul Willatts)

A mascot's view

Having dispatched Maidstone, AFC Wimbledon were drawn at home to Wycombe, two divisions above the Dons and pushing for promotion to League One. The tie was to be screened live on TV and delivered a memorable experience for a 10-year-old mascot. It's a shame the result didn't.

10 November 2008
AFC Wimbledon 1 Wycombe Wanderers 4 FA Cup first round
By Kyran O'Neill (AFC Wimbledon mascot)

I was so excited to be chosen as mascot for the match as I knew the game was on TV! Jealous schoolmates! As I was playing for the AFC Wimbledon Under-10 A team I had spent quite a bit of time at the club, sometimes in and around the dressing room.

On the day of the game we got to the ground really early. It was packed, so Dad had to drop us off and run back from about a mile away. The place was buzzing. I took a friend from the Under-10s, Tom Wensley.

In the matchday programme I had to mention that Andy Little was one of my favourite players. Dad said that if I didn't, Andy would make me run laps of the pitch at my next goalkeeper training session.

I got changed in the changing rooms with the players and went out for the pre-match warm-up, moving the ball around with the Judge and Pully. I tried to avoid Haydon the Womble because he couldn't pass! Danny Kedwell teed me up for a few shots at goal. When he shot he nearly put James Pullen through the net. Luckily I didn't have to do Jason Moriarty's warm-up.

I saw some of the Wycombe Wanderers players warming up, and couldn't believe how tall some of them were. My Dad told me that their manager, Peter Taylor, had managed England once, and introduced me to him in the tunnel. I didn't think he could be that good if he only did it for one game!

I went back into the changing rooms with the squad. My Dad was in there with Jake Leberl and Jason Goodliffe and the FA Cup, so we all had some pictures taken. I started reading the whiteboards in the changing rooms which showed where to stand at corners and who was taking them. Luke Garrard told me that no one took much notice of them anyway!

I then went into the President's Lounge to wait to be called through to lead out the team – and there we were on TV! The referee came over to say "Hi" and gave me a referee's badge and the FA Respect captain's armband.

Adrian and Aideen, who were looking after me as mascot, organised my Remembrance Day poppy and got me back into the dressing room while Terry Brown, Stuart Cash and Simon Bassey said a few words. What an atmosphere!

Out they went, me being led by Jake Leberl straight towards the FA Cup and the cameras. There was a minute's silence, then we shook hands with the opposition and their captain kindly gave me a club pennant. I then sprinted off and kissed the badge for good luck!

The atmosphere was great. I remember Andy making an amazing save, and

AFC Wimbledon mascot Kyran O'Neill leads the
two sides out for the FA Cup first-round tie betwen
AFC Wimbledon and Wycombe Wanderers

Jake Leberl, Kyran O'Neill, Jason Goodliffe
(Phil ONeill)

Chapter Eight

AFC Wimbledon mascot Kyran O'Neill with Andy Little before the cup tie against Wycombe (Paul Willatts)

Kedwell had a decent game. Maybe if Matt Harrold had played for us and not them it might have been different. But it was all a fantastic experience.

I stayed with the club and even had Andy Little as my coach, but I never mentioned that save! I still watch that match from time to time, and it felt great when as the AFC Wimbledon Under-13s, we played Wycombe Wanderers at Bisham Abbey and beat them 4-3. Dad used the word "revenge".

As a youth team, we've gone from playing the likes of Kew Park and Ditton over the years to Millwall and Queens Park Rangers. It just shows how far the club have come.

By Phil O'Neill (AFC Wimbledon fan and father of the mascot)

I remember talking to some of the other youth team coaches in the run-up to the game and reading all the publicity it generated on the back pages. It certainly led to a lot of chat among the younger players at the club. It was great to be drawn at home against a side riding high in League Two. But couldn't the Football Gods have drawn us against another small fish to give us the chance of another round?

At the time, some aspects of the club's youth-set up were not particularly good, and there were some conflicting attitudes to resolve in the younger age groups. We needed to reflect the growing professionalism of the first team's set-up so that by the time we achieved League Two status the youth set-up could be transformed into a Centre of Excellence capable of producing our own high-calibre players.

Fortunately common sense prevailed, and at Christmas of that season the log jam was gone and the footprint for our Centre of Excellence was established. Jeremy Sauer – who I brought into the club to work with the Under-9s as a skills coach with the philosophy of "touch and technique" in the early years and not "hoof it and win" – is now the club's Head of Youth. From my time in sport I know there is a factor that many people overlook – momentum. When you have it, you use it, and we did. Jeremy, with the backing of Nigel Higgs, pushed on and made sure that the club was 80 per cent ready to be granted Centre of Excellence status.

But back to the game. It was a miserably damp evening under floodlights, but the atmosphere crackled. I remember the Tempest End being full of colour and noise – some of the fans' flags were amazing. This was our first huge TV exposure, and with the momentum we had in the Conference South, would there be a sniff of a replay? Knowing that we would be in the President's Lounge before the game, as our son was the mascot, smartly dressed was the order of the day. I ended up chatting to Trevor Brooking, who obviously looked at my suit and thought my role at the club was more than that of a youth coach. Thanks to Ivor Heller for rescuing Trevor or me, whichever way you look at it!

A couple of things really stood out that night – why, with nothing to lose, was the marauding young Chris Hussey, who had been on fire in recent games, dropped for the steady but far more conservative Mickey Haswell? Tony Finn was dropped too, for a patently half-fit Elliott Godfrey, great lad though Godders was.

It just seemed that we were trying to play to keep the score down rather than play with the line-up that had us flying in the league. When the team was read out I heard a number of fans say that Terry Brown had "bottled it". Jon Main didn't get a decent kick all night – their centre-halves didn't have his pace, but they read the game so well. Tom Davis played the best game I'd ever seen from him at the Dons. It was clear that they were just too strong for us, well set up by Peter Taylor to hit us on the break and we couldn't tame Matt Harrold.

Hussey and Finn came on and the game livened up again briefly, but by then it was already lost. But given that Wycombe were a League side, it wasn't the worst result. And to me the game seemed to be a taster. It was the club's first televised evening game under the floodlights and momentum – my favourite buzzword – was gathering pace. There was an obvious appetite for more of these matches.

When I was sitting with my lad Kyran before the match in the changing rooms, the mood was relaxed, but upbeat and pulsing. Then Cashy and Bass started cranking the tempo up. Little and Judge were reading the matchday programme – a totally different approach to James Pullen's, who you would certainly want in your corner if things got bad. I knew him from my time around the club. He may have been a little hot-headed, but he was a diligent trainer and prepared very well every time he played. I remember the big lump who was there to "guard" the FA Cup, and Danny Kedwell teasing him that he was going to "have it". My money was on Danny!

A few lighter moments during the evening stick in my mind. A few players were telling Hussey that he was dropped because the kick-off was just too late for him. Hussey's riposte was that Hatton was playing. Cue group reply: "Ah, but he's family!" Then there was the anchorwoman from Setanta who really only had eyes for the club's jester, Luke Garrard! How many times was he interviewed that night? Afterwards, I enjoyed a cold beer in the lounge after the game with a couple of the players and staff as we watched Little's save on TV over and over again. And no sign of Luke Garrard anywhere.

Reynolds Gate

On 27 November 2008, the past footballing achievements of Wimbledon were finally secured for eternity. It was the culmination of five years of hard work. Plough Lane was the ground Wimbledon FC had graced for decades, home to fond memories for generations of supporters. The battle to keep it as a football stadium had long been lost, but, through the determination of WISA, as a small consolation the new buildings on the site would honour what had been there before.

27 November 2008
Reynolds Gate, Plough Lane
By Gail Moss (WISA Press and Publicity Officer)

It all began in the autumn of 2003, when the news we'd all been dreading finally arrived. After 12 years as an empty site, which many of us had hoped could still see the return of the Dons, Plough Lane's new owner, David Wilson Homes (DWH), revealed plans for a massive development of nearly 600 flats on the land.

WISA submitted a strongly worded objection to the council. And we soon found ourselves in an unlikely alliance with our old friends, the Haydons Bridge Residents Association (HBRA). The HBRA and the Koppelgate tapes had been one of the bizarre twists in the story of our campaign against Wimbledon FC's proposed move to Milton Keynes.

A key argument of WISA's campaign had been that Plough Lane was big enough to build a new stadium for the club – and we had an architect's design to prove it. This so scared Charles Koppel that he attended a secret meeting with a small number of HBRA members in January 2002. He hoped to encourage opposition to the club's return to Plough Lane, and got most of the 20 or so people there to sign a petition. But the proceedings were exposed, thanks to a tape recording of the meeting made by someone sympathetic to our cause.

Two years down the line, those residents who had supported Koppel must have felt that a football stadium would have been far preferable to the massive housing complex now being planned. HBRA organised meetings and a write-in campaign to object. But because of the need for new housing, the development was always likely to go ahead. So our efforts turned to securing some commemoration of Wimbledon FC's history to be included in the development.

Not everyone believed it was the right thing to do. It was really difficult for our fans. Some wanted to forget the whole thing, some just wanted to concentrate on AFC Wimbledon, and others were still too upset about Plough Lane's demise to get involved. But for most there was still an underlying desire to reclaim our history.

One or two individuals came on the chatrooms saying they'd be happy to contact the developers about commemoration. But it sounded like a job for WISA – we had the clout of a few hundred members, and felt we could get results by acting in a co-ordinated way. And it fell to me to contact the director of DWH responsible for the Plough Lane site.

He was friendly and open to suggestions, but was adamant that naming the buildings after former players was impossible. The address and postcode had already been registered with the Post Office, and the buildings were simply going to be numbered: 1, 3, 5 Plough Lane, etc However, the deal between DWH and Merton Council stipulated that the site should contain a commemorative artwork to be funded by the developers.

Clearly, the best people to advise on this would be our fans. There had also been chatroom suggestions that a time capsule should be buried on the site. The developers were receptive to both ideas. But we still hadn't given up on the names. By now, the flats were getting built, and we were anxious not to miss the boat. In spring 2007 our friendly director suggested that we write to him with our ideas, which we did.

Then DWH were taken over by Barratt, and several senior staff left the company, including our friendly director. We heard nothing for weeks – presumably our letter was sitting in a pending pile on someone's desk. We discovered that responsibility for Plough Lane had passed to Barratt's regional headquarters in Guildford, but the development was being handled temporarily by an outside project manager, who we were assured had us on their "to do" list.

In August 2007, WISA Treasurer Sean Fox and I met Mike Tutill of Bruce Shaw Management Services at Plough Lane, which was still very much a building site. Mike suggested we resubmit our ideas to Barratt, this time to Lynnette St Quintin, sales and marketing director, Barratt Southern Counties. He seemed hopeful we'd get what we wanted.

We couldn't quite believe that, but we were aware that Barratt would probably welcome constructive solutions to what for them was the problem of what to provide as a suitable commemoration for Wimbledon FC. Building the flats had not been popular with locals, and Merton Council was becoming increasingly supportive of both AFC Wimbledon and its past history. So Barratt wanted to be seen to be doing the right thing.

We decided that now was the time to get fans voting on their favoured names for the buildings, choosing from players, managers, directors, even fans, who had played a role in the Dons' history at Plough Lane. We were honest in saying there was no guarantee the names would be used – but we reckoned that carrying out the poll at this stage would give us the best chance of getting our wish granted. From several hundred votes, a dozen names came head and shoulders above the rest. We put them forward, together with potted biographies, to Barratt. This would give them flexibility and maximise our chances of getting at least some of the names used.

The next few months saw a nail-biting wait to see what would happen. Barratt couldn't give us any news, as they were still liaising with Merton Council. Then, on 21 February 2008, we heard from Barratt that the buildings would be named after players Harry Stannard, Lawrie Sanchez and Alan Cork, managers Allen Batsford and Dave Bassett and club chairman Stanley Reed. Furthermore – and this was a bonus – the whole development was to be known as Reynolds Gate, after our legendary striker Eddie Reynolds.

And on 27 November 2008 the naming ceremony took place, with 40 people crammed into the Barratt marketing suite on the corner of Plough Lane and Durnsford Road to applaud speeches by Barratt Homes South East managing director Trevor Sawyer, Mayor of Merton Cllr Martin Whelton, and Sean Fox. Former Wimbledon director Peter Miller, Allen Batsford, Lawrie Sanchez and Eddie's brother Victor Reynolds and his wife Iris from Belfast, along with Eddie's cousin Joan, were all there. Sean read out a letter from Eddie's widow Patsy, now living in Canada, expressing her joy at the accolade for her late husband and thanking those fans who voted for Eddie's name.

As for the names of the houses, they are not only words on a plaque – they are addresses on envelopes, on electoral registers, and on estate agents' listings on the internet. These names may not (yet) be gracing a new ground for Wimbledon's football club, but at least they are now once more part of people's lives on Plough Lane. And we, the fans, made it happen.

Wimbledon legends, WISA representatives and Wimbledon historians gather with the contents of the Reynolds Gate time capsule (WISA)

Reynolds Gate takes its name from the Wimbledon striker,
Eddie Reynolds (Player, 1958-1966),
who took the club to victory in 1963 when it won the FA Amateur Cup.
The home of Wimbledon Football Club for 79 years (1912 - 1991),
the six buildings that comprise Reynolds Gate have been named after
notable Wimbledon Football Club players, managers and directors.

Batsford House	Allen Batsford	Manager	1974 - 1978
Reed House	Stanley Reed	Chairman	1983 - 2000
Stannard House	Harry Stannard	Player & Vice President	1935 - 2000
Bassett House	Dave Bassett	Player, Coach & Manager	1974 - 1987
Lawrie House	Lawrie Sanchez	Player & Coach	1984 - 1999
Cork House	Alan Cork	Player	1978 - 1992

BARRATT
HOMES *built around you*

The plaque at Reynolds Gate on the site of Wimbledon's old stadium at Plough Lane (Gail Moss)

The turning point

Back on the pitch, the race for the Conference South title seemed once again to be a battle between the Dons and Chelmsford City. Chelmsford had become the scourge of AFC Wimbledon. They had run away with the Ryman Premier title the season before and were now threatening to do the same with the Conference South. This was a huge match between the top two, and the result would turn the battle Wimbledon's way.

---

31 January 2009
AFC Wimbledon 3 Chelmsford City 1 Blue Square Bet South
By Jon Main (AFC Wimbledon player)

I was still reeling from the 1-0 home defeat by Chelmsford the year before. That really rankled the whole team, and now we wanted to get one over on them. They were flying at the time and were something like nine points above us, but we were on form too. It was the most crucial game of the season – they were our biggest threat then.

I remember doing an interview just before the match. I said: "Right now I wouldn't want to be playing us, it doesn't matter who you are." I really fancied us to turn them over.

The ground itself was buzzing. The crowd were tremendous. They were always good at AFC Wimbledon, but this time was a little bit special. It was a sellout, and you could feel the difference. They were our 12th man, lifting us up. Everyone feels it – it does gee you up and spur you on. We were up for it and the crowd were up for it.

Our first goal came from a long clearance by James Pullen. Keds flicked it on, and I got beyond the defender and slotted it home. My second came 10 minutes later. Elliott Godfrey set me up. He took it past the keeper and I tapped home for 2-0.

We were in total control and then they got one back. It was totally my fault. Tom Davis was screaming at me to mark Kevin James, but he got one on me. And that made it a lot more interesting! I missed a good chance for my hat-trick. I had a clear one-on-one. The ball came back to me and I managed to get it back to Sam Hatton, but he blasted over.

Then Browny took me off. I was gutted because I so wanted my hat-trick, especially as this was Chelmsford and I wanted to make amends for my mistake. I hate being taken off – no one likes it. And if you look at my record, I reckon about half of my goals come in the last 10 minutes. Some players row with the manager when they get subbed, I didn't do that, but he knew I wasn't happy.

Luckily Tom got a third at the death as they pushed forward, and that killed all the nerves. 3-1 didn't flatter us, but it set us on our way. There were a couple of dodgy games – as there always are – but we were basically unstoppable after that.

By Ben Judge (AFC Wimbledon player)

Chelmsford at home was built up as a massive game, they were flying high and we were on a fantastic run. It was a sellout, and a game I was really pleased to be involved in. I played alongside Jason Goodliffe at the back – I think we only played a few times together.

The atmosphere was really something special. Chelmsford bought a fair few with them. I remember in the first 10 minutes turning to Jason and saying, "Blowing here!" – meaning I was feeling tired already – and he replied that he was too. It just shows how nervous energy can take over even the two most experienced players in the team. Mainy scored two of his typical goals, and we weren't being put under too much pressure at the back.

The second half was a different story. We had to defend for long periods of the game, and personally I would put it down as one of my best performances in a Dons shirt. They got a goal back from a free-kick, which was really disappointing. Then it was real backs-to-the-walls stuff, with us trying to hit back on the break. We had a great chance to finish it off but Sammy Hatton unfortunately missed.

A couple of minutes from the end we cleared another Chelmsford attack. I volleyed the ball away as high and as far as possible (doing myself no justice) and, as luck would have it, it landed straight with Keds. He crossed it, and there were three people who could have tapped it in; after what seemed like an eternity, Tom Davis duly obliged. The place went crazy, and then it was all over and we had a crucial three points.

It was a massive moment in the season which proved to be an amazing one for the club and for me personally – one I'll never forget.

By Martin Fielding (AFC Wimbledon fan)

This game mattered so much because we had been through the agony and ecstasy of the play-offs in each of the previous three seasons, and I don't think any Dons fan wanted to face that prospect again. We wanted to win the Blue Square South outright. Chelmsford had been Ryman Premier champions the previous season, beating us into third place by 12 points and doing the double over us.

Even in January, this really seemed like it would be the championship decider – not least because someone had been calling Chelmsford the "champions elect" on the Blue Square website ever since the start of the season!

We knew it would be a capacity crowd, and my son Michael, his mate and I got to the ground early enough – so we thought – only to find that the Tempest End, for which we had season tickets, was already full and we would have to go into the Kingston Road End. I managed to squeeze the boys to the front of the stand, right behind the goal, so they were guaranteed a close-up view of two typical Jon Main side-footed goals in the first half an hour.

It seemed like we were cruising, but a scrambled goal for Chelmsford on 64 minutes meant that we would face a nervous final quarter. And so it proved, with the tension only finally relieved after an 89th-minute breakaway by Danny Kedwell. His cross found an unmarked Tom Davis waiting to apply the final touch. There is always something magical about getting a late goal in a really tight game to put you two goals up. The Tempest erupted, and the ground seemed to shake even at the Kingston Road End.

Someone grabbed my coat collar, and for a while I was struggling to stay on my feet while making sure the boys stayed on theirs. It was the game that gave most people the belief that we could win our first league title since 2005.

Jon Main hits the first against Chelmsford on 31 January 2009 (Paul Willatts)

AFC Wimbledon's Ben Judge in action (Getty Images)

Jon Main celebrates scoring against Chelmsford in January 2009 (Paul Willatts)

Tom Davis, left, goes crazy after scoring the
crucial third goal against Chelmsford on
31 January 2009 (Paul Willatts)

A late Hall nightmare at Hayes Lane

The Dons had been on a fine run since the victory over Chelmsford, but when the title finally seemed to be within reach, the club developed the jitters. The likes of Hampton & Richmond were sensing blood. The week before, "a helping hand" had seen the Dons slip up at another promotion rival, Eastleigh. And controversy was again going to deny the Dons at Hayes Lane. After Jay Conroy went down injured, instead of returning the ball in a sportsmanlike manner Bromley's Ryan Hall lobbed the Dons goalkeeper to secure a point for the home side.

---

13 April 2009
Bromley 2 AFC Wimbledon 2 Blue Square Bet South
By Lewis Taylor (AFC Wimbledon player)

I remember that goal at Bromley – who wouldn't! It was such a massive game. We were within touching distance of the title – 2-1 up with seconds to go. A win, and the trophy would be as good as ours. And then…

I had been out for about nine to 10 months. It was so frustrating – I had got injured in pre-season and missed everything. Watching the boys week in week out was so painful. As a footballer, all you want to be is out there playing.

Before the game, I was told by the gaffer that I was going to get the last 10 or 20 minutes at most. I really didn't expect to be called into the action, so I'd stayed out at half-time, warming up with the other substitutes as usual. Then Bassey came out and called me in. I was thinking: "What's going on, what have I done?"

Terry told me I was replacing Elliott Godfrey for the second half. Elliott had given us the perfect start with a volley after two minutes, and we seemed all set for a comfortable victory. We were in control. However, at some point in the first half, Elliott had picked up a shoulder injury. I hadn't noticed it. Of all the players on the bench, I was the most obvious replacement for him.

The second half began like the first. We were still in control, and then out of nowhere Ryan Hall levelled it. It must have been their first shot of the game, and it changed everything. Suddenly they were up for it, and it became a real battle in midfield. But as the game wore on we began to reassert ourselves.

I was a bit cross about our second goal – it should have been mine! My shot was going in – no doubt about it – right into the corner. And then Rocky Baptiste got a touch on it. I didn't even see him. He stuck out a foot and nicked it off me, but that's what goal poachers do and I have to live with it. We had banter about that for weeks and weeks after. We would joke about it in training. Every time I took a shot, it would be: "You got on the end of the one at Bromley, but you couldn't get on the end of that."

There were just three minutes left, and we just wanted to close out the game. You always want to concentrate on the game in front of you and focus on that, but it was going through our heads what a win would mean. Three points here and we would be as good as champions. We kept asking the ref: "How long's left? How long's left?"

Then Jay Conroy went down injured, and we kicked the ball out for a throw-in.

That really should have been it. Time was more or less up. Bromley took the throw. The ball went to Ryan Hall near the halfway line…and the rest is history.

I don't think he really meant to score. I think he hit it far more sweetly than he meant to. James Pullen was off his line, and the ball sailed right over his head. Everyone was gutted. Some things you can take in football, but not that. If Hall had scored a blinder, then fair enough. But when it's a goal like that, when it could have cost us the league… It hurt, but what could we do? In hindsight they should have allowed us to walk one in, but in the mayhem that followed it didn't happen. We couldn't start a fight or anything like that, we had to accept it.

Certain players you come up against time and time again, and Ryan Hall was one of those. The two of us never saw eye to eye before that, and this didn't help.

Now we knew we had to go to Hampton the week after and get a result.

By Terry Brown (AFC Wimbledon manager)

I recently gave a talk to a referees' society and before I went they asked me to name the two worst decisions I have ever experienced in football: both of them came at the end of that season in the Conference South.

The first was away at Eastleigh, who were chasing for promotion as well. And their captain Tom Jordan – a giant of a man, he must have been six foot six – jumps up and with his arm way above the crossbar bats the ball into the net. It was as clear as day, and you would have to be blind or just too old to referee not to see it. The referee knew he had made the biggest clanger in his life and had about 3,000 people berating him for it. So it was no surprise he took himself off. When you see it on the video it's simply embarrassing. I can't see how the referee or his assistant didn't see it. It was blatant cheating and what was even more embarrassing was the way Jordan celebrated. It was more blatant than Maradona in '86, yet he celebrated as though it was him who just won the World Cup. We lost 2-1.

And then there was Bromley. It was the worst display by a management team I have ever witnessed. Mark Goldberg, the club's owner, was a complete disgrace.

Now I know Ryan Hall very well. He's a very talented player. He's got a great left foot and he smashes the ball into the top corner. He could try and do that 100 times and he'd be lucky to do it once, but it was the reaction afterwards that was a disgrace.

He was jumping about like an idiot. It was shocking. I was dumbfounded. Credit to the referee and his staff. They all tried to get the numskull in the dugout to change his mind and allow us to walk the ball in, but he was a brain-dead idiot.

In the ensuing 10 minutes, I asked their captain to do the honourable thing, but he said no. Then I asked the assistant manager and he said no too. Then there was Goldberg. He was on crutches or something like that after a recent operation and he was cock-a-hoop with the goal. I told him in no uncertain terms that he was an utter disgrace, but he wouldn't move.

There's no doubt that their actions that day tarnished the reputation of Bromley. It brought their club into disrepute and I still don't like Bromley to this day.

I wanted to knock someone out but, to be honest, I was more worried about Simon Bassey, Dwane Lee and Luke Moore. Dwane had lost it and I wouldn't want to be on the wrong side of him in a fight. We had the crunch game against Hampton next up and we had to make sure it didn't end up in a mass brawl like Bradford against Crawley. It would have meant nothing to Bromley, but it could have destroyed our season.

I'm lucky, I'm in my fifties and I had enough sense not to get involved and I dragged other people away.

We used it to motivate our players. Our players were so keen to right that wrong. In the end all Ryan Hall's goal did was delay the celebration. We were never going to lose to Hampton or St Albans after that.

By Ivor Heller (AFC Wimbledon commercial director)

I'd "had problems" at Eastleigh, after Tom Jordan punched the ball into the Wimbledon net and the goal was allowed. So I was on my best behaviour at Bromley. I was sitting with Dickie Guy – and, after that goal by Ryan Hall, it was his turn to lose the plot. Completely.

There were fans behind us watching through the window that separated our box from the bar. And when they saw how disgruntled we were, they started banging on the glass – and that was too much for Dickie. He started gesticulating at them, and if he could he'd have waded in and there would have been fisticuffs.

My entire job then was to stop him, calm him down and make sure none of our other people got into any problems of the physical kind. It was the worst atmosphere I have ever experienced in a directors' box. After the final whistle, I stayed for no more than a minute. Even Erik, who is normally the dignified one, didn't shake hands with anyone afterwards.

By Dickie Guy (AFC Wimbledon president)

I don't think I'll ever go there again. I felt we were cheated. It was not the right thing to do, but the referee was powerless to do anything about it. It was down to their management, simple as that. They should have let us walk the ball in. To do nothing – that for me was just cheating. And the guy who scored took great pleasure in celebrating, along with most of his team-mates.

I was incensed about it. I was at fault – I should not have let those people bring me down to their level, but I did. Since then I have promised myself I won't let it happen again. You should never get dragged down to that level.

By Matthew Couper (AFC Wimbledon fan)

If I never go to Hayes Lane again it will be too soon. We lost our unbeaten record at Hayes Lane – although that was against Cray Wanderers. There was the battle against Coney Hall there. And we had also lost a play-off semi there a couple of years earlier. It's just a place full of bad experiences, and this just about topped the list.

My natural belief is that in every game we play we are always in a position to mess things up, so even at 2-1 up with a few minutes left I thought we could still throw it all away. I expected a bad back-pass or a momentary lapse of concentration. But I certainly didn't believe we'd get cheated out of a win.

One of our players goes down injured. We put the ball out so he can get attention. They take the throw-in. All our players stand off. Their player collects the ball. Does he return it to us or kick it out of play? No. Instead, he spots Pullen off his line – he would be, because he wouldn't have been expecting what happens next – their player lobs him from all of 30 yards. A pretty spectacular goal, yes, except it's not quite right, is it?

Elliott Godfrey is squeezed by Ryan Hall, right, at Bromley on 13 April 2009 (Paul Willatts)

AFC Wimbledon President Dickie Guy, who was enraged by Bromley's behaviour (Terry Buckman)

AFC Wimbledon supporters react in disgust after Bromley's Ryan Hall's controversial late equaliser on 13 April 2009 (Paul Willatts)

A fuming James Pullen, in red, is pulled back by Terry Brown after the controversial equaliser at Bromley (Paul Willatts)

AFC Wimbledon frist-team coach Simon Bassey vents his displeasure at Bromley (Paul Willatts)

But the bit that really gets me is they see no fault with their actions. There's no offer for us to walk the ball into their goal, and that's when people start getting angry. Angry in a Wimbledon way, that is. No one storms the pitch, or punches one of their players, because we're just not like that. But we're pretty p***ed off, and their players are so damn smug. Unsporting, cheating, "not in the wider interests of football" are words that spring to mind.

I still check Bromley's results to make sure they're not getting any closer to us, because I couldn't face another trip down there!

The Main event

The race for the title became tighter in the final few weeks of the season. Chelmsford had faded, and Eastleigh and Hayes & Yeading had emerged as serious challengers. But it was near-neighbours Hampton & Richmond who provided the stiffest opposition. Defeat for the Dons against them would have put the two sides level on points with a game to go. A draw and, with the Dons' superior goal difference, the title would be as good as theirs.

18 April 2009
Hampton & Richmond 1 AFC Wimbledon 1 Blue Square Bet South
By Dickie Guy (AFC Wimbledon President)

I honestly thought I was going to have a heart attack from the time I took my seat. My heart was banging, and I could feel it the whole time right through the game. I have never felt like that before. I have always been excited about games, but at Hampton & Richmond my heart was pounding from the moment I sat down until afterwards in the boardroom when I calmed down a bit.

By Terry Brown (AFC Wimbledon manager)

The Hampton game was a very nervy affair. I dropped Jon Main for Lewis Taylor. Mainy's form had gone off the boil and I wanted to change things around. Almost straight away their big lump of a centre back Dean Wells tried to decapitate Lewis – and I thought: "Right, I can see how they are going to try and play it." Despite that, we tried to play football. We played three up front and battered them. Lewis was absolutely electric and their goal came against the run of play. We lost concentration at a corner and that was enough. They had a good chance to make it 2-0 shortly after, and that's when I turned to Jon Main.

When you have a player like Jon Main to take off the bench anything is possible. Wimbledon fans hold him in such high regard and I was delighted that he got the crucial goal. I remember it really well. There were some fans saying it was just like Bromley, but I didn't see it like that. Their bloke has tried to smash Chris Hussey into Row Z, he misses and takes out his own man. As far as I was concerned, I thought: "You paid the price for trying to wipe our boy out."

And it was great that Jon got the decisive touch. He had a bit of the Crazy Gang about him. You wouldn't be surprised to hear that he had been out on a Friday night, that was just Jon Main. The likes of Ben Judge, Andy Little and Alan Inns they all liked a good drink after the game. And all of them were vital to AFC Wimbledon's success that year.

But there's no doubt AFC Wimbledon wouldn't be where they are now without Jon Main. His goalscoring record was absolutely phenomenal. He deserves all the plaudits he gets.

It was a fantastic night in Wimbledon Village. It seemed like the entire crowd were out there with us celebrating and we would do it all over again a few days later after the last game of the season against St Albans.

The players really enjoyed playing in the Blue Square South. Some of the games were really good games of football, we were getting the ball down and passing it. We were playing football the way I wanted it to be played.

By Jon Main (AFC Wimbledon player)

Yes, there was a slight element of controversy about our goal, but we'd had our bad luck against Eastleigh and Bromley. There were only a couple of minutes left and we were losing. I saw the two players down injured, but the referee waved play on. Chris Hussey threw the ball to Keds, and he crossed it to me. My first thought was to flick it to the other corner, but I changed my mind. The keeper didn't stand a chance.

Everyone went mental – the crowd and the players. But it just didn't sink in. I just kept thinking there's still one more game. It kept going round and round in my mind – there's another game to go.

The TV cameras were there, so it wasn't going to be an ordinary game. I was really disappointed not to be starting the game. I knew on Tuesday I wasn't going to be starting. Terry had set up training in a 4-3-3 and I don't fit into that. I was going through a dry patch at the time, but it was still disappointing. I was still the club's top scorer.

Francis Quarm gave Hampton the lead just after half-time, and that made it even more frustrating. I wanted to be out there. I wanted to make a difference. Terry threw me on with just under 20 minutes to go. He said to me: "Just play and score goals – that's your job." I was pumped up and I managed to get the chance.

It only really sank in at the Dog and Fox afterwards, seeing a thousand fans spilling out onto the streets and singing loudly. The whole team were there (except Danny Kedwell, who had to do something else that night), celebrating and celebrating.

It was a fantastic night. I didn't spend a penny all night. I remember waking up on the floor of some fan's kitchen with Alan Inns. That night was one of the best of my life. It was just unbelievable.

By Simon Bassey (AFC Wimbledon first-team coach)

That night in the Dog and Fox will live in the memories of all the players and fans who were there. They were a great squad, and they deserved it.

But the way we had scored really bothered me. It didn't feel right with those two guys down injured. We'd been on the wrong end of the incidents at Eastleigh and Bromley, but that didn't make it right. Terry was jumping up and down and going mental. The whole place had gone mad, but I just sat down and said: "I ain't sure about that." It put a little doubt in his mind, but the goal stood and we were up.

Promotion... Jon Main's header hits the back of the net to get the goal that more or less secures promotion to the Conference (Terry Buckman)

Jon Main celebrates his vital goal at Hampton & Richmond on 18 April 2009 (Getty Images)

Dons fans celebrate at Hampton (Getty Images)

AFC Wimbledon's Jon Main pushes through the crowds at the final whistle at Hampton (Getty Images)

Kennedy Adeji joins in celebrations
(Getty Images)

By Mark Lewis (AFC Wimbledon fan)

Every football team has its own bogey opponent – someone they just cannot beat, no matter how well they perform or how lucky they are. For a few seasons in the Ryman Premier and the Conference South, it seemed that Alan Devonshire's uncultured Hampton & Richmond side had the Indian sign on Terry Brown's Dons. A run of wins for Hampton left Wimbledon looking nervously over their shoulders as they travelled to the Beveree late in the season needing a positive result.

It was perhaps no surprise to see the Dons largely freeze on the pitch, despite the warm weather. In the closing minutes the home side were inching to a deserved victory, until two of their defenders collided with each other and went down injured. Seconds later, as I am taller than the average bear, I was probably one of the first of many Dons fans squeezed in behind the goal to see that the only place Mainy's flicked header was going was into the top corner.

Goodliffe's perfect finale

Jason Goodliffe had been an inspirational captain for AFC Wimbledon. His final game was to be the perfect send-off.

25 April 2009
AFC Wimbledon 3 St Albans City 0 Blue Square Bet South
By Jason Goodliffe (AFC Wimbledon captain)

I scored four goals during my two seasons at AFC Wimbledon. But it had been a long time since I'd scored – the first three were in my first season. This one, my last, came in the last minute of my last Dons game. It was a nice moment for me, a fitting end to a great season and a great time.

It wasn't a classic strike. We were 2-0 up at the time. The ball went out on the right-hand side, and I started to head up the pitch. I can't remember whether it went out for a corner or not, but instead of heading back I just kept going forward. The ball was eventually whipped in by Tony Finn, and it went through two or three players. I got my knee on to the ball and it went in.

It wasn't a classic – far from it. It was all about being in the right place at the right time. But I didn't care. For me it was perfect. It was great to score right in front of the Tempest End. The camaraderie and the team spirit at Wimbledon were great. All the players swamped me, they were just as glad that I'd scored as I was. Elliott Godfrey, Sam Hatton, Danny Kedwell, everyone – they all knew what it meant to me.

After the Hampton game, everyone was celebrating. But the devil in me couldn't quite let go. Mathematically, we weren't champions. What if Hampton did score 13 and we lost?

It was 0-0 at half time against St Albans and we were looked tight. I shouted at a few people to turn on the style and show everyone what we were capable of doing. I wanted us to give everyone in the ground a good season's send-off. And in the second half, we were different. Kennedy Adjei scored a good goal early on and that lifted everyone. Gone were any fears of the mathematical nightmare.

Kennedy Adjei opens the scoring for
AFC Wimbledon in the final game of the
Conference South season (Martin Tomlin)

AFC Wimbledon captain Jason Goodliffe scores in the
final minute against St Albans on 25 April 2009. It was
to be his last game for the club (Paul Willatts)

Jason Goodliffe lifts the Conference
South trophy (Martin Tomlin)

It was brilliant afterwards. The game at Hampton in most people's eyes was the winning game – and the atmosphere that night in Wimbledon was unbelievable. But as a captain, to lift the championship trophy in front of your own fans – that's a special feeling.

I had my son with me, and after the game they read out the names of each of the players one by one. As captain I was last to go up, and I remember turning to my boy and saying to him: "Remember this moment, son, remember this day. These don't come along very often." It was special.

I was realistic enough to know that it was going to be my last game for AFC Wimbledon. I had missed the first 10 or so games with an injury I'd picked up in pre-season. Alan Inns and Ben Judge were playing really well, so I had to bide my time. I kept on picking up niggles and the whole season was stop/start. Time was catching up with me. But there could be no better way to stop the clock than that win over St Albans and everything that came with it.

The battle of AFC Wimbledon

Off the pitch, matters were not quite so rosy. And in the close season, an argument over the club's desire to move back to Merton exploded. By 2009, AFC Wimbledon had been at Kingsmeadow for seven years. The arrangement had become cosy, and the Dons Trust Board was edging towards a stronger commitment to the ground. That angered WISA, and led to acrimony on the Board and the resignation of the Dons Trust chair.

18 May 2009
By Simon Wheeler (WISA chair)

The Dons Trust Board had been presented with a draft stadium review document that put forward a number of options, and the Board passed it unanimously. But we were far from happy. It was far too Kingston biased, and all the feedback I got showed that supporters and WISA members felt the same.

WISA has a long-standing commitment to ensure that the long-term future of the club lies in Merton and nowhere else. We believed (and still do) that we need a purpose-built stadium in our home borough. We couldn't stand by, so we sent a strongly worded letter. We welcomed the idea of a review, but we wanted the Dons Trust Board to look at it all again.

It ruffled a lot of feathers and led to some heated exchanges. Some Board members changed their minds and called for a rewrite of the review. David Cox, the chair of the Board, resigned. He was very upset by it all. He spoke of all the possibilities at Kingsmeadow.

The review changed when it was finally presented to a Dons Trust meeting, at which it became clear that the supporters backed a return to Merton. For WISA this was monumental. Several people had questioned the need for an independent supporters' association at a fans-owned club. The Stadium Review was a clear example of why WISA remained important.

From the very start of AFC Wimbledon the biggest issue was always going to be our stadium.

Wimbledon's former home in Merton, Plough Lane
(Getty Images)

Chapter Nine:

Some things money can't buy

THERE ARE SOME THINGS MONEY CAN'T BUY

Jon Main fires home from the penalty spot to level the scores against Luton Town on 8 August 2009 (Getty Images)

Jon Main is congratulated by his team-mates after his goal against Luton on 8 August 2009 (Getty Images)

Dons overcome nerves to hold Hatters in debut

Promotion from the Conference South put Wimbledon back on the national stage for the first time in seven years. First up was Luton Town, a team the Dons had met numerous times in the top flight two decades earlier. Luton were now in the Conference, failing to survive in League Two after being deducted 30 points by the FA for irregularities. The media interest was immense and the Dons went into the match as huge underdogs.

---

8 August 2009
AFC Wimbledon 1 Luton Town 1 Blue Square Premier
By Steven Gregory (AFC Wimbledon player)

I had just joined from Hayes & Yeading. Hayes were in the same league as AFC Wimbledon and I had played against the Dons a couple of times. I'd had a good season, and I scored twice in the play-off final. It turned out that Browny and Cashy were at that game, so I must have done something right. I loved my time at Hayes but, given the difference in size of the two clubs, it didn't take me long to make up my mind. Even then I didn't quite know what sort of club I was joining.

Early on we had an evening on the history of the club. There were a number of us who had joined at the same time, and this was a key part of getting to know what the club was all about and, most importantly, how much it meant to the fans. AFC Wimbledon is a special club and that night you really got to know it. It's the only club I know of that does something like that. It's brilliant. It makes you realise what it truly means to pull on the yellow and blue shirt.

My first competitive game for Wimbledon was against Luton in the Conference. It was the biggest game I had ever played in, and I think that went for most of the team too. It meant a lot to the club to be back on the national stage. The match was originally going to be shown on Setanta, but they had hit financial difficulties and had to pull out. However, there was still a huge amount of interest in it. It was eagerly anticipated.

Coming up to the ground, I could see that the place was awash with yellow and blue. It was one of those games when you could sense the excitement in the air, and you just wanted to get out on the pitch. To be honest, I was happy just to be picked for the game. I'd had a good pre-season, but there was still no guarantee I would start.

For the first half-hour we couldn't string a pass together and Luton were all over us. I think the whole occasion had got to us, and it was no real surprise that we were a goal down at the break. But the second half was different. Terry got hold of us. Jon Main levelled with about 10 minutes to go, and we could have nicked it at the end. But before the game, we would have taken a point.

Luton had been given their points deduction because of the actions of a former regime, so they too had a sense of injustice – they felt they shouldn't be playing Conference football. They were firm favourites to go straight back up. And we had just come up – so to get a point was pretty good.

Living with the Lions

AFC Wimbledon continued to hold their own in the League, but it was the FA Cup that caught the imagination of the Dons' supporters when they were handed a mouthwatering first-round tie at high-flying Millwall. The final scoreline was an injustice. AFC Wimbledon, barely six years old, held their own for 80 minutes against a club on the brink of a return to the nation's second tier of football. It gave the Dons a new belief in what could be – and it was an unforgettable night for Lewis Taylor, who scored the Dons' goal.

---

9 November 2009
Millwall 4 AFC Wimbledon 1 FA Cup first round
By Lewis Taylor (AFC Wimbledon player)

It was a sweet goal. We were 2-0 down at the time, but we were giving it a go and we felt we still had a chance. Derek Duncan sent out a strong ball to Danny Kedwell. Danny was storming down the left. I know his game well, and I ran round the back of him. Danny spotted me and found me with a neat back-heel. I took one touch and went for the far post.

That gave me a massive, massive buzz. It's every boy's dream to play in the FA Cup. I'd played for Horsham against Swansea before, but Millwall away was as big as that at the time – and to score as well! That was a bit special, especially in front of all of our fans.

At 2-1, most of us thought we were getting back at them. Then they brought on a sub and that made the difference. In the end, fitness told. We were in bits. We had to keep pushing, but we ran out of steam and they hit us on the break, twice.

Everyone knows that in football, fitness is everything. We were still semi-professional. They were full-time, and that was the difference. But let's not forget that, for 75 minutes, we were as good as them.

By Steven Gregory (AFC Wimbledon player)

I thought we played really well in the game. It was about the toughest tie we could have got. Millwall were flying in League One, and we matched them. We held them at 0-0 for 45 minutes. The final scoreline was no reflection of the game. Until the last couple of minutes we were still in it. They got two late goals that flattered them, we knew it and they knew it. But it gave us belief in how good we really were.

It was a great experience. The Dons fans that night were unbelievable. There was well over 3,000 of them there filling one end. And the noise – they were so loud. It was the biggest match I had ever played in at the time, and easily the biggest stadium, and I think that was the same for most of the lads.

We had been immense in the first half. Alan Inns, Paul Lorraine and Brett Johnson were stopping every attack that was coming through, and in the midfield we were winning the battles too.

But they weren't near the top of League One for no reason. We made one mistake and they punished us. And then with about 15 minutes left we were all caught ballwatching, and it was two. We were gutted – it didn't reflect what was happening.

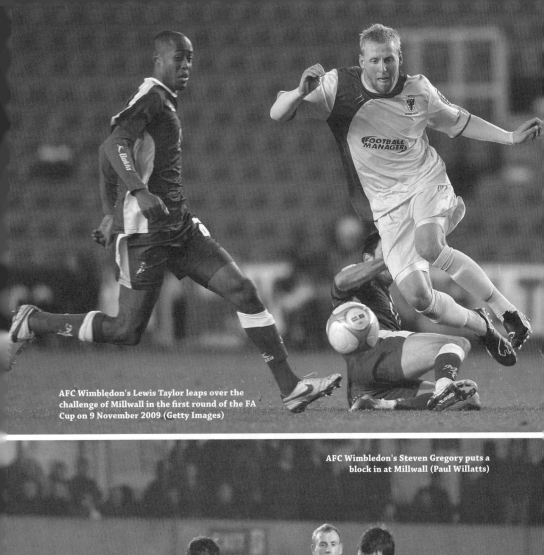

AFC Wimbledon's Lewis Taylor leaps over the challenge of Millwall in the first round of the FA Cup on 9 November 2009 (Getty Images)

AFC Wimbledon's Steven Gregory puts a block in at Millwall (Paul Willatts)

AFC Wimbledon fans fill the North stand at Millwall (Paul Willatts)

When Lewis got one back, I honestly thought we would kick on and get the replay. It was a neat goal too. Keds' neat back-heel found Lewis, who fired home. But at 2-1 down in a cup tie you have to go for it. As we pushed forward we left gaps, and that was that.

Unveiling the "Landmark"

Back at Plough Lane, early 2010 also saw the unveiling of the first public statue to honour the achievements of Wimbledon.

---

22 January 2010
Reynolds Gate, Plough Lane
By Gail Moss (WISA press and publicity officer)

Reynolds Gate, the new development on Plough Lane, had been completed, but there was still the issue of what the commemorative artwork on the site would look like.

The time capsule was already sorted. It would contain an array of items including a shirt from the 1989-90 centenary season, a Wimbledon scarf, pin badges, a copy of the Centenary Book, programmes from the 1988 FA Cup and 1963 Amateur Cup finals, an FA Cup final DVD, DVDs containing highlights of other memorable

The Landmark used as a shrine for Wimbledon fans (Gail Moss)

The Landmark outside Reynolds Gate on Plough Lane (WISA)

matches, and photographs of the ground and teams. But that would be buried without any reference point. The artwork would be something more permanent and more visible.

AFC Wimbledon supporter David Miller put us in touch with a contact at the Wimbledon College of Art, where he'd been a governor. The college, now part of the University of the Arts London, plugged us in to the Engine Room, its specialist unit advising on community-related artwork projects. And in early November 2008, WISA chair Simon Wheeler and I met with the developers Barratt and Engine Room staff to start the process.

At that meeting it was decided that there should be two sculptures, one representing Wimbledon FC's history at Plough Lane, the other celebrating local history. The Engine Room team were very sensitive to what we wanted -a fitting landmark outside the development that would serve as a shrine-like memorial for fans. It was the final piece in the jigsaw. Sam Burford, the sculptor, spent weeks with club historians Mick Pugh and Dave McKnight, and by June 2009 Sam had his prototype. After a few modifications it was all go.

Then on a cold and wet day in January 2010, under a flimsy gazebo erected between the blocks of flats in the new development, the sculpture, named "Landmark", was formally unveiled by Merton's Mayor, Cllr Nick Draper. Present at the ceremony were Roy Law and John Martin, from the 1963 FA Amateur Cup-winning team; Jeff Bryant, who scored our first goal in the Football League; Dickie Guy and Ian Cooke; John Scales, from the 1988 FA Cup-winning team, and Mrs Maureen Batsford, the widow of former Wimbledon manager Allen.

Those huddled under the gazebo listened to a poignant speech by Mick Pugh, in which he relived his memories of the Dons' finest triumphs and expressed the anger over the sale of the site, and the subsequent betrayal of the club and its fans and the theft of its league place. But he thanked Barratt for their sensitivity towards our wishes for permanent recognition, when other developers could well have ignored us. He also pointed out that Merton Council had been more supportive than ever in our last few years as AFC Wimbledon. This indeed was a community coming together.

The sculpture, cast from molten bronze, was made by the Chelsea College of Art & Design Foundry, with the finish from Benson-Sedgwick Engineering, some of whose staff were Dons fans and kindly sponsored it. The sculpture itself has a separate design on each face. The side facing Durnsford Road shows the double-headed eagle from the Wimbledon FC crest inset in stainless steel, which reflects the light and can be clearly seen by pedestrians and passing traffic. On the other side is a minute-by-minute timeline of the events of the 1988 FA Cup Final.

Eighteen months later, the sculpture became a shrine after our historic promotion to the Football League, covered in shirts and scarves from Wimbledon, both FC and AFC.

Kedwell upsets the Hatters

AFC Wimbledon had begun life in the Conference National overwhelmed by the whole experience. But five months in, the nerves had gone and victory at Luton gave the first hint of what was to come the following season.

---

20 February 2010
Luton Town 1 AFC Wimbledon 2 Blue Square Bet Premier
By Danny Kedwell (AFC Wimbledon captain)

It was a great game. They got off to a flyer and were all over us. It was real back-to-the-walls stuff, and then against the run of play we nicked one. Nathan Elder got it. I'm not quite sure how – I think it came off his bum, but it sneaked in.

And then it was us in the ascendancy even after they levelled. I didn't want that first half to end – we were buzzing. At half-time Terry Brown just told us to keep playing the way we had. Terry believes in his players – he really gets the best out of them. And we went out determined to get the three points.

I remember getting the ball on the halfway line, and the game opened up for me. No one came to me, so I just kept running and running. The keeper came out, I just caught the ball perfectly and it flew into the top corner.

It was so significant. When we had played them at home in the first game of the season, we had all come off the pitch exhausted and thinking: "Bloody hell, they were a good side and they are going to win the league." This result really gave us a lift – it showed how far we had already come.

From a personal perspective, at the time it was the most important goal in my Wimbledon career. There was only going to be one that would beat that, and that was to come 15 months later at the City of Manchester Stadium from the penalty spot.

AFC Wimbledon's Danny Kedwell, scorer of the decisive goal at Luton on 20 February 2010 (Martin Tomlin)

AFC Wimbledon's Jon Main, who never truly fulfilled his promise in the Conference (Andy Nunn)

The step up to professionalism

As the Dons climbed up through the leagues, inevitably conversations on the terraces and behind the scenes turning increasingly to when the club would finally make the decision to turn fully professional. The key vote came in mid-April 2010. The announcement, however, was a bungled mess.

---

13 April 2010
AFC Wimbledon 0 Grays Athletic 2 Blue Square Bet Premier
By Erik Samuelson (AFC Wimbledon Chief Executive)

The decision to turn professional was one big PR disaster. It was a Tuesday night, and we had just lost badly at home to already-relegated Grays Athletic. We were sixth at the time, and the defeat more or less killed any lingering hopes that we would make the play-offs. Terry Brown was fuming. He came out to the press and blurted it out: "It'll all be different next year when we go full-time."

That would have been OK but for the fact that 24 hours earlier Terry had been told in no uncertain terms to keep the decision to turn professional to himself so that we could announce it with an appropriate explanation. "Erik, Erik," he said afterwards, "I f***ed up." He was crestfallen. He knew he wasn't supposed to have said anything, but in the heat of the moment he had forgotten. I don't think it would have

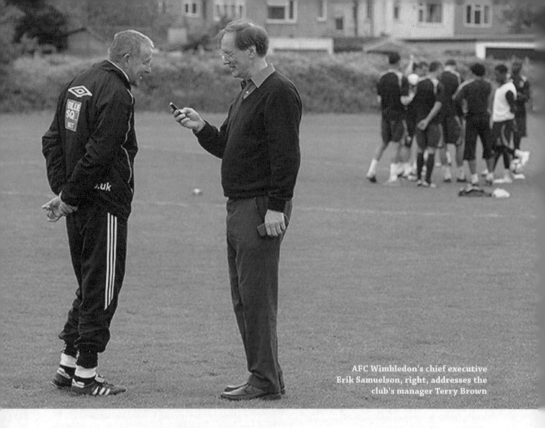

made any difference if I had been standing next to him – he would still have said it.

We wanted to keep the news quiet until we had a press release prepared, so telling BBC Surrey live on air was not part of the script. It was a disaster, a PR mess. We had wanted to tell the players first, sit down with them and discuss their concerns, look at contracts and sound a few other people out. But the deed was done. At the end of the day we had to stop, survey the scene and ask ourselves: "OK, has anyone died? No. So let's dust ourselves down, move on and treat that as a lesson learned."

The debate about whether to turn professional had actually started several months earlier when we started planning for the 2010-11 budget. And credit to Terry, he was very persuasive. He used to be a salesman, and he can be very, very good at getting his point across. He can be great at managing a conversation.

He said to me: "We could very easily be having this discussion at this time next season – and will we be in a better position to decide then?" The answer was obvious and Terry went on: "So why don't it we do it now and get on with it?"

He was right, we'd need to make the decision sooner or later and while we might have had a slightly better season with a part-time squad, we would have been avoiding the issue. So I took it to the football-club board and we agreed.

Terry can be very persuasive, even when you realise he is manipulating you. Halfway through listening to him, I suddenly imagined myself as an ice-skating judge. Terry was doing superbly on artistic impression, and, to be fair, he was also doing well on the technical excellence of his argument. We looked at the budget over the next few weeks and worked out how it could be done.

It should really have been me who presented the case for going full-time to the Dons Trust Board on the Monday night, but Terry had been so persuasive that I asked him to put the same argument to the Board that he'd put to me. And when it came to it he won them over – with the proviso that we did everything right first.

We all agreed – but then came the press conference after the Grays defeat 24 hours later. We made the formal announcement the next day.

By Terry Brown (AFC Wimbledon manager)

I remember being interviewed straight after the defeat to Grays. I was annoyed, I was wound up. We had played abysmally and I just blurted it out. I had it agreed in principle by Nigel, Erik and Ivor to go full-time but there were still a few hoops they wanted to go through first. Erik went into meltdown after I let it slip.

I said: "Bugger off, you try and run the club part-time." It was always going to happen, the club was going to have to become full-time sooner or later, it just came out a bit sooner than Erik wanted.

Erik is a fiery character. He loses the plot every time we lose. We came to an early agreement that we don't talk about football on match days. He will go away and come in on Monday with a list of 14 things that went wrong with the game. "As you know Terry," he will say, "I don't know a lot about football…" And that's when you know you are in a lot of trouble. It's just a prelude.

To be fair Erik, like a lot of other directors I have worked for, is really knowledgeable about football. The likes of Erik, Ivor, Nigel and Dave will question and argue about things, but they will always allow me to manage.

That said, it was a major decision to go professional. I had to bend a lot of arms to go full-time. You nearly double your costs. You need proper training facilities. I was going to go full-time, the players were going to go full-time. And that's all a very big deal. Players like Brett Johnson might be earning £300 a week from us and another £400 a week from their other job, so we'd have to effectively double their wages to keep them. So it changes your whole recruitment policy. You have to make your budget, which at AFC Wimbledon is already small, go even further. We had to find the best young boys we could, players who were living at home with mum and dad and didn't have to fork out for lodgings. It was a tough ask, but the benefits of being professional, with all the extra training and fitness that delivers, far outweighed the risks.

By Lewis Taylor (AFC Wimbledon player)

I never wanted to leave the club. I'd had two spells there and I loved it, but I was plagued with knee injuries. Terry Brown was in two minds about what to do with me. I could tell he was worried. We were going full-time, and he didn't really want to take any risks. We had talks and he wanted me to stay, but it was difficult. He couldn't offer me what I needed. He had the knees in his head. He couldn't offer me what I needed to go full-time.

I had a family to support, so it was not just a case of just "go for it". It's such a big step from semi-professional to full-time, and in the end it was a jump too far financially for me. I needed to offer my family security.

The first new Don to don the three Lions

Steven Gregory, AFC Wimbledon's first England C international (Andy Nunn)

As AFC Wimbledon sped up the pyramid, international recognition from England was inevitable. It was to become a race as several names continued to be linked with a call-up. In the end, Steven Gregory narrowly beat Sam Hatton to the honour.

---

26 May 2010
Republic of Ireland 1 England C 2
International Challenge Trophy (Waterford United FC, Co Kilkenny)
By Steven Gregory (AFC Wimbledon player)

It was a great honour to get the call. Every schoolboy dreams of pulling on the England shirt, and I am no different. The England C level had become more and more prestigious in recent years, and I was delighted.

I actually found out during a presentation night at the club. Sam Hatton and I had got called up to the training squad. All the boys were delighted for us and congratulated us. Sadly Sam failed to make it to the final 18 that travelled up for the game.

We actually had a warm-up game a couple of days before, against an East of Scotland XI, but that didn't count as an international match. It was the Ireland match that mattered. I was fully aware I was the first AFC Wimbledon player to pull on an England football shirt. It was definitely a proud moment for me.

My dad is no longer with us, but my mum was really happy for me. She wanted to go over to Ireland, but I wasn't sure whether I'd get a game, so I told her not to bother. Luckily she was to get her chance to see me in an England shirt a few months later when we played a game at Luton. And while Sam missed out against Ireland, he was to get his chance later. Seb Brown was to get a call up not longer after too.

As for the game itself, we hadn't really impressed in Scotland, and Paul Fairclough, the England C manager, was none too pleased. He got hold of us and we played far better against Ireland. Wrexham's Andrew Fleming put us ahead, and then Max Porter made it two (Max and I would later pass each other in and out of AFC Wimbledon). Ireland got one back, but to be honest we were always in control.

I've still got my shirt from that game. One thing a lot of people don't know is that you get two shirts every time you play for England. I've got four red and four white ones now. I'm going to get them framed along with the cap that came with it.

AFC Wimbledon's manager Terry Brown, who worked with the club's vice-presidents in June 2010 to get a much-needed cash injection (Andy Nunn)

Digging deep

The move to full-time meant costs would soar – and in simple terms there would be less money for Terry Brown to add to the squad. The outlook was bleak, and it took the generosity of the club's vice-presidents to ensure that the club's second season in the top flight of non-league would not become a battle against relegation.

June 2010
By Iain McNay (AFC Wimbledon vice-president)

Erik had done budgets for the new season, and the playing budget was even lower than the previous season. "Some of the costs have gone up and I can't budget for the unexpected. It's a relegation budget as it is," Erik stated bluntly. Mike Richardson and I were meeting with him to talk about our expectations for next season. Erik always does very detailed budgets and refuses to factor in possible income from cup runs or transfers.

I had now joined Mike Richardson as a vice-president, which involved helping out the club financially. Mike and I were an odd pair in one way. We were very different in how we saw things; I was more in the Erik camp of being as ethical as possible, while Mike was more "win at any cost". We still got on pretty well, though, and bounced ideas off each other.

We told Erik we would both renew our vice-president's commitment of £50,000 each, but that still wasn't enough to bring the budget up to where it needed to be to give us any chance of promotion. The previous season Mike had guaranteed a further amount which would be payable only if we didn't make any extra out of a cup run or transfer fee. The only way we could give Terry any kind of reasonable budget was to do something similar, so we agreed to guarantee a further £100,000 between us. Now, we all thought, at least we shouldn't get relegated.

Mike and I as vice-presidents have lunch with Terry and Erik every three months or so, and at the next lunch the figures still weren't quite adding up as far as Terry was concerned. He felt he needed two more players and had a list of who was available and how much he thought they would cost. Mike had just had some good news that morning and was feeling very generous, so again he dug deep into his pocket and gave Terry the extra. That still only gave us something like the 14th highest wage bill in the Conference, but now Terry thought that, with a bit of luck, we could have a crack at making the play-offs.

Kedwell takes the armband

Danny Kedwell had just completed his most successful season of his career – top goalscorer for the club and a catalogue of awards – but he had his eyes on one more prize: the club captaincy

July 2010
By Danny Kedwell (AFC Wimbledon captain)

That year I swept the board with the Player of the Year trophies. I got 24 league goals; the year after I scored the same number, but I didn't get a thing. And that showed how quickly the club was moving on. In 12 months, Sam Hatton had improved by leaps and bounds and Seb Brown had proved to be the best goalkeeper in the league – they were both worthy winners.

The whole issue of captaincy surfaced when Terry and I sat down to discuss my contract in 2010. I told Terry in no uncertain terms that I wanted to be captain of the club. I said that I could lead the boys to promotion. I wanted the armband. He said he'd think about it, and after pre-season he turned to me and said: "It's yours."

The role of a captain has always meant a lot to me. As I've grown up I've always looked up to my captain. And I wanted people to look up to me as captain to follow my example. If my captain works hard, I work hard. If my captain runs around like a lunatic and refuses to give up, then I run around like a lunatic and refuse to give up. And that was the example I always tried to set. I always gave 120 per cent.

But I'm not a captain who shouts and hollers at players. I'm an arm-around captain, trying to get the best out of the team, trying to find the words that will lift them, inspire them and talk to them. I do sometimes get aggressive and tell them to give their all and win the battle, but that's what I believe in.

By Terry Brown (AFC Wimbledon manager)

It is never easy to make a forward a captain, but Danny Kedwell is a different breed. He led on the field, he always gave 100 per cent on the pitch, much more than he ever did in training. Making him captain took him to another level. The year before it had been the Jon Main show and now Danny took over.

I felt terribly sorry for Mainy – he had terrible luck. He would hit the post, miss chances he'd normally tuck away. It wasn't going for him. And then he would pick up injuries. I never had any doubt that he was more than capable of playing in the Conference, but Jon's lifestyle meant he was never going to have a long career in football.

Danny Kedwell who became the club's new captain in summer of 2010 (Andy Nunn)

Sunny days as Dons go top

A trip to the coast showed exactly what the new professional AFC Wimbledon were all about. And things were looking good – a few games into the new season and the Dons were top of the league.

---

28 August 2010
Eastbourne Borough 2 AFC Wimbledon 3 Blue Square Bet Premier
By Darren Abbabil (AFC Wimbledon fan)

A trip down to the South Coast on August Bank Holiday weekend in glorious sunshine and three points for the Dons to go top of the Conference – days just don't get much better.

I hadn't intended going to the game, but a late change of plans gave me a free afternoon. After what seemed like an interminably long train ride down to Pevensey & Westham station, and a not inconsiderable walk from there to the Priory Lane ground, I got to the ground half an hour before kick-off.

Eastbourne began brightly, and had a few chances to take the lead. After the hosts' initial salvo, the Wombles' passing game came to the fore. Eastbourne were clearly set up to score goals rather than avoid conceding them, so it made for an open game, and we went in at the break one goal to the good thanks to a long-range effort from Danny Kedwell their keeper appeared to dive over.

For the first 20 minutes of the second half we played some glorious football, continually cutting through the Eastbourne defence. In the space of 10 seconds Lee Minshull and Steven Gregory both hit the woodwork with long-range efforts. A second goal arrived from a Minshull header, and it seemed a question only of how many more we would rack up.

But the champagne football suddenly gave way to misplaced passes and panicky defending. Eastbourne scored twice, leaving the fans wondering whether we would hold on for a point. The songs from the Dons choir was replaced with cries of "Man on!" "Clear it!" and "Get rid of the bloody thing!" What had happened? It was like we were watching a different game.

Luckily for us, Eastbourne were not content with a point and were leaving gaps at the back in the search of a winner. And as the game ticked into injury time, a lovely through ball from Sam Hatton found Kedwell, who rounded the keeper and slotted the ball into the empty net. Cue pandemonium, both on and off the pitch. There were wild celebrations behind the goal – people flying all over the place. I must apologise to the girl who was in front of me – I accidentally elbowed her on the top of her head.

A few minutes of injury time seen out and victory was ours. News filtered through of results from elsewhere, and the chant of "We are top of the league" rang out as the players came over to celebrate with us.

Wonderful scenes, wonderful game. I floated back to the train station and the return journey didn't seem nearly as long. I was back in Clapham by 7.30pm to meet a friend for a few pints. "Good game?" he asked. "Yeah, not bad," I replied. Just another Saturday in the life of a Wimbledon fan.

Danny Kedwell scores the winner at Eastbourne on 28 August 2010 (Terry Buckman)

Sammy Moore, left, and Luke Moore, right, congratulate Danny Kedwell, centre, after his winner at Eastbourne (Terry Buckman)

Some things money can't buy

AFC Wimbledon captain Danny Kedwell had been the target of an audacious bid from Crawley Town – and he turned it down. It was a decision that rankled the Sussex club and cemented Kedwell's place in Dons folklore. And when Crawley – clear favourites for the league title – arrived at Kingsmeadow they were met with a sea of T-shirts with Danny Kedwell's face on it and the slogan "Some things money can't buy". The Dons came into the game with several key players injured and were forced to field an inexperienced back four. Defeat seemed on the cards – but the Dons captain would have the final say.

23 September 2010
AFC Wimbledon 2 Crawley 1 Blue Square Bet Premier
By Mike Richardson (AFC Wimbledon Vice-President)

When the whole Crawley approach came in, I knew we had to keep Danny Kedwell. So I agreed, with the club's consent, to fund a goal bonus which made it advantageous for him to stay. Danny was essential to us – we had to keep him.

By Ed Harris (AFC Wimbledon player)

I had only played three or four times before this game. I had been doing quite well, and I was set to start alongside Ismail Yakubu in central defence. I was 19; Yaks was 26 and had hundreds of League games behind him. He was a perfect player to learn from. But just before the match Yaks pulled up injured, and suddenly Fraser Franks was in for the first time. Here we were, about to play the biggest game of the season and, with Chris Bush also making his debut, I had to take control.

The build-up to the game was huge, and all those Keds T-shirts added to the buzz in the stadium. The atmosphere was really good. It was intense – and we were pumped up, it got us all going. The adrenalin was flowing. All that combined to push us on the extra 10 per cent we needed to get a result.

With all the Keds stuff going on it was going to be a bit tasty. Keds was a great captain. The squad was one of the best I have ever been in. Our togetherness was unique – no one could break us. We were all in it together and Keds was our leader. He would step up and take one for the team if it was needed. But that night everyone was a leader – all Keds had to do was lead us out onto the pitch.

I made the mistake for their goal. I was trying to let the ball run out of play. I didn't want to kick it out for a throw – they had this guy who could launch them into the box. I should have risked it, but that's easy to say with hindsight. I waited for the ball to go out, but their big striker shoved me over and squared it to Matt Tubbs to slot home. I was 19, and that was a big lesson for me – I've never made the same mistake again. I still get flashbacks of that even now, but I can also recall some of the better moments of the game. There was Sammy's equaliser, and I can picture as clear as day how the place erupted when Keds got the winner.

On a personal level, I was really down at half-time. We were losing 1-0 and I kept thinking about my mistake. It was haunting me. But Keds and Simon Bassey came up to me and told me to keep going. They told me that apart from that one error I'd

AFC Wimbledon's Fraser Franks and Ed Harris leap into action against Crawley Town on 3 September 2010 (Terry Buckman)

AFC Wimbledon players reel away in celebration after Sam Hatton fires in the equaliser against Crawley (Terry Buckman)

Danny Kedwell, out of shot, scores the winner against Crawley (Terry Buckman)

played really well. Even Marcus Gayle told me to keep going. It's rare for Marcus to put his head round the changing-room door. He showed that he had faith in me, and that really helped and gave me the confidence I needed. In the second half I stood up tall. I won every header, every tackle. I think the second half was probably the best I have ever played.

The bar after the game was great. Mingling with the fans, the feedback was brilliant. It lifted me even more. But as a team we couldn't celebrate too much. We had another game coming up fast. We had to rest, gather ourselves and go again.

By Steven Gregory (AFC Wimbledon player)

It's hard to think of a game during my time at AFC Wimbledon where we were such underdogs. Crawley were flying, and we had just lost 3-0 away at Luton. The talk was all about us crumbling away after our good start. And then there were the injuries.

In defence we had Fraser Franks, who hadn't played, paired with Ed Harris, who couldn't have been more than 20. At left back was Chris Bush in his debut game.

For the first 45 minutes we were chasing the game and went one down. But the second half we just went at them. It was just one of those games for which the script had already been written. And after everything that had gone on before involving Keds, it was inevitable that he would get the winner.

By Danny Kedwell (AFC Wimbledon captain)

It had all been spiced up a few weeks before by Steve Evans' bid to buy me. I came into training one day, and Terry Brown took me to one side and said Crawley had made an offer for me. He added that he didn't think it was the best move for me at that time. But it wasn't a hard decision for me. I still felt there was so much I wanted to do at Wimbledon, and I said: "No way." There wasn't even a chance I'd agree. Crawley came back in with another bid, but there was never any chance of me moving there.

Steve Evans spiced it up a bit after that with a few crude comments, and then there were the T-shirts with my face on them. It really heated up the atmosphere. Everyone there on the night must have thought we were going to get beaten. We had a load of injuries. Ed Harris and Fraser Franks were paired in central defence. In the end they did brilliantly, but there was no experience there. When the team-sheet came out, everyone must have thought we would get hammered.

They went ahead just before half-time, and we were on the back foot. But Terry lifted us at the break and we went out determined to give it a go. Sam Hatton scored a great equaliser.

A couple of minutes later, Sammy Moore put the ball into the box. I'd already seen their goalie coming out. As I jumped, the two Crawley defenders went into each other. I was thinking: "All I've got to do is get my head on the ball and loop it over, and it'll go in." Of course it all happens a lot quicker than that, and you don't really get that much time to think, but I did get my head on the ball and it dropped in. It was a great feeling – the whole ground erupted. There were about 10 minutes left, but it felt like at least 20.

It was so sweet to get the winner – especially after all those comments. Steve Evans had made a big mistake. Everything he said had just inspired me. Once people criticise me, I want to get even to prove a point. If you say things like that, they have a habit of coming back to bite you on the bum, and that night Steve Evans suffered one big bite.

The T-shirt really made me smile. After the game I was interviewed wearing one. I will always remember that – my face on a T-shirt. Bloody amazing!

Power play as Dons impress

Newly professional, sitting pretty at the top, things looked bright. But the performances hadn't been that great, and there were doubts about whether Wimbledon were the real deal. A 5-2 win away at title-chasing Mansfield changed all that.

---

5 October 2010
Mansfield Town 2 AFC Wimbledon 5 Blue Square Bet Premier
By Ed Harris (AFC Wimbledon player)

There are times in football when everything clicks, and away at Mansfield was one of those. We were simply untouchable. We scored three in the first half, but it could have been seven or eight. And what made it even more impressive was that Mansfield were flying at the time. Like us, they were in the top five and full of confidence, but that day they just couldn't live with us.

Some of the football we played was simply brilliant. That day a lot of people realised that we were a real threat. Before that game, the likes of Luton and Crawley had really dismissed us. They hadn't taken us seriously, but after our win at Mansfield they knew that we were true contenders. We knew we were good, but we hadn't often shown it. We had been winning, but sometimes not too impressively: it had taken two late goals to beat Histon.

We got off to the best possible start at Mansfield. Sammy Moore scored after just 11 seconds – apparently that that was the Dons' fastest ever goal – and we were flying. Christian Jolley made it two inside 10 minutes. They got one back, but that was just a blip. Keds added our third just before the break.

The whole team was on fire. We kept the ball on the floor and created a lot of chances. I didn't make a mistake all game. Ryan Jackson played brilliantly – he added our fourth. Keds was excellent, and Sammy Moore was awesome. He was spraying the ball over the park and played really well. He got the fifth. Those three were the real standout players that day. They made us tick.

On the way up on the coach we'd felt good. Most of us found it easy to relax. A couple of players kept to themselves, but that's how it always was. On the way back we were tired and wanted to sleep, but the adrenalin was still flowing.

Coach journeys were always good. Bass, Keds and Main were the big characters on the coach. They kept us going and were always full of banter. The spirit was always good. Even when we lost they could lift us. Anyone could sit anywhere. We all got on. It is very unusual to have a squad like that – there were no outsiders.

There's no single reason why that was the case. AFC Wimbledon is just a special club. Browny chose the players to fit in, and certain individuals like Keds, Lee Minshull and Steven Gregory helped everyone to get along.

AFC Wimbledon's Ryan Jackson scores at Mansfield on 5 October 2010 (Paul Willatts)

Ryan Jackson celebrates his goal at Mansfield on 5 October 2010 (Paul Willatts)

AFC Wimbledon's Ed Harris. His commanding peformance helped the Dons grind out a 2-1 victory at Wrexham on 9 October 2010 (Andy Nunn)

Dons put up the blockades to show the resolve of champions

Wrexham had been tipped by many to go up, and the trip to Wales was a tough test for the Dons. They passed it with flying colours, showing the mettle of true title contenders. The Dons won ugly.

---

9 October 2010
Wrexham 1 AFC Wimbledon 2 Blue Square Bet Premier
By Ed Harris (AFC Wimbledon player)

It was a massive, massive game – not many teams would go to Wrexham and win. They came at us, they threw everything at us and we took it all. Bush, Yaks, Sammy and I were pinned back non-stop. It seemed like every time we got the ball away it would come straight back. Their forwards kept continually coming at us.

But as a defence we really stepped up. Yaks just kept talking – as he always did – offering non-stop tips. We both like our headers and our challenges, and I learnt a lot from him. I looked up to him. And then there was Sam Hatton. He did give advice, but he let his performances do the talking. At the time he was on fire every game. Every week he would be putting in an eight or nine out of 10. It was hard not to be inspired by performances like that.

Andy Mangan gave Wrexham the lead in the first half, but I think the battle and the spirit we showed in defence started to inspire the rest of the team. Christian Jolley scored with a neat volley straight after half-time and we were back in it.

Wrexham kept coming. But even though we were pinned back, we were not going to give them any clear chances, and even if they did get through we had Seb Brown behind us. He made a couple of excellent saves. Having someone like that behind you gives you such confidence. Seb is such a great goalkeeper. Then with five minutes left, Keds headed the ball into the path of Rashid Yussuff, and he slotted home from 10 yards.

It was a steal, but for me this was the game when AFC Wimbledon really arrived. We didn't play all that well, but it gave us the belief that we could go places. Wrexham were always going to be in the play-offs or thereabouts, and we left feeling that now we had the upper hand over them. We had nothing to fear. It showed that we could win games under pressure and take the three points – that's the key for any good side.

I remember speaking to Ryan Jackson after the game. I said: "We have achieved something here." The Mansfield game the week before had shown that we had the talent to go up. The game against Wrexham showed that we had the steel.

The dreaded draw

AFC Wimbledon or Ebbsfleet United will play Milton Keynes Dons or Stevenage Borough. It was the draw the wider world of football had wanted for eight years. ITV instantly made it their live FA Cup game, irrespective of the result of the two replays. It was also the draw that WISA, the Dons Trust Board, the AFC Wimbledon Board and the majority of the fanbase feared most.

---

6 November 2010
By Simon Wheeler (WISA chair)

I got a text message from Jill Stratton. It just said: "Bloody hell, it's happened." "Bugger!" was my initial reaction. I knew exactly what she meant. Thankfully the fixture didn't happen that year. But it opened up the question again of what would we do. I had no real answer.

The club would have to fulfil the fixture. We couldn't be a martyr. If we refused to play it, the football authorities would come down on us like a ton of bricks. The option of playing the tie at a neutral venue also felt like a non-starter. Only if the police had serious concerns about safety would that be a possibility.

So what do you do? Do you call for a boycott of the game? The fanbase is split. There is a group of supporters who are desperate for the two clubs to meet, and there are others who would boycott it at all costs. The most important thing is that, as a group of fans, we don't rip ourselves apart over it. We need to find a solution that satisfies all supporters. And I have no idea what the answer might be.

We would have to do something. It would depend on where the meeting is scheduled to take place. And that's the reality: it is no longer a matter of if, it is a matter of when.

There are so many problems. Under Football League rules we have to send at least one director to the game if it's at Milton Keynes, and they would have to do likewise if it's at Kingsmeadow. None of our directors would ever want to be in the same room as one of theirs.

And then there's the issue of the fans. There is little doubt that the fans of Milton Keynes would be keen on antagonising us. It would be hell.

By Kris Stewart (Dons Trust Board member)

My reaction was "F***!" That was my only reaction for about five minutes. It was just horrible. There were two parts to it. The first was personal – "F***ing hell, that's horrible!" – but then there was the question for the club: "How the f*** do we handle this?"

I can't quite describe how thankful I was a few days later when Stevenage won and the possibility was put off for another day. But it really brought it into sharp focus – it is bound to happen at some point. I just wasn't ready for it.

We all know now that when it happens we will have to play the game, and that's going to hurt. And that presents us with a huge logistical problem: how can we do it? It has to be safe, and if we don't think it can be…well, tough, it has to be safe. If we think it can't reasonably be played at Kingsmeadow, then it can't be played at Kingsmeadow. If the FA says it has to be played at Kingsmeadow, and if we know it is not going to be safe, then we are not going to play at Kingsmeadow. But then what's the alternative? Our place, behind closed doors? That's horrible. Our place, not behind closed doors? That's horrible too.

We talked about it with Erik. Where could you put Winkelman? Where would the directors be? Up there it would be easier. No one in the boardroom, no comps.

The police don't really understand. We've spoken to them about it – and they always go on about the "big" matches they deal with, and always mentioning Millwall. But this is different. Wimbledon does have its few idiots, but we all know who they are and it's not too difficult to control them. But if we played Franchise, trouble could come from anywhere. It isn't a football thing, it's not Everton v Liverpool or Millwall v West Ham. This is different. No one really understands it except us.

Thankfully they lost, and the prospect of playing them disappeared. So thank you, Stevenage. But now we are in the Football League, the clubs will meet each other sooner rather than later.

By Richard Brazier (AFC Wimbledon supporter)

After reading various websites and speaking with fellow fans, I realised I was very much in the minority in wanting the dreaded game played. I appreciated the awkward position Erik and the club would be put in, and, more importantly, the violence that would most likely have happened. I am not necessarily pointing at our own fans, but certainly there would have been plenty with no affiliation to either side who would want to go to the game.

On the pro side, I just felt that the best way to put it up them was to beat them and also to out-sing them (out-abuse them, if you like) on a live televised match. However much as we loathe the club, they are a team there to be beaten. I also felt that it was a bit self-indulgent for people to say that we could not possibly play them. "Give them a bye to the next round of the FA Cup and cop out of it ourselves" sounded

to me like cutting our noses off to spite our face. There are plenty of incredibly intense rivalries in football. Portsmouth don't refuse to play Southampton; Cardiff don't refuse to play Swansea. They never say they could not play each other because they hate each other so much.

By Lou Carton-Kelly (AFC Wimbledon fan)

I sometimes wonder just how many Wimbledon fans still feel strongly about Milton Keynes. Take Lee Willett. He was a huge figure in the protest movement. He takes his boy to games now. When I spoke to him about the prospect of playing them in 2010, his answer was clear: "How can you cheer on the team one week and stop the next, especially in a game when they need you more than ever?" It was amazing – he had changed his tune dramatically over the years, but I could see his point of view. I also spoke to Kris Stewart and Nicole Hammond about it, and I think they still couldn't go into a game against the Franchise.

I'd still certainly find it difficult, but for Lee's son, for the new generation of AFC Wimbledon fans, it's different. Yes, they know why we were formed, and yes, a Wimbledon shirt is now a badge of honour – kids across London can wear it alongside their friends in Chelsea and Manchester United shirts and know they won't get the p*** taken out of them in the way that we of the older generation used to suffer. But it's not mainly about the history for them, it's about the football.

My big concern is that now we're in the League, we don't become just another football club.

By Rob Dunford (Webmaster, SW19's Army)

We all remember certain things when it comes to Wimbledon. Some are obvious, like Beasant in 1988, or Danny Kedwell's penalty at Eastlands. Or, unfortunately, 28 May 2002.

And strangely enough, most of those who witnessed the FA Cup second-round draw on ITV in 2010 will have the words that appeared on the screen etched in their mind forever more. Think back to your reaction when you saw this:

AFC WIMBLEDON or EBBSFLEET UNITED v STEVENAGE or MILTON KEYNES DONS

I remember exactly where I was that fateful minute. Not at home, or out shopping, or doing anything one would normally do on a quiet Sunday. Instead, I was in a hotel room in a place called Olive Branch in Mississippi, a typical Mid-South community where they still allowed smoking in bars.

Although I was about to go out, I decided to quickly check the live feed to see who we would get in the draw, expecting it to be, say, Walsall or Burton Albion. To this day, I'm convinced somebody was telling me something when my feed buffered, then came back on that very image.

Even though I was a good 4,000 miles from home, I felt bewildered and, most of all, in shock. The one fixture we never wanted to face up to was now all too real, and just two replays separated us from the unthinkable.

It didn't help that I was due to drive through the flat, isolated farmlands of Arkansas and Missouri that day. Thankfully, I didn't break down or crash, as trying to explain my state of mind to a policeman would have been impossible. Would they have understood? I would have probably been put in jail for my own safety.

We hated the thought of the game, but what shocked a lot of AFC Wimbledon fans was how the rest of the football world licked its lips. They wanted the tie to happen, and assumed we did too. Funnily enough, after yet more soul-searching, I ended up agreeing with them.

Why? One word – catharsis. I wanted to play them so the whole circus would be over and done with, and we could move on. If we lost, so be it, I could take it on the chin. If we won, what better way of sticking it to them? As much as I didn't want to admit it, they existed and weren't going away.

When Stevenage went up to Buckinghamshire for the replay, they suddenly found over 4,000 new supporters. The resulting penalty shootout was as bad and as nerve-wracking as our own spot-kicks at Eastlands a few months later. It wasn't helped by the BBC website being slow to update, especially when it went to sudden death. But Franchise missed, Stevenage scored, and we celebrated as much as we would have done had we been the ones up there that evening.

We dodged a bullet back then, although with us being in the Johnstone's Paint Trophy now it makes a meeting more likely. Even so, the draw did us a favour – it forced us to be mentally tougher in dealing with them. Few will ever like the Franchise. We all want them to disappear forever, and I hope we never have to play them. But it's not quite such a big deal any more, relatively speaking. The loathing remains, but the fear seems to have gone.

Though we remain thankful that Stevenage won, especially after Sammy Moore's injury-time strike at Ebbsfleet...

Getting that little bit Moore (twice)

The prospect of an FA Cup tie with MK Dons had hung over the replay, though thankfully 24 hours before this match Stevenage put an end to that particular scenario with a penalty shoot-out victory in Buckinghamshire. That left only the prospect of a live TV game dangling over the tie. But even that was enough, and nerves took over. For over 90 minutes Wimbledon were staring defeat in the face. Twice it would be Sammy Moore who rescued the Dons, leaving it late – very, very late – both times.

---

18 November 2010
Ebbsfleet United 2 AFC Wimbledon 3 (aet) FA Cup first round
By Sammy Moore (AFC Wimbledon player)

After we were held 0-0 at home, we all knew what might be lying in front of us. But I didn't really want to think about the consequences of what would happen if we defeated Ebbsfleet. It was a big deal, with all that history, but I wanted to focus on the game in front of us – and let what happens next happen.

Thankfully, in the end Stevenage played their part and made sure that by the time we had our replay the meeting we didn't want was no longer on the cards. But I was always focused on Ebbsfleet. They had given us a tough game at home, and we knew it would be difficult there.

The FA Cup is special to Wimbledon fans, and that night there was the big carrot of a live ITV television game if we won. But at 2-1 down and deep, deep into injury time we were dead and buried. And then the ball came to Luke Moore – he'd only been on for about 10 minutes. As soon as he put the ball across to me I knew exactly what I wanted to do with it. It would need to be inch-perfect, and one quick contact would be enough. There wouldn't be another chance, the clock was up. This was the last kick of the game. I got a touch with the outside of my right boot and thankfully it went in.

I had a couple more chances in extra time, but I missed them and it looked like the game was going to penalties. Time was nearly up again. And then, out of nowhere, I got another chance. As the ball looped up, I nipped in and slotted it home. To see the ball hit the back of the net in the last seconds and with the big TV game to come – it was perfect, a dream come true. I still watch that match over and over again. It was superb – you could really feel the emotion of the fans.

There are two games in my career that stick out for me: my debut and that game at Ebbsfleet, and the Ebbsfleet one shades it. When I made my debut, I was so proud to put on the shirt. But for a midfielder, to score two goals in any game is memorable and to get them in the FA Cup, and at the times I scored them – well, that's simply unforgettable.

I was absolutely delighted, and so pleased for the fans as well. The fans have always been like a 12th man at AFC Wimbledon, and against Ebbsfleet they never gave up – even when we looked doomed. At the end, when they were singing my name, I got goose pimples all over. You can live off moments like that forever.

I came to Wimbledon from Dover. Andy Hessenthaler had been the manager there, but he left. I was offered a new contract, but I wanted full-time football and I wanted

Sammy Moore celebrates his
90th minute equaliser at Ebbsfleet on
18 November 2010 (Paul Willatts)

AFC Wimbledon's Sammy Moore enjoys the
television spotlight at Ebbsfleet in the first round
of the FA Cup after scoring the Dons' late winner
(Paul Willatts)

to play in the Football League, so I didn't sign. I'd been following AFC Wimbledon for a while. I was good mates with Jake Leberl, and I spoke to him about it and he was really positive about the club. And in the end my dad picked up the phone and called Terry Brown to see if I could come down for a trial. Terry said: "I have all the midfielders I need, but come down and we'll have a look at you." And the rest is history.

It's amazing how the players, the management and the fans are all so supportive. It's like one big family. You can really feel the support all the way through. If I could stay forever, I would. And if I could bring people in to help strengthen the team, I wouldn't hesitate for a second. I would recommend AFC Wimbledon to anyone.

Broughton's arrival sparks a bout of soul searching

The moment came 66 minutes into a game in Staffordshire. Coming off the bench to replace Christian Jolley was journeyman striker Drewe Broughton on loan from Lincoln City. The controversy came from his CV: among his former clubs was a certain team from Buckinghamshire. His arrival was to spark a huge row among Wimbledon fans. Nine minutes into his debut, he scored. What would the fans think now?

19 February 2011
Tamworth 2 AFC Wimbledon 5 Blue Square Bet Premier
By Adam Beal (AFC Wimbledon fan)

I have always backed any player in the yellow and blue, and have stuck up for many despite some pretty harsh criticism from fellow fans. But even I had to reach pretty deep to muster support when Drewe Broughton stepped onto the pitch at Tamworth.

Glancing at images on the internet of him in that soulless white shirt, and then seeing him in ours, was something I just couldn't come to terms with. Some might say that is an immature viewpoint. After all, players are just mercenaries who will go anywhere for a couple of quid more. But for me the transition from them to us is simply not right.

It also had me asking questions of Terry Brown. For Drewe to succeed he would have to be one hell of a player, and then some. But to bring in a player with that baggage and whose football style seemed almost the opposite to ours – that baffled me. Surely there must have been players at least as good as him without that dark stain on their CV?

By Kyle Bond (AFC Wimbledon fan)

On the train back from Tamworth, he was most definitely the hot topic of conversation. The issue was clearly divisive. Some said it was time to move on and get real about the world of professional football; others took the uncompromising line that one game for the Franchise was one game too many for any potential Wimbledon signing.

Drewe Broughton in the colours of his former club Franchise FC before his loan move to AFC Wimbledon

Controversial striker Drewe Broughton in the blue of AFC Wimbledon (Paul Willatts)

One fan asked me: "What does this say about us and what we stand for, what we started all this for in the first place?" It struck me that he was right. AFC Wimbledon is just that: the football team of Wimbledon first and foremost. But for me, to deny it a hard-line anti-Franchise stance is wrong and always will be.

By Robert Dunford (Webmaster, SW19's Army)

The strikers who have turned out for AFC Wimbledon are a somewhat mixed bag. For every Danny Kedwell, Shane Smeltz or Jon Main to have worn the shirt, there's been a Nathan Elder, a Giuliano Grazioli or a Seb Kneissl. However, nothing could come close to the sheer weight of opinion that Drewe Broughton generated.

When a team is on a restricted budget, getting the right striker in is always a challenge. You either have to spend big, get extremely lucky or go cheap and – more often than not – nasty. Even so, the arrival of Broughton on loan raised more than a few eyebrows. Firstly, his record wasn't that special – three clubs in two years (Wrexham on loan, Rotherham and Lincoln), close to 100 appearances for them and just 11 goals in that time.

But that wasn't the issue: he had also played 13 games for Milton Keynes Dons. The fact that he didn't score for them, and it was only a stop-gap for him, didn't matter – he'd broken the taboo of playing for them. He, and we, crossed that line.

It's hard for anyone outside the club to imagine such a negative reaction that was evident on internet message-boards. The language was highly emotive – people really did feel that the club had betrayed them. It's unlikely that Broughton joined the Franchise for ideological reasons. Jon Main had a trial in Buckinghamshire, and no such animosity was directed at him. But people were in no mood to welcome Broughton. For some, it was just one step short of dealing directly with Peter Winkelman.

The proof of the pudding, as the old cliché goes, is in the eating. And we got the chance to see Broughton in action at Tamworth. Just as it had been in cyberspace, the reaction in the real world to our new loanee was mixed – some politely applauded, while others were clearly seething. Indeed, one Womble stated that even if he scored a hat-trick it still wouldn't be enough.

The second half came, and our new hero (or villain) made his debut. And almost inevitably, he scored. It was a shot from outside the box, and he finished it well. His goal seemed to bring out the humour in everyone. One group of fans were even joking that we ought to sign more players from Winkelman if they were so good.

Iain McNay (Dons Trust Board member)

I knew that Terry was trying to get a striker in on loan to help our promotion push. But it came as something of a shock to hear that the candidate was none other than the much-travelled Drewe Broughton. While at Lincoln City, he had gone on loan to the Franchise operation. I couldn't believe we were about to sign a player that had played for them. All the chants that had been directed over the years from the terraces at ex-Franchise mercenaries, and here we were about to have one play for us. For me this just wasn't acceptable.

I called David Charles, the club secretary. "Have we actually signed him yet?" I asked. "He's having a medical at the moment, and if he passes we'll sign him straight afterwards," David replied. "No, we won't. I can't believe this. An ex-Franchise player playing for Wimbledon – it's just not on. I have a really bad feeling about this," I retorted. "I am bringing this up at the Dons Trust Board meeting tonight. Hold the signing till then."

A few hours later the Dons Trust Board discussed the matter. I was really surprised and frustrated, I wasn't getting much support from my fellow Board members – in fact, I wasn't really getting any. In the end I proposed a motion stopping the club from signing him. I lost by eight votes to one. It was a strange feeling to be so out on a limb. But I felt I was right: we shouldn't sign players that had played for them, even if they had only been there on loan.

When Broughton scored in his first game, I was caught completely unawares. I was out of my seat celebrating when David Charles, who was sitting next to me, said: "Iain, do you realise who has just scored?" I hadn't. I sat down and thought about it. I decided that I couldn't not support a player wearing a Wimbledon shirt, but I still hated the fact that he was playing for us. When he disappeared back to Lincoln City a few weeks later, I was more than happy.

By Terry Brown (AFC Wimbledon manager)

I felt really sorry for Drewe. The crowd were never going to have him. He had played for the garbage up the road and that was enough. He was never going to endear himself to the Wimbledon population. But I don't view Drewe's time at AFC Wimbledon as a failure. Look at the stats – I am the only manager to get him to score a goal in something like five years.

I had actually followed Drewe's career for a while. I remember him playing against one of my teams and he had been a real handful. His CV was impressive and I needed a foil for Danny Kedwell – someone who could take the burden off him and on paper Drewe was that man.

The problem is he was getting towards the end of his career and I hadn't had the chance to see him. And that's the big advantage of having a lot of money, you can get a decent scouting system in place. I'd seen Jon Main three times in person before I signed him and Danny Kedwell twice. I couldn't afford to do that with Drewe. That said, Drewe was nowhere near the worst signing I ever made. And if people are going to remember me by Drewe Broughton then I'll take that – he came on for his debut in a difficult game against Tamworth and scored with his first touch.

By Drewe Broughton (AFC Wimbledon player)

I have always been keen to play football and that's the bottom line. Did it make a difference that I played for MK Dons? Well for a number of AFC Wimbledon fans, yes it did. Given the history there's no doubt that it matters. But it's far more intense from the AFC Wimbledon side. For the fans of MK Dons there isn't too much feeling – a rivalry yes and I have no doubt they would like to see the two teams in the same division, but hatred? I'm not so sure.

I've seen and experienced both sides of the argument.

I enjoyed my time at both clubs. Unfortunately I didn't score any goals while I was at MK Dons, but they had a good team with a good young manager. In my opinion, MK Dons need to do the decent thing and drop the 'Dons' bit from their name now that AFC Wimbledon are on the rise. Things have moved on, as long as they continue to use the term Dons they are claiming an identity that they no longer lay claim to. Milton Keynes has its own team now, with its own colours and its own badge, the Dons belong to Wimbledon.

Dons turn on the style

As the season drew to a close, AFC Wimbledon were beginning to discover a swagger. Their form was becoming scintillating, as was evident on a trip to Cambridge.

9 April 2011
Cambridge United 1 AFC Wimbledon 2 Blue Square Bet Premier
By Tim Hanson (AFC Wimbledon fan)

9 April 2011. That's the day I started to believe we really could gain promotion to the Football League. We had done pretty well before then, of course. We'd shown that we could beat the top teams (Crawley at home), that we could "win ugly" (York and Fleetwood at home) and that we could bounce back from a run of defeats (the wins against Rushden & Diamonds and Barrow, following three consecutive losses culminating in defeat at Crawley). But Cambridge was the first time we really took a team apart playing Terry Brown's preferred brand of neat, pacy, attacking football.

The occasion was ideal – a beautiful spring day, a perfect playing surface and a great

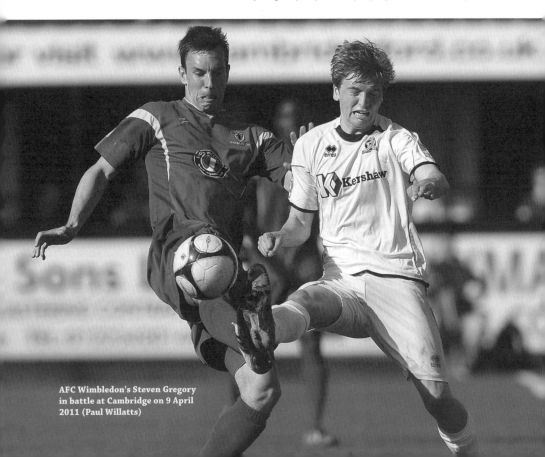

AFC Wimbledon's Steven Gregory in battle at Cambridge on 9 April 2011 (Paul Willatts)

atmosphere among the Dons fans, already all but assured of a play-off place. Forget the scoreline: 2-1 comes nowhere near reflecting our dominance for the majority of the game. The performance suggested that we had what it takes to go on a run that could end in glorious promotion.

We were unstoppable over the next six games, recording five wins and a draw while knocking in 16 goals and conceding just three. The seventh game was the play-off final and the culmination of our unforgettable rise to League Two.

Looking back now, I'm in no doubt that Cambridge was a massive turning point in our season – and in the history of AFC Wimbledon. The way we performed that day instilled a confidence in the players that we did have what it takes to go all the way – and to do so playing our way.

Advantage Dons

After the Cambridge game, the Dons dropped just two points in their last four games to finish in second place, 12 points ahead of play-off semi-final opponents Fleetwood Town. Nerves were on edge for the trip up to Fleetwood. They had the money and had been on a late surge. But AFC Wimbledon turned in a professional performance, and by the end of 90 minutes had one foot in the play-off final.

---

6 May 2011
Fleetwood Town 0 AFC Wimbledon 2
Blue Square Bet Premier play-off semi-final, first leg
By Kaid Mohamed (AFC Wimbledon player)

The trip to Fleetwood didn't faze me. I'd been in the same situation the year before with Bath in the Conference South play-offs. I scored in both the semi-finals and in the final as well, so I was confident.

I'd joined Wimbledon just a couple of months before. I had had a big fall-out with Bath City. It was a bit stupid – I refused to sit on the bench, and that was that. I was finished with Bath and I was left without a club. That was on the Saturday, and on the Sunday morning my phone was buzzing. The top eight clubs in the Blue Square Bet Premier were all interested in me, but once I heard Wimbledon's message that was it.

It was a little messy, I was on a non-contract deal with Bath and I had to go back to them to sign some formal terms to be able to go on loan to Wimbledon. I think they had to pay a small fee for me, but I wasn't involved in any of that.

I had such a great time at AFC Wimbledon. I think I played only nine or 10 games there, and we won all but one. They'd been on a bit of a dodgy run when I joined, but from the moment I arrived at training I knew they were a good side. By the time of the play-off semis I was feeling really good, and as a team we were on a great run of form.

I felt so sharp. I was tearing Fleetwood apart down the right, causing them so many problems. I wanted the ball at every turn. It was end-to-end stuff, but as soon as Luke Moore got the first goal just before the break, that felt like it – job done. And from then on we were buzzing.

AFC Wimbledon's Luke Moore fires in the Dons' first goal in the first-leg of the play-off semi-final at Fleetwood on 6 May 2011 (Paul Willatts)

As for my goal, well that came at the perfect time for us, right after half-time. Luke Moore was plugging away down the right and cut it back. I knew he was going to chop it back, so I made the run and it was a good finish. I was delighted to score. I love scoring goals – it's what I live for. But this was live on TV and a big match, and that made it all the more special.

It was a great performance but we weren't there yet. We didn't get carried away. Terry kept telling us this was just half-time. And I knew that too. We had put ourselves in a great position, but there were still 90 minutes to go.

By Paul Harrison (AFC Wimbledon fan)

I live in Preston, and I turned up for my most local Dons fixture both nervous and confident. I was nervous because Fleetwood had players who could score goals, but confident as I was well aware of Sean Gregan's lack of mobility at the back.

The game really couldn't have gone much better – though it was a pity that the heavens opened to dampen the enthusiasm of the home fans in their shiny new stand, which had leaks. The goals were well taken, the half-time TV highlights didn't show us with the ball at all, and I got to meet a Geordie Womble. Of the games I saw that season it was the most disciplined performance especially given some of the tactics of Fleetwood, which bordered on the Neanderthal.

I travelled back with someone who had watched from the bar in the ground, courtesy of a free ticket from a Fleetwood player. He was that impressed with how

we played that he promised to watch the second leg in a pub in Preston, and to come to Manchester if we got there. The result the Wednesday after made my season. He came to Manchester for the final – and we know the rest.

By Anita Gibbons (AFC Wimbledon fan)

Full of nervous excitement, my daughter Elina and I arrived at Euston around midday. Wanting something good to eat on the train to Blackpool, we took a short tube ride to the Angel and a sprinted up to Ottolenghi for a packed lunch of cold salmon and a massive mixture of salads – far too much for the two of us, but delicious.

We hurried back and caught the 2.30pm train to Preston, where we changed for Blackpool North. We wandered through a damp and semi-closed Blackpool to our B&B before getting the bus to Fleetwood, arriving 15 minutes ahead of kick-off.

The journey had not been uneventful. We chatted with other AFC fans, and met some Fleetwood fans on the Preston to Blackpool train – most of them more nervous than we were, and one of them we later spotted as the "fans blogger" in the matchday programme.

Standing on the terrace with a fair view of the excellent Fleetwood pitch we felt more than lucky to be standing within chatting distance of Kris Stewart. We heard him loud and clear when he lambasted a fan for racist abuse, going further up in my daughter's eyes for being so strong and forthright.

As for the match, we, like the players, relaxed into it after the first goal was scored on 39 minutes, rather against the run of play, but when the second went in just after half-time there was only one team in it.

Elina was far too excited for bed, so we got a bus back to Blackpool and headed for a warm pub. There we found plenty of happy Dons fans discussing the game in the midst of a huge crowd of well dressed-up young farmers at a weekend convention. It was one of the best weekends away ever. A Saturday spent on Blackpool's rollercoasters rounded it off nicely.

Dons seal final berth in style

The Dons' 2-0 win in Lancashire made them favourites to progress. Kaid Mohamed's early strike in the second leg put an end to any nerves – and allowed Wimbledon to turn on the style. It was arguably their best performance of the season.

11 May 2011
AFC Wimbledon 6 Fleetwood Town 1
Blue Square Bet Premier play-off semi-final, second leg
By Kaid Mohamed (AFC Wimbledon player)

Before the game Terry told us how important it was, what it meant to the club. He reminded us of the history – and it sunk in. He kept saying: "You are just 90 minutes away from the City of Manchester Stadium – an hour and a half away from a shot at the Football League." But that game sticks with me more than any other – far more than the final that followed.

It was a sellout, and the crowd were right behind us. At that point of my career it was the best team I had ever played in. And it wasn't too bad a start – 35 seconds in, I put us one up. That's the fastest goal I've ever scored. I got the turn on Sean Gregan and slotted it in. Then it was 2-0, then 3-0 – Luke Moore set me up for that one. The performance was professional. There were a few nerves when they pulled one back, but with a 5-1 aggregate lead there were always more chances for us.

I hadn't scored a hat-trick for a long, long time. So when the ball was bouncing around the area, I was delighted to get the decisive touch to make it 4-1. I was buzzing. I would have been happy to just get one as long as we got the job done. Just to be a part of it, it was the best day of my life. Jolley made it five and Mulley added the sixth. We were unstoppable.

As I left the pitch, I saw my dad. He goes to every one of my games, and he had the biggest smile. At first I thought he was just delighted that I'd got a hat-trick. But I know he always has a sneaky bet on me before most games. He'd had £20 on me to score in the first leg, and I thought he'd done the same again. But he'd had a little look at the other bets on offer, and one caught his eye – 50-1 for me to get a hat-trick. He stuck £50 on that, and now he was all cashed up. A great day for me and a great day for him.

The atmosphere that night was amazing. I walked around the stadium afterwards and the fans were all going crazy. It was mental. It was amazing. Nothing can beat the memories of that night. I gave a little speech afterwards.

We had got to the stage that every game we played in we felt we could win. We were dominating everything, we were flying. And now Manchester was calling.

As for the ball? I asked a friend of mine who had got some of my shirts framed what

Kaid Mohamed gets mobbed by his team-mates after scoring in under a minute in the second leg of the play-off final (Terry Buckman)

Danny Kedwell fires in the Dons second against Fleetwood on 11 May 2011 (Terry Buckman)

Kaid Mohamed rolls in the Dons' third in the play-off semi against Fleetwood (Terry Buckman)

AFC Wimbledon's Kaid Mohamed taps in to
complete his hat-trick against Fleetwood
(Terry Buckman)

AFC Wimbledon's Christian Jolley
flicks in the Dons' fifth on 11 May 2011
(Terry Buckman)

Kaid Mohamed celebrates against Fleetwood on 11 May 2011 (Terry Buckman)

AFC Wimbledon's Christian Jolley celebrates his goal against Fleetwood (Terry Buckman)

he could do with it, and well he put it in a glass case. It's signed and there's a nice plaque to go with it too. It's in pride of place in my bedroom.

By James Mulley (AFC Wimbledon player)

We had done so well in the first leg to go 2-0 up. At home we didn't give away too many goals, but it was still a semi-final and the job was only half-done. So yes, there were nerves. But then Mo changed everything. That early goal after 30 seconds settled us down and got rid of the nerves. In the end, it was easily our best performance of the season. They had to come at us and we just punished them time and time again.

I didn't play in the first leg. I was on the bench, itching to get on, but the boys on the pitch were doing such a great job. In the return, we were already coasting when I got my chance to come on. Terry turned to me and said: "Go out there, enjoy yourself and do what you do best." It was the perfect time to come on. My form had dipped in the weeks before, and it was a great relief to get a goal. I had set myself a number of targets when I joined, and the goal sealed one of them.

I was helping out the defence, and won the ball back on the edge of our box and soared forward. They kept backing off, so I carried it further and further upfield, then popped it inside to Toks [Rashid Yussuff]. I know how Toks thinks. He's totally left-footed. I ran across in front of him and he laid on the perfect ball for me. I took on the defender and saw the keeper coming out. I thought about chipping him, but then changed my mind, took it round him and tucked it in. It was a great goal going from one end to the other, a great team goal and a great way to sign off the season at home. It gave us all a lift and set us up perfectly for the play-off final.

I joined from Chelmsford, but it is mainly thanks to Steven Gregory that I got my chance. I am good friends with Steven from my time at Hayes & Yeading. And I always played well against AFC Wimbledon. Hayes always seem to beat them at home, and AFC Wimbledon would do the same at Kingsmeadow. I knew Terry Brown, and that helped too.

I was released by Hayes in October over a footballing disagreement. I was only 22 at the time and had already played over 150 times for their first team. I went on to Chelmsford, but didn't really fit in there and couldn't nail down a first-team place.

So I took a chance. I spoke to Gregs, and Terry Brown said there might be an opportunity as there was a number of injuries at the time. So I went down to training, and was basically on a month's trial. And the sweetest of ironies is that I got my chance against Hayes just a couple of months after they released me. I played well, scored and we won. Wimbledon was a club I wanted to join. When the chance came, I was so happy to take it.

Haydon the Womble joins in the celebrations after the final whistle on 11 May 2011 (Terry Buckman)

Chapter Ten:

This is our time

The City of Manchester Stadium comes into view on matchday (Terry Buckman)

Wimbledon fans begin to gather at the bar outside the stadium (Caroline Kingston-Lynch)

This is our time

So it all came down to this. A trip to Manchester, and after a nine-year journey the promised land of the Football League was at last within reach. What follows is the build-up to the game, the action and the post-match celebrations through the eyes of the AFC Wimbledon squad.

21 May 2011
Luton Town 0 AFC Wimbledon 0
(AFC Wimbledon win 4-3 on penalties)
Blue Square Bet Premier play-off final
City of Manchester Stadium

Seb Brown: I am a lifelong Wimbledon fan. I was there when we voted for the season-ticket boycott in 2002. My dad and uncle were Plough Lane regulars. AFC Wimbledon means a lot to me. I spent four years in the family section at Kingsmeadow watching the miracle unfurl. And then I left school and joined Brentford's youth team as a goalkeeper. It was a bit of a pain – we travelled with the first team on matchdays, and that ruled out any chance of getting to watch the Dons. The games always seemed to clash – Tuesdays and Saturdays all the time. It was only when I was injured that I could get down to watch. And then Wimbledon came in for me, and I leapt at the chance. For the first year in the Conference I had the best seat in the house, the substitutes' bench. And then I got my chance. And this – the play-off final at Manchester – was the pinnacle of it all.

Steven Gregory: I was really relaxed. We had had such a good win in the semis. We were full of confidence, and I don't think for one moment we thought we wouldn't win.

Seb Brown: The preparations for the final had actually begun six weeks earlier, after the defeat at Crawley. We'd been practising penalties ever since. As a goalie, it had got to the point where it was a bit awkward as I knew exactly where the players liked to put their kicks.

Lee Minshull: Despite that, everyone was scoring. Then on the Thursday before the final, when the TV cameras were down to film us, we were awful. Everyone was missing. Terry must have been in a panic! Perhaps, though, we needed to have one bad session to get it out of our system.

James Mulley: After the Thursday training session it was straight on the coach for the journey north. On the way up, the coach was full, which was unusual. It was great to have everyone on board. We were all there to support each other. We were totally relaxed.

Jon Main: It was great to be back in the fold. I loved it that I'd had my loan at Dover cut short, and the club had given me a game and a great send-off in the last game of the regular season against Grimsby. I wanted to be in the squad for the final, but it wasn't to be.

Sammy Moore: Terry wanted everybody to be there, everybody who had taken part in the season. He wanted to do things properly. I shared a room with Jon Main. Neither of us would be playing, and we were both trying to help the rest of the lads in any way we could. Terry did everything right. The preparation, the unity of team – it was all perfect. Of course I was sad not to be playing – I was out injured – but the fans and the players made me feel every bit a part of it. Terry and Cashy kept saying: "You've played your part already. Sammy, your job now is to help the lads through it."

Christian Jolley: We were all given these new polo shirts and that was a problem in itself. Me, Luke Moore and Sammy Moore always want the small – and well there wasn't enough to go round and that caused a bit of a palaver.

Seb Brown: We checked in at the Village Hotel in Ashton-under-Lyne. All season, I'd been sharing with Jack Turner – it's a lot easier to share with another goalkeeper. Goalies are a special breed. It might seem weird, but there was no rivalry between us. I always wanted him to have a good run somewhere. But we are different characters. Jack likes gallivanting round the hotel searching for someone with an Xbox or something else to mess about with, whereas I couldn't be more content just sitting in my room like an old man and watching TV. However, on the Thursday night even I went out.

Terry Brown: We always prepare properly. We have a set pre-match routine. We stay in proper hotels now, but the problem this time is that we had arrived considerably earlier than normal, so we knew we had to give the players the chance to unwind and take their minds off things. But there wasn't really much near the hotel, so we sent them across the road to the bowling complex.

Sam Hatton: We had a lot of time to waste, and just across from the hotel there was a bowling alley complex. So it was obvious we'd go there. I had a game of bowling – I was in the sensible group with Seb.

Steven Gregory: I didn't bowl – I was too busy in the arcades. It would have been easy for the manager to tell us not to leave our hotel rooms, but they let us out to socialise and relax, and that was the right thing to do. Reece Jones was on inspired form. He is the funniest kid I've ever known. He kept everyone entertained. He found one of those dance machines and he was unbelievable on it. He took it all so deadly seriously. It was all part of the perfect build-up to the game. It made me smile and helped us all relax.

Seb Brown: Me, Keds, Mo, Jack, Fraser, Ed, Sammy, Mike Rayner, Jamie Stuart and our kitman Robin Bedford, better known as Rocket, took to the bowling. It was all a good laugh. We had two games and I won one of them on my lane. But the other lane was where all the action was. Keds and Mo were on there, and those two are super-competitive.

Danny Kedwell: On my lane it was basically between me and Mo. I nicked £40 off him. I won the first game. The second one went down to the last ball, and I nicked it by one point. Mo was gutted and challenged me to pool. He kept losing, but kept saying double or quits. I think I was about £80 up at one point and should have walked away, but Mo pinched one and we ended level.

Seb Brown: The next morning it was off to the ground. It was intriguing to see the new stadium. We were all buzzing on the coach ride down there – it was like being on a school trip. Terry had told us to bring our cameras, and we were all staring out the window desperate to get the first glimpse of Eastlands. And then there it was, riding up on the horizon, looming large. In that one moment it hit me how big this was all going to be. It was pretty surreal.

Kaid Mohamed: Seeing the stadium for the first time was just too good to be true. I was thinking: "What the hell are we doing here?" This is the richest club in the country, if not the world, and I'm going to be playing here. The stadium, the entrance, everything was amazing.

Lee Minshull: When you walk up to a ground like that, it's just "Wow!" – what else can you say? Everyone was taking photographs and looking up at the stands. It's hard not to be in awe of a place like that.

Terry Brown: I was really surprised Luton didn't take the option to go up a day early. But I can understand it. They wanted to have the same routine as a normal matchday, but that wasn't the same for us. This was everything we had been working for in the last six weeks.

   We had been building up for the game ever since the defeat at Crawley. I gave the team a massive bollocking after that. We didn't do ourselves justice and I was fuming. We all sat down and gave them a target: the City of Manchester Stadium. That was our focus. From the Crawley defeat, it was the be-all and end-all. Nothing else mattered. And from then on we were magnificent.

Danny Kedwell: I remember seeing the stadium for the first time and thinking "Bloody hell!". We all thought we were going to have the away dressing room, but I think the decision by Luton not to come up the day before and train on the pitch had p***ed off the Manchester City authorities, so they gave us the home dressing room instead. And that gave us a little lift.

Seb Brown: That was a big surprise. We'd all thought we'd be given the away one, but when we arrived we were ushered in the other direction.

Terry Brown: In football memories last a long time and a number of the Manchester City staff were still haunted by the image of the then Luton manager David Pleat dancing on the pitch when Luton Town sent them down on the final day of the season at Maine Road all those years ago. So when Luton began to mess them around, the groundsman decided to usher us into the home dressing room instead.

Simon Bassey: We wanted to get the tourist bit done the day before. Our players

2.30 Terry Brown recieves some words of
comfort from Haydon the Womble during
the pre-match warm-up (Terry Buckman)

2.31 The players take to the pitch to warm-up
(Caroline Kingston-Lynch)

2.40 The anxious wait for kick-off
(Terry Buckman)

2.53 The play-off trophy is put on display
(Terry Buckman)

2.54 The fire is lit as the players run-out for kick-off (Terry Buckman)

2.55 Dons fans in full song before kick off at the City of Manchester Stadium (Getty Images)

2.55 The Wimbledon players are introduced to the dignitaries (Terry Buckman)

went out there saw the size of the pitch and the stadium, and got their mementos. We wanted no surprises. And it worked: we were able to treat it like any other game. It was a no-brainer for me. I was astonished when I heard that Luton had passed up the opportunity. Man City had offered them two slots to train on the pitch, and they wanted a different one – and that really rankled the City officials. Originally Luton had been allocated the home dressing room, but after all that they gave it to us.

Terry Brown: The Manchester City home changing room has all these inspirational messages and pictures in it. And above each of the players' pegs is an iconic image of that player scoring a vital goal or making a vital tackle. We replaced them all with pictures of our players and changed all the names on the pegs. I remember we gave Tevez's spot to Jon Main.

Seb Brown: When Trev Williams and Rocket had finished with it – putting photographs up and the kits all out – it looked pretty good.

Jon Main: They had my kit hanging up, and that was special for me. I wanted to be there for the youngsters, to gee them up and encourage them.

Danny Kedwell: The decision to go up a day early, really took the nerves off us. But there were other benefits too. We got used to the surroundings, the speed of the ball on the pitch, the width. It was great for Terry to do that – a real insight into what a well-prepared manager he is. If we hadn't done that we would have had to overcome our nerves as well as Luton on the day. We didn't need that extra hurdle.

Terry Brown: It really helped us to train on the pitch beforehand. The pitch was immaculate. It was greasy on top, but rock hard underneath, so choosing the right footwear for the match became a big thing.

James Mulley: There is no doubt that the Friday-morning training session was important. It got us used to the aura of the place. Jamie Stuart and a couple of others had played in a few big stadiums, but for most of us this was something different, the biggest stage we'd ever played on. We took pictures, we got all the excitement out of our system. Friday was about calming us down. Saturday was going to be about business.

Sam Hatton: It gave us an idea of what to expect. Luton didn't take up that option – and maybe that was a factor in their defeat.

Danny Kedwell: But it wasn't all a bed of roses. I picked up an injury in training. No one was near me, but I just felt my knee go. I couldn't believe it – it was a real jolt of pain, and I honestly thought there and then that I was out of the final. It was a real scare, but I had a painkilling injection and I was ready to go.

James Mulley: I roomed with Gareth Gwillim. He was only 50-50 for the game, but he was so determined to be involved. He was confident he would be fit. He was doing everything, all the right physio, lots of swimming.

Ed Harris: I was just back from being on loan at Dover and had just got back to full fitness. I knew Gareth was struggling, so there was a chance I might make it onto the bench. It was just after the Friday training session that I knew that I wasn't going to make the cut. I saw Gareth doing a fitness test on his own. He got through it, so I gathered he was going to pull through. I was 90 per cent sure I wouldn't be playing. But I had to be prepared just in case.

James Mulley: Gareth was delighted. He knew then that all the hard work he had put in had paid off and he was going to be starting. It was at the end of the same session that Terry named the subs and I was told then that I was one of them. To know I'd be involved was fantastic news.

Ed Harris: Actually it didn't make too much difference whether you were going to be involved or not. Even those who knew they weren't going to play didn't feel left out.

Seb Brown: After training on the pitch, we went back to the hotel. We had a bit of lunch and some of the lads went into town. I was a bit Victor Meldrew and stayed at the hotel, had a little nose around the pool and got a couple of hours' kip.

Christian Jolley: I room with Toks and we just went for a wander around the city centre the day before just to try and relax a little.

Lee Minshull: I had hoped to spend most of the day relaxing after that, but I'd forgotten my contact lenses. I was in a bit of a panic, so I was on the phone to my optician to try and get a prescription sent up to Manchester, and then I spent most of the afternoon dashing around trying to find a store that would make them up for me. It was proper chaos, but it was all right in the end.

Seb Brown: We had dinner around 7pm, then it was on to the club tradition. The night before your first big away game you have to sing a song. First up was Delano Sam-Yorke, who sang Rihanna's "What's My Name?".

Lee Minshull: Poor Delano. I'd done my turn earlier in the season with "Champagne Supernova" by Oasis. To be honest, it's about the only song I can do. The one to look for is Sammy Moore – he's the real expert.

Christian Jolley: Delano did quite well. But then it was Natalie's turn. She's our physio and sang "Dancing In The Moonlight". She was so nervous and we were really egging her on. It was hilarious, but in the end she had the whole squad singing. It was real fun.

Lee Minshull: Then it was back to the room. I was sharing with Luke Moore, and we just chilled out.

James Mulley: I just relaxed in the hotel with Gareth. We just chatted about general stuff. I was asking him what he thought his chances were of being OK, and he was confident. I'd taken the box set of Heroes with me and we watched that.

Danny Kedwell: I shared with Jamie Stuart. Jamie is the same off the pitch as he is on it. I've known him for years. I used to play against him all the time when I was at Welling and he was at Grays, and then I had two years with him when I was at Grays and we became really good friends. We went down together for the pre-match meal and it was all over to Terry.

Terry Brown: I knew more or less what I was going to say. I always draft a few bullet points before every major match. In reality most of the players switch off after a minute or two. I'd given a big speech before the Fleetwood game – that had worried me more as I always thought the big pitch at the City of Manchester Stadium would suit our style. If we got to the final, I thought, we would win. What I wanted to do now was fill the boys with confidence. I wanted them to come away thinking: "Wow, we are here, now let's deliver" and not "Oh my God, this is it."
  The speech is all on the DVD. I said: "This is our day. This is our moment. This is our time. Over the last six weeks it's been about when we get to Eastlands. This is our day. It is made for us. The pitch is made for us. It's big. It's beautiful. Everyone down there loves us and hates Luton. We are unbeaten in the last nine games. We sat down after Crawley and we said we had to improve. This is where you get to show 30,000 people or however many it is how good we are and set a marker to League Two managers saying: 'S*** me, they can play some stuff.' We are fitter, sharper, we are hungrier, we are unbeaten. We have one game to go. You have done all the hard graft. This is a glory day. This is where you get to show how good you are. We've got the home dressing room. It's our pitch. It's our tempo. Good luck, gentlemen."

Danny Kedwell: Terry had set us targets throughout the year, and each time we had met them. He ended his speech by saying: "Go out and give your best. You have just one target left, don't mess it up." Me and Jamie kept saying that night that we couldn't imagine messing it up, not now we'd got this far.

Simon Bassey: By Saturday, there was so little left to do. That's the beauty of being full-time – we had already done all the preparation. We had a meeting at the hotel beforehand. It was all about relaxing then, about making it just another game. We talked about the set pieces, who was taking them, who was marking who – all the usual stuff we would do before a game.

Seb Brown: At breakfast there was an option to have more or less what you wanted. I try and watch what I have. So it was eggs, beans and toast. I'm really picky with my eggs. I can't have fried eggs and I'm really fussy about my scrambled eggs. Poached is perfect, but that wasn't on offer. There was a light pre-match meal at 11am of chicken breast and pasta, followed by a short walk to stretch our legs and keep us ticking over and then it was on to the bus. The police escort turned up at 12.30 to take us to the ground. They were stopping everything to make sure we had a smooth ride.

Sam Hatton: Travelling down to the stadium was a buzz, seeing all the fans. It just added to the day.

Seb Brown: It was weird, given the magnitude of the game – there were no nerves. We did everything we normally do and stayed focused.

Steven Gregory: I felt more excited than nervous on the way to the stadium. Seeing all the flags and the fans, that's when the realisation of what a special day it was started truly hitting home.

James Mulley: Walking out on matchday was amazing. It was a dream stadium, a dream atmosphere. I remember thinking that this was what playing football was all about – this sort of atmosphere, this sort of stage. Seeing all our fans who had made the journey up, and paid all that money. Now it was all about one thing – winning. That was all we needed to do.

Seb Brown: On a personal level, the only thing that went wrong was my warm-up. We were told that we couldn't get out on the pitch until 1.50pm. Normally, I'm out way earlier than that. But we had the big dressing room and there were exercise bikes in there, so I made do with one of those.

Simon Bassey: The Luton players had their cameras out, taking photographs and looking around the stadium and everything. We'd got that all out of the way the day before.

Sam Hatton: Back in the changing room, some players were bubbling and chatting away. I just sat down quietly in the corner, dealing with it all in my own way.

Terry Brown: It wasn't anything long. We had already done all our preparations. I just said: "Are they fitter than you? No. Are they better than you? No. We didn't finish second in the league for no reason. I'm proud of you. Go out and enjoy it. Most of you will never get another opportunity like this. Go out and do what you've been doing for the last few months."

Sam Hatton: I didn't listen to what was being said. I was thinking about my own personal goals. I just blanked everything out and thought about my own game. And then it was into my little routine. It's the same every game. My socks go on in a set way. I have set places to put all my bottles, all that sort of stuff. If someone messes with my routine…well, let's put in this way: no one messes with my routine.

Simon Bassey: After the run we had been on, the team were in such a good place that we really didn't have to say much. But personally, I was really nervous. The last five minutes before kick-off I was in the toilet. It was all too much. I'd been at the club almost from the start. I knew that the Conference was a bloody hard league to get out of. And we had achieved a chance to get out of it in two years – a fantastic achievement. I kept thinking we might never get another chance, especially with the budget we had. It was small compared to all the other teams around us. I was really scared of failure.

Steven Gregory: I thought I would be really nervous. I was really surprised how I felt going into the stadium. Walking down the tunnel, all the formal handshakes, and

2.56 The players sing the national anthem
(Caroline Kingston-Lynch)

2.58 Handshakes before the hostilities begin
(Terry Buckman)

3.02 AFC Wimbledon fans prepare for kick-off (Terry Buckman)

3.08 Luke Moore's effort flicks towards an onrushing Danny Kedwell (Terry Buckman)

3.15 Sammy Hatton gets back in the zone after a lack lustre start with a classic sliding tackle (Andy Nunn)

3.14 AFC Wimbledon's Jamie Stuart gets his point across (Andy Nunn)

3.33 Stuart Cash and Terry Brown in conversation during the play-off final (Terry Buckman)

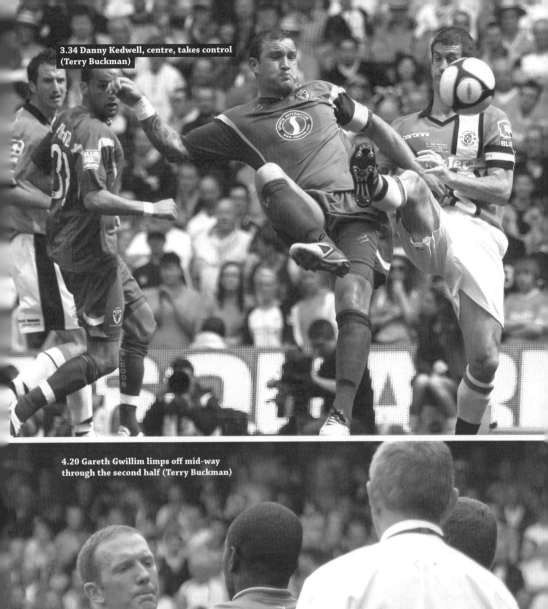

3.34 Danny Kedwell, centre, takes control
(Terry Buckman)

4.20 Gareth Gwillim limps off mid-way
through the second half (Terry Buckman)

then the national anthem – that was the only time I had a few nerves, but other than that I was calm.

Sam Hatton: The first thing that hit me when I ran out onto the pitch was the huge flames that were part of the welcome for the cameras. It was roasting hot. And then there was the noise, the roar. You could barely hear the person next to you.

Seb Brown: Once we were out there, all you could hear was a general roar. In a normal league game you can hear every word. We just had to try to shut it out and stay focused.

Danny Kedwell: Before the kick-off, I talked to the lads for two or three minutes in a huddle. I said: "This is our time, we've worked hard for it." I walked around. "We can do these," I said. "Believe in yourselves. Let's not be disappointed, let's win our battles. If we play as we have done in the last 10 matches they won't be able to live with us. If you win individual battles, you win games."

Ed Harris: For the game itself I was sitting on the bench. Me, Mainy and Jacko were all there. We weren't in the squad, but we were involved. It was far worse watching than playing. When you are on the pitch you are caught up in it all, but when you are watching you can see everything. It was horrible!

Kaid Mohamed: I remember we had the ball in the net within the first 10 minutes. I was up celebrating, but it was offside. Everything was going at 100 miles an hour.

Steven Gregory: The first few minutes were frenetic – end to end, like a basketball match. Then there was Keds' disallowed goal. Luke Moore got the initial shot in, the keeper saved it, and it came back to Keds who fired it in, but he was standing in an offside position. I didn't see the flag and it took me a while to realise – I had already run off celebrating.

Ed Harris: When we scored, me and Mainy went mental. We were jumping up and down. Luke Moore had had a shot saved and Keds put in the rebound. We were celebrating for ages – we had all the Dons fans behind us, and it felt great. And then we turned round, saw the ball was already back in play, and reality kicked in. It was a big downer, a bit depressing and yes, OK – slightly embarrassing.

Terry Brown: For once in my life I didn't look at the linesman. I was jumping about. When I realised what had happened, I didn't get low from it, instead I thought: "Blimey we nearly scored there." It made me think: "We can score against this lot." Danny was offside and that was the end of it.

Sammy Moore: Watching the game was really hard. I've never been so nervous in all my life. I must have kicked and headed every ball. I was screaming and shouting. I'd lost my voice way before the end.

Sam Hatton: The whole game was non-stop. It was end to end from the first kick to the last.

4.24 AFC Wimbledon's Jamie Stuart in action (Getty Images)

4.26 Ricky Wellard applauds the Dons faithful after being substituted (Terry Buckman)

4.32 Luke Moore, right, battles in midfield (Terry Buckman)

4.47 Jason Walker gets the jump on AFC Wimbledon's Jamie Stuart, left, and Brett Johnson (Terry Buckman)

4.48 Kaid Mohamed can't contain his relief as Jason Walker's effort ends up safely in Seb Brown's hands (Terry Buckman)

4.50 AFC Wimbledon's Seb Brown grasps the ball in the final minute of normal time (Terry Buckman)

5.01 James Mulley prepares to shoot in the first period of extra time (Terry Buckman)

Seb Brown: My one abiding memory from the start of the match is Jamie Stuart laying into Sammy Hatton. Sam had been so consistent all season, but he looked almost lost for the first 15-20 minutes. He was nervous, he just wasn't himself and they were tearing strips off him down that side of the pitch.

Sam Hatton: I was off the pace for the first 15 minutes or so. I can't explain why. I was just a little off the pace – half a yard or so. It was just positioning. I don't know why – I just wasn't with it.

Seb Brown: Jamie just told him to switch on – well, in slightly more mouthy terms than that. Jamie's an experienced lad and he knows how to reach people. And it worked. It shook Sammy out of it and from then on I can't remember them getting any luck from his side.

Sam Hatton: I needed Jamie to get me out of it. He started shouting and bellowing at me, and that woke me up. Then we started to dominate the game.

Terry Brown: That's what Jamie Stuart was there for. He's a born leader, when we signed him in January 2011 we were heading for a play-off spot at best, we weren't heading for second. And before every game he did a take on the Al Pacino speech from The Godfather, he was really inspirational. He brought a determination to the club. He is a fanatical winner. He put a little bit of fear into the back four and at the City of Manchester Stadium that day some of our players needed it.

Lee Minshull: I am the worst sub ever. I get so nervous watching. I want to kick every ball – it must be just like being a fan. I spent nearly the entire time warming up.

James Mulley: Managers always seem to make a substitute around the 65-70 minute mark. Minsh, Jolls and me – we all thought it was likely to be one of us coming on. The tempo was so high.

Christian Jolley: I had been coming off the bench a lot since getting back from injury and that was the initial plan. I was expecting to get the nod about 60 or 70 minutes, but then Gareth got injured and that changed everything. We had to shuffle things around a bit and Yaks came on.

Terry Brown: Gareth Gwillim was a gamble. He had been great for us and we needed him to be fit. He was a big player to lose. Gareth was an integral part of the team. Brett's all right there, he's a solid full-back, but he didn't have the same marauding style as Gareth.

In the end we got over an hour out of him. So on balance I suppose that was worth the risk. The problem was that we had to bring on Yakubu and that wasn't really planned. We wanted to use Jolley as a substitute. He would have been perfect, but every substitution we made that day was made out of necessity and not out of choice.

James Mulley: Five minutes later Ricky Wellard went down injured. Terry could have

5.02 Lee Minshull replaces Steven Gregory
(Andy Nunn)

5.03 A distraught Steven Gregory
cuts a lonely figure on the substitute
bench (Andy Nunn)

5.27 Luke Moore goes close as time starts to run out (Terry Buckman)

5.30 Kaid Mohamed, out of shot, sees his effort hit the post (Terry Buckman)

turned to any of us. I was just hoping to hear my name so I could get involved. Minsh and Jolls were probably thinking the same. I just wanted to get on and help us get into League Two. There was no special message. It was like: "Good luck Muls, have a good game." He just wanted me to get on and do well. I'd been out injured for a bit and that had coincided with a change in formation. I had been used to playing in a 4-3-3 with Toks and Gregs. And now we were playing in a new diamond shape, that was something I'd been used to playing at Hayes. And it suited me against Luton. And that's probably why I got the nod ahead of Minsh and Jols.

Being a winger, I just kept going out wide and got lots of space to attack. I could feel we were putting them on the back foot. After the injury, I wasn't as sharp as I wanted to be, but I could sense the opportunity was there. I had a chance to seal it. We had the ball for around 10 passes. Toks got on the ball, I peeled off him and he fed it back to me. I had a touch with my right, saw the defender coming across and decided to hit it first time on the half-volley, low and hard. Perhaps, if I had hit it lower or harder… I don't think the keeper knew a lot about it. If I could do it again, maybe I would have gone across him. It was a good save.

Kaid Mohamed: The big turning point was that header a minute before the end. Jason Walker's effort. That was the moment when the game swung our way. I was biting my nails. That would have knocked us out…

Steven Gregory: There's no doubt that was the moment. The header. It was heart-stopping. If everyone in football has just one heart-stopping moment, then this was it for me. It was a perfect header. It should have gone in, but it didn't. And when it bounced back out we all knew it was going to be our day. Luck was on our side.

James Mulley: I was right behind Walker's header. The game was so stretched at the time. Walker peeled off his marker and he hit it too well. It was textbook, everything the coaches tell you to do – head it down and back across the keeper.

Terry Brown: I had the best view in the house of Jason Walker's header. I was in line with the post and it looked for the world like it was going in. I remember thinking in that split second that's another play-off final I have lost, having lost with Aldershot before. But then when it came back out, I thought fate is with us and maybe just maybe this was going to be our day. It would have been nigh on impossible to come back from that.

Simon Bassey: My heart hit me on the foot. I was down on my knees. "Jesus Christ!" I thought, "This is it." And then the ball was in Seb's hands.

James Mulley: The relief as it bounced back into Seb's arms. That would have been game, set and match. It would have destroyed us mentally, there would have been no way back. Instead, it gave us a new belief – this, you could sense, was going to be our day. You could sense their heads drop.

Sam Hatton: There's a picture in our gym of Seb clutching the ball in sheer relief and Jason holding his head in his hands. It's a permanent reminder to all of us about how close we came to losing that day.

5.31 An unmarked Ismail Yakubu, centre, beats Danny Kedwell to the ball to power in a header in final minute (Terry Buckman)

5.32 Ismail Yakubu holds his head in his hands as his last-minute effort goes wide (Andy Nunn)

5.33 The final whistle goes and the players have to settle for penalties (Terry Buckman)

5.34 Nail-biting stuff for the Dons faithful (Terry Buckman)

5.38 Alex Lawless fires in the first penalty of the shoot-out (Getty Images)

Seb Brown: It was horrible. But I still wonder to this day how a five-foot three-inch striker managed to win the header. It was the perfect header: as soon as it hit his forehead, I was beaten all ends up. Everything then went into super-slow motion. I was convinced that was it. You could feel the whole stadium just watching the ball. As a goalkeeper you would normally never admit it, but I thought it was in. And then it hit the post, everything cut back to full-speed again and I pounced on it. I could hear the huge sigh of relief from all the Dons fans.

Ed Harris: Then there was the penalty appeal late on. I felt physically sick watching it.

Seb Brown: I've seen it a few times since and it looks pretty bad on video, but the photo stills show clearly that he passed the ball before my momentum took me through him. There was no intent on my part and, though I've seen them given for that, it wasn't a penalty. Luton still had a chance. First Jamie Stuart threw himself in front of the ball, and then Sam got a block in and we managed to scramble the ball away. Those last few minutes were manic, and we needed the whistle.
Terry got hold of the lads after that. I can't remember exactly what he said – I was chatting with the other goalkeepers. But it was along the lines of: "Keep going, believe in yourselves and be more calculated in your decisions." We all knew we were at least as fit as them, or fitter. So we went for it. You are never going to go into extra time with the aim of playing for penalties.

Ed Harris: We always had a feeling we were going to win it but you can't go on gut instinct all the time.

Steven Gregory: I got injured with about 20 minutes left of normal time. Mike Rayner strapped it up well and I carried on. What killed me really was when the 90 minutes were up. Waiting for extra time to start I just stiffened up. I was gutted to come off. I wanted to stay out there, but luckily it didn't matter in the end.

Lee Minshull: I honestly didn't think I was going to get on. I kept thinking Christian Jolley would get the run, but when Gregory pulled up injured, Terry turned to me. But to be honest, I can't really remember much about being on the pitch – it went by in a blur.

James Mulley: In extra time we had two great chances to win it. First there was Mo's chance. I was maybe one or two metres behind him and maybe better placed. I called for it. But Mo's a striker and he went for it. And it so nearly went in.

Kaid Mohamed: Luke Moore nipped the ball back and I felt I caught it right – I don't want my effort to go down as a scuff or a deflection. It felt good, but it came off the post and the chance was gone.

Seb Brown: The Luton goalkeeper Mark Tyler told me later that Mo's shot had taken a slight deflection – and he was well beaten.

Kaid Mohamed: With about 10 minutes to go, cramp hit and I could barely move. I was limping all over the place. We had made three substitutions already so I had no choice – I knew I had to stay on. Every time I got the ball I had to give it to someone else as soon as I could.

Terry Brown: When Kaid got injured it would have been perfect to bring on Christian Jolley. He would have eaten up the ground, but we had already used our three subs by then. I had never thought Kaid would have been the one to get injured. I was far more worried about Danny Kedwell breaking down than Kaid. Danny is not the fittest bloke. And I always thought it would be a bonus if Danny was still walking at the end of extra time let alone running. And then there was also Luke Moore. He was an absolute phenomenon that day. I have no idea how he was still full of running at the final whistle.

James Mulley: Then there was Yaks' chance. I think Sam crossed it. If you wanted anybody to be at the back post at the end of it, it would be Yaks or Minsh. Keds can talk for ever about it going to him, but Yaks attacked the ball. He wanted it. For Yaks to miss it was just so unusual. I can still see his face now – he couldn't believe it, I couldn't believe it. The game was there for the taking.

Seb Brown: I saw the net rustle and I thought it was in, I really did. But it had hit the side netting.

Sam Hatton: Keds will curse him forever more.

Danny Kedwell: He should have left it. The keeper was on my side. I saw the ball coming over and kept thinking we need this, this is it. I knew where I was going to go, I'd already decided what I was going to do. And then out of nowhere came Yaks. He came flying in and the chance went. I could have absolutely killed him!

James Mulley: Two golden chances, two chances gone and that made it even more tense. It was probably one of the best 0-0 games you could ever watch.

Seb Brown: And then penalties. As a keeper there's little anyone can say to you at that point.

James Mulley: I had my arms around Sam Hatton and Brett Johnson on the halfway line. We were all together. We were confident: we had great penalty takers in our team, and such a great goalkeeper in Seb Brown.

Sam Hatton: I was so confident we would win the penalties.

Terry Brown: We had been practising penalties for months. I have been through enough play-offs in my time to know that they nearly always come down to penalties. I think it is massively negligent of any manager not to practise penalties. It a) helps players get used to taking them, b) helps goalkeepers get used to facing them, and most importantly c) stops your players getting frightened of the whole experience.
I had my five. Danny Kedwell was always going to take one. Jon Main would have taken another, but he was out of form. Luke Moore was another definite. Kaid Mohamed was another, apart from on the day he was absolutely cream crackered.

Seb Brown: Terry knew his five penalty takers – depending on who was on the pitch. Gareth Gwillim would have taken one if he had still been on. He had been excellent in training.

Steven Gregory: I'm sure they would have put me forward if I had still been on the pitch. But to be honest, I'm not too sure about me and penalties!

Simon Bassey: We had been practising penalty kicks for at least six weeks, and at every session I had taken notes. I knew exactly who had the best record: we had the five. But the problem was that Gareth was in the five, and Gregory was another. So Yaks came into it. Mo was touch and go with his injury, but he had been the best one in practice and he wanted to step up. We ended up with eight who were up for it – and then we had the ones who didn't want to know.

Seb Brown: The only thing Terry had to really worry about was the order. I had my notes – everyone's seen that I had a bit of paper with me. It was a little chart with the goal and a noughts and crosses grid overlaid on top of it. I did my research, looking on the net and reading reports of how many of the Luton players' penalties had gone to the keeper's left, right or centre, and how many they had taken. I was looking not just at their time at Luton, but also their past clubs as well. But I only had only managed to research four potential penalty takers: Danny Crow, Matthew Barnes-Homer, Claude Gnapka and Jason Walker. In the end, only one of them was to take a penalty – but that was to prove crucial.

Terry Brown: I knew Seb had down his research, but I swear the piece of paper Simon gave him was blank. It was all about putting a little bit of extra doubt in their minds. The Luton goalkeeper was a fantastic goalkeeper – easily one of the best in the league, but he didn't have the presence of Seb Brown. I remember looking at Seb before Alex Lawless stepped up for the first one and thinking how big he looked.

Seb Brown: The first one – Alex Lawless. It was a massive buzz to save it. The noise, I remember the noise behind me – it went through the roof. I was a bit wary of going too crazy as there was still a long way to go. But we were now in pole position.

James Mulley: Seb made the save and then Sam put us on the front foot. You couldn't have a better penalty taker. There was never any doubt he was going to score.

Sam Hatton: When it came to me, I was calm, surprisingly so. I knew where I was going to hit it. I was more nervous watching everyone else than I was about my own penalty. But a lot of emotion came out, once it went in. It was four years of emotion. Four years of being at AFC Wimbledon. It all came out in that one kick.

Steven Gregory: It was horrible watching it all unfold. After the second and third penalties I was ready to cry.

James Mulley: Luton scored comfortably with their second effort. Mooro sent one in to the top corner, and then they made it 2-2.

Seb Brown: I'd said to Luton's keeper, Mark Tyler, that the standard of penalties had been unbelievable – four had gone into the top corner. It takes a lot of nerve to do that in a game of such importance. And then came Mo.

Sam Hatton: When I saw Kaid walk up, I was worried. He had cramp and that's never easy.

Kaid Mohamed: I was always going to take a penalty. It didn't matter if I had cramp. I had scored eight penalties for Bath City earlier that season. I got all the goals in the semi – so there was never any doubt. I just wanted to get it over, and I think I rushed it. The cramp would be just an excuse. It was the longest walk back to the halfway line. I was thinking: "I have just missed a penalty and we've lost everything." It was horrible – I wanted the world to swallow me up.

Seb Brown: You congratulate the opposing keeper for saving it – that's what goalkeepers do – but I was gutted for Mo. I looked at the boys on the halfway line. Luke Moore had sunk to his knees, and the Luton fans were going mad.

Christian Jolley: I remember Mo's miss. He had been suffering with severe cramp with about 20 minutes to go. By the time it came to penalties, he could barely stand up. I would have been willing to take one if I had been on the pitch. Maybe I would have got Mo's spot.

Danny Kedwell: When Mo missed, I really felt for him. He was distraught. I tried to lift him, but it's impossible at moments like that. I said to him: "Don't worry, Seb will save us." But I don't think he was listening to me.

James Mulley: Mo had had a tough 120 minutes. He ended with cramp in both of his legs, but he's a penalty taker – that was his job at Bath. But even when he missed I still felt we'd win: with Seb in goal, you knew he would save another one.

Danny Kedwell: And then it was back to Seb. We knew he was a great penalty stopper. He'd had special training sessions and had even got a few tips from Dave Beasant. He is a passionate man, and a Wimbledon fan. It was written that he'd be a hero.

Seb Brown: So to Jason Walker. I had studied six penalties of his. Four had gone down the centre and two to the right. I told myself to hold back for that extra half a second before going – and that was enough to get a claw to it and keep it out. Had I gone too soon, it would have sailed over me. That half a second, that research, that's what did it. It was the perfect reward for all my homework. Afterwards a lot of people told me they had thought the ball was going to spin back in. But I knew that once I got my hand to it, it was going to stay out. I knew it was going to be all right. It looks a lot slower on video than it felt in real life. I was about to put my boot through the ball and kick it as far away as possible to celebrate, but I stopped myself and picked it up and threw it instead. I've looked at that moment a few times since and can't help thinking I looked a bit of a doughnut! I can't describe how important that penalty was. Straight after Mo's miss, the momentum had been with them – so there couldn't have been a better time to stop one. It just swung everything back our way.

Kaid Mohamed: When Seb saved it, relief. That's all I could think of – relief.

Steven Gregory: Watching Seb's save was amazing. I can't describe the feeling. No words can do it justice.

Terry Brown: Then it came to Yaks. Out of all our penalty-takers he was the one I was most worried about. He takes one step, which I hate. He waits for the goalie to move and then sticks it to the other side. You try and do that – it takes an enormous amount of skill and confidence to do that. If it goes in you look like a clever bastard, but if you miss you look like a doughnut. It worried the life out of me.

Sam Hatton: Yaks was the calmest one of us all. I thought I was relaxed, but he was even more so. He wasn't going to miss.

Ed Harris: Yaks took an age to walk up. He seemed to take forever to take it. It was nerve-wracking. He slowly put the ball down and then took a massive deep breath. He only took a couple of steps back. I kept thinking: "He's taking too long, he's taking too long." I was convinced he was going to miss. And then, whack. It was probably the best penalty of the night.

Terry Brown: Once Yaks scored I knew we'd win. I know more than anyone that anything can happen in penalties. I've been 3-0 up before and seen my team lose, but Danny was up next for us.

Christian Jolley: I think Luton's Jack Howells' penalty was the best of the lot. He was a young lad and with all that pressure, knowing that if it doesn't go in the game's over, I honestly thought he'd miss. He put it right in the top corner.

Sam Hatton: Then Keds stepped up and I just knew. He was never going to miss.

Danny Kedwell: I watched from the halfway line as Jake Howells hammered in Luton's third, but all I was thinking about was what I was going to do. I hadn't really kept track of the score. We were all in a line, and I asked the other lads: "Is this the one to win it?" And the answer came back firmly: "Yes." I turned and said to them all, simply: "This is our time." And I set off to the penalty spot.

Lee Minshull: My one abiding memory was standing there – all of us on the halfway line, arms locked, watching Danny.

Ed Harris: Danny had his socks pulled down as he began his walk to the penalty spot. I was about five yards from him and Bass shouted: "Keds, pull your socks up. If you're going to do it, for God's sake look professional!" That comment just drew a look of disgust from Keds. And Sammy Moore shouted: "Just leave him alone, let him do what he wants." The rest is history.

Simon Bassey: I had faith in Keds, but I really didn't like the way he looked. I shouted: "Dan, Dan," and then I thought, "Bloody hell – what am I doing? Just let him get on with it." I didn't like the socks. In 1982 I remember seeing Jean Tigana going up to

5.38 AFC Wimbledon's Seb Brown gets down to his right to stop Alex Lawless' effort (Terry Buckman)

5.38 A jubiliant Seb Brown celebrates his penalty save (Andy Nunn)

5.39 Sam Hatton fires home the Dons' first penalty (Getty Images)

5.39 Sam Hatton celebrates after his penalty finds the net (Andy Nunn)

5.40 Luton's Adam Newton levels the scores (Andy Nunn)

5.41 An injury-hit Kaid Mohamed walks up to take his penalty (Andy Nunn)

5.41 Luton's Mark Tyler saves Kaid Mohamed's effort (Terry Buckman)

5.42 Seb Brown flicks out his left arm to save Jason Walker's effort (Terry Buckman)

5.42 Jason Walker hits his penalty goalwards (Getty Images)

5.42 AFC Wimbledon's Seb Brown saves
Jason Walker's effort (Andy Nunn)

5.42 Seb Brown celebrates his decisive
penalty save (Andy Nunn)

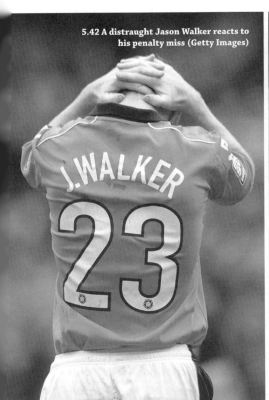

5.42 A distraught Jason Walker reacts to his penalty miss (Getty Images)

5.42 Seb Brown celebrates his second penalty save (Getty Images)

5.44 Danny Kedwell fires his penalty goalwards (Andy Nunn)

The Heart of the City

take a penalty for France. He had his socks rolled down and he looked scruffy. I must have been only about six, but when he missed in my mind it was because he looked scruffy. Now Keds looked the same, and it all came back to me.

Danny Kedwell: We had been taking penalties in training ever since the Crawley defeat. Early on it was just one a day, but in the last couple of weeks it moved up to three a day. I missed only two in that whole period. And when you get a goalkeeper who knows which way you are going to go, it gets a lot harder!

Ed Harris: No one knew Danny was going to hit it that hard. I thought he was going to place it.

Danny Kedwell: Normally I place them, but Jamie Stuart knew their keeper from his Rushden & Diamonds days, and he said to me that he was great at getting down to penalties. So I knew I was going to smash it.

Sammy Moore: When it came to Danny's penalty, I said to Bass: "We are through to the Football League." I had no doubts. I used to travel to the ground with Danny, and this was his dream – to take the penalty, the last penalty, the one that would send us into the Football League. This was his moment, this is what he had lived for.

Terry Brown: Then it came to Danny. By then it was painful, it had gone way beyond nerves. It was such a pivotal moment for myself, for the players, for the supporters and for the club. It was an awful experience. I have watched it a hundred times since and I still get just as tense.

Danny Kedwell: I remember walking towards the spot and seeing the ball in the referee's hands. All I could think was: "Drop it, drop it". I didn't want to get the ball out of his hands. It's a little superstition I have. I just don't like that – I'd rather get the ball myself. The ref threw it to me and I let it bounce before catching it. And from then I was completely focused. I'd had a feeling for a long time that my penalty kick would be the winner. I smashed the ball and I knew it was home before it hit the back of the net. I hit it nice and perfect.

Seb Brown: When it came to Danny, the only doubt I had was whether Tyler had done his homework. Danny always liked to put the ball in the same spot. But in the end it didn't matter – Tyler went the right way, but Danny hit it so hard that no one could have saved it. It was just pure power and accuracy. And then all hell broke loose.

Christian Jolley: I can't even remember Keds' penalty, I couldn't look. I didn't doubt for one second it wasn't going to go in. I was already half way down the pitch running to celebrate before the ball had hit the back of the net.

Lee Minshull: After Danny, I would have been next up. I was going to go the same way as him and smash it. When he whacked it in, there was only one emotion for me – relief. We'd done it.

Steven Gregory: It was an amazing, amazing feeling. I was overwhelmed with emotion.

5.44 Danny Kedwell hits his penalty
(Terry Buckman)

5.44 The Wimbledon players react in delight
after Danny Kedwell's effort secures victory
(Getty Images)

5.44 Delirious Dons players react to Danny Kedwell's decisive kick (Andy Nunn)

5.46 It only took nine years. AFC Wimbledon fans celebrate promotion to the Football League (Getty Images)

5.48 The Wimbledon players acknowledge the Dons faithful after securing promotion to the Football League (Caroline Kingston-Lynch)

5.49 Terry Brown and an emotional Seb Brown moments after the Dons secured promotion to the Football League (Getty Images)

5.50 Jon Main with tears in his eyes looks up at the Wimbledon support after the final whistle (Terry Buckman)

5.52 An emotional Simon Bassey applauds the Wimbledon supporters (Andy Nunn)

5.56 Up goes the cup. Danny Kedwell lifts the trophy (Terry Buckman)

**5.59 Jon Main lifts the trophy
(Getty Images)**

6.00 Time for fireworks (Andy Nunn)

THE SIXTH DAY GOD CREATED MANCHESTER CITY
PLAY-OFF
YAKUBU
5
TURNER
20
JAGUAR

6.01 The Dons players charge towards the club's supporters (Andy Nunn)

6.03 The AFC Wimbledon squad celebrate madly after securing promotion (Andy Nunn)

There was no way Keds was going to miss his penalty. When it hit the net I just dropped to my knees and cried.

James Mulley: The shoot-out – the whole game – was one of the most emotional moments of my life. I have never cried like that. It's one of the happiest ways to win – and it must be the worst way to lose. I will never forget it as long as I live.

Sammy Moore: When the ball went in, I was just so pleased for the boys and for everything the club had achieved.

Kaid Mohamed: When Danny scored, that was it. There was no better feeling in the world. It was party time.

Simon Bassey: At the end I left all my notes behind, along with the details of all our set plays. I went back for them afterwards, but they were gone. Some Wimbledon fan must have taken them – they will make a great souvenir. They might be worth a few bob now.

Terry Brown: I felt sorry for Luton afterwards. They had played some brilliant stuff. Their managerial team were so dignified and deserved promotion too – but just not at our expense. I felt that if they could have kept that side together they would have gone up as champions the year after, but that was not to be.

It was to be our day, and overall we deserved it, we had created the better chances.

Christian Jolley: The celebrations afterwards were unbelievable. It was great to have the whole squad there. Everyone who had helped, all the staff, all in one place. There was no one missing, it was just brilliant.

Ed Harris: Being part of such a special club and the way we did it… It was probably the happiest day of my life. As an outcome it couldn't have been better. I can't imagine what it would have been like if we hadn't won.

Steven Gregory: It was a massive achievement. We had played 50-odd games that season, and it all came down to those five penalties. To do it in that fashion…well, it was relief, happiness, ecstasy – all those emotions rolled into one.

Seb Brown: I agreed with Mark Tyler before the game that we'd swap shirts afterwards. Keds and Jack Turner ran over to me, but I was desperately trying to get my shirt off and swap it. Ed Harris was trying to help get it over my gloves while I was trying to get Mark's shirt off him. Full credit to Mark for staying there – if I had been him, I would have just wanted the world to swallow me up. After that I let the boys do the running and celebrating. I wanted to take it all in.

James Mulley: The whole team were on the halfway line and went sprinting off to the fans and Keds to celebrate. I didn't even make it five yards before my legs gave way and I broke down in tears of joy.

Lee Minshull: We all sprinted towards Danny, and it was mayhem. There was that feeling of relief. It felt like it was our destiny.

Sam Hatton: I just ended up running. It was everything I had worked for in my career – it had all came true. It was a great feeling.

Lee Minshull: It was weird though, I never felt worried. Not even when Mo missed – there was just this calm. I never doubted we'd win.

James Mulley: One fan ran up to me and tried to rip my shirt off. But I kept saying: "I want to keep it, I want to keep it." Eventually he left and I think he ripped off Jamie's shirt instead. I wanted mine – I wanted to frame it and have it for ever more. About five or 10 seconds later, I got up and ran up to the other boys.

Danny Kedwell: And then after that, agony. I had a really bad stitch, and all the lads piled on top of me. I kept shouting at them all to get off, get off. I couldn't breathe. But then it hit me – what we had done, what we had achieved. Looking at all the fans going mental, I thought about the club's history. What had happened to the fans was awful – and now they had this. It was amazing, you could see the emotion. Wimbledon were back where they belonged. And forever more I will take great pride in saying that I took the last kick for Wimbledon as a non-league club.

Simon Bassey: I didn't shout, I didn't scream. It's funny because I am pretty vocal most of the time. But I have never been a good celebrator. You will rarely find a picture of me celebrating. For me, it's always been a case of "I have achieved my goal, and that's it – job done." After the Staines play-off game, I went straight down the tunnel and into the changing room. I look back at that and felt that perhaps I had missed out. So this time I wanted to take it in. I didn't feel the need to run and jump.

  I was on my own in the middle of the pitch, with no one near me. I just wanted to soak it all in. We had achieved something that was unbelievable, something I'd been a part of from the start. It was all mind-blowing, being there on the pitch with all that going through my mind. It was for the supporters, it was for them. It was a massive moment. It was justice for everything that had happened before. It was righting a massive wrong. I sat back and looked at everyone in the stands and the players. And I took it all in.

Sam Hatton: I just remember going crazy. Some fans were on the pitch and we were all going mental. It was such a good feeling.

Steven Gregory: I was on the pitch at the end, trying to take it all in. I looked up at my family and they were cheering. It was all too much.

Simon Bassey: Steven Gregory – I loved him to pieces. The previous season, he had been determined to play in a game a day or so after he had lost his father. But he couldn't get through the game, and we took him off at half-time. He was so close to his family. You have to remember footballers are human beings as well. I remembered the date, and one year after I'd pulled him aside to check that he was OK. Steven was the first person I went to after the penalties. He was crying. I put

6.05 Wimbledon fans celebrate promotion to the Football League (Andy Nunn)

6.06 AFC Wimbledon captain Danny Kedwell celebrates (Andy Nunn)

6.06 Terry Brown, left, and Stuart Cash, conduct the Dons faithful (Terry Buckman)

6.09 Fraser Franks, Ed Harris and James Mulley celebrate promotion to the Football League (Andy Nunn)

my arm around him and said: "He would be really proud of you." I knew what he was thinking, and he bawled his eyes out even more after that.

Jon Main: After Danny's winning penalty, as I walked around the pitch, everything hit me. I have never cried at a football match before, never. I opened up that day, it was so emotional. I was so happy. I knew how it felt for the fans because I knew the journey they had been on, how much it meant to them. It was just overwhelming.

Danny Kedwell: The celebrations that followed were a blur. I remember talking briefly to Terry and then going up to lift the cup.

James Mulley: Keds had this picture on his phone for months after. It's of him running away while the ball was nestling in the net, all the players running up to him and the joy of the fans' faces in the background. It's the best picture I've seen. It captures the whole moment. I had 25 or 30 friends and family there. I went over and waved at them and took loads of pictures. It was perfect. The fireworks, the music, getting the trophy – I will remember every moment. It was such an achievement. It all started in the Combined Counties League, so low compared to the Premier League. To have achieved so much – for all those fans who made the journey to Manchester, for those fans that went to Gateshead and everywhere else over all those years. I was so happy for all of them.

Danny Kedwell: All the hard work, everything that had gone into the season, all that passion. You could see the emotion in the faces of all the lads. It got very emotional.

Seb Brown: When they played "We Are Wimbledon" that just set me off. I was in tears, thinking of the whole journey, the whole adventure. We had done it in nine years, just nine years, and now it was pure, raw emotion. You could see it in everyone's faces in the photographs, but it was that song that finished me off. It was just a crazy moment. The fireworks, the trophy, everything.

Jon Main: I just couldn't believe that outpouring of emotion. And then that song from the fans: "It only took nine years." It sent a tingle down my back and will forever stick in my mind. You could see what it meant. It was just brilliant. The Dons fans had been so great to me. They sang my name even though I hadn't played, and that was special. It would have been great to have played and scored, but this was as close as it could come.

Simon Bassey: And then there was Mainy. I took him across to the fans, and he was suffering too. He had lost his mum recently. And he deserved the accolade – he deserved it as much as anyone else. We would never have been there without him – all the goals he had scored in getting us up into the Conference. He knew his time at the club was coming to an end, but it felt right that he was there. I knew how much it meant to him. He was crying too.

Lee Minshull: We went mad in the dressing room. Music was blaring. Trevor Williams had made this special CD with one song chosen by each of the players, and we were dancing around to it and spraying champagne everywhere.

Sammy Moore: After leaving the pitch, it was a bit of a blur. The champagne was flowing. I left the ground with "It only took nine years" ringing in my ears.

Danny Kedwell: The biggest disappointment of the day was what happened once I walked off the pitch. I wanted to be in the dressing room, celebrating. I wanted to be with my team. And if I had been one of them, I would have wanted my captain there. But I was dragged off for a drugs test.

Lee Minshull: The hardest bit was waiting for Keds to reappear from his drugs test. He took an age.

Danny Kedwell: The test took about half an hour, and then there were a dozen press interviews – that was just horrible. I was itching to be with the lads. Everything in my Wimbledon career had led to this moment, and here I was doing interview after interview. I was getting very p***ed off... But that was what was expected of me as captain and what we had just achieved will probably never be repeated again. By the time it was all done, the rest of the lads were already on the coach – and that's when the drinking really started!

James Mulley: On the way back to the hotel, we were all bouncing up and down. "We are going up, we are going up!" It was non-stop.

Seb Brown: We drove back to the hotel and there were a lot more tears when we got there – all the families and significant others were there waiting for us. It was really nice to come off the coach to the hugs from all the families. My mum, my dad, my sister, my auntie and two of my cousins were all there to greet me – it was pretty emotional. I hugged my mum and dad. They all stayed with us till about 11pm. Some of the other families had started to drift off before then. Then it was the team's time to celebrate.

Terry Brown: I was completely and utterly drained after the final. I had two beers after the game. I was completely cream crackered. My wife had to go to bed by 8pm. My whole family was exhausted. Once we knew we were in the play-offs we had basically been killing time waiting for this game. And everything we had worked for for three months came down to one penalty. Once that went in – utopia. It was a momentous achievement. The players were full of it, but I was exhausted. I lasted till about 11. My brother was caning me for going to bed before him, but there was nothing left. Everything had gone into that game.

Sam Hatton: We took taxis into central Manchester. I don't know exactly where we went, but we ended up in some bar and then a night club.

Seb Brown: We started off in the Slug and Lettuce. Somehow or other we got split up and went off in different directions for a while, but at the end of the night we were all in the same club. I'll not say much about what went on, but needless to say it was a pretty hectic night!

6.20 Jon Main with the play-off trophy in the City of Manchester changing rooms (Jon Main)

6.30 Job done. Dons fans head home (Caroline Kingston-Lynch)

AFC Wimbledon fans wait for the return of the victorious Dons (Caroline Kingston-Lynch)

Sam Hatton: I am not a drinker, so I have a pretty vivid recollection of the evening. Everyone was buzzing. Kaid was playing DJ. We have a bit of video from that night, and it's pretty entertaining!

Kaid Mohamed: It was just carnage after that, with all the partying and singing. Me, Jamie Stuart and Danny Kedwell – we were the crazy ones and partied wild.

Jon Main: That night the whole squad took over the dance floor, singing and dancing until the early hours. That's the thing with Wimbledon – you are always guaranteed a good night.

Danny Kedwell: I couldn't really get drunk, with all the adrenalin still pumping around my body.

Kaid Mohamed: We went to a night club – the whole team was there. I went up to the DJ and grabbed the microphone off him and started singing "We are going up!" The whole club joined in. The strange thing is, I think one or two of the Luton players were there too.

Ed Harris: The one memory from the night that sticks out was all of us together at 3am. We'd been singing: "We are going up" for ages, but by the end of the night we'd got the whole club joining in. Even Bass was there singing.

Jon Main: That day was unbelievable. My time at Kingsmeadow, my memories of everything that is AFC Wimbledon. I am a Wimbledon fan now – no two ways about it. It was the perfect end to my Wimbledon career. When I had signed, Terry Brown said to me: "I want you to score the goals that take us into the Football League." I might not have played that afternoon, but I had played my part in getting the club back where it belongs.

Sam Hatton: The next day was amusing. The rest of the team were suffering, but my head was fairly clear. Jon Main for one was an absolute mess – he was throwing up in the toilet!

James Mulley: The amazing thing is that we were all up early the next day. We left at 11 – even though some of the lads had been up all night.

Kaid Mohamed: I didn't get the coach back down to Kingsmeadow with everyone else. I went back down to Cardiff – although I got my girlfriend to drive as I was obviously ruined. I didn't feel too much like I missed out, as a few days later the whole team went on a trip together to Vegas. It was one of the best holidays in my life. All I can say about it is that whatever happened in Vegas stays in Vegas!

Lee Minshull: The next day it was all a bit quiet on the coach – we'd got back in the early hours, so a lot of us were sleeping.

Seb Brown: We were struggling the next morning on the coach back.

Steven Gregory: I have never been so hung over in my life!

Seb Brown: At Warwick Services, Burger King and KFC didn't know what hit them. Even after that there were still a few sore heads.

James Mulley: It took five hours to get back to Kingsmeadow. And at 4pm we arrived to see the fans there – there must have been over a thousand of them.

Seb Brown: The worst thing that could happen was to have around 1,000 people shouting to welcome us back! But we got over it, and it gave us all a second wind.

Steven Gregory: I was a mess, but that feeling went as soon as we got back to Kingsmeadow.

Lee Minshull: When we got back to the ground it all started again. That's when I really began to start realising how much we had achieved and how much it really meant to the fans.

Sam Hatton: It was just amazing to see so many people there, chanting our names and still buzzing from the night before.

Steven Gregory: The reception, the fans, the colours and then to be introduced on the pitch – that was really special.

Lee Minshull: I saw people crying. Ivor tried to put it all into words, but he couldn't really do it. It was the faces of the fans that said it all. And then of course there's Seb. He really helped me understand what it all meant. We all knew that the club is in his heart, and for him to save those two penalties – it was like it was meant to be.

Seb Brown: Hearing all those songs, the emotion in the voices. It reminded us all of what we had all lost and what we had achieved. It was a part of the club's history, and no one will ever be able to take that achievement away from us.

James Mulley: We went into the changing room, and we were all lined up in the corridor – and then every one of us went out onto the pitch to be introduced to the fans, one by one. You could see how much it meant to so many people. It was great to see that everything we had worked for had made so many people so happy. It was just amazing. And for me it capped a remarkable season, a remarkable turnaround. From rejection at Hayes to this. It was unbelievable.

Seb Brown: At the start of that season, I wrote down some dreams, some goals and targets. Top of the list was winning promotion to the Football League with Wimbledon. I had given myself a couple of seasons to do it – and we did it in one.

Simon Bassey: To achieve all we had in nine years was amazing. To be a part of it was brilliant. To be a part of it as a Wimbledon fan – it was even more so.

Seb Brown: "It only took nine years." It's just amazing. There are so many people to

The Wimbledon coach arrives back at Kingsmeadow (Caroline Kington-Lynch)

The play-off final trophy arrives back at Kingsmeadow (Caroline Kingston-Lynch)

AFC Wimbledon players in jubiliant mood on the pitch at Kingsmeadow (Caroline Kingston-Lynch)

Danny Kedwell shows off his medal (Caroline Kingston-Lynch)

Danny Kedwell and the AFC Wimbledon squad are swamped by well-wishers (Caroline Kingston-Lynch)

thank, so many faces. Trevor, Ivor, Kris, Jonesy…the list goes on. They put everything in. You see the people, the volunteers who help out on the turnstiles, the people selling stuff in the club shop, helping clean up – this was what it was all for. It was for them. There were plenty of doubters, plenty of people who said it could never be done. People who thought it would be a flop, people who thought we would never escape non-league. We proved them all wrong. It can be done.

Terry Brown: Nothing will ever transcend the emotions and the importance of the victory to AFC Wimbledon. Winning League Two won't even touch it, perhaps beating Milton Keynes might come close.

Chapter Eleven:

It only took nine years

AFC Wimbledon fans celebrate promotion to the
Football League (Terry Buckman)

WE'RE NOT REALLY HERE

Wimbledon fans at the bar outside the stadium
(Caroline Kingston-Lynch)

A light refreshment for Dons fans Mike Willis, Andy
Gritton, Mark Jacob, Bobbie Gillip and Steve Hale
(front) before the match starts (Emily Gritton)

It only took nine years

AFC Wimbledon had formed back in 2002, and one of the early goals had been to get the club back into the Football League by 2013. Victory at the City of Manchester Stadium ensured that that goal was achieved two years early. The news reverberated across the football world.

By Dave Anderson (former AFC Wimbledon manager)

I covered the second leg of the semi-final against Fleetwood for BBC London. After the game Ivor got me up on the stage, and the reception I got from the fans was immense. It was a moment that will live with me forever. The BBC wanted me to do the final as well, but I had a commitment to play golf in Portugal as part of a team competition. If there was a way I could have got back, I would have.

I spent the whole day of the final having flashbacks to my time at Wimbledon, remembering the cup final at Woking, winning the title, the disappointment at Fisher and Bromley and all those great evenings at Kingsmeadow. I was on the course when the game kicked off, and I was getting constant texts from Aideen Rochford. I was a nervous wreck.

There was nothing for ages and then 0-0 at half-time, and then...nothing again. I thought my phone was broken! I had finished the course and was back in the villa – the same villa where I had been told seven years ago that I got the Wimbledon job – when I heard it was down to penalty kicks.

I remember turning to the lads and saying: "You know, I fancy Seb Brown to save one." And he went and saved two! I was numb when Aideen told me AFC had won. I can talk the hind legs off a donkey at the best of times, but right then I was absolutely gobsmacked. It was a strange feeling. The journey the club had been through – all that pain. It was unbelievable. To do all that in nine years. No one will ever repeat that.

The BBC eventually got through to me and patched me through to Manchester to talk about it all. It was all a bit too much.

To get promotion – it was destiny. It was like it was always going to happen. The Football Gods understood that there had been a great miscarriage of justice – that people had suffered. If you look back at it all now and everything that has been achieved, you can't help thinking it should be made into a movie. Nothing in football will ever beat this story.

By Dave Bassett (former Wimbledon manager and player)

I was at the play-off final, with my fingers and just about everything else crossed hoping for a Wimbledon win. It was a nightmare as well: I had to leave early to get down to Hereford. There was a dinner there that I had promised to attend months before. I had no choice.

The game was tense, the atmosphere was brilliant. I wanted to stay, but there was no way I would have made it for 7.30 if I had. So well before the end I had to dash out of the stadium. I jumped into the car and frantically searched for a radio station that had the game on. But nothing. It was infuriating. I wanted Wimbledon to be 2-0 up and coasting so I could drive on happy. I didn't want extra time.

And then just as I pulled in for petrol, my phone went. It was a text from one of my mates. Short and sweet: "Wimbledon 4-3 on penalties". I was delighted, so pleased. After all that hard work, Wimbledon were back in the Football League.

I've been a player, an assistant manager and a manager of Wimbledon. I knew the people who had done all the hard work. All the people that had made it happen. I witnessed Wimbledon's demise, the move away. This was a different Wimbledon now, but it was still the same people, the same supporters, the same passion.

Yes, there were some new faces and new players, and some of the old boys had died. But this was the spirit of Wimbledon. And the best thing of it all – they made it back even quicker than they thought they would. It was a great day and a great result.

By Dave Beasant (former Wimbledon captain)

I was delighted to hear the news. The chairman had invited me to the game. I wanted to go, but I was playing in a benefit game in Northampton for Alzheimer's, so I couldn't make it. But I went looking for the result – and it was fantastic. It's good for football.

A lot of young kids used to get confused when I said I won the FA Cup with Wimbledon. They'd look through the tables and they couldn't see a Wimbledon – they just hadn't heard of the club. And now they are back. I am so pleased for the fans, the supporters. The players have changed, but the fans are still there.

I am adamant that I never played for MK Dons. I felt sorry for the players when they moved, as they had no choice in the matter – they weren't given the chance to leave. Suddenly they were playing for a club in a new place under a new name. It wasn't Wimbledon.

And for me, the club I played for, the club that had won the FA Cup, had gone. The remarkable climb I had been part of was followed by a disappearance that was even more dramatic. The fact that the fans have a club they can call their own back in the Football League is great for everyone.

By Jim Brittain (AFC Wimbledon supporter)

I came to football late. I was 21 and Wimbledon had just got into the First Division. I went along to the first home match of the season against Villa and never looked back. The FA Cup win cemented my passion and I was hooked for life. Wimbledon and football soon became my life's backbone.

I remember when all the players had skinhead haircuts – it was around the time Carl Leaburn scored two against Palace. But actually watching the game was only a small part of the whole occasion for me. It was as much about meeting friends, having somewhere to be, feeling part of something and importantly getting one over on bigger clubs and feeling like a bit of a thorn in football's side. I've always had a small rebellious streak, and this element fed that.

I took it for granted. It was only when the Unique Solution booklet came through my letterbox that I realised it might all be taken away from me. I played my small part in the protests – bought the T-shirts, turned my back – still thinking it would never really happen. Even on 28 May 2002 I thought it would be an opportunity for everyone to see sense. I didn't know what I would do if they moved Wimbledon away. To be honest, I think I would have given up football altogether.

Once I heard about AFC Wimbledon, I had to go along. All my friends were going too. By the second season I'd bought a season ticket. I've always enjoyed going to AFCW games, but in my heart of hearts it was never quite the same. The element that was missing was being the underdog, the punching above our weight and giving people pause for thought. It was only when we reached the Conference that we came up against opposition of a similar strength. But even then it was similar strength, not superior. Crawley had the finances, but it wasn't like the difference between us and Man United, Arsenal, Liverpool. That all changed for the final at the City of Manchester Stadium.

I couldn't wait for the day. My nine-year-old son was coming with us, for only his second away game. He'd patiently put up with my stories about Wimbledon in the top flight for all of his life. Finally he could see us play in a big stadium. Handily, the ticket agent for the game, Seetickets, had delayed sending me my tickets, so I had that to fret about rather than worry about team fitness, team selection and the team choking on the day. The Thursday evening before, tickets finally in my hands, I could relax and look forward to it.

I quite liked the fact that the game was in Manchester, which made it a whole day event. I know more people would have gone if it was at the Emirates or some other venue in London, but if it had been I would have been hanging around waiting for it to happen, probably going to Sainsbury's first, a normal Saturday morning. As it was, I was up at 6.30am and home by half past midnight – a complete day of AFC Wimbledon. I can't really remember that much about the match: I was concentrating so hard that I could only remember a couple of minutes at a time. It gave me the memory of a goldfish!

Penalties are horrible, but it did seem fitting for our story. From Dickie Guy to Dave Beasant to the move to MK, there was always some official happy to go against us. The other thing about penalties is the focus they give you. You know when they are coming and what they mean. When Kedwell scored it was rapturous. You could scream and shout, secure in the knowledge that that was it, there couldn't be an equaliser. We were back in the League. I hadn't really cared much about that before it happened. Sure, I wanted AFCW to progress and I was confident that it would happen eventually. I didn't think this would be our only chance. There is nothing like having your club stolen to give you an appreciation of the long game.

By winning that game and achieving Football League status, the "thorn in the side" part of it was back and bigger than before. This time it wasn't other clubs getting pricked, but the FA themselves. It was a massive "F*** you, I won't do what you tell me" to them. I felt whole again. I won't forget or forgive, but it has given me a satisfying conclusion.

By Richard Brazier (AFC Wimbledon supporter)

I was really worried about playing Luton. Anyone else I felt fairly confident of beating, but not them. We had played them four times previously and been outplayed in every game, yet we had got as many points from them as they had from us. They also still felt very aggrieved about the huge points deduction that effectively relegated them from the League, and I thought this would be make-up time for them.

We played well in the final, but I always felt they would score and win at some point. I hate penalty shoot-outs but this was one I was very confident about. Seb Brown is a great shot-stopper. I knew he would save some, but we still had to score – and thankfully we generally stood up superbly in that department. The quality of our penalties was almost Germanic, they were so good.

For the last couple of years I'd had this fantasy of Jonny Main on a 50-yard run slotting home the winner in injury time at Wembley, with 20,000 Dons going bonkers. I had also wondered just how I would react when and if – no, when – we got back in the League and just how much noise one person could make. As Danny went up to take the final kick, I wanted to make sure my wife, standing next to me, knew the significance. I said: "This kick for the Football Le—" and that was all that came out. After much absurd noise and jumping into everyone's arms, what had happened really sunk in. The motorway journey home could have not have produced a starker contrast – cars with Wimbledon scarves and flags flying overtaking minibuses of Luton fans looking as depressed as it is possible to look.

This kind of achievement was exactly what Wimbledon had always been about – more than for any other club, anywhere. From non-league to the top division in nine years, staying there for 14 and winning the FA Cup in 11. This time, the non-league journey had resulted in what for me was the greatest moment of watching football in 43 years, something far greater than the FA Cup win. This was as good as it got, and the previous nine seasons flashed through my head as an amazing, joyful experience that I would not have missed for the world.

By Matt Breach (Dons Trust chair)

For me the play-off final was a real family event, with the Mancunian and Wrexham branches of my dispersed clan providing me with an extra six Dons fans for the occasion. They included my secret weapon: Sarah, my sister, has been to nearly a hundred matches either with me (to see Wimbledon or England) or with her son Sam (to watch Manchester United) and still never seen "her" team lose, whichever one it was at the time. This streak had just been extended when she accompanied me into the boardroom at our first-leg semi-final victory in Fleetwood, so Ivor had demanded that she be there at Eastlands!

Although Luton probably shaded the game, I felt strangely calm throughout and was quietly confident heading into the penalty shoot-out. Never being behind helped the nerves, but I finally succumbed to the tension as Danny stepped up for that final kick. I thought the sheer joy I felt as the net bulged and Danny ran to us screaming was unsurpassable, but when the refrain of "It only took nine years!" took hold, I have to confess to being moved to tears. Not in the wider interests of football? Yeah, right.

By Terry Burton (former Wimbledon FC manager)

For the guys who were there at the start, this was for them. We've seen it grow, it's happened in our time. I suspect that in the summer of 2002 very few people thought they would still be around when AFC Wimbledon got back into the Football League. It would have been a dream, a fairytale. And now it had happened.

Wimbledon have always been good to me, and hopefully there will be a part of me

Lois Collett and Anton Collett at the City of Manchester Stadium (Emily Gritton)

Lee Trathan, left, and Gary Kingston-Lynch at the City of Manchester Stadium (Caroline Kingston-Lynch)

Anxious Wimbledon fans watch the action unfold on 21 May 2011 (Getty Images)

Wimbledon fans Lois Collett, Emily Gritton and Andy Gritton at the City of Manchester Stadium (Andrew Collett)

that will always be close to them. I'm a football man and I have a great affinity with the club, so if at some point down the line there was an opportunity for me to help in some capacity – chairman, manager, who knows? Perhaps when Terry Brown becomes mayor and is given the freedom of the city!

By Richard Butler (AFC Wimbledon player of the season 2004-05)

I was away on holiday when the match was played, but a few friends were there and they kept me in the loop. I was chuffed for them. Terry Brown had done a great job and deserved it. I was delighted for everyone involved in the club – not just the players, but the fans, the stewards, the volunteers, everyone. I still bump into a few ex-AFC players in the Conference South, and we always talk about our times at the club.

By Lou Carton-Kelly (AFC Wimbledon supporter)

The day after the play-off final I bought the Non League Paper which had a special feature on the game. A few weeks later I saw the paper on my desk at home and thought to myself: "That will have to go into one of the boxes of Dons stuff in the loft, on top of the box containing the WISA papers and leaflets and the Dons Trust papers." It felt like closure.

I still enjoy taking non-Wimbledon fans to games and watching their expressions as they look in awe at everything this bunch of fans have achieved. But I don't bust a gut to go to every game now. I'm quite happy sitting at home for some of the midweek games listening on Radio WDON. It's a fait accompli – we have achieved everything we set out to do.

I bumped into Erik Samuelson on Wimbledon Common a few weeks after the play-off final at the Wimbledon Village Fair. We gave each other a hug and a kiss and both of us said the same thing: "We did it, it only took nine years." We did what we set out to do. Now it's time for the football. Hopefully the club is now set up in such a way that it will always be secure for the fans.

Dave Boyle got it spot on. It is the greatest story ever told. It's certainly the best sporting story this country has ever heard.

By Roger Casale (former MP for Wimbledon)

AFC Wimbledon had got into my heart and I was glued to the internet to watch it all. I would love to have been there in person, but I had made a decision when I lost my seat in 2005 to take a step back from all things Wimbledon. When it came to the game at the City of Manchester Stadium though, I was absolutely there in spirit and followed it at home with my family.

When the winning penalty went in, it was absolutely great. I felt so happy for all the people who had put all that hard work in and for all those supporters who had suffered such pain nine years earlier. It was inspirational – onwards and upwards. It showed that great things can be achieved, and achieved again.

By Ian Cooke (AFC Wimbledon director and former Wimbledon captain)

My wife and I, (former player) Tom McCready and his wife all stayed in a hotel in Stockport. We had wanted to stay in the same hotel as Dickie Guy, but by the time we had got our act together the hotel was fully booked. It was the same hotel that the team were staying in. We had a meal and wondered around the area on the Friday night, but even then you could feel the atmosphere building.

The day of the game was fantastic. We were in the boardroom, and they made a real fuss of us. There were loads of ex-Manchester City legends who were introduced to us. The Blue Square Bet Premier laid on a magnificent meal, and there were representatives from every club (although Crawley had their own table). However, they had absolutely no concept of time.

I was on a table with Marcus Gayle and his wife, and Dickie Guy and his wife. And the meal didn't start until 1pm. After the starter they brought out this Welsh singer to sing some opera-style songs. Apparently he was quite famous, but he just went on and on. I kept looking at my watch. It was 2pm before the main meal arrived, and the whole thing didn't finish until 10 minutes before kick-off. I would love to have been out there earlier, at least by 2.30, to soak in all the atmosphere and get a feel for the occasion.

The stadium was great, but with two southern sides the game would have been better played at Wembley or the Emirates – I think if that had happened the crowd would have been at least twice as big. We hadn't played that well against Luton in either of the two league games that season. But in the weeks leading up to the final we'd got some of our injuries sorted out and had hit some form – we'd been playing some magnificent stuff.

As for the game itself, we really played well. The big pitch suited our style of play. There were excellent performances all across the pitch – Steven Gregory and Rashid Yussuff stood out for me in midfield. I thought all our lads did really well. It was a shame Christian Jolley didn't get on, as I thought the game was suited perfectly for him as an impact sub. The game was getting stretched, they were getting tired and he would have given them a run-around. But injuries hit, and Terry didn't have much choice in the matter.

When it came to penalties, I was very confident. I knew Seb would save at least one – he's a good shot-stopper and he's very calm in those situations. And when it came to Danny I expected him to score – he never suffers from nerves. When the ball hit the net it was absolutely fantastic – there's no other word to describe it. I was very emotional, and everyone around me had tears in their eyes. Erik, me and Dickie were all hugging each other.

It was history repeating itself. Wimbledon had battled through and made it into the Football League. But this time round, it was different: the celebrations were instant and the emotions more dramatic. Back when I was captain, there was no automatic promotion to the Football League; you had to get voted in, and there was no certainty that we would make it. We had won the Southern League three times in a row, but in the previous two years had got nowhere near enough votes to get elected to the League.

So when we clinched the title in 1977 there was no great celebration. There were efforts still to be made in the boardrooms and politics behind the scenes. When the vote came through and we had got elected to the League, it

Wimbledon fans before kick-off at the City of Manchester Stadium (Terry Buckman)

Luton's Jason Walker sees his last minute-header bounce off the post and fall safely into the hands of Seb Brown (Andy Nunn)

Seb Brown stretches out a hand to save Jason Walker's penalty (Terry Buckman)

Seb Brown celebrates his second penalty save at theCity of Manchester Stadium (Getty Images)

Danny Kedwell striking AFC Wimbledon's final kick as a non-league club (Terry Buckman)

was mixed emotions for me. I was delighted for the club, but for me it spelt the end of my Wimbledon career.

As a non-league side we were part-time. And I knew that if we got into the Football League we'd eventually have to go full-time. I had known for a long time that I couldn't make the switch. I was 32 and I had a good job at the Westminster Bank. So that was that. But even then I always felt Wimbledon would remain a part of me.

I first got involved with AFC Wimbledon thanks to a phone call from Ivor. I had been to some matches but I wasn't a week-in, week-out man. But Ivor asked whether, in view of my history, I would be prepared to become a non-executive director. It was completely out of the blue, but I didn't have to be asked twice – I was delighted to say yes. It was a difficult time for the club. Terry Eames had just left, and I think they wanted someone with a bit of football knowledge on the Board. After those early days, my role became more of a meeter and greeter rather than a decision-maker. I was happy to leave the big decisions to younger brains.

I watched promotion after promotion all the way to the fateful day at the City of Manchester Stadium.

After the play-off final, we went back to the players' hotel with Dickie and we went downstairs to have a few drinks. The club had laid on some food, and the mood was total euphoria.

I was really angry with the decision to move to Milton Keynes. It was wrong. But that is history, and we can't change it. It is time to forget about all that anger, Koppel, Milton Keynes and move on. It's time for AFC Wimbledon to move onwards and upwards.

What the club have achieved is nothing short of fantastic. Nine years earlier, the FA Panel had said we were "not in the wider interests of football". AFC Wimbledon had proved what a lie that was.

By Kevin Cooper (former AFC Wimbledon player)

I really wanted to go to the game, but I had promised months before to take part in an England representative 11-a-side team in the inner city World Cup.

On the day, I kept checking my phone to get updates. And then when we were driving back with a few mates in the car, I was listening to it all on LBC. I was getting constant updates by text as well. And at 0-0 I was praying for a miracle. When it came to penalties, I was sitting outside my apartment in my car. I couldn't leave the commentary for one second.

That said, the commentator was awful. There was no emotion in his voice – he just didn't seem to understand the importance of it all. "Up steps Sam Hatton and he scores," he said, all in one tone. And that just made the tension worse. When Kedwell sealed it, I just screamed and screamed. For me to have played a part in such an incredible journey – it all felt so special.

It was scary to think just how much had been achieved in such a little space of time. All the memories shot through my mind in seconds. To think I had been there when we started it all off. We had a dream back then, a dream to win our league and get promoted, and this bunch of players had had the same dream. And now it was reality. All that pressure, all that heartache. And now Wimbledon were back. Amazing.

By Robert Cornell (Radio WDON presenter)

It had been my debut season on Radio WDON (the club's Internet service for those all around the world who can't make it to games) and matters couldn't have been scripted any better by the end of it.

I'd recently past the 30 years mark as a supporter and the extremely dedicated Mikey T, who follows the club the length and breadth of the land week in, week out and our cake-loving technical genius, producer Geoff Hawley (Bigfatcat) had got me to try out down at the memorable August Bank Holiday victory at Eastbourne Borough where we scaled the summit of non-league football for the first time. "Can you come back next week?" they asked, and so began a life behind the mike.

Flash forward nine months. The night of the semi-final second leg had been an emotional one and one I'll never forget. I spent it gathering interviews with president Dickie Guy, who is clearly passionate about the club; Ben Judge, who told me "he'd die to be out there in front of this crowd again", and Sammy Moore, who was so "buzzin'" after spending time during the match with the home support that I thought I'd stumbled across a new energy source. But in particular I remember going pitchside after, at a near-deserted stadium, with Jon Main. He knew his time was coming to an end as a player for the club, but would see it through professionally.

And so to the trip to Manchester, a Saturday that started at 5am and involved little sleep. I went up there not cocky, but not nervous either. Maybe it was what Marcus Gayle told me a few days before: "Hey, you wake up on the right side of the bed – it's your day."

We'd arrived and set up early and a pre-production meeting in the plush surroundings of the City of Manchester press room identified what areas our five-strong team – including another stalwart Barry James and our North of England correspondent, Yorkshire Womble – needed to look out for in commentary.

After Danny had struck the winning penalty, though, matters went out the window in the commentary box, as they did on the pitch. Briefly, a female steward came to the rescue of five hysterical Wimbledon fans, reminding us that our commentary position was actually very much in Luton territory.

With the screaming and shouting going on and chairs knocked back in celebration and Geoff typing furiously about the penalty shoot-out to the outside world, I just remember one of us needed to confirm it to those listening in and so I just repetitively let out – in a high-pitched voice, which I've never been made to forget since – "They've done it...they've done it!"

Gareth Gwillim somehow found the energy to make it up to our commentary position to chat with us and then after I dashed down to grab fitness coach Jason Moriarty – whose work at helping the team into the full-time era shouldn't be underestimated – dressed only in his shorts as he wandered around in a daze at the side of the pitch. It is times like that you remember all the hard-working people behind the scenes who put in so much.

I then made it down to the tunnel area and saw the club secretary David Charles as level-headed as ever. Soon after, my travel companions Geoff and Luke McKenzie and I were in the car. The national radio was talking about our success, AFC Wimbledon was "trending" in the top 10 worldwide on Twitter, and there was the story directly in front of us – the team coach. We followed it down the back streets back to the hotel where we witnessed Seb fall off the coach and straight into the arms of loved

Wimbledon players celebrate after Danny Kedwell's spot kick finds the net to secure the club's promotion to the Football League (Getty Images)

John and Chris Jarrett celebrate victory at the City of Manchester Stadium (Nick Jarrett)

Danny Kedwell celebrates after the final whistle
(Terry Buckman)

Matthew Couper acclaims
promotion (Niall Couper)

Mike Harris, left, and Ray Armfield
celebrate promotion (Mike Harris)

ones and another key character behind the scenes, Trevor Williams, clutching the base of the play-off trophy.

Time soon became a blur, but the memories will always remain. I made it down to Kingsmeadow on the Sunday with voice recorder in hand to capture the moments in history for the website again. We were all packed in around the main stand – the pitch strictly off limits to slightly the worse for wear footballers, its sandy base already showing signs of life – for what would now be League Two football.

As Ivor Heller gave each of the staff the individual reception they deserved in front of the stand, Chris Phillips showed me Ivor's phone that he was looking after as he'd missed a call – it was Vinnie. When I got around to speaking with Ivor I made a point – thinking back to when the line had been drawn at Selhurst and I wasn't going to cross it again and felt life had been kicked out of me – "Thanks for giving me back a football club".

By Mark De Bolla (former AFC Wimbledon player)

I was at home in Lake Hamilton, Orlando, watching the game. I now work in my parents' pub, The Red Lion, and we've got the Soccer Channel there. I was watching every moment. I may have left the club three years before, but I've never stopped following AFC Wimbledon.

And when the final penalty went in, I was over the moon. I knew so many of the fans, I knew the history. It was so s***ty what happened to them, it was wrong. And this was justice, this was redemption, for all the players I knew during my time there, for all the fans and for the club. They deserved this.

By Wally Downes (former Wimbledon player)

When I heard the news, there was just one thought in my mind: "Brilliant." For everyone concerned, it shows that players, managers and owners come and go, but the fans are the most important.

By Roscoe Dsane (former AFC Wimbledon player)

I was at work when the game was on, but I listened to the whole match on the radio. A few of my colleagues were tuning in as well – they all knew what AFC Wimbledon was about.

In the end, I think the result was inevitable. You have to feel sorry for Luton – there has to be someone there to make up the numbers. But it was written in the stars that AFC Wimbledon were meant to go up. There's so much positivity, so much willing and so much hope at AFC Wimbledon – and that is a power in itself.

I had trained with a few of the boys a couple of months earlier. I felt I could have added a different dimension to AFC Wimbledon's attack – they didn't have a player like me then. But it wasn't to be. It would have been nice to play with Kedwell. He is a quality player and he deserved his moment in the sun with the winning penalty.

But I'll admit I was a little bit jealous – I wanted it to be me scoring the winning penalty. But Danny's got his place in history now, and no one will ever forget it. I would love to have been in the stadium that day, but then again I would have probably been kicked out for trying to get on the pitch.

The club is just amazing. All that positivity does filter through to the players. As players we are just employees, but it was great to have worked for a company that had such great morals and such a good foundation.

By Steve Elson (AFC Wimbledon fan)

Ever since I got locked out of the Leeds replay in 1975 I have had a recurring anxiety dream where I can't get to or into an important Wimbledon match. Happily, in the years since '75 it has just been a bad dream as I have got to see pretty much every Wimbledon game I wanted to.

Then one night early in 2011 my wife came home from work very excited. She had won an outstanding achievement award at work, and she and her partner were to get a luxury trip to St Petersburg. I already knew which weekend it would be before I even asked. "Why worry?" she said. "We might not even be in the play-off final." She was right, we might not. We weren't playing well at the time, and some pessimists were predicting another eighth-place finish. I knew though. I had thought from the first weeks of the season that we would finish third and play Luton in the play-off final. I was nearly right – we finished second.

I went to the Fleetwood games knowing I was cheering for something I wouldn't get to see. Not that it spoiled those games for me. The home game was, for me, AFC Wimbledon's best-ever performance, and I celebrated hard after that one. Then the feeling of loss set in even as I celebrated, and my friends starting planning their trips to Manchester.

Even as we boarded the plane to Russia I was hoping for something to halt the trip. That way I would still get to see the match without upsetting Krystyna or without it being my fault. Then the plane took off, and I finally accepted the inevitable. To be fair, the trip was astonishing, and a great way for a company to reward its high achievers.

But as we drove through St Petersburg I quickly realised that there wouldn't even be a bar showing the game. Then I found that the hotel's wi-fi was non-existent, so my cunning plan of watching it on my iPad was stymied. As the game started I tried listening though an internet radio station on my iPhone. That went well, and I heard a full minute of the game before I got a text from O2 telling me I had spent £40 in five minutes. After that I decided to check at half-time and full-time before we went off to the ballet.

That was how I spent the extra time and penalty shoot-out of the most important game in Wimbledon's history: watching the Kirov Ballet at the Hermitage Museum in St Petersburg. I managed to get onto Twitter as we got onto the coach back to the hotel, and I burst into tears when I realised what had happened. Krystyna's work friends must have thought I was very sensitive for being so affected by the ballet.

By Nicky English (ex-AFC Wimbledon caretaker manager)

I listened to the final on Talksport, and it was nerve-wracking. There was the early disallowed AFC Wimbledon goal and then all those near misses. And then it went to penalties I just remember thinking: "Jesus Christ, please come through it!" It was the completion of an amazing story. Terry Brown's achievements are on a par with those of any coach – José Mourinho has barely a patch on what Terry's achieved.

I feel a deep affinity with the club, and I hope they keep getting better and better. I'm deeply proud to be associated with the story. It's simply magnificent to be part of that success. And the more it grows, the more it will mean to me.

By Matt Everard (former AFC Wimbledon player)

I bought a ticket for the final. I wasn't going to miss it. I went with my son Harvey, my wife Zoë and her parents, Alan and Josie Titmuss. My mother- and father-in-law still go to watch Wimbledon. They used to support Aldershot, but when I started playing for AFC they went there instead, and they've never looked back. So they were always going to go.

And then Erik rang me up and offered me hospitality with all the other players who had won past AFC Wimbledon Player of the Year awards: Lee Sidwell, Ben Judge, Richard Butler, and so on.

I went to the corporate section for about an hour before kick-off, but it didn't feel quite right. It would have been wrong not to have watched the match with my son. He was more excited about watching the game than going on holiday! I'm not the cleverest about picking tickets. I think Harvey wanted to be behind the goal, but we were on the side. We were still surrounded by Dons fans, of course, and it was a brilliant atmosphere.

At the end, I was like any other Dons fan – a nervous wreck. I don't know how anyone can enjoy penalties. My mother-in-law was as white as a ghost, and I honestly thought she was going to have a heart attack. She couldn't watch. But it so nearly never got to that. I can picture clearly Jason Walker's 89th-minute header. To this day I don't know how it stayed out. I'm not a believer in divine intervention or fate, but…

Then there was Ismail Yakubu's effort in the last seconds of extra time. I think even Niall Couper would have scored it. He probably still doesn't know how he missed it. What made it worse was that he had nicked it off the head of Danny Kedwell. But then I have to admire his courage. He had the bollocks to step up and take a penalty. I never fancied him, but he tucked it away neatly.

And then it came to Danny. I can't even imagine the pressure he must have been under. After everything Wimbledon had been through, it all came down to this, and he knew it. And to be honest, I don't think I've ever seen someone take a better penalty. If one kick could epitomise AFC Wimbledon, that was it.

Down on the pitch, celebrating with the players, I saw Simon Bassey. I was chuffed to bits for him. He had been there from day one. He'd seen players, managers, board members and physios all come and go. He'd been a really good player, but like me he had succumbed to a knee injury. It was a hell of an achievement.

Wimbledon made it back in nine years, and that will never be repeated. I played a small part in it and of that I'm deeply proud. But the hard times came after I left: getting out of the Ryman Premier and through the Conference South and the Conference. That was the real achievement.

By Lord Faulkner of Worcester

Others have written about AFC Wimbledon's astonishing progression up the non-league pyramid, winning promotion after promotion. I have particular memories of two play-off finals, both nerve-wracking, nail-biting affairs. The first was the victory at Staines on 5 May 2008, which secured our place in the southern section of the Football Conference. With 10 minutes to go, we were losing 1-0, and it looked as if the dream would have to be put on hold for another season. Then two late goals and we were up.

Promotion from the Conference South took just one season, and the Dons found themselves in the Blue Square Bet Premier. This was a competition in which loads of former Football League clubs played, all of them trying to win back their League status but finding it incredibly hard. Surely we wouldn't be able to win yet another promotion?

We kept pace with Crawley for much of the season, but once we were into 2011 they pulled away. Promotion via the play-offs was the only feasible ambition – and winning that seemed a far-fetched proposition once it was known that Luton Town would be our opponents in the final.

I had a huge personal problem with the date and venue. I was already committed on 21 May to chair the annual meeting of the Cotswold Railway Line's Promotion Group (I am their President) in Moreton-in-Marsh, and I wasn't prepared to let them down. There was no way I could get from Gloucestershire to Manchester in time for the game if I went by train (Wembley would have been a piece of cake), so I'd have to drive.

To begin with it all went fine. After doing what was required of me at the railway meeting, I jumped in the car and drove steadily north-westwards. I made excellent progress and was on the outskirts of Manchester when I hit stationary traffic – there had been an accident. I diverted through Altrincham and got to the stadium just 10 minutes late.

Breathlessly I asked my neighbour the score, and was told that there was none. And that's the way it stayed, for 90 minutes and then another 30. When it came to penalties, Eileen, Erik Samuelson's wife – I'd been sitting by her for the second half – said she couldn't watch, and disappeared somewhere.

The rest you all know. It took some while for the truth to dawn on me. Danny Kedwell had scored the decisive penalty and AFC Wimbledon had achieved what no club had managed in recent memory. They had won a place in the Football League on merit, without the help of massive financial backers, owned not by oligarchs, property companies or egomaniac businessmen but by their supporters – the people who in football really matter.

By Martin Fielding (AFC Wimbledon supporter)

We were on one of the two "lost" coaches from Kingsmeadow that decided to go the wrong way round the Manchester ring road. This became clear when we saw Old Trafford on our right and the solid queues of shopping traffic for the Trafford Centre coming back on the other carriageway. We had passed the point of no return and had no option but to carry on round another two-thirds of the ring road to the other side of Manchester. We finally arrived at 2.36pm, and after a dash to the ticket office we eventually got into our seats at 2.52!

Only one of my mates couldn't be at the final or in front of a TV on the day, and I said I'd send him text updates. I hadn't had to do much texting during the 120 minutes of play, but now I was faced with the problem of how to text a penalty shoot-out in progress. I copped out and texted him to say that I would only send the

Delirious Dons fans celebrate promotion to the
Football League (Terry Buckman)

Danny Kedwell lifts the trophy at the City of
Manchester Stadium (Getty Images)

Wimbledon fans provide a simple message to the
Football Association (Emily Gritton)

The Wimbledon players spray the
champagne in celebration on 21 May 2011
(Terry Buckman)

final outcome. I made use of the time before the first penalty to set up a draft text saying "Lost on pens but we can be proud of our overall performance". When Keds hit the winner my hands were shaking so much that I very nearly sent the prepared text, but composed myself enough to replace it with the single word "YES!"

The most touching moment after the last pen was when Keds set off for the corner flag, the first person to catch him was Mainy. He must have been gutted not to have played, but he was still first out of the technical area and first to grab Keds round the neck before they were rapidly swamped by the rest of the playing and non-playing staff. Jon Main will be an AFC Wimbledon legend forever.

The overall feeling after the play-off win, other than relief, was that it had all been scripted: from the big things like Crawley getting their cash injection, which probably stopped us winning the league, to the smaller things like Mo having his penalty saved which meant that Keds would have to take the winning penalty. It was simply written in the script that we would win promotion that way. I reckon no one present that afternoon would have changed that script even if they had been able to.

By Luke Garrard (former AFC Wimbledon player)

I was in Vegas when the game was played. We were seven hours behind Manchester, but I was awake and keeping up with what was going on.

I had my brother watching the game and sending me constant text updates: "0-0 at half time", "Luton hit the post in 88th", "AFC hit the post". And then the last text: "Kedwell to win it". It was all too much to take, so I phoned him.

And then in it went. I was f***ing buzzing. I was over the moon. After everything that had happened, this was brilliant. The likes of Ivor, Trev, Erik, Kris, all the supporters, all the volunteers, everyone – finally they had done it. I was buzzing. My Facebook page went mental.

I am so proud to been part of that history. I do feel a part of it. I played 120-odd games for the club. And I thoroughly enjoyed it: I loved training, I loved matchdays. I haven't felt like that anywhere else. Wimbledon is a unique club, and I've said this many times since I left – if, by the time I'm 35, I'm not a manager somewhere, I will buy a season ticket and stand on the terraces. I mean that 100 per cent: I'm a lifelong supporter now. It was such a privilege to pull on the shirt.

By Chris Gell (former AFC Wimbledon captain)

I follow AFC now. I'm a big supporter. AFC Wimbledon – good times, mad times. I watched the whole game in Sweeneys in Ruislip. I was the only Dons fan in there – it was one against 15. No one would believe me when I said I used to play for them! And God, I loved it when Danny hit the winner. It was a good feeling to watch the Luton fans crying that afternoon. They had been so confident, but for me – a Wimbledon fan – it was relief. It was the end of a journey.

I'd wanted to get Wimbledon as high up as I could. Whenever I pulled on the shirt, it meant so much to me. It meant even more to wear the captain's armband. I knew how much the fans had been through. To be their captain was a great honour. I saw the passion in the fans' faces, the way they encouraged us, their never-say-die attitude. That's Wimbledon.

By Jason Goodliffe (former AFC Wimbledon captain)

Erik Samuelson phoned me up the week before the final and asked if I wanted to come up and watch the game. I hadn't been able to get down to Wimbledon since I left, and I wanted to go. But my wife was away that weekend and I couldn't get any childcare.

I was going to watch the game on TV, but when I settled down on the sofa just before 3pm I couldn't find it on any of my channels. I went into a mild panic and in the end I had to settle for listening to it on radio. And that's not the best way – you don't get a full sense of what's going on and you keep hearing the crowd in the background. It was really nervy – I must have kicked every ball. And then when Danny's penalty went it, it was like I had scored the goal myself. I jumped off the sofa and punched the air.

I am so pleased for the club, it's a big part of me. To have captained the club to two successive promotions makes me so proud. I consider myself to be a Wimbledon supporter. The fans at Wimbledon are second to none, what with everything they have been through and everything they have achieved. AFC Wimbledon is a special club.

I stay in touch with a couple of the ex-players such as Sam Hatton, and I still speak regularly to Simon Bassey and Terry Brown.

By Gareth Graham (former AFC Wimbledon player)

I knew the game was on. AFC Wimbledon is one of those results I always keep an eye out for. I was out with friends that day, and as soon as I got back I put the telly on. I was expecting to see it on Sky Sports, but there was nothing. And then I saw the ticker on the bottom of the screen: "AFC Wimbledon promoted".

It sent a little tingle down my spine. I'd played a small part in Wimbledon's revival, and now they were back in the League. It was an amazing feeling. Every club I've played for has got to my heart, but it was AFC Wimbledon that gave me that unique tingle when I heard the news.

By Tony Hill (AFC Wimbledon fan)

My wife and I hated watching that game. I could not see us beating Luton, who in the previous four meetings had run us ragged, even though we had won one and drawn two of them. So it was 90 minutes – and then another 30 – of agony waiting for the blade to drop. I was thinking how well we had done just to get to the final when the final whistle of extra time ended my torment.

But in what now seems like a miraculous premonition, I simply knew we had won it before the first penalty kick was taken. I watched all 10 of them in a calm and pleasant place waiting for our inevitable victory, and even when Mo missed my heart rate stayed the same. I cannot explain how I went straight from 120 minutes of nervous sickness to 10 minutes of warm smugness – I know of no drug that acts as quickly. So when Kedwell's shot struck the net I was pleased but not as euphoric as the mad people around me.

I have the same sense of knowing when I watch the replay now. We ended with 90 points – six more than Luton – and we had a much bigger "family" than them, so why should there have been any other outcome?

Joy at the final whistle on 21 May 2011
(Niall Couper)

Posing with the Cup (Andy Nunn)

Caroline Kingston-Lynch at the play-off final

Wimbledon fan Seb Brown poses with the play-off final trophy (Getty Images)

By Paul Hodges (former Wimbledon FC captain)

AFC Wimbledon has totally revitalised me. I lost contact with everyone from 1970 to 2008, and then I got a phone call from a small builder. We got talking and he found out I had played for Wimbledon, and he got the club back in touch with me. I went down to watch a game against Team Bath, and saw a lot of my old mates: Ian Cooke, Dickie Guy, Roy Law and Tommy McCready. Since then I've been in touch with the club constantly.

Before the play-off final I spoke to Ian Cooke. He wasn't confident at all – in fact, he was convinced that Luton would win. I wish I had gone. I was invited up there, but I was in the middle of a building job and it just wouldn't have been possible. My brother-in-law kept phoning me up throughout the game, telling me exactly what was happening. It was nerve-wracking.

And when it was all done, it brought tears to my eyes. All the fans, all the hard work that had happened before – they all deserved it. Looking back to 2002, it's absolutely remarkable. I was just so pleased for all of them, and it gave me a huge sense of personal pride. Nowadays, I am proud to say that I played for Wimbledon. In the old days, it used to be "Isn't that just where they play tennis?". But not now.

By Antony Howard (former AFC Wimbledon player)

I was listening in on Radio WDON – I log in all the time. There's also the iPlough Lane virtual matchday stadium, and I'm there for about 60 or 70 per cent of Dons games. As for the final – did I take it seriously? You should ask my wife – she was trying to calm me down.

When it came to penalties, I couldn't even be in the same room as the commentary, and I had my eyes shut even though it was on the radio. But deep down I knew Seb could do it. And then there was Kedwell. He's been phenomenal. He's the one signing that really changed Wimbledon.

When it went in, I called my dad. He got the Wimbledon bug like me, and is now a huge fan. He was singing and dancing. He was crazy. It's amazing how much this club has affected my whole family. My dad was pumped.

By Nicholas Jarrett (AFC Wimbledon fan)

The first Wimbledon game I saw was a 0-0 draw at Plough Lane against Aston Villa. Maybe there is something about them? Certainly you can't imagine many people using the words "6 am", "Manchester" and "nil-nil" when describing the best day of their life and yet We Are Wimbledon, no ordinary club. The day started at six and unlike the Ryman play-off final just three years earlier I felt pretty relaxed. Then, well we had to win: HAD to. Against Luton, we all wanted a win but the Conference wasn't such a bad a league to be in. On the drive to Kingsmeadow "Can't Help Falling In Love" by Elvis Presley came on the radio, it felt like a sign.

There isn't too much that needs to be said about the day, stuck on a coach leaving little time to down two quick beers before 120 minutes of football that could only really be described as stomach churning. On the official video we are captured twice; the first in the second half, my brother's head in his hands, looking quite green. But it wasn't really about the day, or even the match. It was about the previous 10 years, ever since the infamous brochure landed on our doormats. The reaction of my brother and father in the minutes after Danny Kedwell's winning penalty which burnt a small hole into an Eastlands net encapsulate this. Some may find it hard to understand the pure unbridled joy at the moment an average football team won promotion from one average league into another, but then we know it was much more than that.

By the way, the other time we were captured on the official video was a few minutes after the photo was taken. We are seen singing "Can't Help Falling In Love", hearts bursting with emotion.

By Ben Judge (former AFC Wimbledon player)

The Dons getting back their rightful place in the Football League was a great moment, and every single supporter, player and member of staff who has been involved with this great club fully deserves it. I was honoured to be invited to the game as a former Player of the Year. I went up with Andy Little in a minibus (with a few beers along the way). I thought it was a great game and no way should it have finished 0-0.

The penalties were nerve-wracking. I was so pleased for Seb, and when Luton went up to take penalty number five, Andy said to me: "I bet Keds wants them to score so he can smash the winner in" – he was right to believe that. When the ball nearly broke the net the emotion that ran through the place was amazing, grown men were crying and hugging me. It was a great feeling, but there was also a little part of me thinking how I would love to be out there on that pitch and still involved.

Afterwards we spoke to many fans who told us that we played a massive part in what was achieved on that day. That's something I will never forget. I will always be proud to have played for such a fantastic club.

By Luke Kirton (Brentford Independent Association of Supporters Committee member)

It was absolutely brilliant. I was delighted when I found out. But it's not over yet. Getting back into the Football League was a great achievement, but there's still one target left: MK Dons.

I am not a Wimbledon fan and I never will be. As a Brentford fan, I have my traditional enemies: QPR and Fulham. I have never stepped foot in Loftus Road. I am even reluctant to watch us play them in the cup as I know half of the revenue will go to them. Yet, when QPR played MK Dons, I wanted QPR to win.

I look forward to the day when Wimbledon meet MK Dons as equals in the League and then when they hopefully sail past them.

Any decent football fan who knows their history, will look forward to that day and cherish it.

By Roy Law (former Wimbledon FC captain)

I was lucky to be up there in Manchester watching the game. It was such an emotional time. A lot of my neighbours knew how important it was and how much it all meant to me. When we got home afterwards, two of them – a couple in their eighties – had made a yellow and blue rosette and pinned it to our door. We've still got it and we'll treasure it.

At the game there were a few of us old boys altogether – Ian Cooke, Dickie Guy

The Wimbledon faithful celebrate promotion (Emily Gritton)

Job done. Dons fans head home

and Tom McCready. It was just wonderful. I don't get to watch much football, but this was a special occasion. My son Gary had got us the tickets. It wasn't the most entertaining of games, but when the winning penalty went in – well, I was very, very happy.

By Andy Little (AFC Wimbledon Player of the Season, 2005-06)

Erik phoned me and invited me to watch from the posh seats. That just showed what sort of club Wimbledon are, they don't forget. I travelled up with Ben Judge, and we were quite relaxed.

It was a good game for a 0-0. We got more on the edge of our seats during the game. There was Luton's header that hit the inside of the post – I thought that was in, and then it bounced out. After that I really fancied our chances – and the boys came up with the goods.

When Danny got the winning penalty we were jumping up and down like a couple of numpties. I saw the tears from the fans. It was a bit emotional, to be honest. It was one of those "get in there" moments. I caught Erik's eye. He was 20 yards away and he's not really an emotional chap, but he had a smile on his face. I mouthed "Well done!" and he gave me a little thumbs-up.

But the real emotion was in the car park on the way back to our minibus. All the Dons fans were coming up and hugging us. They kept saying we were just as much a part of the story as the players who had been out on the pitch that afternoon, and that meant the world to me. It was just another example of the fact that Wimbledon fans don't forget.

By Brian Lomax (former Supporters Direct chief executive)

I was absolutely delighted and overjoyed when I heard the news. There wasn't anything I wanted more in football apart from the welfare of my own club. This was the proper Wimbledon back where they belonged. It was the start of righting a horrific wrong.

The Dons Trust, the owners of AFC Wimbledon, have become very influential in the supporters trust movement, an inspiration to supporters everywhere. And that can only be good for the future of football.

By Iain McNay (AFC Wimbledon vice-president)

My wife has only been to about seven or eight AFC Wimbledon matches, but she had a 100 per cent record – she had only seen us win. She had to come to this game.

What we did that season was outstanding. We got promoted on a mid-table budget. The job that Terry and Stuart did on the money they had to spend was extraordinary, and we should never forget that. The whole success of Wimbledon FC was built on over-performance: the sum of the parts hardly ever really made sense in the final outcome. We had done that again.

There was a spirit, an energy, behind us that was so special, and once again we had confounded the doubters. What we represent to all football fans whose clubs are underperforming is massive. We are living proof that it can be done. The little David

AFC Wimbledon supporters (from left to right)
Bert Dale, David Growns, Simon Bath, Wagner
Gimenes, Bernie Baldwin, Peter Proto celebrate
the Dons promotion to the Football League at
Warwick Services (David Gowns)

of AFC Wimbledon can come back and beat the Goliath of the FA to prove that there is a Football God alive and well and shining on us.

When Luton hit the post towards the end of full-time and the ball bounced out again, it was so clear to me that this really was our time. It was the force of good and fairness coming home again.

By Paul Millington (Enfield Town chairman)

I was in Spain, but I was keeping in touch with how things were going over the internet. When it went to penalties it became utterly nerve-wracking. And then it was over. I tottered off to the nearest bar and raised a quiet glass to AFC Wimbledon and the fans' movement.

By Glenn Moore (Independent football editor)

When I heard that AFC Wimbledon had beaten Luton Town to get into the Football League I did feel some sympathy for Luton and for Nick Owen, who I'd interviewed the previous week. But that was outweighed by my joy for AFC, for Erik Samuelson – who I'd also spoken to – and for the rest of the club's indomitable fans.

As someone who's lived in and around the area for years, and first covered Wimbledon at Plough Lane, I've followed the club's rise and fall closely – and it is a wonderful story. Rejoining the Football League (mentally I've always regarded AFC as an extension of the original club, rather than a new one) is an incredible achievement and an example to fans and administrators everywhere of what can be done. There was been a sense of inevitability to the Dons getting back into the League, but I know that a lot of hard work went into it, and nothing would have happened without that. I hope the club continues to prosper, and hold on to what makes it unique in the League.

By Gary Peters (former Wimbledon FC captain)

I was in Spain when I heard the news and I was absolutely delighted. It couldn't have been better, switching on Sky Sports News and seeing the breaking news scrolling across the bottom of the screen.

I've always been Wimbledon through and through. I must be one of the most successful players in the club's history. I was there for two seasons as captain; in the first we won the Fourth Division title and in the second we were promoted. It was such an enjoyable time. Everything about being at Wimbledon was fun – I just loved the place. So to see them get back into the Football League meant the world to me.

I've faced MK Dons as a manager at Shrewsbury, and remember their local paper asking me what it felt like having been the captain of their club – and I was livid. I said I'd never played for them. As far as I was concerned they were a franchise club that had appeared from nowhere, and the sooner they disappeared again the better. AFC Wimbledon are the real Dons. They absolutely hated that. At the game I got slaughtered by them, but come the end of the season we faced them in the play-offs and beat them to get to Wembley – and that felt very sweet.

My love is for Wimbledon, the proper Wimbledon. The other lot are just a franchise.

Wimbledon is a unique club. It's a club that comes from the heart. It was an absolute delight to see them back in the Football League. Anything can happen now – but that's Wimbledon. No one can talk about the spirit of football without talking about Wimbledon.

By Mike Richardson (AFC Wimbledon vice-president)

In the 2010-11 season the club lists about £190,000 in donations, I must have put in about half of that.

In 2009, I said I would take Danny Kedwell and Jon Main to Las Vegas if they could get 40 goals for us between them. I think they managed 39, but I still took them there for a couple of days.

Then in 2011, I said I would take the whole squad there if we got promoted. I wanted to go, but my wife didn't want me to go there on my own. So it was a perfect arrangement. I took 30 people along with me, and it was a price well worth paying.

By Erik Samuelson (AFC Wimbledon chief executive)

As soon as we realised we had reached the play-offs we got all the players together in the back bar for a series of presentations. Terry Brown went first. His presentation was all about how good they, the players, had been and what they had achieved and how they were going to win promotion.

I followed Terry, and I spoke about how important the match was to the fans. Then I reminded the players that just a couple of months earlier Bobby Gould and Lawrie Sanchez had been at the ground and had been lauded as heroes. I told them: "Win on 21 May and you will be the next generation of heroes. It will be you that will be invited back in 23 years from now, and it will be you that will be getting a standing ovation."

Then there was Mark Francis, a sports psychologist. He did this whole thing on being a lion or dog – sometimes you can dominate like a lion and sometimes you just need to fight and hang on, like a dog refusing to let go of a bone. It is now quite a famous comparison within the club, and it obviously hit home as one of the players went out and brought a toy lion and dog, and they went up to Manchester on the coach as a club mascot.

I remember after all the presentations overhearing Lee Minshull. He had taken it all in, and said: "God, I'm so hyped-up now, I want to go out and kick someone!"

I travelled up the night before the game and stayed with my sister in Congleton. I remember doing an interview live from there with Sky Sports on the Saturday morning. The Sky van was parked in their street and my brother-in-law was delighted to be able to recount the tale of the broadcast from their garden and our story!

I recall being monumentally calm. I was 100 per cent convinced that if we got to the final we would win it. It was a massive pitch and a perfect surface, and I fancied us to beat anyone there – there was no one in the league who could play football as well as us. I'd been more worried about the Fleetwood game and the conditions we would face in Lancashire than about the final in Manchester. I was amazingly calm during the game, even when they hit the post. I only jumped up when Danny scored (I didn't see the flag).

When it came to the penalties, my wife Eileen went and hid in the toilets – she hates penalties. There was a flicker of doubt for me when I saw Kaid walking up to take a penalty. He didn't look right. But even when he missed I still had faith in Seb and the rest of the team.

Meanwhile in the toilets, all Eileen could hear was the cheering. She thought that the louder cheers were from the Luton fans, so she was getting increasingly depressed. And she was vaguely aware of someone else in the cubicle next door. Eventually she stepped out and asked a steward if it was over. He said: "Yes, Wimbledon won" and just as she burst into tears someone in a blue shirt went running by in jubilation. And then someone else emerged from the Ladies . It was Josie Guy, the wife of AFC Wimbledon president and Wimbledon legend Dickie Guy. When they got back to their seats, I just said: "What was all the fuss about?"

The whole day had been like an out-of-body experience. I have never felt as calm as that at a match before or since. But I remember the noise when Danny scored. For me, it was the noise of relief. It was the completion of something that, looking back, we were destined to achieve. My elder son told me it was the worst football day of his life, until the last kick.

I did something I never normally do after the final whistle: I went down to the changing room. I remember being worried about getting photographed hugging naked players!

Then there were the Luton Town directors. Never have I met so nice a bunch of people in defeat. Gary Sweet, the managing director, and Nick Owen were so gracious. Their goodwill towards us knew no bounds. I'm sure I could never be like that in the same situation. They are truly good people.

I spent the next week in the Lake District. But it was no holiday. I spent the first two days filling in an online grant application for the new control room we now needed to build at Kingsmeadow to meet Football League requirements and the rest of the week on the phone and email as the scale of what we needed to do in the close season to be ready for the Football League sunk in. But it was what we'd aspired to for years, so I wasn't going to complain.

By Shane Smeltz (former AFC Wimbledon player)

I knew straight away. I was on the websites following the game. I was really pleased. Ever since I left, I check the website regularly to see how AFC Wimbledon are getting on. And I was following the final avidly. I'm absolutely delighted how far they have progressed since I've gone. I always felt as a club they could go places. It's a fantastic club. I wish them all the best.

They have always attracted good players, but I don't know anyone there now. The players and coaches from my time have long since gone, but I'd love to go back one day and pop my head in and say hello.

They have fantastic support and the club is run really well. Getting back into the Football League was always just a matter of time.

By Campbell Smith (Chester City Trust)

That day I was in Chester city centre. It was a sea of blue and white all afternoon following the open-top bus victory parade and civic reception held earlier in the day to mark Chester FC's promotion in our first season as a fan-owned club. The local hostelries were doing plenty of trade.

As soon as I heard about Wimbledon's success I called Kevin Rye to congratulate him, and a few of us decided on the spur of the moment to get the first train to Manchester to make it a joint celebration. I was still wearing my Chester FC top, so I had to borrow a pullover from Andy Walsh of FCUM, who was with Kevin Rye, so I could stay in one of the pubs. It was a great day, start to finish. I think I slept on the train most of the way home.

By Kris Stewart (Dons Trust Board member)

I had been off work for a bit and I wasn't even sure whether I was going, but in the end I couldn't miss it. I booked my hotel the day after the first leg of the semi-final – I don't buy any of the superstition bollocks.

I didn't want to be with a big group of people before the game. I wanted to be just a fan, to be vaguely anonymous. I met up with a couple of people and had a couple of drinks on Canal Street. It wasn't far from kick-off by the time I got to the ground. It seemed like everyone was there. The atmosphere was weird – great, but weird.

I'd managed to convince myself that losing wouldn't matter – we had achieved so much just in getting there. Yes, winning would be amazing, but if we missed out this time it would be a shame, but not the end of the world – we'd go up eventually. A win would be a defining moment and a defeat wouldn't be. And then the game started, and all that changed.

It was so tense. I'm not very good at 0-0 – and this was a very hard 0-0. There was a lot happening. The longer it went on the worse it got – we could have been destroyed at any moment. I had this horrible headache, a pure tension headache. It was there right until the end of the game.

When we got to penalties, I thought, well, we hadn't lost, and I relaxed a bit. And then the shoot-out started. And then…and then…and then…and then…and then your man took the penalty and that was that. And suddenly there was just happiness.

It was a lot of things in one moment. I didn't realise how important it was until it happened. I kept saying: "F***ing hell!", I don't know how many times. I was stuck repeating those words again and again. It was one of those strange, really drawn-out moments. The odd little tear sneaked out.

I didn't really celebrate afterwards. People said: "You must be really proud", but that wasn't how I felt. Other people said: "It must have been all worthwhile" But that wasn't it. It's been worthwhile since the trials, since the first game. In fact since 28 May 2002 it's all been worthwhile.

By Lewis Taylor (AFC Wimbledon player)

After I left AFC Wimbledon I kept looking out for their results. The stature of the club made it already a League club in all but name. When I found out they'd won the play-off final I was over the moon. I had a few good mates at the club, the likes of Sam Hatton and Brett Johnson. It was great to see them all back where they belong.

By Alan Turvey (Ryman League chairman)

It showed everyone that if you want something enough, you can achieve it. It is silly to say that any team that wants to get into the Football League can do it, but AFC

Wimbledon is a special club. I was very pleased for them. I like to think that our league played a part in their progress. I was very proud of them – and of every team that leaves our league. And there are few people that deserve success more than Terry Brown.

By Violet Wallis (wife of former Wimbledon captain Jack Wallis)

Jack would have been delighted to hear about AFC Wimbledon getting promoted. My son, Sean, goes to a few games now and there is still that connection. Wimbledon brings back a load of happy memories. Jack was an amateur footballer through and through. He would never take any money. He had huge rows with the chairman back then, but he loved the community aspect of the club. And in some ways that's what AFC Wimbledon has now.

By Andy Walsh (FC United of Manchester chief executive)

I was in the ground and what I witnessed was nothing short of momentous. In nine years, what AFC Wimbledon achieved was an inspiration to everyone – to all those who want to see supporters have a greater say in the future of football. To get promoted to the Football League from nothing, from playing on a pitch with a rope around it, shows what can be achieved when fans come together.

The example of AFC Wimbledon constantly inspires us at FC United of Manchester. The achievement of promotion while remaining true to your values is an inspiration to everyone and one in the eye for all those who doubt that the model of supporter ownership can work.

The way the game was played and the level of the support and passion from the Wimbledon supporters that day showed the strength of the bond between the fans and the players. And then there was the penalty shoot-out. Nobody seemed to doubt the outcome – it was almost like destiny. Luton were better resourced and more experienced, but AFC Wimbledon fought hard. The Wimbledon supporters I spoke to told me it was going to happen. It was fantastic to be there and I was glad to see it all.

AFC Wimbledon, especially Kris Stewart and Ivor Heller, were instrumental in the formation of FC United. It was Kris's honesty and his ability to get across to us as United fans about what it meant to him and the difficulties that would lie ahead that inspired and informed our supporters. Even now, people quote to me what Kris said in the Apollo Theatre in Manchester the night FC United was formed.

His honesty has stood us well. He told us there would be ups and downs, and he was frank about AFC Wimbledon's mistakes. We know what a difficult journey lies ahead for us and clubs like us. But the Wimbledon story shows us all just how big those ups can be.

By Simon Wheeler (WISA chair)

Jill Stratton and I travelled up on the Friday night before the game. We went for a coffee in the morning and then drove down to the stadium. There was a surreal feeling about the whole day. I desperately wanted us to get promoted, but it didn't really seem to matter whether we did it that day. We knew we were going to get promoted at some point. We felt no real pressure in the build-up – we could really enjoy the game.

But when it kicked off, it all changed: the tension was there. I seem to remember we had slightly more chances than Luton – but that could just be me seeing it from a fan's perspective.

And when Kedwell smashed in the final penalty kick, the emotion just poured out. People all around me were in tears. It was just an unbelievable experience, an unbelievable achievement. It was justice, it was mission impossible – all rolled into one. It was the greatest statement against football franchising you could ever make.

By Rob Ursell (former AFC Wimbledon player)

I knew all about it. The night before I played against Montenegro for the England Futsal team, and when I got back I called Dave Anderson to see if he was going. I'd have gone if he was, but he was away on holiday.

I listened to Dave Anderson's interview after the 6-1 win at Fleetwood. He was bubbling. It would have been great to have been there with him. It is almost unbelievable what Terry Brown has achieved. And it was lovely to see a club I played for now in the Football League.

By Tony White (former Wimbledon player)

I am proud to have been the first black player to wear the Wimbledon shirt and thus share a little piece of this wonderful club's history. The well-documented 'demise' of my club and the decision to relocate literally turned my world upside down.

I had been at the club for 13 years, so it is obviously a big part of my life, as it is for so many AFC fans. I celebrated Marcus' goal against Man Utd like a kid. I watched my daughter in floods of tears after losing the FA cup semi-final to Chelsea (the team I supported as a boy). I was at Robbie Earle's hospital bedside when we lost at Bradford. I cried at Southampton when we were relegated from the Premier League. So many memories, so many friends made and the sadness of seeing it all fall apart.

The fantastic achievement of AFC Wimbledon in getting back into the Football League put a big smile back on my face. I listened to the play-off final on the internet at my new home in Paris and celebrated like a fool. My wife is French and doesn't really understand.

I will always remember a conversation with Ivor Heller in the gents at the Cannizaro House Hotel at Stanley Reed's funeral when he told a very depressed Tony White: "Don't worry – things are being put in place. We'll be back." Ivor was right. A massive well done to everyone who worked so hard to make it happen.

By Jim Wright (former Wimbledon captain)

AFC Wimbledon is one of the results I always look out for. I was chuffed to bits when I saw the result of the play-off final on the BBC. I'd wanted to go, and the coach deal was brilliant, but the ticket prices for the game put me off.

It's fantastic what they have achieved – and who knows what lies ahead? To be honest, my first emotion was fear. The club have adjusted so well to all the challenges that have been placed in front of them, but how long can they keep progressing? AFC Wimbledon – and the likes of Ivor and Erik – are custodians. They have to be so careful about what happens next.

By Jim White (Telegraph football editor)

I'd been following AFC through their Blue Square Bet Premier season to the play-off final. The moment of ascendance was delivered to me in a text message by my friend Herbie Knott, who was there in Manchester, his nerves shredded by the penalty shoot-out. And my immediate thought was this: so it's true – good things really do come to those who wait.

Nine years may not seem a long time in football history, but it's long enough. Long enough, certainly, to demonstrate to those who are meant to be the stewards of the national game how Football League membership should be obtained. You get a team together, you start them off at the bottom of the pyramid and you work your way up. You don't just steal someone else's place. To demonstrate that fact by gaining League status is but one of AFC's many achievements.

But in many ways, history started again that day. There were now new opportunities, not least to prove in, this age of indebted corporate asset stripping, that fan ownership can succeed and prosper in the full-time game.

Chapter Twelve:

Back in the big time

Jamie Stuart leads the Dons out for their first
Football League encounter (Jerzy Dabrowski)

Better than the Bible?

It was just one tweet. But it was one tweet too far. And it would cost the chief executive of Supporters Direct his job and threaten the very future of fan ownership in football. Dave Boyle tweeted simply that the AFC Wimbledon story was better than the Bible.

---

21 May 2011

By Dave Boyle (former chief executive of Supporters Direct)

When Danny Kedwell scored, I went totally, absolutely berserk. I ran around the pub I was in and out into New Cross Road, oblivious to whether anyone was walking past. Then I nearly hyperventilated, and I sent some tweets which ultimately led to me leaving the job that had become my life's work.

That wasn't how it was supposed to happen.

I'd helped to form the Dons Trust back in 2002 when I was a lowly caseworker at the newly formed Supporters Direct. I remember walking into the first meeting to talk about whether there should be a trust at the club and thinking to myself: "This lot will form a new club if they lose their own to Milton Keynes." You could feel the resolve in the room, even if key figures discounted the possibility at that stage.

I'd moved to London a year earlier, and such was the demand from fans across the UK for Supporters Direct's help that I'd spent much of that time on the road. As a result, the weekly meetings to get the Dons Trust going back in November 2001 were the first regular events in London I'd been able to go to, and thanks to the convivial gatherings in the Wibbas Down pub following those meetings, got to know a lot of great people. Slowly, they became friends.

When 28 May happened, I was there at Soho Square, being asked by the FA to see what we could do to make the crowd disperse. "Release the written report of the decision!" was my response. That report showed that behind a stunningly awful decision lay what was perhaps the worst piece of reasoning football has ever seen. Buried in there was the weasel-worded nugget that this re-formed club would not be in the wider interests of English football.

That night we went to the Fox and Grapes, where Marc Jones spoke passionately about that re-formation. Two days later I was at the Wimbledon Community Centre for probably the most electrifying meeting I've ever had the privilege to attend, at which Kris Stewart said he just wanted to watch some football.

I ended up watching most of the first season's matches, and admitted to myself that I was indeed a Don. While I always knew we'd get back into the league, I couldn't quite envisage when it would be or how it would be. But I knew one thing with absolute certainty: it would be in the wider interests of the kind of English football that I, and hundreds of thousands of others, wanted to see.

I spent the next nine years working for those interests, meeting hundreds of committed volunteers who wanted nothing more than a secure, stable team which treated them with respect and gave them the voice their loyalty deserved and the accountability that the terrible state of the game demanded.

Over that time I also became involved in the co-operative movement, and by late 2009 I was starting to see big parallels between the work I was doing with football fans and the world of local newspapers. I wrote a short paper saying that there were opportunities in the media for readers to own their newspapers just as Wimbledon fans owned their club, and people within the co-operative movement were receptive. Get on with it, they said. (In my spare time, I replied.)

So there I was in February 2011, sitting with various media types talking about running a one-day conference to give these issues a good airing. Since we were doing it on a shoestring we couldn't turn down the offer of a free venue for the conference. We'd been told we could use Goldsmith's College for our event as long as it was on 21 May. My memory twitched; I was reasonably sure this meant a clash with the play-off final, but I couldn't be sure. Also, I couldn't look the gift horse of a free conference venue in the mouth, and I didn't want to hex our chances of getting to the play-offs by saying I wasn't free on the 21st.

Goldsmith's College is about an hour from Wembley. I could go to half of the conference at least and still make the game, I reasoned, before quickly apologising to the Football Gods for my impudent thoughts.

By mid-March the media co-op conference agenda was finalised, and I was down to give a speech on the day. I'd also found that, thanks to the Champions League final being held at Wembley, the play-off final was going to be in Manchester instead. I checked the train times – I could make the match, but only if I left the conference half an hour before I arrived. Something had to give.

The football fan reading this is probably wondering what the dilemma was. It's a textbook no-brainer. But I felt all responsible. I'd lobbied for this media conference and got various people together from several organisations. I was representing the co-operative movement, and this could be big. I couldn't back out. I had to be a credible and responsible representative.

I decided to put off making a decision until we were actually in the final, so as to not annoy those Football Gods. But really, it was a decision made because I couldn't back out of the media conference with only a week or so to go. I knew in my heart of hearts that, if AFC Wimbledon reached the play-off final, I wouldn't be there.

There's a famous scene in Goodfellas where Henry Hill has a crazy day racing backwards and forwards across New York before the world comes crashing down around him. The week leading up to the final felt like that.

I'd been interviewed by The Times ahead of the match, talking about what a major achievement it would be for the club and for the cause of supporter ownership, and how wrong it felt to be missing it. The club had then offered me a seat in the VIP area as a representative of Supporters Direct. It felt horribly wrong to have to find someone else to represent the organisation where I'd worked for 11 years to watch the club I'd played a small role in creating, and which I now supported, play in their greatest game since 1988.

After the interview I'd been to Wrexham to speak at a crucial meeting to help a fans' takeover bid, then flown to Dublin for a meeting before flying back to England to pick up my daughter to take her to Manchester where she would be looked after for a week by my parents while my wife and I did some urgent DIY at home in Brighton. Walking into Manchester Piccadilly Station, I bumped into club commercial manager Ivor Heller, who was off to inspect the City of Manchester Stadium. I then got on a train to London. This felt really wrong.

The morning of the play-off final dawns, and I'm back in London for the conference. It's a lovely warm day and I've got a plan. I ask on Twitter if anyone knows of any

The tension begins to unfold. While Dave Boyle is struggling to get a decent internet connection. Sam Hatton blasts the Dons ahead in the penalty shoot out (Andy Nunn)

An emotional Danny Kedwell lifts the trophy in Manchester. It led to a tweet that would cost Dave Boyle his job (Andy Nunn)

pubs in New Cross that might be showing the game, and it's pointed out that Premier Sports also carry Gaelic football. So my task is simply to find an Irish pub in the area and I will be happy. Twitter is my friend!

The conference is going well. I'm used to speaking in front of a football audience about football issues, so I'm outside my comfort zone here, but it's gone well. I'm now buzzing like Gazza after the 1991 FA Cup semi-final. I wait until the interval to work through my list of pubs that might be showing the game. The second one I call assures me they'll have it. They've got two tellies, and they'll see me at 2.45pm.

I start to get a sinking feeling the second I walk into the pub and see a Celtic shirt. It's the same day as the Scottish Cup final. Not only is this pub showing that match, but it takes about 1.24 nanoseconds for me to realise that so will every other Irish pub on my list. The second telly is no help either. It's showing the horseracing for the sole pleasure of a guy who, in due course, will doubtless die as a result of the amount of money he will sink into this pub – and, judging by the look of him, that might not be far away.

I ask the barman if there are any other pubs nearby which show football. He tells me there's one in New Cross Road. I get the number from Google and call. They swear they have Premier Sports and have no Celtic fans in. I beg him to check for me – this is my last hope – and he tells me he can see the teams warming up. I promise to be there in three minutes. Thank goodness for the internet!

I walk in with seconds to spare. This is great. The pub has some lovely-looking pork pies and a great ale selection. I have pride of place in front of the telly and I am taking the kind of contented, smile-encrusted sip that men in beer adverts do. And then it happens. The screen goes blue. It turns out that Premier Sports were showing a Freeview teaser. The pub doesn't, in fact, have the game. They'll have to get a subscription to do that.

I'm not thinking straight by this point, and I offer my debit card to pay for a month's subscription – about fifty quid, I reckon. The guy can't do it, though. Only the manager can do these things, and he, of course, is out. But he feels for me, and says they have free Wi-Fi. Can I maybe watch the game online?

Now, like anyone working in football in any official capacity, I know that watching dodgy football streams is something that No One Should Do Because Copyright Theft Is Very Bad And Could Kill The Game. But by this point I'd sell my nearest and dearest to see the match, and what one should do as a responsible representative of fans with an official capacity is starting to diverge from what I'm actually doing. We'll come back to this one.

So I get out my laptop, connect up, and head for one of the many websites which tell you where to look, and several clicks later I'm watching the game. The internet is the best thing ever!

But the network (BT OpenWorld – you didn't ask, but I'm distributing blame widely here) is (as they say in the city where my beloved Dons are playing) bobbins. It's jerkier than a Eighties schoolboy doing a robot impression, and grainier than a holiday snap from the 1880s. I decide to use my mobile phone as the connection instead. It's more reliable than the Wi-Fi, but no better in terms of the quality. When Luton hit the post on 88 minutes, for about 30 seconds I have no idea whether the ball has gone in or not until the pictures starting moving again. Can you imagine how I felt? The low bitrate was causing a very high heart rate.

I know I can't watch extra time like this, never mind those things that come afterwards and begin with 'p'. No sir. We are going to switch medium: it's time for Radio WDON, where the lack of pictures will mean a reliable and consistent connection.

But now there is sensory underload. I need something to do with my eyes, and my hands can't keep lifting pints to my lips, as lovely as the four I've had by this point have been. After all, I am a responsible and judicious representative of fans. And then I get a bright idea, since my laptop is open: Twitter is my friend!

I can follow the action there. Heck, it's kind of like being there – so many people are tweeting from the ground. There's also a global cuddle of love from all those people around the world who believe that it will be in the wider interests of football if our righteous club is playing in League Two. Wonderfully, Twitter is slightly behind the radio commentary, so it's like we're reacting to the action. This is great, I think, as I embark on pint number five.

And so to penalties (I can't remember a damn thing about extra time) and my drinking/listening/tweeting companion is genuinely worried for me. He sees my face drained of colour, hears my shallow and laboured breathing. A few other people have gathered around us in the pub, probably as intrigued by me and my palpitations as much as the action 250 miles away.

As Danny Kedwell walks forward, I start to cry. This would mean so much, so very, very much. Not just for me, or the club, or for all my friends in the stadium, but for fan ownership and for Supporters Direct, of which I am now chief executive.

I can't help thinking how wonderful a win would be for the idea that there has to be a better way to own and run clubs than for them to be the playthings of rich men. How it would be bloody brilliant news for people who were trying to make it happen at their clubs up and down the country, and often got abuse for their efforts. I think of those who said it was a crazy idea, which wouldn't survive the first flushes of enthusiasm, who predicted that, since fans shouldn't run clubs, fans couldn't run clubs.

Most of all, I think of those who had told Wimbledon fans that what they were trying to do was not in the wider interests of English football, and of all those people I knew who were at the game and had refused to be told what to do and what to think and instead, by force of will, had changed the landscape of the game.

And Kedwell scores. I go crazy. Certifiably, unable-to-tell-you-precisely-what-I-did-next bonkers. Maybe it's work stress. Maybe it's the beer. Maybe it's just the fact that AFC Wimbledon are now a League club. The Twitter hashtag is rolling fast, with messages pouring in from well-wishers who, in our moment of glory, take some vindication as people who share the ideals and ethos of the club.

Now I'd love to say that at this point I left my computer unattended, and someone came in and messed with it (they might well have been the same person who sent emails from Garry Cook's account at Man City). But that's not true. I do the blag myself.

I send three tweets. The first compares our success to the title of the 1963 epic The Greatest Story Ever Told. This would later be said to be disrespectful to the film's subject matter of the Bible, which makes me wish the film title had been used some years earlier to retell a story like Pinocchio.

I send another tweet which reminds people what was said by Pete Winkelman about how never again could a club rise from the lower reaches of non-league football like Wimbledon did before. And I then send something unprintable in a family newspaper about the person who'd chaired the committee which had pronounced that all this was not in the wider interests of English football, and had never publicly acknowledged the horribleness of this remark, never mind apologised.

Actually, I don't send that about him. I send it about a minor TV psychologist who shares several syllables of his name with the panel chairman. I come back from the loo to be informed of my mistake, and I do what any responsible and judicious representative would do. I correct it, and with a flourish of my finger I send the tweet again – and send my career down the gurgler.

As I walked home that night, I was called by the Guardian's David Conn, friend of Wimbledon and fans everywhere. He'd seen my tweets and wanted to share the joy. Neither of us realised that I was a dead man walking.

The tweets were soon deleted and apologised for. When the next two weeks' papers were full of goings-on at FIFA, I thought that on the scale of egregious problems in football administration, what I had done would be even less likely to be newsworthy. Sadly not.

A reporter (who didn't follow me on Twitter) had been sent a copy of my tweets. He ran the story after the media circus had left Sepp Blatter behind, publishing the first tweet and referring to the rest. Several days later, it became clear that what I did had put the job security of my hard-working colleagues in jeopardy. In a surprisingly calm moment amidst the storm, it became clear to me that there was only one course of action I could take, and I fell on my sword.

The moral of the story is that if you find yourself euphoric and inebriated at the realisation of long-hoped for but scarcely imagined success, which validates what you've spent 11 years working for, and you get an urge to share your thoughts with the world, then don't.

And if, rather more prosaically, you see a friend with a drink in one hand, and a tweeting phone in the other, urge them to choose between these two combustible ingredients. Twitter is not, in the end, your friend. It's asymmetrically perceived. Just because it scrolls off your screen in a matter of seconds doesn't mean that it's scrolled off everyone else's.

I don't blame anyone for what happened apart from myself. It wasn't nice, of course, but no one made me send those tweets. Well, apart from Danny Bloody Kedwell.

By Niall Couper ("Supporters Direct Has My Support" Facebook group founder)

Football is a funny old game, someone once said. Tell that to Dave Boyle. While the rest of us were going potty after AFC Wimbledon's glorious victory at the City of Manchester Stadium, he'd got caught up in the emotion too and got busy in the world of social media. What he did would prove costly – and come perilously close to destroying the fans' movement in the UK.

Those of us in the know may well have sympathy – and even wholehearted agreement – with the sentiments of the tweet in question. Yes, the Wimbledon story is good. But there are several bits of advice you get given early in life. Such as, religion – where possible, don't talk about it. That's especially advisable when you happen to be the chief executive of Supporters Direct and lazy journalists are listening.

The consequences were dramatic. Within days the tweet had become the centre of an article published in the Daily Mail, and as a consequence the Government-

The fireworks go off in Manchester. More were set to explode in London a few days later (Terry Buckman)

funded Football Stadia Improvement Fund withdrew its £1.8m annual funding for Supporters Direct. Without that cash, Supporters Direct faced extinction. In one stroke the organisation that had helped over 50 clubs across the UK, and set up hundreds of trusts in football and rugby league across the country, was doomed.

From Swansea City to Liverpool and FC United of Manchester, and of course AFC Wimbledon, there was shock and anger. Dave Boyle fell on his sword and resigned in an attempt to get the decision reversed. It didn't work. But the football world had failed to learn. They had underestimated the power of the movement Dave had helped to shape. Fans were no longer there to be trampled on.

Personally, I was incensed. I knew all the good work Supporters Direct had done and I couldn't stand by and see it all go to waste. I set up a Facebook Group, Supporters Direct Has My Support, and sat back and watched as the whole movement exploded. Within an hour it had 100 members, within 24 hours 1,500 members. Supporters from across the country were calling on their trusts to demand that the FSIF reverse its decision. Press releases were sent and statements posted on the internet. But the main success came through lobbying.

All three main political parties had pledged their support to the growing fans' movement, and now was the time for them to put their words into action. Labour were quick off the mark with a statement, and the LibDems soon followed. An early day motion was put down in the House of Commons, and fans of all colours lobbied their MPs to get them to sign it.

In the end, 121 MPs signed. Out of 2,172 EDMs in that parliamentary session, this one made the top five per cent in terms of support. And the ministers that mattered listened. They took their concerns to the FA and, eight weeks after Dave Boyle's infamous tweet, the funding was back.

So fans can make a difference. But it is a pity that Dave Boyle's indiscretion cost him his job, that a man so instrumental in AFC Wimbledon's development paid such a price on the very day that the Trust he helped to create achieved its most famous goal. It remains the one grey cloud over what should have been a perfect summer.

Three heroes depart

Shortly after the victory in Manchester, the Dons were hit by a bombshell. Danny Kedwell, the club's talisman and hero of the penalty shoot-out, handed in a transfer request. Steven Gregory, a cornerstone of the Dons midfield for two seasons, and Kaid Mohamed, the star of the semi-final, were also to depart.

June 2011
By Danny Kedwell (Gillingham player)

I knew Gillingham were interested in me and I remember talking to Erik about it. It was one of the hardest conversations I've ever had. He explained that there were bound to be several clubs coming in for me, but he was not going to talk to anyone unless I put in a transfer request. It was a compliment, I suppose, as I knew there and then how much he valued me.

But I wanted to know who the offers were from. I so didn't want to do it. It was Erik's club and he didn't want to lose me. There were three or four clubs interested – but as soon as I heard about Gillingham there was only really one choice. And this is why I really understand Wimbledon fans. I used to watch Gillingham when I was seven and I used to say to my family: "I'm going to play for this club one day." It was my boyhood dream, what I had always wanted to do. I know what it means to be a fan.

And then there was the family side to it too. I had been travelling for seven years. I had two kids going to school, and it was always a struggle to get back in time to see them. It wasn't fair on the other lads at AFC Wimbledon – they'd stay on and I'd shoot off. I was nearly 28. If I'd been 21 or 22, maybe it would have been different. But when you have a mortgage and kids it is difficult. I had to think about my family and my security. Gillingham, my home town, my boyhood heroes, had offered me a three-year contract. At Wimbledon there was one year and the option of another year on offer.

I remember Terry once saying to me that I was one of the few players who really understood what Wimbledon was about. He said I was the only one who really knew what the fans felt. I knew what it was to be a fan, and I had grown to really understand the history of AFC Wimbledon.

It was all about the fans – their passion, after everything that had happened to them. Getting into the League meant as much to me deep down as it did to them. That's why I always put in 120 per cent. This club deserved justice.

It was only ever going to be Gillingham that could wrench me away.

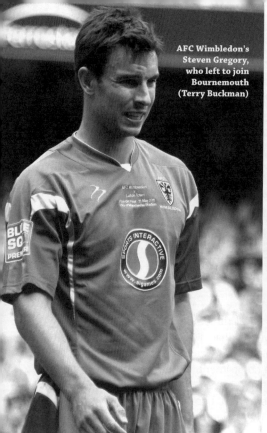

AFC Wimbledon's Steven Gregory, who left to join Bournemouth (Terry Buckman)

Kaid Mohamed, who swapped South London for Cheltenham in the summer of 2011 (Terry Buckman)

By Kaid Mohamed (Cheltenham Town player)

I was speaking to the gaffer. He sat me down in front of my parents and said: "We want him signed up, we need to get him accommodation and we need to get him settled in." I wanted 100 per cent to sign for AFC Wimbledon, but it was taking too long and there were a few other clubs sniffing around. Cheltenham were one of those. They offered me a good deal. It meant I could remain in Cardiff and stay with my girlfriend there. It was a horrible choice to make, but AFC Wimbledon is still the first result I look for when I come off the pitch. I wasn't there for long, but the club got into my heart.

By Steven Gregory (AFC Bournemouth player)

I never wanted to leave. It never really crossed my mind, but then Bournemouth came in with a bid that was rejected. I got wind of it, and I started to think that perhaps it was the right thing to go. It all came down to playing in League One.

I knew the area well. My girlfriend had been studying at the university down there, but she did not really play a part in the decision – she was set to head back anyway. And the issue of money never came into it either. It was about playing at that level. I would never have gone to a club in the same league. I just wanted to see what life was like in League One.

AFC Wimbledon's Danny Kedwell,
who moved to Gillingham to be closer
to his family (Andy Nunn)

By Terry Brown (AFC Wimbledon manager)

I do look back at the side that triumphed in Manchester and wonder how well they would have done in League Two if we had managed to keep them all together. Danny Kedwell, Steven Gregory and Kaid Mohamed were three of our most influential players. It was a massive, massive blow to lose them all. Fair play to the rest of the squad for the way they rolled up their sleeves and worked hard the following year.

We were never going to win the battle with Danny. He was offered a three-year deal and we simply couldn't match that. But it all came down to the fact that Gillingham was his home-town club. He is a very strong-minded player. He had gone to a different level when we made him captain, and if we had stopped him going to Gillingham we would never have seen the same Danny Kedwell.

With Kaid Mohamed we couldn't get anywhere near the money Cheltenham were offering him. He was also based in Wales, and Cheltenham was only up the road.

Steven Gregory was the one I thought we had the best chance to keep, but Bournemouth were an established League One club. We couldn't offer him anything near what they were offering. My budget wasn't even going to get close. So we had to try and get the most we could for him.

The three of them would have made a huge difference for us.

Breach takes the chair

Matt Breach had moved from Wimbledon FC supporter to AFC Wimbledon supporter, and from volunteer to Dons Trust Board member. He had become chair of the Dons Trust in December 2010, but the realisation of what it truly meant dawned on him only after the victory at Manchester

Summer 2011
By Matt Breach (chair of the Dons Trust)

After four years on the Board, I put myself forward for election as chair of the Board in December 2010 and was gratified – not to mention a little nervous – to be unanimously voted into the position by my fellow Board members.

In the year that followed I felt we made great progress – and not just by getting promoted into the League. We became much more organised and professional at all levels of the club. And there was progress on the holy grail of a return back home to a stadium in Wimbledon.

I was amazed at how much energy I found to devote to the role. I no longer had time for much of a social life outside work and football – thankfully, I have an understanding partner! And then there was the buzz of being so involved with my club.

But what the position of being chair of the Dons Trust Board really means was brought home to me when club secretary David Charles handed me a copy of the infamous "Fit and Proper Persons Test" in the summer of 2011 to fill out in readiness for our return to the Football League. After nine years, we, the fans, had our own Football League club, and serving as the chair of the Board made me the "face" of that ownership, a position I was immensely proud to hold.

An excellent development for the Dons

In the afterglow of the victory in Manchester, a momentous announcement came through from the Football League Trust. The club's youth scheme was granted Centre of Excellence status. In eight years the youth set-up had moved from a couple of Sunday League sides run by parents to a fully fledged elite centre for age groups from under-9 to under-18.

19 July 2011
Football League Trust meeting

By Nigel Higgs (AFC Wimbledon youth and community director)

The single biggest achievement for me was the creation of the Centre of Excellence. It was the completion of a long, hard journey that began at the start of the 2003-04 season. I was on the Dons Trust Board at the time and I volunteered (or was volunteered, I can't quite remember which) to look after the youth and community schemes. I think Lou Carton-Kelly was also involved back then, and there was a realisation early on that we needed a youth scheme.

The first youth teams were led by Terry Eames and some of his friends, the likes of John Egan and Paul Bentley. It wasn't anything sophisticated. They looked around the local area and persuaded teams to play under the AFC Wimbledon banner. We started with under-8s, under-9s and under-12s and grew to two teams in each age group from under-7s to under-16s. But basically they were Sunday league sides made up of a coach, his son and his son's mates. The coaches were all friends of Terry Eames. They were all good-standard footballers, but there was no real connection with the Dons Trust. There was a real disconnect, but that shouldn't take anything away from their achievements. Those early teams were our foundations, and without them there would be no Centre of Excellence now.

At the time everything was exciting and passionate, and that went on for two or three years. But it couldn't go on like that: we needed to try and gain some credibility. It was around this time that I was appointed to the AFC Wimbledon Board as youth and community director, and that cranked everything up a notch or two. I was given a budget and I knew things had to change. The club was moving into a new era. The youth system could no longer be run by a bunch of enthusiastic amateurs.

We set up a strategy. We needed to have a fit-for-purpose youth set-up, with professional coaches, good facilities and subscriptions coming in. Most importantly, we needed people who believed in the Dons Trust and AFC Wimbledon.

I knew we couldn't do everything overnight. It was going to be a two or three-year journey. Big changes have to be made in the close season – you can't go changing a youth-team manager in mid-season as you risk losing the team's players. A couple of teams did walk away, but I take great pride that some of those players came back, and some of them went on to become scholars.

We also linked up with Merton College, and that's been really useful in providing a rounded education for our scholars.

Then there was the arrival of some key individuals in key positions. Mark Robinson had been in charge of the under-10s, and he became head of youth. Jeremy Sauer also stepped up to help run the scheme. He had been helping with the younger teams, from under-9 to under-12. David Walsh also volunteered his services. He was perfect. He was an ex-deputy head, a former PE teacher and a fully licensed coach. He is now the education officer at the Centre of Excellence. Those three proved invaluable in our development. We all had a shared vision, and that was crucial.

But there was also the big issue of funding. One of the reasons we had been attracting players was that we didn't charge subscription fees, but that couldn't continue. We needed the extra revenue, and we introduced subscriptions. It set us apart from other clubs who didn't charge, and that made it difficult for us. But we have something extra – we have the AFC Wimbledon story, and we use that as a selling point. I want the kids to buy into it. It's easier to get the younger ones to do that; the older ones can be a bit more cynical.

We have our own set of values, our tradition and our history, and we tell them all about it from day one. We want them to believe in the shirt. So when the crunch comes and a Premier League side, who they have no chance of playing for when they are older, comes in for them, they choose to stay with us. Reece William-Bowers is an excellent example. As an under-13 he turned down Fulham to stay with us. Mark Robinson used to support Chelsea, but he is a fully converted Dons fan now and he tells the Wimbledon story brilliantly. He's probably the best signing the club has ever made. I remember listening in to him telling a parent about the whole journey. It was inspirational. I was almost in tears by the end of it.

But the big step towards a Centre of Excellence came shortly after that momentous day in Manchester. Mark Robinson, Jeremy Sauer, David Walsh and I locked ourselves in a room and set about putting together a business case for the Centre of Excellence. We had told the club what we were trying to achieve, and they were very supportive. The Football League Trust were also very supportive. They gave us all the templates and documents to help us get the funding, but there was still a lot to do.

We still had a few doubts about the training ground, but King's College School too were very supportive and very helpful. The set-up at their sports ground in New Malden is first class. We are their main "external client", and it's a fantastic venue. Without their help we couldn't have fulfilled the criteria to become a Centre of Excellence for the start of the 2011-12 season. It completed a remarkable eight years.

Most of the teams train and play there now. It's a beautiful setting, where you can see three or four games happening simultaneously. I take great pride in the fact that by the end of our first season in the Football League, 90 to 95 per cent of the players in our squads from under-9 to under-16 had been players in the Surrey Youth League. At the end of that first season we staged a series of matches against the Reading and Charlton Academy sides – supposedly a level above our status as a Centre of Excellence – and we more than held our own, winning a couple and drawing some.

It's so rare that I get the chance to look back and see how far we have come. But I will be content in my dotage to be able to say that I have done something for this club. It's all a far cry from my days of selling Yellow and Blue outside Selhurst Park back in 2001!

The long journey to Merton

Ever since AFC Wimbledon came into existence, WISA has campaigned tirelessly to ensure that the club's future lies in the London Borough of Merton – Kingsmeadow is just outside the borough's boundary. It is a battle that has relied on the help and expertise of Dons fans everywhere.

July 2011
By Gail Moss (WISA)

It all began towards the end of 2005. An eagle-eyed Tim Hillyer – Dons fan and long-standing Wimbledon resident – spotted that Merton Council were about to start preparing the borough's long-term development plan. The plan would set out a blueprint for planning strategy for the next 15 years. Tim knew exactly what the implications were for us. This, he said, would be an ideal opportunity to lay the foundations for the club's potential return to Merton. And he thought this was something WISA could get its teeth into.

At the time, it all seemed very abstract. It was only two years since we had bought Kingsmeadow from Mr Khosla, and with crowds comfortably under 3,000 there seemed little need to plan for a new and bigger stadium. But we knew that a commitment by Merton Council to help us return, enshrined in the plan, could be crucial if and when AFC Wimbledon was in a position to consider moving back.

Merton Council issued a call for anyone to suggest what the most important planning issues were, and we leapt on it, putting up a news piece on the WISA website urging our fans to write to the council. We provided a model letter, arguing why it was important to help bring first-class football back to the borough.

The response was big enough for the council to take notice. And in April 2006, they issued a statement that included the observation: "There is a need to consider the creation of a multi-purpose sports stadium in the borough to provide a resource for local sports teams." It was a start.

A further opportunity to lobby the council – in fact, all the local political parties – came with the council elections the following month. All the parties expressed support for bringing the Dons back where they belong. Momentum was building.

A year later, the borough plan was taking shape. Once again, the time had come to ask people to write in for the last round of public consultation.

We needed a big response. WISA held an open meeting in July 2007 at the Wimbledon Community Centre. Steve Cardis, then Merton's planning policy team leader, explained the plans and answered questions. He stressed that any move back to Merton had to be club-led. But, he added, as fans we could still influence the final document, and there were two main sections of the plan which we should address. The council's support for a new multi-purpose sports stadium had to be included as a policy in the Core Strategy document, and a specific reference to AFC Wimbledon as a user of the stadium had to go with it.

By this time we were fortunate to have on board Graham Timms, a WISA member and a planning consultant by profession. Graham provided the model response. The council wanted people to use a specially designed website, but it was extremely

difficult to navigate, as Graham and Sean Fox, then WISA Treasurer, found one evening when it took them several hours to road-test the submission process.

We managed to write a painstaking, step-by-step guide on how to submit a response. The Dons Trust also emailed their members with our instructions, and put a news piece on the club's website.

In the end, around 150 people responded. It made a sizeable impact – the football stadium was by a long way the topic that elicited the most responses.

But there was more to come. As a new process, the plan had encountered teething problems, and the Core Strategy had to be re-drafted. So in September 2009 we geared up for what thankfully did indeed turn out to be the final round.

An informal chat with a council officer revealed that they considered we had already made our point at the previous consultation. But we didn't want to leave anything to chance: we were concerned that a lack of response from us now might give the impression that we were losing interest. So we held another open meeting on 24 September, attended by two members of the council's planning department. Graham once again wrote a model response, calling for the support for a sports stadium to be strengthened by inclusion in the development policy itself, rather than the supporting text.

In the end we managed to get around 200 replies to the consultation – again, a small proportion of the number of fans we know want to get back to Merton, but a significant number given the commitment involved in taking part in such a technical process.

In May 2010 WISA again quizzed the main political parties in the local elections. It was clear that support for the Dons' return had grown. We were winning the battle.

The final version of the Core Strategy was adopted by Merton Council in July 2011. It would include express support for a sports stadium in the borough – support that had not been included in the earlier drafts, which shows just how worthwhile it had been for Wimbledon supporters to get involved. It had taken six years, but for the first time Merton had a firm commitment, in black and white, to bring the club home, and thanks had to go to all those fans who took part. The club, with the co-operation of the council, was now actively looking at sites in Merton.

Rovers ruin the Wombles' return

On 6 August 2011, justice was delivered. Nine years after the club's place in the Football League had been stolen, Wimbledon were back. As with the Sutton friendly in 2002, the result was almost an irrelevance. What mattered most was that this game – the club's first back in the Football League – was taking place at all.

6 August 2011
AFC Wimbledon 2 Bristol Rovers 3 npower League Two
By Erik Samuelson (AFC Wimbledon chief executive)

I remember shaking the hands of all the players and saying: "Welcome to the Football League!"

Terry Brown had lost twice in Conference play-offs, so I knew this match meant a lot to him. In the days before the match I was constantly being interviewed, and I kept on making the point of referring to Terry as "Terry Brown, Football League manager". I wanted to keep reinforcing to him what he had done, what he had achieved.

Meanwhile, there was also Eileen – my wife. She normally organises the teas and coffees in the President's Lounge, which meant she always missed the start of games. I said to her that there was no way she would miss the start of this match. I wanted her to watch our club take the pitch as a Football League side for the first time.

And when the players ran out we were standing at the back of the stand, arms around each other, watching our team – our Football League team.

By Terry Brown (AFC Wimbledon manager)

The first game of the season is always a nightmare. It always takes on a massive importance. You plan and train for the game for six weeks, and it's your one focus. But this was even more significant. It was live on television and it was also Wimbledon's first game back in the Football League.

I wanted to win the game so badly. I didn't really have time to enjoy the occasion – I vaguely remember the white kit being a nice touch – but all I wanted to do was win.

In the end, the game was typical of our season. We looked bright at times, but we

Sam Hatton sends in a cross against Bristol Rovers
(Jerzy Dabrowski)

The AFC Wimbledon team greet their Bristol Rovers counterparts for the club's return to the Football League (Paul Jeater)

AFC Wimbledon's Jamie Stuart flicks in the Dons' first Football League goal in nine years (Paul Willatts)

gave away three sloppy goals. The penalty was a hammer blow: we had worked hard to get back into the game and then that happened. I'm not one for ranting and raving. Brett Johnson didn't intentionally handle the ball: he got one in the back, his hand came out and that was that. I came away from the game thinking that this season was going to be hard. I was asking myself: "If the opposition get the ball into our box, are we physically strong enough to deal with it?" The answer, too often, was "No".

On the plus side, the game also saw the debut of Jack Midson. Jack had been on our radar for two years. He was our main target before he went to Oxford; they had offered him twice as much as we could. But we kept pestering him. We kept telling him how good we thought he was and how well he would fit into AFC Wimbledon, and eventually it paid off. If we had still been in the Conference he wouldn't have dropped down to join us. He would prove to be a revelation for us in our first League season.

The other highlight for me that day was Jamie Stuart's goal. We rarely score from set plays, and to be honest we hadn't practised one where Jamie runs in and flicks the ball into the net at 100 miles per hour. It was fitting that Jamie got it – the first goal for AFC Wimbledon back in the Football League. He had been instrumental in getting us promotion. We would not have got up without him. He was the obvious choice to replace Danny as captain.

By Jack Midson (AFC Wimbledon player)

It was a real pleasure to play for the real Dons and be a part of Wimbledon's history. I already knew about the history of Wimbledon before I signed, and how much it meant to the fans. Once I joined, I listened to Terry's introduction to the club and his explanation about what they were looking to achieve. All that made Wimbledon's first game back in the League very special for me.

I first spoke to Terry Brown and Stuart Cash in 2009, before I signed for Oxford. So when my contract at Oxford came to an end, Wimbledon was top of my list of clubs to go to. Thankfully Terry and Stuart were still interested, and contacted me in the summer of 2011 to ask me to come in for contract negotiations. It didn't take much – I wanted to be part of the story and I wanted to be playing in the Football League, so it all came together perfectly.

I knew that the first game back in the League was going to be a big deal. During the build-up the amount of messages I received on Twitter and Facebook was amazing, and the buzz around the club was something I had never experienced before. I was at Oxford when they got back into the Football League, and that was special, but this seemed very different – this was justice being delivered for the wrongs that had happened nine years before, and it was something I will never forget.

When it came to the match day, it didn't take a genius to realise how much it meant to the fans – you could sense it everywhere. The atmosphere was electric, and it was a great feeling to be a part of it. On the pitch I could hear and feel the fans. It urged us on.

Unfortunately the result didn't go our way, which was disappointing, but the fans were so supportive and continued to cheer throughout the whole game – as they have done ever since.

We started badly, but we managed to turn it round, and then there was the disappointment of conceding a late penalty. I don't blame anyone for the result, and

Brett Johnson was disappointed he had given it away, but the whole game went so fast it was all a bit of a blur. The real achievement was that the match had taken place at all, after all the preceding battles.

I will always treasure the one-off special kit that we wore on the day, and it hangs in pride of place on my wall.

By Joe Blair (AFC Wimbledon fan)

Football close seasons these days seem shorter than an X Factor winner's career. As soon as the dust settled on that phenomenal day out in Manchester, the media frenzy began again, focusing on Wimbledon's first game back in the Football League.

I was forced to follow the build-up from afar as I was working in New York for the summer from literally the day after the play-off final. News of our success had even reached those shores, and I was astonished to see a New York Times report of the play-off final which compared the re-formation of Wimbledon with that of the Cleveland Browns in the NFL.

With the release of the fixture list and confirmation that our first game would be at home against Bristol Rovers, I began to panic. Would I get out of the States in time to be there, and even if I could, would I get a ticket? Desperate times call for desperate measures – and why hadn't I been considering a season ticket anyway? I still wonder if mine was the first or indeed the only season-ticket application the club has ever received from Manhattan. Ticket for the match and indeed the season secured, I could get on with ensuring that I could return home in time for the game.

So the match day came around, and was attended by the usual media blur that had been accompanying Wimbledon promotions during the previous nine years. But it seemed an opening game like any other, until I saw the cover of the matchday programme which quite clearly stated "npower League 2". That's when I realised that we really were back.

By Martin Fielding (AFC Wimbledon fan)

Playing Bristol Rovers in our first game back in the League had a surreal edge to it. The teams had been four divisions apart as recently as three and a half years before, and I was surely not alone in having a worrying feeling that this game might be men versus boys. This queasiness was emphasised by the presence in the Rovers forward line of the enormous Matt Harrold, who we all remembered as one of the Wycombe team that had dismembered us at Kingsmeadow in the FA Cup in 2008. We had also replaced our own departed midfield giant (in all senses) Steven Gregory, with the smaller (and, as it would turn out, lesser) holding midfielder Max Porter.

The men v boys scenario seemed to be confirmed within the first 20 minutes by two pieces of juvenile defending right in front of the horrified Tempest End that gifted Rovers two goals. Both came from us losing possession inside our own half, and the second was, inevitably, scored by Harrold. Fears of a humiliating drubbing in front of the Sky TV cameras passed through my mind before we at last got into the game just before half-time through a free-kick which allowed Jamie Stuart to produce a fine glancing header and narrow the gap to a single goal at the break.

An even start to the second half showed us that maybe we did have a future in this division after all. Terry Brown's substitution of Christian Jolley by Charles

Jamie Stuart, second left, celebrates after scroing
on 6 August 2011 (Jerzy Dabrowski)

AFC Wimbledon captain Jamie Stuart faces
the cameras after defeat to Bristol Rovers
(Jerzy Dabrowski)

Ademeno produced an equaliser within three minutes when the new sub turned on the proverbial sixpence to shoot home from six yards with 20 minutes to go.

I think that every Wimbledon fan present would have settled for a point at that stage – but it was not to be. Having survived over an hour without gifting the visitors a goal, we extended our hospitality with five minutes to go by giving away a soft penalty for handball from an innocuous cross.

We were back – and we had very nearly held our own against a team that was one of the favourites for promotion. I left the ground thinking that perhaps we could do more than just survive at this level after all.

By Nick Jarrett (AFC Wimbledon fan)

"I just want to watch football," Kris Stewart had famously said back in 2002. I don't think he or anyone else could have dreamt we'd be watching our own team play in the Football League just nine years later. I was in too much shock in Manchester to cry, to let the emotion hit me fully, but against Bristol Rovers was the day it struck home.

There are times in life when you can be in the middle of a moment and find it hard to realise that it is not just a dream. Looking around Kingsmeadow in August 2011 I saw the same ground, the same people who had watched Combined Counties League football – and all the memories of the previous nine seasons came flooding back. All I around me I could sense the pride in what we had all achieved. They had stolen our League place but they hadn't stolen our spirit. Four thousand Dons fans were each remembering the journey in their own way.

And that is the beauty of the game. On a day that seemed to be about so much more than football, within 20 minutes we were 2-0 down and just another Football League club with a back four who couldn't defend for toffee and an attack that wouldn't know where the goal was if you gave them a banjo and stuck a barn door on their backside.

But then the spirit we love and expect from our players came to the fore. Goals from captain Jamie "Everyone Loves a Nutter" Stuart and Charles Ademeno pulled it back to 2-2, and, for a while, we even dreamt about winning the game. A desperate handball and penalty with five minutes left put paid to that, but it didn't really matter. We had proved we could live with one of the pre-season title favourites, and after just nine years we had taken back what had been taken from us. We started the day as a story, as part of a journey, and we ended the day as just another Football League club. And didn't it feel great?

By Fazal Ahmad (AFC Wimbledon fan and Dons Trust volunteer)

Getting promoted in Manchester was the maddest day ever as a Dons fan, but it only really sunk in that we were back in the League at our first match in August, when Bristol Rovers and Sky TV came to Kingsmeadow.

The day was a bit crazy, with the TV crews to accommodate and lots of new rules to comply with as a League club, so we couldn't set up the Dons Trust gazebo. But the day was mainly about the buzz, the nostalgia of seeing the team running out in replicas of the old Seventies kit, and seeing a full away end. It reminded me of the old Plough Lane days – in fact Selhurst Park now seemed like a long-lost memory.

Nine years of non-league had brought us to this. You couldn't help thinking of where we had been – Sandhurst, Chessington, Merstham, Dorking, Leatherhead, Chelmsford, Walton – even (ahem) Bromley. Would I have swapped that for nine years in the Premier League? No way. Against Bristol Rovers, this was our club, playing in our ground, with stewards and club staff who were fans. What a difference!

So here we were – over 4,600 fans seeing five goals and lots of defensive foul-ups (a sign of what was to come all season). Off we go again!

It never rains but it pours

AFC Wimbledon's season had begun brightly. The defeat to Bristol Rovers was followed by two away wins, and Dons fans were starting to look towards the play-offs. Those hopes and dreams were derailed in spectacular fashion away at Macclesfield.

27 August 2011
Macclesfield 4 AFC Wimbledon 0 npower League Two
By Stephen Crabtree (AFC Wimbledon supporter)

Just when I thought the day couldn't get any worse, it started raining. Things had begun to unravel the moment our train from Euston left Stoke. We were set fair to reach Macclesfield early enough for a gentle stroll down to the ground, but no sooner had we pulled out of the Potteries than a flustered guard alerted us to a problem ahead. A man was threatening to throw himself off the Stockport railway viaduct, so the train was being rerouted. Our next stop would be in Manchester.

The small group of Dons fans on board put our heads together. We worked out that if we got off at Wilmslow we could catch a cab and still arrive in time for kick-off. We cajoled, pleaded with and then harangued the harassed guard – but he would not budge. No stopping would be allowed on what had now become a very busy line. Inevitably, having shot through Wilmslow station at high speed, we slowed down and then stood motionless in the Cheshire countryside for what seemed like an age.

By the time our train eventually crawled into Manchester Piccadilly just after three o'clock, several of us were receiving texts from those at the game telling us that Terry Brown's boys had conceded an early goal. As we waited anxiously on the concourse we were joined by a couple of Leeds-based Wombles who were attempting to take in their first game of the season. We swapped stories while the potential suicide was talked down from the viaduct. Then, at last, the line south was reopened.

Our mobile phone updates relayed the news that the Dons were going in two down at the break just as we were disgorged at Macclesfield station. A couple of cabs got us down to Moss Lane in record time, but we then had to endure another frustrating delay, this time outside the away end. When the steward finally got radio confirmation that we should be all be allowed in for free, the news was greeted with cheers. Mine were muted by the fact that I had bought my ticket in advance.

Once through the gate we raced up the steps just in time to see Emile Sinclair slide home the Silkmen's third goal. Our northern-based fans responded to seeing a team in blue scoring by leaping madly into the air. Twenty-four hours later, viewing the

A resigned look on Terry Brown's face as AFC Wimbledon slip to defeat at Macclesfield (Paul Willatts)

AFC Wimbledon's Brett Johnson is called over by the referee at Macclesfield (Paul Willatts)

highlights on TV, I could see the funny side of two guys wildly celebrating while the rest of the occupants of the well-populated terrace looked on in sullen silence.

I found my brother wallowing in his customary gloom. "I was just about ready to give up and go home," he said to me, apparently without irony. Then, as if to match the mood in the away end, the skies began to darken and those of us on the open terrace were drenched by a short deluge of almost biblical proportions. There was still time for us to witness some more comedy defending as the home team were handed their fourth goal on a plate before the referee's whistle called time on a dismal display.

Damp, defeated and dejected, we departed for home. Whoever it was who said "It is not the destination but the journey that matters" clearly never had that trek to Moss Rose in mind.

Jolley turnaround seals first home League win

Christian Jolley had begun the day expecting to watch the game from the stands. By 5pm he was being lauded as a hero by a delirious Kingsmeadow crowd. His injury-time strike had given AFC Wimbledon their first Football League home win.

3 September 2011
AFC Wimbledon 3 Port Vale 2 npower League Two
By Christian Jolley (AFC Wimbledon player)

I remember the day really well. It was a massive rollercoaster for me – a real mixed bag of feelings. It was also our first home win as a Football League club.

I got to the ground and was called into the manager's office. That happens before every game, and he tells you whether you are in or out. Sometimes you get the nod beforehand, but mainly it's on the day. And Terry told me straight that not only was I not in the team, I hadn't even made the squad. I was gutted. I wanted to be involved and it was really hard to take.

So I went out and did a session with fitness trainer Jason Moriarty. And I took all my frustration out. I pounded and pounded. It's not unusual to do a big session like that when you are not playing. It's all about keeping your fitness up. I wanted to get my lungs going.

By the time I got out of the showers, there was Charles Ademeno seeing the physio and it was clear he wasn't going to make it. He'd taken a knock in the five-a-side warm-up, which is part of our usual pre-match routine. I think Jamie Stuart had clipped him. And suddenly I was back in the squad, on the bench.

Watching from the dugout, I could see that we were a bit hot and cold. Port Vale had really dominated the first half and stopped us from playing our game. They were on top, but they hadn't scored. Then Kieran Djalili sprinted clear and got upended, and we had a penalty. Luke Moore's effort was saved, but Jack Midson reacted first to give us a 1-0 lead at the break.

We had been lucky, and Terry wanted to shuffle things about, so he brought me on

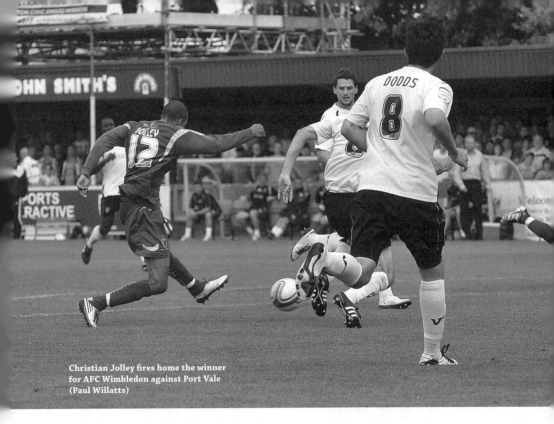

Christian Jolley fires home the winner
for AFC Wimbledon against Port Vale
(Paul Willatts)

for Luke at half-time. I was so motivated. After being dropped from the squad a few hours earlier, I had a point to prove. But the problem was I had nothing left in my legs, I'd put too much into the fitness session. It was a matter of getting myself into the right place and trying to cause as many problems as possible.

I hadn't even got into my stride when they pulled level. Then Gareth Gwillim gave us the lead again with an excellent left-foot volley. It looked like we were all set for three points again, but they scrambled one home with a few minutes left. We were deflated – their goal had come against the run of play. I was knackered, the referee had indicated six minutes of added time, and suddenly we were hanging on at 2-2. But then there was Lee Minshull. He hit a massive diagonal ball from the middle of the pitch. I was in the right place at the right time. I picked up the ball on the touchline, cut inside a couple of players and hit the target – and the club had its first Football League home win. The crowd went mental.

It was a great day. Going from the disappointment of not playing to getting the opportunity to play, and then getting on the pitch, was a complete turnaround. And then to score the winning goal in the final minute – that was just perfect.

Jack and Jolley shine at the seaside

Wimbledon were on the rise, but few predicted the Dons would get three points away at early pace-setters Morecambe, especially after the home side had taken an early lead. But the doubters had failed to take account of the blossoming strike partnership of Jack Midson and Christian Jolley.

A delighted Christian Jolley is
congratulated by Sam Hatton after scoring
on 3 September 2011 (Paul Willatts)

8 October 2011
Morecambe 1 AFC Wimbledon 2 npower League Two
By Christian Jolley (AFC Wimbledon player)

Morecambe were flying. They were the real surprise package at the start of the season. They had trashed Crawley 6-0 the week before, and most people would have thought we would be on a hiding to nothing.

But we soon found ourselves on top. Rashid Yussuff hit the post, and then Luke Moore had a penalty saved. It seemed just a matter of time before we would take the lead. We were keeping the ball and spraying it around brilliantly – and then we went one down from a corner. But we kept going, and Jack Midson brought us level with a neat strike not long after.

It was an easy team talk from the gaffer at half-time. He knew we were playing well, and he just told us to keep going. It was one of those days when it all came together.

The thing with Wimbledon then was that we had so much in the tank. We would always come on strong late in the game. If matches lasted 180 minutes, we would have won every one. We knew that if we just kept going we would get a goal – it was just a case of whether or not we would beat the clock.

The winner came with five minutes to go. Sammy Hatton sent over a great cross. I get a lot of stick for my headers at the club – they can go anywhere. But I got up at the back post, got a jump on the big lad marking me and headed the ball straight across the goal and into the bottom corner.

I had been at the club for just over a year, and everything was working out for me. I had been at Kingstonian before – and there was the obvious connection to AFC Wimbledon. I had got a run in the Kingstonian team and we'd reached the Ryman Premier play-off final. There were a couple of other clubs interested in me. But as soon as I met Terry Brown and Erik Samuelson, and they told me about their ambitions to get into the Football League, I knew that going to AFC Wimbledon was the right move to make. It also helped that I knew there were going to be a number of other new faces coming in, which would make it a lot easier for me to slot in. So I signed on the dotted line.

But it really came together for me when the Dons signed Jack Midson. Jack and I get on really well. We both have high energy levels and we like to harass defenders. Jack's brilliant to play with, and it's amazing watching him. There can be 90 minutes on the clock and he'll still be there making 50-yard runs. He earns every goal he gets.

Back then, it seemed like one of us would score every week. At Morecambe we both got on the scoresheet and the fans were loving it. They stuck around for a good half-hour afterwards lapping it up.

The journey back was full of smiles – it always is after a win. On the way back from away games we put on the DVD of the game and cringe at ourselves for any mistakes we make. If we lose it's totally different – it can be a long, sore journey back. You just want to get home and get that Saturday over with. But the trip back from Morecambe was just one long craic.

Christian Jolley roars away in delight. His goal secured victory for the Dons at Morecambe (Paul Willatts)

By Jack Midson (AFC Wimbledon player)

The Morecambe game was arguably our best all-round performance of the season, and I was very happy with my goal and the win. We played our best football, never gave up, and came out deserved winners from a tough away game against a club on top form.

Their manager apparently said that we were the best footballing side he had seen in the past two years in League Two. That was a great compliment. All through the game, whatever they tried to do and however many times they changed their formation, we had the answer and they couldn't break us down.

Luke missed a penalty, and then they took the lead against the run of play, so it felt great to get the equaliser just before half-time. I remember getting the ball out wide, cutting in on my right foot and hitting a shot from just on the edge of the box. It was a great strike, but I was honestly surprised to see it nestle in the bottom corner. The goal set us up for the rest of the game, and we were all ecstatic when Jolls scored the winner.

Stewart's manifesto exposes Trust division

In the autumn of 2011, there was the annual election for the Dons Trust Board. Among the five candidates were Kris Stewart – one of the club's founders and the former club chairman. Another candidate was former Dons Trust chairman Tom Adam. Both should have been favourites to take one of the four spots available. But a bitter campaign saw Kris appeal to the Dons Trust electorate to use their four votes to vote for everyone except Tom. The result would see Kris finish last and finally sever his direct involvement in the club after 10 years. Tom was elected.

Tuesday 6 December 2011
Dons Trust Board election result Kingsmeadow
By Kris Stewart (AFC Wimbledon supporter)

Yes I was disappointed, but I wasn't shocked by the result. I had been thinking it wasn't going well. I was getting that vibe from people who were speaking to me and even more so from the people that weren't.

It was the scale of it that surprised me. Let's be honest – it wasn't nip and tuck. I was smashed. I finished last with 412 votes. Zoë Linkson did fantastically well to finish above two incumbents, and Nicole Hammond topped the poll with 693 votes. Tom Adam got 522 votes and took the last of the four spots.

I had been on or around the Board for nearly 10 years. Tom became chair of the Stadium Working Group very early on. Since then, in my eyes, not enough progress had been made in getting the club back to Merton. There were a number of things I think we could have done. It was an issue that had bothered me increasingly.

It came to the fore with the draft stadium review document that the Board had put together two years earlier. If that had gone through, it would have more or less committed AFC Wimbledon to Kingsmeadow and seen the club give up on a move back to Merton – and that's where the likes of Simon Wheeler and WISA deserve a lot of credit. They persuaded enough of the Board members to look at the draft again, and the original document was kicked into the long grass.

At the time it seemed every mention was of Kingston, and Tom was very enthusiastic about it. When it came to Merton, I wasn't sure whether he had the same level of enthusiasm. Yet until the election, I had never talked about it publicly.

I was undecided about whether to stand again. There were some positives and some negatives. I didn't want to be on the Board and not be able to tell people about my feelings. So I made the decision to air my concerns openly in my manifesto, and, well, it didn't work out for me. It was obviously the key issue in the campaign. But I don't regret what I did.

The whole campaign was also tiring and unpleasant for me, and I'm not sure I was up for that.

There was a relief of some kind when I lost. I genuinely think people shouldn't be able to be on the Board for a long time. People go stale, they get used to the process, they can't see the woods for the trees. I'd done my time. But there were other issues that needed to be addressed.

There are some people who think the Dons Trust is like a company and we should be running ourselves like BP. But for me that's the very antithesis of everything we should be. A couple of the people on the Board are of the opinion that the Board should operate on collective responsibility – that whatever is agreed by the Board, all Board members should champion it whether they agree with the policy or not. But AFC Wimbledon is a different beast: we only exist because of our members. In my view, if there are issues or differences then they should be discussed in the wider world. After December 2011, I was finally free of those politics. I could say what I liked.

By Tom Adam (Dons Trust Board member)

As far as I am concerned, the election was a success. It was more vibrant than any before. The format of having an on-line forum and a broadcast debate added a lot to the value of our usual election arrangements. And the on-line voting scheme was also a success.

However, the professionalism of the Dons Trust Board may have been, for a brief moment, slightly tarnished when a suggestion was made as to who members should vote for. But it was clear from the election results that Dons Trust members were quite able to decide for themselves, and that was a good sign for the future.

Ever since the inception of the Board, it has been a great pleasure and honour to represent all Dons Trust members' interests and it's been a delight to be chairman of the Stadium Working Group. And the SWG achieved a lot in the first 10 years.

It was the SWG that helped to ensure that a stadium was included in Merton's Local Development Framework, published in 2011 – and that is key. The framework is a blueprint for all development in the borough for the next 15 years. And it was the hard work by the SWG members and the tremendous support given by London Borough of Merton councillors and officers that helped the club move closer to identifying a location in Merton suitable to meet our long-term stadium needs and against which the design process could be initiated.

Then there is Kingsmeadow. It was the SWG that evaluated and secured the approval of the purchase of the stadium. It was fantastic when we ultimately secured

£1.1 million to purchase the Kingsmeadow stadium.

And there is always the issue about making sure that Kingsmeadow is fit for purpose – both in terms of meeting Football League requirements and being a pleasant environment for our supporters. We have to make it work for as long as we are there.

These are all huge achievements and ones I'm deeply proud of. But the work can never stop and, from the high turnout of the election in 2011, I believe our members know that more than anyone.

A Jolley departure as Dons slump

Back on the pitch, AFC Wimbledon were in the middle of a dismal run. They needed hope, and the return from injury of Christian Jolley, who had been so instrumental in the club's fine early-season form, offered that. But that hope was extinguished in a moment of madness in which a two-footed lunge led to the 23-year-old striker seeing red.

31 December 2011
AFC Wimbledon 1 Southend United 4 npower League Two
By Christian Jolley (AFC Wimbledon player)

I can't defend it. It was over-enthusiasm. I had been out for a long time. The annoying thing was that I had been playing well. Jack Midson and I were everywhere, we were harassing their defenders, causing mayhem. Jack had given us the lead and we were worthy of it. They'd levelled, but I still thought we were the better team. And then I did that.

Going into the tackle, I wasn't 100 per cent sharp – my body was a yard slower than my head. I couldn't pull out of it as I would have got hurt. It was stupid, it was reckless, it was inexperience showing through, and I paid for it.

Nothing was going right for us. We were in the middle of a dismal run and were starting to feel sorry for ourselves. We almost couldn't buy a win. It was such a big difference from the year before. Now we were getting punished for our mistakes, which hadn't always happened in the Conference. It made me realise how special the season before had been. Sometimes you don't appreciate the heights until you hit the lows.

It's horrible to watch from the sidelines. I had been out injured. The problem had started back in October when I picked up a dead leg against Morecambe. I didn't think much of it at the time, but a couple of weeks later I pulled up against Torquay. It felt like a hamstring tear, but the symptoms suggested otherwise. So I kept going. I played against Scunthorpe, but broke down against Swindon. I came back against Bradford, only to break down again. It was only then that that I finally went for a scan. In hindsight I should have gone after the Morecambe game, but we'd done everything right – a dead leg normally clears up quickly. But for those three months I just didn't have a fifth gear.

By the time of the Southend game I was back, and I wanted to make a difference. Instead I made a fool of myself. The referee had no choice. With only 10 men it is always going to be hard. Not long after the break the ball ricocheted in off Jamie

Christian Jolley, No 12, sees red for his lunge at
home to Southend United on 31 December 2011
(Paul Willatts)

Stuart for Southend's second. After that, we were chasing it and we got caught. And caught again.

Not long after, the gaffer brought in a bunch of new players, and the whole atmosphere changed almost overnight. Suddenly there was a new energy around the place.

Dons wilt in Wiltshire

Defeat to champions-elect Swindon Town was to signal the end of the road for a number of Wimbledon players. Terry Brown saw that he had to make some changes.

Monday 2 January 2012
Swindon Town 2 AFC Wimbledon 0 npower League Two
By Nick Jarrett (AFC Wimbledon fan)

Swindon isn't the most uplifting of places to visit at the best of times, even less so when you haven't won in what feels like years. So it was more in hope than expectation that 500 Dons made the trip there on a cold and wet January afternoon.

The teamsheet showed what can only be described as an experimental line-up with what felt like (and turned out to be) a number of players at the last-chance saloon. The team battled but never really looked like scoring, and at half-time the mood on the terrace (or rather, in the £25-a-ticket stand) was that we'd do well to finish with nil.

They say that football careers can be defined by a matter of inches. While that probably wasn't true in this instance, with the score at 0-0 and 10 minutes into the second half Charles Ademeno manufactured a clever turn and shot, and his finish whistled just wide of the post. It was to be the last time he touched the ball in a Wimbledon shirt. Not long after that Swindon broke away, won a free-kick and got a deflection. At 1-0, we all knew it was over.

The small amount of confidence left in the players drained away, and even the hitherto noisy away support struggled to pick themselves up. The game ended 2-0, but if it were not for the post and the crossbar (just behind eventual Player of the Season Sammy Moore in the Man of the Match stakes) Swindon could have scored six or seven. As the team trudged off the pitch and the fans headed off into the Wiltshire rain, everyone was wondering just where the next win would come from.

By Terry Brown (AFC Wimbledon manager)

We are a footballing side, and we had started the season bright and bubbly. Christian Jolley had been on fire. No one works harder or trains harder than him, and when he's on his game he's brilliant. But he was picking up injuries. And as a team we were having problems with the physicality of League Two.

I look back now and I can see that the problem I didn't address quickly enough was the centre-half situation. In almost every game we were conceding the most hideous goals. In the back of my mind, Mat Mitchel-King was always on the verge of a return. He was the one with the Football League experience, and to lose him had been a massive blow. I kept thinking he'd be back in a couple of weeks, no need to panic.

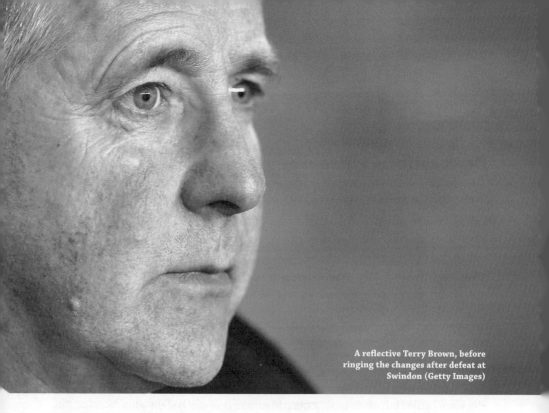

But he had glandular fever and was out until Christmas. In his absence we never handled the six-foot four inch strikers.

I also seemed to have made a mistake in signing Callum McNaughton. He played well for us when he was still on West Ham's books, but when they let him go it knocked the stuffing out of him and he wasn't the same player. He'll be back, though. I am sure of that.

As a manager you are always looking at potential new players. I always have a list – two full-backs, two centre-backs, two midfielders, and so on. By the time of the Swindon away game it was really the last chance for a number of our squad. We had tried a lot of things. We had been putting square pegs in round holes to try and find a solution. I had rewarded the players who had got us up, but I'd now given them as much time as I could afford. It wasn't lack of effort that cost us at Swindon – we just weren't good enough.

We needed to hit the bottom before we made big changes, and this was the bottom. And credit to the Board – they allowed me to do what I felt I had to.

Would Euell believe it?

After a run of 12 games without a win, Terry Brown had to act. So in came several new players, including ex-Wimbledon FC legend Jason Euell. While his presence made little difference on the pitch, it gave the club a new lift and helped inspire the Dons to put an end to their dismal run.

New AFC Wimbledon recruit Jason Euell
points the way to victory for the Dons at
Port Vale (Paul Willatts)

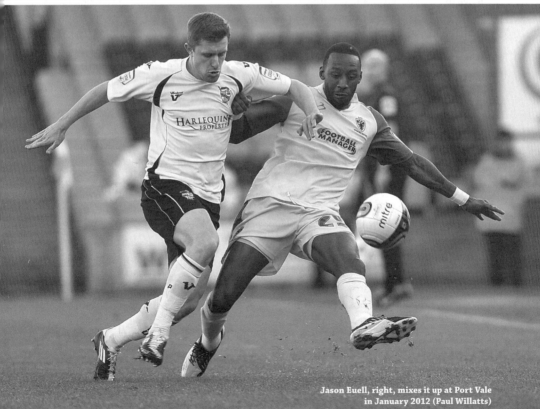

Jason Euell, right, mixes it up at Port Vale
in January 2012 (Paul Willatts)

Saturday 14 January 2012
Port Vale 1 AFC Wimbledon 2 npower League Two
By Terry Brown (AFC Wimbledon manager)

This was a massive game for us. It was the first of a run of three victories that would prove vital at the end of the season. Port Vale were no mugs. They were one of the best sides we played against in 2011-12. Were it not for their 10-point deduction and the six points lost to us, they would have made the play-offs ahead of Crewe. I'd brought in a whole bunch of new players. That's always a gamble, but behind the scenes it had given us a real lift.

On the pitch, we were really unlucky with Jason Euell. He had hardly played at Blackpool or Charlton – a period stretching back almost two years. He needed a couple of games to settle in, to get back up to speed. He lasted 42 minutes before limping off. But there was another side to having Jason around. His arrival gave us a massive morale boost. Here was a Wimbledon legend, a strong character, mixing it with the squad. And of course, he also lifted the morale of the supporters. There is no way we would have taken that many away to Port Vale without him in the squad.

But Jason Euell wasn't the only key signing I made then. Getting Billy Knott and George Moncur in also made a huge difference. They brought with them that little bit of extra confidence and arrogance of youth. They wanted the ball at their feet – they wanted to play the game the way I wanted to play it. All of them together bucked us up enormously.

It wasn't just about the talent they brought with them – it also delivered a kick up the backside to some of our existing players. Sammy Moore had just seen some of his friends, including Max Porter and Lee Minshull, leave the club, but he took it well and welcomed us signing players. The new arrivals gave him a new challenge and took him to a new level. As for the game itself, I dropped Rashid Yussuff, and when he came on near the end he was brilliant. Luke Moore was also on the bench. He came on for Jason Euell and scored the winner.

By Nick Jarrett (AFC Wimbledon fan)

On 9 January, just a week after the defeat at Swindon, and with the only "new" player one who had been part of the team since September, it's fair to say that the mood on the internet forums was a mixture of consternation, worry and downright despondency. By Wednesday morning we had the son of a West Ham legend, a new record signing and a Premier League player (sort of). Oh yeah, and someone called Jason Euell.

I'm a few years younger than Jason. I remember his debut well as it coincided with my 14th birthday, and after he scored that goal – an overhead kick against Southampton from 20 yards – he was a hero of mine. I had his name on the back of my shirts and I almost spoke to him once. I say "almost" because when I met him I was in too much awe to say anything.

Heroes can sometimes let you down, but on top of all this Jason comes across as an unbelievably nice human being and top bloke. Marcus Gayle came back to the Dons – and what an experience that was – but this felt different. We really needed something, and there was the feeling that Jason could be a real asset in his old position, rolling back the years in a Wimbledon shirt.

Even the players talked about the buzz of having him around at training. I had my suspicions about that – did they have his poster on their wall as well? But everything about his second debut had a good vibe about it. There was a buzz on the train up to Port Vale and in the pub beforehand, and the away end was positively bouncing 10 minutes before kick-off. I love our away support – we always make a lot of noise and we're good-natured – but that day was different because, for the first time in a long while, we had belief.

OK, the homecoming maybe wasn't as romantic as Thierry Henry's at Arsenal. There was no goal from Jason, and apart from a few glimpses of class the only thing notable about his debut was him limping off in the 42nd minute after Jack Midson had bundled in the equaliser. But part of you felt that even if Jason Euell played no other part on the pitch again, maybe he'd already done enough.

In fact it was the two young loanees who really caught the eye. Billy Knott looked a class above the rest when he was on the ball, and George Moncur supplied the cross that Luke Moore – ironically dropped for Jason Euell, but now on as his replacement – controlled and placed into the top corner to send the away support into raptures. It had been a long time coming, but boy, was it worth the wait?

Midson seals the return of the Dons

After a catastrophic run Brown had signed a swathe of new players. A victory at Port Vale stopped the rot, and a remarkable comeback at Gillingham a week later helped lift the club even further.

Saturday 21 January 2012
Gillingham 3 AFC Wimbledon 4 npower League Two
By Jack Midson (AFC Wimbledon player)

We had played really well away at Morecambe, but the most memorable game of the season was away at Gillingham. We had been on the most horrendous run of form. We had come off the back of a run of six straight defeats, and Terry had decided to ring the changes. In came Byron Harrison from Stevenage, and on loan we signed two England Under-19 internationals in Sunderland's Billy Knott and West Ham's George Moncur. And then of course there was Jason Euell from Charlton – Wimbledon fans didn't need too much of an introduction to him.

Euell's arrival created a buzz around the place, but the talent of the other three helped massively as well. The run of defeats came to an end straight away with the 2-1 win at Port Vale the week before the trip to Gillingham.

Despite all that, it still takes something special to come back from 3-1 down with just over quarter of an hour to go – and to be honest, if the match had been two weeks earlier I don't think we would have. But after strengthening the squad in the January transfer window and gaining a great result at Port Vale we were back on track, and we showed patience, heart and desire to draw level and go on to win the game.

AFC Wimbledon's Jack Midson slots him a penalty to restore parity at Gillingham on 21 January 2012 (Paul Willatts)

Jack Midson stabs home the Dons' fourth and their late winner at Gillingham to complete a remarkable comeback (Paul Willatts)

Jack Midson celebrates his winner at Gillingham (Paul Willatts)

We got one back through an own goal. And then came the penalty. I'll be honest – I was surprised when I got the decision. I've watched it several times since and it still doesn't look like a penalty – I actually played on, but I'm glad the ref gave it. I'm not normally on penalty duty, but I stepped up and took it and put it in the top left corner. The crowd went wild – the away support that day was amazing, and they were even louder when I scored the winner. I just tried to get to the ball before the defender and it flew off my foot and into the net.

It just showed our progression. We didn't want to settle for a draw: we went for the win and we got what we wanted – and deserved. It was a great day out for everyone, and it will stick with me for a long time.

By Ray Armfield (AFC Wimbledon supporter)

It might be hyperbole, but for me this game was right up there with the great Dons comebacks of yore – think 4-3 at West Ham in 1998, the late drama of the Ryman Premier play-off final at Staines or the injury-time recovery to beat Sunderland at Plough Lane.

Terry Brown's side looked dead and buried at Priestfield at 1-0 down, let alone when they trailed 3-1 with just 17 minutes left on the clock. But as the song goes, "We are Wimbledon", and it was typical of us that, urged on by vociferous support and with the hosts looking increasingly nervous, the Dons – in unfamiliar blood-red shirts – went for the jugular, and it paid off handsomely. When Sam Hatton's cross thundered in off Gills defender Gary Richards, there was still little to indicate how the remaining 10 minutes would pan out.

Jack Midson was manhandled by their struggling Status Quo roadie lookalike, and the referee's assistant lived up to his job description by making a decision of his own. Our leading scorer – serenaded for scoring goals with both his left, his right and for making his predecessor look, um, inadequate by comparison – blasted home the spot-kick and, in the words of the excitable man in the Ladbrokes adverts, it was "Game on!"

And when the winner went in with "89" on the scoreboard it was like being down the coast at Herne Bay in the FA Vase eight years earlier, with grown men embracing each other as only football fans who've just seen their team score a last-minute winner can do. At the final whistle, the unbridled joy on the faces of Brown and his players – even the recent arrivals – mirrored our own and reinforced what a special club we have.

It was a poignant victory for me. I live only half an hour's drive from Gillingham, so local bragging rights are very important when you are a relatively faraway Womble and you've had to grimace and bear it when your nearest League club has bagged your talismanic captain. Over the years I've seen us make our debut as a Football League club at Priestfield (in the League Cup), and get hammered 6-1 in 1982, and I watched Alan Cork nick an important win two seasons later. But none of those afternoons will live quite as long in the memory as this one.

Oh, and I had a fiver on us to win at 15 to 4.

Rampant Dons ease relegation fears

The spectre of relegation still hung over Kingsmeadow, but a performance inspired in part by second-half substitute and record signing Byron Harrison put paid to those fears and edged the Dons closer to their pre-season target of 50 points.

Saturday 24 March 2012
AFC Wimbledon 4 Burton Albion 0 npower League Two
By Terry Brown (AFC Wimbledon manager)

The Burton match was hugely significant. Our form had been hit and miss, and we needed a win. Luke Moore gave us an early lead after going clean through, but it was still very tight. And I certainly didn't see 4-0 coming.

But once George Moncur made it two midway through the second half, we looked like we could have gone on to get six or seven. In the end we showed more character than Burton, and that was enough.

Looking back now, I have no doubt that this was the game that took us to safety. A couple of weeks later we beat promotion-chasing Torquay 2-0, and they were a far better side than Burton. That was a good win, but it is easier to play when the fear has been taken away. The win over Burton was totally different. Then, the pressure was on.

It was also a big day for Byron Harrison. I had signed him from Stevenage and he was the club's most expensive signing. He came in at a difficult time for us. Jack Midson was shouldering nearly all the responsibility up front and needed support. But Byron is a different type of player – he thrives on deliveries into the box, and some of the fans had got on his back, saying he didn't really try. Fans like busy players, such as Danny Kedwell and Jon Main, so when Byron shut down Burton's left-back seconds after coming on for Luke Moore he got the biggest cheer of the night, and that lifted him.

About six minutes later he set up George Moncur for our second, before adding the third himself. Sammy Moore added the fourth with a neat finish at the death, and with that I knew we had reached our target. We were safe. AFC Wimbledon was still a Football League club.

Sun sets on the Dons' first season back

AFC Wimbledon ended their first season back in the Football League with a comfortable win over already promoted Shrewsbury Town. The end-of-season feel was a perfect backdrop for the matchday mascot, and it inspired club icon Haydon the Womble to make a leap of faith. But in the days that followed, there was a cull of players and the chief executive began to ponder the future.

George Moncur eases the tension as he hits the second against Burton (Paul Willatts)

AFC Wimbledon's George Moncur celebrates his goal that more or less secured safety (Paul Willatts)

Byron Harrison, left, celebrates against
Burton Albion (Paul Willatts)

Byron Harrison heads his first goal for the
Dons and their third on the day against
Burton (Paul Willatts)

Saturday 5 May 2012
AFC Wimbledon 3 Shrewsbury Town 1 npower League Two
By Jerzy Dabrowski (AFC Wimbledon fan)

When it comes to watching Wimbledon, I have pretty much seen it all. Since 1976 I haven't witnessed an uneventful season.

As a father of two girls, I never expected either of them to grow to share my love of football and the Dons, but I have been very lucky in that respect. My eldest, Isa, loved football from an early age, and when she was four she was a mascot for the first time, running out of the tunnel with Joe Sheerin, before Wimbledon beat Southall 4-2.

It was several years later that she made her second appearance as a mascot, this time with her sister Anya, when they both ran out against Tamworth in August 2010. Wimbledon won 3-0. Now, I'm not one who lives my life vicariously through my children, but their appearance as mascots that day was a birthday present from my wife to me, not my daughters!

Back in the League, Isa was a mascot for the last time, having reached the age of 12. On the last day of the season she led the team out, alongside Jamie Stuart, against already promoted Shrewsbury Town. The moment she came out, and the intense noise of the crowd, increased my already heightened feeling of elation, and I really did feel my smile widen from ear to ear.

Three mascot days and three wins couldn't be beaten, I thought, but the club managed to go one better. After the game, when Isa was up on stage for the Man of the Match awards, Ivor Heller asked her if she played football. "Yes", she said, and then Ivor asked her who she played for. Well, I was already the proud father when she made her debut in my club's colours, but when the packed bar roared its approval I nearly burst with pride and tears of joy. It's amazing what effect the words "AFC Wimbledon" can have on you.

By Haydon the Womble

Paul Goode had been begging me to do it all season. And I couldn't think of a better way of a celebrating a tough but great first season back in the League. The Dons fans were decked out in yellow and blue. The Shrewsbury fans, celebrating promotion, were also in yellow and blue. It was a fabulous party atmosphere. So what better way to show my appreciation than with a party trick to make everyone smile?

So I climbed up and leapt. Crowd-surfing is great, but for a six-foot fluffy Womble it might not be the safest of activities. Yes, it meant putting my trust in others, but I never feared that I would be dropped. It was great fun, and it was great to see the smiles on everyone's faces – even if the stewards were in a bit of a panic!

By Terry Brown (AFC Wimbledon manager)

I had two objectives for the Shrewsbury game. I wanted to reward some of the players who had been good servants to the club – it's the dream of every non-league player to play in the Football League, and they deserved a League Two start. But I had to balance that with success – every manager wants to end on a high.

The end of the season is a very difficult time of year. It's not easy to motivate players for what on paper is often a meaningless fixture. But we had a full house, and that meant it was far from meaningless.

I was delighted with our performance. Not only did we play well, but we played in the right manner. We kept the ball on the floor and we passed it. We scored three good goals. Luke Moore scored twice – though it made little difference to his future at the club, as I was always going to try and keep him. Everyone went home happy. The only disappointment was that we didn't keep a clean sheet.

It marked a successful year. We finished 18 points off the play-offs and 10 points clear of relegation. For the supporters, used to win after win in the first nine years, it might seem strange to call that a success. But for me, if you would have offered me that at the start of the season I would have bitten your hand off.

The hard work really began in the days that followed. I always call the first day back after the last game of the season Black Monday, as it's the day I call the players in one by one and tell them whether they have a future at the club. In 2012 it was actually Black Tuesday, because of the Bank Holiday, but it was still the same feeling.

I always try and give each player a reason. In 2011 it had been really tough – it's very difficult to break up a winning side. And I remember how hard I found it to tell Alan Inns, for example, that we would be letting him go. In 2012 the side needed freshening up – and the squad knew it. With a couple of exceptions we had given them all a chance to see if they could cope with League Two football – perhaps Reece Jones and Fraser Franks could have done with more game time, but the rest had had their chance. We got all the players down to the training ground. Stuart Cash and Simon Bassey were with me, and we ran through the reasons with each member of the squad.

It is a tough call to know exactly what to say. Some wanted to know all the reasons down to the smallest detail about what they had got wrong and how they could improve. But others didn't want to hear it – they switched off and wanted to be out of the room as fast as possible. I also wanted to have the chance to thank them. They all deserved that at the very least. Most of them had been instrumental in our promotion season, but we had to move on. And that's the thing with management: you have to be able to make the tough decisions as well as the easy ones.

In the end, we released 14 players, six of them were defenders. We simply hadn't had enough clean sheets.

By Erik Samuelson (AFC Wimbledon chief executive)

I enjoyed the fact we won the game, but it was very much end-of-season fare. My mind was already on the huge challenges we had to face for our second season in the Football League. Yes, there were a few individuals out there with a point to prove, but I felt no real tension in the game. Shrewsbury were already up. It was a little bit of an anti-climax. It would have been nice if the sun had been out, but instead it was a cold and cloudy day. Somehow that seemed appropriate.

There were a few highlights. The chants aimed at their goalkeeper, Chris Neal, after he dropped the ball at Byron Harrison's feet for our first goal: "One Neal". And then Haydon the Womble crowd surfing at the Athletics End at the final whistle. I was only about 15 yards away from him at the time and while I was laughing

Mascot Isa Dabrowski prepares to lead out the Dons for their final game of the debut season back in the Football League (Jerzy Dabrowski)

Haydon the Womble goes crowd surfing on 5 May 2012 (Jerzy Dabrowski)

Byron Harrison, centre, in action against
Shrewsbury Town (Niall Couper)

I was also concerned that his head might come off – that's not allowed in public under the terms of his licence. But the reality was that for me the season ended the moment we were safe and it was time to think about the many other things we had to consider.

I think quite a few fans saw the season as a bit of a disappointment because of finishing 16th after our fantastic start. But it was a success, perhaps not quite as good as I would have liked, but that is because I too am a fan and I want to win every game. Being realistic, to finish 16th was a great result given our limited resources. Having started in a field in Sandhurst, to finish comfortably in mid-table in League Two 10 years later was a remarkable achievement.

Yes we had one horrible period when we only won three points in 12 games and people were coming up with all sorts of reasons: Terry had gone beyond his level; he'd kept the wrong players; we didn't have full-time staff at the training ground. Understandably everyone looks for a reason when they are disappointed by performances but I'm always amazed how adamant they are that 'they know'. I too have a theory but it's supported by analysis. There is a book by Simon Kuper and Stefan Szymanski called Why England Lose and the one main theme throughout is simple: there is a direct link between how much you spend on players' wages and where you finish in the league table. And on that criterion we have consistently over-performed since we arrived in the Conference National.

In our first season in the Football League, as I told anyone who would listen, we were fourth from bottom in the wages league, yet we finished 16th. The year before in the Conference, we started with the 14th highest wage bill and we finished second. The year before that we were part-time and had the one of the lowest bills in Conference National, yet we finished eighth. You have to go back to the Conference South and the Ryman League to find a time when our wage bill was competitive with most of the top teams – and even then there were one or two big spenders we couldn't match. Even in our first season – remember AFC Wallingford and Withdean 2000?

So in my opinion people should be praising Terry Brown for his achievement in ending up five places above where our budget suggested we should. For me, it is irrational to believe we can consistently outperform our budget so regularly and we will need to find more money if we are to progress.

Looking back on the season, and many seasons in fact, there are many other people who deserve credit – all the club's backroom staff and directors. And people like Tim Hillyer, Roger Dennis, Mags Hutchison, Neil Messenbird and my wife Eileen who has worked as a volunteer and supported me selflessly in doing my job. They are just a few of the army of volunteers.

The work our volunteers have put in day-after-day over 10 years has been extraordinary. Many have worked way beyond their remits and often late into the night, or deep into a game they desperately wanted to watch. They have slaved away in an almost religious way. They are astonishing. They are fantastic.

In the days that followed the Shrewsbury game I felt sorry for Terry Brown. On the Tuesday after, he called all the players in. Superficially it was for the players to hand in their old kit – their tracksuits and everything – but Terry was using the opportunity to tell each one of them whether they were going to stay or go. It is a task I know he hates. It happens every year, and every year I think about the young men who are going to be released, not knowing where their careers will take them next.

Matthew Couper with Haydon
the Womble at the final game
of the Dons' first season in the
Football League (Niall Couper)

The players are all personable, decent young men. Yet he needed to make changes to strengthen the side. He needed to be ruthless and it's part of his role that I don't envy. Meanwhile, the Board had the job of trying to create a budget good enough to enable Terry to build on our first year in the League.

It was a huge challenge just to match the budget from that first season in the Football League. In the first year we had benefited from transfer fees, live television games and a reasonable cup run. None of these were certain to be available in year two, and there was also going to be a £45,000 reduction in central funding from the League. And then we also had the extra cost of building work. All that left a hole of £350,000 in our playing budget, and we spent the summer trying to work out how we could fill it. But we had no choice, we had to find a way.

Meanwhile some fans were looking for more. They wanted full-time training staff, they wanted better facilities in the stadium, they wanted better communications, but each time we spend on those things it potentially takes a player away from Terry's budget. It is a dreadfully hard task to balance the conflicting needs. I'm not looking for sympathy – it's my job, and that of Nigel, David and Ivor – and of course the fans want the best, but it is a difficult challenge.

After a long season, everyone is very tired, players, management, staff and volunteers alike. But the pace is as relentless in the summer as during the season and there were other things going on as well. There were a number of developments on the stadium front. We were entering a critical stage of discussions about a new stadium, while trying to fund the essential changes in the current one. These things were going to take a lot of time and energy, more than ever before. To make it

Byron Harrison, No 27, takes advanatage
to stab the ball home on 5 May 2012
(Jerzy Dabrowski)

Luke Moore slides the ball home for
his second and the Dons' third against
Shrewsbury (Jerzy Dabrowski)

clear, I absolutely love it, 95 per cent of the time. If I didn't like it, I would just stop. But the close season is a time to stop and take stock of where you are and where you are going.

My thinking has been going along these lines for a year or so now. I was in my 65th year and Eileen had decided to give up her voluntary roles at the club after 9 years. We're grandparents now and to make sure we get to know our granddaughter, Lexie, I take every Thursday off work and we spend all day with her. So the end of the season was a good time to think about what I want to do.

I wanted to get other people thinking so earlier in the season I met Matt Breach, the chair of the Dons Trust Board, and raised the subject about how much longer I should go on.

I have thought about this quite a lot. I want to be the person who decides when I leave – I'd hate to be told I had outstayed my welcome and be shown the door, however politely it might be done. During my career at PricewaterhouseCoopers in the city, I witnessed many colleagues who had been, as they described it, "tapped on the shoulder", in other words told to go. I don't want to end up like that. I want to be able to choose my own time and go when I'm ready – hopefully with not too many people muttering "About time too". At the moment, I still have the energy to go on.

The way I look at it, we have been on a sharp upward climb for 10 years, but at sometime we will start to plateau. Before we do, we need to find a person with the skills to take over and re-set the club on an upward curve: whether it is to look at reaching the Championship, to get a new stadium or just to maintain the momentum.

For me, it's about judging when I can no longer play my part in pushing us forward towards our goals and making sure I go before we reach that plateau. I will need to move over and give the new person the chance to put new energy in and keep the momentum going. I'm not certain when that time will be, but I plan to spot it before other people do.

Shane Warne once said: "The secret is to go at the right time. You want everybody to say: 'Why did he go now?'" I couldn't agree more.

Epilogue:

Where do you go from here?

T he past 10 years have been a remarkable journey for AFC Wimbledon. To end with managers associated with Wimbledon offer their thoughts and opinions on the club's achievements and what the future might hold.

By Lawrie Sanchez
(former Northern Ireland, Fulham and Barnet manager and former Wimbledon FC player)

It's been phenomenal: five promotions and then becoming established in League Two, all in the first 10 years. It's a credit to everyone connected with the club. It's been a team effort from the top to the bottom. I still speak to a lot of people at Wimbledon, and I know there is a great drive to continue the journey. It's not finished yet. I look at AFC Wimbledon and I can only seeing it going one way – and that's up.

AFC Wimbledon is a truly great fans' club. And it is the supporters that hold the best promise for the club's future.

So much has changed over the past 20 or 30 years. When Wimbledon first reached the top flight in 1986, we had around 6,500 or 7,000 fans. It wasn't much, but we had our own stadium in Wimbledon and it felt like home. It was an intimidating place for opposing teams to come to.

Plough Lane suited us, and once we moved to Crystal Palace I always said it was like playing 38 away games a season. It just wasn't home, and that's why the Milton Keynes thing never really bothered me as much as it did most Wimbledon fans. Wimbledon should never have been allowed to leave Plough Lane. I felt we had already been shafted once. What we needed was our own ground in Wimbledon.

Yes, we had bigger gates at Selhurst, but most of the spectators were either away fans or Palace fans wanting to watch Premier League football on a regular basis. They didn't have the depth of emotion connected to the club. And that's the great achievement of the club now. They have a brilliant community scheme. There are children throughout the area who are proud to wear the AFC Wimbledon shirt, children who have little or no experience of Wimbledon in the Premier League but have been on the 10-year journey. There are new Wimbledon fans who only know AFC Wimbledon and have grown up with the club at Kingsmeadow.

Back in the Combined Counties League the gates were huge for that level, but you could still get a ticket, and now that can be really difficult. AFC Wimbledon is building a strong fanbase. Games are regularly sold out, and the fanbase may even now be bigger than it was 20 years ago. The potential to grow is massive.

That demand means not only that the club can develop, but that it needs to. The club has to let Milton Keynes go and put all their efforts in to getting their own ground, and I already see that happening. Everybody is working together to help AFC Wimbledon: the players, the manager, the fans, the council and the sponsors. At the City of Manchester Stadium in May 2011 I spoke to the Mayor of Merton, and he was adamant that he wanted to have the club back in the Borough of Merton. And I know now that there are plans on the table – that has to be the next step.

I can see only a bright future. I look at all the other clubs in the lower leagues, and yes, there are a couple that can go forward, such as Swindon. But even they don't have the same strong foundations of AFC Wimbledon. Wimbledon is capable of going places. They are a Championship side in waiting.

You need 20,000 people coming through the turnstiles to make you viable in the Championship, but I can see that easily happening. A new stadium and Championship football: that's where I see Wimbledon in the next 10 years. The step after that is huge, from the Championship to the Premier League. But even then, clubs such as Blackpool and Swansea have shown what can be done. With the resources, who knows what can happen – perhaps AFC Wimbledon can even get back to the Premier League.

Wimbledon went from Amateur Cup winners to FA Cup winners in 25 years. They went from non-league to the top flight in nine years, and then from the CCL to the Football League also in nine years. Anything is possible.

But let's not get ahead of ourselves. Now is the time to consolidate, push for the play-offs, get into League One and secure that ground in Wimbledon. The Premier League can wait.

By Keith Curle (Notts County manager and former Wimbledon captain)

It's been another success story. The old Wimbledon was a fairy tale, which climaxed with the winning of the FA Cup – and it might all be about to be rewritten.
I have a lot of affinity with Wimbledon. They were the first top-flight club to show faith in me. Wimbledon back then were willing to invest in youth. The likes of Terry Phelan, Roger Joseph and John Scales epitomised exactly what the culture of the football club was all about.
AFC Wimbledon is similar now. They have a progressive management team and they have to keep that in place. They need to build the desire to succeed from within the football club. It is so much tougher to buy it in.

And then of course there is the Milton Keynes thing. It is difficult, but AFC Wimbledon cannot allow themselves to be distracted by it.

Back in the day, Wimbledon was a club that did things its own way. We never wanted to be Tottenham, Chelsea or Arsenal. We were Wimbledon and we were proud of it. That was always where the strength of the club was. There can't be any distractions. AFC Wimbledon need to replicate that.

Would I manage AFC Wimbledon one day? Well, in football never say never!

By Dario Gradi (Crewe Alexandra director of football and Wimbledon manager 1978-81)

AFC Wimbledon's journey is a remarkable achievement. To get into the Football League is amazing; to do it twice is phenomenal. In my playing days I was at Sutton United in the Southern League. Wimbledon were in the Isthmian League. Both leagues were where the Conference is now in the pyramid, but nowhere near as good in terms of standard.

Ron Noades took Wimbledon into the League and then Sam Hammam took them up the divisions. I remember talking to Sam back then. He wanted to take the club into the top four in the country, and he was willing to do whatever it took to achieve his ambition – even if that meant relocating to Dublin. That idea was ridiculous. But Sam was right in some ways. Money was coming into football, and he didn't have limitless resources – he was no Saudi sheikh.

Sam needed to find extra resources to survive and build, but Dublin was not the right option. He turned to the Norwegians, and that didn't work out either. The club then relocated to Milton Keynes – hopefully that wouldn't be allowed now. Milton Keynes got a Football League club through the back door, and that was wrong.

Most Wimbledon fans, myself included, regard AFC Wimbledon as the proper Wimbledon. I remember when they first started out, they issued an appeal for cash, and I sent a couple of hundred quid. My allegiances have always been to the new Wimbledon and I was truly thrilled to get a great reception when I went to the ground.

What they have achieved has been good, but there is a limit to what they can do. And that limit is set by crowds and money. They need their own ground in Merton. It's basically back to where Sam was all those years ago, except that they don't have the same level of support yet. They are not even as big as Crewe yet! So they need to set their sights accordingly. If they stay in the League, that will be a big achievement in itself. Macclesfield, Burton and Morecambe have all been in the same boat.

As for Milton Keynes? Well, they are a separate club and have absolutely nothing to do with Wimbledon any more. AFC Wimbledon should forget all about them. The focus should be on getting their own ground where their support is. Wimbledon people will support Wimbledon in Wimbledon. And Wimbledon has a bigger population than Crewe. It really is about gates. If you look all the way down, there is a pretty good correlation: the bigger the gates, the better the league position.

By Dave Bassett (media commentator and Wimbledon manager 1981-87)

It's been a remarkable journey for AFC Wimbledon, and I have nothing but praise for everything they have achieved. Having started from the very bottom of the pyramid, they have been backed by fanatical supporters who didn't want to see their club die.

And they were determined. They wanted to make sure Wimbledon existed close to Wimbledon. They didn't want one owner to have the power to do whatever he wanted. They wanted control. And they got all those things.

And through four managers and many players they have progressed through the leagues and kept going. They got to the Conference play-off final and they won it. That's a tremendous achievement. Since then they have consolidated their League position – and that's not to be sniffed at either. To go straight back down would not have been a disaster, but it would have been a major setback.

It is all such a great reward for the fans, for the people who have put in all the hard work – people like Ivor Heller, who I remember from my days at Plough Lane. And, through it all, the fanbase has grown and become stronger.

The problem now is how to step forward. Raising money will become increasingly important if they want to attract the players they need to progress to get into League One and beyond. The immediate priority has to be to consolidate. Wimbledon might have to spend five or six years to build a side that's capable of getting promotion and staying up.

And it's made tougher by the stance the club takes. AFC Wimbledon has its principles – and good on them for that – but there are some clubs they are never going to be able to compete with. There are always going to be some club owners who are happy to throw money away, and Wimbledon didn't want to go down that route. But the reality is that a fans-owned club will struggle to compete against the rest.

So what does the future hold? If they want to move on, then AFC Wimbledon need to find a wealthy benefactor who will buy into that ethos, but I'm not sure that there are many people like that around.

Then there's the stadium. That's vital. They need somewhere in Merton where they can conduct their own commercial activities. They need their own offices and function rooms in a location where people want to be. The club needs to constantly search for new ways of raising money.

Then there's the issue of the capacity. If they can get gates over 5,000, that would help. And more would be even better.

And finally there's the underlying ethos of the club. If they want to be the community club they have set themselves out to be, then they need to invest in youth and gamble on the future. The youth scheme at Wimbledon back in my day was the secret to our success. We produced the likes of Wally Downes, Kevin Gage, Glyn Hodges, Andy Thorn, Andy Sayer, Paul Fishenden and Mark Morris – and that was a great help to the club. Those boys all grew up at Wimbledon and they were proud of their club. It's harder now as the modern player rarely fits into that mould, but that's what AFC Wimbledon need to strive to achieve.

By Bobby Gould (TalkSport pundit and Wimbledon FC manager 1987-90)

Sometimes you have to take stock and look at what you have achieved. The way this club was treated back in 2002 was pitiful. I have watched the story unfold since then with awe. It is nothing short of incredible – that's my word of the moment, and it describes AFC Wimbledon perfectly.

After the FA's decision, the fans rolled up their sleeves and got on with it. You have to remember that the club basically started in parks football with nothing. They went up through all the leagues – and God knows where they can go now.

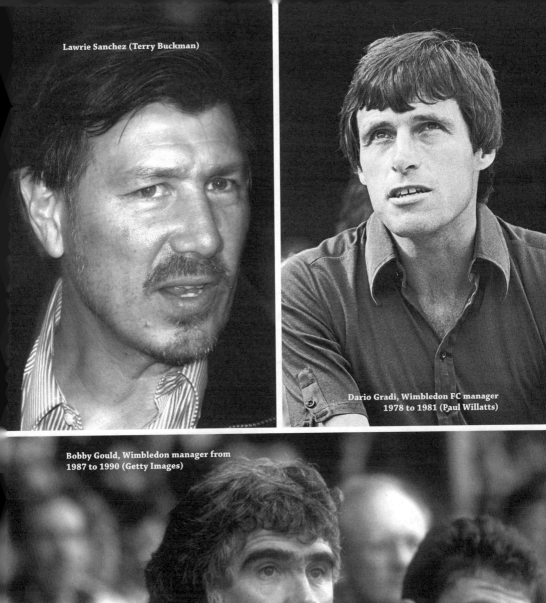

Lawrie Sanchez (Terry Buckman)

Dario Gradi, Wimbledon FC manager 1978 to 1981 (Paul Willatts)

Bobby Gould, Wimbledon manager from 1987 to 1990 (Getty Images)

Terry Burton, manager of Wimbledon from 2000 to 2002 (Paul Willatts)

Dave Anderson, AFC Wimbledon manager 2004 to 2007 (Terry Buckman)

Nicky English, left, with Gareth Graham (Marcus Massey)

Niall Couper: A Dream Come True

Terry Brown has to be really pleased with his achievements. The Football League is not like the Conference. Every team is full-time and that changes everything. The pressure is constant, week after week: there are no easy games, there's no break. It takes a lot out of you. The aim must now be to survive, build, balance the books and go for it.

When I first started as a football manager, I phoned Brian Clough to ask him for some advice. "Brian," I said, "what would be your tip for a young manager just starting out?" And I remember his reply as clear as day. He said: "First thing you do, young man, is call me Mr Clough." And then he added: "What you need to do, young man, is make sure you get your backroom staff right. You'll get nowhere without that."

I now work for TalkSport, and I remember speaking to Brian McDermott moments after he had guided Reading back to the Premier League. I asked him then what he thought was the secret to the club's success, and he said the same thing: "It's all about getting the right backroom staff." Thirty years separate the comments by Mr Clough and Mr McDermott, yet the advice remains the same.

Brian Clough first gave me the benefit of his wisdom back in 1981, when I was at Bristol Rovers. It took me seven years to get the right people together, and by then I was at Wimbledon. It was the best backroom staff I ever assembled. I had Don Howe, Joe Kinnear, Terry Burton, Stevie Allen...the list just goes on and on. I would never have achieved even half of what I did at Wimbledon without them. Sam Hammam's influence was also vital. He was a 24/7 pal, supporting everything we were trying to do. We all had the same drive and ambition. We wanted to make Wimbledon the best we could.

To continue to succeed, AFC Wimbledon need to have that belief at every level of the club. Can they go as far as the Wimbledon of my day? Well, why not?

AFC Wimbledon have already written a new chapter in Wimbledon's history. They have built upon the glory days of the past – not my glory days, but our glory days, the glory days of all the supporters, players and managers of Wimbledon, and rightly so. With their determination the club have already achieved so much, but there are still many more great chapters to write.

The first time around, that same determination led to the club winning the FA Cup. My one regret is that we were denied the opportunity to play in Europe. Now that would be a nice target for AFC Wimbledon to set.

By Terry Burton (Sheffield Weds assistant manager and Wimbledon manager 2000-02)

AFC Wimbledon's journey has been a fantastic achievement. I was there from day one, and I remember vividly the trials on Wimbledon Common. If someone had said then that in 10 years' time AFC Wimbledon would be playing League football, I would have said: "It's a great idea, but I can't see it happening."

What has made the achievement even more impressive is the way they have done it. It's not been done with the cash from some rich benefactor – you see that time and time again, and that's just not sustainable in the long term. This has been all about the hard work and determination of the supporters, and that makes it even more amazing.

AFC Wimbledon has been built on a passion. At the start it was Terry Eames. Without people like him, without their enthusiasm, it could have faltered before it had even started. And that's the message to take to the wider world: it is amazing what people can do when they come together.

I have followed this club very closely over the years. David Barnard, the former Wimbledon FC chief executive, still texts me quite regularly with all the latest updates, and I try and get down to the ground at least once a season.

AFC Wimbledon is a unique club. It's built on people's enthusiasm and a determination to make amends for the wrongs of the FA.

AFC Wimbledon is blessed. There is an ambition at the club. It's being run by some very intelligent and loyal men. They know what they can achieve and what their limitations are. They won't be thinking about being in the Champions League in four years' time. They are sound people. They are happy to have a football club they can call their own.

It's very difficult to see where they can go from here. From now on it's all about budgets, and at present there are too many clubs bankrolled by individuals for it to be a fair fight. That might seem a bleak outlook, but there is a glimmer of hope in UEFA's fair-play financial rules. If they are implemented, that will help to level the playing field and help those clubs with a strong fanbase – and AFC Wimbledon has developed that at League Two level.

And then of course there is an element that sets AFC Wimbledon apart: Milton Keynes. It is a driving force behind the club. It is said that you shouldn't look back, but sometimes you need to use a negative to inspire you, to drive you on. And there can't be more of an inspiration to AFC Wimbledon than the injustice that the FA dealt to Wimbledon supporters back in 2002.

That's where the ambition started, that's where the journey started. The ill-feeling may have diminished a bit, but it is still raw in the hearts of Wimbledon fans. There is no doubt that they were done wrong by the Football Gods at the time, and hopefully now the Football Gods are making amends for their error and are looking after them now. I blame the people who ran the club at the time – the Norwegians, Koppel and his crew – and I blame the FA. It was a disgusting decision, and AFC Wimbledon need to use the memory of it to drive them on and right the injustice they were dealt.

In the meantime, the club need to know their strengths and weaknesses and act within those. Terry Brown is a wily manager who knows his stuff. Recruitment is the basis of how well they will do in the League. And that works on two levels: promoting a good youth system and mixing it with some clever acquisitions. That is the old Wimbledon way.

Football is a strange game. I didn't know that one week I was going to be working with West Bromwich Albion in the Premier League and the next I would be at Sheffield Wednesday as an assistant helping them get promotion to the Championship. So you never know what is around the corner. AFC Wimbledon? Who knows?

By Nicky English (Whyteleafe manager and AFC Wimbledon manager 2004)

The AFC Wimbledon story is as good as any story can be. And that should never be forgotten. The club has been ruthless when they needed to be. You only have to look at what happened to both Dave Anderson and myself. Dave came within a whisker of taking the club up to the Conference South and they got rid of him. I won everything I could have in the short time I was in charge, and I was replaced as well. But in hindsight they were right both times.

Terry Brown, AFC Wimbledon manager
2007- (Getty Images)

Being manager of AFC Wimbledon was relatively easy for me. All I had to do was pick up the phone to players a division or two above us and they would be at training with us the next week. There was never any question back then of money. Wimbledon had that draw because of who they were, but it was fading even then. They needed someone with experience of the Ryman League and I didn't have that, so they brought in Dave. As for his replacement, you can't really argue with Terry Brown's achievements from the moment he took over.

The club has been steered and administered immensely well by Erik Samuelson and the Board. Their aim has been to keep moving forward, and that has served AFC Wimbledon well. To go even further would be amazing. Don't get me wrong – everything that has happened so far has been superb – but to reach an even higher level would be like Bolton Wanderers winning the Champions League.

The support of 4,000 or 5,000 fans is great, but in fairness that's mid-table League Two figures. AFC Wimbledon need to work on those Premier League supporters who are disillusioned with the way money rules the game and the cost to themselves of following top-flight football. They need to attract those fans and tap into their disillusionment – take some of those Chelsea, Arsenal or Fulham fans and put an AFC Wimbledon shirt on their backs. That's the harsh reality. Unless AFC Wimbledon get a bigger stadium and find another 10,000 supporters, they are really going to struggle to progress much further.

But then there's money – if you don't have it, you have no chance of moving on. I speak to a lot of ex-players, and AFC Wimbledon just don't have the budget. There are clubs around them that can spend perhaps £100,000 or £200,000 a week – and I doubt Wimbledon have much more than £20,000 a week to spend.

When Wimbledon went from the Fourth Division to the top flight, money wasn't such a big factor. I'm good mates with Jim Cannon, who was captain of the Crystal Palace team that was dubbed the team of the Eighties. He played under the likes of Terry Venables and Steve Coppell, and he earned £500 a week. The equivalent player, perhaps the centre-half at Spurs or Newcastle now, is probably on around £60,000 a week.

However good a manager AFC Wimbledon can get, the money side is always going to come into play. Unless they can borrow José Mourinho for a couple of seasons, I can't really see them moving on. Perhaps Erik should make that call. Sadly, that's the brutal truth.

But I don't want to sound too pessimistic. What people forget is how much of a phenomenal achievement it has been so far. It's been an absolute dream. I don't think anyone will truly realise what an amazing story it is until 10 or 15 years from now. Then, with the aid of hindsight, you will be able to look back and really grasp what has been achieved. AFC Wimbledon have come from the Combined Counties League, which is basically parks football, to the professional ranks of the biggest domestic league in the world. It is a story that will never be repeated again.

If you wrote it all down and gave it to an American, they would say it was just a fantasy story.

By Dave Anderson (Harrow manager and AFC Wimbledon manager from 2004 to 2007)

It's been an unbelievable achievement. When Ivor Heller said all those years ago that he wanted the club to be in the Football League within 10 years, he should have been committed to a mental institution. It was beyond ridiculous.

No one will ever be able to match it. It's massive. It is Hollywood stuff. I've got Brad Pitt down to play the Dave Anderson role. I think Ivor would have to be played by Danny DeVito, no doubt about it. As for Erik, well it would have to be some famous Shakespearean actor. I've got it all worked out. It would make a great film.

On a more serious note, I can't offer the club any more tips, and why should they listen to a non-league manager anyway? It would be absolutely wrong of me. As for the supporters, there's only one bit of advice I can give them – be patient.

It's easy to get used to winning games and leagues each year, but if the club can maintain their status in the Football League that will be as big an achievement as anything they achieved in their first 10 years. It will be massive if they can become a recognised Football League club.

Perhaps if everything goes right one year they could make it to League One, but that's a big ask. Finances now are so much more a determining factor than when Wimbledon first broke the mould and reached the top flight all those years ago.

My big worry is that Terry Brown could become a victim of his own success. He has constantly overachieved. And once the success stops, it is easier for people to turn on the manager.

I remember Erik telling me that the club had something like the fourth-lowest budget in the Football League. The club can't continue to overachieve. And that's the problem with getting to the next level: AFC Wimbledon need more finance, and that puts pressure on the club's ethos as a fans-owned club.

But in my personal opinion, AFC Wimbledon is far better being a fans-owned club, a part of the community and constantly honouring their own history, than gambling that all by selling up and throwing away everything they have built up in the past 10 years. It would be wrong to go the other way.

Yes, you should always try and reach for the stars, but there has to be a sense of realism about it now.

By Terry Brown (AFC Wimbledon manager)

No one can really question the remarkable success of AFC Wimbledon in the first 10 years of the club's existence. But it means very little to the manager of the club. Football is a results' game, and Stuart Cash and I were always aware of that brutal truth. Every year has to be a winning year. It only takes one bad three-month spell and it is over.

Promotion from the Ryman League in my first season in charge won over the fans – although we managed it only by the skin of our teeth. After that first year it was about creating a legacy. It wasn't just about winning, it was about winning in style. We were never going to emulate the Crazy Gang either in style or spirit. I have great respect for their achievements, but we wanted to do it our way. We wanted to get the ball down and pass it, and we wanted to be disciplined. I take great pride that in four of the first five years of my time in charge we topped the Fair Play League – and that is reflected right through the club, through all the youth teams.

However, the first 10 years are history. The difficult phase begins now, protecting what we have created and working within a limited budget. There is still so much the club wants to achieve. There are two main short-term targets: to get the ground up to Football League standard as quickly as possible, while at the same time ensuring that we have the quality of players on the pitch to thrive. That's a difficult juggling act and requires a minor miracle from Erik Samuelson.

In the long term there is a bigger issue. The club has a great fanbase that has been immensely patient. The problem is that we live in an increasingly impatient society in which, for many, supporting a football club means expecting to win all the time. Even for AFC Wimbledon fans, the patience may run out eventually. So the challenge is to manage expectations.

And that's the one thing that scares me most – ambition. Just about every club that has got into financial difficulties or gone bankrupt has done so because of ambition. Rangers, Leeds and Portsmouth are just three. I am truly wary of that word "ambition".

At Kingsmeadow, maybe we can reach League One, but we will hit a glass ceiling when it comes to wages. And there's no hiding from the fact that in every league and in every division, 90 per cent of the time the big payers finish at the top and the worst payers finish at the bottom. There will always be a few anomalies like Everton, but realistically it is all about finances.

AFC Wimbledon's biggest success was buying its own ground and constantly growing the fanbase. For many games you can't get a ticket now, and the reality is that Kingsmeadow restricts us. The only way I believe that the club can truly push on and thrive is to get a home back in SW19, and become an even bigger club, in a bigger stadium with bigger gates. All that needs to be done without risking the security of the club, and while Erik remains in charge the security of the club will be never put in jeopardy. But the future has to be a fans-owned Wimbledon in Wimbledon.

The Fans Remember:

Darren Abbabil
Missed the game at Sutton, so went to Dulwich to see what the fuss was about. I was hooked.

Colin Adkins
The big family reunion which was the play off final – it was emotional.

Fazal Ahmad
North Greenford United final at Woking. What an atmosphere! Drove round Woking all day waiting for the game.

Raymond Ardley
Nicky English's first game in charge was a 9-0 away win at Chessington Utd which I happily witnessed.

Ashley and Kev
Fantastic ten years; from Sutton to the Football League and just being able to support our team.

John Balchin
Whistle goes, supporters embrace
Watery eyed, smiley faced
Jump the fence the Play Off's won
Conference South here we come!

John Bliss
Attending AFC Wimbledon's first non-league match at Sandhurst and finding 2500 other supporters there crowded round the pitch.

Malcolm Brackley
Carrie, Billy and Tasha collecting signatures in the player's lounge from the amateur to the professional. Quality club and people.

Malcolm Brackley
Being proud to tell people about your football club and being part of this wonderful story.

Richard Brazier
The best ten years I've ever had watching football. I would not have missed it for the world.

Jim Brittain
My son Robert, scoring in a penalty shoot out at half time during the Crewe game in 2011.

Terry Buckman
21st May 2011. A never to be forgotten privilege, sharing the day with the players and fans in Manchester.

Toby Buckman
I've made some good friends. They're all called Nick. I remember Millwall away. And Manchester. And sneaking into Feltham Arena…

John Butcher
I will always remember that from sylvan Sandhurst to electric Eastlands we willed our wronged club onwards and rebuffed our detractors.

J.K. Callow
Sponsoring our first match in December 2005 and making lots of new friends.

David Carpenter
Fifty years! Amateur cup, Southern League, Burnley, Leeds, Premier League, 1988. Betrayed! Away Grounds! Referees! Eastlands! FL! A wonderful experience!

Steve Cook
Haydon's warm up at Wembley when playing Corinthian Casuals: one armed press ups, high knee lifts, great fun, great day.

Robert Cornell
From disillusionment with the game to times of great experiences, valuable memories and good people once again.

Alan Cotterill
That last day in May, last kick of the season, what a football story like no other.

Jerzy Dabrowski
I had tears in my eyes at Sutton. We had our club back, and it was OURS.

Isa Dabrowska
My favourtie game was against Shrewsbury, as I was mascot. I loved the warm up and leading the team out.

Bert Dale
Ten years? Bloody hell.

Alex Davis
What greater feeling than the Dons fans swarming the pitch as we secured promotion to the Conference South? That match had it all!

Robert Day
Walking through Fleetwood the morning after the semi-final, spotting our win headlined on the news stands.

Ashley Dell
My favourite memory is the play-off final at Staines. I'll remember the last ten minutes forever.

Russel Earl
Godalming and Guildford Oakins' goal, sendings off and a Wimbledon win. AFC Wallingford with police helicopters! Welcome to non-league.

The Eccles Family
Belief as Keds stepped up to take 'that pen' and sheer elation as the ball rocketed into the net!

Richard Edwards
'It only took nine years' reverberating around the City of Manchester stadium as Kedwell's penalty took us into League Two.

Thomas Emanuel
Hearing 'We are Wimbledon' in Manchester as the players and fans celebrated. An emotional, joyful, magical moment – we were back.

Sami Everett
Staines; heavy legs; pain my stomach; blinded by the sun; goal; mêlée; goal; raptures; Marcus atop a Don dwarfed trophy aloft.

Neal Exall
Wimbledon FC and AFC Wimbledon. Womble till I die.

Bob Farrance
Shane Smeltz's strike in the fourteenth minute of the Surrey Senior Cup final – what a goal.

Michael Field
First game at Sandhurst, steam train to Wallingford. Five promotions in ten years. Danny Kedwell's final kick. Fantastic times.

Bob Ford
Hope at Sandhurst, cheese rolls at Mersham, last minute at Herne Bay, late at Staines, Eastlands ecstasy – WHAT A BLAST.

Howard Fry
Drewe Broughton scoring, to restore the lead, within minutes of coming on as sub on his Wimbledon debut at Tamworth.

Neil, Libby and Georgie
Fantastic club – lots of goals, lots of fun – wouldn't change a thing!

Wagner Gimenes
Thanks for eight great years (late to the party) of memories. Looking forward to the next thirty. Love the Dons!

Paul Goode
Southall v AFC Wimbledon, 0-0, Tuesday evening 03/09/02. Cigar and beer in one hand, curry in the other, watching the team then drinking the bar dry. FANtastic!

Derek and Susan Goodhew
The day AFC Wimbledon beat Staines Town to win promotion to the Blue Square South. Momentous.

Colin Graham
The tremendous hospitality and welcome given to our team and supporters by all the clubs in the Combined Counties league.

Brian Halliday
Away to Mersham in the Combined Counties and getting free cheese rolls handed out at the end of the game.

Rory Harding
Fans 1 Establishment 0.

Karen Hardy
Meeting up with my two children for the first game at Sutton – four thousand people could not be wrong.

David and Jane Hart
At Staines, ten minutes from the end, seeing sad faces, thinking that we would never go up – and then...

Matt Jennings
Seb Brown's home debut against Cambridge. Who would've thought that nervous debut could lead to such legendary heroics in Manchester!

David Heller
I missed the 1977 game against Halifax, so was excited at KM against Bristol Rovers. A fantastic achievement for all Dons.

Mark Hillyer
Together on and off the field, we've shown that fans can run football clubs

Tim Hillyer
'Mes que un club' (More than a club) relates to AFC Wimbledon as much as to Barca.

Matthew Hunt
Watching from the terraces with my dad in 2003, as we courageously battled back to beat AFC Wallingford 3-2.

Gareth Hughes
So many great memories but that first game versus Sutton Utd said emphatically that we ARE Wimbledon and we ARE back!

Paul Hughes
My memory of 21st May 2011 is crystal clear, it was one of pride, immense pride. Our club was back.

Terry Hunt
My son being born on May 20th 2011, AFC Wimbledon winning the playoffs on the 21st, what a weekend!

Rupert Jeffery
All the first two seasons' games were brilliant. Best ever, though: December 17th 2011, Rotherham away; 'Terry Brown's having a party'.

Ben Jones
Quite simply, City of Manchester Stadium, Danny Kedwell steps up... bang... the hurt is over, we are back.

Sue Knight
Matt Martin presented a framed pair of gloves to Jordan, pitchside in 2004. They still hang proudly above our fireplace.

Peter Leng
I flew over from Singapore in December 2002 to see my first game, Chipstead away. 0-2 down, win 3-2. Sheer joy.

Michael Lewis
Starting my computer in Sydney to see the result against Luton Town – doing it the hard way, but doing it!

Jonathan Ling
17th July 2002: AFCW's first ever goal at Bromley on a beautiful summer evening. The moment when I thought: 'we can do this'.

Anders Lundqvist
AFC Wimbledon, my second home when living in Reigate 2006-07, and for always in my heart!

Ian Lyden
Sandhurst Town on a brilliant summer's day, standing on straw bales and a wonderful victory. It was a great game. COYD!

John Lynch
Flying back for Conference play-off semi, staying for Eastlands, Kedwell's penalty, tears of joy, we're back in the league.

John Marshall
Promotion, FA cup winners, relegation, heartbreak, promotion, promotion, promotion, promotion, promotion, back in league football, my life as a Dons fan.

Geoff Mason
Jack being mascot for Newport game in the Blue Square Premier – thirty one years after his Dad's first Dons game against… Newport!

Iain McNay
Our first win; Enfield Town on 12th August 2002 After losing our first nine matches we finally managed a 3-2 win to set us up for the first league game against Sandhurst.

Nick Miller
Being on the pitch when my daughter Ella presented Kevin Cooper with the Junior Dons Player of the Year Award 2003.

Peter Morey
The penalty shoot-out at the play-off final in Manchester – a sheer roller coaster of emotion.

Patrick Mysliwek
"It only took nine years" we sing, what will the next nine bring. Joy, despair, elation, we'll still sing in jubilation.

Stan, Jean and Maddy Nicholls
What a 'fan'tastic journey! … and getting better and better.

Steve Nuttall
Danny Kedwell's penalty at CMS encapsulated not just the moment, but the whole wonderful journey back into the league.

Michael Padmanathan
Being so welcomed by the management, players and fans in producing the film "Common Ground" which heavily featured AFC Wimbledon.

Eric Page
Returning from Asia to see my first ever AFC game at Croydon and realising that everything was possible, again.

Greg Parker
Anger and despair turned to eager anticipation by those who had the vision for AFCW – 2002. Joyful tears, Manchester 2011!

Doug Preece
From supporter to stewarding. Thirty five years following the Dons. Never a dull moment. Long may it last.

Vinnie Preece
Mum and Dad are Dons, Uncle's a Don, named after a Don, forever a Don.

Jim (JamPot) Potter
My proud ten years supporting AFC Wimbledon encourages continued belief - our club is at the vanguard reclaiming football for all dispossessed!

Huw Powell
Spending the weekend in Manchester watching Wimbledon v Luton was one of the best weekends ever.

Kevin Robbins
At the Surrey Senior Cup final 2005, seeing the stand at Woking's ground a sea of yellow and blue.

Matthew Robbins
A fan doing a jig down Wheatsheaf Lane after the Ryman League play-off final, in relief and celebration!

Nigel Standish
Sandhurst for the first game with my wife and children and all feeling we were part of something very special.

Andrew Staker
Southern League to Premier League, Combined Counties to the Football League, David and Andrew Staker are Wombles till we die!

Howard & Helen Stevens
(Paramlimni Wombles)
Our inspirational captain proclaims "This is our time" It hits the back of the net, The Euphoria is sublime!

Richard Stobbs
Final game of 2002-2003, we beat Raynes Park 5-1. Many supporters ended up celebrating in the same nightclub as the team!

Richard Thomas
The first game I took my son to, Folkestone, we won 4-1 in 05/06 season. He became a Dons supporter!

Greg Valentine
The unique story of AFC Wimbledon will live long in football history. I'm simply proud that they're my team.

Adam Velasco
Kedwell's winning penalty – City Of Manchester Stadium. A special moment and great to know that sometimes in life you can get what you deserve, the good guys won.

Peter Ware
Club franchised/stolen. Formed AFC Wimbledon. Decade alter reclaimed Football League status. What a rise! Come on you Dons!

Nick Whitley
Those Manchester penalties – That free kick at Staines – Jon Main's goals – Kevin Cooper's goals – Great memories – Great anticipation. Our club.

Angela Widdup
Iain's dream to see Wimbledon regain Football League status was achieved on my birthday weekend, the best present ever.

Nesta Wood
A curry house in Manchester, evening, 21st May 2011 – two blokes leaving as we were waiting for a table: 'You've had a wonderful day. Now you're going to have a wonderful meal.'

Mark Worledge
De Bolla (Staines), Main (H&R), Kedwell (Luton) – all exhilarating but AFC's very existence brings me happiness and pride every day.

With thanks to the above, all of whom took advantage of an offer to pre-order the book from the club's website and include a few words of their own. Greatly appreciated!

ALSO AVAILABLE FROM CHERRY RED BOOKS:

Nina Antonia: Johnny Thunders – In Cold Blood

Andy Blade: The Secret Life Of A Teenage Punk Rocker: The Andy Blade Chronicles

Craig Brackenbridge: Hells Bent On Rockin': A History Of Psychobilly

Jake Brown: Tom Waits: In The Studio

Steve Bruce: Best Seat In The House – A Cock Sparrer Story

David Burke: Heart Of Darkness – Bruce Springsteen's 'Nebraska'

David Cartwright: Bittersweet: The Clifford T Ward Story

Jeremy Collingwood: Kiss Me Neck – A Lee 'Scratch' Perry Discography

Campbell Devine: All The Young Dudes: Mott The Hoople & Ian Hunter

Malcolm Dome / Jerry Ewing: Celebration Day – A Led Zeppelin Encyclopedia

Sean Egan: Our Music Is Red – With Purple Flashes: The Story Of The Creation

Sean Egan: The Doc's Devils: Manchester United 1972-77

Martin Elliott: The Rolling Stones: Complete Recording Sessions 1962-2012

Ian Glasper: The Day The Country Died: A History Of Anarcho Punk 1980 To 1984

Ian Glasper: Burning Britain – A History Of UK Punk 1980 -1984

Ian Glasper: Trapped In A Scene - UK Hardcore 1985-89

Ian Glasper: Armed With Anger – How UK Punk Survived the Nineties

Stefan Grenados: Those Were The Days – The Beatles' Apple Organization

Phil Harding: PWL: From The Factory Floor

Colin Harper / Trevor Hodgett: Irish Folk, Trad And Blues: A Secret History

Dave Henderson: A Plugged In State Of Mind: The History of Electronic Music

Nick Hodges / Ian Priston: Embryo – A Pink Floyd Chronology 1966-1971

Jim Bob: Goodnight Jim Bob – On The Road With Carter USM

Barry Lazell: Indie Hits 1980 -1989

Mark Manning (aka Zodiac Mindwarp): Fucked By Rock (Revised and Expanded)

Mick Mercer: Music To Die For – International Guide To Goth, Goth Metal, Horror Punk, Psychobilly Etc

Alex Ogg: Independence Days – The Story Of UK Independent Record Labels

Alex Ogg: No More Heroes: A Complete History Of UK Punk 1976 To 1980

David Parker: Random Precision – Recording The Music Of Syd Barrett 1965 - 1974

Mark Powell: Prophets and Sages: The 101 Greatest Progressive Rock Albums

Terry Rawlings / Keith Badman: Good Times Bad Times – The Rolling Stones 1960-69

Terry Rawlings / Keith Badman: Quite Naturally – The Small Faces

John Repsch: The Legendary Joe Meek – The Telstar Man

John Robb: Death To Trad Rock – The Post-Punk fanzine scene 1982-87

Garry Sharpe-Young: Rockdetector: A To Zs of '80s Rock / Death Metal / Doom, Gothic & Stoner Metal and Power Metal

Garry Sharpe-Young: Rockdetector: Black Sabbath – Never Say Die

Garry Sharpe-Young: Rockdetector: Ozzy Osbourne

Mick Stevenson: The Motorhead Collector's Guide

Dave Thompson: Truth... Rod Stewart, Ron Wood And The Jeff Beck Group

Dave Thompson: Number One Songs In Heaven – he Sparks Story

Dave Thompson: Block Buster! – The True Story of The Sweet

Dave Thompson: Children of the Revolution: The Glam Rock Story 1970 -75

Paul Williams: You're Wondering Now – The Specials from Conception to Reunion

Alan Wilson: Deathrow: The Chronicles Of Psychobilly

Terry Wilson: Tamla Motown – The Stories Behind The Singles

PLEASE VISIT WWW.CHERRYREDBOOKS.CO.UK FOR FURTHER INFO AND MAIL ORDER

THE BLUE AND YELLOW CLUB

For AFC Wimbledon to consolidate its position in the Football League the club needs to raise substantially more money for the playing budget, which is currently one of the lowest in League Two. Even if we are successful on the field and move forward to League One, the increase in non-gate revenue would not be large and the wage bill would very probably increase, so the problem will be made more pronounced by success. At the same time, the club needs to find more funds to bring our current stadium up to Football League standards and help pay the costs of exploring our proposed move back to Merton.

We have a very different business model and structure from other Football League clubs. Almost without exception they have directors who put substantial sums of money in to help subsidise the playing budget and keep their clubs afloat. In return they often receive shares, a seat on the board and are involved with all the big decisions. We, on the other hand, elect our Dons Trust Board, which oversees our four man Football Club Board on behalf of the supporters. The majority of shares in the club are held by the Trust, with the residue being held by fans directly so we cannot follow the model of these other clubs.

A group of supporters has therefore decided to launch 'The Blue and Yellow Club' with the intention of raising money to assist in building the best team possible. It will be run by us and will donate money back to the club to assist with the playing budget as needed and as agreed by us the members.

The cost of membership of the club will be £1,000 per season and two alternative packages of benefits have been devised to recognise the differences between members who can regularly attend games (the Yellow Package) and those who cannot (the Blue Package).

The benefits of the Blue membership for supporters who attend matches regularly include:

1. A pass to the President's lounge for home matches (but not match day tickets)
2. Two tickets for the end of season dinner
3. Dinner with the football management team and club CEO twice a season (for the cost of the meal)
4. Access to reserved table(s) for the Blue and Yellow Club in the carvery before home matches (for the cost of the meal)
5. Invitation to the occasional Wimbledon celebrity dinner each season (again for the cost of the meal)

The benefits of the Yellow membership for those who don't attend matches regularly includes:

1. VIP treatment for you and a guest at two home games a season. This would include a special welcome from the CEO, The Dons Trust Chairman, and the manager; a pre-match meal in the carvery plus access to the President's lounge and seats in the Directors' box next to a former player, such as Club President Dickie Guy or former Captain Ian Cooke. (If you can't make two home games but can get to one or two away games we will do our best to arrange a similar package for you there).
2. A tour of the training ground and opportunity to meet the players
3. A club shirt signed by the whole squad, plus a club tie
4. Invitation to at least one scheduled telephone briefing each season with the CEO and Manager

You will see from the above that the idea is to give members unique benefits that have low direct costs, so as not to consume the membership fees in order that they are available as far as possible entirely for the playing budget.

Whichever package you choose, where possible we will help facilitate Club members sharing travel and meeting up at for lunch at away games; hopefully this will, in time, also include specially arranged luxury coach travel to important games. We will also hold Club meetings during the year to explore how else we can help the club.

The idea is that the Yellow and Blue Club will run itself independently of the football club and would form a small group of Club members to manage it.

If you would like to join or know more please email Martin Fielding martin@cardextras.com or Iain McNay at iain@cherryred.co.uk saying which package you are interested in, and we'll send you more information or talk you through any details which are not clear to you. We look forward to hearing from you!

The AFC Wimbledon Album

This Is Our Time

To coincide with and support the release of this book Cherry Red Records is releasing a download album of tracks about the club, all recorded by Wimbledon supporters. Tracks featured include:

The Big Blast Band (see details below) – featuring Sammy Moore, Luke Moore, Jack Midson, Byron Harrison and Christian Jolley - 'We Are Wimbledon' / Steven Bor - 'This Is Our Time' / The Fans' Club Band – 'All I Want To Do (Is Watch Football)', 'More Important Than That' and 'A Fans' Club' / I, Ludicrous - 'From The Lane To The Meadow' / Kevin Holland and Wills McGuigan - 'Nine Years' / The Jumble - 'History' / On Trial UK - 'Not In The Wider Interest of Football' / Paul Jeffrey - 'This Wimbledon' / Thomas Barnes - 'In The Dons We Trust' / Lion O' Brien - 'Rise' / Chris Mears - 'Look At Us Now (A Fans Club)' / John Power - This Is Our Time

The Big Blast Band – The project explained by Clive Yelf:
The band consists of twelve adults with learning disabilities form the High Path Day Centre in Merton. As part of an innovative community project with AFC Wimbledon they were encouraged to explore music through the chants and percussive rhythms of the football terraces under the expert guidance of Elisabeth Wigly and John Merriman of the Merton Music Foundation and Crown Lane recording studios respectively. After ten weeks' hard work they premiered their version of the Wimbledon FA Cup Final song 'We Are Wimbledon' to an appreciative half time audience during The Dons' League Two game against Burton Albion, inspiring the players to a 4 – 0 victory!

Having started their career with a sell-out stadium gig, they then retired to the studio to record a more polished version of the song for posterity, aided and abetted by some of the AFC Wimbledon first team squad. The enthusiasm, dedication and sheer exuberance the band bought to the task made the whole project a real pleasure, both to work on and to participate in, and it was the real sense of community engendered by such a performance which makes the High Path 'Super Dons' such a valued part of the AFC Wimbledon community. So settle back, crank the volume up to eleven and enjoy the vocal sledgehammer that is The Big Blast Band and the AFC Wimbledon players.

Cherry Red Records is home to the world's largest known football-related music catalogue. To find out more and access this AFC Wimbledon album go to www.cherryred.co.uk/ cherryredfootball.asp